MATHEMATICS

for Edexcel GCSE

Foundation Tier

Tony Banks and David Alcorn

Causeway Press Limited

Published by Causeway Press Ltd
P.O. Box 13, Ormskirk, Lancashire L39 5HP

First published 2002

British Library Cataloguing-in-Publication Data.
A catalogue record for this book is available from the British Library.

ISBN 1-902796-26-8

Acknowledgements
The authors and publisher wish to express their thanks and gratitude to Tony Fisher, Paul Newton, Peter Balaam and Bruce Balden for their contributions to this book.

Exam questions
Past exam questions, provided by *London Examinations, A division of Edexcel*, are marked Edexcel. The answers to all questions are entirely the responsibility of the authors/publisher and have neither been provided nor approved by Edexcel.

Every effort has been made to locate the copyright owners of material used in this book. Any omissions brought to the notice of the publisher are regretted and will be credited in subsequent printings.

Page design
Billy Johnson
Alan Fraser

Readers
Anne Alcock
Heather Doyle
David Hodgson

Artwork
David Alcorn
Alan Fraser

Cover design
Waring-Collins Partnership

Typesetting by Billy Johnson, San Francisco, California, USA

Printed and bound by Scotprint, Haddington, Scotland

preface

Mathematics for Edexcel GCSE - Foundation Tier has been written to meet the requirements of the National Curriculum and provides full coverage of **Edexcel Specification A** and **Edexcel Specification B (Modular)**.

The book is suitable for students preparing for assessment at the Foundation Tier of entry on either a 1-year or 2-year course or as a revision text.

In preparing the text, full account has been made of the requirements for students to be able to solve problems in mathematics both with and without a calculator. Whilst there has been no artificial division of subject content into calculator and non-calculator work, non-calculator questions and exercises have been incorporated throughout the book where appropriate.

The planning of topics within chapters and sections has been designed to provide efficient coverage of the specifications. Depending on how the book is to be used you can best decide on the order in which chapters are studied.

Chapters 1 - 10	Number
Chapters 11 - 17	Algebra
Chapters 18 - 27	Shape, Space and Measures
Chapters 28 - 33	Handling Data

Each chapter consists of fully worked examples with explanatory notes and commentary; carefully graded questions, a summary of key facts and skills and a review exercise.
The review exercises provide the opportunity to consolidate topics introduced within the chapter and consist of exam-style questions, which reflect how Edexcel intend to assess the work, plus lots of past examination questions (marked Edexcel).

Further opportunities to consolidate skills acquired over a number of chapters are provided with section reviews. There is a final exam questions section with a further compilation of exam and exam-style questions, organised for non-calculator and calculator practice, in preparation for the exams.

Some chapters include ideas for investigational, practical and statistical tasks and give the student the opportunity to improve and practice their skills of using and applying mathematics.

contents

CHAPTER 18 · Angles

CHAPTER 19 · Triangles

CHAPTER 20 · Symmetry and Congruence

CHAPTER 21 — Quadrilaterals

CHAPTER 22 — Polygons

CHAPTER 23 — Direction and Distance

CHAPTER 24 — Circles

CHAPTER 1

Whole Numbers 1

The numbers 0, 1, 2, 3, 4, 5, … can be used to count objects.

"I have 3 pound coins in my pocket."
"There are 8 tables in the room."
"There are 0 students absent today."

Such numbers are called **whole numbers**.

There are other types of numbers, including fractions, decimals and negative numbers which you will meet in later chapters.

Place value

Our number system is made up of the digits 0, 1, 2, 3, 4, 5, 6, 7, 8 and 9.

The position a digit has in a number is called its **place value**.

In the number 5384 the digit 8 is worth 80, but in the number 4853 the digit 8 is worth 800.

$$17 = 10 + 7 \qquad = 1 \times 10 + 7$$
$$23 = 20 + 3 \qquad = 2 \times 10 + 3$$
$$567 = 500 + 60 + 7 = 5 \times 100 + 6 \times 10 + 7$$
$$2060 = 2000 + 60 \qquad = 2 \times 1000 + 6 \times 10$$

EXAMPLES

1 What is the value of the digit 2 in the number 6234?

The 2 is worth 200.

2 Which of these numbers is the largest?
374, 276, 375, 357, 283.

The largest number is 375.

3 Write the following numbers the in descending order.
54, 49, 123, 98, 1001.

1001, 123, 98, 54, 49.

4 Using the digits 5, 6 and 8 (do not use the same digit more than once) make as many three-digit numbers as you can. Place your numbers in ascending order.

568, 586, 658, 685, 856, 865.

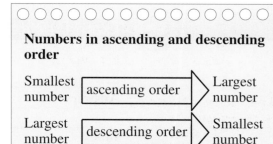

Numbers in ascending and descending order

Smallest number → ascending order → Largest number

Largest number → descending order → Smallest number

Exercise 1.1

1 Copy and complete the following.
(a) $923 = 900 + 20 + 3 = 9 \times 100 + 2 \times 10 + 3$
(b) $456 = \qquad =$
(c) $\quad 54 = \qquad =$
(d) $\qquad = 700 + 60 + 5 =$
(e) $\qquad = \qquad = 4 \times 100 + 9 \times 10 + 2$
(f) $1872 = \qquad =$
(g) $\qquad = 1000 + 20 + 3 =$
(h) $\qquad = \qquad = 3 \times 1000 + 4 \times 100 + 5$

2 In the number 173:
the digit 1 is worth 100,
the digit 7 is worth 70,
the digit 3 is worth 3.
Give the value of each digit in the
following numbers.
(a) 53
(b) 341
(c) 673
(d) 987
(e) 333
(f) 1897
(g) 1052
(h) 1520

3 In the number 3<u>8</u>4 the value of the
underlined figure is 80.
Give the value of the underlined figure
in the following.
(a) 62<u>3</u>4
(b) <u>2</u>003
(c) 95 6<u>7</u>0
(d) 423<u>6</u>

4 For these pairs of numbers say which
digit has the greater value.
(a) The 1 in 512 or the 8 in 648.
(b) The 7 in 745 or the 9 in 892.
(c) The 5 in 599 or the 6 in 769.

5 Look at these numbers.
97, 32, 23, 28, 302, 203.
(a) Which is the largest number?
(b) Which is the smallest number?

6 Write the following numbers in
ascending order.
(a) 74, 168, 39, 421.
(b) 555, 545, 544, 554.
(c) 3842, 5814, 3874, 3801, 4765.

7 Write the following numbers in
descending order.
(a) 399, 425, 103, 84, 429.
(b) 234, 239, 349, 324.
(c) 9434, 9646, 9951, 9653.

8 Using the digits 2, 3 and 7 make as
many three-digit numbers as you can.
Use each digit just once in each
three-digit number, e.g. 237.
Put your three-digit numbers in
descending order.

9 Using the digits 8, 5, 4 and 3 make as
many four-digit numbers as you can.
Use each digit just once in each
four-digit number, e.g. 8543.
Put your numbers in ascending order.
How many numbers begin with eight?

10 By using each of the digits 5, 4 and 7
(a) make the largest three-digit
number,
(b) make the smallest three-digit
number.
In each case explain your method.

11 By using each of the digits 5, 1, 6
and 2
(a) make the largest four-digit
number,
(b) make the smallest four-digit
number.

12 By using each of the digits 4, 6, 7, 1
and 5
(a) make the largest five-digit
number,
(b) make the smallest five-digit
number.

Reading and writing numbers

$8543 = 8 \times 1000 + 5 \times 100 + 4 \times 10 + 3 \times 1$

The number 8543 is written or read as, "eight thousand five hundred and forty-three."

For numbers bigger than one thousand split the number into groups of three digits, starting from the units column.

EXAMPLES

1 Write these numbers in words.

32	thirty-two
514	five hundred and fourteen
45237 = 45 237	forty-five *thousand* two hundred and thirty-seven
1234567 = 1 234 567	one *million* two hundred and thirty-four *thousand* five hundred and sixty-seven

2 Write these numbers in figures.

Sixty-eight	68
Four hundred and seventy	470
Two thousand five hundred and seventeen	2517
Two million eight hundred and fifty thousand four hundred and sixty-one	2 850 461

1. Split the numbers into groups of 3 digits.
2. Combine the numbers of millions and thousands with the number less than 1000.

Exercise 1.2

1 Write these numbers in words.
- (a) 17
- (b) 88
- (c) 187
- (d) 2045
- (e) 5612
- (f) 7802
- (g) 8888
- (h) 92000
- (i) 132045
- (j) 1500000

2
- (a) Write these numbers in figures.
  - (i) one
  - (ii) ten
  - (iii) one hundred
  - (iv) one thousand
  - (v) ten thousand
- (b) What do you notice?
- (c) What are the next two numbers in the sequence?
  Write them in words as well.

3 Write the following numbers in figures.
- (a) five hundred and forty-six
- (b) six hundred and seven
- (c) one thousand and ten
- (d) seventy thousand two hundred
- (e) one million two hundred thousand and fifty-two

4 One million is 1 000 000.
Write these numbers in figures.
- (a) two million
- (b) ten million
- (c) half a million
- (d) one and a half million

5 In the following report numbers are written in words.
Rewrite the report showing the numbers as figures.
The attendance at the football match was *forty-eight thousand*. The pitch measured *one hundred and nineteen* yards by *sixty-two* yards. After *twenty-five* minutes the centre forward (who cost *fifteen million* pounds) scored from *eighteen* yards.

6 Write answers to the following using figures.
- (a) ten more than seven thousand and twenty
- (b) one hundred less than five hundred and sixty-three
- (c) one thousand more than ten thousand

Non-calculator methods for addition

Writing numbers in columns

Write the numbers in tidy columns according to place value.
Add together the numbers of units, tens, hundreds, etc.
If any of these answers comes to more than 10 then something is carried to the next column.

EXAMPLE

Work out $4567 + 835$.

$$\begin{array}{r} 4\,5\,6\,7 \\ +\ \ 8\,3\,5 \\ \hline 5\,4\,0\,2 \\ \hline \scriptstyle 1\ \ 1\ \ 1 \end{array}$$

$7 + 5 = 12$ which is 2 carry 1.
$6 + 3 + \text{carried } 1 = 10$,   which is 0 carry 1.
$5 + 8 + \text{carried } 1 = 14$,   which is 4 carry 1.
$4 + \text{carried } 1 = 5$.

Using a number line

A number line shows a different method for adding numbers.
With practice you should not need to draw a number line.

EXAMPLE

Work out $26 + 37$.

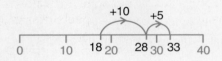

$$\begin{array}{c} \overset{+20}{\frown} \qquad \overset{+6}{\frown} \\ \hline 0 \quad 10 \quad 20 \quad 30 \quad \overset{37}{|}\ 40 \quad 50 \quad \overset{57}{|}\ 60\ 63 \quad 70 \end{array}$$

$26 + 37$ is the same as $37 + 26$.
$37 + 20 = 57$ (adding 20)
$57 + 6 = 63$ (adding 6)
So $26 + 37 = 63$.

Working in context

1. Identify the calculation required by the question.
2. Do the calculation.
3. Give the answer to the question using a short sentence.

EXAMPLE

In Year 7 the class attendances were as follows:
    28   30   27   30   25
What was the total attendance?

The total attendance was 140.

$$\begin{array}{r} 2\,8 \\ 3\,0 \\ 2\,7 \\ 3\,0 \\ +\ 2\,5 \\ \hline 1\,4\,0 \\ \hline \scriptstyle 1\ \ 2 \end{array}$$

Exercise **1.3**

Do not use a calculator for this exercise.

1   Here is a number line for $18 + 15$.

$$\begin{array}{c} \overset{+10}{\frown} \qquad \overset{+5}{\frown} \\ \hline 0 \quad 10 \quad \overset{18}{|}\ 20 \quad \overset{28}{|}\ 30\ 33 \quad 40 \end{array}$$

(a)   What is $18 + 10$?
(b)   What is $18 + 15$?

2   Draw a number line for each of the following sums and work out the answers.
(a) $14 + 15$
(b) $18 + 25$
(c) $7 + 36$
(d) $24 + 29$

3   Work these out in your head.
(a) $7 + 5$ (b) $9 + 6$
(c) $15 + 12$ (d) $24 + 32$
(e) $19 + 16$ (f) $26 + 48$
(g) $29 + 41$ (h) $13 + 99$

4   What must be added to each of these numbers to make 100?
(a)   9   (b)   96   (c)   45   (d)   37
(e)   62   (f)   83   (g)   24   (h)   77

5   This signpost is between Poole and London.

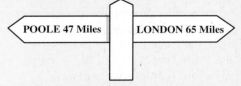

POOLE 47 Miles   LONDON 65 Miles

How far is it from Poole to London?

6

Holiday Special
CYPRUS

| B & B 7 Nights | £249 |
| Insurance | £27 |

What is the total cost of the holiday?

7 Here is part of a price list.

Café Enfant
Price List

Drink.................. 35p
Doughnut........... 27p
Packet of Crisps.. 19p

(a) What is the cost of a drink and a doughnut?
(b) What is the cost of a drink and a packet of crisps?
(c) What is the total cost of buying one of each item?

8

Computer Package

PC   £349
Printer   £125
Software £65

What is the total cost of this computer package?

9 The class attendance in Year 7, Year 8 and Year 9 is shown.

Year 7		Year 8		Year 9	
7A	25	8A	27	9A	26
7B	29	8B	30	9B	25
7C	29	8C	25	9C	27

What is the total attendance
(a) in Year 7,
(b) in Year 8,
(c) in Year 9,
(d) in all nine classes?

10 Work these out by writing the numbers in columns.
(a) 765 + 23
(b) 27 + 56
(c) 76 + 98
(d) 324 + 628
(e) 1273 + 729
(f) 3495 + 8708
(g) 67 + 89 + 45
(h) 431 + 865 + 245

11 What is the total weight of these packages?

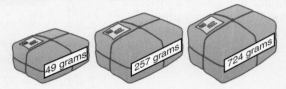

49 grams   257 grams   724 grams

12 The table shows the number of tickets sold each day last week at a cinema.

Mon	Tue	Wed	Thu	Fri	Sat	Sun
125	87	95	105	278	487	201

How many tickets were sold altogether?

13 The last four attendances at a football stadium were:
     21 004,   19 750,   18 009,   22 267.
What is the total attendance?

14 Last month Mr Ahmed had the following household bills to pay.

Mortgage	£429
Gas	£ 39
Insurance	£ 26
Electricity	£ 18
Council Tax	£135
Telephone	£ 23

What is the total cost of these bills?

15 The chart shows the distances in kilometres between some towns.

Bath		
153	Woking	
362	367	York

Kathryn drives from Bath to Woking and then from Woking to York.
Calculate the total distance she drives.

Non-calculator methods for subtraction

Writing numbers in columns

Write the numbers in columns according to place value.
The order in which the numbers are written down is important.
Then, in turn, subtract the numbers of units, tens, hundreds, etc.
If the subtraction in a column cannot be done, because the number being subtracted is greater, borrow 10 from the next column.

Work out 7238 − 642.

$$\begin{array}{r} {}^{6}\;{}^{11}\;{}^{1}\;\,7\,2\,3\,8 \\ -\;\;\;6\,4\,2 \\ \hline 6\,5\,9\,6 \end{array}$$

Units: 8 − 2 = 6
Tens: 3 − 4 cannot be done, so borrow 10 from the 2 in the next column. Now 10 + 3 − 4 = 9.
Hundreds: 1 − 6 cannot be done, so borrow 10 from the 7 in the next column. Now 10 + 1 − 6 = 5.
Thousands: 6 − 0 = 6.

You can use addition to check your subtraction.
Does 6596 + 642 = 7238?

$$\begin{array}{r} 6\,5\,9\,6 \\ +\;\;6\,4\,2 \\ \hline 7\,2\,3\,8 \\ {}_{1}\;\;{}_{1} \end{array}$$

EXAMPLES

1
$$\begin{array}{r} {}^{0}\,{}^{16}\,{}^{15}\,{}^{1}\;1\,7\,6\,2 \\ -\;\;\;\;8\,7\,3 \\ \hline 8\,8\,9 \end{array}$$

2
$$\begin{array}{r} {}^{2}\,{}^{9}\,{}^{9}\,{}^{1}\;3\,0\,0\,6 \\ -\;\;1\,8\,4\,7 \\ \hline 1\,1\,5\,9 \end{array}$$

3
$$\begin{array}{r} {}^{8}\,{}^{9}\,{}^{10}\,{}^{1}\;9\,0\,1\,2 \\ -\;\;5\,6\,7\,8 \\ \hline 3\,3\,3\,4 \end{array}$$

Addition is the opposite (inverse) operation to subtraction.
If $a − b = c$,
then $c + b = a$.

Check the answers by addition.

Subtracting numbers in context

EXAMPLE

The table shows the milometer readings for three cars at the start and end of a year.

	Start	End
Car A	2501	10980
Car B	55667	67310
Car C	48050	61909

Which car has done the most miles in the year?

Car A
$$\begin{array}{r} {}^{7}\,{}^{1}\;1\,0\,9\,8\,0 \\ -\;\;\;2\,5\,0\,1 \\ \hline 8\,4\,7\,9 \end{array}$$

Car B
$$\begin{array}{r} {}^{6}\,{}^{12}\,{}^{10}\,{}^{1}\;6\,7\,3\,1\,0 \\ -\;\;5\,5\,6\,6\,7 \\ \hline 1\,1\,6\,4\,3 \end{array}$$

Car C
$$\begin{array}{r} {}^{5}\,{}^{1}\,{}^{8}\,{}^{1}\;6\,1\,9\,0\,9 \\ -\;\;4\,8\,0\,5\,0 \\ \hline 1\,3\,8\,5\,9 \end{array}$$

Car C has done the most miles.

Do not use a calculator for this exercise.

1 Here is a number line for 43 − 16.

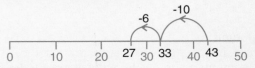

(a) What is 43 − 10?
(b) What is 43 − 16?

2 Draw a number line for each of the following questions and work out the answers.
(a) 58 − 26   (b) 44 − 17
(c) 37 − 19   (d) 51 − 25

3 Write down the answers to the following by working them out in your head.
(a) 100 − 95   (b) 100 − 8
(c) 100 − 57   (d) 100 − 32
(e) 100 − 24   (f) 100 − 83
(g) 100 − 41   (h) 100 − 79

4 Sylvia takes £100 on holiday.
On the first day she spends £13.
How much money has she got left?

5 Work these out in your head.
(a) 9 − 5   (b) 26 − 10
(c) 26 − 9   (d) 87 − 37
(e) 87 − 38   (f) 200 − 110
(g) 204 − 99   (h) 500 − 350
(i) 500 − 199   (j) 1003 − 999

6 Ivan has saved £53. He spends £27.
How much has he got left?

7 Mandy wins £1000.
She spends £385 on a DVD player.
How much has she got left?

8 Work these out by writing the numbers in columns. Use addition to check your answers.
(a) 978 − 624   (b) 843 − 415
(c) 1754 − 470   (d) 407 − 249
(e) 5070 − 2846   (f) 2345 − 1876
(g) 8045 − 1777   (h) 10 000 − 6723

9 A secretary has 67 letters to post.
She has nineteen stamps.
How many more stamps does she need?

10 A car park has spaces for 345 cars.
On Tuesday 256 spaces are used.
How many spaces are not used?

11 A school has 843 pupils.
How many are boys if there are 459 girls?

12 Look at these prices.

Salad Specials

Cucumber	34p each
Lettuce	35p each
Spring onions	27p a bunch

(a) Ricky buys a bunch of spring onions.
He pays with 50p.
How much change is he given?
(b) Liz buys a cucumber and a lettuce.
She pays with £1.
How much change is she given?

13 A shop records the number of tins of soup it has on its shelves.

	Start of the week	End of the week
Tomato	67	28
Oxtail	54	36
Chicken	81	26

(a) How many of each type of soup did the shop sell?
(b) How many tins of soup did the shop sell altogether?

14 Here is a price list for some electrical goods.

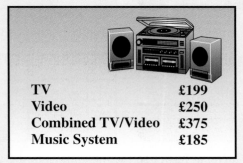

TV	**£199**
Video	**£250**
Combined TV/Video	**£375**
Music System	**£185**

(a) How much more does it cost to buy the TV and Video separately than to buy the Combined TV and Video?
(b) I have £500. How much more do I need to buy the Combined TV and Video, and the Music System?

Multiplication of whole numbers

It is very useful to know your Multiplication Tables up to 10×10.

×	1	2	3	4	5	6	7	8	9	10
1	1	2	3	4	5	6	7	8	9	10
2	2	4	6	8	10	12	14	16	18	20
3	3	6	9	12	15	18	21	24	27	30
4	4	8	12	16	20	24	28	32	36	40
5	5	10	15	20	25	30	35	40	45	50
6	6	12	18	24	30	36	42	48	54	60
7	7	14	21	28	35	42	49	56	63	70
8	8	16	24	32	40	48	56	64	72	80
9	9	18	27	36	45	54	63	72	81	90
10	10	20	30	40	50	60	70	80	90	100

Activity

How quickly can you answer the following questions?

9×5	6×6	7×4	9×6
8×7	9×7	8×8	

Working with a partner ask each other questions from the table.

Non-calculator method for short multiplication

Short multiplication is when the multiplying number is less than 10, e.g. 165×7.
One method multiplies the units, tens, hundreds, etc. in turn.

```
  1 6 5
×     7
-------
1 1 5 5
  1 4 3
```

Units: $7 \times 5 = 35$, which is 5 carry 3.
Tens: $7 \times 6 = 42 +$ carried $3 = 45$, which is 5 carry 4.
Hundreds: $7 \times 1 = 7 +$ carried $4 = 11$, which is 1 carry 1.
There are no more digits to be multiplied by 7, the carried 1 becomes 1 thousand.

EXAMPLES

1
```
  1 6 2
×     4
-------
  6 4 8
    2
```

2
```
  9 0 7 1
×       7
---------
6 3 4 9 7
      4
```

3
```
  4 8 3 5
×       8
---------
3 8 6 8 0
    6 2 4
```

Multiplying numbers in context

EXAMPLE

A minibus holds 16 people. How many people will 6 minibuses hold?

```
    1 6
×    6
------
    9 6
    3
```

6 minibuses hold 96 people.

Do not use a calculator for this exercise.

1 I get 8 doughnuts for £1.
How many doughnuts will I get for £5?

2 When John uses a store card he gets 4 points for every pound he spends.
He spends £18.
How many points does he get?

3 A machine makes 24 jigsaws in an hour.
How many jigsaws will it make in 6 hours?

4 Linda is paid 3p for each leaflet she delivers.
She delivers 184 leaflets.
How much is she paid?

5 Here are the prices of some school equipment.

Pencil	8p
Rubber	12p
Ruler	15p
Protractor	23p

(a) What is the cost of 5 pencils?
(b) What is the cost of 6 rubbers?
(c) What is the cost of 6 rubbers and 4 rulers?
(d) What is the cost of 5 pencils and 7 protractors?
(e) I buy 4 rubbers and 6 rulers.
How much change do I receive from £2?

6 Work these out.
(a) 21×4 (b) 68×2
(c) 17×5 (d) 42×9
(e) 36×7 (f) 183×3
(g) 264×8 (h) 3179×5
(i) 4012×6 (j) 6012×7

7 The table shows the maximum number of people that can be carried on some buses.

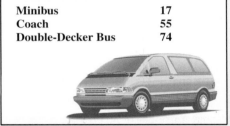

Minibus	17
Coach	55
Double-Decker Bus	74

(a) How many people can 4 minibuses carry?
(b) How many people can 5 coaches carry?
(c) How many people can 9 double-decker buses carry?
(d) A trip for 174 people is planned.
4 coaches are ordered.
How many empty seats will there be?

8 A caretaker puts out 7 rows of chairs.
There are 13 chairs in each row.
How many more chairs are needed for 120 chairs to be put out?

Multiplying a whole number by 10, 100, 1000, . . .

When you multiply a whole number by:
10 The units become 10s, the 10s become 100s, the 100s become 1000s, and so on.
100 The units become 100s, the 10s become 1000s, the 100s become 10 000s, and so on.
1000 The units become 1000s, the 10s become 10 000s, the 100s become 100 000s, and so on.

EXAMPLES

$753 \times 10 = 7530$
$753 \times 100 = 75\ 300$
$753 \times 1000 = 753\ 000$

We can show these multiplications in a table.

100 000s	10 000s	1000s	100s	10s	Units	
			7	5	3	
		7	5	3	0	←753 × 10
	7	5	3	0	0	←753 × 100
7	5	3	0	0	0	←753 × 1000

Explain any patterns you can see.

$100 = 10 \times 10$
Multiplying a number by 100 is the same as multiplying the number by 10 and then by 10 again.

Multiplying a whole number by multiples of 10 (20, 30, 40, . . .)

Work out 753 × 20.

This can be written as:

$$753 \times 20 = 753 \times 10 \times 2 \qquad (20 = 10 \times 2)$$
$$= 7530 \times 2$$
$$= 15\,060$$

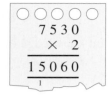

$$\begin{array}{r} 7\,5\,3\,0 \\ \times\quad 2 \\ \hline 1\,5\,0\,6\,0 \\ 1 \end{array}$$

Exercise 1.6

Do not use a calculator for this exercise.

1 Work out.
  (a) 132 × 10
  (b) 123 × 100
  (c) 47 × 1000
  (d) 384 × 100

2 What number should be put in the box to make each of these statements correct?

  (a) 231 × 10 = ☐

  (b) ☐ × 1000 = 514 000

  (c) 172 × ☐ = 17 200

3 Here is a price list from an office catalogue.

| Desk | £120 |
| Chair | £59 |

  (a) What is the cost of 10 desks?
  (b) What is the cost of 100 chairs?
  (c) What is the total cost of 100 desks and 1000 chairs?

4 A packet of 24 custard cream biscuits costs 39 pence.
I buy 10 packets.
  (a) How many biscuits do I buy?
  (b) How much will they cost altogether?

5 I get 10 French francs for £1.
How many French francs will I get for £25?

6 A bag of compost costs £12.
1 m² of turf costs £7.
  (a) What is the cost of 10 bags of compost?
  (b) What is the cost of 100 m² of turf?
  (c) What is the total cost of 100 bags of compost and 1000 m² of turf?

7 There are 7 classrooms in a school.
In each classroom there are 30 chairs and 20 tables.
Find the total number of
  (a) chairs,
  (b) tables.

8 Calculate the number of seconds in
  (a) 5 minutes,
  (b) 9 minutes.

9 A farmer has 32 bags of turnips.
Each bag weighs 50 kg.
What is the total weight?

10 Work out.
  (a) 357 × 20
  (b) 632 × 30
  (c) 537 × 40
  (d) 260 × 50
  (e) 186 × 70
  (f) 239 × 90

11 (a) Describe a method of multiplying by 200, 300, 400, and so on.
  (b) Work out (i) 67 × 200,
              (ii) 35 × 300.

12 There are 400 metres in one lap of a running track.
How many metres are there in 25 laps?

Non-calculator method for short division

The process of dividing a number by a number less than 10 is called **short division**.
Short division relies on knowledge of the Multiplication Tables.
What is $32 \div 8$, $42 \div 7$, $72 \div 9$, $54 \div 6$?

Work out $882 \div 7$.

$7\overline{)8\,{}^18\,{}^42}$ Starting from the left:
$\quad$ 1 2 6 $8 \div 7 = 1$ remainder 1, which is 1 carry 1.
$\qquad\qquad$ $18 \div 7 = 2$ remainder 4, which is 2 carry 4.
$\qquad\qquad$ $42 \div 7 = 6$, with no remainder.
$\qquad\qquad$ So $882 \div 7 = 126$.

You can check your division by multiplying.
Does $126 \times 7 = 882$?

EXAMPLES

1 $6\overline{)1\,4\,{}^27\,{}^30}$
$\qquad$ 2 4 5

2 $9\overline{)2\,7\,6\,{}^63}$
$\qquad\qquad$ 3 0 7

Dividing numbers in context

EXAMPLES

1 8 children share 112 sweets.
How many sweets does each child receive?

$112 \div 8$ $\qquad$ $8\overline{)1\,1\,{}^32}$
$\qquad\qquad\qquad$ 1 4

Each child receives 14 sweets.

2 Pencils are boxed in packs of 5.
I have 87 pencils.
How many boxes can I fill?

$87 \div 5$ $\qquad$ $5\overline{)8\,{}^37}$
$\qquad\qquad\qquad$ 1 7 $\quad$ remainder 2

I can fill 17 boxes.
There will be 2 pencils left over.

Exercise **1.7**   Do not use a calculator for this exercise.

1 Here is a price list for drawing instruments:

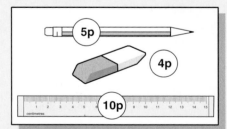

I have 80p.
(a) How many pencils can I buy?
(b) How many rubbers can I buy?
(c) How many rulers can I buy?

2 How many chews costing 6p each can I buy for 90p?

3 Calculate these divisions.
Show your working clearly.
State the remainder if there is one.
Use multiplication to check your answers.
(a) $85 \div 5$
(b) $471 \div 3$
(c) $816 \div 6$
(d) $455 \div 6$
(e) $3146 \div 8$
(f) $824 \div 4$
(g) $9882 \div 9$
(h) $80\,560 \div 4$

4 An icepole costs 9p.
Bernard has 93p.
(a) How many icepoles can he buy?
(b) How much money will he have left?

5 A lollipoop costs 7p.
Maxine has 95p.
(a) How many lollipops can she buy?
(b) What amount of money will she have left?

Dividing a whole number by 10, 100, 1000, . . .

When you divide a whole number by:
10 The 10s become units, the 100s become 10s, the 1000s become 100s, and so on.
100 The 100s become units, the 1000s become 10s, the 10 000s become 100s, and so on.
1000 The 1000s become units, the 10 000s become 10s, the 100 000s become 100s. and so on.

Examples

10 000s	1000s	100s	10s	Units	
	7	5	3	0	
		7	5	3	←753 ÷ 10

$7530 \div 10 = 753$
$12\,400 \div 100 = 124$
$631\,000 \div 1000 = 631$

Draw tables to show the other division sums. Explain any patterns you can see.

Dividing a whole number by multiples of 10 (20, 30, 40, . . .)

Work out $7530 \div 30$.

$7530 \div 30$
$= (7530 \div 10) \div 3$
$= 753 \div 3$ (dividing by 10)
$= 251$ (dividing by 3)

○○○○○○○○○○○○○○○○
$30 = 10 \times 3$
Dividing by 30 is the same as
dividing by 10 and then dividing by 3.

Exercise **1.8**

Do not use a calculator for this exercise.

1 Work out.
(a) $4560 \div 10$
(b) $465\,000 \div 1000$
(c) $64\,000 \div 1000$
(d) $65\,400 \div 100$

2 What number should be put in the box to make each of these statements correct?

(a) $56\,400 \div \square = 564$

(b) $\square \div 1000 = 702$

(c) $35\,000 \div \square = 3500$

3 How many £20 notes are needed to pay a bill of £240?

4 A coach can carry 50 people.
How many coaches are needed to carry 350 people?

5 A box holds 40 matches.
How many boxes are needed to hold 1000 matches?

6 Hannah completes a puzzle in 420 seconds.
How many minutes is this?

7 Work out.
(a) $7590 \div 30$ (b) $7110 \div 90$
(c) $21\,480 \div 40$ (d) $7560 \div 60$
(e) $900 \div 20$ (f) $30\,650 \div 50$

8 (a) Describe a method to divide by multiples of 100 (200, 300, 400, …)
(b) Work out:
(i) $13\,000 \div 500$
(ii) $329\,600 \div 800$

Long multiplication

Long multiplication is used when the multiplying number is greater than 10, e.g. 24×17.

Work out 24×17.

$$\begin{array}{rl} 24 & \\ \times\ 17 & \\ \hline 168 & \leftarrow 24 \times 7 = 168 \\ +\ 240 & \leftarrow 24 \times 10 = 240 \\ \hline 408 & \\ \hline \end{array}$$

A standard non-calculator method for doing long multiplication multiplies the number by:

- the units figure, then
- the tens figure, then
- the hundreds figure, and so on.

All these answers are added together.

EXAMPLES

1

$$\begin{array}{rl} 145 & \\ \times\ 62 & \\ \hline 290 & \leftarrow 145 \times 2 \\ +\ 8700 & \leftarrow 145 \times 60 \\ \hline 8990 & \\ \hline \end{array}$$

2

$$\begin{array}{rl} 273 & \\ \times\ 234 & \\ \hline 1092 & \leftarrow 273 \times 4 \\ 8190 & \leftarrow 273 \times 30 \\ +\ 54600 & \leftarrow 273 \times 200 \\ \hline 63882 & \\ \hline \end{array}$$

Long division

Long division works in exactly the same way as short division, except that all the working out is written down.

Consider $952 \div 7$.

$$\begin{array}{r} 136 \\ 7\overline{)952} \\ 7 \\ \hline 25 \\ 21 \\ \hline 42 \\ 42 \\ \hline 0 \\ \hline \end{array}$$

$9 \div 7 = 1$ and a remainder.
What is the remainder?
$1 \times 7 = 7$ (write below the 9).
$9 - 7 = 2$ (which is the remainder).
Bring down the next figure (5) to make 25.
Repeat the above process.
$25 \div 7 = 3$ and a remainder.
$3 \times 7 = 21$, $25 - 21 = 4$ (remainder).
Bring down the next figure (2) to make 42 and repeat the process.
$42 \div 7 = 6$, but there is no remainder.
$6 \times 7 = 42$, $42 - 42 = 0$ (remainder).
There are no more figures to be brought down and there is no remainder.
So $952 \div 7 = 136$.

Using short division:

$$\begin{array}{r} 7\overline{)9^{2}5^{4}2} \\ 136 \end{array}$$

Long division process

→ ÷ (obtain biggest answer possible)
× } calculates
− } the remainder
Bring down the next figure

Repeat process until there are no more figures to be brought down.

EXAMPLE

How many 27p stamps can I buy for £5? What change am I given?
£5 is the same as 500p.

$500 \div 27$

$$\begin{array}{r} 18 \\ 27\overline{)500} \\ 27 \\ \hline 230 \\ 216 \\ \hline 14 \\ \hline \end{array}$$

27 goes into 50 once with a remainder of 23.
Bring down the 0 to make 230.
$27 \times 8 = 216$, so $230 \div 27 = 8$ remainder 14.

18 stamps with 14p change.

Exercise 1.9

Do not use a calculator for this exercise.

1 Work out:
(a) 17×12 (b) 23×15
(c) 42×32 (d) 76×32
(e) 143×34 (f) 718×54

2 A box holds 12 tins of soup.
How many tins will 18 boxes hold?

3 A computer prints 17 symbols on a line.
How many symbols will it print on
15 lines?

4 A restaurant charges £23 for dinner.
What is the total charge for 42 dinners?

5 A company has 47 shops.
Each shop employs 28 people.
How many people are employed
altogether?

6 A coach trip costs £29 per person.
48 people go on the trip.
How much money is paid altogether?

7 Here is a price list for some office
furniture:

Office Supplies

Desk	£126
Cabinet	£149

What is the total cost of 14 desks and
23 cabinets?

8 Work out:
(a) $473 \div 11$ (b) $480 \div 15$
(c) $324 \div 12$ (d) $544 \div 17$
(e) $624 \div 13$ (f) $943 \div 23$
(g) $777 \div 37$ (h) $841 \div 29$

9 Work these out and state the remainder
each time.
(a) $410 \div 25$ (b) $607 \div 24$
(c) $800 \div 45$ (d) $754 \div 57$

10 A pint of milk costs 29 pence.
How many pints of milk can be bought
for £5?
How much change will there be?

11 Tins of beans are packed in boxes of 24.
A supplier has 1000 tins of beans.
(a) How many full boxes is this?
(b) How many tins are left over?

12 Here is a price list.

Price List

Packet of Crisps	25p
Biscuit	14p
Can of Drink	35p

I have £5.
In each case state the change if there is any.
(a) How many packets of crisps can I buy?
(b) How many biscuits can I buy?
(c) How many cans of drink can I buy?

What you need to know

You should be able to:
- Read and write whole numbers expressed in figures and words.
- Order whole numbers.
- Recognise the place value of each digit in a number.
- Use mental methods to carry out addition and subtraction.
- Carry out accurately non-calculator methods for addition and subtraction.
- Know the Multiplication Tables up to 10×10.
- Carry out multiplication by a number less than 10 (short multiplication).
- Multiply whole numbers by 10, 100, 1000, . . .
- Multiply whole numbers by 20, 30, 40, . . .
- Carry out division by a number less than 10 (short division).
- Divide whole numbers by 10, 100, 1000, . . .
- Divide whole numbers by 20, 30, 40, . . .
- Carry out long multiplication.
- Carry out long division.

IDEAS FOR INVESTIGATION

Write down a three-digit number.
   Write in words.
   Count the letters.
   Write this number in words.
   Count the letters.
   Write this number in words
and so on.

Example
569, five hundred and sixty-nine
 23, twenty-three
 11, eleven
  6, six
  3, three
  5, five
  4, four

❶ Start with the number 207.
What number do you end up with?

❷ Repeat the process starting with a different number.

❸ Do you always end up with the same number?

Review Exercise

Do not use a calculator for this exercise.

❶ (a) Write the number 807 in words.
  (b) Write the number one hundred thousand and fifty-seven in figures.
  (c) Write these numbers in order.
      Start with the smallest number.
      5342, 2104, 483, 2901, 712

❷ In the number 3549 the 4 represents 4 tens. What does the 5 represent?

❸ (a) What must be added to 33 to make 100?
  (b) What numbers are needed to complete these sums?

   (i) $100 - 17 = \square$

   (ii) $55 + \square = 100$

   (iii) $100 - \square = 29$

  (c) (i) Work out 5×100.
      (ii) Work out $2500 \div 100$.

❹ (a) The number 3 is multiplied by 1000.
      Write the answer in words.
  (b) The number seven is multiplied by one million.
      Write the answer in figures.

❺ (a) Continue this pattern of additions.
      Stop when the answer is greater than 100.
         $6 + 20 = 26$
        $26 + 20 = 46$
        $46 + 20 = 66$
        $\ldots + \ldots = \ldots$
        $\ldots + \ldots = \ldots$
        $\ldots + \ldots = \ldots$

  (b) Jane said: "If you start with a number between 1 and 10 and keep adding 20, you will always get over 100 in 5 additions."

      Try to explain **why** it is true or false.
                                        Edexcel

❻ By using each of the digits 7, 2, 8 and 5,
  (a) write the largest four-digit number you can,
  (b) write the smallest four-digit **odd** number you can.

❼ Work out.
  (a) $99 + 9$ (b) $500 - 9$ (c) $465 + 12 + 1582$ (d) $2465 - 1878$

❽ The chart shows the distances in miles between some towns.

Liverpool				
35	Manchester			
109	70	Nottingham		
77	37	44	Sheffield	
102	71	87	61	York

Isaac drives from Liverpool to Nottingham, from Nottingham to York and then from York back to Liverpool.
Calculate the total distance he drives.

9 In the game of darts the scores of the three darts are added together. These are then taken away from the current total to calculate the new total. In each case work out the score of the three darts and the new total.

	Current Total	1st dart	2nd dart	3rd dart	Score	New Total
(a)	501	60	18	19	[ ]	[ ]
(b)	420	19	57	38	[ ]	[ ]
(c)	301	50	25	17	[ ]	[ ]

10 Work out.
(a) 78×3 (b) $78 \div 3$ (c) 718×9 (d) $1446 \div 6$

11 Write down the answers to these questions.
(a) 735×100 (b) 214×30 (c) $3\,020\,000 \div 1000$ (d) $18\,480 \div 40$

12 Find the cost of 15 cameras at £145 each.

Edexcel

13 Lauren does a paper round.
She delivers 47 newspapers, 6 days a week for 52 weeks a year.
How many newspapers does she deliver altogether in one year?

14 A supermarket orders 1800 kg of potatoes.
The potatoes are delivered in 15 kg bags.
How many bags are delivered?

15 One thousand chocolate biscuits are packed in boxes of 6.
(a) How many full boxes will there be?   (b) How many biscuits will be left over?

16 A group of 43 people pay £379 each to go on a skiing holiday.
What is the total cost of the holiday?

17 The table shows the value of each prize and the number of winners in a lottery.

Value of each prize	Number of winners
£1 000 000	1
£ 100 000	4
£ 50 000	10
£ 25 000	17
£ 10 000	44
£ 5000	87

(a) Work out the total number of winners.
(b) Work out the total amount of prize money won.

Edexcel

18 Bob is taking 26 boys to watch a football match.
The total cost is £442.
What is the cost for each boy?

19 Sylvia has collected £1632 to provide Christmas meals for retired people.
Each meal costs £12. How many meals can she provide?

20 A lorry is loaded with 25 boxes. Each box weighs 55 kg.
(a) Work out what the boxes weigh altogether.
The maximum load the lorry can take is 5000 kg.
(b) Work out how many more boxes can be loaded onto the lorry.

Edexcel

2 Whole Numbers 2

Order of operations in a calculation

What is $4 + 3 \times 5$*?*   It is not sensible to have two possible answers.
It has been agreed that calculations are done obeying certain rules:

First	Brackets and Division line
Second	Divide and Multiply
Third	Addition and Subtraction

EXAMPLES

1 $4 + 3 \times 5$ $= \quad 4 + 15$ $= \quad 19$

2 $10 \div 2 + 3$ $= \quad 5 + 3$ $= \quad 8$

3 $10 \div (2 + 3)$ $= \quad 10 \div 5$ $= \quad 2$

4 $(5 + 6) \times 3 + 4$ $= \quad 11 \times 3 + 4$ $= \quad 33 + 4$ $= \quad 37$

5 $\dfrac{12}{11 - 8} - 3$ $= \quad \dfrac{12}{3} - 3$ $= \quad 4 - 3$ $= \quad 1$

This is the same as $12 \div (11 - 8) - 3$.

Exercise **2.1**   Do not use a calculator for this exercise.

1 Work these out.

(a) $7 + 6 \times 5$ (b) $7 - (6 - 2)$ (c) $24 \div 6 + 5$

(d) $7 \times 6 + 8 \times 2$ (e) $10 \div 5 + 8 \div 2$ (f) $(5 - 2) \times 7 + 9$

(g) $60 \div (5 + 7)$ (h) $60 \div 5 + 7$ (i) $4 \times 3 + 2$

(j) $4 \times (3 + 2)$ (k) $12 \times (20 - 2) \div 9$ (l) $36 \div (5 + 4)$

(m) $4 \times 12 \div 8 - 6$ (n) $\dfrac{15}{18 - 3} + 4$ (o) $\dfrac{22 - 4}{9} + 12 \div 3$

2 Choose from the four signs $+$, $-$, $\times$ and $\div$ to make these sums correct.

(a) $5 \quad 6 \quad 7 = 37$ (b) $5 \quad 6 \quad 7 = 47$ (c) $15 \quad 8 \quad 9 = 87$

(d) $15 \quad 8 \quad 9 = 129$ (e) $15 \quad 8 \quad 9 = 111$ (f) $15 \quad 5 \quad 3 = 6$

(g) $5 \quad 24 \quad 6 = 1$ (h) $19 \quad 19 \quad 7 = 8$ (i) $4 \quad 4 \quad 7 \quad 2 = 30$

3 Using all the numbers 6, 3, 2 and 1 in this order, brackets and the signs $+$, $-$, $\times$ and $\div$ make all the numbers from 1 to 10.

$6 - 3 \times 2 + 1 = 1$, $6 - 3 - 2 + 1 = 2$,   and so on.

Problems involving number

The number skills you have met in Chapter 1 and Exercise 2.1 can be applied to practical situations.

EXAMPLES

Set your working out clearly so that someone else can follow what you are doing.

Harold loads 5 parcels each weighing 3 kg and 4 parcels each weighing 7 kg onto a trolley. The unloaded trolley weighs 18 kg. What is the total weight of the trolley and the parcels?

$$\text{Total weight} = (5 \times 3) + (4 \times 7) + 18 \text{ kg}$$
$$= 15 + 28 + 18 \text{ kg}$$
$$= 61 \text{ kg}$$

The total weight of the trolley and parcels is 61 kg.

How could a calculator be used to answer this problem?

Exercise 2.2

You should be able to do this exercise without using your calculator.
Having completed the exercise use a calculator to check your working.

1 Claire is 16 cm taller than Rachel. Their heights add up to 312 cm. How tall is Rachel?

2 Look at this price list.
   (a) What is the total cost of a can of drink and a packet of crisps?
   (b) What change does Alec get from £2, if he buys 2 bars of chocolate, a doughnut and 3 packets of biscuits?
   (c) How much does Lisa save if she buys 2 packets of crisps and a can of drink instead of a pack of biscuits and 2 bars of chocolate?

School Tuck Shop
Price List

Can of drink	36p
Packet of crisps	22p
Bar of chocolate	28p
Doughnut	25p
Pack of biscuits	39p

3 The caretaker set out 17 rows of chairs. There are 15 chairs in each row.
How many more chairs are needed to provide seats for 280 people?

4 The total weight of a carton which contains 6 eggs is 520 g. The carton weighs 70 g.
What is the weight of each egg?

5 A cupboard is 90 cm wide. It is placed between two walls which are 160 cm apart. The gap between the cupboard and each wall is the same. What is the size of the gap?

6 A roll of wire is 550 cm long. From the roll, Hilary cuts 3 pieces which each measure 85 cm and 4 pieces which each measure 35 cm. How much wire is left on the roll?

7 A box, which contains 48 matches, has a total weight of 207 g.
If each match weighs 4 g, what is the weight of the empty box?

8 The admission charges to a zoo are £4 for a child and £7 for an adult. Zoe is organising a trip to the zoo for a group of people and worked out that the total cost would be £336.
She collected £84 from the adults in the group.
   (a) How many children are in the group?
   (b) What is the total number of people in the group?

Approximation

In real-life it is not always necessary to use exact numbers. A number can be **rounded** to an **approximate** number. Numbers are rounded according to how accurately we wish to give details. For example, the distance to the Sun can be given as 93 million miles.

Can you think of other situations where approximations might be used?

Rounding to the nearest 10, 100, 1000

If there were 21 152 people at a football match the newspaper report could say, "21 000 at the football match".

Consider the number 7487.
The same number can be rounded to different degrees of accuracy depending on the situation.

Rounding to the nearest 10

7487 is between 7480 and 7490,
but it is closer to 7490.
7487 rounded to the nearest 10 is
7490.

7480   7487   7490

Rounding to the nearest 100

7487 is between 7400 and 7500,
but it is closer to 7500.
7487 rounded to the nearest 100 is
7500.

7400   7487   7500

Rounding to the nearest 1000

7487 is between 7000 and 8000,
but it is closer to 7000.
7487 rounded to the nearest 1000
is 7000.

7000   7487   8000

The number 7487 can be approximated as 7490, 7500 or 7000 depending on the degree of accuracy required.

It is a convention to round a number which is in the middle to the higher number.
75 to the nearest 10 is 80.
450 to the nearest 100 is 500.
8500 to the nearest 1000 is 9000.

EXAMPLES

	Rounded to the nearest 10	Rounded to the nearest 100	Rounded to the nearest 1000
7547	7550	7500	8000
973	970	1000	1000
62 783	62 780	62 800	63 000
9125	9130	9100	9000

1 (a) Which of these numbers:
4850, 4860, 4870, 4880, 4890
is closest to 4872?

(b) Which of these numbers:
4600, 4700, 4800, 4900, 5000
is closest to 4872?

(c) Which of these numbers:
3000, 4000, 5000, 6000
is closest to 4872?

2 Round the number 7425
(a) to the nearest 10,
(b) to the nearest 100,
(c) to the nearest 1000.

3 Round each of the following numbers to
the nearest ten.
(a) 42   (b) 76   (c) 85
(d) 132   (e) 736   (f) 1843

4 Round each of the following numbers to
the nearest hundred.
(a) 432   (b) 550   (c) 409
(d) 1437   (e) 53   (f) 2584

5 Copy and complete this table.

Number	Round to the nearest 10	Round to the nearest 100	Round to the nearest 1000
7613	7610	7600	8000
977			
61 115			
9714			
623			
9949			
5762			
7501			
7500			
7499			

6 Round each of the following numbers to
the nearest thousand.
(a) 7482   (b) 3765   (c) 18 500
(d) 21 084   (e) 49 832   (f) 132 498

7 Write down these figures to appropriate
degrees of accuracy.
(a) There were 19 141 people at the
football match.
(b) There were 259 people on the plane.
(c) Tom had 141 marbles.
(d) The class raised £49.67 for charity.
(e) There are 129 students in Year 7.
(f) The population of the town is
24 055.
(g) The land area of the country is
309 123 km^2.
(h) The distance to London is 189 km.
(i) Sarah spent £50.99 on CDs.
(j) There were 693 students in the
school.

8 Write down a number each time which
fits these roundings.
(a) It is 750 to the nearest 10 but 700 to
the nearest 100.
(b) It is 750 to the nearest 10 but 800 to
the nearest 100.
(c) It is 8500 to the nearest 100 but
8000 to the nearest 1000.
(d) It is 8500 to the nearest 100 but
9000 to the nearest 1000.

9 "43 000 spectators watch thrilling Test
Match."
The number reported in the newspaper
was correct to the nearest thousand.
What is the smallest possible number of
spectators?

10 Carl has 140 postcards in his collection.
The number is given to the nearest ten.
What is the smallest and greatest number
of postcards Carl could have in his
collection?

11 "You require 2700 tiles to tile your
swimming pool."
This figure is correct to the nearest 100.
What is the greatest number of tiles
needed?

Rounding in real-life problems

In a real-life problem a rounding must be used which gives a common sense answer.

Penny is arranging a BBQ.
50 people have been invited.
She caters for everyone to have one burger.
Burgers are sold in packs of 12.
How many packs of burgers should she buy?

The answer is found by working out $50 \div 12$.
In 4 packs, there are $4 \times 12 = 48$ burgers.
In 5 packs, there are $5 \times 12 = 60$ burgers.
$50 \div 12 = 4$ remainder 2.
Penny must buy 5 packs in order that everybody has one burger.
(In fact she will have 10 left over for those who might want a second burger.)

EXAMPLES

1 A Year group in a school are going to Alton Towers. There are 242 students and teachers going.
Each coach can carry 55 passengers.
How many coaches should be ordered?

$242 \div 55 = 4.4$
This should be rounded up to 5.

4 coaches can only carry 220 passengers
($4 \times 55 = 220$).

2 Filing cabinets are to be placed along a wall.
The available space is 460 cm.
Each cabinet is 80 cm wide.
How many can be fitted in?

$460 \div 80 = 5.75$
This should be rounded down to 5.

Although the answer is nearly 6 the 6th cabinet would not fit in.

Exercise 2.4

Do not use a calculator for this exercise.

1 49 students are waiting to go to a stadium.
A minibus can take 15 students at a time.
How many trips are needed?

2 A classroom wall is 700 cm long.
How many tables, each 120 cm long, could be fitted along the wall?

3 76 people are waiting to go to the top of Canary Wharf.
The lift can take 8 people at a time.
How many times must the lift go up?

4 A group of 175 people are going to Margate by coach.
Each coach can carry 39 people.
How many coaches are needed?

5 There are 210 students in a year group.
They each need an exercise book.
The exercise books are sold in packs of 25.
How many packs should be ordered?

6 Car parking spaces should be 2.5 m wide. How many can be fitted into a car park which is 61 m wide?

7 A sweet manufacturer puts 17 sweets in a bag. How many bags can be made up if there are 500 sweets?

8 How many 26p stamps can be bought for £5?

9 How many grapefruits, each costing 29p, can be bought for £1.50?

10 Kim needs 26 candles for a cake.
The candles are sold in packs of 4.
How many packs must she buy?

11 Lauren needs 50 doughnuts for a party.
Doughnuts are sold in packs of 12.
How many packs must she buy?

Rounding using significant figures

Another kind of rounding uses **significant figures**.
The **most** significant figure in a number is the figure which has the greatest place value.

Consider the number 237.
The figure 2 has the greatest place value. It is worth 200.
So 2 is the most significant figure.

12 is between 10 and 20 but it is closer to 10.
12 rounded to one significant figure is 10.

267 is between 200 and 300 but it is closer to 300.
267 rounded to one significant figure is 300.

Noughts which are used to locate the decimal point and preserve the place value of other figures are not significant.

> **To round a number to one significant figure:**
> - Identify the most significant figure.
> - Look at the next figure to the right of this and
>   if the figure is 5 or more round up,
>   if the figure is less than 5 round down.
> - Add noughts, as necessary, to preserve place value.

EXAMPLES

Number	Rounded to 1 sig. fig.
26	30
135	100
1478	1000
2890	3000
75	80
150	200
2500	3000

Notation
Often significant figure is shortened to sig. fig.

Estimation

It is always a good idea to find an **estimate** for any calculation.
An estimate is used to check that the answer to the actual calculation is of the right magnitude (size).
If the answer is very different to the estimate then a mistake has possibly been made.

Estimation is done by approximating every number in the calculation to 1 significant figure.
The calculation is then done using the approximated values.

EXAMPLES

 Estimate 421×48.

Round 421 to one significant figure: 400
Round 48 to one significant figure: 50
$400 \times 50 = 20\,000$

Use long multiplication to calculate
421×48.
Comment on your answer.

 Estimate $608 \div 19$.

Round the numbers in the calculation to one significant figure.
$600 \div 20 = 30$

Use long division to calculate
$608 \div 19$.
Comment on your answer.

Do not use a calculator for this exercise.

1 Copy and complete this table.

Number	Rounded to 1 sig. fig.
17	
32	
467	
523	
350	
2400	
620	
99	

2 Bernard plans to buy a conservatory costing £6328 and furniture costing £1784.
By using approximations to one significant figure, estimate the total amount Bernard plans to spend.

3 Make estimates to these calculations by using approximations to 1 sig. fig.
(a) (i) 39×21 (ii) 115×18 (iii) 797×53 (iv) 913×59
(b) (i) $76 \div 18$ (ii) $597 \div 29$ (iii) $889 \div 61$ (iv) $3897 \div 82$

4 Chairs are arranged in rows.
There are 18 chairs in each row.
Estimate the total number of chairs in 27 rows.

5 A book contains 576 pages which are grouped into 32 chapters of equal length.
Estimate the number of pages in each chapter.

6 (a) When estimating the answer to 29×48 the approximations 30 and 50 are used.
Why can you tell that the estimation must be bigger than the actual answer?
(b) When estimating the answer to $182 \div 13$ the approximations 200 and 10 are used.
Will the estimate be bigger or smaller than the actual answer? Explain your answer.

Using a calculator

A calculator is a very useful piece of equipment.
But you must know how to use it properly.

Calculators vary but almost all do calculations in the right order.
Use your calculator to work out
    $3 + 4 \times 5$
by entering the following key sequence:

| 3 | + | 4 | × | 5 | = |

You should get the answer 23.

If you wish to work out
    $(3 + 4) \times 5$
then you must use the brackets on your calculator.
Try entering the following key sequence:

| (| 3 | + | 4 |) | × | 5 | = |

You should get the answer 35.

If your calculator works in a different way refer to the instruction booklet supplied with the calculator or ask someone for help.

EXAMPLES

Work out the following without using a calculator.
Then use a calculator to check your answers.

Question	Without a calculator	Using a calculator

(a) $\dfrac{5 \times 6}{1 + 2}$ $\dfrac{5 \times 6}{1 + 2} = \dfrac{30}{3} = 10$

Answer: 10

(b) $\dfrac{50}{22 - 12}$ $\dfrac{50}{22 - 12} = \dfrac{50}{10} = 5$

[5] [0] [÷] [(] [2] [2]
[−] [1] [2] [)] [=]

Answer: 5

(c) $\dfrac{8 \times 9}{6 \times 6}$ $\dfrac{8 \times 9}{6 \times 6} = \dfrac{72}{36} = 2$

[(] [8] [×] [9] [)] [÷]
[(] [6] [×] [6] [)] [=]

Answer: 2

Exercise 2.6

1 Work out the following without using a calculator.
Then use a calculator to check your answers.
Write down the key sequence you pressed on your calculator.

(a) $\dfrac{20}{22 - 18}$ (b) $\dfrac{4 \times 6}{7 + 5}$ (c) $\dfrac{21 - 9}{3 \times 2}$ (d) $\dfrac{48}{10 + 6}$ (e) $\dfrac{56 - 30}{13}$ (f) $\dfrac{12 + 18}{11 - 5}$

2   (a)   Write down the numbers you could use to get an approximate answer to 196×311.
    (b)   Write down your approximate answer.
    (c)   Use a calculator to find the difference between your approximate answer and the exact answer.

3 Make estimates to these calculations by using approximations to 1 sig. fig.
Then carry out the calculations accurately using a calculator.
Compare your estimates with your answers.
   (a) 32×41 (b) 12×66 (c) 58×34 (d) 72×45
   (e) 34×78 (f) 17×219 (g) 291×56 (h) 312×23

4 Make estimates to these calculations by using approximations to 1 sig. fig.
Then carry out the calculations accurately using a calculator.
Compare your estimates with your answers.
   (a) $594 \div 18$ (b) $609 \div 21$ (c) $256 \div 16$ (d) $840 \div 35$

5 Make estimates of the following by rounding each number in the calculation to one significant figure.
Then use a calculator to carry out an accurate calculation.
Compare the answer given by the calculator to the estimate.
   (a) $\dfrac{51 \times 199}{22}$ (b) $\dfrac{581}{12 \times 29}$ (c) $\dfrac{18 \times 57}{38 \div 4}$ (d) $\dfrac{62}{86 \div 9} + 48$

- The **order of operations** in a calculation.
  First   Brackets and Division line
  Second   Divide and Multiply
  Third   Addition and Subtraction

- A number can be rounded to an **approximate** number.

- How to round numbers to the nearest 10, 100, 1000.

- In real-life problems a rounding must be used which gives a commonsense answer.

- How to approximate to one **significant figure**.
  1. Identify the most significant figure.
  2. Look at the next figure to the right of this and
       if the figure is 5 or more round up,
       if the figure is less than 5 round down.
  3. Add noughts, as necessary, to preserve place value.

- How to use approximations to **estimate** that the actual answer to a calculation is of the right magnitude (size).

- How to use a calculator to check answers to calculations.

Review Exercise

Do not use a calculator for this exercise.

1 Round 8475
  (a) to the nearest 10   (b) to the nearest 100   (c) to the nearest 1000

2 The actual number of people who watched an election broadcast was 3 967 234.
  (a) A radio report gave the number to the nearest thousand.
      What number did they use?
  (b) A newspaper headline gave the number to the nearest million.
      What number did they use?

3 The price of a sofa is **eight hundred and seventy-nine** pounds.
  (a) Write the price of the sofa in figures.
  (b) Write this price to the nearest hundred pounds.

Edexcel

4 (a)

> ### THE HERALD
> **6000 ATTEND RALLY**

The number in the newspaper was given to the nearest 1000.
What is the smallest possible number of people that attended?

  (b) 38 569 people attended a concert.
    (i) Copy and complete this newspaper headline using a suitably rounded number.

> "....................... ATTEND CONCERT"

    (ii) Copy and complete this sentence.
          My number is rounded to the nearest …… people.

5 Jonathan buys a new car for £9495.
His friend says, "That's £10 000 to the nearest £1000."
Is he correct?
Explain your answer.

6 Calculate these.
Remember to do the operations in the right order.
(a) $2 + 6 \times 8$ (b) $3 \times 6 - 4$ (c) $72 \div 8 + 1$ (d) $(9 - 4) \times (3 + 7)$

7 Alys is given this sum: $84 + 16 \times 5$
She works out the answer as 500.
Is she right?
Explain your answer.

8 Anton pays 84 pence for a cucumber and a lettuce.
The lettuce costs 6 pence more than the cucumber.
How much does the cucumber cost?

9 A plank of wood is 396 cm in length.
The plank is cut into two pieces.
One piece is 28 cm longer than the other.
How long is the shorter piece of wood?

10 George needs 100 tiles to cover his kitchen floor.
The tiles are sold in boxes of 15.
How many boxes does he need to buy?

11 A school is planning a disco for 936 pupils.
Each pupil will be given 1 can of drink.
Cans of drink are sold in trays of 24.
Work out how many trays of drinks will be needed.
                                         Edexcel

12 Round these numbers to 1 significant figure.
(a) 72   (b) 138   (c) 754   (d) 650   (e) 78   (f) 987

13 A concert hall has 22 rows of seats. Each row has 69 seats.
The total number of seats is 22×69.

(a) Write down the numbers you could use to get an approximate answer to 22×69.
(b) Write down your approximate answer.
(c) Using a calculator find the difference between your approximate answer and the exact answer.
                                         Edexcel

14 (a) Write down the numbers you could use to get an approximate answer to 593×312.
(b) Write down your approximate answer.
(c) Use a calculator to find the difference between your approximate answer and the exact answer.

15 Alf is set this problem: $686 - 41 + 398$
Alf works out the answer to be 247.
(a) Use estimation to show that Alf's answer is wrong.
(b) Work out the correct answer.

16 Jo has to calculate $\dfrac{481 + 97}{32}$.
She calculates the answer to be 180.625.
By rounding each number to one significant figure estimate whether her answer is of the right order of magnitude.
Show your working.

CHAPTER 3

Decimals

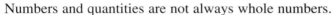

Numbers and quantities are not always whole numbers.
The number system you met in Chapter 1 can be extended to include **decimal numbers**, such as tenths, hundredths, thousandths, and smaller numbers.
A **decimal point** is used to separate the whole number part from the decimal part of the number.

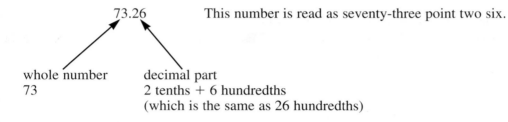

73.26   This number is read as seventy-three point two six.

whole number   decimal part
73   2 tenths + 6 hundredths
                               (which is the same as 26 hundredths)

Place value

In the number 1.53 the digit 1 is worth 1 unit = 1
                          the digit 5 is worth 5 tenths = 0.5
                          the digit 3 is worth 3 hundredths = 0.03

$1.53 = 1 + 0.5 + 0.03$

> 1 unit = 10 tenths
> 1 tenth = 10 hundredths
> 1 hundredth = 10 thousandths
> … and so on.

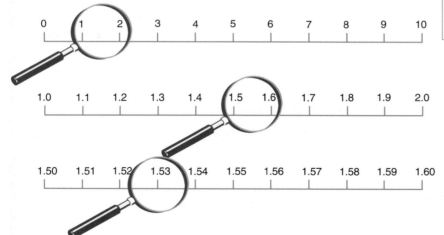

The first digit after the decimal point represents **tenths**.

The second digit after the decimal point represents **hundredths**.

The number 1.53 can be represented by a diagram.

1 unit

5 tenths

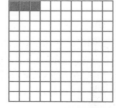

3 hundredths

Ordering decimals

Compare the numbers 52.359 and 52.36. Which number is the bigger?

You can use a grid to compare the numbers.

tens	units	tenths	hundredths	thousandths
5	2 .	3	5	9
5	2 .	3	6	

Start by comparing the digits with the greatest place value, the tens.
Both numbers have 5 tens, so move down to compare the units.
Both numbers have 2 units, so move down to the tenths.
Both numbers have 3 tenths, so move down to the hundredths.
52.359 has 5 hundredths but 52.36 has 6 hundredths.
So 52.36 is bigger than 52.359.

A similar method can be used to place a list of decimal numbers in order.

Decimals . . . Decimals . . . Decimals . . .

EXAMPLES

1 What numbers are arrows *A*, *B* and *C* pointing to on this scale?

There are 10 marks between 2 and 3.
Each mark represents 0.1.
Arrow *A*: 2.2   Arrow *B*: 2.6   Arrow *C*: 2.9

The scale shows the main numbers.
The distance between the main numbers is divided up using marks.
To read a scale you must first work out what the distance between two marks represents.

2 What numbers are arrows *P*, *Q* and *R* pointing to on this scale?

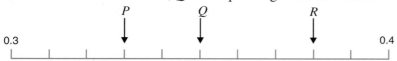

There are 10 marks between 0.3 and 0.4.
Each mark represents 0.01.
Arrow *P*: 0.33   Arrow *Q*: 0.35   Arrow *R*: 0.38

Exercise **3.1**

1 2.564 = 2 + 0.5 + 0.06 + 0.004.
Write these numbers in the same way.
(a) 4.7   (b) 5.55   (c) 7.62   (d) 37.928   (e) 7.541

2 In the number 17.4<u>6</u>2 the value of the underlined figure is 0.06.
Give the value of the underlined figures in the following.
(a) 2.<u>7</u>   (b) 3.5<u>2</u>   (c) 27.<u>4</u>3   (d) 36.42<u>9</u>   (e) 28<u>5</u>.03

3 Write down the numbers shown by these diagrams.

 (a)   (b)

4 (a) Copy the diagram.
   (b) Show the number 1.25 on your diagram.

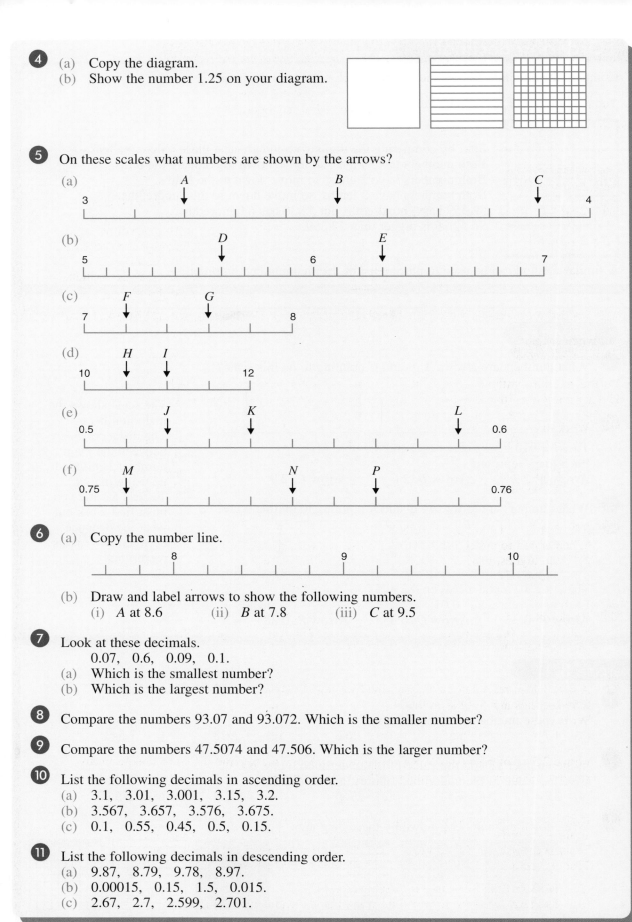

5 On these scales what numbers are shown by the arrows?

(a)

(b)

(c)

(d)

(e)

(f)

6 (a) Copy the number line.

   (b) Draw and label arrows to show the following numbers.
      (i) *A* at 8.6   (ii) *B* at 7.8   (iii) *C* at 9.5

7 Look at these decimals.
      0.07, 0.6, 0.09, 0.1.
   (a) Which is the smallest number?
   (b) Which is the largest number?

8 Compare the numbers 93.07 and 93.072. Which is the smaller number?

9 Compare the numbers 47.5074 and 47.506. Which is the larger number?

10 List the following decimals in ascending order.
   (a) 3.1, 3.01, 3.001, 3.15, 3.2.
   (b) 3.567, 3.657, 3.576, 3.675.
   (c) 0.1, 0.55, 0.45, 0.5, 0.15.

11 List the following decimals in descending order.
   (a) 9.87, 8.79, 9.78, 8.97.
   (b) 0.00015, 0.15, 1.5, 0.015.
   (c) 2.67, 2.7, 2.599, 2.701.

Non-calculator method for addition of decimals

Write the numbers in tidy columns according to place value.
This is easily done by keeping the decimal points in a vertical column.
Start the addition from the right, just as you did for whole numbers.
Use the same method for carrying as well.

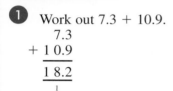

EXAMPLES

1 Work out 7.3 + 10.9.

```
   7.3
+ 1 0.9
  1 8.2
    ₁
```

2 Work out 42.6 + 0.75 + 9.

```
  4 2.6
    0.7 5
+   9.0
  5 2.3 5
    ₁ ₁
```

> You can write 9 as 9.0 or 9.00 to keep your figures tidy. This does not change the value of the number. 42.6 can be written as 42.60

Exercise 3.2

Do this exercise without using your calculator, showing your working clearly.
Having completed the exercise you can use a calculator to check your answers.

1 Work out.
(a) 3.6 + 15.2	(b) 2.6 + 3.8	(c) 14.8 + 3.5
(d) 23.4 + 9.7	(e) 5.14 + 3.72	(f) 8.36 + 4.74
(g) 6.48 + 5.9	(h) 11.8 + 5.69	(i) 7.065 + 5.384
(j) 17.93 + 8.09	(k) 5.06 + 27.3	(l) 12.7 + 5.463

2 3.2   4.1   1.6   2.5   0.8
When added together, which two of these numbers give:
(a) the highest total,   (b) the lowest total,
(c) a total of 6.6,   (d) a total closest to 5?

3 Work out.
(a) 6.54 + 0.27 + 0.03	(b) 2.22 + 0.78 + 0.07	(c) 79.1 + 7 + 0.23
(d) 5.564 + 0.017 + 10.2	(e) 9.123 + 0.71 + 6.2	(f) 16 + 2.98 + 5.9

4 A 4 × 100 m relay team complete the four legs in 10.05 seconds, 10.13 seconds, 9.89 seconds and 9.92 seconds.
What is the total time for the team?

5 I have 2.5 kg of potatoes, 0.5 kg of butter, 0.75 kg of grapes and 0.6 kg of cheese in my shopping bag. What is the total weight of my shopping?

6 In bobsleigh the times of four runs are added together.

Team A records	37.03 sec	37.76 sec	36.89 sec	37.25 sec
Team B records	36.87 sec	37.51 sec	37.03 sec	38.12 sec
Team C records	37.27 sec	37.45 sec	37.64 sec	36.72 sec

(a) Work out the total time for each team.
(b) The team with the lowest time wins. Put the teams in order 1st, 2nd and 3rd.

Non-calculator method for subtraction of decimals

Write the numbers in tidy columns according to place value.
This is easily done by keeping the decimal points in a vertical column.
Start the subtraction from the right, just as you did for whole numbers.
Use the same method for borrowing as well.

EXAMPLES

 Work out $5.6 - 3.8$.

$$\begin{array}{r} \overset{4}{\cancel{5}}.\overset{1}{6} \\ -\ 3.8 \\ \hline 1.8 \end{array}$$

> You can use addition to check your subtraction.
> Does $1.8 + 3.8 = 5.6$?

 Work out $17.1 - 8.72$.

$$\begin{array}{r} 1\,\overset{6}{\cancel{7}}.\overset{10}{\cancel{1}}\,\overset{1}{0} \\ -\ 8.7\,2 \\ \hline 8.3\,8 \end{array}$$

> **Useful tip:**
> Writing 17.1 as 17.10 can make the working easier.
> This does not change the value of 17.1.

Check the answer by addition.

Money

1360p can be written as £13.60

£13.60

complete number   number
of pounds, 13   of pence, 60

£6 can be written as £6.00
There must be exactly **two** figures after the decimal point when a decimal point is used to record amounts of money.

EXAMPLE

I buy a newspaper for 45p, a set of batteries for £2.50 and a book of stamps for £2.
What is the total cost?
How much change should I get from £5?

Working in pounds.

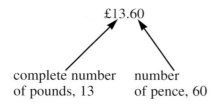

The total cost is £4.95. The change is £0.05 or 5p.

Other uses of decimal notation

Many measurements are recorded using decimals, including time, distance, weight, volume, etc.
The same rules for addition and subtraction can be applied if all the measurements involved are recorded using the same units.

Exercise 3.3

Do this exercise without using your calculator, showing your working clearly.
Having completed the exercise you can use a calculator to check your answers.

 (a)   Work out.

    (i) $6.7 - 2.3$ (ii) $9.47 - 3.24$ (iii) $7.4 - 2.8$
    (iv) $24.5 - 9.7$ (v) $12.48 - 7.52$ (vi) $37.6 - 16.8$
    (vii) $14.15 - 3.07$ (viii) $45.04 - 20.36$

  (b)   Show how addition can be used to check each of the answers to part (a).

2 Work out.
(a) $4.7 - 2.56$ (b) $10 - 4.78$ (c) $9.57 - 4.567$ (d) $9.13 - 7.89$
(e) $17.1 - 8.82$ (f) $9.123 - 2.85$ (g) $14.2 - 5.16$ (h) $3.1 - 1.204$

3 Add these amounts of money. Calculate the change from the given amount.
(a) (i)   45p, 63p, 79p, £1.43   (ii) What is the change from £5?
(b) (i)   £2.47, £6, £1.50, £1.27   (ii) What is the change from £15?
(c) (i)   31p, £0.25, 27p   (ii) What is the change from £10?
(d) (i)   £12, £3.57, 67p   (ii) What is the change from £50?

4 Fred cuts three pieces of wood of length 0.95 m, 1.67 m and 2.5 m from a plank 10 m long. How much wood is left?

5 Kevin is 0.15 m shorter than Sally. Sally is 1.7 m tall. How tall is Kevin?

6 Swimmer A finishes the 100 m freestyle in 51.371 seconds. Swimmer B finishes in 52.090 seconds. How long after Swimmer A does Swimmer B finish?

Working mentally

Addition and subtraction of decimals can be carried out mentally, in your head.
For example, using place value, we know that $2.5 = 2 + 0.5$.
So, adding 2.5 to a number is the same as adding 2 and then adding 0.5.

EXAMPLES

1 Work out $8.31 + 3.58$.

$3.58 = 3 + 0.5 + 0.08$
$8.31 + 3.58$
$= 8.31 + 3 + 0.5 + 0.08$
$= 8.39 + 3 + 0.5$ (adding 8.31 and 0.08)
$= 8.89 + 3$ (adding 8.39 and 0.5)
$= 11.89$

$3.58 = 3 + 0.5 + 0.08$
The adding of 3, 0.5 and 0.08 can be carried out in any order.
Here, we have added the numbers in order of size, starting with the smallest.
Choose a method you find easiest.

2 Work out $25.4 - 8.7$.

$25.4 - 8.7$
$= 25.4 - 8 - 0.7$
$= 24.7 - 8$ (subtracting 0.7 from 25.4)
$= 16.7$

$8.7 = 8 + 0.7$
To subtract 8.7, first subtract 0.7 and then **subtract** 8.
Alternatively, first subtract 8 and then **subtract** 0.7.

Exercise **3.4**

Work these out in your head.
Having completed the exercise you can use a calculator to check your answers.

1 $0.7 + 0.6$ **2** $2.5 + 8.4$ **3** $0.7 + 0.95$

4 $0.36 + 0.54$ **5** $6.47 + 4.53$ **6** $12.06 + 5.72$

7 $2.7 - 1.5$ **8** $1.3 - 0.7$ **9** $2.6 - 0.9$

10 $0.48 - 0.16$ **11** $15.87 - 6.43$ **12** $4 - 0.8$

Multiplying and dividing decimals by powers of 10 (10, 100, 1000, . . .)

When you multiply a decimal by:
10 Each figure moves 1 place to the left.
100 Each figure moves 2 places to the left.
1000 Each figure moves 3 places to the left.
... and so on.

When you divide a decimal by:
10 Each figure moves 1 place to the right.
100 Each figure moves 2 places to the right.
1000 Each figure moves 3 places to the right.
... and so on.

EXAMPLES

276 has the same value as 276.0

Noughts can be used as place fillers to locate the decimal point, as in 2.76 × 1000 = 2760.
If the nought was omitted the value of all other figures would change.

Multiplication

			2 .	7	6
		2	7 .	6	
	2	7	6 .		
2	7	6	0 .		

← 2.76 × 10 = 27.6
← 2.76 × 100 = 276
← 2.76 × 1000 = 2760

Division

3 .	4	5			
0 .	3	4	5		
0 .	0	3	4	5	
0 .	0	0	3	4	5

← 3.45 ÷ 10 = 0.345
← 3.45 ÷ 100 = 0.0345
← 3.45 ÷ 1000 = 0.00345

Exercise 3.5

Do this exercise without using a calculator.

1 Work out the following.
(a) 25.06 × 10
(b) 25.06 × 100
(c) 25.06 × 1000
(d) 0.93 × 10
(e) 0.93 × 100
(f) 0.93 × 1000
(g) 0.0623 × 10
(h) 0.0623 × 100
(i) 0.0623 × 1000
(j) 9.451 × 10
(k) 9.451 × 100
(l) 9.451 × 1000

2 Work out the following.
(a) 37.7 ÷ 10
(b) 37.7 ÷ 100
(c) 37.7 ÷ 1000
(d) 0.27 ÷ 10
(e) 0.27 ÷ 100
(f) 0.27 ÷ 1000
(g) 189.02 ÷ 10
(h) 189.02 ÷ 100
(i) 189.02 ÷ 1000
(j) 9 ÷ 10
(k) 9 ÷ 100
(l) 9 ÷ 1000

3 (a) Multiply 0.064 by (i) 10 (ii) 100 (iii) 1000
(b) Divide 6.4 by (i) 10 (ii) 100 (iii) 1000

4 A biro costs 25 pence.
(a) How much will 10 cost? (b) How much will 100 cost? (c) How much will 1000 cost?

5 One lap of a cycling track is 0.504 km.
(a) How far is 10 laps? (b) How far is 100 laps? (c) How far is 1000 laps?

6 (a) 100 calculators cost £795. How much does one cost?
(b) 1000 pencils cost £120. How much does one cost?
(c) 10 litres of petrol cost £6.69. How would the cost of 1 litre be advertised?

7 Write down pairs of calculations which give the same answer.
12.3 × 1000   12.3 ÷ 100   12.3 × 0.1   12.3 ÷ 0.01   12.3 × 10   12.3 ÷ 0.1
12.3 × 100   12.3 × 0.001   12.3 ÷ 0.001   12.3 ÷ 10   12.3 ÷ 1000   12.3 × 0.01

Multiplying decimals

The result of multiplying two numbers is called the **product**.

Activity

Use a calculator to multiply these decimals.

5.924×2.34 5.2×6.4 6×3.7 5.1×6.02 2.16×5.79

Count the total number of decimal places in the numbers to be multiplied together.
For example, 5.924 has three decimal places (there are three figures to the right of the decimal point) and 2.34 has two decimal places. The product of 5.924 and 2.34 has five decimal places.
Can you find a rule?

How many decimal places does your rule predict 0.5×0.5 should have?

Non-calculator method for multiplying decimals

To multiply decimals without using a calculator:

1 Ignore the decimal points and multiply the numbers using long multiplication.

2 Count the total number of decimal places in the numbers being multiplied together.

3 Place the decimal point so that the answer has the same total number of decimal places.

EXAMPLES

1 Work out 1.7×0.4.

$$
\begin{array}{r}
1.7 \\
\times\, 0.4 \\
\hline
0.6\,8 \\
\hline
{\scriptstyle 2}
\end{array}
$$

1.7 has 1 decimal place.
0.4 has 1 decimal place.
The answer has 2 decimal places.

$1.7 \times 0.4 = 0.68$

2 Work out 4.25×0.18.

$$
\begin{array}{r}
4.2\,5 \\
\times\, 0.1\,8 \\
\hline
3\,4\,0\,0 \\
4\,2\,5\,0 \\
\hline
0.7\,6\,5\,0 \\
\hline
\end{array}
$$

$\leftarrow 425 \times 8$
$\leftarrow 425 \times 10$

The answer must have 4 decimal places because 4.25 has 2 and 0.18 has 2.

$4.25 \times 0.18 = 0.7650$ This can be written as 0.765 which has the same value as 0.7650.

3 Work out 0.2×0.4.

$$
\begin{array}{r}
0.2 \\
\times\, 0.4 \\
\hline
0.0\,8 \\
\hline
\end{array}
$$

0.2 has 1 decimal place.
0.4 has 1 decimal place.
The answer has 2 decimal places.

$0.2 \times 0.4 = 0.08$

$4 \times 2 = 8$
The answer must have 2 decimal places.
Noughts are used in the answer to locate the decimal point and to preserve place value.

Do this exercise without using a calculator, showing your working clearly.
Having completed the exercise you can use a calculator to check your answers.

1 Work these out in your head.
   (a) 0.6 × 2   (b) 1.7 × 5   (c) 3.2 × 4   (d) 12 × 0.3   (e) 5 × 2.6
   (f) 8 × 2.2   (g) 6 × 1.8   (h) 4.3 × 7   (i) 3 × 9.6   (j) 87 × 0.4

2 A puzzle costs £1.90.
   How much will 4 puzzles cost?

3 A cup of coffee costs £1.15.
   How much will 7 cups cost?

4 I buy 5 kites which cost £1.99 each.
   (a) What is the total cost?
   (b) How much change will I get from £10?

5 Here is a price list:
   (a) What is the cost of 5 geometry sets?
   (b) What is the cost of 7 basic calculators?
   (c) I buy 3 geometry sets, 4 basic calculators
        and 5 scientific calculators with £50.
        What is my change?

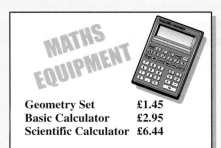

MATHS EQUIPMENT

Geometry Set	£1.45
Basic Calculator	£2.95
Scientific Calculator	£6.44

6 Calculate these products.
   (a) 0.7 × 0.6   (b) 0.2 × 0.3   (c) 2.5 × 3.5   (d) 8.7 × 1.9
   (e) 54 × 0.36   (f) 4.1 × 0.25   (g) 0.9 × 4.32   (h) 13.4 × 0.7
   (i) 0.7 × 5.4   (j) 0.06 × 0.72   (k) 0.35 × 0.08   (l) 0.07 × 0.02

7 (a) Multiply each of these numbers by 0.6.
        (i) 5   (ii) 2.5   (iii) 0.4   (iv) 25
   (b) What do you notice about the original numbers and each of your answers?

8 Work out the cost of these vegetables.
   (a) 0.6 kg of carrots at 35p per kilogram.
   (b) 4.6 kg of potatoes at 40p per kilogram.
   (c) 1.2 kg of cabbage at 65p per kilogram.

9 What is the cost of each of these lengths of material?
   (a) 7 metres of sheeting at £1.99 a metre.
   (b) 4.5 metres of linen at £2.24 a metre.
   (c) 7.8 metres of satin at £6.95 a metre.
   (d) 3.2 metres of silk at £8.20 a metre.

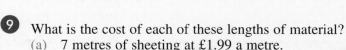

10 Work out the cost for each of these portions of cheese.
   (a) 0.7 kg of Stilton.
   (b) 1.6 kg of Cheddar.
   (c) 0.8 kg of Sage Derby.
   (d) 0.45 kg of Cotherstone.

Select CHEESES

Price per kilogram

Cheddar	£3.20
Cotherstone	£5.20
Sage Derby	£3.25
Stilton	£6.20

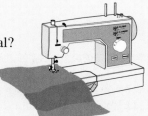

Dividing decimals

Non-calculator method for dividing decimals

Work out $2.4 \div 0.4$.

$2.4 \div 0.4$ can be written as $\dfrac{2.4}{0.4}$

$\dfrac{2.4}{0.4} = \dfrac{2.4 \times 10}{0.4 \times 10} = \dfrac{24}{4} = 6$

It is easier to divide by a whole number than by a decimal.

To divide by a decimal:
1. Multiply the dividing number by a power of 10 (10, 100, 1000, …) so that it becomes a whole number.
2. Multiply the number to be divided by the same number.
3. If necessary the answer will have a decimal point in the same place.

EXAMPLES

1 Work out the following.
   (a) $4 \div 0.8$
      Multiply both numbers by 10.
      $40 \div 8 = 5$

   (b) $9 \div 4$

   $4)\overline{9.0\,^10\,^20}$
   $2.2\,5$

Noughts are added until the division is finished.

2 8 video tapes cost £14.
   How much does each tape cost?

   You must work out $14 \div 8$.

   $8)\overline{1\,4.^60^40}$
   $1.7\,5$

   One video tape costs £1.75.

Noughts can be added to the end of a decimal. Adding noughts does not change the value of the number. 14 has the same value as 14.00.
Continue dividing until either there is no remainder or the required accuracy is obtained.

3 Work out $11.06 \div 0.7$.

   $0.7 \times 10 = 7$ $11.06 \times 10 = 110.6$
   $110.6 \div 7$ has the same value as $11.06 \div 0.7$.

   $7)\overline{1\,1\,^40\,^50.6}$
   $1\,5.8$
   So $11.06 \div 0.7 = 15.8$

Use the same method of working as you used for dividing whole numbers.
The decimal point moves vertically to the same position in the answer.

Exercise 3.7

Do this exercise without using a calculator, showing your working clearly.
Having completed the exercise you can use a calculator to check your answers.

1 Work these out in your head.
   (a) $0.9 \div 3$
   (b) $7.5 \div 5$
   (c) $6.8 \div 4$
   (d) $22.4 \div 7$
   (e) $35.2 \div 8$

2 Work out.
   (a) $7 \div 4$
   (b) $8 \div 5$
   (c) $1.2 \div 8$
   (d) $18.2 \div 7$
   (e) $10.5 \div 6$

3 What number should be put in the box to make each of these statements correct?
   (a) $8 \div 0.5 = 80 \div \square$
   (b) $1.2 \div 0.3 = \square \div 3$
   (c) $3.5 \div 0.07 = \square \div 7$

4 Work out.
   (a) $2 \div 0.5$
   (b) $3 \div 0.2$
   (c) $6 \div 0.4$
   (d) $10 \div 2.5$
   (e) $60 \div 1.2$

5 Work out.
(a) $2.46 \div 0.2$ (b) $0.146 \div 0.05$
(c) $2.42 \div 0.4$ (d) $100.1 \div 0.07$
(e) $0.0025 \div 0.05$ (f) $0.05 \div 0.004$
(g) $4.578 \div 0.7$ (h) $0.3 \div 0.008$

6 Use long division to work out the following.
(a) $81.4 \div 2.2$ (b) $15.12 \div 2.7$
(c) $7 \div 0.16$ (d) $11.256 \div 0.24$
(e) $0.1593 \div 0.15$

7 (a) Divide each of these numbers by 0.6.
     (i) 6   (ii) 3.6   (iii) 0.18
(b) What do you notice about the original numbers and each of your answers?

8 A 3-litre bottle of lemonade costs £1.41. What is the cost of 1 litre of lemonade?

9 A pack of 7 tape cassettes costs £9.45. How much does each tape cassette cost?

10 13 oranges cost £1.43. How much does each orange cost?

11 12 rolls cost £1.08. How much does each roll cost?

12 25 litres of petrol cost £16.70. What is the cost of 1 litre of petrol?

13 A bottle holds 0.25 litres. How many bottles can be filled from a tank holding 30 litres?

14 A steel bar is 12.73 metres long. How many pieces, each 0.19 metres long, can be cut from it?

15 A jug holds 1.035 litres. A small glass holds 0.023 litres. How many of the small glasses would be required to fill the jug?

Changing decimals to fractions

How to change a decimal to a fraction:

Change 0.12 to a fraction.   0.12

Write the decimal without the decimal point.   12
This will be the numerator (top number).

The denominator (bottom number) is a power of 10. $\frac{12}{100}$
The number of noughts is the same as the number of decimal places in the original decimal.

Fractions are covered in further detail in Chapter 6.

Divide both the numerator and denominator by   Divide
the largest possible number.   by 4

This gives the fraction in its simplest form. $\frac{3}{25}$

EXAMPLE

Write the following decimals as fractions in their simplest form.

(a) $0.3 = \frac{3}{10}$ (b) $0.6 = \frac{6}{10} = \frac{3}{5}$ (c) $0.45 = \frac{45}{100} = \frac{9}{20}$

(d) $1.5 = 1 + 0.5$

$ = 1 + \frac{5}{10}$

$ = 1 + \frac{1}{2}$

$ = 1\frac{1}{2}$

$1\frac{1}{2}$ is called a **mixed number**.
It is a mixture of whole numbers and fractions.

1 Write the following decimals as fractions in their simplest form.
    (a) 0.25   (b) 0.5   (c) 0.75   (d) 0.1

2 Write the following decimals as fractions in their simplest form.
    (a) 0.7   (b) 0.4   (c) 0.01   (d) 0.2
    (e) 0.05   (f) 0.15   (g) 0.52   (h) 0.07
    (i) 0.125   (j) 0.65   (k) 0.6   (l) 0.95

3 Change these decimals into mixed numbers.
    (a) 1.7   (b) 2.3   (c) 1.4   (d) 3.25
    (e) 4.8   (f) 12.1   (g) 16.75   (h) 5.05

Rounding using decimal places

What is the cost of 1.75 metres of material costing £1.99 a metre?
    $1.75 \times 1.99 = 3.4825$
The cost of the material is £3.4825 or 348.25p.
As you can only pay in pence, a sensible answer is £3.48 correct
to two decimal places (nearest penny).
This means that there are only two decimal places after the
decimal point.

> Often it is not necessary to use an exact answer. Sometimes it is impossible, or impractical, to use the exact answer.

To round a number to a given number of decimal places

When rounding a number to one, two or more decimal places:
    1. Write the number using one more decimal place than asked for.
    2. Look at the last decimal place and
        • if the figure is 5 or more round up,   • if the figure is less than 5 round down.
    3. When answering a problem remember to include any units and state the degree of
        approximation used.

EXAMPLES

1 Write 2.76435 to (a) 2 decimal places,   (b) 1 decimal place.

    (a) Look at the third decimal place. **4**   (b) Look at the second decimal place. **6**
        This is less than 5, so round down.   This is 5 or more, so round up.
        Answer 2.76   Answer 2.8

2 Write 7.104 to 2 decimal places.
    $7.104 = 7.10$ to 2 d.p.
    The zero is written down because it shows the
    accuracy used, 2 decimal places.

> **Notation**
> Often decimal place is shortened to d.p.

3 Estimate $\dfrac{78.5 \times 0.51}{18.7}$
    Approximating: $78.5 = 80$ to 1 sig. fig.
                    $0.51 = 0.5$ to 1 sig. fig.
                    $18.7 = 20$ to 1 sig. fig.

    $\dfrac{80 \times 0.5}{20} = \dfrac{40}{20} = 2$ (estimate)

    Using a calculator $\dfrac{78.5 \times 0.51}{18.7} = \dfrac{40.035}{18.7} = 2.140909\ldots$

    Is 2.140909 reasonably close to 2? Yes.

> **Remember**
> When you are asked to estimate, write each number in the calculation to one significant figure.

1 Write the number 3.9617 correct to
   (a)   3 decimal places,   (b)   2 decimal places,   (c)   1 decimal place.

2 Write the number 567.654 correct to
   (a)   2 decimal places,   (b)   1 decimal place,   (c)   the nearest whole number.

3 Copy and complete this table.

Number	2.367	0.964	0.965	15.2806	0.056	4.991	4.996
d.p.	1	2	2	3	2	2	2
Answer	2.4						

4 The display on a calculator shows the result of 34 ÷ 7.

What is the result correct to two decimal places?

5 Carry out these calculations giving the answers correct to
   (a)   1 d.p.   (b)   2 d.p.   (c)   3 d.p.
     (i)   6.12 × 7.54   (ii)   89.1 × 0.67   (iii)   90.53 × 6.29
    (iv)   98.6 ÷ 5.78   (v)   67.2 ÷ 101.45

6 In each of these short problems decide upon the most suitable accuracy for the answer.
Then work out the answer.
Give a reason for your degree of accuracy.
   (a)   1.74 metres of cloth at £6.99 a metre.
   (b)   1.74 metres of cloth at £2.05 a metre.
   (c)   0.454 kg of cheese at £5.21 a kg.
   (d)   7 equal sticks measure 250 cm in total when lying end to end.
       How long is each stick?
   (e)   A packet of 6 videotapes costs £7.99.
       How much does one cost?
   (f)   Petrol costs 81.4 pence a litre. I buy 15.6 litres.
       How much will I have to pay?

7 By using approximations to one significant figure find estimates to these products.
Then carry out the calculations with the original figures.
Compare your estimate to the actual answer.
   (a)   4.2 × 1.8   (b)   8.9 × 3.1   (c)   48.1 × 4.2   (d)   103.4 × 2.9

8 Find estimates to these divisions by using approximations to one significant figure.
Then carry out the calculations with the original figures.
Compare your estimate to the actual answer.
   (a)   10.78 ÷ 4.9   (b)   19.68 ÷ 4.1   (c)   30.4 ÷ 3.2   (d)   203.49 ÷ 5.1

9 Find estimates to these calculations by using approximations to one significant figure.
Then carry out the calculations with the original figures.
Compare your estimate to the actual answer.

   (a) $\dfrac{9.9 \times 4.1}{4.8}$ (b) $\dfrac{11.6 + 49}{6.2}$ (c) $\dfrac{400 \times 0.29}{6.2}$ (d) $\dfrac{81.7 \times 4.9}{1.9 \times 10.3}$

What you need to know

You should be able to:
- Place decimals in order by considering place value.
- Add and subtract decimals.
- Use decimal notation for money and other measures.
- Multiply and divide decimals by powers of 10 (10, 100, 1000, …).
- Multiply and divide decimals by other decimals.
- Change decimals to fractions.
- Round a decimal to a given number of decimal places.
- Carry out a calculation to a given number of decimal places.

Review Exercise

Do not use a calculator for questions 1 to 11.

1 List the following decimals in ascending order.
0.7,   0.5,   0.8,   0.85,   0.55.

2 Write 0.45 as a fraction.
Give your answer in its simplest form.

3 Work out.
(a)   2.94 + 9.47   (b)   10 − 5.67
(c)   Check the subtraction in part (b) with an addition.

4 Work out.
(a) 3.6×4 (b) 14×0.3
(c) $7.8 \div 6$ (d) $8 \div 0.4$

5 Four parcels weigh 1.6 kg, 0.8 kg, 0.55 kg and 1.25 kg.
What is the total weight of the parcels?

6 Two pieces of wood of length 0.97 m and 1.78 m are sawn from a plank 5.12 m long.
How much wood is left?

7 (a)   Multiply 87.3 by 30.
(b)   Divide 87.3 by 30.

8 (a)   A calculator costs £4.95.
How much do 50 cost?
(b)   20 textbooks cost £159.80.
How much does one cost?

9 Tom uses his calculator to multiply 17.8 by 0.97.
His answer is 18.236.
Without finding the exact value of 17.8×0.97, explain why his answer must be wrong.
Edexcel

10 The display on the calculator shows the result of $179 \div 7$.

$$\boxed{25.57142857}$$

What is the result correct to
(a)   two decimal places,
(b)   one decimal place?

11 The Williamson family went into a café.
The table shows what they ordered.

| Three cans of cola at 63 pence each |
| Two cups of tea at 54 pence each |
| Five buns at 32 pence each |

Mr Williamson paid the bill with a £10 note.
How much change did he get?
Edexcel

12 (a)   Calculate the cost of 6.3 metres of material at £7.40 per metre.
(b)   2.3 metres of ribbon costs £1.61.
What is the cost of ribbon per metre?

13 Calculate the value of $\dfrac{21.7 \times 32.1}{16.20 - 2.19}$
Give your answer correct to two decimal places.
Edexcel

14 Here is a flow chart to change pounds to dollars.

| Enter number of pounds | → | Subtract £2.50 | → | Multiply by 1.8 | → | Number of dollars |

Use the flow diagram to find the number of dollars Chuck would get if he changed £225 to dollars.
Edexcel

CHAPTER 4

Working with Number

Multiples

Numbers in the 4 times table are called **multiples** of 4.
Numbers in the 10 times table are called **multiples** of 10.

EXAMPLES

1 Write down the first five multiples of 5.

$1 \times 5 = 5$
$2 \times 5 = 10$
$3 \times 5 = 15$
$4 \times 5 = 20$
$5 \times 5 = 25$
The first five multiples of 5 are 5, 10, 15, 20 and 25.

2 What is the eighth multiple of 9?

The eighth multiple of 9 is $8 \times 9 = 72$.

3 The fifth multiple of a number is 30. What is the number?

$5 \times 6 = 30$.
So, the number is 6.

A table of multiples

	1	2	3	4	5	6	7	8	9	10
1	1	2	3	4	5	6	7	8	9	10
2	2	4	6	8	10	12	14	16	18	20
3	3	6	9	12	15	18	21	24	27	30
4	4	8	12	16	20	24	28	32	36	40
5	5	10	15	20	25	30	35	40	45	50
6	6	12	18	24	30	36	42	48	54	60
7	7	14	21	28	35	42	49	56	63	70
8	8	16	24	32	40	48	56	64	72	80
9	9	18	27	36	45	54	63	72	81	90
10	10	20	30	40	50	60	70	80	90	100

The shaded numbers in the table are the **multiples** of 2.
Multiples of 2 are called **even numbers** and end in 0, 2, 4, 6 or 8.
Odd numbers end in 1, 3, 5, 7 or 9.
6, 12, 18, 24, … are **multiples** of 6.
The 8th **multiple** of 7 is $8 \times 7 = 56$.
3×8 has the same value as 8×3.

Exercise **4.1**

Do not use a calculator.

1 Write down the first five multiples of:
    (a)   10   (b)   3   (c)   7   (d)   6   (e)   9   (f)   20

2 Copy and complete the following.
    (a)   The fifth multiple of 4 is ….
    (b)   The seventh multiple of 6 is ….
    (c)   The …… multiple of 6 is 18.
    (d)   The …… multiple of 8 is 56.
    (e)   The sixth multiple of … is 60.
    (f)   The eighth multiple of … is 72.

3
    (a)   What multiple of 6 is the third multiple of 4?
    (b)   What multiple of 8 is the fourth multiple of 4?
    (c)   What multiple of 20 is the tenth multiple of 10?
    (d)   What multiple of 3 is the sixth multiple of 4?
    (e)   What multiple of 12 is the fourth multiple of 9?

4
    (a)   Write down a multiple of 7 between 30 and 40.
    (b)   Write down a multiple of 8 between 40 and 50.

 5 (a) Look at the table of multiples on Page 40.
What can you say about the following?
    (i)   Even multiples of an even number.   (ii) Even multiples of an odd number.
    (iii) Odd multiples of an even number.   (iv) Odd multiples of an odd number.

(b) Using **O** for an odd number and **E** for an even number copy and complete these multiplication tables.

(i)

×	2	3	6	7	9
2	E				
3		O		E	
6					
7					
9					

(ii)

×	O	E
O	O	
E	E	

(c) Why are there more even numbers than odd numbers in the table of multiples?

Activity

The product of 1 and 12 is $1 \times 12 = 12$.
Write down **all** the other pairs of **whole numbers** that have a product of 12.
Write down all the pairs of whole numbers that have a product of 6.
Write down all the pairs of whole numbers that have a product of 5.
Write down all the pairs of whole numbers that have a product of 48.

> When numbers are multiplied together the answer is called the **product** of the numbers.

Factors

Pairs of **whole numbers** which have a product of 6 are 1×6 and 2×3.
1, 2, 3, and 6 are called **factors** of 6.

EXAMPLES

 1 Find all the factors of 30.

Find **all** the pairs of whole numbers that have a product of 30.
$$30 \times 1 = 30 \qquad 15 \times 2 = 30$$
$$10 \times 3 = 30 \qquad 6 \times 5 = 30$$
1, 2, 3, 5, 6, 10, 15 and 30 are all factors of 30.

2 Find all the factors of 7.

Only one pair of numbers has a product of 7.
$$1 \times 7 = 7$$
7 has just two factors, 1 and 7.

> Numbers like 7 are called **prime numbers**.
> A prime number has exactly **two** factors, 1 and the number itself.
> The first few prime numbers are: 2, 3, 5, 7, 11, 13, ...
> The number 1 is not a prime number because it has only one factor.

Common factors

The factors of 20 are: **1**, **2**, 4, **5**, **10**, 20.   The factors of 50 are: **1**, **2**, **5**, **10**, 25, 50.

1, 2, 5 and 10 are factors of both 20 **and** 50.
They are called the **common factors** of 20 and 50.

Do not use a calculator.

1 These pairs of numbers have a product of 12.
         1 × 12   2 × 6   3 × 4
    (a) List all the factors of 12.
    (b) Explain why 8 is not a factor of 12.

2 (a) Find all the pairs of whole numbers that
           have a product of 18.
    (b) Write down all the factors of 18.

3 (a) Find all the pairs of whole numbers that
           have a product of 20.
    (b) Write down all the factors of 20.

4 Find all the factors of:
    (a) 16   (b) 28   (c) 36   (d) 45
    (e) 48   (f) 50   (g) 60   (h) 80

5 (a) Find all the factors of:
         (i)   2   (ii) 3   (iii) 5
         (iv) 7   (v)   11   (vi) 13
    (b) Find two more numbers with only two
         factors.

6 (a) Find all the factors of:
         (i) 4   (ii) 9   (iii) 25   (iv) 49
    (b) Find two more numbers with only three
         factors.

7 (a) Find all the factors of:
         (i)   6   (ii) 10   (iii) 14
         (iv) 26   (v)   55   (vi) 38
    (b) Find two more numbers with only four
         factors.

8 Which of these numbers have common factors
    of 1, 2 and 3?
         6, 16, 26, 36, 46.

9 Find the common factors of
    (a) 10 and 15,   (b) 12 and 20,
    (c) 16 and 18,   (d) 24 and 36,
    (e) 12, 18 and 36.

10 Consider these numbers.
         3, 4, 5, 14, 20, 27, 35, 60.
    (a) Which number is a factor of 10?
    (b) Which number is a multiple of 9?
    (c) Which number is a prime number?

11 (a) How many multiples of 6 are factors of 36?
    (b) How many multiples of 5 are factors of
         120?
    (c) How many factors of 100 are multiples of 2?
    (d) How many factors of 96 are multiples of 4?

12 Draw a 100 square on squared paper.

1	2	3	4	5	6	7	8	9	10
11	12	13	14	15	16	17	18	19	20
21	22	23	24	25	26	27	28	29	30
31	32	33	34	35	36	37	38	39	40
71	72	73	74	75	76	77	78	79	80
81	82	83	84	85	86	87	88	89	90
91	92	93	94	95	96	97	98	99	100

    (a) On your 100 square shade all the
         multiples of 2 **except** 2.

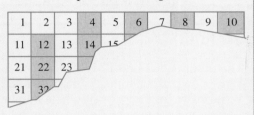

    (b) Next, shade all the multiples of 3
         except 3.

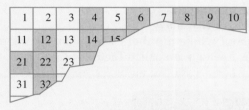

    (c) All the multiples of 4 are already
         shaded. Explain why.

    (d) Shade all the multiples of 5
         except 5.

    (e) Why have all the multiples of 6
         already been shaded?

    (f) Shade all the multiples of 7
         except 7.

    (g) Explain why 11 is the next
         unshaded number.
         Shade all the multiples of 11
         except 11.

    (h) Continue to shade multiples of
         unshaded numbers (except the
         unshaded number).

    (i) Write a list of all the unshaded
         numbers less than 50 (except 1).
         How many factors has each of
         the numbers in your list?

Powers

Products of the same number, like 3×3, $5 \times 5 \times 5$, $10 \times 10 \times 10 \times 10 \times 10$,
can be written in a shorthand form using **powers**.

For example:
$3 \times 3 = 3^2$ This is read as   '3 to the power of 2'. 3^2 has the value 9.
$5 \times 5 \times 5 = 5^3$ This is read as   '5 to the power of 3'. 5^3 has the value 125.
$10 \times 10 \times 10 \times 10 \times 10 = 10^5$ This is read as   '10 to the power of 5'. 10^5 has the value 100 000.

Index form

Numbers written in shorthand form like 3^2, 5^3 and 10^5 are said to be in **index form**.

Square numbers

Whole numbers raised to the power of 2 are called **square numbers**.

$1^2 = 1 \times 1 = 1$ 1^2 is read as '1 squared'.   1 is a square number.
$2^2 = 2 \times 2 = 4$ 2^2 is read as '2 squared'.   4 is a square number.
$3^2 = 3 \times 3 = 9$ 3^2 is read as '3 squared'.   9 is a square number.

To **square a number** multiply it by itself.

Square numbers can be shown as square patterns of dots.

$1^2 = 1$ $2^2 = 4$ $3^2 = 9$

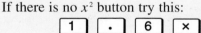
Squaring on a calculator
1.6^2 is read as '1.6 squared'.

To calculate 1.6^2 use this sequence of buttons: [1] [.] [6] [x^2] [=]

If there is no x^2 button try this:
[1] [.] [6] [×] [=]

Find the next two square numbers.
Numbers that are not whole numbers can also be squared.
For example:
    $1.6^2 = 1.6 \times 1.6 = 2.56$
    2.56 is **not** a square number. *Why not?*

Cube numbers

Whole numbers raised to the power of 3 are called **cube numbers**.

$1^3 = 1 \times 1 \times 1 = 1$ 1^3 is read as '1 cubed'.   1 is a cube number.
$2^3 = 2 \times 2 \times 2 = 8$ 2^3 is read as '2 cubed'.   8 is a cube number.
$3^3 = 3 \times 3 \times 3 = 27$ 3^3 is read as '3 cubed'.   27 is a cube number.

Cube numbers can be shown using small cubes.

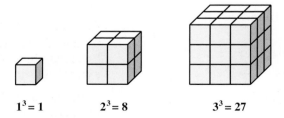

$1^3 = 1$ $2^3 = 8$ $3^3 = 27$

Draw a diagram to show 4^3.
What is the value of 4^3?

Numbers that are not whole numbers can also be cubed.
For example:
    $1.6^3 = 1.6 \times 1.6 \times 1.6 = 4.096$
    4.096 is **not** a cube number. *Why not?*

1.6^3 is read as '1.6 cubed'.

Do not use a calculator for questions 1 to 6.

1 Copy and complete.
(a) $5^2 = \ldots\ldots \times \ldots\ldots$ (b) $2^3 = \ldots\ldots \times \ldots\ldots \times \ldots\ldots$
(c) $10^5 = \ldots\ldots \times \ldots\ldots \times \ldots\ldots \times \ldots\ldots \times \ldots\ldots$ (d) $2.8^3 = \ldots\ldots \times \ldots\ldots \times \ldots\ldots$
(e) $0.4^2 = \ldots\ldots \times \ldots\ldots$

2 Write each of the following as a power.
(a) $4 \times 4 \times 4$ (b) 8×8
(c) $0.3 \times 0.3 \times 0.3$ (d) 1.6×1.6
(e) $10 \times 10 \times 10$ (f) $10 \times 10 \times 10 \times 10 \times 10 \times 10 \times 10$

3 Copy and complete this table of the powers of 10.

Expression	Index form	Value
$10 \times 10 \times 10 \times 10 \times 10 \times 10$	10^6	1 000 000
$10 \times 10 \times 10 \times 10 \times 10$	10^5	
	10^4	
$10 \times 10 \times 10$		
		100
10		

4 Work out the value of:
(a) 2^3 (b) 6^2 (c) 3^3 (d) 12^2 (e) 5^3 (f) 10^7

5 (a) Complete this list of square numbers from 1^2 to 20^2.
$1^2 = 1 \times 1 = 1$
$2^2 = 2 \times 2 = 4$
$3^2 = 3 \times 3 = 9$

(b) Copy and continue the difference pattern shown below for your list of square numbers.

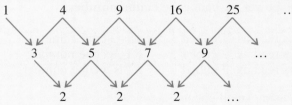

What do you notice?
(c) Use the pattern to find 21^2 from 20^2.

6 Complete this list of cube numbers from 1^3 to 10^3.
$1^3 = 1 \times 1 \times 1 = 1$
$2^3 = 2 \times 2 \times 2 = 8$
$3^3 = 3 \times 3 \times 3 = 27$

7 Calculate the value of:
(a) 1.3^2 (b) 1.7^3 (c) 5.4^2 (d) 4.8^3

8 Calculate the value of:
(a) $3.4^2 - 1.6^3$ (b) $2.3^2 \times 8.5^2$ (c) $3.6^3 \div 2.4^2$

Square roots

The opposite of squaring a number is called finding the **square root**.
For example:
The square root of 16 is 4 because $4^2 = 16$.

$$4 \xrightarrow{\text{square}} 16$$

$$4 \xleftarrow{\text{square root}} 16$$

The square root of 3.24 is 1.8 because $1.8^2 = 3.24$.

$$1.8 \xrightarrow{\text{square}} 3.24$$

$$1.8 \xleftarrow{\text{square root}} 3.24$$

$\sqrt{}$ This special symbol stands for the square root.

For example:

$\sqrt{9} = 3$ $\sqrt{2.56} = 1.6$

Square roots on a calculator

To calculate $\sqrt{2.56}$ use this sequence of buttons:

If your calculator works in a different way refer to the instruction booklet or ask someone for help.

Cube roots

The opposite of cubing a number is called finding the **cube root**.
For example:
The cube root of 27 is 3 because $3^3 = 27$.

$$3 \xrightarrow{\text{cube}} 27$$

$$3 \xleftarrow{\text{cube root}} 27$$

The cube root of 0.125 is 0.5 because $0.5^3 = 0.125$.

$$0.5 \xrightarrow{\text{cube}} 0.125$$

$$0.5 \xleftarrow{\text{cube root}} 0.125$$

$\sqrt[3]{}$ This special symbol stands for the cube root.

Square roots and cube roots can be worked out on a calculator without using special buttons.
A method called **trial and improvement** can be used.

EXAMPLE

You are asked to find the cube root of 18.6 but your calculator does not have a cube root button.
You know that $2^3 = 8$ and $3^3 = 27$.
Use trial and improvement, and a calculator, to find the cube root of 18.6 to an accuracy of one decimal place.
Show your method clearly.

2^3 $= 2 \times 2 \times 2$ $= 8$ so the cube root of 8 is 2
3^3 $= 3 \times 3 \times 3$ $= 27$ so the cube root of 27 is 3   So try 2.5 *Why?*
2.5^3 $= 2.5 \times 2.5 \times 2.5$ $= 15.625$ so the cube root of 15.625 is 2.5   So try 2.6 *Why?*
2.6^3 $= 2.6 \times 2.6 \times 2.6$ $= 17.576$ so the cube root of 17.576 is 2.6   So try 2.7 *Why?*
2.7^3 $= 2.7 \times 2.7 \times 2.7$ $= 19.683$ so the cube root of 19.683 is 2.7   So try 2.65 *Why?*
2.65^3 $= 2.65 \times 2.65 \times 2.65 = 18.609625$ so the cube root of 18.609625 is 2.65

This shows that the cube root of 18.6 lies between 2.6 and 2.65.
So correct to one decimal place the cube root of 18.6 is 2.6.

Remember
When using trial and improvement:
(a) Work methodically using trials first to the nearest whole number, then to one decimal place etc.
(b) Do at least one trial to one more decimal place than the required accuracy to be sure of your answer.

1 Write down the value of:

(a) $\sqrt{25}$ (b) $\sqrt{100}$ (c) $\sqrt{64}$ (d) $\sqrt{49}$

2 Write down the value of:

(a) $\sqrt[3]{8}$ (b) $\sqrt[3]{64}$ (c) $\sqrt[3]{125}$ (d) $\sqrt[3]{27}$

3 Work out.

(a) $\sqrt{3^2 + 4^2}$ (b) $\sqrt[3]{6^2 - 3^2}$

4 (a) Use the method of trial and improvement to find the square roots of:

(i) 20   (ii) 108   (iii) 7.6

Give your answers to an accuracy of one decimal place.

(b) Check each of your answers using the square root button.

5 Use the method of trial and improvement to find the cube roots of:

(a) 45   (b) 200   (c) 4.6

Give your answers to an accuracy of one decimal place.

6 Use the method of trial and improvement to find the length of the side of a square carpet of area 55 m². Give your answer to an accuracy of one decimal place.

7 Use the method of trial and improvement to find the length of the side of an ice cube of volume 4500 mm³. Give your answer to an accuracy of two decimal places.

Using a calculator

Powers

The **squares** of numbers and the **cubes** of numbers can also be calculated using the $\boxed{x^y}$ button on a calculator. The $\boxed{x^y}$ button can be used to calculate the value of a number x to the power of y.

EXAMPLE   Calculate (a) 7^3,   (b) 5.6^2.

(a) To calculate 7^3 enter this sequence into your calculator:

$\boxed{7}$ $\boxed{x^y}$ $\boxed{3}$ $\boxed{=}$

This gives $7^3 = 343$

(b) To calculate 5.6^2 enter this sequence into your calculator:

$\boxed{5}$ $\boxed{.}$ $\boxed{6}$ $\boxed{x^y}$ $\boxed{2}$ $\boxed{=}$

This gives $5.6^2 = 31.36$

Reciprocals

The **reciprocal** of a number is the value obtained when the number is divided into 1.

The reciprocal of a number x is $\dfrac{1}{x}$.

To find the reciprocal of a number on a calculator use the $\boxed{\frac{1}{x}}$ button.

EXAMPLE   Find the reciprocal of   (a) 5,   (b) 0.5.

(a) The reciprocal of 5 is $\dfrac{1}{5}$.

$1 \div 5 = 0.2$

The reciprocal of 5 is 0.2.

To find the reciprocal of 5 on your calculator use the sequence:

$\boxed{5}$ $\boxed{\frac{1}{x}}$

(b) The reciprocal of 0.5 is $\dfrac{1}{0.5}$.

$1 \div 0.5 = 2$

The reciprocal of 0.5 is 2.

Use your calculator to check your answer.

Exercise 4.5 — Use your calculator for the questions in this exercise.

1 Use the x^y button on your calculator to find the value of:

(a) (i) 13^2 (ii) 17^2 (iii) 2.5^2 (iv) 0.8^2 (v) 9.7^2

(b) (i) 6^3 (ii) 15^3 (iii) 2.4^3 (iv) 0.7^3 (v) 5.6^3

2 (a) Find the reciprocals of these numbers without using a calculator, then use a calculator to check your answers.

     (i) 2   (ii) 5   (iii) 10   (iv) 0.5   (v) 0.1   (vi) 0.2

(b) Use the $\frac{1}{x}$ button on your calculator to find the reciprocals of:

     (i) 4   (ii) 20   (iii) 25   (iv) 0.25   (v) 0.4   (vi) 0.16

3 Work out.

(a) $10^4 - 7.5^2$ (b) $2.4^2 + 0.6^3$ (c) $10^5 \times 2.5^3$ (d) $\dfrac{8.1^2}{2.7^3}$

4 Find the reciprocal of 0.5^3.

5 Work out these calculations.
Give your answers correct to two decimal places.

(a) $4.7 + 2.4^2$ (b) $9.5 - \sqrt{86}$ (c) $2.6 - \dfrac{1}{2.6}$ (d) $4.8^3 + 1.9^2$

(e) $3.5^2 - \sqrt{95}$ (f) $\dfrac{1}{2.7^2}$ (g) $3.4^2 \times \sqrt{4.6 - 2.9}$ (h) $\sqrt{\dfrac{1}{1.4^3}}$

What you need to know

- **Multiples** of a number are found by multiplying the number by 1, 2, 3, 4, . . .
  For example: the multiples of 8 are $1 \times 8 = 8$, $2 \times 8 = 16$, $3 \times 8 = 24$, $4 \times 8 = 32$, . . .

- You can find **all** the **factors** of a number by finding all the multiplication facts that give the number.
  For example: the factors of 6 are 1, 2, 3 and 6.

- An expression such as $5 \times 5 \times 5$ can be written in a shorthand way as 5^3.
  This is read as '5 to the power of 3'.

- Numbers raised to the power of 2 are **squared**.
  Whole numbers squared are called **square numbers**.
  Squares can be calculated using the x^2 button on a calculator.
  The opposite of squaring a number is called finding the **square root**.
  Square roots can be calculated using the $\sqrt{\ }$ button on a calculator.

- Numbers raised to the power of 3 are **cubed**.
  Whole numbers cubed are called cube **numbers**.
  The opposite of cubing a number is called finding the **cube root**.

- **Powers**
  The squares of numbers and the cubes of numbers can be worked out on a calculator by using the x^y button.
  The x^y button can be used to calculate the value of a number x to the power of y.

- **Reciprocals**
  The reciprocal of a number is the value obtained when the number is divided into 1.
  The reciprocal of a number can be found on a calculator by using the $\frac{1}{x}$ button.

- Square roots and cube roots can be found using a method called **trial and improvement**.

Do not use a calculator for questions 1 to 10.

1 Find all the factors of 12.

2 Write down three multiples of 7.

3 Look at these numbers.

2   3   4   5   6   7   8   9

Which of these numbers are
(a)   even,
(b)   multiples of 3,
(c)   factors of 6?

4 What is the square of 6?

5 Here is a number sequence

4, 8, 12, 16, 20, 24, 28.

Use one of these words

factor, square, multiple, cube,

to complete these sentences about the sequence.
(a)   Each number is a .... of 4.
(b)   The numbers 4 and 16 are ....
       numbers.
(c)   Each of the numbers 4 and 8 is a
       .... of 16.   Edexcel

6 This question is about the ten numbers in the box.

9010	68	764
390	71	
85	437	253
105	829	

(a)   Write down all the numbers that divide **exactly**
       (i) by 2, (ii) by 5, (iii) by 10.
(b)   Explain how you picked out the numbers in (a) (i), (ii) and (iii).
(c)   Explain how you know when numbers divide exactly by
       2 **and** 5 **and** 10.   Edexcel

7 Consider only the numbers

2   4   8   16   32   64

(a)   Which of these numbers are square numbers? Give the square root of each square number.
(b)   Which of these numbers are cube numbers? Give the cube root of each cube number.

8 What is the value of $2^3 - \sqrt{25}$?

9

Lighthouse A   Lighthouse B

Lighthouse A flashes every 10 seconds.
Lighthouse B flashes every 14 seconds.

Lighthouses A and B both flash at the same time.
How many seconds will it be before they both flash at the same time again?   Edexcel

10 Work out the value of
(a) 5^3,   (b) $\sqrt{36}$,   (c) $2^3 \times 3^2$
          Edexcel

11 Which is smaller $\sqrt{400}$ or 4^3?
Show working to explain your answer.

12 What is the value of $\sqrt{50}$?
Give your answer correct to two decimal places.

13 Calculate the value of $0.7^3 + \sqrt{30}$.
Give your answer correct to one decimal place.

14 (a)   Calculate the exact value of 1.5^3.
(b)   Find the reciprocal of 6.
       Give your answer correct to
       3 decimal places.

15 (a)   Write each of the following as a power of 10.
       (i)   100   (ii)   1 000 000
(b)   Work out 1 000 000 ÷ 100.
       Give your answer as a power of 10.

16 Karen is using a trial and improvement method to find the cube root of 23.
She calculates:

$3 \times 3 \times 3 = 27$	too big
$2 \times 2 \times 2 = 8$	too small

Continue this method to find the cube root of 23 correct to one decimal place.
You **must** show all your working.

17 Calculate $2.6^3 \times \sqrt{4.3 + 2.8}$.
Give your answer correct to one decimal place.

Negative Numbers

In Chapter 1 we used a number line to show whole numbers.
This number line can be extended to include **negative whole numbers**.

Negative whole numbers, zero and positive whole numbers are called **integers**.
−5 can be read as "minus five" or "negative five".
A number written without a sign before it is assumed to be positive. +5 has the same value as 5.
Real-life situations which use negative numbers include temperature, bank accounts and depths below sea-level.
Can you think of any other situations where negative numbers are used?

Ordering numbers

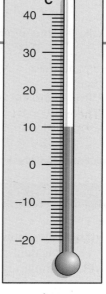

The thermometer

−5°C is colder than −1°C.   2°C is warmer than −3°C.
−3°C is colder than   1°C.   4°C is warmer than −5°C.
−4°C is colder than   0°C.   0°C is warmer than −3°C.
  2°C is colder than   4°C.   5°C is warmer than   2°C.

As you move up the   As you move down the
thermometer the   thermometer the
temperatures become   temperatures become
warmer.   colder.

The number line

−5 is less than −1.   2 is more than −3.
−3 is less than   1.   4 is more than −5.
−4 is less than   0.   0 is more than −3.
  2 is less than   4.   5 is more than   2.

As you move from left to   As you move from right to
right along the number line left along the number line
the numbers become bigger.   the numbers become smaller.

EXAMPLES

1 List these temperatures from coldest to hottest:

3°C,   5°C,   −2°C,   0°C,   −4°C.

−4°C,   −2°C,   0°C,   3°C,   5°C.

2 List these numbers from lowest to highest:

50,   −41,   −18,   −11,   28,   9.

−41,   −18,   −11,   9,   28,   50.

49

1. Copy and complete these sentences using the words 'colder' or 'warmer' as appropriate.
   (a) $-2°C$ is ...... than $-5°C$.
   (b) $-1°C$ is ...... than $4°C$.
   (c) $2°C$ is ...... than $-4°C$.
   (d) $-10°C$ is ...... than $-5°C$.

2. Copy and complete these sentences using the words 'less' or 'more' as appropriate.
   (a) -3 is ...... than 2.
   (b) 1 is ...... than -5.
   (c) -4 is ...... than -1.
   (d) -4 is ...... than -10.

3. At midnight on New Year's Day the temperatures in some cities were as shown:
   (a) Which city recorded the highest temperature?
   (b) Which city recorded the lowest temperature?
   (c) List the temperatures from coldest to hottest.

Edinburgh	$-7°C$
London	$0°C$
Moscow	$-22°C$
New York	$-17°C$
Rome	$3°C$
Colombo	$21°C$
Cairo	$15°C$

4. List these temperatures from coldest to hottest.
   (a) $23°C, -28°C, -3°C, 19°C, -13°C.$
   (b) $-9°C, -11°C, 12°C, 10°C, -7°C, 0°C.$
   (c) $27°C, 18°C, -29°C, -15°C, 2°C.$
   (d) $20°C, -15°C, -20°C, 0°C, -5°C, 10°C.$

5. List these numbers from lowest to highest.
   (a) $31, -78, 51, -39, -16, -9, 11.$
   (b) $5, 1, -1, -3, -5, -2, 0, 2, 4.$
   (c) $99, -103, 104, 5, -3, 52, -63, -19.$
   (d) $30, 10, -30, -50, -20, 0, 40.$
   (e) $27, -30, 17, 0, -15, -10, 8.$

Subtracting a larger number from a smaller number

Work out $3 - 5$.
To work out smaller number $-$ larger number:
   (i) Do the calculation the other way round. $3 - 5$ becomes $5 - 3$.
   (ii) Put a minus sign in front of the answer. So $3 - 5 = -2$.

This is the same as starting at 3 on a number line and going 5 places to the left, to get to -2.

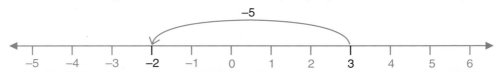

EXAMPLES

1. Work out $7 - 13$.
   Do $13 - 7 = 6$.
   Then $7 - 13 = -6$.

2. Calculate $21 - 34$.
   Do $34 - 21 = 13$.
   Then $21 - 34 = -13$.

3. Alec has £50 in his bank account. He writes a cheque for £80. What is his new balance?

   His new balance is given by the calculation £50 $-$ £80.
   $80 - 50 = 30$.
   So $50 - 80 = -30$.
   The new balance is $-£30$.
   This means that Alec's account is overdrawn by £30.

Exercise **5.2**   Do not use a calculator for this exercise.

1 Use the number line to work out the following.

(a) 4 − 3   (b) 1 − 3   (c) 2 − 4   (d) 5 − 9   (e) 3 − 6

2 Draw a number line to show each of these statements.
(a) 7 − 10 = −3   (b) 4 − 6 = −2   (c) 3 − 4 = −1

3 Work out the following.
(a) 1 − 4   (b) 3 − 5   (c) 5 − 8
(d) 10 − 12   (e) 4 − 7   (f) 8 − 12
(g) 13 − 20   (h) 24 − 36   (i) 10 − 20
(j) 23 − 30   (k) 29 − 50   (l) 20 − 21

4 What number should be put in the box to make each of these statements correct?
(a) 7 − ☐ = −2   (b) ☐ − 6 = −5   (c) 9 − ☐ = −3
(d) −3 − 7 = ☐   (e) ☐ − 50 = −20   (f) 10 − ☐ = −5

5 Mr Armstrong has £25 in the bank. He writes a cheque for £100.
What is his new balance?

6 The temperature inside a fridge is 6°C above zero.
The temperature inside a freezer is 5°C below zero.
By how many degrees is the temperature inside the freezer below the temperature inside the fridge?

7 At midnight, the temperature in York is 3°C below freezing and in Bath the temperature is 2°C above freezing.
What is the difference in temperature between York and Bath?

8 Brad is 8 cm shorter than Alex and Cath is 9 cm taller than Alex.
By how many centimetres is Cath taller than Brad?

9 Adrian is 5 kg heavier than Tim. Matt is 3 kg lighter than Tim.
What is the difference in weight between Matt and Adrian?

10 Negative numbers can be used for depths below sea level.
Use negative numbers to answer the following.
(a) At what depth is the diver?
(b) At what depth is the treasure chest?

What is the difference in height between
(c) the helicopter and the parachutist,
(d) the diver and the jellyfish,
(e) the diver and the treasure chest,
(f) the bird and the jellyfish,
(g) the parachutist and the treasure chest,
(h) the kite and the jellyfish,
(i) the helicopter and the kite,
(j) the diver and the helicopter,
(k) the bird and the treasure chest?

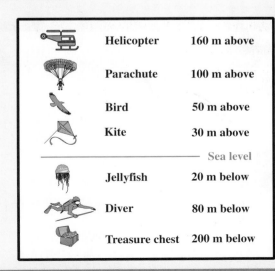

Helicopter	160 m above
Parachute	100 m above
Bird	50 m above
Kite	30 m above
	Sea level
Jellyfish	20 m below
Diver	80 m below
Treasure chest	200 m below

Addition and subtraction using negative numbers

Think of the number line as a series of stepping stones.

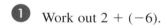

What is $-4-5$?
Using the number line:
Start at -4 and move 5 to the **left**.
The answer is -9.
$-4-5 = -9$

$-4-5$ can be written as:
$-4 + (-5)$ or $-4 -(+5)$.
So $-4 + (-5) = -9$,
and $-4 - (+5) = -9$.

What is $-3 - (+7)$?
$-3 - (+7)$ is the same as $-3-7$.
Using the number line:
Start at -3 and move 7 to the **left**.
$-3 - (+7) = -10$

$-3 - (-7)$ must start at -3 and move 7 to the **right**.
$-3 - (-7)$ is the same as $-3 + 7$.
So $-3 - (-7) = 4$,
and $-3 + 7 = 4$.

What is $-5 + (+7)$?
$+7$ can be written as 7.
$-5 + (+7)$ is the same as $-5 + 7 = 2$.

To add or subtract negative numbers:
Replace double signs with a single sign.
Start on the number line with the first number.
Then move left or right according to the single sign.

> $+ \ +$ can be replaced by $+$
> $- \ -$ can be replaced by $+$
> $+ \ -$ can be replaced by $-$
> $- \ +$ can be replaced by $-$

EXAMPLES

1 Work out $2 + (-6)$.

$+-$ can be replaced with $-$.
Start at 2 and move 6 to the left.
$2 + (-6) = 2 - 6 = -4$

2 Work out $-2 - (-8)$.

$--$ can be replaced with $+$.
Start at -2 and move 8 to the right.
$-2 -(-8) = -2 + 8 = 6$

3 Work out $-4 - (+6)$.

$-+$ can be replaced with $-$.
Start at -4 and move 6 to the left.
$-4 -(+6) = -4 - 6 = -10$

4 Work out $-4 + (-3) + 6 - (-5) - (+3)$.

Replace signs.
$= -4 - 3 + 6 + 5 - 3$
$= 1$

Do not use a calculator for this exercise.

1 Work out.
    (a) $-3 + (+5)$ (b) $5 + (-4)$ (c) $-2 + (-7)$
    (d) $-1 + (+9)$ (e) $7 + (-3)$ (f) $15 + (-20)$
    (g) $-11 + (+4)$ (h) $11 + (-4)$ (i) $8 + (-7)$
    (j) $-8 + (-7)$ (k) $3 + (+3) + (-9)$ (l) $-7 + (-5) +6$

2 Work out.
    (a) $8 - (-5)$ (b) $-4 - (-10)$ (c) $10 - (+3)$
    (d) $6 - (-1)$ (e) $-5 - (-10)$ (f) $-4 - (+8)$
    (g) $-7 - (-6)$ (h) $7 - (-6)$ (i) $-2 - (+9)$
    (j) $2 - (-9)$ (k) $5 - (+5) + 9$ (l) $-10 - (-6) + 4$

3 Work out.
(a) $-3 - (-8)$
(b) $5 + (-2)$
(c) $7 - (+4)$
(d) $-9 - (-5) + (-3)$
(e) $7 + (-8) - (+5)$
(f) $-2 - (-7) - 6$

4 Work out.
(a) $10 + 5 - 8 + 6 - 7$
(b) $12 + 8 - 15 + 7 - 20$
(c) $30 - 20 + 12 - 50$
(d) $6 + 12 - 14 - 4$
(e) $37 - 23 - 24 - 25$
(f) $12 + 13 + 14 - 20$

5 What is the difference in temperature between
(a) London and Rome,
(b) Edinburgh and Rome,
(c) Moscow and New York,
(d) Cairo and Colombo,
(e) Moscow and Cairo?

Edinburgh	$-7°C$
London	$0°C$
Moscow	$-22°C$
New York	$-17°C$
Rome	$3°C$
Colombo	$21°C$
Cairo	$15°C$

6 The temperature inside a freezer was $-23°C$.
After two hours the temperature had risen by $8°C$.
What is the temperature in the freezer then?

7 The temperature inside an igloo is $-5°C$.
The temperature outside the igloo is $17°C$ cooler.
What is the temperature outside the igloo.

8 The temperature of an iceberg is $-13°C$.
The temperature of the sea is $15°$ warmer than the iceberg.
What is the temperature of the sea?

Multiplying and dividing negative numbers

You will need to know these rules for
multiplying and dividing negative numbers:

When multiplying:
$+ \times + = +$
$- \times - = +$
$+ \times - = -$
$- \times + = -$

When dividing:
$+ \div + = +$
$- \div - = +$
$+ \div - = -$
$- \div + = -$

The multiplication table can be
extended to include negative
numbers.

*Describe any patterns you
can see in the table.*

Division is the opposite (inverse)
operation to multiplication.
If $a \times b = c$,
then $c \div b = a$ and $c \div a = b$.

If $(+5) \times (-2) = -10$,
then $(-10) \div (-2) = +5$
and $(-10) \div (+5) = -2$.

Second number

F	×	−5	−4	−3	−2	−1	0	1	2	3	4	5
i	−5	25	20	15	10	5	0	−5	−10	−15	−20	−25
r	−4	20	16	12	8	4	0	−4	−8	−12	−16	−20
s	−3	15	12	9	6	3	0	−3	−6	−9	−12	−15
t	−2	10	8	6	4	2	0	−2	−4	−6	−8	−10
	−1	5	4	3	2	1	0	−1	−2	−3	−4	−5
n	0	0	0	0	0	0	0	0	0	0	0	0
u	1	−5	−4	−3	−2	−1	0	1	2	3	4	5
m	2	−10	−8	−6	−4	−2	0	2	4	6	8	10
b	3	−15	−12	−9	−6	−3	0	3	6	9	12	15
e	4	−20	−16	−12	−8	−4	0	4	8	12	16	20
r	5	−25	−20	−15	−10	−5	0	5	10	15	20	25

1 Work out $(+7) \times (-5)$.

Signs: $+ \times - = -$
Numbers: $7 \times 5 = 35$
So $(+7) \times (-5) = -35$.

2 Work out $(-4) \times (-8)$.

Signs: $- \times - = +$
Numbers: $4 \times 8 = 32$
So $(-4) \times (-8) = 32$.

3 Work out $(+8) \div (-2)$.

Signs: $+ \div - = -$
Numbers: $8 \div 2 = 4$
So $(+8) \div (-2) = -4$.

4 Work out $(-36) \div (-3)$.

Signs: $- \div - = +$
Numbers: $36 \div 3 = 12$
So $(-36) \div (-3) = 12$.

○○○○○○○○
Work logically
Work out the sign first.
Then work out the
numbers.

Exercise **5.4**

Do not use a calculator for this exercise.

1 $(+7) \times (+5)$

2 $(-7) \times (+5)$

3 $(-7) \times (-5)$

4 $5 \times (+2)$

5 $(+5) \times (-2)$

6 $(-5) \times (-2)$

7 $(-1) \times (-1)$

8 $8 \times (-3)$

9 $(-8) \times (+3)$

10 $(-5) \times 9$

11 $(-8) \times (-8)$

12 $(-7) \times 6$

13 $(-7) \times (-6)$

14 $8 \times (-10)$

15 $(-8) \times (+10)$

16 $(+5) \times (-2) \times (+2)$

17 $(+4) \times (-3) \times (-5)$

18 $(-3) \times (-2) \times (-5)$

19 $(-5) \times (+3) \times (-4)$

20 $(-5) \times (+3) \times (+4)$

21 $(-8) \div (+2)$

22 $(-8) \div (-2)$

23 $(+20) \div (+4)$

24 $(+20) \div (-4)$

25 $(-20) \div (+4)$

26 $(-20) \div (-4)$

27 $(+18) \div (+3)$

28 $(-18) \div (+3)$

29 $(-24) \div (-6)$

30 $(+24) \div (-3)$

31 In a multiple choice test there are 5 marks for a right answer and -3 marks for a wrong answer.

For example: A student has 8 questions right and 17 wrong.
What is his overall mark?
$8 \times 5 + 17 \times -3 = 40 + -51 = 40 - 51 = -11$

In a 25-question test these students have the following right and wrong answers.
They can leave a question out rather than guess a wrong answer.

	Ahmed	Bridget	Chris	Dileep	Evan
Right	10	12	6	7	9
Wrong	8	13	17	18	16

(a)   How many marks did each student score?
(b)   Put the students in order from first to fifth.

You should be able to:
- Use **negative numbers** in context such as temperatures, bank accounts.
- Realise where negative numbers come on a **number line**.
- Put numbers in order (including negative numbers).
- Add $(+)$, subtract $(-)$, multiply $(\times)$ and divide $(\div)$ with negative numbers.

You will also meet negative numbers further on:
They may be solutions to equations.
Negative coordinates on graphs.
They may be substituted into algebraic formulae.

Review Exercise   Do not use a calculator for this exercise.

1 Place the following numbers in order of size starting with the smallest.
15   -5 25   0 -20

2 The table shows the midday temperatures in these towns one day.

Town	Selby	Poole	Woking
Temperature (°C)	-8	-2	-5

(a)   Which town has the highest midday temperature?
(b)   Which town has the lowest midday temperature?

3 Calculate.
(a) $-7 - 11$ (b) $-7 + 11$ (c) $-7 - (-11)$

4 A miner is 924 metres below the ground.
A plane is 3267 metres above the ground.
How many metres is the plane above the miner?

5
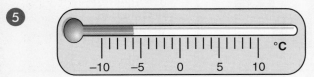

(a)   What temperature is shown on the thermometer?

One Autumn morning the temperature went up from $-4°C$ to $5°C$.
(b)   By how many degrees did the temperature rise?

During the afternoon the temperature then fell by seven degrees from $5°C$.
(c)   What was the temperature at the end of the afternoon?   Edexcel

6 Dan has £26.40 in his bank account.
He buys a jacket for £59.95 and pays by cheque.
If the cheque is accepted by his bank how much will his account be overdrawn?

7 One winter's day the temperatures in 3 cities were measured at the same time.
The results were:

London	$-3°C$
Paris	$+5°C$
Moscow	$-21°C$

Work out how many degrees difference there was between the temperatures in
(a)   London and Paris,
(b)   Moscow and London,
(c)   Moscow and Paris.   Edexcel

8 Work out.
(a) $6 \times (-5)$ (b) $(-3) \times (-4)$
(c) $18 \div (-3)$ (d) $(-12) \div (-2)$

9 (a)   Work out.
(i) $(-3) - (-2)$
(ii) $(-2) \times (-3)$

(b)   Complete the boxes.
(i) $\boxed{} \div (-2) = -3$
(ii) $(-5) + \boxed{} = -3$

10 A multichoice test has 20 questions.
For each question the mark given is:

$+2$ for a correct answer
-1 for a wrong answer
0 if the question is not attempted

(a)   What is the lowest mark that could be scored on the test?
(b)   Tim attempts all the questions and gets 8 correct.
Naomi attempts 13 questions and gets 8 correct.
Who scores the better mark?
Explain your answer.

Activity

(a) Each diagram shows a different way of shading one half of a square.

 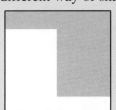  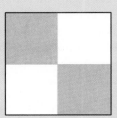

Find some more ways of shading one half of a square.

(b) Each diagram shows a different way of dividing the square into quarters.

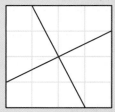 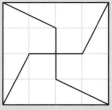 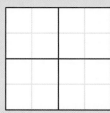 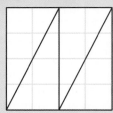

Find some more ways of dividing a square into quarters.

Shaded fractions

What fraction of this rectangle is shaded?

The rectangle is divided into **eight** squares.
The squares are all the same size.
Three of the squares are shaded.

$\frac{3}{8}$ of the rectangle is shaded.

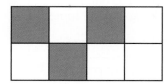

In a fraction:
The top number is called the **numerator**.
The bottom number is called the **denominator**.

EXAMPLES

1 What fraction of this rectangle is shaded?

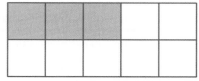

The rectangle is divided into 10 equal parts.
Three of the equal parts are shaded.

So $\frac{3}{10}$ of the rectangle is shaded.

2 Shade $\frac{2}{5}$ of a rectangle.

Draw a rectangle and divide it into 5 equal parts.
Then shade two of the parts.

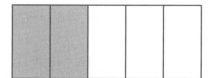

56

1 What fraction of each of these rectangles is shaded?

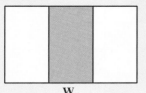 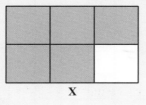 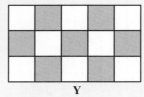 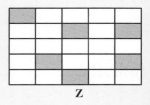

W   X   Y   Z

2 Make two copies of each rectangle.

(a) Shade $\frac{1}{4}$ of rectangle A.

(b) Shade $\frac{3}{4}$ of rectangle A.

(c) Shade $\frac{1}{5}$ of rectangle B.

(d) Shade $\frac{3}{5}$ of rectangle B.

(e) Shade $\frac{1}{2}$ of rectangle C.

(f) Shade $\frac{3}{4}$ of rectangle C.

(g) Shade $\frac{2}{3}$ of rectangle D.

(h) Shade $\frac{6}{9}$ of rectangle D.

(i) Shade $\frac{1}{3}$ of rectangle E.

(j) Shade $\frac{3}{12}$ of rectangle E

(k) Shade $\frac{3}{7}$ of rectangle F.

(l) Shade $\frac{12}{28}$ of rectangle F.

Rectangle A 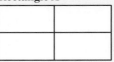   **Rectangle B**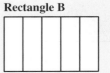

Rectangle C 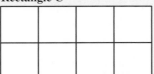   **Rectangle D**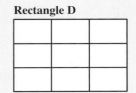

Rectangle E 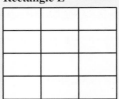   **Rectangle F**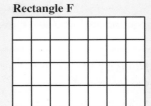

3 What fraction of each of these diagrams is shaded?

(a)    (b) 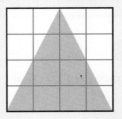   (c)

4 What fraction of each of these shapes is shaded?

(a)   (b)   (c)   (d)   (e)

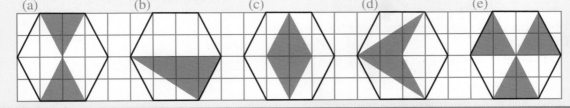

5 Look at these diagrams.

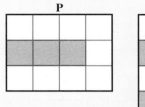 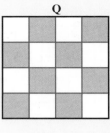 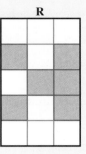 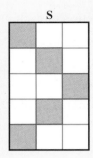

P   Q   R   S

(a) Which diagram has $\frac{3}{12}$ shaded?

(b) Which diagram has $\frac{1}{4}$ shaded?

(c) Which diagram has $\frac{6}{15}$ shaded?

(d) Which diagram has $\frac{2}{5}$ shaded?

(e) Which diagram has $\frac{1}{2}$ shaded?

(f) Which diagram has $\frac{1}{3}$ shaded?

6 You are asked to design a flag.

(a) In one design, $\frac{1}{2}$ of the flag is red and $\frac{1}{3}$ of the flag is blue. The rest of the flag is white.

    (i) On squared paper, draw some 2 by 3 rectangles and design some possible flags.
    (ii) What fraction of the flag is white?

(b) In another design, $\frac{2}{3}$ of the flag is red and $\frac{1}{4}$ of the flag is blue. The rest of the flag is white.

    (i) On squared paper, draw some 3 by 4 rectangles and design some possible flags.
    (ii) What fraction of the flag is white?

Activity

What fraction of each of these shapes is shaded?

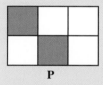 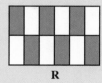 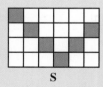

P   Q   R   S

Which rectangles have the same fraction shaded?

Equivalent fractions

Fractions which are equal are called **equivalent fractions**.

Rectangle Q has $\frac{3}{12}$ shaded, $\frac{3}{12} = \frac{1}{4}$.

Rectangle S has $\frac{6}{24}$ shaded, $\frac{6}{24} = \frac{1}{4}$.

Each of the fractions $\frac{1}{4}, \frac{3}{12}, \frac{6}{24}$, is the same fraction written in different ways.

These fractions are all equivalent to $\frac{1}{4}$.

Write down two more fractions equivalent to $\frac{1}{4}$.

To write an equivalent fraction:
Multiply the numerator and denominator by the **same** number.

For example. $\frac{1}{4} = \frac{1 \times 3}{4 \times 3} = \frac{3}{12}$

$\frac{1}{4} = \frac{1 \times 6}{4 \times 6} = \frac{6}{24}$

EXAMPLES

1 Write down three fractions equivalent to $\frac{5}{7}$.

The numerators are any multiples of 5.
For example: 5, 10, 15, 20, …

The denominators are the same multiples of 7: 7, 14, 21, 28, …

This gives the fractions: $\frac{5}{7}, \frac{10}{14}, \frac{15}{21}, \frac{20}{28}, \ldots$

2 The fraction $\frac{2}{3}$ is equivalent to the fraction $\frac{?}{12}$.

Find the value of the unknown numerator.

3 has been multiplied by 4 to get 12.
So 2 must also be multiplied by 4 to get the unknown numerator.
The unknown numerator is 8.

3 Write the fractions $\frac{3}{4}, \frac{2}{5}$ and $\frac{7}{10}$ in ascending order.

Find equivalent fractions for $\frac{3}{4}, \frac{2}{5}$ and $\frac{7}{10}$ with the same denominators.

$$\frac{3}{4} = \frac{6}{8} = \frac{9}{12} = \frac{12}{16} = \mathbf{\frac{15}{20}} \qquad \frac{2}{5} = \frac{4}{10} = \frac{6}{15} = \mathbf{\frac{8}{20}} \qquad \frac{7}{10} = \mathbf{\frac{14}{20}}$$

The fractions in ascending order are: $\frac{2}{5}, \quad \frac{7}{10}, \quad \frac{3}{4}$.

Simplifying fractions

Fractions can be **simplified** if both the numerator and denominator can be divided by the **same number**.

To write a fraction in its **simplest form** divide both the numerator and denominator by the largest number that divides into them both.

This is sometimes called **cancelling** a fraction.

Remember:
Multiplication and division are inverse (opposite) operations.

Equivalent fractions can also be made by dividing the numerator and denominator of a fraction by the same number.

EXAMPLES

1 Write the fraction $\frac{25}{30}$ in its simplest form.

The largest number that divides into both the numerator and denominator of $\frac{25}{30}$ is 5.

$$\frac{25}{30} = \frac{25 \div 5}{30 \div 5} = \frac{5}{6}$$

$\frac{25}{30} = \frac{5}{6}$ in its simplest form.

2 In a class of 28 pupils there are 12 boys.
What fraction of the pupils are boys?
Write this fraction in its simplest form.

There are 12 out of 28 boys.
The fraction of boys $= \frac{12}{28}$

$$\frac{12}{28} = \frac{12 \div 4}{28 \div 4} = \frac{3}{7}$$

$\frac{12}{28} = \frac{3}{7}$ in its simplest form.

3 Simplify $\frac{24}{30}$.

The largest number that divides into both 24 and 30 is 6.

$$\frac{24}{30} = \frac{24 \div 6}{30 \div 6} = \frac{4}{5}$$

4 Write 42 as a fraction of 70.
Give your answer in its simplest form.

42 as a fraction of 70 is $\frac{42}{70}$.

2 divides into both 42 and 70.

$$\frac{42}{70} = \frac{42 \div 2}{70 \div 2} = \frac{21}{35}$$

7 divides into both 21 and 35.

$$\frac{21}{35} = \frac{21 \div 7}{35 \div 7} = \frac{3}{5}$$

$\frac{42}{70} = \frac{3}{5}$ in its simplest form.

Do not use a calculator.

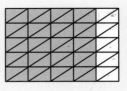

1 Write three equivalent fractions for the shaded part of this rectangle.
What is the simplest form of the shaded fraction?

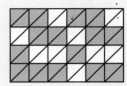

2 Write three equivalent fractions for the shaded part of this rectangle.
What is the simplest form of the shaded fraction?

3 The diagrams show that:

$$\frac{1}{2} = \frac{2}{4} = \frac{3}{6}$$

Copy the diagrams.
Add two more diagrams to show that: $\frac{1}{2} = \frac{2}{4} = \frac{3}{6} = \frac{4}{8} = \frac{5}{10}$

4 Copy and draw more diagrams to show that:

(a) $\frac{2}{3} = \frac{4}{6} = \frac{6}{9} = \frac{8}{12} = \frac{10}{15}$

(b) $\frac{3}{4} = \frac{6}{8} = \frac{9}{12} = \frac{12}{16} = \frac{15}{20}$

(c) $\frac{5}{6} = \frac{10}{12} = \frac{15}{18} = \frac{20}{24} = \frac{25}{30}$

5 The diagram shows a 6 by 4 rectangle with a fraction of the rectangle shaded.

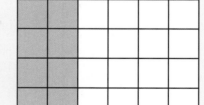

(a) How many $\frac{1}{3}$'s are shaded?

(b) How many $\frac{1}{6}$'s are shaded?

(c) How many $\frac{1}{24}$'s are shaded?

6 Write down three fractions equivalent to:

(a) $\frac{1}{3}$ (b) $\frac{2}{9}$ (c) $\frac{5}{8}$ (d) $\frac{4}{5}$ (e) $\frac{3}{10}$ (f) $\frac{7}{12}$

7 Each of these pairs of fractions are equivalent.
In each case find the value of the unknown numerator.

(a) $\frac{1}{3}$ and $\frac{?}{6}$ (b) $\frac{?}{8}$ and $\frac{6}{16}$ (c) $\frac{?}{4}$ and $\frac{12}{16}$

8 Each of these pairs of fractions are equivalent.
In each case find the value of the unknown denominator.

(a) $\frac{5}{?}$ and $\frac{15}{18}$ (b) $\frac{24}{64}$ and $\frac{3}{?}$ (c) $\frac{7}{?}$ and $\frac{56}{96}$

9 Write these fractions in ascending order.

$$\frac{5}{8} \qquad \frac{3}{4} \qquad \frac{7}{16}$$

10 Write these fractions in descending order.

$$\frac{2}{3} \qquad \frac{3}{5} \qquad \frac{7}{10} \qquad \frac{8}{15}$$

11 Which of these fractions is the largest?

$$\frac{4}{5} \qquad \frac{13}{20} \qquad \frac{7}{10} \qquad \frac{3}{4}$$

12 Write each of these fractions in its simplest form.

(a) $\frac{6}{8}$ (b) $\frac{12}{15}$ (c) $\frac{18}{27}$ (d) $\frac{22}{99}$

(e) $\frac{50}{75}$ (f) $\frac{16}{40}$ (g) $\frac{12}{50}$ (h) $\frac{52}{65}$

13 Write the first number as a fraction of the second.
Write the fractions in their simplest form.

(a) 4, 20   (b) 3, 12   (c) 8, 12
(d) 24, 60   (e) 60, 105

14 In a class of 32 there are 4 left-handed students.
What fraction of the students are left-handed?
Write this fraction in its simplest form.

15 A box of 50 chocolates includes 30 soft-centred chocolates.
What fraction of the chocolates are soft-centred?
Write this fraction in its simplest form.

16 In each hour a television channel shows:
programmes for 48 minutes and adverts for 12 minutes.
For what fraction of an hour are
(a) programmes shown,
(b) adverts shown?
Give each answer in its simplest form.

17 Mr Jones plans a car journey.
(a) The journey is 50 km long.
Mr Jones plans to stop after 35 km.
What fraction of the total distance is this?
Give your answer in its simplest form.

(b) The journey takes 60 minutes which includes a 12-minute stop.
For what fraction of the total time does Mr Jones stop on his journey?
Give your answer in its simplest form.

18 A group of students were asked some questions about how they travelled to school.

$\frac{1}{2}$ of the students said they walked.

$\frac{1}{3}$ of the students said they travelled by bus.

In the group there were more than 20 students and less than 30.
(a) How many students were in the group?

The rest of the group came by car.
(b) What fraction of the group came by car?
Give your answer in its simplest form.

Types of fractions

This diagram shows that when 5 cakes are shared equally between 2 people they get $2\frac{1}{2}$ cakes each.

The diagram below shows that when 5 cakes are shared equally between 4 people they get $1\frac{1}{4}$ cakes each.

Numbers like $2\frac{1}{2}$ and $1\frac{1}{4}$ are called **mixed numbers** because they are a mixture of whole numbers and fractions.
Mixed numbers can be written as **improper** or **'top heavy'** fractions.
These are fractions where the numerator is larger than the denominator.

EXAMPLES

1 Write $3\frac{4}{7}$ as an improper fraction.

$$3\frac{4}{7} = \frac{(3 \times 7) + 4}{7} = \frac{21 + 4}{7} = \frac{25}{7}$$

2 Write $\frac{32}{5}$ as a mixed number.

$32 \div 5 = 6$ remainder 2.

$$\frac{32}{5} = 6\frac{2}{5}$$

Finding fractions of quantities

EXAMPLES

1 Find $\frac{2}{5}$ of £65.

Divide £65 into 5 equal parts.
£65 ÷ 5 = £13.

13	13	13	13	13

Each of these parts is $\frac{1}{5}$ of £65.

Two of these parts is $\frac{2}{5}$ of £65.

13	13	13	13	13

So $\frac{2}{5}$ of £65 = 2 × £13 = £26.

2 A coat costing £138 is reduced by $\frac{1}{3}$.
What is the reduced price of the coat?

Find $\frac{1}{3}$ of £138.

$\frac{1}{3}$ of £138 = £138 ÷ 3 = £46

So reduced price = £138 − £46
$$= £92$$

Exercise 6.3

Do not use a calculator in questions 1 to 3.

1 Change the following improper fractions to mixed numbers:

(a) $\frac{13}{10}$ (b) $\frac{3}{2}$ (c) $\frac{17}{8}$ (d) $\frac{15}{4}$ (e) $\frac{23}{5}$ (f) $\frac{34}{7}$ (g) $\frac{7}{2}$ (h) $\frac{11}{3}$ (i) $\frac{16}{9}$

2 Change the following mixed numbers to improper fractions:

(a) $2\frac{7}{10}$ (b) $1\frac{3}{5}$ (c) $5\frac{5}{6}$ (d) $3\frac{3}{20}$ (e) $4\frac{5}{9}$ (f) $7\frac{4}{7}$ (g) $3\frac{1}{4}$ (h) $4\frac{2}{3}$ (i) $2\frac{3}{8}$

3 Calculate:

(a) $\frac{1}{4}$ of 12 (b) $\frac{1}{5}$ of 20 (c) $\frac{1}{10}$ of 30 (d) $\frac{1}{6}$ of 48 (e) $\frac{2}{5}$ of 20

(f) $\frac{3}{10}$ of 30 (g) $\frac{2}{7}$ of 42 (h) $\frac{5}{9}$ of 36 (i) $\frac{5}{6}$ of 48 (j) $\frac{3}{8}$ of 32

4 Richard has 30 marbles.
He gives $\frac{1}{5}$ of them away.
(a) How many marbles does he give away?
(b) How many marbles has he got left?

5 Stella has collected 48 tokens.
She needs $\frac{1}{6}$ more to claim a prize.
What is the total number of tokens she needs to claim a prize?

6 Aisha has 36 balloons.
She sells $\frac{2}{9}$ of them.
How many balloons has she got left?

7 Alfie collects £12.50 for charity.
He gives $\frac{3}{5}$ of it to Oxfam.
How much does he give to other charities?

8 Ken has saved £5.60.
Paula has saved $\frac{3}{8}$ more than Ken.
How much has Paula saved?

9 In a sale all prices are reduced by $\frac{3}{10}$.
What is the sale price of a microwave which was originally priced at £212?

10 Lauren and Amelia share a bar of chocolate.
The chocolate bar has 24 squares.
Lauren eats $\frac{3}{8}$ of the bar.
Amelia eats $\frac{5}{12}$ of the bar.
(a) How many squares has Lauren eaten?
(b) How many squares has Amelia eaten?
(c) What fraction of the bar is left?

Adding and subtracting fractions

There are 12 sweets in a packet. Alena eats $\frac{2}{3}$ of the sweets and Sead eats $\frac{1}{4}$ of the sweets. What fraction of the packet of sweets have they eaten altogether?

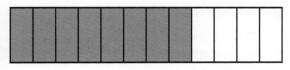

Alena eats $\frac{2}{3}$ of the sweets in the packet.

$$\frac{2}{3} \text{ of } 12 = 8 \qquad \frac{2}{3} = \frac{8}{12}$$

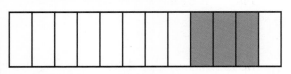

Sead eats $\frac{1}{4}$ of the sweets in the packet.

$$\frac{1}{4} \text{ of } 12 = 3 \qquad \frac{1}{4} = \frac{3}{12}$$

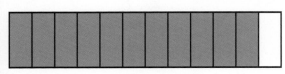

Together Alena and Sead eat $\frac{2}{3} + \frac{1}{4}$ of the packet.

$$\frac{2}{3} + \frac{1}{4} = \frac{8}{12} + \frac{3}{12} = \frac{11}{12}$$

Together Alena and Sead eat $\frac{11}{12}$ of the packet.

How to add (and subtract) fractions

Calculate $\qquad 1\frac{3}{4} + \frac{5}{6}$

Change mixed numbers to improper ('top heavy') fractions. $\qquad 1\frac{3}{4} = \frac{7}{4}$

The calculation then becomes $\qquad \frac{7}{4} + \frac{5}{6}$

Find the smallest number into which both 4 and 6 will divide.
Multiples of 4: 4, 8, 12, 16, …
Multiples of 6: 6, 12, 18, …
So 12 is the smallest.

Change the original fractions to equivalent fractions using the smallest number as the new denominator.
$$\frac{7}{4} = \frac{21}{12} \quad \text{and} \quad \frac{5}{6} = \frac{10}{12}$$

Add the new numerators. Keep the new denominator the same.
$$\frac{21}{12} + \frac{10}{12} = \frac{21 + 10}{12} = \frac{31}{12}$$

Write the answer in its simplest form. $\qquad \frac{31}{12} = 2\frac{7}{12}$

> Fractions must have the **same denominator** before addition (or subtraction) can take place.
>
> *What happens when you use a common multiple that is **not** the lowest?*

EXAMPLE

1. Work out $\frac{5}{8} - \frac{7}{12}$.

Multiples of 8 are: 8, 16, 24, …
Multiples of 12 are: 12, 24, …
24 is the smallest number into which both 8 and 12 divide.

$$\frac{5}{8} = \frac{5 \times 3}{8 \times 3} = \frac{15}{24}$$

$$\frac{7}{12} = \frac{7 \times 2}{12 \times 2} = \frac{14}{24}$$

$$\frac{5}{8} - \frac{7}{12} = \frac{15}{24} - \frac{14}{24}$$

$$= \frac{1}{24}$$

EXAMPLE

2 Work out $\frac{3}{4} + \frac{2}{3}$.

$$\frac{3}{4} + \frac{2}{3} = \frac{9}{12} + \frac{8}{12} = \frac{17}{12} = 1\frac{5}{12}$$

Remember
- Add the numerators only.
- When the answer is an improper fraction change it into a mixed number.

Exercise 6.4

Do not use a calculator in this exercise.

1 Work out:

(a) $\frac{1}{4} + \frac{1}{8}$ (b) $\frac{1}{3} + \frac{1}{4}$ (c) $\frac{1}{2} + \frac{1}{5}$ (d) $\frac{1}{3} + \frac{1}{5}$ (e) $\frac{1}{2} + \frac{1}{7}$ (f) $\frac{1}{4} + \frac{1}{5}$

2 Work out:

(a) $\frac{1}{4} - \frac{1}{8}$ (b) $\frac{1}{3} - \frac{1}{4}$ (c) $\frac{1}{2} - \frac{1}{5}$ (d) $\frac{1}{3} - \frac{1}{5}$ (e) $\frac{1}{2} - \frac{1}{7}$ (f) $\frac{1}{4} - \frac{1}{5}$

3 Work out:

(a) $\frac{1}{2} + \frac{3}{4}$ (b) $\frac{2}{3} + \frac{5}{6}$ (c) $\frac{3}{4} + \frac{4}{5}$ (d) $\frac{5}{7} + \frac{2}{3}$ (e) $\frac{3}{8} + \frac{5}{6}$ (f) $\frac{2}{5} + \frac{3}{4}$

4 Calculate:

(a) $\frac{5}{8} - \frac{1}{2}$ (b) $\frac{13}{15} - \frac{1}{3}$ (c) $\frac{5}{6} - \frac{5}{24}$ (d) $\frac{7}{15} - \frac{2}{5}$ (e) $\frac{3}{4} - \frac{5}{12}$ (f) $\frac{7}{8} - \frac{2}{3}$

5 Calculate:

(a) $2\frac{3}{4} + 1\frac{1}{2}$ (b) $1\frac{1}{2} + 2\frac{1}{3}$ (c) $1\frac{3}{4} + 2\frac{5}{8}$ (d) $2\frac{1}{4} + 3\frac{3}{5}$ (e) $4\frac{3}{5} + 1\frac{5}{6}$ (f) $3\frac{3}{10} + 2\frac{3}{20}$

6 Calculate:

(a) $2\frac{1}{2} - 1\frac{2}{5}$ (b) $1\frac{2}{3} - 1\frac{1}{4}$ (c) $3\frac{3}{4} - 2\frac{3}{8}$ (d) $5\frac{2}{5} - 2\frac{1}{10}$ (e) $4\frac{5}{12} - 2\frac{1}{6}$ (f) $3\frac{3}{8} - 2\frac{5}{16}$

7 Colin buys a bag of flour. He uses $\frac{1}{3}$ to bake a cake and $\frac{1}{2}$ to make a loaf.

(a) What fraction of the bag of flour has he used?
(b) What fraction of the bag of flour is left?

8 Kathryn and Matt share a bottle of cola.

Kathryn drinks $\frac{1}{4}$ of the cola. Matt drinks $\frac{1}{5}$ of the cola.

What fraction of the bottle of cola is left?

9 Both Lee and Mary have a packet of the same sweets.

Mary eats $\frac{1}{3}$ of her packet. Lee eats $\frac{3}{4}$ of his packet.

(a) Find the difference between the fraction Mary eats and the fraction Lee eats.

Lee gives his remaining sweets to Mary.
(b) What fraction of a packet does Mary now have?

10 Jon, Billy and Cathy are the only candidates in a school election.

Jon got $\frac{7}{20}$ of the votes. Billy got $\frac{2}{5}$ of the votes.

(a) What fraction of the votes did Cathy get?
(b) Which candidate won the election?

How to multiply fractions

Calculate $\dfrac{3}{8} \times \dfrac{1}{9}$

Simplify, where possible, by cancelling.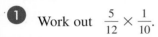

Multiply the numerators.
Multiply the denominators. $\dfrac{1 \times 1}{8 \times 3} = \dfrac{1}{24}$

Write the answer in its simplest form. $\dfrac{3}{8} \times \dfrac{1}{9} = \dfrac{1}{24}$

To simplify:
Divide a numerator **and** a denominator by the **same number.**

In this case:
3 and 9 can be divided by 3.
$3 \div 3 = 1$ and $9 \div 3 = 3$.

EXAMPLES

1 Work out $\dfrac{5}{12} \times \dfrac{1}{10}$.

$$\dfrac{5}{12} \times \dfrac{1}{10}$$

Simplify by cancelling.

$$= \dfrac{\overset{1}{\cancel{5}}}{12} \times \dfrac{1}{\underset{2}{\cancel{10}}}$$

Multiply out.

$$= \dfrac{1 \times 1}{12 \times 2}$$

$$= \dfrac{1}{24}$$

2 Calculate $\dfrac{3}{8} \times 12$.

$$\dfrac{3}{8} \times \dfrac{12}{1}$$

Simplify by cancelling.

$$= \dfrac{3}{\underset{2}{\cancel{8}}} \times \dfrac{\overset{3}{\cancel{12}}}{1}$$

Multiply out.

$$= \dfrac{3 \times 3}{2 \times 1} = \dfrac{9}{2}$$

Write the answer in its simplest form.

$$\dfrac{9}{2} = 4\dfrac{1}{2}$$

Any whole number can be written as a fraction with denominator 1.

$$12 = \dfrac{12}{1}$$

Dividing fractions

Activity

The diagram shows $1\dfrac{1}{2}$ divided into $\dfrac{1}{6}$'s.

Use the diagram to explain why …

(a) $1\dfrac{1}{2} \div \dfrac{1}{6} = 9$

(b) $1\dfrac{1}{2} \div \dfrac{1}{3} = 4\dfrac{1}{2}$

(c) $1\dfrac{1}{2} \div \dfrac{2}{3} = 2\dfrac{1}{4}$

Think of each of these as …

(a) How many $\dfrac{1}{6}$'s in $1\dfrac{1}{2}$?

(b) How many $\dfrac{1}{3}$'s in $1\dfrac{1}{2}$?

(c) How many $\dfrac{2}{3}$'s in $1\dfrac{1}{2}$?

Fractions . . . Fractions . . . Fractions . . . Fractions . . .

How to divide fractions

The method normally used when a fraction is divided by a whole number is to change the division to a multiplication. Then multiply in the usual way.

Calculate $\dfrac{6}{7} \div 10$

Write the whole number as a fraction. $\dfrac{6}{7} \div \dfrac{10}{1}$

Change the division to a multiplication. $\dfrac{6}{7} \times \dfrac{1}{10}$

Simplify, where possible, by cancelling. $\dfrac{\cancel{6}^{3}}{7} \times \dfrac{1}{\cancel{10}_{5}}$

Multiply the numerators.
Multiply the denominators. $\dfrac{3 \times 1}{7 \times 5} = \dfrac{3}{35}$

Write the answer in its simplest form. $\dfrac{6}{7} \div 10 = \dfrac{3}{35}$

EXAMPLE

Work out $\dfrac{2}{3} \div 5$.

$\dfrac{2}{3} \div 5$

$= \dfrac{2}{3} \times \dfrac{1}{5}$

$= \dfrac{2}{15}$

Divide by 5 is the same as multiply by $\dfrac{1}{5}$.

Exercise 6.5

Do not use a calculator in this exercise.

1 Work out. Give your answers as mixed numbers.

(a) $\dfrac{1}{2} \times 7$ (b) $\dfrac{1}{3} \times 8$ (c) $\dfrac{3}{5} \times 3$ (d) $\dfrac{5}{8} \times 10$ (e) $\dfrac{6}{7} \times 8$

2 Work out. Give your answers in their simplest form.

(a) $\dfrac{1}{2} \div 5$ (b) $\dfrac{3}{4} \div 2$ (c) $\dfrac{2}{3} \div 2$ (d) $\dfrac{2}{5} \div 4$ (e) $\dfrac{6}{7} \div 3$

3 Work out:

(a) $\dfrac{1}{2} \times \dfrac{1}{3}$ (b) $\dfrac{1}{4} \times \dfrac{1}{5}$ (c) $\dfrac{3}{5} \times \dfrac{1}{6}$ (d) $\dfrac{5}{7} \times \dfrac{1}{3}$ (e) $\dfrac{2}{3} \times \dfrac{1}{4}$

4 Calculate:

(a) $\dfrac{1}{2} \times \dfrac{3}{4}$ (b) $\dfrac{3}{4} \times \dfrac{2}{5}$ (c) $\dfrac{2}{5} \times \dfrac{5}{6}$ (d) $\dfrac{2}{3} \times \dfrac{1}{2}$

(e) $\dfrac{3}{10} \times \dfrac{5}{8}$ (f) $\dfrac{2}{5} \times \dfrac{1}{7}$ (g) $\dfrac{3}{4} \times \dfrac{2}{3}$ (h) $\dfrac{3}{10} \times \dfrac{5}{6}$

5 Bradley needs $\dfrac{3}{8}$ of a kilogram of flour to make one cake.

How many kilograms of flour does he need to make 4 cakes?

6 Neil uses $\dfrac{1}{2}$ of a block of paté to make 5 sandwiches.

What fraction of the block of paté does he put on each sandwich?

7 Spencer has $\dfrac{1}{4}$ of a pint of milk. He uses $\dfrac{1}{2}$ of the milk.

(a) What fraction of a pint does he use?   (b) What fraction of a pint is left?

8 Kylie has $\dfrac{2}{3}$ of a litre of orange. She drinks $\dfrac{2}{5}$ of the orange.

(a) What fraction of a litre does she drink?   (b) What fraction of a litre is left?

9 Tony eats $\dfrac{1}{5}$ of a bag of sweets.

He shares the remaining sweets equally among Bob, Jo and David.
(a) What fraction of the bag of sweets does Bob get?
(b) What is the smallest possible number of sweets in the bag?

Fractions on a calculator

Fraction calculations can be done quickly using the fraction button on a calculator.

On most calculators the fraction button looks like this …

EXAMPLES

1 Use a calculator to work out $\frac{4}{5} + \frac{2}{3}$.

This can be calculated with this calculator sequence.

$$\boxed{4}\ \boxed{a^b/_c}\ \boxed{5}\ \boxed{+}\ \boxed{2}\ \boxed{a^b/_c}\ \boxed{3}\ \boxed{=}$$

This gives the answer $1\frac{7}{15}$.

2 Calculate $\frac{7}{12}$ of 32.

This can be calculated with this calculator sequence.

$$\boxed{7}\ \boxed{a^b/_c}\ \boxed{1}\ \boxed{2}\ \boxed{\times}\ \boxed{3}\ \boxed{2}\ \boxed{=}$$

This gives the answer $18\frac{2}{3}$.

Use a calculator to check your answers to some of the questions in Exercises 6.4 and 6.5.

Fractions and decimals

All fractions can be written as decimals and vice versa.

Changing decimals to fractions

$0.7 = \frac{7}{10}$ $\qquad$ $0.03 = \frac{3}{100}$ $\qquad$ $0.009 = \frac{9}{1000}$

0.35 can be written as a fraction.
Using place value:

$0.35 = \frac{3}{10} + \frac{5}{100} = \frac{30}{100} + \frac{5}{100} = \frac{35}{100}$

This can be written as a fraction in its simplest form.

$\frac{35}{100} = \frac{35 \div 5}{100 \div 5} = \frac{7}{20}$

$0.35 = \frac{35}{100} = \frac{7}{20}$

> Write equivalent fractions with denominator 100.
>
> $\frac{3}{10} = \frac{3 \times 10}{10 \times 10} = \frac{30}{100}$

EXAMPLES Change the following decimals to fractions in their simplest form.

1 0.02 $\qquad$ $0.02 = \frac{2}{100} = \frac{2 \div 2}{100 \div 2} = \frac{1}{50}$

2 0.225 $\qquad$ $0.225 = \frac{225}{1000} = \frac{225 \div 25}{1000 \div 25} = \frac{9}{40}$

Changing fractions to decimals

EXAMPLES

Change the following fractions to decimals.

1 $\frac{1}{5} = 1 \div 5 = 0.2$ $\qquad$ **2** $\frac{11}{20} = 11 \div 20 = 0.55$

> $\frac{1}{5}$ means $1 \div 5$.
>
> $1 \div 5$ can be worked out using: short division, long division or a calculator.
>
> **Remember:**
> $11 \div 20 = 11.00 \div 20$
>
> $$\begin{array}{r} 0.5\,5 \\ 20\overline{)1\,1.\overset{11}{0}\overset{10}{0}} \end{array}$$

Do not use a calculator for questions 1 to 3.

1 Change the following decimals to fractions in their simplest form.
(a) 0.12 (b) 0.6 (c) 0.32 (d) 0.175
(e) 0.45 (f) 0.65 (g) 0.22 (h) 0.202
(i) 0.28 (j) 0.555 (k) 0.625 (l) 0.84

2 Change the following fractions to decimals.

(a) (i) $\frac{1}{4}$ (ii) $\frac{1}{2}$ (iii) $\frac{3}{4}$

(b) (i) $\frac{1}{10}$ (ii) $\frac{3}{10}$ (iii) $\frac{7}{10}$

(c) (i) $\frac{2}{5}$ (ii) $\frac{3}{5}$ (iii) $\frac{4}{5}$

3 Change the following fractions to decimals.

(a) (i) $\frac{3}{20}$ (ii) $\frac{7}{20}$ (iii) $\frac{19}{20}$

(b) (i) $\frac{4}{25}$ (ii) $\frac{9}{25}$ (iii) $\frac{23}{25}$

(c) (i) $\frac{7}{100}$ (ii) $\frac{23}{100}$ (iii) $\frac{106}{200}$

4 Change these fractions to decimals.
(a) $\frac{1}{8}$ (b) $\frac{5}{8}$ (c) $\frac{9}{40}$ (d) $\frac{29}{40}$

5 Change these fractions to decimals.
Give your answers correct to two decimal places.
(a) $\frac{1}{3}$ (b) $\frac{2}{3}$ (c) $\frac{3}{7}$ (d) $\frac{5}{11}$ (e) $\frac{7}{9}$

What you need to know

- The top number of a fraction is called the **numerator**, the bottom number is called the **denominator**.

- To write **equivalent fractions**, the numerator and denominator of a fraction are multiplied (or divided) by the **same** number.
  e.g. $\frac{3}{8} = \frac{3 \times 4}{8 \times 4} = \frac{12}{32}$

- In its **simplest form**, the numerator and denominator of a fraction have no common factor, other than 1.

- $2\frac{1}{2}$ is an example of a **mixed number**. It is a mixture of whole numbers and fractions.

- $\frac{5}{2}$ is an **improper** (or '**top heavy**') fraction.

- Fractions must have the **same denominator** before **adding** or **subtracting**.

- When dividing a fraction by a number, change the division to a multiplication.
  Then multiply in the usual way.
  e.g. $\frac{6}{7} \div 10 = \frac{6}{7} \times \frac{1}{10}$

- Mixed numbers must be changed to **improper fractions** before **multiplying** or **dividing**.

- Decimals can be written as fractions.
  e.g. $0.7 = \frac{7}{10}$

- Fractions can be written as decimals.
  e.g. $\frac{11}{20} = 11 \div 20 = 0.55$

Review Exercise   Do not use a calculator for questions 1 to 12.

6

1 (a)   What fraction of this shape is shaded?

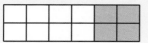

Copy this shape.

(b)   Shade $\frac{2}{5}$ of your shape.

Edexcel

2   Which of these fractions is equivalent to two fifths?

$\frac{3}{9}$ $\frac{4}{12}$ $\frac{8}{20}$ $\frac{12}{25}$

3 $\frac{2}{3} = \frac{a}{6} = \frac{8}{b}$

Find the values of a and b.   Edexcel

4   Andy and Pat share a bar of chocolate.
It has 15 pieces.

(a)   Andy eats $\frac{1}{5}$ of the bar.
How many pieces has he eaten?

(b)   Pat eats 5 pieces.
What fraction of the whole bar has she eaten?

(c)   What fraction of the bar is left?

5   A packet contains 24 biscuits.
Emily eats $\frac{3}{8}$ of the biscuits.
How many biscuits are left?

6   Brenda's dog eats $\frac{5}{8}$ of a tin of dog food each day.
How many tins of food does the dog eat each week?

7   Write down two different fractions that lie between $\frac{1}{4}$ and $\frac{1}{2}$.   Edexcel

8   (a)   Write $\frac{1}{6}$ as a decimal.
Give your answer correct to two decimal places.

(b)   What fraction is equal to 0.4?
Give your answer in its simplest form.

9   An examination in French is marked out of 80.

(a)   Jean scored $\frac{4}{5}$ of the marks.
How many marks did she score?

(b)   Tony scored 35 marks.
What fraction of the total did he score?
Give your answer in its simplest form.

10 (a)   Work out $\frac{7}{10}$ of £5.

(b)   Work out $\frac{3}{4}$ of £24.   Edexcel

11   Janice is saving to buy this camera.

£77.40

She saves $\frac{2}{3}$ of the cost.
Her father gives her the rest.
How much does Janice's father give her?
Edexcel

12   Work out.

(a) $\frac{1}{4} + \frac{2}{3}$ (b) $\frac{2}{5} - \frac{1}{8}$

13   A necklace is made from 60 beads.
$\frac{3}{10}$ of the beads are red.
$\frac{9}{20}$ of the beads are blue.
The rest of the beads are white.
What fraction of the beads are white?
Give this fraction in its simplest form.

14   In a school $\frac{8}{15}$ of the pupils are girls.
$\frac{3}{16}$ of the girls are left-handed.
What fraction of the pupils in the school are left-handed girls?

15   36 girls and 24 boys applied to go on a rock climbing course.
$\frac{2}{3}$ of the girls and $\frac{3}{4}$ of the boys went on the course.
What fraction of the 60 students who applied went on the course?
Write the fraction in its simplest form.

CHAPTER 7

Percentages

The meaning of a percentage

A fraction with denominator 100 has the special name - **percentage**.
'Per cent' means 'out of 100'.
The symbol for per cent is %.
A percentage can be written as a fraction with denominator 100.

> 10% means 10 out of 100.
>
> 10% can be written as $\frac{10}{100}$.
>
> 10% is read as '10 percent'.

EXAMPLE

What percentage of this diagram is shaded?

The large square is divided into 100 smaller squares.
5 of the squares are shaded.

$\frac{5}{100}$ of the diagram is shaded.

$\frac{5}{100} = 5\%$

So 5% of the diagram is shaded.

What percentage of each of these diagrams is shaded?

Changing percentages to decimals and fractions

To change a percentage to a decimal or a fraction: **divide by 100**

EXAMPLES

1 Write 38% as a fraction in its simplest form.

38% means '38 out of 100'.

This can be written as $\frac{38}{100}$.

$\frac{38}{100} = \frac{38 \div 2}{100 \div 2} = \frac{19}{50}$

$38\% = \frac{19}{50}$

> **Remember**
> To write a fraction in its **simplest form** divide both the numerator and denominator of the fraction by the **largest** number that divides into them both.

2 Write 38% as a decimal.

$38\% = \frac{38}{100} = 38 \div 100 = 0.38$

3 Write 2.5% as a decimal.

$2.5\% = \frac{2.5}{100} = 2.5 \div 100 = 0.025$

> **Remember**
> To change a fraction to a decimal divide the numerator by the denominator.

Do not use a calculator for questions 1 to 3.

1   What percentage of each diagram is shaded?

(a) 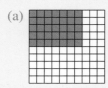   (b)   (c) 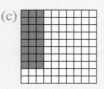   (d)

(e) 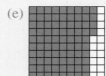   (f)   (g) 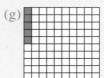   (h)

2   (a)   Draw a 10 by 10 square on squared paper.

    (i)   Calculate $\frac{2}{5}$ of 100.

    (ii)   Shade $\frac{2}{5}$ of a 10 by 10 square.

        What percentage of the square is shaded?

  (b)   Repeat (a) for the following fractions.

    (i) $\frac{3}{5}$ (ii) $\frac{7}{10}$ (iii) $\frac{9}{20}$ (iv) $\frac{6}{25}$ (v) $\frac{23}{50}$ (vi) $\frac{17}{25}$

3   Copy and complete this table to show the percentages given as:
(a)   fractions in their simplest form,
(b)   decimals.

Percentage	10%	20%	25%	50%	75%	80%
Fraction	$\frac{1}{10}$					
Decimal	0.1					

4   Change these percentages to fractions in their simplest form.
  (a) 15%   (b) 5%   (c) 18%   (d) 52%   (e) 23%   (f) 12.5%

5   Change these percentages to decimals.
  (a) 15%   (b) 5%   (c) 47%   (d) 72%   (e) 87.5%   (f) 150%

Changing decimals and fractions to percentages

To change a decimal or a fraction to a percentage: **multiply by 100**

EXAMPLES

1   Change 0.3 to a percentage.

$0.3 \times 100 = 30$
So 0.3 as a percentage is 30%.

2   Change 0.875 to a percentage.

$0.875 \times 100 = 87.5$
So 0.875 as a percentage is 87.5%.

3   Change $\frac{7}{10}$ to a percentage.

$\frac{7}{10} \times 100 = 7 \times 100 \div 10$
$\qquad\qquad = 700 \div 10 = 70\%$

4   Change $\frac{11}{25}$ to a percentage.

$\frac{11}{25} \times 100 = 11 \times 100 \div 25$
$\qquad\qquad = 1100 \div 25 = 44\%$

Comparing fractions

Fractions can be compared by first writing them as percentages.

EXAMPLE

Ben scored 17 out of 20 in a Maths test and 21 out of 25 in a History test.
Which is Ben's better mark?

Change each mark to a percentage.

Maths: $\frac{17}{20}$
$$\frac{17}{20} \times 100$$
$$= 17 \times 100 \div 20$$
$$= 85\%$$

History: $\frac{21}{25}$
$$\frac{21}{25} \times 100$$
$$= 21 \times 100 \div 25$$
$$= 84\%$$

So Ben's better mark was his Maths mark of 85%.

Exercise 7.2

Do not use a calculator for questions 1 to 3.

1 Copy and complete this table to work out the percentage equivalents of the fractions given.

Fraction	Percentage
$\frac{3}{10}$	
$\frac{2}{5}$	
$\frac{3}{25}$	
$\frac{7}{20}$	

2 Copy and complete this table to work out the percentage equivalents of the decimals given.

Decimal	Percentage
0.7	
0.45	
0.05	
1.2	

3 What is $\frac{1}{3}$ as a percentage?

4 Change these fractions to percentages.
(a) $\frac{17}{50}$ (b) $\frac{12}{25}$ (c) $\frac{30}{200}$ (d) $\frac{4}{5}$
(e) $\frac{135}{500}$ (f) $\frac{13}{20}$ (g) $\frac{2}{3}$ (h) $\frac{2}{9}$

5 Change these decimals to percentages.
(a) 0.15 (b) 0.32 (c) 0.125
(d) 0.07 (e) 1.12 (f) 0.015

6 Write in order of size, lowest first:
(a) $\frac{1}{2}$ 60% $\frac{2}{5}$ 0.55
(b) 43% $\frac{9}{20}$ 0.42 $\frac{11}{25}$
(c) $\frac{23}{80}$ 28% $\frac{57}{200}$ 0.2805

7 Peter scores 96 out of 120.
What percentage did he get?

8 Change each of these marks to a percentage.
(a) Maths: 27 out of 30.
(b) French: 34 out of 40.
(c) Science: 22 out of 25.
(d) Art: 48 out of 60.

9 Which rectangle has the greater percentage shaded?

A

B

10 In an ice hockey competition Team A won 8 out of the 11 games they played whilst Team B won 5 of their 7 games.

Which team has the better record in the competition?

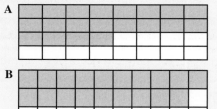

72

Expressing one quantity as a percentage of another

To work out one number as a percentage of another there are two steps.

| Step 1 | Write the numbers as a fraction. |
| Step 2 | Change the fraction to a percentage. |

EXAMPLES

*The numbers in the fraction must be in the **same** units.*

1 What is 30p as a percentage of £2?

£2 = 200p

Step 1

30p as a fraction of 200p is $\frac{30}{200}$.

Step 2

$\frac{30}{200} \times 100 = 30 \times 100 \div 200 = 15\%$

So 30p as a percentage of £2 is 15%.

2 A newspaper contains 48 pages, 6 of which are Sports pages.
What percentage of the pages are Sports pages?

Step 1

6 out of 48 pages are Sports pages.

$\frac{6}{48} = 6 \div 48 = 0.125$

Step 2

$0.125 \times 100 = 12.5$

12.5% of the pages are Sports pages.

Exercise 7.3

Do not use a calculator for questions 1 to 6.

1 What is
   (a) 30 as a percentage of 50,
   (b) 4 as a percentage of 25,
   (c) 7 as a percentage of 10,
   (d) 42 as a percentage of 200,
   (e) 63 as a percentage of 300?

2 What is
   (a) 64 pence as a percentage of £2,
   (b) 6 minutes as a percentage of 1 hour,
   (c) 30 mm as a percentage of 5 cm,
   (d) 150 g as a percentage of 1 kg,
   (e) 18 pence as a percentage of £0.60?

3 There are 8 yellow fruit drops in a packet of 25 fruit drops.
What percentage of the fruit drops are yellow?

4 James saved £30 and then spent £9.
What percentage of his savings did he spend?

5 A Youth Club has 200 members.
80 of the members are boys.
   (a) What percentage of the members are boys?
   (b) What percentage of the members are girls?

6 240 people took part in a survey.
30 of them were younger than 18.
What percentage were younger than 18?

7 A bar of chocolate has 32 squares.
Jane eats 12 of the squares.
What percentage of the bar does she eat?

8 Billy earns £4.50 per hour.
He gets a wage rise of 27 pence per hour.
What is his percentage wage rise?

9 What is
   (a) £2 as a percentage of £6,
   (b) 80 km as a percentage of 120 km,
   (c) 20 cm as a percentage of 160 cm,
   (d) £1530 as a percentage of £3600,
   (e) £105.09 as a percentage of £186?

10 A new car costs £13 500.
The dealer gives a discount of £1282.50.
What is the percentage discount?

11 There are 600 pupils in Years 9 to 13 of a High school.
360 pupils are in Years 10 and 11.
15% of pupils are in Years 12 and 13.
What percentage of pupils are in Year 9?

Finding a percentage of a quantity

1 Find 20% of £56.

Step 1   Divide by 100.
£56 ÷ 100 = £0.56

Step 2   Multiply by 20.
£0.56 × 20 = £11.20
So 20% of £56 is £11.20.

To find 1% of a quantity divide the quantity by 100.
To find 20% of a quantity multiply 1% of the quantity by 20.
This is the same as the method you would use to find $\frac{20}{100}$ of a quantity.

2 The price of a car is £12 500.
A car salesman offers a 7% discount.
How much is the discount?

Discount = 7% of £12 500
1% of £12 500 = £12 500 ÷ 100 = £125
7% of £12 500 = £125 × 7 = £875
The discount is £875.

3 David invests £500 in a building society.
He earns 6% interest per year.
How much interest does he get after one year?

Interest = 6% of £500
1% of £500 = £500 ÷ 100 = £5
6% of £500 = £5 × 6 = £30
The interest is £30.

Exercise 7.4

Do not use a calculator in this exercise.

1 Find:
(a) 10% of 500
(b) 5% of 800
(c) 20% of 700
(d) 30% of 200
(e) 40% of 600
(f) 20% of 550
(g) 5% of 50
(h) 15% of 80
(i) 65% of 30
(j) 85% of 20
(k) 12% of 500
(l) 32% of 200

2 Find:
(a) 20% of £80
(b) 75% of £20
(c) 30% of £220
(d) 15% of £350
(e) 5% of £500
(f) 20% of £150
(g) 9% of £300
(h) 20% of 20 m
(i) 30% of 80 kg
(j) 35% of 800 m
(k) 45% of £25
(l) 60% of 20 pence

3 Garry has 300 marbles.
20% of the marbles are blue.
35% of the marbles are red.
The rest of the marbles are white.
(a) How many marbles are blue?
(b) How many marbles are red?
(c) What percentage of the marbles are white?

4 Tim invests £400 in a building society.
He earns 5% interest per year.
How much interest does he get in one year?

5 There are 450 seats in a theatre.
60% of the seats are in the stalls.
How many seats are in the stalls?

6 A salesman earns a bonus of 3% of his weekly sales.
How much bonus does the salesman earn in a week when his sales are £1400?

7 Jenny gets a 15% discount on a theatre ticket.
The normal cost is £18.
How much does she save?

8 Dipak earns £150 per week.
He gets a wage rise of 3%.
How much extra does he earn each week?

9 In a school of 1200 pupils 45% are boys.
(a) How many are girls?

30% of the girls are under 13.
(b) How many girls are under 13?

10 A dozen biscuits weigh 720 g.
The amount of flour in a biscuit is 40% of the weight of a biscuit.
What is the weight of flour in **each** biscuit.

Percentage change

EXAMPLES

1 Increase £25 by 30%.

First find 30% of £25.
$$\frac{30}{100} \times 25 = 0.3 \times 25 = 7.5$$
30% of £25 is £7.50.
£25 increased by 30% = £25 + £7.50
                     = £32.50

2 Decrease £600 by 12%.

First find 12% of £600.
$$\frac{12}{100} \times 600 = 0.12 \times 600 = 72$$
12% of £600 is £72.
£600 decreased by 12% = £600 − £72
                      = £528

3 A shirt normally priced at £24 is reduced by 15% in a sale.
How much does this cost in the sale?

Reduction in price = 15% of £24
$15 \div 100 \times 24 = 0.15 \times 24 = 3.6$
15% of £24 = £3.60
The shirt costs £24 − £3.60 = £20.40.

4 A packet of cereals weighs 440 g.
A special offer packet contains 30% more.
What is the weight of a special offer packet?

Extra contents = 30% of 440 g
               = 440 ÷ 100 × 30
               = 132 g
440 + 132 = 572

A special offer packet weighs 572 g.

Exercise 7.5

Do not use a calculator for questions 1 to 5.

1 Increase:
  (a) £400 by 20%   (b) £300 by 40%
  (c) £2000 by 40%   (d) £600 by 80%
  (e) £3000 by 15%   (f) £900 by 40%
  (g) £50 by 60%   (h) £10 by 30%
  (i) £15 by 10%   (j) £50 by 15%

2 Decrease:
  (a) £600 by 30%   (b) £800 by 25%
  (c) £2500 by 20%   (d) £250 by 40%
  (e) £12 000 by 15%   (f) £7000 by 35%
  (g) £600 by 15%   (h) £55 by 90%
  (i) £42 by 20%   (j) £63 by 35%

3 A mobile telephone company offers a 20% discount on calls made in March.
The normal cost of a peak time call is 50 pence per minute.
How much does a peak time call cost in March?

4 Abdul earns £200 per week.
He gets a wage rise of 7.5%.
What is his new weekly wage?

5 A packet of breakfast cereal contains 660 g.
A special offer packet contains an extra 15%.
How many grams of breakfast cereal are in the special offer packet?

6 Prices in a sale are reduced by 18%.
The normal price of a shirt is £22.50.
Calculate its sale price.

7 The price of a gold watch is £278.
What does it cost with a 12% discount?

8 The price of a used car is £5200.
What does it cost with a 9.5% discount?

9 The price of a new kitchen is £3650.
What does it cost with a 35% discount?

10 Jane's salary of £14 000 is increased by 4%.
Calculate her new salary.

11 A car was valued at £13 500 when new.
After one year it lost 22% of its value.
What was the value of the car after one year?

12 Louisa puts £480 into a bank account.
At the end of one year interest at 2.5% is added to her account.
How much is in her account at the end of one year?

Percentage increase and decrease

$$\text{Percentage increase} = \frac{\text{actual increase}}{\text{initial value}} \times 100\%$$

$$\text{Percentage decrease} = \frac{\text{actual decrease}}{\text{initial value}} \times 100\%$$

EXAMPLES

1 A shop buys pens for 15 pence and sells them for 21 pence.
What is their percentage profit?

Actual profit = 21 pence − 15 pence
= 6 pence

$\%\ \text{profit} = \dfrac{\text{actual profit}}{\text{initial value}} \times 100$

$= \dfrac{6}{15} \times 100 = 40\%$

2 Pam buys a micro-scooter for £24.
She sells the micro-scooter for £15.
What is her percentage loss?

Actual loss = £24 − £15
= £9

$\%\ \text{loss} = \dfrac{\text{actual loss}}{\text{initial value}} \times 100$

$= \dfrac{9}{24} \times 100 = 37.5\%$

Exercise 7.6   Do questions 1 to 5 without a calculator.

1 A shop buys calculators for £5 and sells them for £6.
Find the percentage profit.

2 John's weekly wage rises from £150 to £165.
What is John's percentage wage rise?

3 On Monday peaches cost 15p each.
On Tuesday peaches cost 12p each.
What is the percentage reduction in price?

4 The price of a book increases from £8 to £9.
What is the percentage increase in price?

5 A man buys a boat for £2500 and sells it for £1800. Find his percentage loss.

6 During 1998 the rent on Karen's flat increased from £80 to £90 per week.
(a) Find the percentage increase in her rent.
In the same period Karen's wages increased from £250 per week to £280 per week.
(b) Find the percentage increase in her wages.
Comment on your answers.

What you need to know

- 'Per cent' means 'out of 100'.
  The symbol for per cent is %.

- A percentage can be written as a fraction with denominator 100.
  For example: 10% can be written as $\dfrac{10}{100}$.

- To change a decimal or a fraction to a percentage - **multiply by 100**.
  For example:
  0.12 as a percentage is $0.12 \times 100 = 12\%$.
  $\dfrac{3}{25}$ as a percentage is
  $\dfrac{3}{25} \times 100 = 3 \times 100 \div 25 = 12\%$.

- To change a percentage to a decimal or a fraction - **divide by 100**.
  For example:
  18% as a decimal is $18 \div 100 = 0.18$.
  18% as a fraction is $\dfrac{18}{100}$ which in its simplest form is $\dfrac{9}{50}$.

- $\text{Percentage increase} = \dfrac{\text{actual increase}}{\text{initial value}} \times 100\%$

- $\text{Percentage decrease} = \dfrac{\text{actual decrease}}{\text{initial value}} \times 100\%$

Review Exercise   Do not use a calculator for questions 1 to 10.

1 Copy and complete the following.

Fraction Decimal Percentage

(a) $\boxed{\dfrac{1}{4}}$ = $\boxed{0.25}$ = $\boxed{}$

(b) $\boxed{}$ = $\boxed{0.7}$ = $\boxed{70\%}$

(c) $\boxed{\dfrac{2}{5}}$ = $\boxed{}$ = $\boxed{40\%}$

2 Helen eats five doughnuts from a packet of ten.
What percentage has she eaten?

3 Match the pairs.

10% of £20		£10
50% of £10		£2
25% of £40		£5

4 Write in order of size, lowest first:

0.41 $\dfrac{2}{5}$ 39% $\dfrac{21}{50}$

5 A packet contains 20 biscuits.
(a) Graham eats 20% of the biscuits.
How many biscuits does he eat?
(b) Sylvia eats 9 of the biscuits.
What percentage of the biscuits does she eat?

6 Jo did a maths test.
There was a total of 40 marks for the test.
Jo got 65% of the marks.

(a) Work out 65% of 40.

Jo got 36 out of 80 in an English test.
(b) Work out 36 out of 80 as a percentage.   *Edexcel*

7 Of 50 plants in a flower bed,
15 had white flowers,
20 had pink flowers,
12 had blue flowers,
3 had no flowers.

(a) What percentage of the plants had pink flowers?
(b) What fraction of the plants had white flowers?
(c) Write, as a decimal, the fraction of the plants that had no flowers.
    Edexcel

8 A train has 1200 seats.
85% of the seats are occupied.
How many seats are empty?

9 Tim invests £650 in a building society.
He earns 5% interest in the first year.
How much interest does he earn?

10 A roll of carpet is 20 m long.
Beryl buys 18 m of carpet from the roll.
What percentage of the roll did she buy?

11 For selling a house an estate agent makes a charge of 1.5% of the sale price.
What is the charge on a house sold for £225 000?

12 $\dfrac{5}{8}$ of the cost of building a house is labour.
What percentage of the cost of building a house is labour?

13 In a sale rolls of wallpaper are sold at a 30% discount.

DISCOUNT ON ALL WALLPAPERS 30%

A roll of wallpaper normally costs £12.60.
How much will a roll of wallpaper cost in the sale?

14

Sue buys a pack of 12 cans of cola for £4.80.
She sells the cans for 50p each.
She sells all of the cans.
Work out her percentage profit.   *Edexcel*

15 (a) A year ago Paul was 150 cm tall.
He is now 6% taller.
Calculate his height now.
(b) A year ago Paul weighed 50 kg.
He now weighs 55 kg.
Calculate the percentage increase in his weight.

Time and Money

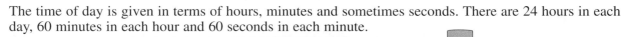

The time of day is given in terms of hours, minutes and sometimes seconds. There are 24 hours in each day, 60 minutes in each hour and 60 seconds in each minute.

24-hour clock and 12-hour clock times

The time can be given using the 12-hour clock or the 24-hour clock.

The watch and the digital clock both show the same time.
The time on the watch is 5.45 pm using 12-hour clock time.
The digital clock shows 5.45 pm as 1745 using 24-hour clock time.

12-hour clock times Times before midday are given as am. Times after midday are given as pm.	**24-hour clock times** The first two figures give the hours. The last two figures give the minutes.

EXAMPLES

1 A video recorder uses 24-hour clock times.
  (a) What time is shown by the video recorder at 6.30 pm?
  (b) The video is set to record programmes from 1120 to 1645.
      What are these times in 12-hour clock time?

  (a) 6.30 pm is equivalent to 1830.

  (b) 1120 is equivalent to 11.20 am.
      1645 is equivalent to 4.45 pm.

12-hour to 24-hour clock times
Times before midday:
  use the same figures.
Times after midday:
  add 12 to the hours.
	24-hour to 12-hour clock times
	Times before midday:
	  use the same figures and
	  include **am**.
	Times after midday:
	  subtract 12 from the hours and
	  include **pm**.

2 A motorist left Liverpool at 10.50 am and arrived in Birmingham at 1.20 pm.
How long did the journey take?

Method 1 (subtraction)

$$
\begin{array}{r}
1\,3.2\,0 \\
1\,0.5\,0 \\
\hline
\end{array}
$$

1. Write the times as 24-hour clock times.
2. Subtract the minutes.
    20 − 50 cannot be done.
    Exchange 1 hour for 60 minutes.
    60 + 20 − 50 = 30 minutes.

$$
\begin{array}{r}
1\,\overset{2}{\cancel{3}}.\overset{6}{2}\overset{0}{0} \\
1\,0.5\,0 \\
\hline
2.3\,0 \\
\hline
\end{array}
$$

3. Subtract the hours.
    12 − 10 = 2.

Method 2 (adding on)

10.50 to 11.00 =	10 minutes
11.00 to 13.00 = 2 hours	
13.00 to 13.20 =	20 minutes

Total time   = 2 hours 30 minutes

The journey took 2 hours 30 minutes.

Exercise 8.1

1 Write these 12-hour clock times in 24-hour clock time.
  (a) 10.30 am   (b) 10.30 pm   (c) 1.45 am   (d) 1.45 pm   (e) 11.50 pm

2 Write these 24-hour clock times in 12-hour clock time.
  (a) 1415   (b) 0525   (c) 2320   (d) 1005   (e) 1705

3 The clock shows the time an alarm
goes off in the morning.
What time does the alarm go off
  (a) in 12-hour clock time,
  (b) in 24-hour clock time?

4 The clocks show the time a school starts
in the morning and finishes in the afternoon.
  (a) Write these times in 12-hour clock time.
  (b) Write these times in 24-hour clock time.
  (c) How long is the school day?

Start

Finish

5 A video is set to record a film using 24-hour clock time.
The start and finish times are shown.
  (a) Write these times in 12-hour clock time.
  (b) How long did the film last?

START: 11:54
FINISH: 13:35

6 The times of some Sunday evening BBC 1
programmes are shown.
  (a) Give the times of these programmes
       using 24-hour clock time.
  (b) How many minutes does
       "Holiday Guide to Australia" last?
  (c) How many minutes does
       "Antiques Roadshow" last?

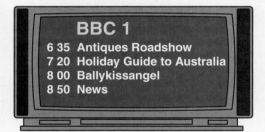

BBC 1
6 35 Antiques Roadshow
7 20 Holiday Guide to Australia
8 00 Ballykissangel
8 50 News

7 The times of some Monday afternoon ITV programmes are shown.
  (a) Give the times of these programmes using 24-hour clock time.
  (b) How many minutes does Shortland Street last?

12 30	News
12 55	Shortland Street
1 20	Three minutes
1 25	Home and Away

8 A coach left Poole at 1340 and arrived in Swanage at 1428.
  (a) What was the arrival time in 12-hour clock time?
  (b) How many minutes did the journey take?

9 A train left Paddington at 1315 and arrived in Exeter at 1605.
  (a) At what time did the train leave in 12-hour clock time?
  (b) How long did the journey take?

10 A train left Manchester at 9.10 am and arrived in Reading at 1.25 pm.
  (a) What was the arrival time in 24-hour clock time?
  (b) How long did the journey take?

11 A bus leaves Corfe Castle at 12.25 pm and arrives in Weymouth at 1.18 pm.
  (a)   What was the arrival time in 24-hour clock time?
  (b)   How long did the journey take?

12 A coach leaves Bournemouth at 10.50 am to travel to London.
  The journey takes 2 hours 40 minutes.
  At what time does the coach reach London?
  Give your answer in   (a)   12-hour clock time,   (b)   24-hour clock time.

13 A motorist leaves York at 2.35 pm to travel to Scarborough.
  The journey takes 50 minutes.
  At what time does the motorist reach Scarborough?
  Give your answer in   (a)   12-hour clock time,   (b)   24-hour clock time.

14 A plane flies from Southampton to Jersey.
  The plane leaves Southampton at 1255.
  The flight takes 48 minutes.
  At what time does the plane arrive in Jersey?
  Give your answer in   (a)   the 24-hour clock,   (b)   the 12-hour clock.

15 Mrs Hill took 3 hours 56 minutes to drive from Bath to Blackpool.
  She left Bath at 1045. At what time did she arrive in Blackpool?
  Give your answer in   (a)   the 24-hour clock,   (b)   the 12-hour clock.

Timetables

Bus and rail timetables are usually given in 24-hour clock time.
Here is part of a rail timetable.

Kidderminster	1035	1115	1155	1240	1325	1410
Bewdley	1050	1130	—	1300	—	1430
Arley	1105	1148	—	1318	1403	1448
Highley	1114	1158	—	1328	—	1458
Hampton Loade	1125	1210	—	1340	1425	1510
Bridgnorth	1140	1225	1310	1355	1440	1525

Some trains do not stop at every station. This is shown by a dash on the timetable.

How many minutes does the journey take on the 1035 train from Kidderminster to Arley?

Jean catches the 1155 train from Kidderminster to Bridgnorth.
What is her arrival time in 12-hour clock time?
How long does the journey take?

Alex lives in Bewdley.
What is the time of the last train he can catch to keep an appointment in Bridgnorth at 1.15 pm?

Exercise 8.2

1 The times of rail journeys from Guildford to Reading are shown.

Guildford	1415	1428	1515	1528
North Camp	1427	1444	1527	1544
Wokingham	1441	1508	1541	1608
Reading	1450	1524	1550	1624

  (a)   Richard catches the 1415 from Guildford to Reading.
    (i)   How many minutes does the journey take?
    (ii)   What is his arrival time in 12-hour clock time?
  (b)   Kate catches the 1444 from North Camp to Wokingham.
    (i)   How many minutes does the journey take?
    (ii)   What is her arrival time in 12-hour clock time?

2 The times of some bus journeys are shown.

Poole	1210	1225	1240	1255
Ashley Cross	1218	1233	1248	1303
Branksome	1228	1243	1258	1313
Westbourne	1233	1248	1303	1318
Bournemouth	1240	1255	1310	1325

(a) Terry catches the bus at 1258 from Branksome to Westbourne.
    (i)   How many minutes does the journey take?
    (ii) What is his arrival time in 12-hour clock time?
(b) Adrian has to be in Westbourne by 1 pm.
    What is the time of the latest bus he can catch from Ashley Cross?

3 The table shows the train services from Oxford to Birmingham.

Oxford	1109	1204	1313	1413	1503	1628	1736
Banbury	1142	1239	1337	—	1521	1652	1800
Leamington	1201	1300	1359	1454	1542	1713	1822
Coventry	1218	1317	1416	1512	1559	1730	1839
Birmingham	1247	1345	1445	1540	1635	1758	1911

(a) Carol catches the 1142 from Banbury to Coventry.
    How long does the journey take?
(b) Arnold needs to be in Birmingham before ten to five in the afternoon.
    What is the latest train he can catch from Oxford?
(c) Debbie arrives at Leamington station at 4.30 pm.
    What time is the next train to Birmingham?

4 The times of some trains from Hastings to Charing Cross are shown.

Hastings	0702	0802	0857	0900	0957	1102	1257
Crowhurst	—	—	0908	—	1008	—	1308
Battle	0715	0815	0912	—	1012	—	1312
Tunbridge Wells	0745	0845	0943	0940	1043	1141	1342
Sevenoaks	0805	0905	1003	—	1103	1201	1403
Charing Cross	0834	0934	1032	1025	1132	1230	1432

(a) John catches the 0745 from Tunbridge Wells to Charing Cross.
    How many minutes does the journey take?
(b) Aimee catches the 0857 from Hastings to Charing Cross.
    How long does the journey take?
(c) Sarah catches the 1257 from Hastings to Tunbridge Wells.
    What is her arrival time using the 12-hour clock?
(d) Keith wants to be in Charing Cross by 1030.
    What is the latest train he can catch from Battle?

5 The timetable shows some rail journeys from Waterloo to Brookwood.

Waterloo	1510	1520	1523	1538	1540
Clapham Junction	1516	—	1529	—	—
Surbiton	1528	—	—	—	1558
Woking	1542	1546	1549	1603	1612
Brookwood	1547	—	—	—	1617

(a) Nick catches the 1538 from Waterloo to Woking.
    (i)   What is his time of arrival in 12-hour clock time?
    (ii) How long does the journey take?
(b) Anne-Marie arrives at Waterloo station at 3.30 pm.
    What time is the next train to Surbiton?

Spending

Spending money is part of daily life. Every day people have to deal with many different situations involving money. Money is needed to buy fares for journeys, for purchases at shops, for hiring cars and equipment and for buying large items such as furniture.

When a large sum of money is needed to make a purchase, **credit** may be arranged. This involves paying for the goods over a period of time by agreeing to make a number of weekly or monthly repayments. It may also involve paying a **deposit**. The cost of credit may be more than paying cash.

EXAMPLES

1 Hamish pays £2.73 for 1 kg of pears and 2 kg of apples.
Pears cost 89p per kilogram.
How much per kilogram are apples?

2 kg of apples cost 273 − 89 = 184p
1 kg of apples costs 184 ÷ 2 = 92p
Apples cost 92p per kilogram.

Use the same units:
£2.73 is 273p

2 A motor home costs £6450. It can be bought on credit by paying a deposit of £1500 and 36 monthly payments of £150.
How much more is paid for the motor home when it is bought on credit?

Deposit: £1500
Payments: £150 × 36 = £5400
───────────────────────
Credit Price: £6900

Difference: £6900 − £6450 = £450
Credit price is £450 more.

Exercise 8.3

Do not use a calculator questions 1 to 7.

1 Esther pays £30.47 for a wheelbarrow, a fork and a spade.
The fork costs £7.49.
The spade costs £6.99.
How much did the wheelbarrow cost?

2 Gail pays £2.32 for a packet of cereal, a bag of sugar and a carton of milk.
The packet of cereal costs £1.38.
The sugar costs 65p.
How much did the carton of milk cost?

3 Mr Grey pays £3.40 for 2 adult fares and 3 child fares on the bus.
The fare for an adult is 95p.
How much is the fare for a child?

4 Amy pays £1.52 for celery, cucumber and lettuce.
The lettuce costs 27p.
The cucumber costs 39p.
How much did the celery cost?

5 Mrs Connor pays £3.12 for 2 kg of bananas and 1.5 kg of apples.
Apples cost 80p per kilogram.
How much per kilogram are bananas?

6 A family pay £6.35 for 4 cups of coffee and 3 cups of tea.
A cup of coffee costs 95p.
How much is a cup of tea?

7 Sam pays £56.40 for 200 bricks and 9 paving slabs.
The bricks cost 21p each.
How much is a paving slab?

8 Mushrooms cost £2.10 per kilogram.
Tomatoes cost 96p per kilogram.
James buys 0.2 kg of mushrooms and 0.5 kg of tomatoes.
How much does James have to pay?

9 Mr Jones pays £3.32 for 0.4 kg of Brie and 0.25 kg of Stilton.
Stilton costs £5.60 per kilogram.
How much per kilogram is Brie?

10 A building supplier hires out cement mixers.
There is a delivery charge of £15 and a hire charge of £8 per day.
(a) How much would it cost for the delivery and hire of a cement mixer for 4 days?
(b) A builder pays £95 for the delivery and hire of a cement mixer.
For how many days did he hire it?

11 The cost of hiring a carpet cleaner is £4 per day plus a delivery charge of £5.
(a) What is the cost of hiring a carpet cleaner for 2 days, including delivery?
(b) Gus pays a total of £33 to hire a carpet cleaner, including delivery.
For how many days did he hire the cleaner?

12

£30 per day
+
20p per mile driven

VAN FOR HIRE

(a) Alex hires a van for one day and drives 45 miles.
How much is the total hire charge?
(b) Bob hires a van for 3 days.
The total hire charge is £114.
How many miles did Bob drive?

13 The price of a pram is £299. It can be bought on credit by paying a deposit of £50 and 10 monthly payments of £27.50. How much more is paid for the pram when it is bought on credit?

14 A car costs £4950. It can be bought on credit by paying a deposit of £2000 and 24 monthly payments of £149.50.
How much more is paid for the car when it is bought on credit?

15 The cash price of a settee is £900. It can be bought on credit by paying a deposit of 10% of the cash price and 30 monthly payments of £32.50.
How much more is paid for the settee when it is bought on credit?

16 A washing machine costs £475. It can be bought on credit by paying a deposit of 10% of the cash price and 24 monthly payments of £19.50.
How much more is paid for the washing machine when it is bought on credit?

Best buys

When shopping we often have to make choices between products which are packed in various sizes and priced differently. If we want to buy the one which gives the better value for money we must compare prices using the same units.

EXAMPLE

Peanut butter is available in small or large jars, as shown.
Which size is the better value for money?

Compare the number of grams per penny for each size.
Small: 250 ÷ 58 = 4.31… grams per penny.
Large: 454 ÷ 106 = 4.28… grams per penny.

The small size gives more grams per penny and is better value.

SMALL
250 g
58p

LARGE
454 g
£1.06

In each question you must show all your working.

1 Milk is sold in 1 pint, 2 pint and 4 pint containers.
The cost of a 1 pint container is 28p, the cost of a two pint container is 55p and the cost of a 4 pint container is 89p.
(a) How much per pint is saved by buying a 2 pint container instead of two 1 pint containers?
(b) How much per pint is saved by buying a 4 pint container instead of two 2 pint containers?

2 Mushroom soup is sold in two sizes.
A small tin costs 43p and weighs 224 g.
A large tin costs 89p and weighs 454 g.
Which size gives more grams per penny?

3 Strawberry jam is sold in two sizes.
A small pot costs 52p and weighs 454 g.
A large pot costs 97p and weighs 822 g.
Which size gives more grams per penny?

4 Jars of pickled onions are sold at the following prices: 460 g at 65p or 700 g at 98p.
Which size is better value for money?

5 Honey is sold in two sizes.
A large pot costs £1.28 and weighs 454 g.
A small pot costs 56p and weighs 185 g.
Which size is better value for money?

6 Toothpaste is sold in small, medium and large sizes.
The small size contains 72 ml and costs 58p.
The medium size contains 125 ml and costs 98p.
The large size contains 180 ml and costs £1.44.
Which size is the best value for money?

7 Oscar wants to buy a camcorder.
He looks at two different advertisements.

8 Cottage cheese costs 85p for 120 g, £1.55 for 250 g and £6 for 1 kg.
Which size is the best value for money?

9 Two bottles of sauce are shown.

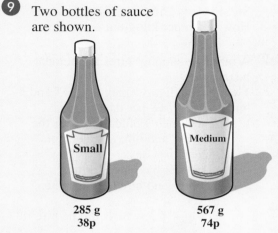

Small — 285 g — 38p

Medium — 567 g — 74p

Which size gives better value for money?

10 Which of these two bottles of "Active" drink is better value for money?

1.5 litre — ACTIVE — 90p

2 litre — ACTIVE — £1.30

DAISY'S
OUR PRICE 30% OFF
Recommended price £640

ALFIE'S
OUR PRICE 1/3 OFF
Recommended price £657

(a) Find the actual selling price of each camcorder.
(b) Which camcorder has the bigger discount?

VAT

Some goods and services are subject to a tax called **value added tax**, or **VAT**, which is calculated as a percentage of the price or bill. Total amount payable = cost of item or service + VAT

For most purchases the rate of VAT is 17.5%.
For gas and electricity the rate of VAT is 5%.
Some goods are exempt from VAT.

EXAMPLE

A bill at a restaurant is £24 + VAT at 17.5%.
What is the total bill?

VAT: £24 × 0.175 = £4.20

Total bill: £24 + £4.20 = £28.20

The total bill is £28.20.

Remember:
$$17.5\% = \frac{17.5}{100} = 0.175$$

Exercise 8.5

Do not use a calculator for questions 1 and 2.

1. Naomi's gas bill is £120 plus VAT at 5%. How much VAT does she have to pay?

2. Joe receives an electricity bill for £70 plus VAT at 5%.
   (a) Calculate the amount of VAT charged.   (b) What is the total bill?

3. A washing machine costs £340 plus VAT at 17.5%.
   (a) Calculate the amount of VAT charged.
   (b) What is the total cost of the washing machine?

   £340 + VAT

4. A car service costs £90 plus VAT at 17.5%.
   (a) Calculate the amount of VAT charged.   (b) What is the total cost of the service?

5. Mrs Swan receives a gas bill for £179.53. VAT at 5% is added to the bill.
   (a) How much VAT does she have to pay?   (b) What is the total bill?

6. A bike costs £248 plus VAT at 17.5%. What is the total cost of the bike?

7. A ladder costs £145 plus VAT at 17.5%. What is the total cost of the ladder?

8. Joyce buys a greenhouse for £184 plus VAT.
   VAT is charged at 17.5%. What is the total cost of the greenhouse?

9. James receives a telephone bill for £37.56 plus VAT at 17.5%. How much is the total bill?

10. George buys vertical blinds for his windows.
    He needs three blinds at £65 each and two blinds at £85 each.
    VAT at 17.5% is added to the cost of the blinds.
    How much do the blinds cost altogether?

11. A car is hired for two days and driven 90 miles.
    VAT at 17.5% is added to the hire charges.
    How much does it cost to hire the car altogether?

RENT A CAR

£25 per day
plus
10 pence per mile

Foreign currency

When we go abroad we have to pay for goods and services in the currency of the country we are visiting. We therefore need to change pounds (£) into other currencies. The rate of exchange varies from day to day.

The table below shows the exchange rates on one day.

EXCHANGE RATE Each £ will buy	
European currency	1.55 euros
Japan	173 yen
Malta	0.63 liri
Norway	12.48 krone
Switzerland	2.30 francs
USA	1.42 dollars

EXAMPLE

What is the value, in £s and pence, of 500 Norwegian krone?
$$12.48 \text{ krone} = £1$$
$$500 \text{ krone} = 500 \div 12.48$$
$$= £40.0641\ldots$$
$$500 \text{ krone} = £40.06, \text{ to the nearest penny.}$$

Exercise 8.6

Use the table of exchange rates above to answer these questions.

1 How much will I receive if I change £200 into
   - (a) European euros,
   - (b) Japanese yen,
   - (c) Maltese liri,
   - (d) Norwegian krone,
   - (e) Swiss francs,
   - (f) United States dollars?

2 How much would each item cost in £s?
   Give your answers to the nearest penny.
   - (a) A vase in Switzerland for 90 francs.
   - (b) A radio in Japan for 5000 yen.
   - (c) A pair of shoes in Italy for 75 euros.
   - (d) A meal in Norway for 225 krone.
   - (e) A pair of jeans in the United States for 35 dollars.

3 (a) A tourist changes £25 into euros. How many euros does she receive?
   (b) She pays 23.25 euros for a gift. What is the cost of the gift in £s?

4 Norman travels to Switzerland. He changes £120 into francs.
   - (a) How many francs does he receive?
   - (b) He pays 24.50 francs for a box of chocolates.
     What is the cost of the chocolates in £s?

5 Dolores travels to England from Spain. She changes 600 euros into £.
   - (a) How much, in £s and pence, does she receive?
   - (b) She buys a theatre ticket for £30.
     What is the cost of the theatre ticket in euros?

6 Marcel travels to England from Norway. He changes 3000 krone into £.
   - (a) How much, in £s, does he receive?
   - (b) He pays £45 for bed and breakfast.
     What is the cost of bed and breakfast in krone?

7 Sue changes £500 into dollars for a trip to the USA.
   - (a) How many dollars does she receive?
   - (b) On holiday she spends 680 dollars. She changes the remaining dollars back into £s.
     There is a £3 charge for changing the money.
     How much, in £s, will she receive?

8 Jeff has just returned from Malta. He changes 85 liri back into £s.
   There is a £3 charge for changing the money.
   How much, in £s, will he receive?

9 In France a car costs 9000 euros.
   In Japan the same car costs 1 million yen.
   In which country is the car cheaper? By how much?

What you need to know

- Time can be given using either the **12-hour clock** or the **24-hour clock**.
  When using the 12-hour clock:
     times **before** midday are given as am,
     times **after** midday are given as pm.

- **Timetables** are usually given using the 24-hour clock.

- When considering a **best buy**, compare quantities by using the same units. For example, find which product gives more grams per penny.

- **Value added tax**, or **VAT**, is a tax on some goods and services and is added to the bill.

- **Exchange rates** are used to show what £1 will buy in foreign currencies.

	00.00	
11.00 / 23.00	12.00	01.00 / 13.00
10.00 / 22.00		02.00 / 14.00
09.00 / 21.00		03.00 / 15.00
08.00 / 20.00		04.00 / 16.00
07.00 / 19.00	06.00 / 18.00	05.00 / 17.00

Review Exercise

Do not use a calculator for questions 1 to 6.

1 A train left London at 0855 and arrived at Manchester at 1202.
How many **minutes** did the journey take?

Edexcel

2 Some of the rail services from Manchester to Birmingham are shown.

Manchester	0925	1115	1215	1415	1555
Stockport	0933	—	1223	—	1603
Stoke	1007	1155	1255	1459	1636
Stafford	1027	—	1318	—	1656
Wolverhampton	1056	1234	1336	1535	1716
Birmingham	1121	1257	1359	1558	1742

(a) David has to be in Wolverhampton by 2 pm.
What is the time of the latest train he can catch from Manchester?
(b) What time does the 1555 from Manchester arrive in Birmingham in 12-hour clock time?

3 Edward pays 81p for 2 pencils and 3 pens.
A pencil costs 12p. How much does a pen cost?

4 Mrs Wye pays 89p for 0.5 kg of carrots and 1 kg of onions.
The onions cost 55p per kilogram.
How much per kilogram are carrots?

5 A bottle of white wine costs £3.80.
Kay buys 2 dozen bottles.
How much does she have to pay?

6 Kim went to Paris.
(a) She changed £200 into euros.
The exchange rate was £1 = 1.60 euros.
Work out the number of euros Kim got.

(b) Kim brought 4.50 euros back from Paris.
The exchange rate was now £1 = 1.50 euros.
Work out how much Kim got in pounds.

7 (a) Last year Ray had to pay four bills for his car.

Tax	£145.00
Insurance	£512.00
MOT test	£ 28.66
Repairs	£368.27

Work out the total cost.

(b) Last year Ray used 950 litres of petrol.
1 litre of petrol costs 67.9 pence.
Work out the total cost of the petrol.
Give your answer in pounds and pence.

Edexcel

8

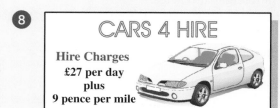

CARS 4 HIRE

Hire Charges
£27 per day
plus
9 pence per mile

(a) Elle hires a car for one day.
She drives 165 miles
What is the total hire charge?

(b) Brett hires a car for 3 days.
The total hire charge is £101.79.
How many miles did he drive?

9 The cash price of the saxophone is £740.
Tom buys the saxophone using a Credit Plan.
He pays a deposit of 5% of the cash price
and 12 monthly payments of £65.
Work out the difference between the cost
when he used the Credit Plan and the cash price.

Saxophone

£740 for cash

*Credit Plan
available*

Edexcel

10

Foodstuff's supermarket sell their own brand of
instant coffee in two sizes of jar.
Which jar is the better value?

11 Two shops sell the same make of calculator.
At **Calculators are Us**, the price of the calculator is £7.50 plus VAT.
At **Top Calculators**, the price is £8.75. This includes VAT.
VAT is charged at a rate of 17.5%.
Work out the difference in cost between the two prices.

Edexcel

12 The table shows the amount of foreign currency
that a tourist can buy with £1.

Pepe travels from Spain to the USA for a holiday.
He changes 400 euros into dollars.
Calculate how many dollars he will get.

TOURIST RATES	
Spain	1.60 euros
USA	1.40 dollars

CHAPTER **9** **Personal Finance**

People need money to pay for accommodation, household bills, food, clothing, transport, entertainment, etc. To get money people do many different types of job and receive payment, or wages, for their work.

Wages

Hourly pay

Many people are paid by the hour for their work. In most cases they receive a **basic hourly rate** for a fixed number of hours and an **overtime rate** for any extra hours worked.

> **EXAMPLE**
>
> A car-park attendant is paid £4.20 per hour for a basic 40-hour week.
> Overtime is paid at time and a half.
> One week an attendant works 48 hours.
> How much does he earn?
>
> Basic Pay: £4.20 × 40 = £168.00
> Overtime: 1.5 × £4.20 × 8 = £50.40
> Total pay = £218.40
>
> Overtime paid at 'time and a half' means 1.5 × normal hourly rate.
> In this example, the hourly overtime rate is given by:
> 1.5 × £4.20
>
> Common overtime rates are 'time and a quarter', 'double time', etc.

Commission

As an incentive for their employees to work harder some companies pay a basic wage (fixed amount) plus commission. The amount of commission is usually expressed as a percentage of the value of the sales made by the employee.

> **EXAMPLE**
>
> An estate agent is paid a salary of £11 000 per year plus commission of 0.5% on the sales of all houses.
> In 1998 the estate agent sold houses to the value of £2 040 500.
> How much did the estate agent earn?
>
> Annual salary: £11 000
> Commission: 0.005 × £2 040 500 = £10 202.50
> Total pay = £21 202.50
>
> **Remember:**
> $0.5\% = \frac{0.5}{100} = 0.005$

Exercise **9.1**

1 Helen is paid £4.20 per hour.
She works 20 hours a week.
How much does she earn each week?

2 John does a part-time job for 7 hours a week.
He is paid £31.50 a week.
What is his hourly rate of pay?

3 Mike earns £364.80 a week.
He is paid £9.60 per hour.
How many hours a week does Mike work?

4 Jean earns a basic £7.20 an hour.
When she works overtime she is paid at time and a half.
How much is she paid for 1 hour of overtime?

5 A secretary is paid a basic £192 for working 30 hours a week.
If she works overtime she is paid at one and a half times her basic hourly rate.
How much is she paid for 1 hour of overtime?

6 Tom is paid at time and a half for overtime.
His overtime rate of pay is £9.90 per hour.
What is his basic rate of pay per hour?

7 A chef is paid £5.60 per hour for a basic 38-hour week.
Overtime is paid at time and a half.
How much does the chef earn in a week in which she works 50 hours?

8 A mechanic is paid £6.40 per hour for a basic 40-hour week.
Overtime is paid at time and a quarter.
One week the mechanic works 42 hours. How much does he earn?

9 A hairdresser is paid £4.80 per hour for a basic 35-hour week.
One week she works two hours overtime at time and a half and $3\frac{1}{2}$ hours overtime at time and a quarter.
How much is she paid that week?

10 A driver is paid £68.85 for $4\frac{1}{2}$ hours of overtime.
Overtime is paid at time and a half.
What is his basic hourly rate of pay?

11 A furniture salesperson is paid an annual salary of £9600 plus commission of 2% on sales.
In 2001 the salesperson sold £300 000 worth of furniture.
How much did the salesperson earn?

12 A car salesperson is paid an annual salary of £10 200 plus commission of 1.5% on sales.
How much does the salesperson earn in a year in which cars to the value of £868 000 are sold?

13 A double glazing salesperson is paid £480 per month plus commission of 5% on sales.
How much does he earn in a month in which he makes sales of £12 600?

14 An estate agent is paid 1.5% commission on the sales of houses.
How much commission does he earn for a house sold for one million pounds?

Income tax

The amount you earn for your work is called your **gross pay**.
Your employer will make deductions from your gross pay for income tax, National Insurance, etc.
Pay after all deductions have been made is called **net pay**.

The amount of **income tax** you pay will depend on how much you earn.
Everyone is allowed to earn some money which is not taxed, this is called a **tax allowance**. Any remaining money is your **taxable income**.

The rates of tax and the bands (ranges of income) to which they apply vary.

EXAMPLE

George earns £5800 per year. His tax allowance is £4385 per year
and he pays tax at 10p in the £ on his taxable income.
How much income tax does George pay per year?

Taxable income: £5800 − £4385 = £1415
Income tax: £1415 × 0.10 = £141.50

George pays income tax of £141.50 per year.

> An income tax rate of
> 10% is often
> expressed as '10p in
> the pound (£)'.

Exercise 9.2

1 Joan earns £12 400 per year. Her tax allowance is £4385 per year.
What is her taxable income?

2 Tony is paid £274 per week for 52 weeks a year.
His tax allowance is £6095 per year.
What is his annual taxable income?

3 Lyn earns £5600 per year. Her tax allowance is £4385 per year and she pays tax at 10p in the
£ on her taxable income.
(a) What is her taxable income?
(b) How much income tax does she pay per year?

4 Brian earns £594 per month. His tax allowance is £5765 per year and he pays tax at 10p in
the £ on his taxable income.
(a) What is his annual taxable income?
(b) How much income tax does he pay per year?
(c) How much income tax does he pay per month?

5 Kay has an annual salary of £23 700. Her tax allowance is £4385 per year. She pays tax at
10p in the £ on the first £1500 of her taxable income and 22p in the £ on the remainder.
How much income tax does she pay per year?

6 Julie earns £865 per month. Her tax allowance is £4385 per year and she pays tax at 10p in
the £ on the first £1500 of her taxable income and 22p in the £ on the remainder.
How much income tax does she pay per month?

7 Jim is paid £186 per week for 52 weeks a year. His tax allowance is £4385 per year.
He pays tax at 10p in the £ on the first £1500 of his taxable income and 22p in the £ on the
remainder.
How much income tax does he pay per week?

Household bills

The cost of living includes many bills for services provided to our homes. Electricity, gas and telephone
charges are all examples of **quarterly bills** which are sent out four times a year. Each bill is made up of
two parts:
A fixed (standing) charge, for providing the service.
A charge for the quantity of the service used (amount of gas/electricity, duration of telephone calls, etc.)

Other household bills include taxes payable to the local council, water charges and the cost of the
insurance of the house (structure) and its contents.

Mrs Davis receives a quarterly bill for electricity.
The standing charge for the quarter is £9.30 and she has used
264 units of electricity at 6.16p per unit.
How much is her electricity bill?

Cost of units used: $264 \times 6.16p = 1626.24p$
$= 1626p$, to the nearest penny.

Electricity bill = standing charge + cost of units used
$= £9.30 + £16.26$
$= £25.56$.

Her electricity bill is £25.56

> The actual cost is rounded down to the nearest penny.
>
> Change the cost of units to £.

Exercise 9.3

1 Last year the Evans family received four quarterly gas bills.

March £134.26   June £52.00   September £33.49   December £80.25

(a) What was their total bill for the year?
(b) The family can pay for their gas by 12 equal monthly instalments.
How much would each instalment be?

2 In 2001 the Price family used 2734 units of electricity.
Each unit costs 6.16 pence.
Calculate the cost of the units used in £ and pence.

3 Mrs Cotton uses 1064 units of electricity during one quarter.
Find the cost of her electricity bill if each unit costs 6.16 pence and the quarterly charge
is £9.30.

4 During one quarter Mr Singh uses 1481 kWh of gas.
Calculate the cost of his gas bill if each kWh costs 1.295 pence and there is a standing
charge of £6.58.

5 Mr Jones receives an electricity bill for £59.20.
The bill includes a quarterly charge of £9.30 and the cost per unit is 6.16 pence.
Calculate to the nearest whole number, the number of units he has used.

6 Mrs Madan receives a gas bill for £179.53. The bill includes a standing charge and the
cost of the gas used. During the quarter the gas used is equivalent to 13 377 kWh at
1.295 pence per kWh.
How much is the standing charge?
Give your answer to an appropriate degree of accuracy.

7 John pays his council tax by 10 instalments.
His first instalment is £98.65 and the other 9 instalments are £97 each.
How much is his total council tax?

8 Mr Peters has an annual council tax of £1123.05.
He pays the council tax in 10 instalments.
The first instalment is £115.05 and the remaining amount is payable in 9 instalments of
equal value.
How much is the second instalment?

9 Mrs Dear checks her water bill.
She has used 46 cubic metres of water at 77.76 pence per cubic metre and there is a standing charge of £11.
How much is her bill?

10 The table shows the premiums charged by an insurance company to insure a house and its contents.

(a) Jim has bought a house valued at £154 000.
How much would he pay to insure the house?

(b) The cost for Mr Brown to insure his house is £126.
What is the value of his house?

(c) Mrs Crow insures the contents of her house for £19 000.
What is the annual premium?

Buildings and Contents Insurance		
	Buildings	Contents
Annual premium for each £1000 insured.	£1.50	£5.00
	Minimum £20 per year	

(d) Andy insures his flat valued at £42 000 and its contents valued at £9000.
Calculate the total cost of the insurance premium.

11 George insures his house valued at £134 000 and its contents valued at £27 500.
The annual premiums for the insurance are:
Buildings: £1.35 per £1000 of cover,
Contents: 56p per £100 of cover.
Calculate the total cost of the insurance premium.

12 Naomi rents a flat and pays £69.44 to insure its contents.
Contents insurance costs 56p for each £100 insured.
For how much are the contents insured?

13 The table shows the monthly payments for loans.

	12 MONTHS	24 MONTHS
LOAN, £	Monthly repayment	Monthly repayment
5000	492.95	287.20
3000	295.79	172.32
2000	197.15	114.88

Marc takes out a loan for £3000 over a period of 12 months.
Holly takes out a loan for £5000 over a period of 24 months.

(a) What is the difference in their monthly repayments?
(b) What is the total amount that Holly is charged for her loan?

What you need to know

- **Hourly pay** is paid at a **basic rate** for a fixed number of hours.
  Overtime pay is usually paid at a higher rate such as time and a half, which means each hour's work is worth 1.5 times the basic rate.

- Everyone is allowed to earn some money which is not taxed. This is called a **tax allowance**.

- Tax is only paid on income earned in excess of the tax allowance. This is called **taxable income**.

- Gas, electricity and telephone bills are paid **quarterly**.
  The bill consists of a standing charge plus a charge for the amount used.

Do not use a calculator for questions 1 to 3.

1 David works 30 hours at £5.60 per hour.
How much does he earn?

2 Mr Blaney gets four telephone bills each year.
He pays for his bills by 12 equal monthly payments.
Last year his telephone bills were:
£46.48, £49.36, £45.65 and £50.51.
How much was each monthly payment?

3 Jessica has an annual income of £5824.
She has a tax allowance of £4535.
(a) Calculate Jessica's taxable income.

She pays tax at 10p in the £ on her taxable income.
(b) How much tax does Jessica pay per year?

4

CHARGES
Standing charge: £9.70
Cost per unit: 6.4 pence

Alan receives a quarterly electricity bill.
It is made up of a standing charge and the cost of the units of electricity used.
What is the total bill if he has used 462 units of electricity?

5 Marie insures her house and its contents with Insure Direct.

INSURE DIRECT
Annual Insurance Premiums
BUILDINGS . . . . £1.20 per £1000 of cover
CONTENTS . . . . 45p per £100 of cover

She insures the house for £180 000 and the contents for £24 000.
Calculate her total annual insurance premium.

6 Yasmine earns £5.20 per hour for working a basic week of 38 hours.
Overtime is paid at time and a half.
The table shows the hours Yasmine worked last week.

Day	Monday	Tuesday	Wednesday	Thursday	Friday
Hours	10	8	7	9	12

(a) How many hours overtime did she work last week?
(b) Calculate her total pay for last week.

7 Bernadette has to pay tax at the rate of 10p in the £ on the first £1500 of her taxable income
and 22p in the £ on the remainder.
Her taxable income is £1967.
How much tax does she have to pay?

Ratio and Proportion

Ratio

 Some faces are SMILERS.

Some faces are GLUMS.

In a group of 10 faces the **ratio** of SMILERS to GLUMS is 3 : 2. This means that for every three SMILERS there are two GLUMS.

For the ratio 3 : 2 say 3 to 2.

In the group there are 6 SMILERS and 4 GLUMS.

EXAMPLES

1 In a group of 16 faces there are 10 SMILERS and 6 GLUMS.

What is the ratio of SMILERS to GLUMS?

For every 5 SMILERS there are 3 GLUMS. So the ratio of SMILERS to GLUMS is 5 : 3.

2 Draw 15 faces where the ratio of SMILERS to GLUMS is 4 : 1.

For every 4 SMILERS there is 1 GLUM.
So draw sets of 4 SMILERS and 1 GLUM until there are a total of 15 faces.

How many sets of 4 SMILERS and 1 GLUM *are there?*

Exercise **10.1**

1 In a group of 14 faces there are 10 SMILERS and 4 GLUMS.

Copy and complete the following.
(a)   For every 5 SMILERS there are …… GLUMS.
(b)   The ratio of SMILERS to GLUMS is 5 : ….

2 In a group of 12 faces there are 9 SMILERS and 3 GLUMS.

Copy and complete the following.
(a)   For every …… SMILERS there is 1 GLUM.
(b)   The ratio of SMILERS to GLUMS is … : 1.

3 In a group of 24 faces there are 15 SMILERS and 9 GLUMS.
Copy and complete the following.
(a) For every 5 SMILERS there are …… GLUMS.
(b) The ratio of SMILERS to GLUMS is 5 : ….

4 In a group of 30 faces there are 21 SMILERS and 9 GLUMS.
Copy and complete the following.
The ratio of SMILERS to GLUMS is … : 3.

5 (a) Draw 10 faces where the ratio of SMILERS to GLUMS is 4 : 1.
(b) Draw 12 faces where the ratio of SMILERS to GLUMS is 1 : 3.

6 The ratio of SMILERS to GLUMS is 5 : 2.

(a) How many SMILERS are there when there are 30 GLUMS?
(b) How many GLUMS are there when there are 30 SMILERS?
(c) How many FACES are there when there are …
(i) 40 SMILERS, (ii) 40 GLUMS?

7 The ratio of SMILERS to GLUMS is 4 : 3.

(a) How many SMILERS are there when there are 12 GLUMS?
(b) How many GLUMS are there when there are 12 SMILERS?
(c) How many FACES are there when there are …
(i) 48 SMILERS, (ii) 48 GLUMS?

8 How many SMILERS and how many GLUMS are there when …
(a) the ratio of SMILERS to GLUMS is 7 : 3 and there are 20 faces?
(b) the ratio of SMILERS to GLUMS is 3 : 2 and there are 15 faces?

9 (a) Look at this group of faces.

(i) What fraction of the faces are GLUMS?
(ii) What fraction of the faces are SMILERS?
(iii) What is the ratio of GLUMS to SMILERS?

(b) In another group of faces $\frac{1}{4}$ are GLUMS.
What is the ratio of SMILERS to GLUMS?

10 (a) In this group of faces the ratio of SMILERS to GLUMS is 7 : 3.

(i) What percentage of the faces are GLUMS?
(ii) What percentage of the faces are SMILERS?
(b) In another group of faces 40% are GLUMS.
What is the ratio of SMILERS to GLUMS?

11 In a group of faces the ratio of SMILERS to GLUMS is 2 : 3.
What fraction of the faces are SMILERS?

12 In a group of faces the ratio of SMILERS to GLUMS is 3 : 1.
What percentage of the faces are SMILERS?

Equivalent ratios

Ratios are used only to **compare** quantities.
They do not give information about actual values.

For example.
A necklace is made using red beads and white beads in
the ratio **3 : 4**.
This gives no information about the actual numbers of
beads in the necklace.
The ratio **3 : 4** means that for every 3 red beads in the necklace there are 4 white beads.
The **possible** numbers of beads in the necklace are shown in the table.

Red beads	White beads	Total beads
3	4	7
6	8	14
9	12	21
12	16	28

*Make similar tables when the ratio of red
beads to white beads in the necklace is:*
(a)   4 : 5   (b)   2 : 3   (c)   3 : 1

The ratios   3 : 4,   6 : 8,   9 : 12,   … are
different forms of the **same** ratio.
They are called **equivalent** ratios.
They can be found by multiplying or dividing
each part of the ratio by the **same** number.

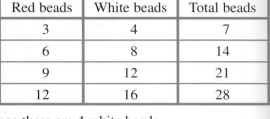

For the beads in this necklace:
The number of red beads is a **multiple** of 3.
The number of white beads is a **multiple** of 4.
The total number of beads is a **multiple** of 7.

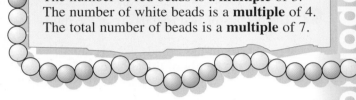

Simplifying ratios

To simplify a ratio divide both of the numbers in the ratio by the **same** number.
A ratio with whole numbers which cannot be simplified is in its **simplest form**.

EXAMPLES

1 Find 3 ratios that are equivalent to the ratio 2 : 1.
$$2 \times 2 : 1 \times 2 = 4 : 2$$
$$2 \times 3 : 1 \times 3 = 6 : 3$$
$$2 \times 4 : 1 \times 4 = 8 : 4$$
3 ratios equivalent to the ratio 2 : 1 are 4 : 2, 6 : 3 and 8 : 4.

Finding equivalent ratios

To find equivalent
ratios multiply or
divide each number
in the ratio by the
same number.

2 These ratios are equivalent.
2 : 5 and ? : 20
Find the missing number.

$20 \div 5 = 4$
To find a ratio equivalent to 2 : 5 where
the second number in the ratio is 20
multiply each number in the ratio by 4.
$2 \times 4 : 5 \times 4 = 8 : 20$
The missing number in the ratio is 8.

3 Write the ratio 15 : 9 in its simplest form.

15 and 9 can both be divided by 3.
$15 \div 3 : 9 \div 3 = 5 : 3$
5 : 3 cannot be simplified.
The ratio 15 : 9 in its simplest form is 5 : 3.

In its simplest form a
ratio contains **only** whole
numbers.
There are **no units**.
In order to simplify the
ratio both quantities in
the ratio must be in the
same units.

4 Write the ratio 2 cm : 50 mm in its simplest form.

2 cm : 50 mm = 20 mm : 50 mm = 20 : 50
Divide both parts of the ratio by 10.
$20 \div 10 : 50 \div 10 = 2 : 5$
The ratio 2 cm : 50 mm in its simplest form is 2 : 5.

Do not use a calculator in this exercise.

1 Give three ratios equivalent to each ratio.
(a) 6 : 1   (b) 7 : 2   (c) 3 : 5

2 Give the simplest form of each of these ratios.
(a) 3 : 6   (b) 9 : 27   (c) 9 : 12
(d) 10 : 25   (e) 30 : 40   (f) 22 : 55
(g) 9 : 21   (h) 18 : 8   (i) 36 : 81
(j) 35 : 15

3 Each of these pairs of ratios are equivalent.
(a) 3 : 4 and 9 : n.   (b) 2 : 7 and 8 : n.
(c) 8 : n and 2 : 25.   (d) 25 : n and 5 : 4.
In each case calculate the value of n.

4 The heights of two friends are in the ratio 7 : 9.
The shorter of the friends is 154 cm tall.
What is the height of the taller of the friends?

5 Sugar and flour are mixed in the ratio 2 : 3.
How much sugar is used with 600 g of flour?

6 The ratio of boys to girls in a school is 4 : 5.
There are 80 girls.
How many boys are there?

7
I earn £800 per month.

I earn £720 per month.

The amounts Jenny and James earn is in the ratio of their ages.
Jenny is 20 years old.
How old is James?

8 A necklace contains 30 black beads and 45 gold beads.
What is the simplest form of the ratio of black beads to gold beads on the necklace?

9 On Monday a hairdresser uses 800 ml of shampoo and 320 ml of conditioner.
Write in its simplest form the ratio of shampoo : conditioner used on Monday.

10 Denise draws a plan of her classroom.
On her plan Denise uses 2 cm to represent 5 m.
Write the scale as a ratio in its simplest form.

11 On a map a pond is 3.5 cm long.
The pond is actually 52.5 m long.
Write the scale as a ratio in its simplest form.

12 Write each of these ratios in its simplest form.
(a) £2 : 50p   (b) 20p : £2.50
(c) £2.20 : 40p   (d) 6 m : 240 cm
(e) 2 kg : 500 g   (f) 1 kg : 425 g
(g) 90 cm : 2 m   (h) 5 km : 200 m
(i) 20 seconds : 5 minutes
(j) $\frac{1}{2}$ minute : 15 seconds

13 Sam spends 45p a week on comics.
Tom spends £2 a week on comics.
Write the ratio of the amounts Tom and Sam spend on comics in its simplest form.

14 The cards in a pack are marked

 or

25% of the cards are marked

What is the ratio of cards marked

 :

in its simplest form?

15 An alloy is made of tin and zinc.
40% of the alloy is tin.
What is the ratio of tin : zinc in its simplest form?

16 A box contains blue biros and red biros.
$\frac{1}{3}$ of the biros are blue.
What is the ratio of blue biros to red biros in the box?

17 A necklace is made from 40 beads.
$\frac{2}{5}$ of the beads are white.
The rest of the beads are red.
Find the ratio of the number of red beads to the number of white beads in its simplest form.

Sharing in a given ratio

EXAMPLES

1 James and Sally share £20 in the ratio 3 : 2.
How much do they each get?

Add the numbers in the ratio.
3 + 2 = 5
For every £5 shared:
    James gets £3,
    Sally gets £2.
20 ÷ 5 = 4
There are 4 shares of £5 in £20.
James gets £3 × 4 = £12.
Sally gets £2 × 4 = £8.
So James gets £12 and Sally gets £8.

2 A necklace is made using red beads and gold beads in the ratio 7 : 3.
A total of 30 beads are used in the necklace.

Calculate the number of red beads and gold beads used to make the necklace.

Add the numbers in the ratio. 7 + 3 = 10
Number of shares 30 ÷ 10 = 3
Red beads   7 × 3 = 21.
Gold beads   3 × 3 = 9.
There are 21 red beads and 9 gold beads.

Exercise 10.3   Do not use a calculator for questions 1 to 6.

1 (a) Share 9 in the ratio 2 : 1.
(b) Share 20 in the ratio 3 : 1.
(c) Share 35 in the ratio 1 : 4.
(d) Share 100 in the ratio 9 : 1.
(e) Share 100 in the ratio 3 : 2.

2 A box contains gold coins and silver coins.
The ratio of gold coins to silver coins is 1 : 9.
There are 20 coins in the box.
How many silver coins are in the box?

3 Sunny and Chandni share £48 in the ratio 3 : 1.
How much do they each get?

4 Copy and complete this table.

| Quantity | Shared in the ratio | |
	4 : 1	3 : 2
(a) 40 marbles		
(b) 20 sweets		
(c) 80 kg		
(d) 200 g		
(e) £1200		

5 (a) Share £35 in the ratio 2 : 3.
(b) Share £56 in the ratio 4 : 3.
(c) Share £5.50 in the ratio 7 : 4.

6 A necklace contains 72 beads.
The ratio of red beads to blue beads is 5 : 3.
How many red beads are on the necklace?

7 £480 is shared in the ratio 7 : 3.
What is the difference between the larger share and the smaller share?

8 In 1901, the total population of England and Wales was 32 528 000. The ratio of the population of England to the population of Wales was 15 : 1.
What was the population of Wales in 1901?

9 A bag contains red beads and black beads in the ratio 1 : 3.
What fraction of the beads are red?

10 A box contains red biros and black biros in the ratio 1 : 4.
What percentage of the biros are black?

11 In a school the ratio of the number of boys to the number of girls is 3 : 5.
What fraction of the pupils in the school are girls?

12 The ratio of non-fiction books to fiction books in a library is 2 : 3.
Find the percentage of fiction books in the library.

13 John is 12 years old and Sara is 13 years old.
They share some money in the ratio of their ages.
What percentage of the money does John get?

14 In the UK there are approximately 240 000 km² of land.
The ratio of agricultural land to non-agricultural land is 7 : 3.
Estimate the area of land used for agriculture.

15 At the start of a game Jenny and Tim have 40 counters each.
At the end of the game the number of counters that Jenny and Tim each have is in the ratio 5 : 3.
(a)   How many counters do Jenny and Tim have at the end of the game?
(b)   How many counters did Jenny win from Tim in the game?

16 On a necklace, for every 10 black beads there are 4 red beads.
(a)   What is the ratio of black beads to red beads in its simplest form?
(b)   If the necklace has 15 black beads how many red beads are there?
(c)   If the necklace has a total of 77 beads how many black beads are there?
(d)   Why can't the necklace have a total of 32 beads?

Proportion

Some situations involve comparing **different** quantities.
For example, when a motorist buys fuel the more he buys the greater the cost.
In this situation the quantities can change but the ratio between the quantities stays the same.
When two different quantities are in the **same ratio** they are said to be in **direct proportion**.

EXAMPLE

4 cakes cost £1.20.
Find the cost of 7 cakes.

4 cakes cost £1.20
1 cake costs £1.20 ÷ 4 = 30p
7 cakes cost 30p × 7 = £2.10
So 7 cakes cost £2.10.

This is sometimes called the **unitary method**.
(a) **Divide** by 4 to find the cost of **1** cake.
(b) **Multiply** by 7 to find the cost of 7 cakes.

Exercise 10.4   Do not use a calculator for questions 1 to 6.

1 5 candles cost 80 pence.
(a)   What is the cost of 1 candle?
(b)   What is the cost of 8 candles?

2 Georgina works for 4 hours and earns £24.
(a)   How much does she earn in 1 hour?
(b)   How much does she earn in 10 hours?

3 5 bananas cost £1.50.
(a)   What is the cost of 1 banana?
(b)   What is the cost of 8 bananas?

4 Gina works for 10 hours and earns £45.
(a)   How much does Gina earn in 1 hour?
(b)   How much does Gina earn in 20 hours?

5 Alistair pays £1.90 for 2 cups of tea.
How much would he pay for 3 cups of tea?

6 The amount a spring stretches is proportional to the weight hung on the spring.
A weight of 5 kg stretches the spring by 60 cm.
(a)   How much does a weight of 10 kg stretch the spring?
(b)   What weight makes the spring stretch 24 cm?

7 Jean pays £168 for 10 square metres of carpet.
How much would 12 square metres of carpet cost?

8 Alfie is paid £28.80 for working 4 hours overtime.
How much would he be paid for 5 hours overtime?

9 Aimee pays £1.14 for 3 kg of potatoes.
How much would 7.5 kg of potatoes cost?

3 kg   7.5 kg

10 5 litres of petrol costs £4.10.
How much would 18 litres of petrol cost?

11 This recipe makes an apple crumble for 6 people.

> 540 g apples
> 75 g butter
> 150 g flour
> 75 g sugar

(a) How much sugar is needed to make an apple crumble for 4 people?

(b) How much apple is needed to make an apple crumble for 8 people?

12 9 metres of stair carpet cost £41.85.
How much does 9.6 metres cost?

13 190 francs is about the same as £20.
Sue spends 304 francs.
How many pounds is this?

14 Mary phones her uncle in New York.
Phone calls to New York are charged at the rate of £1.10 for a 5-minute call.

(a) How much would a 7-minute call to New York cost?

(b) Mary's call cost £2.64. How long was her call?

15 This recipe makes macaroni cheese for 4 people.

> Macaroni . . . . 120 g
> Cheese . . . . 72 g
> Flour . . . . 30 g
> Milk . . . . 900 ml

(a) How much cheese is needed to make macaroni cheese for 10 people?

(b) How much milk is needed to make macaroni cheese for 3 people?

(c) How much macaroni is needed to make macaroni cheese for 7 people?

16 A car travels 6 miles in 9 minutes.
If the car travels at the same speed:
(a) how long will it take to travel 8 miles,
(b) how far will it travel in 24 minutes?

17 5 litres of paint cover an area of 30 m².
(a) What area will 2 litres of paint cover?
(b) How much paint is needed to cover 72 m²?

18 A school is organising three trips to the zoo.

Our trip is on Monday. There are 45 people going. The total cost is £234.

Our trip is on Tuesday. 25 students are going.

Our trip is on Wednesday. The total cost is £166.40.

(a) How much does Tuesday's trip cost?

(b) How many students are going to the zoo on Wednesday?

What you need to know

- The ratio 3 : 2 is read '3 to 2'.

- A ratio is used only to **compare** quantities.
  A ratio does not give information about the exact values of quantities being compared.

- To simplify a ratio divide both of the numbers in the ratio by the **same** number.
  A ratio with whole numbers which cannot be simplified is in its **simplest form**.
  All quantities in a ratio must have the **same units** before the ratio can be simplified.
  For example, £2.50 : 50p = 250p : 50p = 5 : 1.

- When two different quantities are always in the **same ratio** the two quantities are in **proportion.**
  For example, the amount and cost of fuel bought by a motorist are in proportion.

Do not use a calculator for questions 1 to 8.

1   A packet contains 5 white balloons and 15 red balloons.
What is the ratio of white balloons to red balloons in its simplest form?

2   A tin contains 21 nuts and 28 bolts.
What is the ratio of nuts to bolts in its simplest form?

3   A sewing box contains pins and needles in the ratio 4 : 1.
There are 36 pins in the box.
How many needles are in the box?

4   In a class the ratio of students with dark hair to those with light hair is 3 : 2.
There are 18 students with dark hair.
How many students have light hair?

5   A bag contains white buttons and red buttons in the ratio 1 : 2.
The bag contains 24 buttons.
How many white buttons are in the bag?

6   In a recipe for scones, the ratio of **flour** to **fat** is 4 : 1 and the ratio of **flour** to **sugar** is 8 : 1.

> RECIPE FOR SCONES
> 50 g fat,   … g flour,   … g sugar

Copy and complete the recipe.   Edexcel

7

Mortar is made by mixing 5 parts by weight of sand with 1 part by weight of cement.
How much sand is needed to make 8400 kg of mortar?   Edexcel

8   Here are the ingredients for making 18 rock cakes.

9 ounces of flour	6 ounces of margarine	2 large eggs
6 ounces of sugar	8 ounces of mixed dried fruit	

Mark wants to make 12 rock cakes.
(a)   Write down how much of each ingredient he needs for 12 rock cakes.

Mark only has 9 ounces of margarine. He has plenty of all the other ingredients.
(b)   What is the greatest number of rock cakes he can make?   Edexcel

9   Tracey and Wayne share £7200 in the ratio 5 : 4.
Work out how much each of them receives.   Edexcel

10   A plan is drawn on a scale of **2 cm represents 10 m**.
Write this as a ratio in the form 1 : n, where n is a whole number.   Edexcel

11   The cost of 5 metres of wire is £3.
What is the cost of 8 metres of the same wire?   Edexcel

12   Three kilograms of apples cost £2.31.
What is the cost of two kilograms of apples?

Section Review - Number

Do not use a calculator for questions 1 to 35.

1 The winning numbers in the National Lottery one week were

49   36   46   39   23   7

Write the numbers in order of size.
Put the smallest one first.   Edexcel

2 (a) (i) Write down the number **fifty-two thousand four hundred and six** in figures.
  (ii) Write down **fifty-two thousand four hundred and six** to the nearest thousand.
 (b) (i) Write down 10 292 in words.
  (ii) Write down 10 292 to the nearest hundred.   Edexcel

3 (a) What numbers are needed to complete these sums?

  (i) $100 - 13 = \boxed{}$

  (ii) $44 + \boxed{} = 100$

  (iii) $100 - \boxed{} = 39$

 (b) (i) Work out 70×100.
  (ii) Work out $950 \div 100$.

4 How much bigger is $72 \div 3$ than $72 \div 4$?

5 The table shows the distances between towns in miles.

Dover

347	Holyhead			
77	263	London		
290	347	215	Plymouth	
274	190	209	340	York

 (a) Give the distance from Dover to Holyhead to the nearest hundred miles.
 (b) A lorry travels from Dover to London and then from London to York.
  How far does it travel altogether?

6 Work out (a) $528 + 273$
  (b) $342 - 159$
  (c) $16 - 4 \times 3$
  (d) $12 \div 4 + 2$

7 Ian follows this set of instructions.

Step Number	Instruction
1	Write down the number 3.
2	Add 7 to the last number written down.
3	Write down the answer.
4	If the answer is larger than 30 then go to step number 6.
5	If the answer is smaller than 30 then go to step number 2.
6	End.

Write down the answers that Ian should write down.   Edexcel

8 Place these numbers in order of size, **smallest** first.

0.9 -3 2 -1 2.5

9 (a) Richard has a dental appointment at 1425.
  What time is his appointment using the 12-hour clock?
 (b) Richard leaves home at 1345.
  He gets to the dentist at 1417.
  How long did his journey take?

10 A bus can hold a maximum of 73 people.
Work out the maximum number of people that 7 buses can hold.   Edexcel

11 Navroop bought 6 theatre tickets.
The total cost was £117.
Each ticket cost the same.
Work out the cost of each ticket.   Edexcel

12 (a) Lyn writes down the number 26589.
  What is the value of the 6 in Lyn's number?
 (b) Ben writes down these four numbers:
   9, 8, 5, 2.

  (i)   Which number is a factor of 4?
  (ii) Which number is a multiple of 4?
  (iii) Which number is a square number?
  (iv) Use all four numbers to write down the smallest even number you can make.

13 The table shows the midday temperature in two cities on one day.

London	3°C
Moscow	−8°C

(a) How much colder is Moscow than London?

(b) Paris is 5°C colder than London. What is the temperature in Paris?

14 A school hall is used for a play.

(a) For the Friday evening performance, 25 rows of chairs are put out. Each row has 22 chairs. How many people can be seated?

(b) For the Saturday evening performance, 625 people have bought tickets. How many **whole** rows of 22 seats are needed altogether? *Edexcel*

15 Four friends bought a Chinese take-away meal.
They divided the cost equally between them.
The table shows what they bought.

	Cost per portion	Number of portions
Egg fried rice	£1.50	2
Special chow mein	£2.90	1
Chicken and cashew nuts	£2.70	1
Lemon chicken	£3.30	1
Mushroom chop suey	£2.10	1
Special foo yung	£2.90	2
Crispy prawn crackers	£0.90	4

Work out how much each of the four people paid. *Edexcel*

16

Café
Tea 95p
Slice of cake £1.15

(a) Hamish buys 3 cups of tea and 2 slices of cake. What is the total cost?

(b) Hamish pays with a £10 note. How much change does he get?

17 (a) What fraction of this shape is shaded?

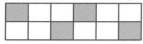

(b) Copy and shade $\frac{2}{5}$ of this shape.

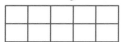

18 On Monday morning a dentist treated 20 patients.

(a) $\frac{1}{4}$ of the patients had a check-up. How many of the patients had a check-up?

(b) 10 patients had a filling. What fraction of the patients had a filling? Give your answer in its simplest form.

(c) $\frac{3}{10}$ of the patients were children. How many patients were children?

19 A calculator gives this list of numbers:
15   23   40   36   42   39

(a) Write down the two numbers that are multiples of five.

(b) Write down the number that has seven as a factor.

(c) Write down the number that is a square number. *Edexcel*

20 Write down the value of
(a) 7^2,   (b) the square root of 81.

21 (a) Write $\frac{1}{4}$, 0.3 and 10% in ascending order.

(b) Find 10% of £50.

(c) Write 0.3 as a percentage.

22 (a) Write down the numbers you could use to get an approximate answer to 59×32.

(b) Write down your approximate answer.

(c) Find the difference between your approximate answer and the exact answer. *Edexcel*

23 Tickets for a concert cost £17 each.
234 people go to the concert.
How much money is paid for tickets?

24 Work out:
(a) $\dfrac{300 \times 200}{300 + 200}$ (b) $\dfrac{100^2}{40}$

25 In a survey, 500 people were questioned about things they recycled.
 (a) 25% of the people said they recycled paper.
  How many people is this?
 (b) $\frac{7}{10}$ of the people said they recycled bottles.
  How many people is this?   *Edexcel*

26 A crowd of 4560 watch a football match.
 (a) Two-thirds of the crowd support the home team.
  How many people support the home team?
 (b) 60% of the crowd are men.
  How many men are in the crowd?

27

Tigers	Cheetahs

Admission: £2.40	Admission: £2.70
Special Offer	**Special Offer**
20% off	$\frac{1}{3}$ off

 Jugdev pays to see the Tigers.
 It normally costs £2.40 but there is 20% off the price.
 (a) Work out how much he pays.

 Jugdev then pays to see the Cheetahs.
 It normally costs £2.70 but there is $\frac{1}{3}$ off the price.
 (b) Work out how much he pays.   *Edexcel*

28 A bag contains 60 beads.
 (a) Emily uses 30% of the beads to make a necklace.
  How many beads does she use?
 (b) Laura uses 12 beads to make a bracelet.
  What percentage of the beads does she use?

29 (a) Work out $2^3 + \sqrt{100}$.
 (b) Which number is smaller, 3^3 or 5^2?
  Show all your working.

30 John pays £2.60 for 200 g of jelly babies and 300 g of toffees.
 100 g of jelly babies cost 37p.
 What is the cost of 100 g of toffees?

31 Ester is given £12 pocket money.
 She spends $\frac{1}{6}$ on magazines and $\frac{2}{5}$ of the remainder on a trip to the cinema.
 (a) How much did it cost to go to the cinema?
 (b) What fraction of her pocket money has she got left?
  Give your answer in its simplest form.

32 (a) Find $\frac{3}{5}$ of 60.
 (b) Work out (i) $\frac{2}{3} + \frac{3}{4}$ (ii) $\frac{1}{2} - \frac{2}{5}$

33 (a) Which of the numbers 2, 4, 6, 8, 9 and 24 are common factors of 12 and 36?
 (b) Work out 12×36.

34 Barry wants to calculate $\dfrac{82.3}{10.2 - 1.98}$.
 (a) Write each of the numbers in Barry's calculation correct to one significant figure.
 (b) Hence, find an estimate of the answer.

35 (a) Write these fractions in ascending order.
  $$\frac{1}{2}, \quad \frac{1}{4}, \quad \frac{1}{3}, \quad \frac{2}{5}, \quad \frac{3}{4}, \quad \frac{2}{3}.$$
 (b) Write down a decimal that lies between $\frac{1}{4}$ and $\frac{1}{3}$.
 (c) Work out $\frac{3}{4} \times \frac{2}{5}$.

36

 The newspaper heading is given to the nearest thousand.
 What is the smallest possible size of the audience?

37 (a) Find the values of
  (i) $\sqrt{36} + \sqrt{64}$, (ii) $3^2 \div 5^2$.
 (b) Given that $37 \times 249 = 9213$, find the exact value of $\dfrac{92130}{37}$.

38 (a) Write $\frac{5}{8}$ as a decimal.
 (b) Write 0.6 as a fraction.
  Give your answer in its lowest terms.

39 Mark has a market stall.

(a) He sells apples at 56p for each kilogram.
Bianca buys 4 kilograms of apples.
She pays for her apples with a £5 note.
How much change should she get?

(b) Mark bought 25 melons for his stall.
He paid £16 for 25 melons.
Work out the price Mark paid for each melon.

(c) Two of the melons were bad.
Mark sold the other 23 melons for 149p each.
Work out the total amount for which Mark sold the melons.

(d) Mark usually sells oranges for 40p each.
He reduces the price to $\frac{7}{8}$ of this.
Work out the new price of an orange.

(e) Mark bought his potatoes for 30p for each kilogram.
He sold the potatoes and made a profit of 40%.
At what price did Mark sell the potatoes? *Edexcel*

40 To cook a leg of lamb, allow 25 minutes per 0.5 kg **plus** 25 minutes.
Dexter wants a leg of lamb, weighing 1.5 kg, to be cooked by 1 pm.
At what time should he put the lamb in the oven?

41 A gas bill is £112.40 plus VAT at 5%.
Calculate the VAT charged.

42 Miss Phillips is organising a trip to London to see the musical "Cats".
195 people decide to go on the trip.

(a) For every 16 tickets that she pays for, Miss Phillips is given a free seat.
Work out how many free seats Miss Phillips will be allowed.

(b) Miss Phillips charges **each person** £27 to cover the cost of the tickets and the coach fare.
Work out the total amount of money collected.

The total cost of the trip was £5000.

(c) Work out the profit that Miss Phillips will make on the trip.

(d) Express the profit as a percentage of the total cost of the trip. *Edexcel*

43 (a) Calculate $2.37^2 - \sqrt{5.8}$.
Give your answer correct to two decimal places.

(b) Calculate $\sqrt{\dfrac{14.7}{(0.7)^3}}$
Give your answer correct to one decimal place.

44 Janet goes on holiday to Spain.
The exchange rate is £1 = 1.6 euros.

(a) She changes £150 into euros.
How many euros should Janet get?

(b) Janet comes back home.
She changes 15 euros back into pounds.
The exchange rate is the same.
How much money should she get?
Give your answer to the nearest penny.
Edexcel

45 A year ago Joan weighed 84 kg.
She now weighs 5% less.
Calculate her weight now.
Give your answer to a suitable degree of accuracy.

46 Starting with $4^3 = 64$, use trial and improvement to find the cube root of 104 correct to 1 decimal place.

47 (a) Calculate the exact value of $4^3 \times 3^3$.
(b) Find the reciprocal of 7.
Give your answer correct to 3 decimal places.

48 Janet invests £50 in a building society for one year.
The interest rate is 6% per year.

(a) How much interest, in pounds, does Janet get?

Nisha invests £60 in a different building society.
She gets £3 interest after one year.

(b) Work out the percentage interest rate that Nisha gets. *Edexcel*

49 Rashid has 35 sweets.
He shares them in the ratio 4 : 3 with his sister.
Rashid keeps the larger share.
How many sweets does Rashid keep?
Edexcel

50 (a) Alika pays £6.46 for some cheese.
She buys 0.3 kg of brie and 0.5 kg of stilton.
The brie costs £7.20 per kilogram.
How much per kilogram is stilton?

(b) The weights and prices of two pots of natural yogurt are shown.

145 g
39 pence

250 g
66 pence

Which pot is better value for money?
Show **all** your working.

51 A shop has a sale of jackets and shirts.
In the sale there are a total of 120 jackets and shirts.
Shirts are to be sold at a price of
£8.00 plus VAT at $17\frac{1}{2}\%$.

(a) What is the cost of buying one shirt, including the $17\frac{1}{2}\%$ VAT?

The jackets and shirts are in the ratio 5 : 3.
(b) Work out the number of jackets.
(c) Calculate the percentage that are shirts. Edexcel

52

MOTOR BOAT

Cash price...£12 800

Credit terms...Deposit of 30% of cash price plus 36 monthly payments of £295

How much more is paid when the motorboat is bought on credit terms instead of cash?

53 Mr Mogg earns £5460 per year.
He has a tax allowance of £4385 per year and tax is paid at 10p in the £ on his taxable income.
How much tax does he pay per year?

54 Calculate the value of $\dfrac{7.84 \times 2.8}{3.28 - 1.04}$ Edexcel

55 Fred has a recipe for 30 biscuits.
Here is a list of ingredients for 30 biscuits.

Self-raising flour	:	230 g
Butter	:	150 g
Caster sugar	:	100 g
Eggs	:	2

Fred wants to make 45 biscuits.
(a) Write a new list of ingredients for 45 biscuits.

The recipe gives the baking temperature as 350° Fahrenheit, F.
A modern oven shows baking temperature in Celsius, C.

(b) Use the formula $C = \dfrac{5(F - 32)}{9}$

to change 350° Fahrenheit to Celsius.
Give your answer correct to the nearest degree.

Gill has only 1 kilogram of self-raising flour.
She has plenty of the other ingredients.
(c) Work out the maximum number of biscuits that Gill could bake. Edexcel

56 A mechanic is paid £7.48 per hour for a basic 35-hour week.
When he works overtime he is paid at one and a half times the basic hourly rate.
(a) One week he has to work 37 hours. How much is he paid that week?
(b) For a different week he is paid £317.90. How many hours overtime did he work that week?

57

EXCHANGE RATES
£1 WILL BUY
GERMANY . . . . 1.60 EUROS
UNITED STATES . . . . . 1.40 DOLLARS

The same computer can be bought in Germany and in the United States.
In the United States it costs 950 dollars.
In Germany it costs 9% more.
How much does it cost to buy the computer in Germany?
Give your answer, in euros, to a suitable degree of accuracy.

58 A farm has 427 acres of land.
135 acres are used for grazing.
What percentage of the land is used for grazing?

Introduction to Algebra

Algebra is sometimes called the language of Mathematics.
Algebra uses letters in place of numbers.
  A class of children line up.
  We cannot see how many children there are altogether because of a tree.
  We can say there are *n* children in the line.
  The letter *n* is used in place of an unknown number.

Three more children join the line.
There are now *n* + 3 children in the line.

This picture shows two lines of *n* children.
So there are *n* + *n* or 2 × *n* children altogether.
The simplest way to write this is 2*n*.

Both *n* + 3 and 2*n* are examples of
algebraic expressions.

Exercise 11.1

Write algebraic expressions for each of the
following questions.

1 There are *n* children in a queue.
4 more children join the queue.
How many children are in the queue
now?

2 There are *n* children in a queue.
3 children leave the queue.
How many children are left in the
queue?

3 There are 3 classes with *n* children in
each class.
How many children are there altogether?

4 I have *m* marbles in a bag.
I put in another 6 marbles.
How many marbles are now in the bag?

5 I have *m* marbles. I lose 12 marbles.
How many marbles have I got left?

6 I have 8 bags of marbles.
Each bag contains *m* marbles.
How many marbles do I have
altogether?

7 There are *p* pencils in a pencil case.
I take one pencil out.
How many pencils are left in the pencil
case?

8 There are *p* pencils in a pencil case.
I put in another 5 pencils.
How many pencils are now in the pencil
case?

9 I have 25 pencil cases.
There are *p* pencils in each pencil case.
How many pencils do I have altogether?

10 I have 6 key rings.
There are *k* keys on each key ring.
How many keys do I have altogether?

11 What is the cost of b biscuits costing 5 pence each?

12 Three cakes cost a total of c pence. What is the cost of one cake?

13 Five kilograms of apples cost a pence. What is the cost of one kilogram of apples?

14 A group of 36 students are split into g groups. How many students are in each group?

15 There are t toffees in a tin. How many toffees are there in
(a)   2 tins,
(b)   10 tins?

Expressions and terms

Consider this situation:
    $2n$ students start a typing course.
    3 of the students leave the course.
    How many students remain on the course?
$2n - 3$ students remain.
$2n - 3$ is an **algebraic expression**, or simply an **expression**.
An expression is just an answer made up of letters and numbers.
$+2n$ and -3 are **terms** of the expression.

> **Note**
> A term includes the sign, $+$ or $-$.
> $2n$ has the same value as $+2n$.

Simplifying expressions

Addition and subtraction

You can add and subtract terms with the same letter.
This is sometimes called **simplifying an expression**.

$a + a = 2a$
$w + 4w = 5w$
$5k + 3k = 8k$
$3p + 2p + 4p = 9p$

$6a - 2a = 4a$
$3d - 2d = d$
$2d - 3d = -d$
$4x - 4x = 0$

$2a + 4b$ cannot be simplified.
$6 + a$ cannot be simplified.
$5p - 2q$ cannot be simplified.
$a - 2a + 5a = 4a$
$3p + 5 + p - 1 = 4p + 4$

> **Note that:**
> A simpler way to write $1d$ is just d.
>
> $-1d$ can be written as $-d$.
>
> $0d$ is the same as 0.
>
> Just as with ordinary numbers you can add terms in any order.
> $a - 2a + 5a = a + 5a - 2a = 4a$

EXAMPLE

Write down an expression for the perimeter of this shape.
Give your answer in its simplest form.

Perimeter is the total distance round the outside of the shape.
$y + 2x - 1 + 2y + 2x + 3$
Imagine that each term is written on a separate card.

The cards can be arranged in any order.

Simplify this expression to get: $4x + 3y + 2$
The perimeter of the shape is $4x + 3y + 2$.

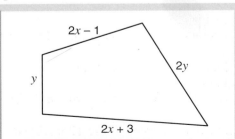

1 Write simpler expressions for the following.

(a) $y + y$

(b) $c + c + c$

(c) $x + x + x + x + x$

(d) $p + p + p + p + p + p + p$

(e) $t + t + t - t$

(f) $d + d + d - d + d$

(g) $2n + n$

(h) $2y + 3y$

(i) $5g + g + 4g$

(j) $2m + 5m + m$

(k) $5z + 4z + z + 3z$

(l) $5r - 3r$

(m) $7t - 2t$

(n) $5y - y$

(o) $5j + 2j - 4j$

(p) $9c - 2c - 3c$

(q) $3x - x + 5x$

(r) $12w - 7w - 4w$

(s) $5d + 7d - 12d$

(t) $-2y - 3y$

(u) $3x - 8x$

(v) $2a - 5a - 12a + a$

(w) $3b + 5b - 4b + 2b$

(x) $m - 2m + 3m$

2 Write an expression for the perimeter of each shape.
Give each answer in its simplest form.

(a)

(b)

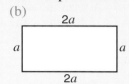

(c)

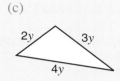

(d)

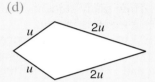

3 Which of these expressions cannot be simplified?
Give a reason for each of your answers.

(a) $v + v$

(b) $v + 4$

(c) $2v + v + 4$

(d) $v + w$

4 Simplify where possible.

(a) $5x + 3x + y$

(b) $w + 3v - v$

(c) $2a + b - 3b$

(d) $2x + 3y + 3x$

(e) $5 + 7u - 2$

(f) $p + 3q + q$

(g) $3d - 5c - 2c$

(h) $3y + 1 - y$

(i) $-a + b + 2a$

(j) $3m + n + m$

(k) $5c + 4c - d$

(l) $2x + y - x$

(m) $-p + 4p + 3p$

(n) $5 - 9k + 4k$

(o) $2a - a + 3$

5 Simplify where possible.

(a) $3a + 5a + 2b + b$

(b) $p + 2q + 2p + q$

(c) $m + 2m - n + 3n$

(d) $2x + 3y - x - 5y$

(e) $3x - x + 5y - 2y$

(f) $2d + 5 - d - 2$

(g) $3a - 5a + 2b + b$

(h) $a - 2a + 7 + a$

(i) $2a - b + 3b - a$

(j) $-f + g - f - g$

(k) $2v - w - 3w - v$

(l) $7 - 2t - 9 - 3t$

(m) $-p + 3q - 3p + q$

(n) $5 - 9k - 4 + 2k$

(o) $2c + d + 4 - c - 2d + 7$

6 Write down an expression for the perimeter of each shape.
Give each answer in its simplest form.

(a)

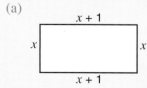

(b)

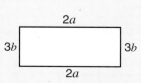

(c)

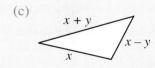

(d)

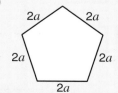

(e)

(f)

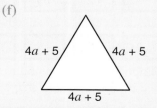

110

Multiplying and dividing terms

$6 \times a = 6a$ $a \times b = ab$ $x \times 2 = 2x$ $b \times b \times b = b^3$ $8a \div 2 = 4a$

$5 \times 2a = 10a$ $3x \times y = 3xy$ $x \times x = x^2$ $5c \times 4c = 20c^2$ $9x \div x = 9$

EXAMPLE

Find an expression for the area of this rectangle.

Area = length $\times$ breadth
    $= 3d \times d$

The simplest way to write an expression for the area is $3d^2$.

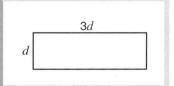

Exercise 11.3

1 Write these expressions in a simpler form.

   (a) $3 \times a$ (b) $7 \times b$ (c) $2 \times 4 \times c$

   (d) $3 \times 3 \times d$ (e) $e \times 4$ (f) $f \times 8$

   (g) $3 \times 2p$ (h) $3q \times 5$ (i) $r \times r$

   (j) $g \times g$ (k) $2g \times g$ (l) $2g \times 3g$

   (m) $t \times t$ (n) $t \times 4t$ (o) $3t \times 4t$

   (p) $5u \times 3u$ (q) $2m \times 5m$ (r) $3d \times 3d$

   (s) $5x \times 3x$ (t) $4y \times 3y$ (u) $3k \times 2k$

2 Simplify.

   (a) $10a \div 2$ (b) $16b \div 4$ (c) $12x \div 3$

   (d) $20y \div 5$ (e) $10a \div a$ (f) $16b \div b$

   (g) $12x \div x$ (h) $20y \div y$ (i) $8y \div 4$

   (j) $8y \div y$ (k) $18p \div 6$ (l) $18p \div p$

3 Simplify.

   (a) $a \times b$ (b) $x \times y$ (c) $y \times y$

   (d) $2 \times p \times q$ (e) $2 \times a \times a$ (f) $3 \times x \times y$

   (g) $3 \times a \times 2 \times b$ (h) $3 \times g \times 4 \times h$ (i) $2 \times d \times 3 \times d$

   (j) $3g \times g$ (k) $a \times 5b$ (l) $2g \times 3h$

   (m) $a \times b \times c$ (n) $m \times m \times m$ (o) $2 \times d \times d \times d$

   (p) $g \times g \times g \times 3$ (q) $2x \times 3x \times x$ (r) $m \times m \times n$

   (s) $3a \times b \times c$ (t) $2p \times 3q \times r$ (u) $5x \times 2y \times y$

4 Write an expression for the area of each shape.
Give your answer in its simplest form.

   (a)   (b)   (c)   (d)

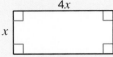
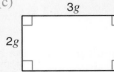

Brackets

Some expressions contain brackets.
$2(a + b)$ means $2 \times (a + b)$.

You can multiply out brackets in an expression either by using a diagram or by expanding.

EXAMPLES

1 Multiply out the bracket $2(x + 3)$.

Diagram method
$2(x + 3)$ means $2 \times (x + 3)$.
This can be shown using a rectangle.

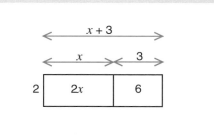

The areas of the two parts are $2x$ and 6.
The total area is $2x + 6$.
$2(x + 3) = 2x + 6$

Expanding
$2(x + 3) = 2 \times x + 2 \times 3$
$\qquad\qquad = 2x + 6$

2 Multiply out the bracket $3(4a + 5)$.

Diagram method

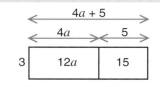

$3(4a + 5) = 12a + 15$

Expanding
$3(4a + 5) = 3 \times 4a + 3 \times 5$
$\qquad\qquad = 12a + 15$

3 Expand $3(2x - 5)$.

$3 \times 2x = 6x$ and $3 \times -5 = -15$
$3(2x - 5) = 6x - 15$

4 Expand $x(x - 5)$.

$x \times x = x^2$ and $x \times -5 = -5x$
$x(x - 5) = x^2 - 5x$

Exercise 11.4

1 Use the diagrams to multiply out the brackets.

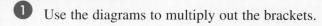

(a)
$2(x + 5) = \ldots$

(b)
$3(a + 6) = \ldots$

(c)
$4(y + 3) = \ldots$

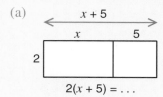
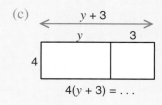

(d)
$2(2a + 1) = \ldots$

(e)
$2(3y + 2) = \ldots$

(f)
$3(a + b) = \ldots$

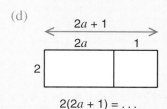
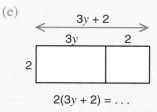
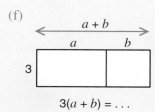

2 Draw your own diagrams to multiply out these brackets.

(a) $3(x + 2)$ (b) $2(y + 5)$ (c) $2(2x + 1)$ (d) $3(p + q)$

3 Match the pairs of cards.

| $2(q + 2)$ | | $2(q - 1)$ | | $2(2q + 1)$ | | $2(2 - q)$ |

| $4q + 2$ | | $4 - 2q$ | | $2q + 4$ | | $2q - 2$ |

4 Multiply out the brackets by expanding.

(a) $2(x + 4)$ (b) $4(b + 1)$ (c) $3(p + 6)$

(d) $5(a + 7)$ (e) $4(2x + 1)$ (f) $2(3a + b)$

(g) $3(t - 2)$ (h) $4(5 - a)$ (i) $3(2 - 4p)$

(j) $6(b + 2c)$ (k) $3(2m - 5n)$ (l) $7(a + b + c)$

5 Use the diagrams to multiply out the brackets.

(a)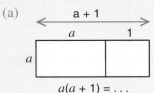

$a(a + 1) = \ldots$

(b)

$d(2 + d) = \ldots$

(c)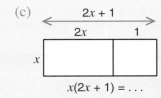

$x(2x + 1) = \ldots$

6 Multiply out the brackets by expanding.

(a) $x(x + 3)$ (b) $y(2 + y)$ (c) $t(t - 5)$ (d) $g(2g + 3)$

(e) $m(2 - 3m)$ (f) $a(3a + 4)$ (g) $p(2p + 3)$ (h) $d(2 - 3d)$

Remember:
Remove brackets first, then simplify by collecting like terms together.

$3(t + 4) + 2$ — Remove the brackets

$= 3t + 12 + 2$ — Simplify

$= 3t + 14$

7 Multiply out the brackets and simplify.

(a) $2(x + 1) + 3$ (b) $3(a + 2) + 5$ (c) $6(w - 4) + 7$

(d) $4 + 2(p + 3)$ (e) $3 + 3(q - 1)$ (f) $1 + 3(2 - t)$

(g) $4(z + 2) + z$ (h) $5(t + 3) + 3t$ (i) $3(c - 2) - c$

(j) $2a + 3(a - 3)$ (k) $y + 2(y - 5)$ (l) $5x + 3(2 - x)$

(m) $4(2a + 5) + 3$ (n) $-2x + 4(3x - 3)$ (o) $3(p - 5) - p + 4$

(p) $3a + 2(a + b)$ (q) $3(x + y) - 2y$ (r) $2(p - q) - 3q$

8 Remove the brackets and simplify.

(a) $2(x + 1) + 3(x + 2)$ (b) $3(a + 1) + 2(a + 5)$ (c) $4(y + 2) + 5(y + 3)$

(d) $2(3a + 1) + 3(a + 1)$ (e) $3(2t + 5) + 5(4t + 3)$ (f) $3(z + 5) + 2(z - 1)$

(g) $3(q - 2) + 5(q + 6)$ (h) $5(x + 3) + 2(x - 3)$ (i) $3(2e - 1) + 4(e - 2)$

(j) $2(5d + 4) + 3(d - 1)$

Factorising

Factorising is the opposite operation to removing brackets.
For example: to remove brackets
$$2(x + 5) = 2x + 10$$

To factorise $3x + 6$ we can see that $3x$ and 6 have a **common factor** of 3 so
$$3x + 6 = 3(x + 2)$$

Common factors
The **factors** of a number are all the numbers that will divide exactly into the number.
Factors of 6 are 1, 2, 3 and 6.

A **common factor** is a factor which will divide into two or more numbers.

EXAMPLES

1 Factorise $4x - 6$.

Each term has a factor of 2.
So the common factor is 2.
$$4x - 6 = 2(2x - 3)$$

2 Factorise $x^2 + 3x$.

Each term has a factor of x.
So the common factor is x.
$$x^2 + 3x = x(x + 3)$$

Exercise 11.5

1 Copy and complete.
- (a) $2x + 2y = 2(\ldots + \ldots)$
- (b) $3a - 6b = 3(\ldots - \ldots)$
- (c) $6m + 8n = 2(\ldots + \ldots)$
- (d) $x^2 - 2x = x(\quad)$
- (e) $ab + a = a(\quad)$
- (f) $2x - xy = x(\quad)$
- (g) $2b - 4a = 2(\quad)$
- (h) $2x^2 + 3x = x(\quad)$
- (i) $g - g^2 = g(\quad)$

2 Factorise.
- (a) $2a + 2b$
- (b) $5x - 5y$
- (c) $3d + 6e$
- (d) $4m - 2n$
- (e) $6a + 9b$
- (f) $6a - 8b$
- (g) $8t + 12$
- (h) $5a - 10$
- (i) $4d - 2$
- (j) $3 - 9g$
- (k) $5 - 20m$
- (l) $4k + 4$

3 Factorise.
- (a) $xy - xz$
- (b) $fg + gh$
- (c) $ab - 2b$
- (d) $3q + pq$
- (e) $a + ab$
- (f) $gh - g$
- (g) $a^2 + 3a$
- (h) $5t - t^2$
- (i) $d - d^2$
- (j) $m^2 + m$
- (k) $5r^2 - 3r$
- (l) $3x^2 + 2x$

What you need to know

You should be able to:
- Write simple algebraic expressions.
- Simplify expressions by collecting like terms together.
  - e.g. $2d + 3d = 5d$ and $3x + 2 - x + 4 = 2x + 6$
- Multiply simple expressions together.
  - e.g. $2a \times a = 2a^2$ and $y \times y \times y = y^3$
- Multiply out brackets.
  - e.g. $2(x - 5) = 2x - 10$ and $x(x - 5) = x^2 - 5x$
- Factorise expressions.
  - e.g. $3x - 6 = 3(x - 2)$ and $x^2 + 5x = x(x + 5)$

1 A lollipop costs t pence.
Write an expression for the cost of 6 lollipops.

2 Tim is x years old.
Naomi is 3 years older than Tim.
How old is Naomi in terms of x?

3 In the triangle PQR, the side PQ has length x centimetres.

Not drawn accurately

x cm

R P Q

(a) PR is twice the length of PQ.
Write an expression for the length of PR.
(b) QR is 3 cm longer than PQ.
Write an expression for the length of QR.

4

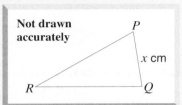

A coach has x passengers upstairs and y passengers downstairs.
(a) Write down an expression, in terms of x and y, for the total number of passengers on the coach.

Tickets for the journey on the coach cost £5 each.
(b) Write down an expression, in terms of x and y, for the total amount of money paid by the passengers on the coach.
Edexcel

5 Write down an expression, in terms of n and g, for the total cost, in pence, of n buns at 18 pence each and 5 bread rolls at g pence each.
Edexcel

6 Simplify
(a) $w + w + w$,
(b) $2w + 5 - w - 3$,
(c) $w \times w$.

7 (a) Simplify (i) $5q + 3q - 4q$,
(ii) $c \times c \times c$,
(iii) $3x \times 4y$.
(b) Multiply out $5(3h + 2)$.
Edexcel

8 (a) Simplify (i) $n + 1 + n + 2$,
(ii) $2n \times 3n$.
(b) Multiply out $2(x + 3)$.
(c) Simplify $3 + 2(x - 1)$.
(d) Factorise $3x - 6$.

9 Simplify (a) $ab + 2ba$,
(b) $a^2 - a + 3a$,
(c) $3(x - 2) - x$.

10 A pint of milk costs m pence.
Write an expression for the cost of p pints of milk.

11 Write an expression in terms of d for the perimeter of this shape.

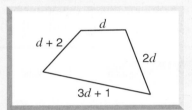

d

$d + 2$

$2d$

$3d + 1$

12 Large sticks of rock cost n pence each.
(a) Write an expression for the cost of 5 large sticks of rock.
(b) A small stick of rock costs 15 pence less than a large stick.
Write an expression for the cost of a small stick of rock.
(c) Alfie buys 2 large sticks of rock and 3 small sticks of rock.
Write an expression for the total cost.
Give your answer in its simplest form.

13 Write these algebraic expressions in a simpler way.
(a) $5a + 6a - 7a$
(b) $7a + 3b - 5a - b$
(c) $3(a + 2) + 5(a - 1)$
(d) $5(2a + 1) + 5(a - 4)$
Edexcel

14 (a) Simplify $2n + 1 - n + 2n - 6$.
(b) Multiply out and simplify
$3(a - 1) + 2(3a + 1)$.
(c) Factorise $2x^2 + xy$.

15 Multiply out $x(x + 3)$.

16 Factorise.
(a) $6x - 15$ (b) $y^2 + 7y$

CHAPTER 12

Solving Equations

Activity

Can you solve these puzzles?

- **Nueve** is a Spanish number.
  If you add 1 to **nueve** you get 10.
  What is **nueve**?

- What number must be put in each shape to make the statements correct?

  $\square + 3 = 8$ $\bigcirc \times 3 = 30$ $2 \times \bigcirc - 3 = 7$

These are all examples of **equations.**
Equations like these can be solved using a method known as **inspection.**
Instead of words or boxes, equations are usually written using letters for the unknown numbers.
Solving an equation means finding the numerical value of the letter which fits the equation.

EXAMPLES   Solve these equations by inspection.

1 $x - 2 = 6$

$x = 8$

Reason: $\mathbf{8} - 2 = 6$

2 $2y = 10$

$y = 5$

Reason: $2 \times \mathbf{5} = 10$

Remember:
A letter or a symbol stands for an unknown number.

$2y$ means $2 \times y$.

Exercise 12.1

1 What number must be put in the box to make each of these statements true?

(a) $\square + 4 = 7$ (b) $15 - \square = 11$ (c) $13 = \square + 4$ (d) $11 = \square - 5$

2 Solve these equations by inspection.

(a) $x + 2 = 6$ (b) $a + 7 = 10$ (c) $y - 4 = 4$

(d) $6 + t = 12$ (e) $h - 15 = 7$ (f) $d + 4 = 5$

(g) $z - 5 = 25$ (h) $p + 7 = 7$ (i) $c + 1 = 100$

3 What number must be put in the box to make each of these statements true?

(a) $3 \times \square = 15$ (b) $\square \times 4 = 20$ (c) $18 = \square \times 2$ (d) $24 = 8 \times \square$

4 Solve these by inspection.

(a) $3a = 12$ (b) $2b = 18$ (c) $4c = 20$

(d) $5e = 30$ (e) $6f = 42$ (f) $4g = 32$

(g) $8 = 2p$ (h) $15 = 5r$ (i) $36 = 6x$

5 What number must be put in the box to make each of these statements true?

(a) $2 \times \square + 3 = 5$ (b) $\square \times 3 + 5 = 17$ (c) $3 + \square \times 2 = 11$

(d) $5 \times \square - 1 = 9$ (e) $4 \times \square - 5 = 7$ (f) $\square \times 3 - 6 = 9$

Solving equations by working backwards

I think of a number and then subtract 3.
The answer is 5.
What is the number I thought of?

Imagine that x is the number I thought of.
The steps of the problem can be shown in a diagram.

$x \longrightarrow$ | subtract 3 | $\longrightarrow$ Answer 5

Now work backwards, doing the opposite calculation.

8 $\longleftarrow$ | add 3 | $\longleftarrow$ 5

The number I thought of is 8.

> The opposite of 'subtracting 3' is 'adding 3'.

EXAMPLES

1 Ken thinks of a number.
He multiplies it by 5.
His answer is 30.
What number did Ken think of?

$x \longrightarrow$ | multiply by 5 | $\longrightarrow$ 30

6 $\longleftarrow$ | divide by 5 | $\longleftarrow$ 30

Ken's number is 6.

> **Remember**
>
> | Forwards | Backwards |
> |----------|-----------|
> | add | subtract |
> | subtract | add |
> | multiply | divide |
> | divide | multiply |

2 I think of a number, multiply it by 3 and add 4.
The answer is 19.
What is my number?

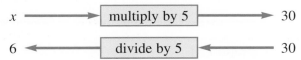

$x \longrightarrow$ | multiply by 3 | $\longrightarrow$ | add 4 | $\longrightarrow$ 19

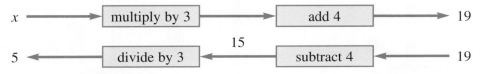

5 $\longleftarrow$ | divide by 3 | $\longleftarrow$ 15 | subtract 4 | $\longleftarrow$ 19

The number I thought of is 5.

Exercise 12.2

Solve the equations by working backwards.

1 I think of a number and then add 4.
The answer is 7.
What is my number?

2 Jan thinks of a number and then subtracts 5.
Her answer is 9.
What is her number?

3 I think of a number and then multiply it by 2.
The answer is 10.
What is my number?

4 Lou thinks of a number.
He multiplies it by 2 and then subtracts 5.
The answer is 7.
What is his number?

5 I think of a number, subtract 5 and then multiply by 2.
The answer is 12.
What is my number?

6 Beth thinks of a number.
She multiplies it by 3 and adds 4.
If the answer is 19, what is her number?

7 I think of a number, add 4 then multiply by 3.
The answer is 24.
What is my number?

8 Steve thinks of a number.
He multiplies it by 5 and then adds 2.
The answer is 17.
What is his number?

9 I think of a number, multiply it by 3 and then subtract 5.
The answer is 7.
What is my number?

10 Solve this puzzle.

> Begin with x.
> Double it and then add 3.
> The result is equal to 17.
> What is the value of x?

11 Kathryn thinks of a number.
She adds 3 and then doubles the result.
(a) What number does Kathryn start with to get an answer of 10?
(b) Kathryn starts with x.
What is her answer in terms of x?

12 Sarah thinks of a number.
She subtracts 2 and multiplies by 3.
(a) What number does Sarah start with to get an answer of 21?
(b) Sarah starts with x.
What is her answer in terms of x?

13 Ali thinks of a number.
He multiplies it by 2 and then adds 3.
(a) What number does Ali start with to get an answer of 15?
(b) Ali starts with x.
What is his answer in terms of x?

The balance method

It is not always easy to solve equations by inspection.
Many equations are harder to solve than those in Exercise 12.1.
To solve harder equations a better method has to be used.
Here is a method that works a bit like a balance.

These scales are balanced.

You can add the same amount to both sides and they still balance.

You can subtract the same amount from both sides and they still balance.

You can double (or halve) the amount on both sides and they still balance.

Equations work in the same way.
If you do the same to both sides of an equation, it is still true.

| EXAMPLES | Use the balance method to solve these equations. Explain what you are doing. |

1 Solve $d - 13 = 5$.

$d - 13 = 5$
Add 13 to both sides.
$d = 18$

2 Solve $x + 7 = 16$.

$x + 7 = 16$
Subtract 7 from both sides.
$x = 9$

3 Solve $4a = 20$.

$4a = 20$
Divide both sides by 4.
$a = 5$

The aim is to find out what number the letter stands for, by ending up with **one letter** on one side of the equation and a **number** on the other side.

4 Solve $4n + 5 = 17$.

$4n + 5 = 17$
Subtract 5 from both sides.
$4n = 12$
Divide both sides by 4.
$n = 3$

Look at the examples carefully.
The steps taken to solve the equations are explained.
Notice that:
Doing the same to both sides means: **adding** the **same number** to both sides.
subtracting the **same number** from both sides.
dividing both sides by the **same number**.
multiplying both sides by the **same number**.

Exercise 12.3

1 Use the balance method to solve these equations.
Write down the steps that you use to solve each equation.

(a) $y + 4 = 7$ (b) $x + 5 = 11$ (c) $a + 10 = 20$
(d) $e + 9 = 24$ (e) $d + 6 = 17$ (f) $c + 15 = 35$
(g) $9 + x = 11$ (h) $2 + y = 21$ (i) $8 + m = 15$

2 Use the balance method to solve these equations.
Explain each step of your working.

(a) $q - 5 = 2$ (b) $m - 2 = 8$ (c) $n - 7 = 9$
(d) $p - 6 = 12$ (e) $x - 11 = 20$ (f) $y - 3 = 14$
(g) $a - 1 = 1$ (h) $g - 3 = 1$ (i) $h - 5 = 7$

3 Use the balance method to solve these equations.

(a) $28 + x = 42$ (b) $t - 15 = 13$ (c) $f + 16 = 34$
(d) $y - 12 = 7$ (e) $14 + b = 21$ (f) $x - 9 = 20$
(g) $7 + m = 11$ (h) $k - 2 = 3$ (i) $5 + y = 12$

4 Use the balance method to solve these equations.
Write down the steps that you use.

(a) $3c = 12$ (b) $5a = 20$ (c) $4f = 12$
(d) $8p = 24$ (e) $6h = 30$ (f) $10u = 20$
(g) $3d = 30$ (h) $2e = 14$ (i) $3f = 27$

5 Use the balance method to solve these equations.
Show each step of your working.

(a) $2p + 1 = 9$ (b) $4t - 1 = 11$ (c) $3h - 7 = 14$
(d) $3 + 4b = 11$ (e) $5d - 8 = 42$ (f) $2x + 3 = 15$
(g) $2 + 3c = 17$ (h) $3n - 1 = 8$ (i) $4x + 3 = 11$

6 Solve these equations.
There is no need to explain your working if you are confident of what you are doing.

(a) $5c + 7 = 42$ (b) $7x = 28$ (c) $8y - 5 = 27$
(d) $3x + 5 = 11$ (e) $4b + 8 = 32$ (f) $6x - 9 = 15$
(g) $6k - 7 = 5$ (h) $7b + 4 = 25$ (i) $9c - 12 = 6$

7 Solve these equations.

(a) $6a = 18$ (b) $4x - 7 = 29$ (c) $8a + 7 = 7$
(d) $1 + 6p = 7$ (e) $8y - 14 = 26$ (f) $12 + 5p = 32$
(g) $3x - 5 = 22$ (h) $5 + 2k = 13$ (i) $5m + 3 = 18$

More equations

All the equations you have solved so far have had whole number solutions, but the solutions to equations can include negative numbers and fractions.

EXAMPLES

1 Solve $5x = 2$.

$5x = 2$
Divide both sides by 5.
$x = \dfrac{2}{5}$

2 Solve $-4a = 20$.

$-4a = 20$
Divide both sides by -4.
$a = -5$

3 Solve $6m - 1 = 2$.

$6m - 1 = 2$
Add 1 to both sides.
$6m = 3$
Divide both sides by 6.
$m = \dfrac{3}{6}$
$m = \dfrac{1}{2}$

4 Solve $5 - 4n = -1$.

$5 - 4n = -1$
Subtract 5 from both sides.
$-4n = -6$
Divide both sides by -4.
$n = 1.5$

Exercise 12.4

1 Solve these equations.
Explain each step of your working.

(a) $4k = 2$ (b) $2a = -6$ (c) $-3d = 12$
(d) $-8n = 4$ (e) $t + 3 = -2$ (f) $n - 3 = -2$
(g) $2m + 1 = 4$ (h) $3x - 2 = 5$ (i) $2y + 5 = 4$

2 Solve these equations.

(a) $5x = -10$ (b) $2y + 7 = 1$ (c) $4t + 10 = 2$

(d) $5 - a = 7$ (e) $2 - d = 5$ (f) $3 - 2g = 9$

(g) $4t = 2$ (h) $2x = 15$ (i) $5d = 7$

(j) $4a - 5 = 1$ (k) $3 + 5g = 4$ (l) $2b - 5 = 4$

3 Solve these equations.

(a) $x - 1 = -3$ (b) $3 + 2n = 2$ (c) $2 - x = 3$

(d) $4 - 3y = 13$ (e) $2x - 1 = -3$ (f) $3 - 5x = 18$

(g) $4x + 1 = -5$ (h) $-2 - 3x = 10$ (i) $2 - 4x = 8$

What you need to know

- The solution of an equation is the value of the unknown letter that fits the equation.

You should be able to:

- Solve simple equations by inspection. e.g. $x + 2 = 5$, $x - 3 = 7$, $2x = 10$

- Solve simple equations by working backwards.

- Use the balance method to solve equations which are difficult to solve by inspection.

Review Exercise

1 What number must be put in the box to make each of these statements correct?

(a) $\square + 5 = 9$

(b) $7 - \square = 4$

(c) $3 \times \square = 18$

(d) $\square \times 2 - 3 = 5$

2 Tim thought of a number.
He doubled the number.
His answer was 24.
What number did Tim think of? *Edexcel*

3 Solve these equations.

(a) $a - 3 = 7$

(b) $6a = 30$

(c) $5 + a = 12$

4 I think of a number, double it and then add 10.
My answer is 32.
Write down the number I am thinking of.
Edexcel

5 Solve these equations.

(a) $3x + 5 = 17$

(b) $5n - 3 = 7$

6 Bob uses this rule.

> Start with a number.
> Multiply it by 3.
> Take away 5.
> Write down the answer.

(a) What is the answer if Bob starts with x?

(b) What is the answer if Bob starts with -1?

(c) What number must Bob start with to get an answer of 16?

7 Solve these equations.

(a) $y + 3 = 5$

(b) $2t + 8 = 2$

(c) $4g = 2$

(d) $5x - 1 = 2$

8 Solve the equation $6x + 25 = 97$.   *Edexcel*

9 Solve the equations

(a) $2x + 3 = -5$,

(b) $5 + 4y = 7$.

10 Solve these equations.

(a) $-5x = 4$

(b) $6 - 2y = 7$

Further Equations

Solving equations was first covered in Chapter 12.
Here are some reminders.

EXAMPLES   Solve the following equations.

1 $5x = 15$
$x = 3$

2 $m - 5 = 3$
$m = 8$

3 $2a + 4 = 7$
$2a = 3$
$a = 1\frac{1}{2}$

4 $3k + 5 = 2$
$3k = -3$
$k = -1$

The aim is to find the numerical value of the letter, by ending up with **one letter** on one side of the equation and a **number** on the other side of the equation.

Exercise 13.1

Solve these equations.
The solutions will not always be a whole number.

1 $4a = 12$

2 $x + 5 = 7$

3 $2m = -6$

4 $6y = 3$

5 $-3y = 15$

6 $3 - k = 5$

7 $2x + 1 = 7$

8 $3 + 4w = 5$

9 $5n + 7 = 3$

10 $2m + 3 = -1$

11 $8 + 2g = 5$

12 $2p + 9 = 18$

13 $-5n - 6 = 19$

14 $4y + 5 = 11$

15 $5 - 2d = 10$

Equations with brackets

Equations can include brackets.
Before using the balance method any brackets must be removed by multiplying out.
This is called **expanding**.

Remember:
$2(x + 3)$ means $2 \times (x + 3)$
$2(x + 3) = 2 \times x + 2 \times 3$
$ = 2x + 6$

Once the brackets have been removed the balance method can be used as before.

EXAMPLES

1 Solve $3(x + 2) = 12$.

$3(x + 2) = 12$
Expand the brackets.
$3x + 6 = 12$
$3x = 6$
$x = 2$

2 Solve $5(3y - 7) = 25$.

$5(3y - 7) = 25$
Expand the brackets.
$15y - 35 = 25$
$15y = 60$
$y = 4$

Exercise **13.2**

1 Solve.
(a) $2(x + 3) = 12$
(b) $4(a + 1) = 12$
(c) $5(t + 4) = 30$
(d) $2(y + 4) = 8$
(e) $3(e + 2) = 21$
(f) $6(3 + x) = 30$

2 Solve.
(a) $3(p - 2) = 9$
(b) $6(c - 2) = 24$
(c) $2(x - 1) = 4$
(d) $4(y - 3) = 24$
(e) $2(g - 3) = 16$
(f) $8(q - 3) = 40$

3 Solve.
(a) $3(a + 1) = 15$
(b) $2(b - 2) = 8$
(c) $4(c + 2) = 12$
(d) $6(d - 3) = 36$
(e) $7(2 + e) = 49$
(f) $5(f + 2) = 30$

4 Solve.
(a) $3(2w + 1) = 15$
(b) $2(4s + 5) = 34$
(c) $4(1 + 3x) = 28$
(d) $6(3g - 7) = 12$
(e) $4(2q - 1) = 28$
(f) $8(3t - 5) = 32$
(g) $3(2w + 1) = 27$
(h) $4(7 - 2x) = 4$
(i) $5(3y - 10) = 25$

5 Solve these equations. The solution will not always be a whole number.
(a) $3(p + 2) = 3$
(b) $2(3 - d) = 10$
(c) $2(1 - 3g) = 14$
(d) $2(x - 5) = 7$
(e) $5(y + 1) = 7$
(f) $2(1 + 3t) = 5$
(g) $2(2t - 1) = 5$
(h) $3(2a - 3) = 6$
(i) $5(m - 2) = 3$

Equations with letters on both sides

In some questions letters appear on both sides of the equation.

EXAMPLES

1 Solve $3x + 1 = x + 7$.

$3x + 1 = x + 7$
Subtract 1 from both sides.
$3x = x + 6$
Subtract x from both sides.
$2x = 6$
Divide both sides by 2.
$x = 3$

2 Solve $2a - 3 = 9 - a$.

$2a - 3 = 9 - a$
Add 3 to both sides.
$2a = 12 - a$
Add a to both sides.
$3a = 12$
Divide both sides by 3.
$a = 4$

Exercise **13.3**

1 Solve the following equations. Write down the steps that you use.
(a) $3x = 20 - x$
(b) $5q = 12 - q$
(c) $2t = 15 - 3t$
(d) $5e - 9 = 2e$
(e) $3g - 8 = g$
(f) $y + 3 = 5 - y$
(g) $4x + 1 = x + 7$
(h) $7k + 3 = 3k + 7$
(i) $3a - 1 = a + 7$
(j) $3p - 1 = 2p + 5$
(k) $6m - 1 = m + 9$
(l) $3d - 5 = 5 + d$
(m) $2y + 1 = y + 6$
(n) $3 + 5u = 2u + 12$
(o) $4q + 3 = q + 3$

2 Solve.

(a) $3d = 32 - d$ (b) $3q = 12 - q$ (c) $3c + 2 = 10 - c$

(d) $4t + 2 = 17 - t$ (e) $4w + 1 = 13 - 2w$ (f) $2e - 3 = 12 - 3e$

(g) $2g + 5 = 25 - 2g$ (h) $2z - 6 = 14 - 3z$ (i) $5m + 2 = 20 + 2m$

(j) $5a - 4 = 3a + 6$ (k) $3 + 4x = 15 + x$ (l) $6y - 11 = y + 4$

3 Solve these equations.
The solution will not always be a whole number.

(a) $3m + 8 = m$ (b) $2 - 4t = 12 + t$ (c) $5p - 3 = 3p - 7$

(d) $5x - 7 = 3x$ (e) $3 + 5a = a + 5$ (f) $2b + 7 = 11 - 3b$

(g) $4 - 4y = y$ (h) $7 + 3d = 10 - d$ (i) $f - 6 = 3f + 1$

Using equations to solve problems

So far, you have been given equations and asked to solve them.
The next step is to **form an equation** first using the information given in a problem.
The equation can then be solved in the usual way.

EXAMPLE

The triangle has sides of length:
x cm, $2x$ cm and 7 cm.

(a) Write an expression, in terms of x,
for the perimeter of the triangle.
Give your answer in its simplest form.

(b) The triangle has a perimeter of 19 cm.
By forming an equation find the value of x.

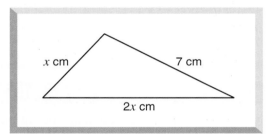

(a) The perimeter of the triangle is:
$x + 2x + 7$ cm
In its simplest form, the perimeter is:
$3x + 7$ cm

(b) The perimeter of the triangle is 19 cm,
so $\quad 3x + 7 = 19$
$\qquad\qquad 3x = 12$
$\qquad\qquad\; x = 4$

Exercise **13.4**

1 (a) Write an expression, in terms of x,
for the sum of the angles of the triangle.
Give your answer in its simplest form.

(b) The sum of the angles is $180°$.
By forming an equation find the value of x.

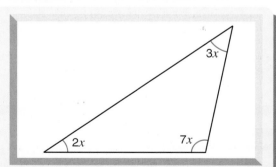

2 The weights of three packages are shown.

(a) Write an expression, in terms of k,
for the total weight of the packages.

(b) The packages weigh 15 kilograms
altogether.
By forming an equation find the
weight of the lightest package.

k kilograms $2k$ kilograms $3k$ kilograms

3 Bernadette pays 96 pence for a newspaper and a magazine.
The magazine costs twice as much as the newspaper.

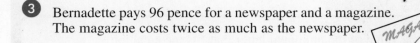

(a) The newspaper costs x pence.
Write an expression, in terms of x, for the price of the magazine.

(b) By forming an equation find the price of the magazine.

4 (a) Write an expression, in terms of y, for the perimeter of this shape.
Give your answer in its simplest form.

(b) The shape has a perimeter of 39 cm.
By forming an equation find the value of y.

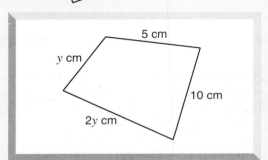

5 cm
y cm
10 cm
$2y$ cm

5 A bag contains the following balls.

a yellow balls
$2a + 1$ red balls
$3a + 2$ blue balls

(a) Write an expression, in terms of a, for the total number of balls in the bag.

(b) The bag contains 45 balls.
How many yellow balls are in the bag?

6 Dominic is 7 years younger than Marcie.
(a) Dominic is n years old.
Write an expression, in terms of n, for Marcie's age.

(b) The sum of their ages is 43 years.
By forming an equation find the ages of Dominic and Marcie.

7 The diagram shows the lengths of three rods.
(a) Write an expression, in terms of y, for the total length of the rods.

(b) The total length of the rods is 30 centimetres.
What is the length of the longest rod?

$y - 5$ centimetres y centimetres

$2y + 3$ centimetres

8 Grace is given a weekly allowance of £p.
Aimee is given £4 a week **more** than Grace.
Lydia is given £3 a week **less** than Grace.

(a) Write an expression, in terms of p, for the amount given to
   (i) Aimee,   (ii) Lydia,   (iii) all three girls.

(b) The three girls are given a total of £25 a week altogether.
By forming an equation find the weekly allowance given to each girl.

9 The cost of a pencil is x pence. The cost of a pen is 10 pence more than a pencil.
(a) Write down, in terms of x, the cost of a pen.

(b) Write down, in terms of x, the total cost of two pencils and a pen.
Give your answer in its simplest form.

(c) The total cost of a pencil and two pens is 65 pence.
Form an equation in x and solve it to find the cost of a pencil.

- The solution of an equation is the value of the unknown letter that fits the equation.

You should be able to:
- Solve equations with brackets.
  e.g. $4(3 + 2x) = 36$

- Solve equations with unknowns on both sides of the equals sign.
  e.g. $3x + 1 = x + 7$

- Use equations to solve problems.

Review Exercise

1 Solve these equations.
(a) $5y = 20$
(b) $3y + 2 = 11$
(c) $2y + 5 = 2 - y$

2 Solve.
(a) $5m - 7 = 28$
(b) $3t + 3 = 5t - 7$

3 Solve these equations.
(a) $2a + 3 = 7$
(b) $3(b + 1) = 15$
(c) $5c + 6 = 2c - 9$ Edexcel

4 Solve the equations
(a) $3(x - 2) = 9$,
(b) $6x + 3 = x - 2$.

5 (a) Solve $3p + 7 = 34$.
(b) Solve $3(2q - 5) = 36$.
(c) Solve $5r + 6 = 2r - 15$.   Edexcel

6 Solve.
(a) $3(a - 5) = 6a$
(b) $5(x + 2) = 14$

7 Solve $4x + 20 = 9x + 5$.

8 (a) Hilda is twice as old as Evie.
Their ages add up to 51 years.
How old is Hilda?

(b) Colin is 2 years older than John.
Their ages add up to 36 years.
How old is Colin?

9 Solve the equation
$5x - 4 = 3x + 15$.   Edexcel

10 (a) Write an expression, in terms of x, for the perimeter of this shape.

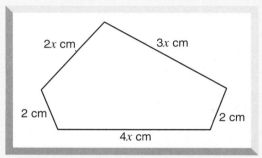

(b) The perimeter is 58 cm.
By forming an equation find the value of x.
(c) What is the length of the longest side of the shape?

11 A drink costs x pence.
A cake costs 7 pence more than a drink.
(a) Write down, in terms of x, an expression for
  (i) the cost of a cake,
  (ii) the total cost of two drinks and a cake.
(b) The total cost of two drinks and a cake is 97 pence.
Form an equation in x and solve it to find the cost of a cake.

12 The diagram shows two cans of oil.

n litres $3n + 1$ litres

The cans hold a total of 3 litres of oil.
By forming an equation find the amount of oil in the larger can.

CHAPTER 14 Formulae ●●●●●●●●●●●●

Most people at some time make use of **formulae** to carry out routine calculations.
A **formula** represents a rule written using numbers, letters and mathematical signs.
When using a formula you will need to **substitute** your own values for the letters in order to carry out
your calculation.

Substitution

Substituting whole numbers

> **EXAMPLE**
>
> Find the value of   (a) $a + 5$,   (b) $a - 3$,   (c) $3a$,   (d) $a \times a$,   when $a = 4$.
>
> | (a) | $a + 5$ | (b) | $a - 3$ | (c) | $3a$ | (d) | $a \times a$ |
> |---|---|---|---|---|---|---|---|
> | | $= 4 + 5$ | | $= 4 - 3$ | | $= 3 \times 4$ | | $= 4 \times 4$ |
> | | $= 9$ | | $= 1$ | | $= 12$ | | $= 16$ |

Exercise 14.1   Do not use a calculator.

1. $m = 3$.   Find the value of   (a) $m + 2$ (b) $m - 1$ (c) $4m$ (d) $m \times m$

2. $t = 5$.   Find the value of   (a) $5 + t$ (b) $3 - t$ (c) $2t$ (d) $t \times t$

3. $x = 4$.   Find the value of   (a) $x + x$ (b) $x - 4$ (c) $3x$ (d) $x \times x \times 2$

4. $a = 6$ and $b = 3$.   Find the value of
(a) $3a + 2b$ (b) $b - a$ (c) $\dfrac{a}{b}$ (d) $a \times b$ (e) $2(a + b)$

5. $p = 10$ and $q = 5$.   Find the value of
(a) $p + q$ (b) $p - 2q$ (c) $\dfrac{p}{q}$ (d) $p \times q$ (e) $3(p - q)$

6. $x = 15$ and $y = 6$.   Find the value of
(a) $x + 2y$ (b) $x - 3y$ (c) $\dfrac{x}{y}$ (d) $x \times y$ (e) $6(x - y)$

Substituting negative numbers

> **EXAMPLE**
>
> Find the value of   (a) $a + 5$,   (b) $a - 3$,   (c) $3a$,   when $a = -4$.
>
> | (a) | $a + 5$ | (b) | $a - 3$ | (c) | $3a$ |
> |---|---|---|---|---|---|
> | | $= -4 + 5$ | | $= -4 - 3$ | | $= 3 \times -4$ |
> | | $= 1$ | | $= -7$ | | $= -12$ |

Do not use a calculator.

1 $m = -3$. Find the value of   (a) $m + 2$ (b) $m - 1$ (c) $4m$ (d) $2m + 9$

2 $t = -5$. Find the value of   (a) $5 + t$ (b) $t - 3$ (c) $2t$ (d) $3t - 1$

3 $x = -4$. Find the value of   (a) $x + x$ (b) $x - 4$ (c) $3x$ (d) $10 + 2x$

4 $a = 6$ and $b = -3$.   Find the value of
(a) $3a + 2b$ (b) $b - a$ (c) $\dfrac{a}{b}$ (d) $a \times b$ (e) $2(a + b)$

5 $p = -10$ and $q = 5$. Find the value of
(a) $p + q$ (b) $p - 2q$ (c) $\dfrac{p}{q}$ (d) $p \times q$ (e) $3(p - q)$

6 $x = 15$ and $y = -6$. Find the value of
(a) $x + 2y$ (b) $y - x$ (c) $\dfrac{x}{y}$ (d) $x \times y$ (e) $6(x + y)$

Writing expressions and formulae

A lollipop costs 15 pence.
How much will n lollipops cost?
Write a formula for the cost, C, in pence, of n lollipops.

Each lollipop costs 15 pence.

So, n lollipops cost $15 \times n$ pence $= 15n$ pence.

> $15n$ is an **algebraic expression**.

If the cost of n lollipops is C pence, then $C = 15n$.

> $C = 15n$ is a **formula**.

Formulae can be used in lots of situations.

The grid shows the numbers from 1 to 50.
An **L** shape has been drawn on the grid.
It is called L_{14} because the lowest number is 14.

What is the sum of the numbers in L_{14}?

The **L** shape can be moved to different parts of the grid.
We can find the sum of the numbers for each shape.

1	2	3	4	5	6	7	8	9	10
11	12	13	14	15	16	17	18	19	20
21	22	23	24	25	26	27	28	29	30
31	32	33	34	35	36	37	38	39	40
41	42	43	44	45	46	47	48	49	50

A formula for the sum of the numbers, S_n,
can be written in terms of n for shape L_n.

$S_n = n + (n + 10) + (n + 20) + (n + 21)$
$S_n = 4n + 51$

$$\begin{array}{|c|c|}
\hline
n & \\
\hline
n+10 & \\
\hline
n+20 & n+21 \\
\hline
\end{array}$$

An **expression** is just an answer using letters and numbers.

A **formula** is an algebraic rule. It always has an equals sign.

EXAMPLES

1 A hedge is l metres long.
A fence is 50 metres longer than the hedge.
Write an **expression**, in terms of l, for the length of the fence.

The fence is $(l + 50)$ metres long.

2 Boxes of matches each contain 48 matches.
Write down a **formula** for the number of matches, m, in n boxes.

$m = 48 \times n$

This could be written as $m = 48n$.

Exercise 14.3

1 A pencil costs *y* pence.
   (a)   What is the cost of 5 pencils?
   (b)   A ruler costs 8 pence more than a pencil.
         What is the cost of a ruler?

2 Egg boxes hold 12 eggs each.
   How many eggs are there in *e* boxes?

3 I am *a* years old.
   (a)   How old will I be in 1 years time?
   (b)   How old was I four years ago?
   (c)   How old will I be in *n* years time?

4 A child is making a tower with toy bricks.
   He has *b* bricks in his tower.
   Write an expression for the number of bricks in the tower after he takes 3 bricks from the top.

5 Paul is *h* cm tall.
   Sue is 12 cm taller than Paul.
   Write down an expression for Sue's height in terms of *h*.

6 John has *d* CDs.
   (a)   Carol has twice as many CDs as John.
         Write down an expression for the number of CDs that Carol has in terms of *d*.
   (b)   Fred has 5 more CDs than Carol.
         Write down an expression for the number of CDs that Fred has in terms of *d*.

7 A packet of biscuits costs *y* pence.
   Write down a formula for the cost, *P* pence, of another packet which costs
   (a)   five pence more than the first packet,
   (b)   two pence less than the first packet,
   (c)   twice the cost of the first packet.

8 David is *d* years old.
   Copy and complete this table to show the ages, *A*, of these people.

Name	Clue	Age
Alec	3 years older than David.	$A = d + 3$
Ben	2 years younger than David.	
Charlotte	Twice as old as David.	
Erica	Half David's age.	

9 Write a formula for the perimeter, *P*, for each of these shapes in terms of the letters given.

   (a)   (b)   (c)   (d)

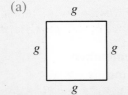
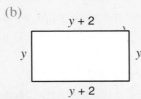
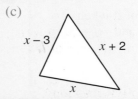

Formulae · · · · Formulae · · · · Formulae

10 A caravan costs £25 per day to hire.
Write a formula for the cost, C, in £s, to hire the caravan for d days.

11 The cost of hiring a ladder is given by:

> £12 per day,
> plus a delivery charge of £8

(a) Bill hired a ladder for 3 days.
How much did he pay?
(b) Sam hired a ladder for 6 days.
How much did he pay?
(c) Fred hired a ladder for x days.
Write down a formula for the total cost, $£C$, in terms of x.

12 The grid shows the numbers from 1 to 50.
A **T** shape has been drawn on the grid.
It is called T_{23} because the lowest number is 23.

Calculate the sum of the numbers in
(a) T_{16} (b) T_{28} (c) T_2

(d) The diagram on the right shows T_n.
Copy and complete the **T** shape in terms of n.

(e) Write a formula for the sum of the numbers, S_n,
in terms of n, for shape T_n.
Write your answer in its simplest form.

1	2	3	4	5	6	7	8	9	10
11	12	13	14	15	16	17	18	19	20
21	22	23	24	25	26	27	28	29	30
31	32	33	34	35	36	37	38	39	40
41	42	43	44	45	46	47	48	49	50

n

Using formulae

The formula for the perimeter of a rectangle is $P = 2L + 2W$.
By **substituting** values for the length, L, and the width, W, you can calculate the value of P.

$P = 2L + 2W$
When $L = 3$ and $W = 5$,
$P = 2 \times 3 + 2 \times 5$
$\quad = 6 + 10$
$\quad = 16$

EXAMPLES

1 $G = 4t - 1$
Find the value of G when $t = \frac{1}{2}$.

$G = 4t - 1$
$\quad = 4 \times \frac{1}{2} - 1$
$\quad = 2 - 1$
$\quad = 1$

2 $A = pq - r$
What is the value of A when
$p = 2$, $q = -2$ and $r = 3$.

$A = 2 \times (-2) - 3$
$\quad = -4 - 3$
$\quad = -7$

3 $H = 3(4x - y)$
Find the value of H when $x = 5$ and $y = 7$.

$H = 3(4x - y)$
$\quad = 3(4 \times 5 - 7)$
$\quad = 3(20 - 7)$
$\quad = 3(13)$
$\quad = 39$

4 $W = x^2 + 2$
Find the value of W when $x = 3$.

$W = x^2 + 2$
$\quad = 3 \times 3 + 2$
$\quad = 9 + 2$
$\quad = 11$

Remember
x^2 means $x \times x$.

Exercise 14.4

Do not use a calculator for questions 1 to 22.

1 The wages earned by an hourly paid person can be worked out using this formula.

> Wages earned = hours worked $\times$ pay per hour

Work out the wages earned by a person who works 8 hours at £6 per hour.

2 The number of points scored by a soccer team can be worked out using this formula.

> Points scored = 3 $\times$ games won + games drawn

A team has won 5 games and drawn 2 games.
How many points have they scored?

3 $A = x + 3.$ Find the value of A when   (a) $x = 5$ (b) $x = 9$ (c) $x = -5$

4 $C = d - 5.$ Find the value of C when   (a) $d = 8$ (b) $d = 5$ (c) $d = -3$

5 $P = 4a.$ Find the value of P when   (a) $x = \frac{1}{2}$ (b) $x = \frac{1}{4}$ (c) $x = \frac{1}{8}$

6 $S = 5t.$ Find the value of S when   (a) $t = 0.2$ (b) $t = 0.3$ (c) $t = 0.4$

7 $M = 4n - 1.$ Find the value of M when   (a) $n = 2$ (b) $n = \frac{1}{2}$ (c) $n = 0.25$

8 $H = 3g - 5.$ Find the value of H when   (a) $g = -1$ (b) $g = 2.5$ (c) $g = \frac{2}{3}$

9 $F = 5(v + 6).$ What is the value of F when   (a) $v = 1,$ (b) $v = 9,$ (c) $v = -9?$

10 $V = 2(7 + 2x).$ What is the value of V when   (a) $x = 3,$ (b) $x = -3,$ (c) $x = \frac{1}{2}?$

11 $P = 3(5 - 2d).$ What is the value of P when   (a) $d = 2,$ (b) $d = 4,$ (c) $d = 0.5?$

12 $C = 8(p + q).$
What is the value of C when
(a) $p = 5$ and $q = 8,$ (b) $p = 6$ and $q = -2,$ (c) $p = 5$ and $q = -8?$

13 $S = ax + 4.$
What is the value of S when
(a) $a = 12$ and $x = 3,$ (b) $a = 3$ and $x = -2,$ (c) $a = 5$ and $x = 0.4?$

14 $T = a(x + 4).$
What is the value of T when
(a) $a = 5$ and $x = 3,$ (b) $a = 2$ and $x = -5,$ (c) $a = -3$ and $x = 2?$

15 $K = ab + c.$
Work out the value of K when
(a) $a = 3,$ $b = 2$ and $c = 5,$ (b) $a = 5,$ $b = 3$ and $c = -2.$

16 $L = xy - z.$
Work out the value of L when
(a) $x = 2,$ $y = 3$ and $z = 4,$ (b) $x = -4,$ $y = 2$ and $z = 3.$

17 $S = a^2$. Find the value of S when (a) $a = 3$, (b) $a = 4$, (c) $a = 10$.

18 $S = 2a^2$. Find the value of S when (a) $a = 3$, (b) $a = 4$, (c) $a = 10$.

19 $T = 2a^2 - 20$. Find the value of T when (a) $a = 3$, (b) $a = 4$, (c) $a = 10$.

20 $A = x^3$. Find the value of A when (a) $x = 2$, (b) $x = 3$, (c) $x = 4$.

21 $S = 2t^3$. Find the value of S when (a) $t = 2$, (b) $t = 3$, (c) $t = 4$.

22 The number of matches, M, needed to make a pattern of P pentagons is given by the formula: $M = 4P + 1$.
Find the number of matches needed to make 8 pentagons.

23 The distance, d metres, travelled by a lawn mower in t minutes is given by the formula: $d = 24t$.
Find the distance travelled by the lawn mower in:
(a) 4 minutes, (b) 30 minutes, (c) 90 seconds.

24 Convert these temperatures from Fahrenheit to Centigrade using the formula: $C = (F - 32) \div 1.8$
(a) 50°F (b) −4°F (c) 77°F (d) −40°F

25 Convert these temperatures from Centigrade to Fahrenheit using the formula: $F = C \times 1.8 + 32$
(a) 10°C (b) −10°C (c) 30°C (d) −40°C

26 $T = 45W + 30$ is used to calculate the time in minutes needed to cook a joint of beef weighing W kilograms.
How many minutes are needed to cook a joint of beef weighing 2.4 kg?

27 The voltage, V volts, in a circuit with resistance, R ohms, and current, I amps, is given by the formula: $V = IR$.
Find the voltage in a circuit when $I = 12$ and $R = 20$.

Writing and using formulae

EXAMPLE

Birthday Party

Specials

£20, plus £5 per person

(a) Nick has a birthday party for 12 people. How much does it cost?

(b) Tony has a birthday party for x people. Write a formula for the cost £T, in terms of x.

(c) Jean pays £100 for her birthday party. How many people went to the party?

(a) Nick's party costs: £20 + 12 × £5
$\qquad\qquad\qquad\qquad = £80$

(b) Cost for x people in £ $= x \times 5 = 5x$
Total cost in £ $\qquad = 20 + 5x$
Total cost is £T
So formula is $\qquad T = 20 + 5x$

(c) Using the formula $T = 20 + 5x$.
Jean's party costs £100, so $T = 100$.
$$100 = 20 + 5x$$
$$5x = 80$$
$$x = 16$$

16 people went to Jean's party.

1 The cost of a taxi journey is:

| £3 plus £2 for each kilometre travelled |

(a) Alex travels 5 km by taxi. How much does it cost?
(b) A taxi journey of k kilometres costs £C.
Write a formula for the cost, C, in terms of k.
(c) Adrian paid £7 for a taxi journey.
Use your formula to find the number of kilometres he travelled.

2 A rule to find the cooking time, C minutes, of a chicken which weighs k kilograms, is:

| multiply the weight of the chicken by 40 and then add 20 |

(a) Find the cooking time for a chicken which weighs 3 kg.
(b) Write a formula for C in terms of k.
(c) Use your formula to find the weight of a chicken which has a cooking time of 100 minutes.

3 An approximate rule for changing temperatures in degrees Celsius, C, to temperatures in degrees Fahrenheit, F, is given by the rule:

| double C and add on 30 |

(a) Find the value of F when $C = 6$.
(b) Write down a formula for F in terms of C.
(c) Use your formula to find the value of C when $F = 58$.

4 A teacher uses this rule to work out the number of exercise books he needs for Year 11 students.

| 3 books per student, plus 50 extra books |

(a) This year there are 120 students in Year 11. How many books are needed?
(b) Using b for the number of books and n for the number of students, write down the teacher's rule for b in terms of n.
(c) For the next Year 11, he will need 470 books.
How many students will be in Year 11 next year?

5 (a) How much does it cost to hire the carpet cleaner for 3 days?
(b) Using T for the total cost in £, and d for the number of days hired, write a formula for T in terms of d.
(c) Sarah paid a total of £96 to hire the carpet cleaner.
For how many days did she hire the carpet cleaner?

CARPET CLEANER HIRE

£15 PER DAY

Plus fixed delivery charge of £6

6 Scaffolding can be hired. The hire charge is calculated using this formula:

| forty-five pounds per day plus a fixed charge of seventy pounds |

(a) How much would it cost to hire scaffolding for 5 days?
(b) Using C for the total cost in £, and n for the number of days, write a formula for C in terms of n.
(c) A builder paid £475 altogether to hire some scaffolding.
For how many days did he hire the scaffolding?

Formule · · · Formule · · · Formule · · ·

You should be able to:
- Write simple algebraic expressions and formulae.
- Substitute positive and negative numbers in expressions and formulae.
- Substitute numbers in simple formulae to solve problems.

Review Exercise

1 What is the value of $2g + 3h$ when $g = 5$ and $h = 2$?

2 Given that $x = 3$ and $y = 4$, find the value of
(a) $x + y$,   (b) $x - y$,   (c) xy.

3 $V = a + bc$.
Find the value of V when $a = 5$, $b = 3$ and $c = 4$.

4 What is the value of $5m + 2n$ when $m = 2$ and $n = -3$?

5 $S = pq + r$.
Find the value of S when $p = -3$, $q = 4$ and $r = -2$.

6 $P = 3(m + n)$.
Find the value of P when $m = 0.5$ and $n = 2$.

7 What is the value of $3x^2$ when $x = 6$?

8 What is the value of $t^3 - t$ when $t = 2$?

9 Neil has a Saturday job.
His wages, in pounds, are worked out using this rule.

> Wages = number of hours worked × 5.

(a) Neil worked for seven hours last Saturday.
Work out Neil's wages for last Saturday.
(b) On a Saturday last month Neil earned £20.
How many hours did Neil work on that Saturday?
Edexcel

10 A roll of wallpaper costs 4 pounds.
Joan buys w rolls of wallpaper.
The total cost is C pounds.
Write down a formula connecting C and w.
Edexcel

11 Daniel buys n books at £4 each.
He pays for them with a £20 note.
He receives C pounds change.
Write down a formula for C in terms of n.
Edexcel

12 The cost, S pounds, of a chest of drawers with d drawers may be calculated using the formula:

$$S = 29 + 15d$$

(a) Calculate the cost of a chest of drawers with 3 drawers.

Another chest of drawers costs £119.
(b) Calculate the number of drawers this chest has.
Edexcel

13 (a) Write, in symbols, the rule:
"To find y, multiply k by 3 and then subtract 1."
(b) Work out the value of k when $y = 14$.
Edexcel

14 The cost of hiring a skip is:

> £15 PER DAY + £45 DELIVERY

(a) Kay hires a skip for 3 days.
How much does she have to pay?
(b) Write a formula for the cost, £C, of hiring a skip for d days.

15 Wilma works h hours a week.
Wilma is paid £x per hour.
Wilma is also paid a loyalty bonus of £20 a week.

(a) Write a formula for her total weekly pay, £T, in terms of h and x.
(b) Each week Wilma works 35 hours and is paid £230.
How much does Wilma get paid per hour?

16 The cost of printing business cards is:

> £5 plus 15 pence a card

(a) What is the total cost of printing 80 cards?
(b) Write a formula for the total cost, £C, of printing n cards.
(c) Fred pays £77 for some business cards to be printed.
How many cards did he have printed?

CHAPTER 15

Sequences

●●●●●●●●●●●●●●●●●

Continuing a sequence

A **sequence** is a list of numbers made according to some rule.
For example:

5, 9, 13, 17, 21, …

The first term is 5.
To find the next term in the sequence, add 4 to the last term.
The next term in this sequence is $21 + 4 = 25$.
What are the next three terms in the sequence?

> The numbers in a sequence are called **terms**.
> The start number is the **first term**, the next is the second term, and so on.

> **To continue a sequence:**
> 1. Work out the rule to get from one term to the next.
> 2. Apply the same rule to find further terms in the sequence.

EXAMPLES

Find the next three terms in each of these sequences.

1 5, 8, 11, 14, 17, …

To find the next term in the sequence, add 3 to the last term.
$17 + 3 = 20$, $20 + 3 = 23$, $23 + 3 = 26$.
The next three terms in the sequence are: 20, 23, 26.

2 2, 4, 8, 16, …

To find the next term in the sequence, multiply the last term by 2.
$16 \times 2 = 32$, $32 \times 2 = 64$, $64 \times 2 = 128$.
The next three terms in the sequence are: 32, 64, 128.

3 1, 1, 2, 3, 5, 8, …

To find the next term in the sequence, add the last two terms.
$5 + 8 = 13$, $8 + 13 = 21$, $13 + 21 = 34$.
The next three terms in the sequence are: 13, 21, 34.
This is a special sequence called the **Fibonacci sequence**.

Exercise **15.1**

1 Find the next three terms in these sequences.

(a) 1, 5, 9, 13, …
(b) 6, 8, 10, 12, …
(c) 28, 25, 22, 19, …
(d) 3, 8, 13, 18, 23, …
(e) 3, 6, 12, 24, …
(f) 32, 16, 8, 4, …
(g) 10, 8, 6, 4, …
(h) 80, 40, 20, 10, …
(i) 1, 3, 6, 10, 15, …
(j) 1, 3, 4, 7, 11, 18, …

2 Find the missing terms from these sequences.

(a) 2, 4, 6, __, 10, 12, __, 16, ...   (b) 2, 6, __, 14, 18, __, 26, ...
(c) 1, 2, 4, __, 16, __, 64, ...   (d) 28, 22, __, 10, 4, __, ...
(e) 1, 4, 9, __, 25, __, 49, ...   (f) 1, 2, 3, 5, __, 13, __, 34, ...
(g) __, 8, 14, __, __, 32, 38, ...

3 Write down the rule, in words, used to get from one term to the next for each sequence.
Then use the rule to find the next two terms.

(a) 2, 9, 16, 23, 30, ...   (b) 3, 5, 7, 9, 11, ...
(c) 1, 5, 9, 13, 17, ...   (d) 31, 26, 21, 16, ...
(e) 64, 32, 16, 8, 4, ...   (f) 1, 3, 9, 27, ...
(g) −2, −4, −6, −8, ...   (h) 10, 7, 4, 1, −2, ...

4 A sequence begins 1, 4, 7, 10, ...
(a) What is the 10th number in this sequence?
(b) Explain how you found your answer.

5 A number sequence begins 1, 2, 4, ...
David says that the next number is 8.
Tony says that the next number is 7.
(a) Explain why they could both be correct.
(b) Find the 10th number in David's sequence.
(c) Find the 10th number in Tony's sequence.

6 Here is part of a number sequence: 3, 9, 15, 21, ...
Is the number 50 in this sequence?
Explain your answer.

Using rules

Sometimes you will be given a rule and asked to use it to find the terms of a sequence.
For example:
A sequence begins: 1, 4, 13, ...
The rule for the sequence is:

> multiply the last number by 3, then add 1

The next term in the sequence is given by:
$$13 \times 3 + 1 = 39 + 1 = 40$$
The following term is given by:
$$40 \times 3 + 1 = 120 + 1 = 121$$

So the sequence can be extended to: 1, 4, 13, 40, 121, ...
Use the rule to find the next two terms in the sequence.

The **same rule** can be used to make different sequences.
For example:
Another sequence begins: 2, 7, 22, ...
Using the same rule, the next term is given by:
$$22 \times 3 + 1 = 66 + 1 = 67$$
The following term is given by:
$$67 \times 3 + 1 = 201 + 1 = 202$$

So the sequence can be extended to: 2, 7, 22, 67, 202, ...
Use the rule to find the next two terms in the sequence.

This rule is used to find each number in a sequence from the number before it.

Subtract 3 and then multiply by 4

Starting with 5 we get the following sequence:
5, 8, 20, 68, …

(a) Write down the next number in the sequence.
(b) Using the same rule, but a different starting number, the second number is 16.
Find the starting number.

(a) $(68 - 3) \times 4 = 65 \times 4 = 260$
Notice that, following the rule, 3 is subtracted first and
the result is then multiplied by 4.
The next number in the sequence is 260.

The method of
working backwards
was first used in
Chapter 12.

(b) Imagine the first number is x.

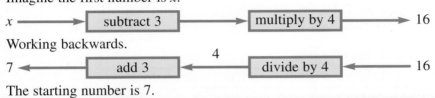

$x \longrightarrow$ subtract 3 $\longrightarrow$ multiply by 4 $\longrightarrow$ 16

Working backwards.

7 $\longleftarrow$ add 3 $\xleftarrow{\quad 4 \quad}$ divide by 4 $\longleftarrow$ 16

The starting number is 7.

Exercise 15.2

1 Write down the first five terms of these sequences.
(a) First term: 1
Rule: add 4 to the last term

(b) First term: 1
Rule: double the last term

(c) First term: 40
Rule: subtract 5 from the last term

(d) First term: 4
Rule: double the last term and then subtract 3

(e) First term: 47
Rule: subtract 1 from the last term and then halve the result

(f) First term: 2   Second term: 6
Rule: add the last two terms and then halve the result

2 This rule is used to get each number from the number before it:

multiply by 2

Use the rule to find the next three numbers when the first number is:
(a) 1,   (b) 3,   (c) −1.

3 This rule is used to get each number from the number before it:

add 1 and then double the result

Use the rule to find the next three numbers when the first number is:
(a) 1,   (b) 3,   (c) −3.

4 This rule is used to find each term of a sequence from the one before:

> subtract 3 then divide by 2

(a) The first term is 45.
   (i)   What is the second term?
   (ii) What is the **fourth** term?
(b) Using the same rule, but a different starting number, the second term is 17.
    What is the starting number for the sequence?

5 This rule is used to find each term of a sequence from the one before:

> add 5 then multiply by 3

(a) The first term is 7.
   (i)   What is the second term?
   (ii) What is the **third** term?
(b) Using the same rule, but a different starting number, the second term is 45.
    What is the starting number for the sequence?

6 A sequence begins 1, -3, ...
The sequence is continued using the rule:

> add the previous two numbers and then multiply by 3

Use the rule to find the next two numbers in the sequence.

7 A sequence begins 4, 7, 13, 25, ...
The next number in the sequence can be found using the rule:

> "Multiply the last term by 2 then subtract 1."

(a) Write down the next **two** terms in the sequence.
(b) The 11th term in the sequence is 3073.
    Use this information to find the 10th term in the sequence.

Sequences of numbers from shape patterns

Activity

These patterns are made using squares.

Pattern 1
3 squares

Pattern 2
5 squares

Pattern 3
7 squares

How many squares are used to make Pattern 4?
How many squares are used to make Pattern 10?
How many squares are used to make Pattern 100?
Which pattern is made using 81 squares?

The number of squares used to make each pattern forms a **sequence**.

Pattern 4 is made using 9 squares.

You could have answered this:
by drawing Pattern 4 or,
by continuing the sequence of numbers   3,   5,   7,   …

It is possible to do the same for Pattern 10, though it would involve a lot of work, but it would be unreasonable to use either method for Pattern 100.
Instead we can investigate how each pattern is made.

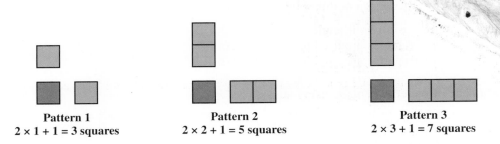

| Pattern 1 | Pattern 2 | Pattern 3 |
| $2 \times 1 + 1 = 3$ squares | $2 \times 2 + 1 = 5$ squares | $2 \times 3 + 1 = 7$ squares |

Each pattern is made using a **rule**.
The rule can be **described in words**.
To find the number of squares used to make a pattern use the rule:

"Double the pattern number and add 1."

$81 = 2 \times 40 + 1$, so the 40th pattern is made using 81 squares.

Pattern number	Rule	Number of squares
4	$2 \times 4 + 1$	9
10	$2 \times 10 + 1$	21
100	$2 \times 100 + 1$	201

The same rule can be **written using symbols**.
We can then answer a very important question:
How many squares are used to make Pattern n?

Pattern n will have $2 \times n + 1$ squares.
This can be written as $2n + 1$ squares.

How many squares are used to make Pattern 6?
Pattern n is made using $2n + 1$ squares.

Substitute $n = 6$.
$$2 \times 6 + 1$$
$$= 12 + 1$$
$$= 13$$

13 squares are used to make Pattern 6.

Draw a diagram to show that the answer is correct.

1 A sequence of patterns is made using equilateral triangles.

  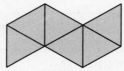 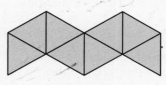

Pattern 1   **Pattern 2**   **Pattern 3**   **Pattern 4**

(a) How many triangles are used to make Pattern 5?
(b) Explain why a pattern in this sequence cannot have 27 triangles.

Pattern n is made using $2n$ triangles.
(c) How many triangles are used to make Pattern 7?
(d) How many triangles are used to make Pattern 12?

2 A sequence of patterns is made using sticks.

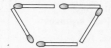 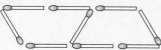 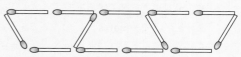

Pattern 1   **Pattern 2**   **Pattern 3**

(a) How many sticks are used to make Pattern 4?
(b) How many more sticks are used to make Pattern 5 from Pattern 4?

Pattern n is made using $4n + 1$ sticks.
(c) How many sticks are used to make Pattern 8?
(d) How many sticks are used to make Pattern 20?

3 A sequence of patterns is made using black and white counters.

1 black   **2 black**   **3 black**
3 white   **6 white**   **9 white**

How many white counters are there in a pattern with
(a) 5 black counters,   (b) 10 black counters,   (c) 100 black counters?

4 These patterns are made using matches.

(a) How many matches are used to make
    (i) Pattern 4,
    (ii) Pattern 20?
(b) Which pattern uses 30 matches?

  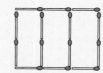

Pattern 1   **Pattern 2**   **Pattern 3**
6 matches   **10 matches**   **14 matches**

5 Fences are made by placing fence posts 1 m apart with 2 horizontal bars between each pair of posts.

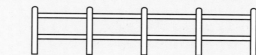

The fence above is 4 m long. It has 5 posts and 8 bars.
A fence is 50 m long.
(a) How many posts does it have?   (b) How many horizontal bars does it have?

6 Linking cubes of side 1 cm are used to make rods.
This rod is made using 4 linking cubes.

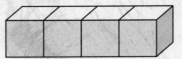

The surface area of the rod is 18 square centimetres.
(4 squares on each of the long sides plus one square at each end.)
(a)   What is the surface area of a rod made using 5 linking cubes?
(b)   What is the surface area of a rod made using 10 linking cubes?

The surface area of a rod made using n linking cubes is $4n + 2$ square centimetres.
(c)   How many linking cubes are used to make a rod with a surface area of
38 square centimetres?

7 A sequence of patterns is made using sticks.

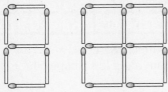 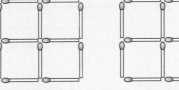 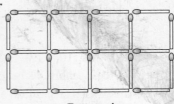

Pattern 1　　　　**Pattern 2**　　　　**Pattern 3**　　　　　　**Pattern 4**

(a)   How many sticks are used to make Pattern 5?

Pattern n uses T sticks.
A formula for T in terms of n is $T = 5n + 2$.
(b)   Use the formula to find the number of sticks used to make Pattern 10.
(c)   Use the formula to find the number of sticks used to make Pattern 50.
(d)   One pattern uses 77 sticks. What is the number of this pattern?

8 These patterns are made using matches.

 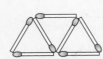

Pattern 1　　　**Pattern 2**　　　**Pattern 3**

(a)   How many matches are used to make Pattern 5?
(b)   Which pattern uses 15 matches?
(c)   Which pattern uses 37 matches?

What you need to know

- A **sequence** is a list of numbers made according to some rule.
  The numbers in a sequence are called **terms**.

- **To continue a sequence:**
  1.   Work out the rule to get from one term to the next.
  2.   Apply the same rule to find further terms in the sequence.

- Patterns of shapes can be drawn to represent a number sequence.
  For example, this pattern represents the
  sequence 3, 5, 7, ...

1 What is the next number in each of these sequences?
(a) 2, 6, 10, 14, ...
(b) 1, 2, 4, 8, 16, ...
(c) 10, 6, 2, −2, ...

2 Here are the first four numbers of a number pattern.
7, 14, 21, 28, ..., ...
(a) Write down the next two numbers in the pattern.
(b) Describe, in words, the rule for finding the next number in the pattern. *Edexcel*

3 (a) Write down the next term in this sequence.
1, 4, 7, 10, 13, ...
(b) Will the number 41 be in the sequence?
Give a reason for your answer.
(c) What is the first number in the sequence which is greater than 100?

4 These sequences all begin with the numbers 3, 6.
Find the third number in each sequence.
(a) 3, 6, ..., 12, ...
(b) 3, 6, ..., 24, ...
(c) 3, 6, ..., 15, ...

5 Here are the rules for a sequence:
If the last number is odd, add 5.
If the last number is even, halve it.
A sequence begins with the number 9.
(a) Write down the next three terms in the sequence.
(b) Explain what will happen to the sequence if you continue.

6
> **Rule:** Add the previous two numbers to get the next one.

(a) Follow the rule given to find the next two numbers in this sequence.
1, 1, 2, 3, 5, ...
(b) Suggest a possible rule for the following sequence.
7, 8, 11, 16, 23, ... *Edexcel*

7 The diagram shows part of a pattern of shapes. The shapes are made from rectangles with a dot at each corner and a dot in the centre.

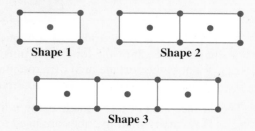

Shape 1   Shape 2

Shape 3

(a) Draw Shape 4.
(b) Copy and complete the table.

Shape number	1	2	3	4
Number of dots	5	8	11	...

(c) Shape 60 has 182 dots.
How many dots has Shape 61? *Edexcel*

8 A sequence of patterns is shown.

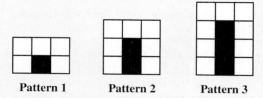

Pattern 1   Pattern 2   Pattern 3

(a) A pattern has 7 black squares.
How many white squares are in the pattern?
(b) How many white squares are used in Pattern 20?

9 Here are the first five terms of a sequence.
17, 14, 11, 8, 5.
(a) Write down the next two terms of the sequence.
(b) Explain how your worked out your answers. *Edexcel*

10 A sequence begins 4, 5, ...
The rule to continue this sequence is:

> Multiply the last number by 2 and then subtract 3.

(a) What is the next number in the sequence?
(b) The same rule is used for another sequence.
The sequence begins with −1.
What are the next two numbers in the sequence?

CHAPTER 16

Coordinates and Graphs

Coordinates

Coordinates are used to describe the position of a point.

Two lines are drawn at right angles to each other.
The horizontal line is called the **x axis**.
The vertical line is called the **y axis**.
The plural of axis is **axes**.
The two axes cross at the point called the **origin**.

On the diagram, the coordinates of point A are (3, 4).
To find point A: start at the origin and go right 3 squares
then up 4 squares.

Notation

A is the name, or label, of the point.

The first number is the **x coordinate**.
  If the number is **positive**, go to the **right**.
  If the number is **negative**, go to the **left**.

The second number is the **y coordinate**.
  If the number is **positive**, go **upwards**.
  If the number is **negative**, go **downwards**.
B is **plotted** at the point with coordinates (3, −4).
What are the coordinates of the points C and D?

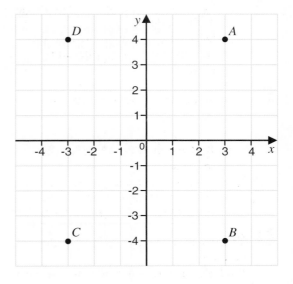

Exercise 16.1

1. Write down the coordinates of points
   A to L shown on this diagram.

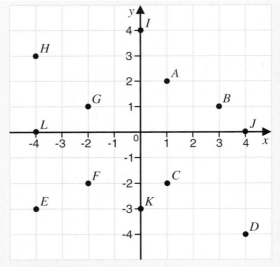

2. Draw x and y axes from −4 to 4, as in Question 1.
   Plot the following points on your diagram.
   A (2, 3)   B (2, −3)   C (−2, 3)   D (−2, −3)   E (3, 0)   F (0, 3)   G (−3, 0)   H (0, −3)

3. Draw x and y axes from 0 to 5.
   (a) Plot the points (2, 1), (5, 1) and (5, 4).
   (b) These are three corners of a square.
       What are the coordinates of the fourth corner of the square?

4 Draw x and y axes from -2 to 4.
  (a) Plot the points $A(3, 2)$, $B(3, -1)$ and $C(-1, -1)$.
  (b) Points A, B and C are three corners of a rectangle.
      Point D is the fourth corner of the rectangle.
      Plot point D on your diagram.
  (c) What are the coordinates of point D?

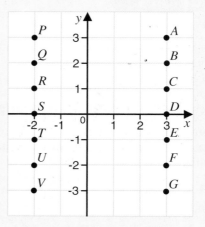

5 (a) What are the coordinates of points A to G?
  (b) What are the coordinates of points P to V?
  (c) What do you notice about the x and y coordinates of each set of points?

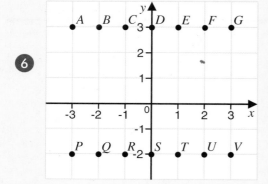

6 (a) What are the coordinates of points A to G?
  (b) What are the coordinates of points P to V?
  (c) What do you notice about the x and y coordinates of each set of points?

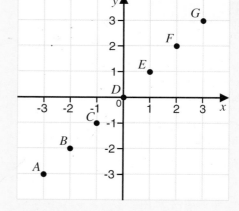

7 (a) What are the coordinates of points A to G?
  (b) What do you notice about the x and y coordinates of each point?

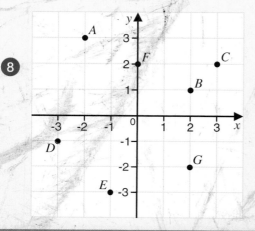

8 Give the letter of the point which matches each of these descriptions.
  (a) The first number of its coordinates is 3.
  (b) The second number of its coordinates is -2.
  (c) The x coordinate is 0.
  (d) The y coordinate is -3.
  (e) The x coordinate is three times the y coordinate.
  (f) The y coordinate is half of the x coordinate.
  (g) The y coordinate is the same number as the x coordinate, **but** has the opposite sign.

Graphs

Look at these coordinates (1, 3), (2, 5), (3, 7), (4, 9).
Can you see any number patterns?

The same coordinates can be shown in a **table**.

x	1	2	3	4
y	3	5	7	9

Notice that as:
  the x coordinate increases by 1,
  the y coordinate increases by 2.

A **rule** connects the x coordinate with the y coordinate.
This rule can be written, in **words**, as:
  "To find the y coordinate, multiply the
  x coordinate by 2 and add 1."
The same rule can also be written, using **symbols**, as an
equation, $y = 2x + 1$.
The coordinates are used to draw the graph of
$y = 2x + 1$, as shown.

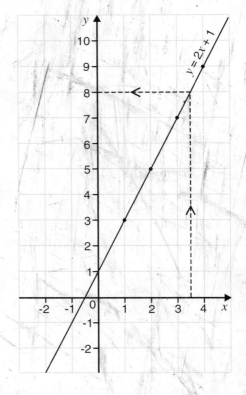

The diagram shows the coordinates plotted on a **graph**.
The points all lie on a **straight line**.
All points on the line obey the rule $y = 2x + 1$.

What is the value of y when $x = 3.5$?
Using the graph:
From 3.5 on the x axis, go up to meet the line $y = 2x + 1$.
Go left to meet the y axis at 8.
So, when $x = 3.5$, $y = 8$.

Using the equation:
Substitute $x = 3.5$ into the equation.
$y = 2x + 1$
$y = 2 \times 3.5 + 1 = 7 + 1 = 8$
So, when $x = 3.5$, $y = 8$.

Drawing graphs

This diagram shows the graphs:

  $x = 4$ $y = 3$
  $x = -2$ $y = -5$

Notice that:
The graph of $x = 4$ is a **vertical** line.
All points on the line have x coordinate 4.

The graph of $y = 3$ is a **horizontal** line.
All points on the line have y coordinate 3.

$x = 0$ is the y axis.
$y = 0$ is the x axis.

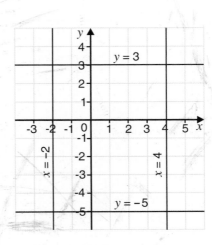

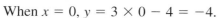

EXAMPLE

Draw the graph of the equation $y = 3x - 4$.

If values of x are not given in the question you must choose your own.

When $x = 0$, $y = 3 \times 0 - 4 = -4$.
This gives the point $(0, -4)$.

When $x = 1$, $y = 3 \times 1 - 4 = -1$.
This gives the point $(1, -1)$.

When $x = 3$, $y = 3 \times 3 - 4 = 5$.
This gives the point $(3, 5)$.

Plot the points $(0, -4)$, $(1, -1)$ and $(3, 5)$.

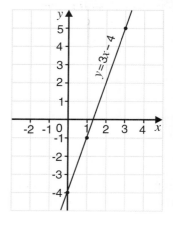

The straight line which passes through these points is the graph of the equation $y = 3x - 4$.

Exercise 16.2

1 Write down the equations of the labelled lines drawn on these diagrams.

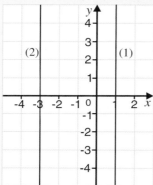 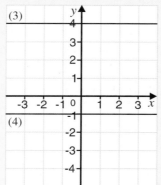 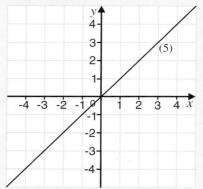

2 Copy this diagram.

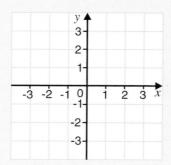

Draw and label the lines:
(a) $x = 3$, (b) $y = 2$, (c) $x = -2$, (d) $y = -1$.

3 Copy and complete a table like the one below for each of these equations.

x	1	2	3
y			

(a) $y = x + 2$ (b) $y = 2x$ (c) $y = 2x + 1$ (d) $y = 3 - x$

4 On separate copies of this diagram draw graphs for each of the equations in Question 3.

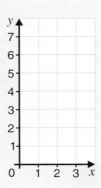

5 Draw tables of values and use them to draw graphs of:
  (a) $y = x - 1$
     Draw and label the x axis from -2 to 3 and the y axis from -4 to 3.
  (b) $y = 3x + 1$
     Draw and label the x axis from -1 to 3 and the y axis from -2 to 10.

6 (a) Draw these graphs **on the same diagram**:
     (i) $y = x + 2$ (ii) $y = x + 1$ (iii) $y = x$ (iv) $y = x - 1$
     Draw and label the x axis from 0 to 3 and the y axis from -1 to 5.
  (b) What do they all have in common?
     What is different?

7 (a) Draw these graphs **on the same diagram**:
     (i) $y = 2x + 2$ (ii) $y = 2x + 1$ (iii) $y = 2x$ (iv) $y = 2x - 1$
     Draw and label the x axis from 0 to 3 and the y axis from -1 to 8.
  (b) What do they all have in common?
     What is different?

8 (a) Draw these graphs **on the same diagram**:
     (i) $y = 3x + 3$ (ii) $y = 2x + 3$ (iii) $y = x + 3$
     Draw and label the x axis from -2 to 2 and the y axis from -3 to 9.
  (b) What do they all have in common?
     What is different?

9 Draw graphs of:
  (a) $y = x - 2$ (b) $y = 3x - 1$ (c) $y = 5 - x$ (d) $y = 6 - 2x$

10 (a) Copy and complete this table and use it to draw the straight line graph of $y = 4 - x$.

x	-2	-1	0	1	2
y		5			2

Draw and label the x axis from -3 to 3 and the y axis from -1 to 6.
  (b) Use your graph to find the value of:
     (i) y when $x = 1.5$,   (ii) y when $x = -0.5$.

11 (a) Draw the graph of $y = 2x + 1$ for values of x from -2 to 3.
  (b) Use your graph to find the value of:
     (i) y when $x = -1.5$,   (ii) x when $y = 2$.

12 (a) Draw the graph of $y = 2x - 1$ for values of x from -2 to 3.
  (b) Use your graph to find the value of x when $y = 0$.

13 (a) Draw the graphs of $y = 3x + 1$ and $y = x + 6$ on the same diagram.
  (b) Write down the coordinates of the point where the two lines cross.

(a) Copy and complete the tables for $y = x + 2$ and $y = 5 - x$.

x		1	2	3
$y = x + 2$				

x		1	2	3
$y = 5 - x$				

(b) Draw the graphs of $y = x + 2$ and $y = 5 - x$ on the same diagram.

(c) Write down the coordinates of the point where the two lines cross.

Further graphs

EXAMPLE

Draw the graph of the line given by the equation $x + 2y = 6$.

> By substituting $x = 0$ into the equation we can find the coordinates of the point where the line crosses the y axis.

$x + 2y = 6$
Substitute $x = 0$.
$0 + 2y = 6$
$\qquad 2y = 6$
$\qquad y = 3$

The line crosses the y axis at the point (0, 3).

> By substituting $y = 0$ into the equation we can find the coordinates of the point where the line crosses the x axis.

$x + 2y = 6$
Substitute $y = 0$.
$x + 2 \times 0 = 6$
$\qquad x = 6$

The line crosses the x axis at the point (6, 0).

To draw the graph of $x + 2y = 6$:
1. Plot the points (0, 3) and (6, 0).
2. Using a ruler, draw a straight line which passes through the two points.

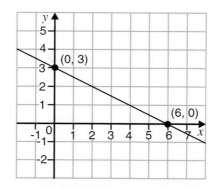

Exercise 16.3

1 A straight line has equation $x + y = 7$.
  (a) By substituting $x = 0$ find the coordinates of the point where the line crosses the y axis.
  (b) By substituting $y = 0$ find the coordinates of the point where the line crosses the x axis.
  (c) Draw the graph of the line $x + y = 7$.

2 (a) Draw these graphs on the same diagram.
      (i) $x + y = 2$ (ii) $x + y = 3$ (iii) $x + y = 5$
  (b) What do they all have in common?

3 A straight line has equation $3x + y = 6$.
  (a) By substituting $x = 0$ find the coordinates of the point where the line crosses the y axis.
  (b) By substituting $y = 0$ find the coordinates of the point where the line crosses the x axis.
  (c) Draw the graph of the line $3x + y = 6$.

4 Draw the graphs of lines with the following equations.
  (a) $x + 2y = 6$ (b) $2y = 4 - x$ (c) $2y = x + 4$

5 A straight line has equation $3y + 5x = 15$.
  (a) By substituting $x = 0$ find the coordinates of the point where the line crosses the y axis.
  (b) By substituting $y = 0$ find the coordinates of the point where the line crosses the x axis.
  (c) Draw the graph of the line $3y + 5x = 15$.

6 Draw the graphs of lines with the following equations, marking clearly the coordinates of the points where the lines cross the axes.
  (a) $5y + 4x = 20$ (b) $4x - y = 4$ (c) $3y + 2x = 12$

What you need to know

- **Coordinates** (involving positive and negative numbers) are used to describe the position of a point on a graph. For example, $A(-3, 2)$ is the point where the lines $x = -3$ and $y = 2$ cross.

- The x axis is the line $y = 0$.
  The y axis is the line $x = 0$.

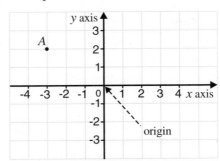

The x axis crosses the y axis at the origin.

- To find the x coordinate of the point where a line crosses the x axis, substitute $y = 0$ into the equation of the line.

  To find the y coordinate of the point where a line crosses the y axis, substitute $x = 0$ into the equation of the line.

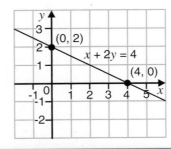

1 The diagram shows points P and Q.

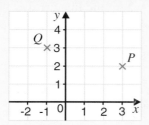

(a) What are the coordinates of P?
(b) What are the coordinates of Q?

2 The diagram shows a square $ABCD$.

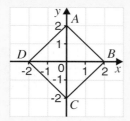

(a) What are the coordinates of A?
(b) What are the coordinates of D?

3 The diagram shows two sides of a rectangle $KLMN$.

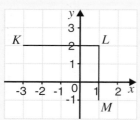

(a) What are the coordinates of M?
(b) Find the coordinates of N.

4 (a) On the same diagram draw and label the lines:
$x = 3$ and $y = 4$.
(b) Write down the coordinates of the point where the lines cross.

5 (a) Complete this table of values for $y = x - 3$.

x	-2	-1	0	1	2	3	4
y	-5	-4	-3	-2			

(b) Plot the points and draw the graph for $y = x - 3$.

Edexcel

6 (a) Copy and complete the table of values for the equation $y = x + 2$.

x	-2	0	2
y			

(b) Plot the points and draw the graph of $y = x + 2$.
(c) The points $P(a, 4)$ and $Q(-1, b)$ lie on the line $y = x + 2$.
Use your graph to find the values of a and b.

7 On a single diagram draw and label the lines:
$y = 3x$ and $y = 4 - x$.
Label the x and y axes from 0 to 6.

8 (a) Copy and complete this table of values for $y = 2x + 3$.

x	-3	-2	-1	0	1	2
y		-1				

(b) Draw the graph of $y = 2x + 3$.
(c) Use your graph to find
(i) the value of y when $x = 1.5$,
(ii) the value of x when $y = -0.5$.

Edexcel

9 (a) Copy and complete the table of values for the equation $y = 2x - 1$.

x	-2	-1	0	1	2	3
y						

(b) Draw the graph of $y = 2x - 1$.
(c) Use your graph to find:
(i) the value of y when $x = -1.4$,
(ii) the value of x when $y = 3.8$.

Edexcel

10 (a) On the same diagram draw and label the lines:
$y = 3$ and $x + y = 5$.
(b) Write down the coordinates of the point where the lines cross.

11 (a) Copy and complete the table of values for the equation $2y + x = 4$.

x	-2	0	2	
y				0

(b) Draw the graph of the line $2y + x = 4$.
Label the x axis from -2 to 4 and the y axis from 0 to 3.

CHAPTER 17

Using Graphs

Graphs are used in many real-life situations to represent information.

Conversion graphs

A **conversion graph** is used to change one quantity into an equivalent quantity.
For example, conversion graphs can be drawn and used to change:

> weight – between pounds and kilograms,
> temperature – between degrees Celsius and degrees Fahrenheit,
> currency – between pounds, £, and euros, €.

EXAMPLE

Use 16 euros = £10 to draw a conversion graph for pounds and euros.

Use your graph to find: (a) 20 euros in £, (b) £4 in euros.

> **Plotting points** and **drawing graphs** is covered in Chapter 16.

16 euros = £10   Plot the point (16, 10).

0 euros = £0   Plot the point (0, 0).

The straight line through the points (0, 0) and (16, 10) is the conversion graph for pounds into euros.

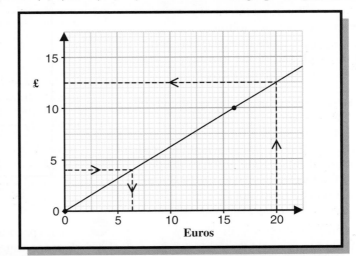

Reading from graph:
(a) 20 euros = £12.50.
(b) £4 = 6.4 euros.

Exercise 17.1

1 This conversion graph can be used to change measurements from inches into centimetres.

Use the graph to find:
(a) 10 centimetres in inches,
(b) 10 inches in centimetres,
(c) 16 inches in centimetres.

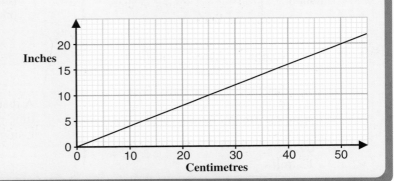

2 Use £10 = 16 dollars to draw a conversion graph for £ and dollars.
Use your graph to find:　(a)　£8 in dollars,　　　　(b)　10 dollars in £.

3 Use 5 miles = 8 kilometres to draw a conversion graph for miles and kilometres.
Use your graph to find:　(a)　3.5 miles in kilometres,　　(b)　5 kilometres in miles.

4 Use 10 kilograms = 22 pounds (lb) to draw a conversion graph for kilograms and pounds.
Use your graph to find:　(a)　4 kilograms in pounds,　　(b)　15 pounds in kilograms.

5 Use 32°F = 0°C and 212°F = 100°C to draw a conversion graph for degrees Fahrenheit and degrees Celsius.
Use your graph to find:　(a)　50°F in degrees Celsius,　　(b)　75°C in degrees Fahrenheit.

Distance-time graphs

Distance-time graphs are used to illustrate journeys.

Speed is given by the gradient, or slope, of the line.
The faster the speed the steeper the gradient.
Zero gradient (horizontal line) means zero speed (not moving).

> **Calculations** involving speed, distance and time are covered in Chapter 27.

EXAMPLES

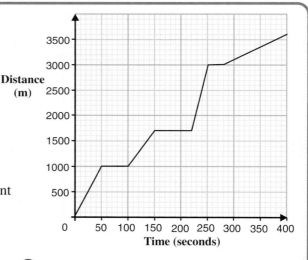

1 The graph shows a bus journey.
(a) How many times does the bus stop?
(b) On which part of the journey does the bus travel fastest?

(a) At zero speed the distance-time graph is horizontal.
So the bus stops 3 times.
(b) The bus travels fastest when the gradient of the distance-time graph is steepest.
So the bus travels fastest between the second and third stops.

2 The graph represents a train journey from Woking.

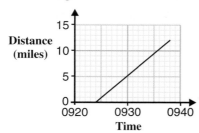

(a) At what time did the train leave Woking?
(b) How far did the train travel?

(a) 0924
(b) 12 miles

3 What speed is shown by this distance-time graph?
Give your answer in metres per second.

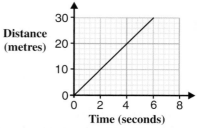

A distance of 30 metres is travelled in a time of 6 seconds.
Using Speed = Distance ÷ Time
　　　　Speed = 30 ÷ 6
　　　　　　　 = 5 metres per second

Exercise 17.2

1 The graph represents a bus journey from Poole.

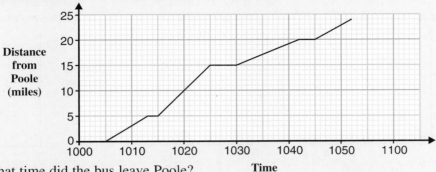

(a) At what time did the bus leave Poole?
(b) How far did the bus travel?
(c) How many times did the bus stop on the journey?

2 The graph represents the journey of a cyclist from Hambone to Boneham.

(a) What time did the cyclist leave Hambone?
(b) The cyclist arrived in Boneham at 1200.
    How far is Boneham from Hambone?
(c) The cyclist made one stop on his journey.
    (i) At what time did the cyclist stop?
    (ii) How far was the cyclist from
         Boneham when he stopped?

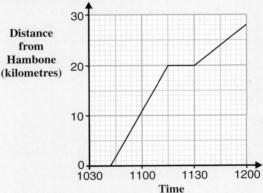

3 The distance-time graph shows the journey of a man from Durham to Leeds and back.

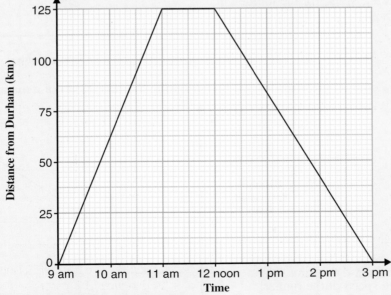

(a) How far is it from Durham to Leeds?
(b) How long did the man stop in Leeds?
(c) Did he travel at a faster speed going to Leeds or on the return journey?
    Explain your answer.

4 (a) The graph represents the journey of a car. What is the speed of the car in kilometres per hour?

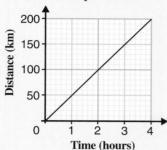

(b) The graph represents the journey of a train. What is the speed of the train in metres per second?

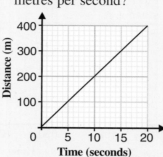

(c) The graph represents the speed of a cyclist. What is the speed of the cyclist in miles per hour?

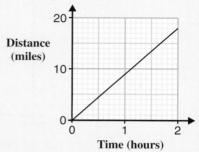

5 The distance-time graph shows the journey of a coach from Hove to Southampton.

(a) At what time did the coach leave Hove?
(b) How long did the coach take to travel from Hove to Southampton?
(c) What is the average speed of the coach in miles per hour?

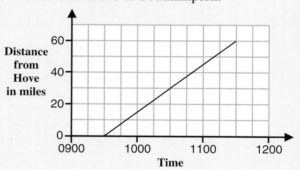

6 Pat cycles from home to the town centre. The graph represents her journey.

Pat takes $\frac{1}{2}$ hour to reach the town centre from her home.
What is her average speed for the journey in kilometres per hour?

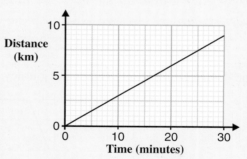

7 This graph shows the progress made by a runner during the first 20 km of a marathon race.

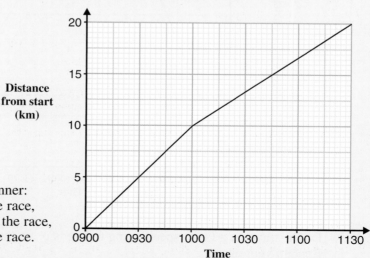

Find the average speed of the runner:
(a) during the first 10 km of the race,
(b) during the second 10 km of the race,
(c) during the first 20 km of the race.

8 A motorist has to travel to Swansea, a distance of 80 kilometres.
He sets off at 0930 and travels at an average speed of 50 km/h for one hour before stopping.
He stops for 30 minutes and then completes the rest of the journey at an average speed of 60 km/h.
    (a)   Draw a distance-time graph to represent his journey.
    (b)   At what time did he reach Swansea?

9 The graph represents the journey of a cyclist from Bournemouth to the New Forest.

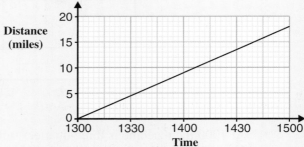

    (a)   What is the average speed of the cyclist in miles per hour?
    (b)   Another cyclist is travelling from the
New Forest to Bournemouth at an
average speed of 12 miles per hour.
At 1300 the cyclist is 15 miles from
Bournemouth.
        (i)   Draw a graph to show the journey
of the cyclist to Bournemouth.
        (ii) At what time does the cyclist
arrive in Bournemouth?

10 Selby is 20 miles from York.
    (a)   Kathryn leaves Selby at 1030 and drives to York.
She travels at an average speed of 20 miles per hour.
Draw a distance-time graph to represent her journey.
    (b)   At 1030 Matt leaves York and drives to Selby.
He travels at an average speed of 30 miles per hour.
        (i)   On the same diagram draw a distance-time graph to represent his journey.
        (ii) At what time does Matt arrive in Selby?

Graphs of other real-life situations

EXAMPLE   Craig drew a graph to show the amount of fuel in the family car as they travelled to their holiday destination. He also made some notes:

Part of Graph	Event
A	Leave home.
A to B	Motorway.
B to C	Car breaks down.
C to D	On our way again.
D to E	Stop for lunch.
E to F	Fill tank with fuel.
F to G	Country roads.
G	Arrive, at last!

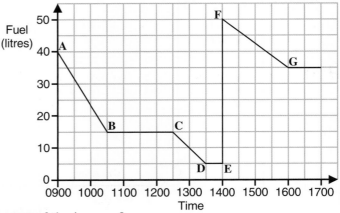

    (a)   How much fuel was in the tank at the start of the journey?
    (b)   At what time did the car break down?
    (c)   How long did the family stop for lunch?
    (d)   How much fuel was put into the tank at the garage?
    (e)   At what time did the journey end?

    (a) 40 litres   (b) 1030   (c) $\frac{1}{2}$ hour   (d) 45 litres   (e) 1600

Use the graph to work out how many litres of fuel were used for the journey.

1　Cans of drink can be bought from a vending machine in the school canteen.
　The graph shows the number of cans in the machine between 1000 and 1500 one day.

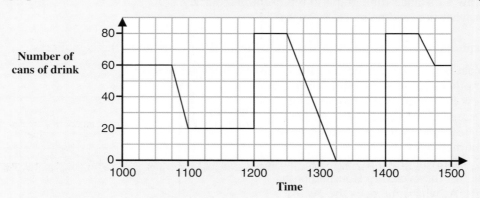

(a)　At 1000 the machine is three-quarters full.
　　How many cans does the machine hold when it is full?

(b)　How many drinks were sold between 1045 and 1100?

(c)　The machine was filled up twice during the day.
　　At what times was the machine filled up?

(d)　Between what times was the machine empty?

(e)　How many cans of drink were sold altogether between 1000 and 1500?

2　Graphs of the average heights and weights for men and women are shown.

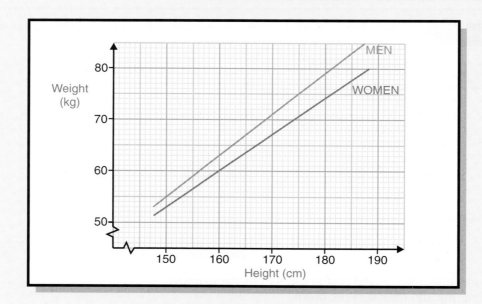

(a)　John and his wife are both 170 cm in height.
　　Use the graphs to estimate the difference in their weights.

(b)　Fred and Mary both weigh 75 kg.
　　Use the graphs to estimate the difference in their heights.

3 In an experiment, weights are added to a spring and the length of the spring is measured. The graph shows the results.

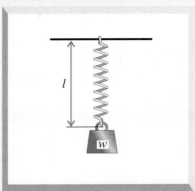

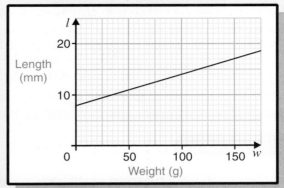

Use the graph to find
(a) the length of the spring when a weight of 100 g is added,
(b) the weight added when the length of the spring is 17 mm,
(c) the length of the spring when no weight is added.

4 The cost of removals includes a fixed amount and a charge per kilometre for the distance moved. The graph shows the cost, in £, for removals up to a distance of 50 kilometres.

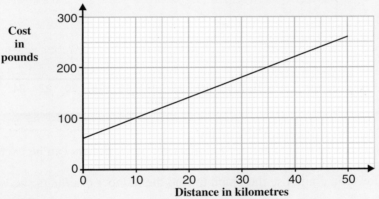

Use the graph to find
(a) the cost of removals for a distance of 20 kilometres,
(b) the distance moved when the cost of removals is £200,
(c) the fixed amount charged.

5 The diagram shows the distance from the starting position of a swimmer in a race in a swimming pool.

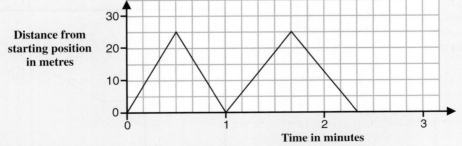

(a) What is the length of the swimming pool?
(b) What is the distance of the race?
(c) How long did the swimmer take to complete the race?

What you need to know

- A graph used to change from one quantity into an equivalent quantity, such as pounds into kilograms, is called a **conversion graph**.
- **Distance-time graphs** are used to illustrate journeys.
  On a distance-time graph: speed can be calculated from the gradient of a line,
  the faster the speed the steeper the gradient,
  zero gradient (horizontal line) means zero speed (not moving).
- Construct and interpret graphs arising from real-life situations.

Review Exercise

1 The diagram shows a conversion graph between pounds (£) and dollars.

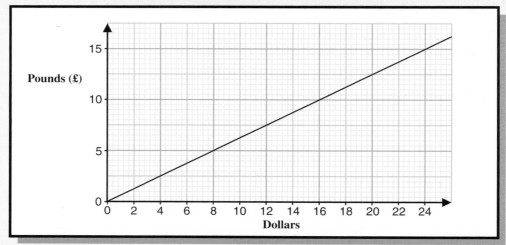

(a) Use the graph to write down how many
  (i) pounds can be exchanged for 8 dollars, (ii) dollars can be exchanged for £12.50.

(b) Kylie changes £300 into dollars.
  Explain how you could use the graph to find the number of dollars she would get.

Edexcel

2 Area of land can be measured in either acres or hectares.
  50 acres is 20 hectares. 300 acres is 120 hectares.

(a) By plotting these values, draw a conversion graph for acres and hectares.

(b) Use your graph to change 180 acres to hectares.

3 A plumber charges a fixed call-out charge and an hourly rate.
The graph shows the charges made for jobs up to 4 hours.

(a) What is the total charge for a
  job which takes 3 hours?

(b) How much is the fixed call-out charge?

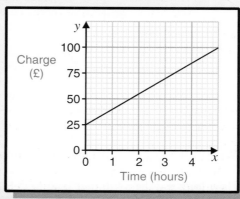

158

4 Mark drives 30 miles to his friend's house.
This travel graph shows Mark's journey.

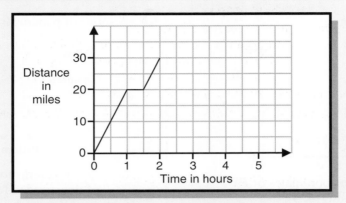

(a) How long does the journey take?
(b) Work out Mark's average speed for the journey from his home to his friend's house.

Mark stays with his friend for 1 hour. He then travels home at 30 miles per hour.
(c) Copy and complete the graph to show this information.   Edexcel

5 Elizabeth went for a cycle ride. The distance-time graph shows her ride.
She set off from home at 1200 and had a flat tyre at 1400.

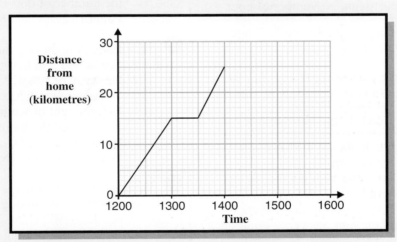

During her ride, she stopped for a rest.
(a) (i) At what time did she stop for a rest?
    (ii) At what speed did she travel after her rest?

It took Elizabeth 15 minutes to repair the flat tyre.
She then cycled home at 25 kilometres per hour.
(b) Copy and complete the distance-time graph to show this information.   Edexcel

6 A motorist has to travel 60 miles.
She sets off at 0900 and travels the first 30 miles at an average speed of 40 miles per hour before stopping.
She stops for 15 minutes and then completes her journey, to arrive at 1030.
(a) Draw a distance-time graph to represent her journey.
(b) What is her average speed for the whole journey?

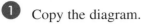

1 Copy the diagram.

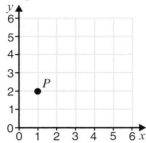

(a) What are the coordinates of P?
(b) Plot the point $Q(5, 4)$.

2 Fill in the missing numbers in these simple sequences.
(a) 8   11   14   17   …   23
(b) 3   …   13   18   …   28

Edexcel

3 Edwina does a part-time job.
Her pay is calculated using this rule.

> Pay = Hourly rate × Number of hours.

Calculate her pay when she works 7 hours at an hourly rate of £6.

4 (a) A number pattern starts   1,   5,   9,   …
The pattern is continued using this rule:

> Add 4 to the last number.

(i) Write down the next two numbers in the pattern.
(ii) What is the 10th number in the pattern?
(iii) Is 100 in this number pattern? Explain your answer.

(b) (i) Write down the next number in this pattern:
30,   26,   22,   18,   …
(ii) Write down a rule that can be used to find the next number.

5

Using the input-output diagram, copy and complete the following table.

Input	Output
7	…
…	24

6 A series of patterns is drawn using dots.

Pattern 1   **Pattern 2**

Pattern 3

(a) Draw patterns to show the number of dots needed for
(i) Pattern 4,   (ii) Pattern 5.

The table shows the number of dots needed for different patterns.

Pattern	1	2	3	4	5	6	7
Number of dots	5	8	11				

(b) Copy and complete the table.
(c) Explain how you would work out the number of dots needed for Pattern 12.

Edexcel

7 (a) Lucy thought of a number.
She added 5 to her number.
Her answer was 12.
What number did Lucy think of?
(b) Bob thought of a number.
He doubled the number.
His answer was 18.
What number did Bob think of?

8 Here is a number pattern.
Two numbers are missing.
6,   12,   18,   …,   …,   36.
(a) Write in the missing numbers.
(b) Describe, in words, the rule that you used to find the missing numbers in the pattern.

Edexcel

9 A sequence of numbers begins
1,   3,   9,   27,   ….
(a) Write in the next **two** numbers in this sequence.
(b) Explain how you found these numbers.

10 (a) On graph paper, plot the points $A(1, 3)$ and $B(-3, -1)$.
(b) M is the midpoint of AB.
What are the coordinates of M?

11 This formula is used to work out Sharon's pay.

> Pay = hours × rate of pay + £10.

Sharon works for 40 hours.
Her rate of pay is £5 per hour.
Work out her pay. *Edexcel*

12 A sequence begins 4, 5, 7, …
The rule for continuing the sequence is:

> Double the last number and subtract 3.

(a) What are the next **two** numbers in this sequence?
(b) Another sequence uses the same rule.
It begins 2, 1, …
What are the next **two** numbers in this sequence?

13 The instructions for cooking a chicken are:

> Cook for 15 minutes per pound,
> plus 15 minutes

Kellie has a 5 pound chicken.
(a) How many minutes will it take to cook?
Kellie wants the chicken to be ready for 2000 hours.
(b) At what time should she start cooking the chicken? *Edexcel*

14 This sequence of diagrams shows patterns of black tiles and white tiles.
(a) Sketch the next two diagrams in the sequence.

(b) Copy and complete the table to show the numbers of black tiles, white tiles and total number of tiles in each diagram.

Black tiles	1	2	3	4		
White tiles	0	1	2	3		
Total tiles						

(c) (i) Describe any patterns that you notice in the table.
(ii) Explain how you could use these patterns to predict the total number of tiles when there are 20 black tiles. *Edexcel*

15 Simplify (a) $g + g + g$,
(b) $3m + 4m + 5m$,
(c) $n \times n$.

16 (a) Pens cost x pence each.
Write an expression for the cost of 3 pens.
(b) A ruler costs 7 pence more than a pen.
Write an expression for the cost of a ruler.

17 Solve the equations.
(a) $y + 3 = 11$
(b) $4a = 32$

18 If $a = 5$, $b = 2$ and $c = 3$, work out the value of
(a) $a + b - c$,
(b) $3a - 2b + c$.

19 n represents any **even** number.
(a) What type of number is $n + 1$?
(b) What type of number is $2n$?
(c) What type of number is $\frac{1}{2}n$?

20 (a) I thought of a number, added 6, then multiplied by 10.
The result was 90.
What was the number I started with?
(b) I thought of a number, multiplied it by 3, then subtracted 8.
My result was 7.
What was the number? *Edexcel*

21 (a) Simplify (i) $3a + a$,
(ii) $3a - 4b + 2a + 3b$,
(iii) $3 \times a \times a$.
(b) Solve the equation $13 - x = 7$.
(c) $d = 3a - 1$.
Find the value of d when $a = 10$.

22 Apples cost t pence per kilogram.
(a) What is the cost of 5 kg of apples?
(b) Pears cost 10 pence per kilogram less than apples.
What is the cost of one kilogram of pears?
(c) Bananas cost twice as much per kilogram as apples.
What is the cost of one kilogram of bananas?

23 Here is a temperature conversion graph.

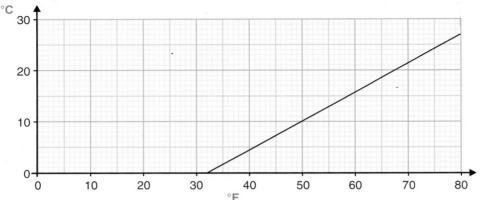

(a) Use the graph to change,   (i)   20°C to °F,   (ii)   12°C to °F.
(b) Use the graph to change,   (i)   60°F to °C,   (ii)   36°F to °C.
                                                                                Edexcel

24 Match the equations to the graphs.

A $x = 3$ **B** $y = 3$ **C** $y = x + 3$ **D** $y + x = 3$

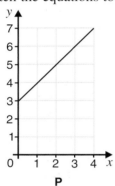
P

Q

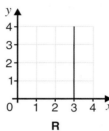
R

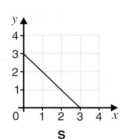
S

25 The graph shows the journey made by a cyclist from Guildford to Brighton.

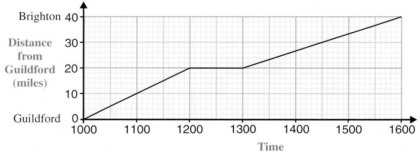

(a) (i)   How far is Brighton from Guildford?
     (ii)   Describe what happened between 1200 and 1300 hours.
     (iii)   Find the average speed of the cyclist between 1000 and 1200.
(b) The cyclist later cycled back to Guildford at an average speed of 16 miles per hour.
     How long did it take the cyclist to get back to Guildford?

26 The cost, C pounds, of a coat rack with h hooks can be worked out using the formula
$$C = 3h + 7.$$
(a) Work out the cost of a coat rack with four hooks.

Another coat rack costs £43.
(b) Use the same formula to work out the number of hooks this coat rack has.   Edexcel

27 (a) What is the value of $2xy$ when $x = 3$ and $y = 4$?
    (b) Work out the value of $ab + c$ when $a = 3$, $b = -2$ and $c = 5$.
    (c) What is the value of $3p - q$ when $p = -1$ and $q = 2$?

28 (a) Solve the equation $3x + 2 = 17$.
    (b) Use the formula $v = at$ to work out the value of v when $a = 3$ and $t = 8$.
    (c) Given that $4y - 3 = 15$, work out the value of $2y - 3$.   Edexcel

29 Solve (a) $8x + 4 = 20$,
         (b) $3x - 2 = 10$.

30 Solve. (a) $3x = 15$
          (b) $4y + 6 = 26$
          (c) $3(z - 4) = 30$ Edexcel

31 (a) Work out the value of $2p^2$ when $p = 3$.
    (b) Simplify $2(x - 3) + 5$.
    (c) Solve $3y - 7 = 5$.

32 The graph represents $y = 3x - 2$.

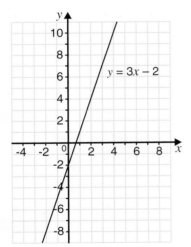

    (a) When $x = 2$, find the value of y.
    (b) When $y = -5$, find the value of x.
    (c) Explain whether or not the line $y = 3x - 2$ passes through the point $(10, 27)$.   Edexcel

33 (a) On the same diagram, draw and label the lines $y = x$ and $y = 6 - x$.
    (b) What are the coordinates of the point where the two lines cross?

34 $y = 5x + 2$.
    (a) Find the value of y when $x = -1$.
    (b) Find the value of x when $y = 17$.

35 Solve the equations
    (a) $2g = 9$,
    (b) $2g + 1 = 9$,
    (c) $2(g + 1) = 9$.

36 (a) Write, as simply as possible, an expression for the total length of these rods.

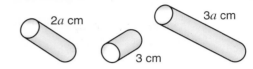

    (b) The total length of the rods is 23 cm. By forming an equation find the value of a.

37 (a) Buns cost x pence each. How much will 2 buns cost?
    (b) A doughnut costs 5 pence more than a bun. How much will 3 doughnuts cost?
    (c) The cost of buying 2 buns and 3 doughnuts is 95 pence. By forming an equation find the cost of a bun.

38 Solve the equations:
    (a) $2x = 10$
    (b) $6y + 1 = 25$
    (c) $8p - 3 = 3p + 13$ Edexcel

39 (a) Complete this table of values for $y = 3x - 1$.

x	-2	-1	0	1	2	3
y			-1			8

    (b) Draw the graph of $y = 3x - 1$.
    (c) Use your graph to find
       (i) the value of x when $y = 3.5$,
       (ii) the value of y when $x = -1.5$.
                    Edexcel

40 (a) Factorise
       (i) $4a + 2b$,
       (ii) $3t - t^2$.
    (b) Multiply out $x(x - 2)$.

Angles ● ● ● ● ● ● ● ● ● ● ● ● ● ● ● ● ● ●

The diagram shows a stopwatch with a second hand.
Every minute the second hand will make one complete turn.
An **angle** is a measure of turn.
Angles are measured in **degrees**.
In one minute the second hand will turn through an angle of 360°.

Types and names of angles

Each of these diagrams shows a quarter-turn.

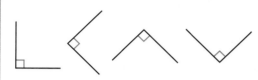

A quarter-turn is called a **right angle**.
A right angle is 90°.

An angle less than 90° is called an **acute** angle.
An angle between 90° and 180° is called an **obtuse** angle.
An angle greater than 180° is called a **reflex** angle.

Exercise 18.1

1 Through what angle will a second hand turn in:

  (a) half a minute,   (b) quarter of a minute,
  (c) three-quarters of a minute,   (d) 15 seconds,
  (e) 20 seconds,   (f) 1 second,
  (g) 7 seconds,   (h) 2 minutes,
  (i) $1\frac{1}{2}$ minutes,   (j) 135 seconds?

2 This clock shows 4.30.

  (a) What size is the acute angle between the hands of the clock?

  (b) What is the size of the reflex angle between the hands?

3 Through what angle will the hour hand of the clock turn between:
  (a) 10.00 am and 11.30 am,
  (b) 10.00 am and 10.00 pm?

4 Say whether each of the marked angles is acute, obtuse, reflex or a right angle.

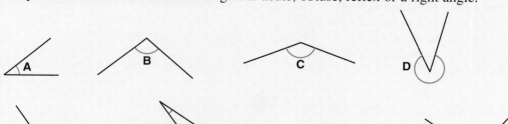

Measuring angles

To measure an angle accurately we need to use a **protractor**.

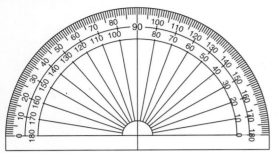

Some protractors have two scales.
Look at the type of angle (acute/obtuse) you are measuring and use the correct scale.

To measure an angle, the protractor is placed so that its centre point is on the corner (vertex) of the angle, with the base along one of the arms of the angle as shown.

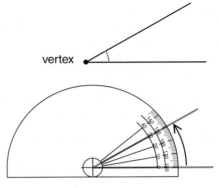

This angle measures 30°.

How can you measure the size of a reflex angle?

Drawing angles

Draw an angle of 74°.

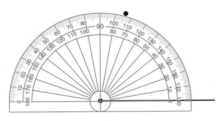

Draw a line.
Mark the vertex of the angle.

Position the protractor as if you were measuring an angle.
Mark a dot at 74°.

Draw a line from the vertex through the dot.

Exercise **18.2**

1 Use a protractor to measure these angles.

(a)

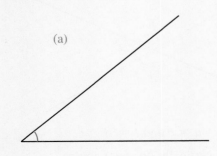

(b)

(c)

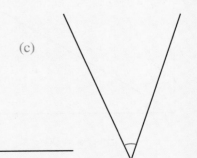

2 Use a protractor to measure these angles.

(a)

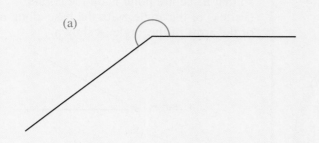

(b)

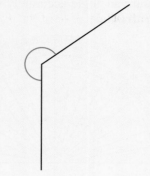

3 Draw these angles accurately.

(a) 20°   (b) 85°   (c) 128°   (d) 205°   (e) 324°

Angles at a point

When angles meet at a point, the sum of all the angles is 360°.

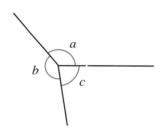

$$a + b + c = 360°$$

Complementary angles

When two angles add up to 90°, the angles are called **complementary**.

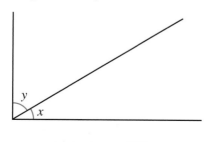

$$x + y = 90°$$

x and y are complementary angles.

Supplementary angles

Angles which can be placed together on a straight line add up to 180°.
When two angles add up to 180°, the angles are called **supplementary**.

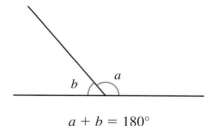

$$a + b = 180°$$

a and b are supplementary angles.

Vertically opposite angles

When two lines cross each other the angles between the lines make two pairs of equal angles.

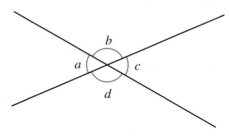

$$a = c \text{ and } b = d$$

a and c are vertically opposite angles.
b and d are vertically opposite angles.

166

EXAMPLES

① Work out the size of the angle marked *a*.

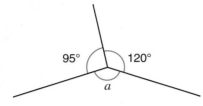

Angles at a point add up to 360°.

$a + 95° + 120° = 360°$

$\qquad a = 360° - 95° - 120°$

$\qquad a = 145°$

② Work out the size of the angles marked with letters.

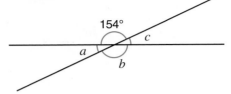

$b = 154°$ (vertically opposite angles)

$a + 154° = 180°$ (supplementary angles)

$\qquad a = 180° - 154°$

$\qquad a = 26°$

$c = 26°$

$a = 26°, b = 154°, c = 26°$

Exercise 18.3

The diagrams in this exercise have not been drawn accurately.
Do not use a calculator for questions 1 to 5.

① These angles are complementary.
Work out the size of angle *p* in each diagram.

(a)

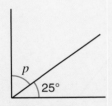

(b)

(c)

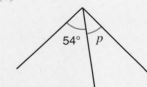

② These angles are supplementary.
Work out the size of angle *q* in each diagram.

(a)

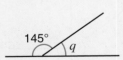

(b)

(c)

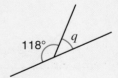

③ *PQ* and *RS* are straight lines.
Work out the size of angle *x* in each diagram.

(a)

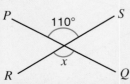

(b)

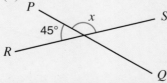

(c)

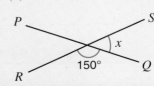

4 Work out the size of angle *y* in each diagram.

(a)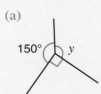

(b)

(c)

5 Work out the size of the angles marked with letters.
Give a reason for each answer.

(a)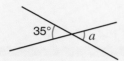

(b)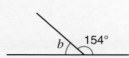

(c)

6 Work out the size of the angles marked with letters.

(a)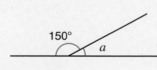

(b)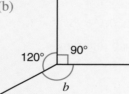

(c)

(d)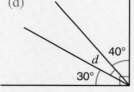

(e)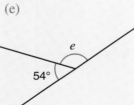

(f)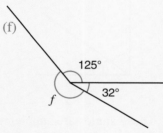

(g)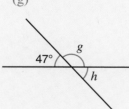

(h)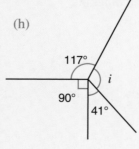

(i)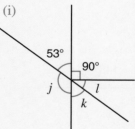

(j)

(k)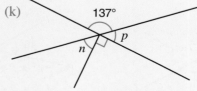

7 Work out the value of x in each diagram.

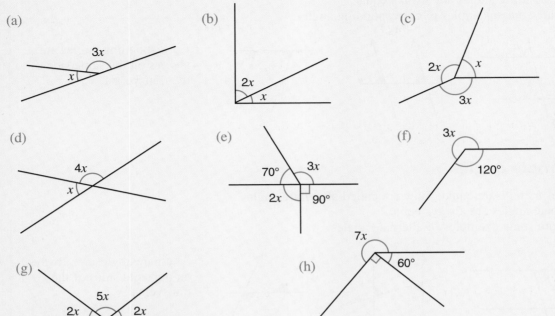

(a)

3x

x

(b)

2x

x

(c)

2x   x

3x

(d)

4x

x

(e)

70°   3x

2x   90°

(f)

3x

120°

(h)

7x

60°

(g)

5x

2x   2x

Parallel lines

Which of the following pairs of lines are parallel?

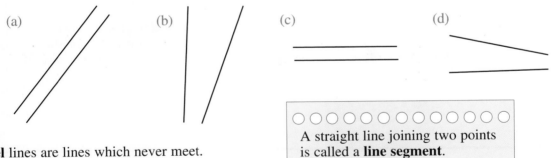

(a)

(b)

(c)

(d)

A straight line joining two points
is called a **line segment**.

Parallel lines are lines which never meet.
The pairs of lines in (a) and (c) are parallel.

The diagram, in the activity below, shows two parallel lines crossed by another straight line called a
transversal.

Activity

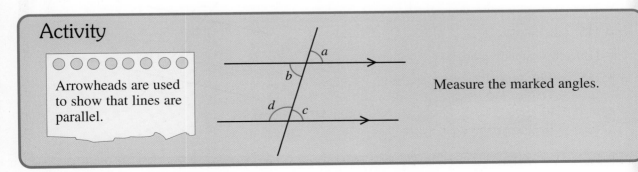

Arrowheads are used
to show that lines are
parallel.

a
b
d   c

Measure the marked angles.

Corresponding angles

Angles a and c are equal. They are called **corresponding** angles.
Corresponding angles are always equal.
Here are some examples of corresponding angles.

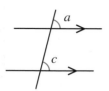 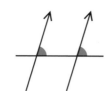 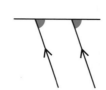

Corresponding angles are always on the same side of the transversal.

Alternate angles

Angles b and c are equal. They are called **alternate** angles.
Alternate angles are always equal.
Here are some examples of alternate angles.

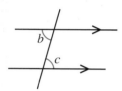 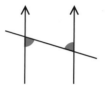

Alternate angles are always on opposite sides of the transversal.

Allied angles

Angles b and d add up to 180°. They are called **allied** angles.
Allied angles are supplementary, they always add up to 180°.
Here are some examples of allied angles.

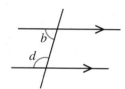

$b + d = 180°$

Allied angles are always between parallels on the same side of the transversal.

EXAMPLE

Work out the size of the angles marked with letters.

$a = 115°$ (vertically opposite angles)

$b = 115°$ (alternate angles)

$c = 115°$ (corresponding angles)

$d + 115° = 180°$ (supplementary angles)
$d = 180° - 115°$
$d = 65°$

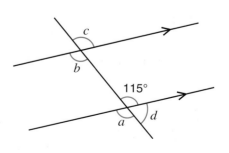

Exercise **18.4**

Do not use a calculator for this exercise.
The diagrams in this exercise are not drawn accurately.

1 Work out the size of the angles marked with letters.
Give a reason for each answer.

(a)
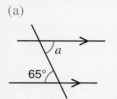

(b)
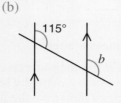

(c)
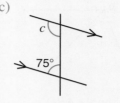

(d)
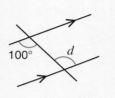

2 Work out the size of the angles marked with letters.

(a)
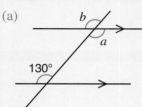

(b)
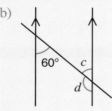

(c)
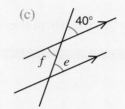

(d)
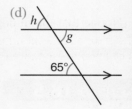

3 Work out the size of the angles marked with letters.

(a)
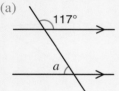

(b)
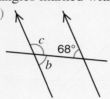

(c)

(d)
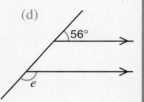

(e)
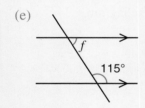

(f)
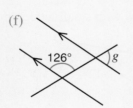

(g)
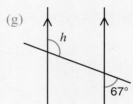

(h)
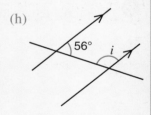

4 Work out the size of the angles marked with letters.

(a)
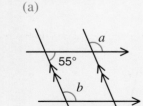

(b)
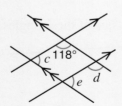

(c)
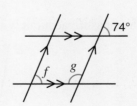

(d)
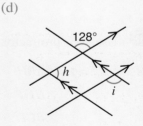

5 Work out the size of the angles marked with letters.

(a)
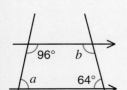

(b)
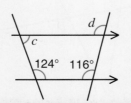

(c)
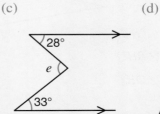

(d)
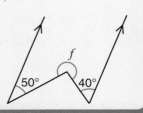

Naming angles

Up to now we have used small letters to name angles. This is not always convenient.
Another method is to use three capital letters.

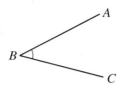

angle *ABC*
∠*ABC*

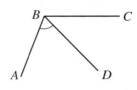

angle *ABD*
∠*ABD*

∠ means 'angle'.

∠*CBA* is the same as ∠*ABC*.
We usually write the letters either side of the
vertex (shown by the middle letter) in
alphabetical order.

Notice that the middle letter is where the angle is made.

Exercise 18.5

1 Use three letters to name the marked angles in each of these diagrams.

(a)

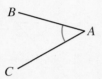

(b)

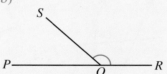

(c)

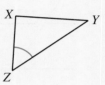

2 Use three letters to name the angles marked with small letters in this diagram.

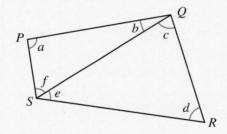

3 Use your protractor to measure accurately the size of these angles.

(a) ∠*ABH*

(b) ∠*HGF*

(c) ∠*BCD*

(d) ∠*AJE*

(e) ∠*GFJ*

(f) reflex ∠*GFJ*

(g) reflex ∠*BHG*

(h) reflex ∠*DEJ*

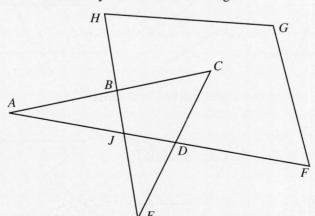

4 These diagrams have not been drawn accurately.
   (i)   Work out the size of the required angles.
   (ii) Give a reason for each of your answers.

(a) *PQ* is a straight line.
    Find ∠*QOR*.

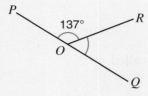

(b) *AB* and *CD* are straight lines.
    Find ∠*AOD*.

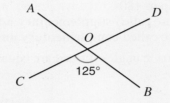

(c) *PQ* and *RT* are parallel.
    Find ∠*XOQ*.

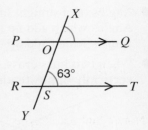

5 These diagrams are not drawn accurately. Work out the size of the required angles.

(a)

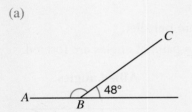

Find ∠*ABC*.

(b)

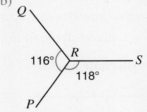

Find ∠*QRS*.

(c)

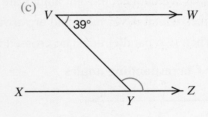

Find ∠*ZYV*.

(d)

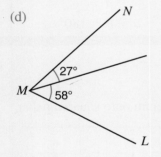

Find ∠*LMN*.

(e)

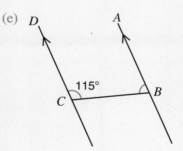

Find ∠*ABC*.

(f)

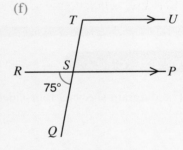

Find ∠*QSP* and ∠*STU*.

6 These diagrams are not drawn accurately. Work out the size of the required angles.

(a)

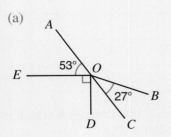

Find ∠*AOB* and ∠*COD*.

(b)

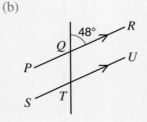

Find ∠*QTU* and ∠*QTS*.

(c)

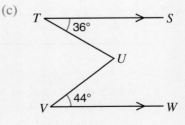

Find reflex angle *TUV*.

- An angle of 90° is called a **right angle**.
  An angle less than 90° is called an **acute angle**.
  An angle between 90° and 180° is called an **obtuse angle**.
  An angle greater than 180° is called a **reflex angle**.

- The sum of the angles at a point is 360°.

- Angles on a straight line add up to 180°.
  Angles which add up to 180° are called **supplementary angles**.
  Angles which add up to 90° are called **complementary angles**.

- When two lines cross, the opposite angles formed are equal and called
  vertically opposite angles.

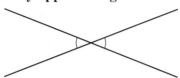

> Vertically opposite angles
> are sometimes called
> **opposite angles at a vertex**.

- Lines which meet at right angles are **perpendicular** to each other.

- Lines which never meet and are always the same distance apart are **parallel**.

- When two parallel lines are crossed by a transversal the following pairs of angles are formed.

Corresponding angles	**Alternate angles**	**Allied angles**
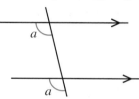	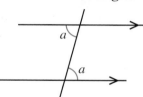	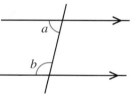
		$a + b = 180°$

Review Exercise

1 The diagram shows a four-sided shape.

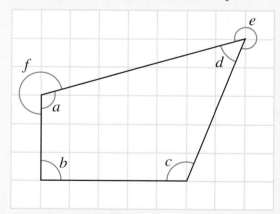

(a) Which of the marked angles are:
  (i) acute,   (ii) obtuse,
  (iii) right-angled,   (iv) reflex?
(b) Find by measurement the size of all the marked angles.

2 Copy the diagram onto squared paper.

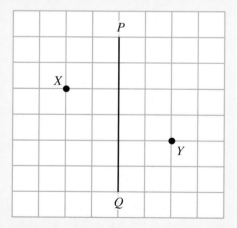

(a) Draw a line through X which is parallel to PQ.
(b) Draw a line through Y which is perpendicular to PQ.

3 (a) What is the size of angle *a*?
Give a reason for your answer.

123° *a*

(b) What is the size of angle *b*?
Give a reason for your answer.

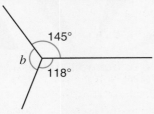

145°
b
118°

(c) What is the size of angle *x*?

x   5*x*

4 *AB* is parallel to *CD*.

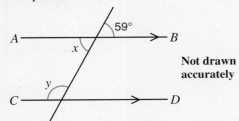

59°
A ————→ *B*
x

Not drawn accurately

y
C ————→ *D*

(a) (i) Write down the size of the angle marked *x*.
  (ii) Give a reason for your answer.
(b) (i) Work out the size of the angle marked *y*.
  (ii) Explain how you worked out your answer.   Edexcel

5 The diagram has two pairs of parallel lines.

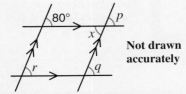

80°   *p*
x
Not drawn accurately
r   *q*

(a) Angles marked *p* and *q* are equal.
What geometrical name is given to this type of equal angles?
(b) Write down the size of angle *r*.
(c) (i) Write down the size of angle *x*.
  (ii) What geometrical name is given to the pair of angles *x* and *q*?   Edexcel

6

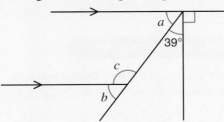

A   *B*
78° 78°
O
129°
D   *C*

(a) What is the size of angle *AOB*?
(b) Work out the size of angle *AOD*.

7 The diagram has one pair of parallel lines.

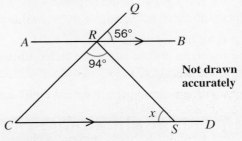

a
39°
c
b

Find the size of
(a) angle *a*,   (b) angle *b*,   (c) angle *c*.

8 In the diagram, the lines *AB* and *CD* are parallel.
CRQ is a straight line.

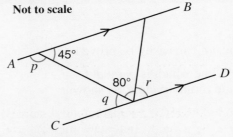

Q
A ———*R* 56°——— *B*
94°
Not drawn accurately
x
C ————————— *S* *D*

Angle *CRS* = 94°.
Angle *QRB* = 56°.
Angle *RSC* = *x*°.

Find the value of *x*.   Edexcel

9 In the diagram the line *AB* is parallel to the line *CD*.

Not to scale

B
45°
A *p*
80° *r*   *D*
q
C

(a) Work out the size of angle *p*.
(b) Work out the size of angle *q*.
(c) Work out the size of angle *r*.

CHAPTER 19

Triangles

A **triangle** is a shape made by three straight lines.

The smallest number of straight lines needed to make a shape is 3. Can you explain why?

Types of triangle

Measure the angles in each of these triangles.
What do you notice?

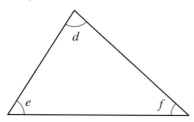 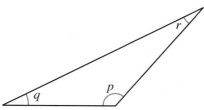 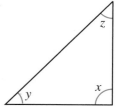

Angles *d*, *e* and *f* are all acute angles.
Triangles with three acute angles are called **acute-angled** triangles.

Angle *p* is an obtuse angle.
Triangles with an obtuse angle are called **obtuse-angled** triangles.

Angle *x* is a right angle.
Triangles with a right angle are called **right-angled** triangles.

The sum of the angles in a triangle

The sum of the three angles in a triangle is 180°.

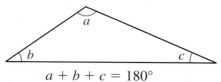

$$a + b + c = 180°$$

Add up the three angles d, e and f in the triangle above. Do the same for the other two triangles. You may not always get 180°. Can you explain why?

This result can easily be proved.

Draw a line which is parallel to one side of the triangle, as shown.

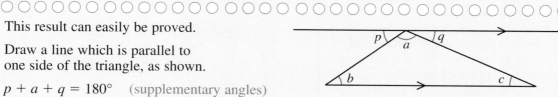

$p + a + q = 180°$ (supplementary angles)
$p = b$ (alternate angles)
$q = c$ (alternate angles)

Substitute $p = b$ and $q = c$ into $p + a + q = 180°$.
So $b + a + c = 180°$, which can be written as $a + b + c = 180°$.

> **Alternate angles** and **supplementary angles** were covered in Chapter 18.

EXAMPLE

Without measuring, work out the size of the angle marked *a*.

The sum of the angles in a triangle is 180°.
$$a + 102° + 37° = 180°$$
$$a + 139° = 180°$$
$$a = 180° - 139°$$
$$a = 41°$$

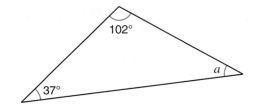

Exercise **19.1**

1 Is it possible to draw triangles with the following types of angles?
Give a reason for each of your answers.
(a) three acute angles,
(b) one obtuse angle and two acute angles,
(c) two obtuse angles and one acute angle,
(d) three obtuse angles,
(e) one right angle and two acute angles,
(f) two right angles and one acute angle.

2 Is it possible to draw a triangle with these angles?
If a triangle can be drawn, what type of triangle is it?
Give a reason for each of your answers.
(a) 95°, 78°, 7°   (b) 48°, 62°, 90°   (c) 48°, 62°, 70°
(d) 90°, 38°, 52°   (e) 130°, 35°, 15°   (f) 27°, 100°, 63°

3 Without measuring, work out the size of the third angle in each of these triangles.

(a)
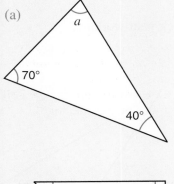

(b)
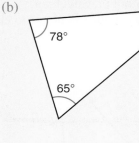

(c)
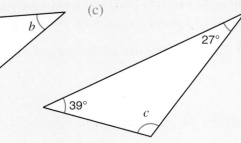

(d)
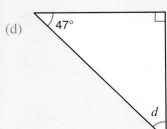

(e)
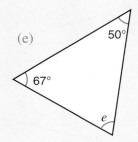

(f)
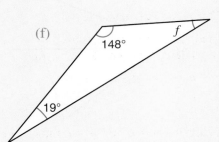

Exterior angle of a triangle

When one side of a triangle is extended, as shown, the angle formed is called an **exterior angle**.

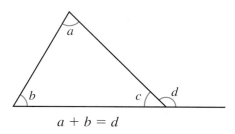

$a + b = d$

In any triangle the exterior angle is always equal to the sum of the two opposite interior angles.
Check this by measuring the angles a, b and d in the diagram.

This result can be easily proved.
$a + b + c = 180°$
(sum of angles in a triangle)
$c + d = 180°$
(supplementary angles)
$a + b + c = c + d$
$a + b = d$

EXAMPLE

Short but accurate
In geometry we often abbreviate words and use symbols to provide the reader with full details using the minimum amount of writing.

Δ is short for triangle.
ext. $\angle$ of a Δ means exterior angle of a triangle.
supp. $\angle$'s means supplementary angles.

Find the size of the angles marked a and b.

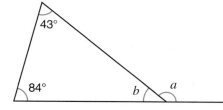

$a = 84° + 43°$ (ext. $\angle$ of a Δ)
$a = 127°$

$b + 127° = 180°$ (supp. $\angle$'s)
$\qquad b = 180° - 127°$
$\qquad b = 53°$

Exercise 19.2

The diagrams in this exercise have not been drawn accurately.
You should be able to do this exercise without a calculator.
Having completed the exercise you can use your calculator to check your working.

1 Work out the size of the marked angles.

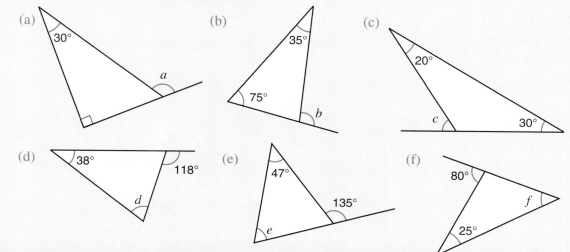

2 Work out the size of the marked angles.

(a)

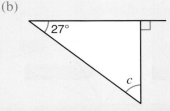

(b)

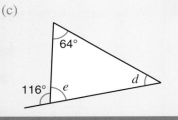

(c)

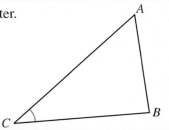

Naming parts of a triangle

Triangles are named by labelling each vertex (corner) with a capital letter.
Triangle *ABC* can be written as △*ABC*.

Triangle *ABC* is formed by the sides *AB*, *BC* and *AC*.
Triangles and lines are often named in alphabetical order.
△*ABC* is the same as △*BCA*.

The angle marked on the diagram is angle *ACB* or ∠*ACB*.
The middle letter is the vertex where the angle is made.

Special triangles

We have already seen that triangles can be described in terms of their angles but they can also be described in terms of their sides.
Measure the lengths of the sides of these triangles.
What do you notice?

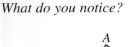

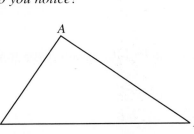

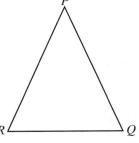

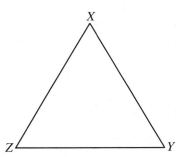

Triangle *ABC* has sides of different lengths. A triangle with sides of different lengths is called **scalene**.

Triangle *PQR* has two equal sides. *PQ* = *PR*. A triangle with two equal sides is called **isosceles**.

Triangle *XYZ* has three equal sides. *XY* = *YZ* = *XZ*. A triangle with three equal sides is called **equilateral**.

Now measure the size of the angles of triangles *PQR* and *XYZ*.
What do you find?

In triangle *PQR*, angle *PQR* = angle *PRQ*.
An **isosceles** triangle has two equal sides and two equal angles.

In triangle *XYZ*, all the angles are equal to 60°.
An **equilateral** triangle has three equal sides and three equal angles.

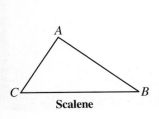

Scalene

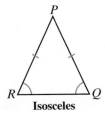

Isosceles

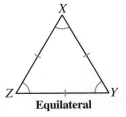

Equilateral

> **Notation used on sketch diagrams**
> A sketch is used when an accurate drawing is not required.
> Dashes across lines show sides that are equal in length.
> Equal angles are marked using arcs.

179

1 Name three different triangles in the diagram.

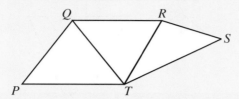

2 In the diagram, $AE = BE = BD = DE$ and CDE is a straight line.

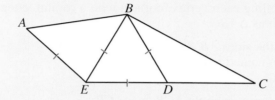

(a) What special name is given to $\triangle ABE$?

(b) What special name is given to $\triangle BDE$?

(c) Triangle BDC is scalene.
Give the three-letter name of another scalene triangle in the diagram.

3 (a) On squared paper, draw triangles with the following coordinates:
(i)   (1, 1),   (6, 1),   (3, 5),
(ii) (1, 1),   (5, 1),   (1, 4),
(iii) (1, 1),   (5, 1),   (3, 4),
(iv) (1, 1),   (6, 1),   (9, 5).

(b) Which of the following words could be used to describe each of the triangles you have drawn?

Acute-angled, Obtuse-angled or Right-angled.

Scalene, Equilateral or Isosceles.

4 On squared paper, draw an isosceles triangle with coordinates:
$A(3, 3)$, $B(9, 3)$ and $C(6, 10)$.
Which two sides are equal?
Which two angles are equal?

5 Triangle PQR is isosceles with angle $RPQ =$ angle QRP.
P is the point $(3, 5)$ and R is the point $(9, 5)$.
Give the coordinates of the two possible positions of Q so that angle PQR is a right angle.

6 These triangles have not been drawn accurately.
Work out the size of angle a in each triangle.

(a)   (b)   (c)   (d)

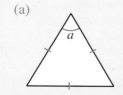   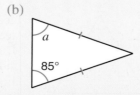   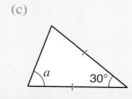   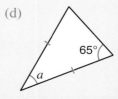

7 The following diagrams have not been drawn accurately.
Work out the size of the angles marked with letters.

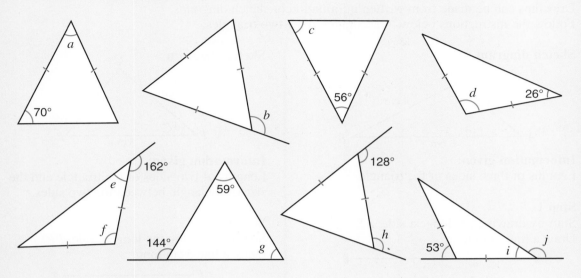

8 In the diagram $AD = DB = BC = CD$.
   (a) What type of triangle is BCD?
   (b) What is the size of angle BDC?
   (c) Work out the size of angle ABC.

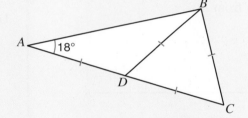

9 In the diagram $AB = BD = DA$ and $BC = CD$.
CD is extended to E.
   (a) What type of triangle is BCD?
   (b) What is the size of angle BDC?
   (c) Work out the size of angle ADE.

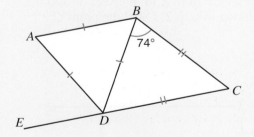

10 These diagrams have not been drawn accurately.
Work out the size of the required angles.

(a)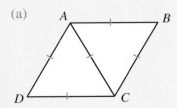

Find $\angle BCD$.

(b)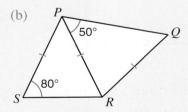

Find $\angle PRQ$ and $\angle QRS$.

(c)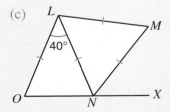

ONX is a straight line.
Find $\angle MNX$.

Drawing triangles

Your ruler, compasses and protractor can be used to draw triangles accurately.
Drawings can be made from written information or sketch diagrams.
Follow the instructions below to accurately draw two triangles.

Sketch diagram

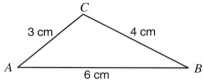

Information given:
Lengths of three sides of the triangle.

Step 1
Start by drawing the longest side, *AB*.
Draw a line 6 cm long.

Step 2
Set your compasses to a radius of 4 cm.
Draw an arc from *B*.

Step 3
Set your compasses to a radius of 3 cm.
Draw an arc from *A* to intersect (cross) the arc drawn in step 2. Label the point *C*.

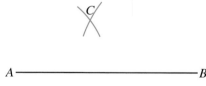

Step 4
Draw the sides *AC* and *BC*.
Add labels.

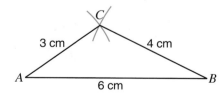

Sketch diagram

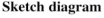
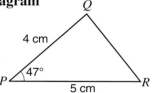

Information given:
Lengths of two sides of the triangle and the size of the angle between the two sides.

Step 1
Start by drawing the longest side, *PR*.
Draw a line 5 cm long.

Step 2
∠*QPR* = 47° (acute angle)
Use your protractor to measure 47°.

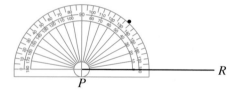

Step 3
Using the dot as a guide, draw a line, 4 cm long, from *P*. Label point *Q*.

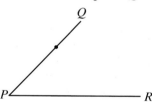

Step 4
Draw the line *QR* to complete the triangle.
Add labels.

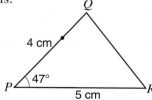

If you are given written information draw a sketch diagram first.

For example, information for triangle *ABC* could be given as:

Draw accurately triangle *ABC* with sides *AB* = 6 cm, *BC* = 4 cm and *AC* = 3 cm.

Activity

Write instructions which someone could follow to draw the following triangles accurately.

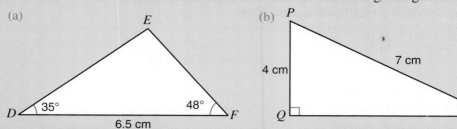

(a)

(b)

Exercise **19.4**

1 Use a ruler and compasses to draw accurately triangles with the following sides.
   (a) 4 cm, 5 cm, 6 cm.
   (b) 3.5 cm, 4.5 cm, 5 cm.
   (c) $AB = 4.8$ cm, $BC = 3.6$ cm, $AC = 6.2$ cm.
   (d) $PQ = 6$ cm, $QR = 6.5$ cm, $PR = 2.5$ cm.

2 Use a ruler and compasses to construct an equilateral triangle of side 5 cm.

3 Draw these triangles accurately using the information given.

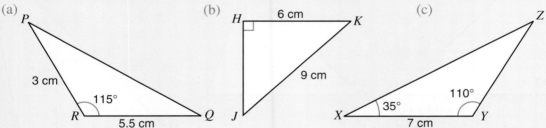

(a) (b) (c)

4 Use a ruler and protractor to draw the following triangles.
   (a) $AB = 4$ cm, $BC = 4$ cm, $\angle ABC = 40°$.
   (b) $PQ = 3.5$ cm, $PR = 5$ cm, $\angle QPR = 100°$.
   (c) $XY = YZ = ZX = 4$ cm.
   (d) $FG = 5$ cm, $FH = 5$ cm, $\angle FGH = 40°$.

5 A sketch of triangle PQR is shown.
   (a) Make an accurate drawing of triangle PQR.
   (b) Measure and write down the length of PR.
   (c) Measure and write down the size of angle QPR.

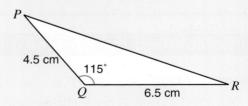

6 A sketch of triangle ABC is shown.
   (a) Make an accurate drawing of this triangle.
   (b) What is the length of CB?
   (c) What is the size of angle ABC?

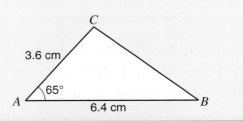

Perimeter of a triangle

The **perimeter** is the distance round the outside of a shape. The perimeter of a triangle is the sum of the lengths of its three sides.

Measure the sides of this triangle.
What is the perimeter?

You should find:
$AB = 4\,\text{cm}$, $BC = 5\,\text{cm}$ and $AC = 6\,\text{cm}$.
Perimeter $= 4 + 5 + 6 = 15\,\text{cm}$.

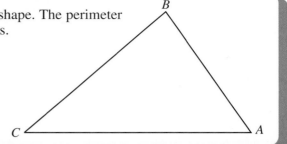

Finding the area of a triangle

Area is the amount of surface covered by a shape.
The standard unit for measuring area is the **square centimetre, cm²**.

Activity

Finding areas by counting squares
The diagram shows three triangles which have been drawn on centimetre-squared paper.

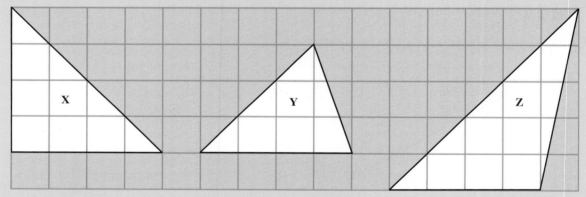

The area of each square on the grid is $1\,\text{cm}^2$.
Triangle X covers a total of 8 squares.
The area of triangle X is $8\,\text{cm}^2$.

1.   What is the area of triangle Y?
2.   What is the area of triangle Z?

> **Can you find a rule?**
> Does your rule work for all triangles?
> Try to explain why your rule works.

Is there a quicker way to find the areas of triangles without having to count squares?

Calculating the area of a triangle

The area of a triangle is given by:
$$\text{Area} = \frac{1}{2} \times \text{base} \times \text{perpendicular height}$$

> The area, A, can be found using the formula:
> $$A = \frac{1}{2} \times b \times h$$

Imagine a rectangle with a diagonal drawn. Area of a triangle can be remembered as:

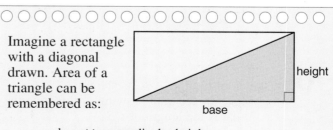

$$\text{Area} = \frac{\text{base} \times \text{perpendicular height}}{2}$$

In these triangles b is the base and h is the **perpendicular height**.

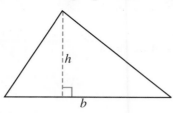

EXAMPLES

1 Calculate the area of this triangle.

$A = \frac{1}{2} \times b \times h$

$= \frac{1}{2} \times 12 \times 7 \, \text{cm}^2$

$= 42 \, \text{cm}^2$

7 cm

12 cm

2 This triangle has area $36 \, \text{cm}^2$.
Find the height of the triangle.

$A = \frac{1}{2} \times b \times h$

$36 = \frac{1}{2} \times 16 \times h$

$36 = 8h$

$h = \frac{36}{8}$

$h = 4.5 \, \text{cm}$

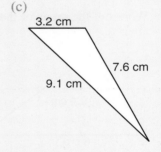

h

16 cm

Exercise 19.5   Do not use a calculator for questions 1 to 5.

1 Work out the lengths of the perimeters of these triangles.

(a)

6 cm

4 cm

3 cm

(b)

4.6 cm

3.5 cm

5.2 cm

(c)

3.2 cm

7.6 cm

9.1 cm

2 Which of the triangles PQR, QRS or RST has the largest perimeter?

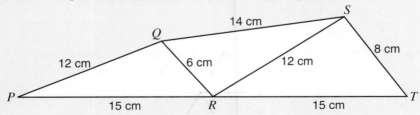

14 cm

S

Q

8 cm

12 cm

6 cm

12 cm

P

15 cm R 15 cm T

3 These triangles each have a perimeter of length 20 cm.
Work out the lengths of the marked sides.

(a)

a

5 cm

8 cm

(b)

6.8 cm

9.4 cm

b

(c)

7.8 cm

c

9.2 cm

4 These triangles have been drawn on 1 cm squared paper.
Find the area of each triangle.

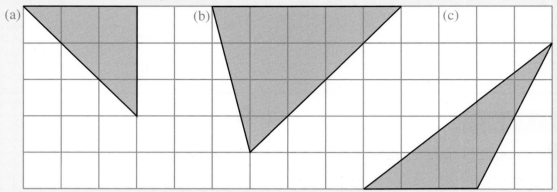

5 Calculate the areas of these triangles.

(a)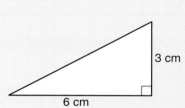

6 cm
3 cm

(b)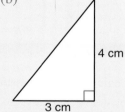

4 cm
3 cm

(c)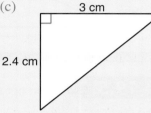

3 cm
2.4 cm

6 Work out the areas of these triangles.

(a)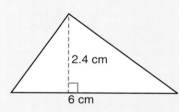

2.4 cm
6 cm

(b)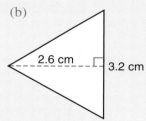

2.6 cm
3.2 cm

(c)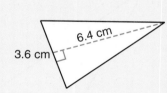

6.4 cm
3.6 cm

7 Find the areas of the shaded triangles.

(a)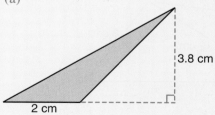

3.8 cm
2 cm

(b)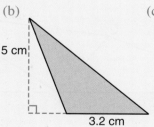

5 cm
3.2 cm

(c)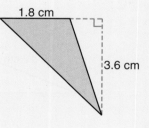

1.8 cm
3.6 cm

8 These triangles each have an area of 24 cm².
Calculate the height of each triangle.

(a)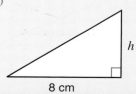

h
8 cm

(b)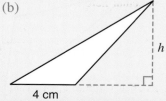

h
4 cm

(c)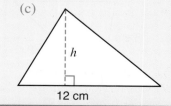

h
12 cm

9 These triangles each have an area of 32 cm². Calculate the lengths of the marked sides.

(a)

8 cm

a

(b)

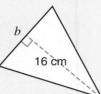

b

16 cm

(c)

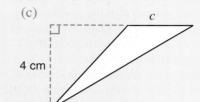

c

4 cm

10 This triangle has a perimeter of 45 cm. Calculate the area of the triangle.

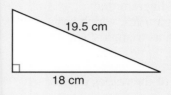

19.5 cm

18 cm

11 This triangle has an area of 150 cm². Calculate the perimeter of the triangle.

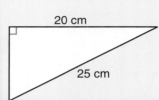

20 cm

25 cm

What you need to know

- Triangles can be: **acute-angled**, **obtuse-angled**, **right-angled**.

- The sum of the angles in a triangle is 180°.
  $$a + b + c = 180°$$

- The exterior angle of a triangle is equal to the sum of the two opposite interior angles.
  $$a + b = d$$

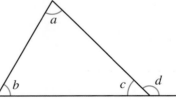

- Types of triangle:

Scalene triangle	**Isosceles triangle**	**Equilateral triangle**

| All sides have different lengths. | Two equal sides. Two equal angles. | Three equal sides. Three equal angles, 60°. |

- Perimeter of a triangle is the sum of its three sides.

- Area of a triangle = $\dfrac{\text{base} \times \text{perpendicular height}}{2}$

  $$A = \frac{1}{2} \times b \times h$$

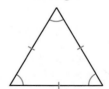

You should be able to:
- Draw triangles accurately using ruler, compasses, protractor.

1 (a) On one centimetre squared paper, plot the points
$P(2, 1)$, $Q(4, 5)$, $R(6, 1)$.
Join the points to form triangle PQR.

(b) (i) What special name is given to triangle PQR?
(ii) What is the area of the triangle?

(c) On the same diagram draw another triangle PRS, which has the same area as triangle PQR.

2 $AB = AC$.
Work out the size of the angles marked
(a) x, (b) y.

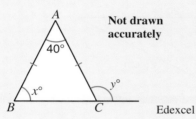

Not drawn accurately

Edexcel

3 In the diagram, triangle ABC is isosceles with $BA = AC$, and triangle ACD is right-angled with angle $CAD = 90°$.

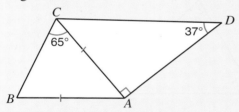

The diagram has not been drawn accurately.

(a) Angle $ADC = 37°$.
Work out the size of angle DCA.

(b) Angle $ACB = 65°$.
Work out the size of angle BAC.
Give a reason for your answer.

4 In the triangle ABC,
$BC = 8$ cm,
angle $CBA = 24°$,
$AB = 10$ cm.

(a) Use the information to draw triangle ABC.

(b) (i) Measure the size of angle BAC.
(ii) What mathematical name is given to angle BAC? Edexcel

5

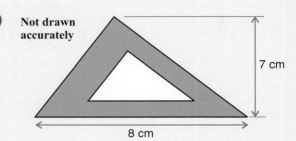

Not drawn accurately

In the diagram, the outer triangle has base 8 cm and height 7 cm.

(a) Calculate the area of the outer triangle.

The base and height of the inner triangle are each half those of the outer triangle.

(b) Calculate the area of the inner triangle.

(c) Hence, calculate the area of the shaded part. Edexcel

6 Calculate the area of triangle ABC.

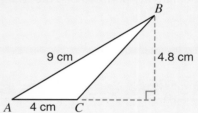

7 The diagram shows a sketch of triangle PQR.

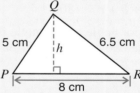

(a) Make an accurate drawing of the triangle.

(b) By measuring the height of your triangle calculate the area of triangle PQR.

8 The diagram shows three triangles, BAE, BED and BDC.

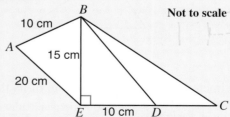

Not to scale

(a) Calculate the perimeter of triangle BAE.

(b) Calculate the area of triangle BED.

(c) The areas of triangles BED and BDC are equal.
Calculate the length of DC.

Symmetry and Congruence

Lines of symmetry

These shapes are **symmetrical**.

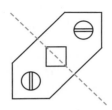

When each shape is folded along the dashed line one side will fit exactly over the other side.
The dashed line is called a **line of symmetry**.

Some shapes have more than one line of symmetry.

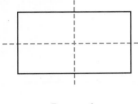
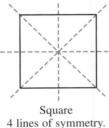

Rectangle
2 lines of symmetry.

Square
4 lines of symmetry.

Circle
Infinite number of
lines of symmetry.
Each diameter is a
line of symmetry.

Shape with no lines of
symmetry.

Rotational symmetry

Is this shape symmetrical?

The shape does not have line symmetry.

*Try placing a copy of the shape over the original
and rotating it about the centre of the circle.*

After 180° (a half-turn) the shape fits into its own outline.
The shape has **rotational symmetry**.
The point about which the shape is rotated is called the **centre of rotation**.
The **order of rotational symmetry** is 2. When rotating the shape through 360° it fits into its own outline
twice (once after a half-turn and again after a full-turn).
A shape is only described as having rotational symmetry if the order of rotational symmetry is 2 or more.

A shape can have both line symmetry and rotational symmetry.

EXAMPLES

Order of rotational symmetry 5.

Order of rotational symmetry 4.
4 lines of symmetry.

Order of rotational symmetry 1.
The shape is **not** described as
having rotational symmetry.

189

1 These shapes have **line symmetry**.
Copy each shape and draw the line of symmetry.

(a)  (b) (c) 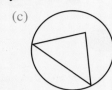 (d)

2 The following diagrams show half a shape.
The dashed line is the line of symmetry for the complete shape.
Copy the diagrams and complete each shape.

(a) 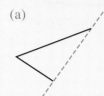 (b)  (c) 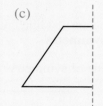 (d)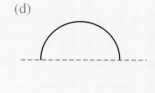

3 These shapes have been drawn accurately.
How many lines of symmetry has each shape?

(a)  (b) 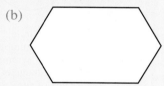 (c)

4 How many lines of symmetry has each of these letters?

A C E H K

5 What is the order of rotational symmetry for each of these shapes?

(a) 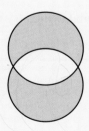 (b) 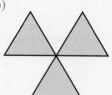 (c)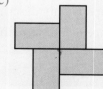

(d) 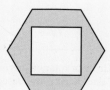 (e) 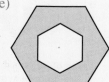 (f)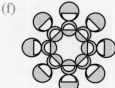

6 Look at these triangles.

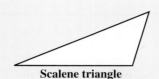 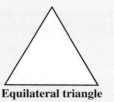

      Scalene triangle   **Isosceles triangle**   **Equilateral triangle**

What is the order of rotational symmetry of each triangle?

7 Look at these letters of the alphabet.

J M N O P X Y Z

(a)   Which two letters have only line symmetry?
(b)   Which two letters have only rotational symmetry?
(c)   Which letters have neither rotational nor line symmetry?

8 Make a copy of this shape.

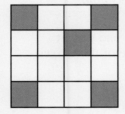

(a)   How many lines of symmetry does the shape have?
(b) (i)   Colour one square so that your shape has rotational symmetry of order 2.
     (ii) Mark the centre of rotational symmetry on your shape.

9 Make a copy of this shape.

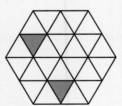

(a)   Colour one triangle so that your shape has rotational symmetry of order 3.
(b)   How many lines of symmetry does your shape have?

10 For each shape state
    (i)   the number of lines of symmetry,
    (ii) the order of rotational symmetry.

(a)   (b)   (c)   (d)   (e)

Symmetry in three-dimensions

Planes of symmetry

So far we have looked at two-dimensional (flat) shapes.
Two-dimensional shapes can have line symmetry.
Three-dimensional objects can have **plane symmetry**.
A **plane of symmetry** slices through an object so that one half is the mirror image of the other half.

A cuboid has three planes of symmetry as shown.

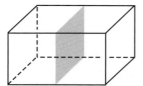 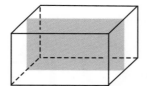 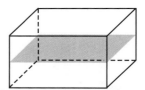

Axes of symmetry

A wall is built using cuboids.

In how many different ways can the next cuboid be placed in position?

If the cuboid can be placed in more than one way, it must have rotational symmetry about one or more **axes**.

A cuboid has three axes of symmetry.
The diagram shows one **axis of symmetry**.
The order of rotational symmetry about this axis is two.

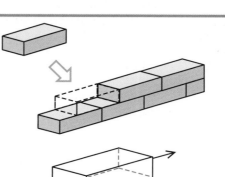

Exercise 20.2

① How many planes of symmetry has a cube?

② State the order of rotational symmetry about the axis shown in each of the following.
   (a) Cube   (b) Square-based   (c) Cylinder   (d) Cone
                          pyramid

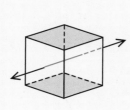  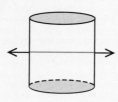

③ Each end of this cuboid is a square.
   The axes of symmetry are labelled *a*, *b* and *c*.
   What is the order of rotational symmetry about
   (a)   axis *a*,
   (b)   axis *b*,
   (c)   axis *c*?

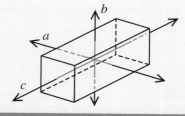

4 The diagram shows a cuboid, with a square base.
On top of the cuboid is a square-based pyramid with
vertex A above the centre of the top of the cuboid.

(a) How many planes of symmetry has the figure?
(b) How many axes of symmetry has the figure?
    Give the order of rotational symmetry about each axis.

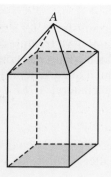

5

The diagram shows a triangular prism.
The ends of the prism are equilateral triangles.

(a) How many axes of symmetry has the prism?
(b) How many planes of symmetry has the prism?

Congruent shapes

When two shapes are the same shape and size they are said to be **congruent**.
A copy of one shape would fit exactly over the second shape.
Sometimes it is necessary to turn the copy over to get an exact fit.
These shapes are all congruent.

Exercise 20.3

1 Look at the shapes below. List five **pairs** of congruent shapes.

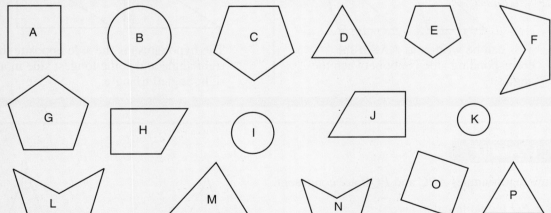

2 Which of these shapes are congruent to each other?

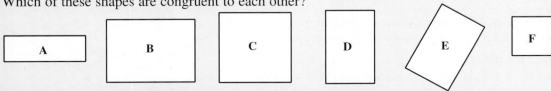

3 The diagram shows a rectangle that has been divided into five triangles.

(a) Which triangle is congruent to triangle *AFG*?

(b) Which quadrilateral is congruent to quadrilateral *ABEF*?

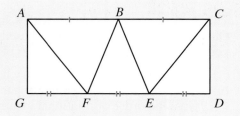

4 Triangle *ABC* has been divided into four smaller triangles as shown.

Name two pairs of congruent triangles.

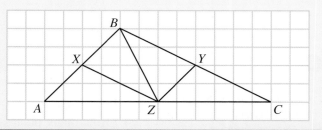

Congruent triangles

There are four ways to show that a pair of triangles are congruent.

1 Three sides.   SSS

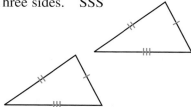

2 Two sides and the included angle.   SAS

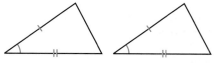

The included angle is the angle between the two sides.

3 Two angles and a corresponding side. ASA

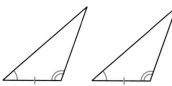

This can be written as AAS if the corresponding side is not between the angles.

4 Right angle, hypotenuse and one side. RHS

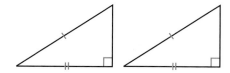

The hypotenuse is the side opposite the right angle and is the longest side in a right-angled triangle.

EXAMPLE

Show that triangles *ABC* and *PQR* are congruent.

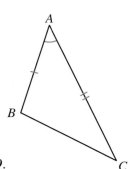
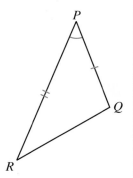

AB = *PQ* (equal lengths, given)
AC = *PR* (equal lengths, given)
∠*BAC* = ∠*QPR* (equal angles, given)

So triangles *ABC* and *PQR* are congruent.
Reason: SAS (Two sides and the included angle.)

Since the triangles are congruent we also know
that *BC* = *QR*, ∠*ABC* = ∠*PQR* and ∠*ACB* = ∠*PRQ*.

194

Exercise 20.4

The triangles in this exercise have not been drawn accurately.

1 Which two of these triangles are congruent to each other?
Give a reason for your answer.

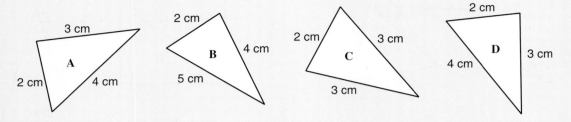

2 Which two of these triangles are congruent to each other?
Give a reason for your answer.

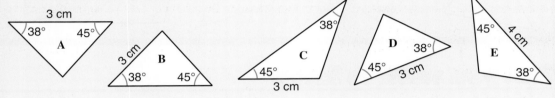

3 State whether each pair of triangles is congruent or not.
Where triangles are congruent give the reason.

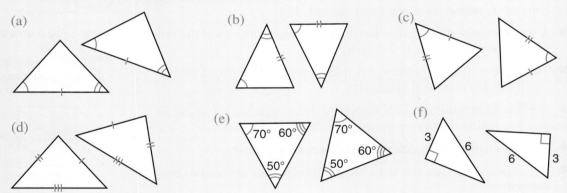

4 For each of the following, is it possible to draw a congruent triangle without taking any other measurements from the original triangle?
If a triangle can be drawn give the reason for congruence which applies.

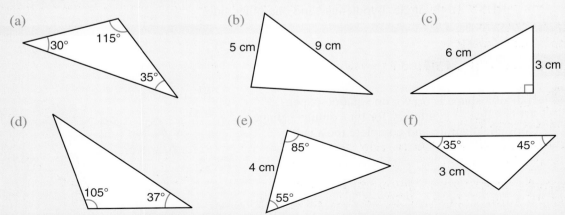

5 Look at the following triangles.
Equal sides and equal angles have been marked.
Using only the information given identify pairs of congruent triangles.
Give a reason for each of your answers.

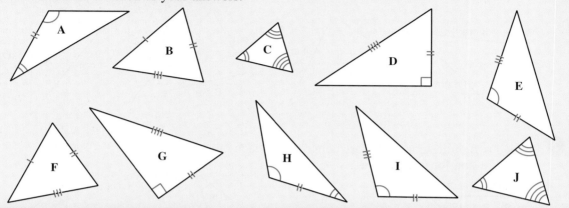

- A two-dimensional shape has **line symmetry** if the line divides the shape so that one side fits exactly over the other.

- A two-dimensional shape has **rotational symmetry** if it fits into a copy of its outline as it is rotated through 360°.

- A shape is only described as having rotational symmetry if the order of rotational symmetry is 2 or more.

- The number of times a shape fits into its outline in a single turn is the **order of rotational symmetry**.

- A **plane of symmetry** slices through a three-dimensional object so that one half is the mirror image of the other half.

- Three-dimensional objects can have **axes of symmetry**.

- When two shapes are the same shape and size they are said to be **congruent**.

- There are four ways to show that a pair of triangles are congruent:
    SSS   Three equal sides.
    SAS   Two sides and the included angle.
    ASA   Two angles and a corresponding side.
    RHS   Right angle, hypotenuse and one other side.

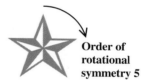
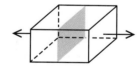

Order of rotational symmetry 5

Review Exercise

1 Half of a shape is drawn on squared paper.
AB is a line of symmetry for the complete shape.
Copy the diagram and complete the shape.

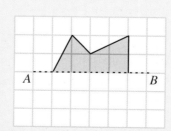

2 Which of these letters have
(a) line symmetry,
(b) rotational symmetry of order 2?

3 Copy these shapes onto squared paper.

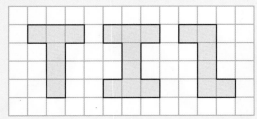

On each of your shapes, draw all of its lines of symmetry, if it has any.

Edexcel

4 Write down the order of rotational symmetry for each of these shapes.

(a)   (b)

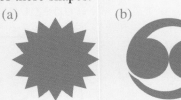

Edexcel

5 Look at these diagrams.

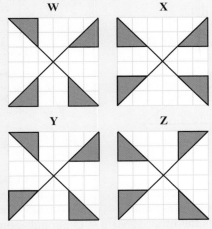

(a) Which diagram has rotational symmetry only?
(b) Which diagram has line symmetry only?
(c) Which diagram has line symmetry **and** rotational symmetry?

6 The diagram consists of three equilateral triangles.

Copy the diagram, and add another triangle so that the final diagram
(a) has rotational symmetry **and** line symmetry,
(b) has rotational symmetry **only**.

7 These shapes have both line symmetry and rotational symmetry.

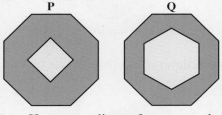

(a) How many lines of symmetry has shape **P**?
(b) What is the order of rotational symmetry of shape **Q**?

8 Copy these shapes and draw in one plane of symmetry for each.

(a)   (b)

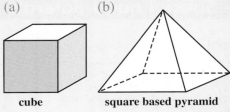

cube   **square based pyramid**

Edexcel

9 Write down the letters of the two pairs of shapes in this diagram that are congruent.

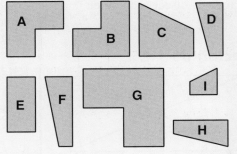

Edexcel

10 This diagram has been drawn accurately.

(a) Which triangle is congruent to triangle *ABC*?
(b) Which triangle is congruent to triangle *ACF*?
(c) Which quadrilateral is congruent to quadrilateral *ABCF*?

CHAPTER 21

Quadrilaterals

A **quadrilateral** is a shape made by four straight lines.

Special quadrilaterals

Parallelogram

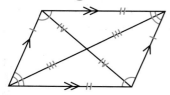

Opposite sides equal and parallel.
Opposite angles equal.
Diagonals bisect each other.

Rectangle

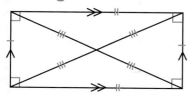

Opposite sides equal and parallel.
Angles of 90°.
Diagonals bisect each other.

Square

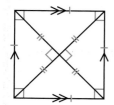

Four equal sides.
Opposite sides parallel.
Angles of 90°.
Diagonals bisect each other at 90°.

Rhombus

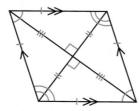

Four equal sides.
Opposite sides parallel.
Opposite angles equal.
Diagonals bisect each other at 90°.

Kite

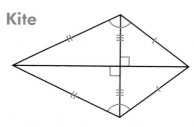

Two pairs of adjacent sides equal.
One pair of opposite angles equal.
One diagonal bisects the other at 90°.

Trapezium

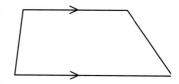

One pair of parallel sides.

Isosceles trapezium

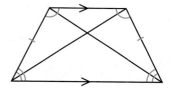

One pair of parallel sides.
Non-parallel sides equal.
Two pairs of equal angles.
Diagonals equal.

Remember:
Sides of equal length are marked with the same number of **dashes**.
Lines which are parallel are marked with the same number of **arrowheads**.
Angles of equal size are marked with the same number of **arcs**.

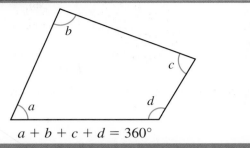

The sum of the four angles of a quadrilateral is 360°.

Measure the angles of this quadrilateral.
Do the angles add up to 360°?

You may not always get 360°.
Can you explain why?

$$a + b + c + d = 360°$$

This result can easily be proved.

Split the quadrilateral into two triangles A and B, as shown.

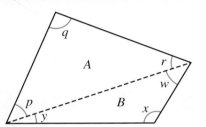

In triangle A:
$$p + q + r = 180° \qquad \text{(sum of angles in a triangle)}$$
In triangle B:
$$w + x + y = 180° \qquad \text{(sum of angles in a triangle)}$$

The sum of the angles of the quadrilateral is given by:
$$p + q + r + w + x + y$$
$$= 180° + 180°$$
$$= 360°$$

The sum of the angles in a triangle is 180°.
This was covered in Chapter 19.

EXAMPLE

PQRS is a parallelogram. Work out the size of the angle marked x.

The opposite angles of a parallelogram are equal.

$$55° + 55° + x + x = 360°$$
$$110° + 2x = 360°$$
$$2x = 360° - 110°$$
$$2x = 250°$$
$$x = 125°$$

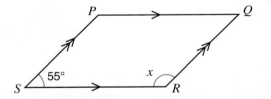

Exercise 21.1

Use squared paper to answer questions 1 to 8.
You should be able to do this exercise without using your calculator.
Having completed the exercise you can use a calculator to check your working.

1 (a) Draw quadrilaterals with the following
coordinates.
    (i) $A(3, 1)$, $B(1, 3)$, $C(2, 6)$, $D(6, 2)$
    (ii) $E(1, 0)$, $F(6, 2)$, $G(8, 9)$, $H(3, 7)$
    (iii) $J(3, 0)$, $K(0, 4)$, $L(3, 8)$, $M(6, 4)$
    (iv) $P(1, 1)$, $Q(2, 4)$, $R(4, 4)$, $S(4, 2)$
    (v) $W(3, 1)$, $X(1, 3)$, $Y(3, 5)$, $Z(5, 3)$
(b) What special name is given to each of
these quadrilaterals?

2 *JKLM* is a square.
J is the point $(1, 1)$, $K(4, 1)$, $L(4, 4)$.
Find the coordinates of M.

3 *PQRS* is a rectangle.
P is the point $(1, 3)$, $Q(4, 6)$, $R(6, 4)$.
Find the coordinates of S.

4 *ABCD* is a rhombus.
A is the point $(3, 0)$, $B(0, 4)$ and $D(8, 0)$.
Find the coordinates of C.

5 *WXYZ* is a parallelogram.
W is the point $(1, 0)$, $X(4, 1)$, $Z(3, 3)$.
Find the coordinates of Y.

6 *OABC* is a kite. *O* is the point (0, 0), *B* (5, 5), *C* (3, 1).
Find the coordinates of *A*.

7 *STUV* is a square with *S* at (1, 3) and *U* at (5, 3).
Find the coordinates of *T* and *V*.

8 Work out the size of angle *a* in each of these quadrilaterals.

(a)

(b)
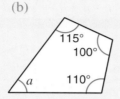

(c)
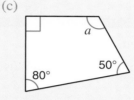

(d)
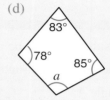

9 Work out the size of the angles marked with letters in each of these rectangles.

(a)
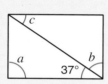

(b)
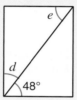

(c)

(d)
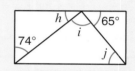

10 Work out the size of the angles marked with letters in each of these parallelograms.

(a)
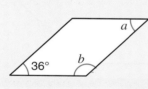

(b)
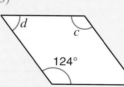

(c)
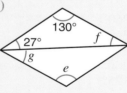

(d)

11 Work out the size of the angles marked with letters in each of these kites.

(a)
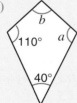

(b)
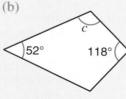

(c)
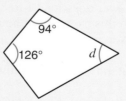

(d)
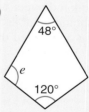

12 The diagram shows a trapezium.
Find the size of angle *a* and angle *b*.

13 *WXYZ* is an isosceles trapezium.
Work out the size of angle *WXY* and angle *XYZ*.

14 The following diagrams have not been drawn accurately.
Work out the size of the angles marked with letters.

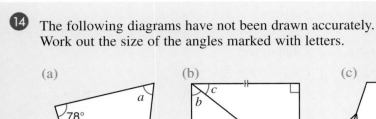

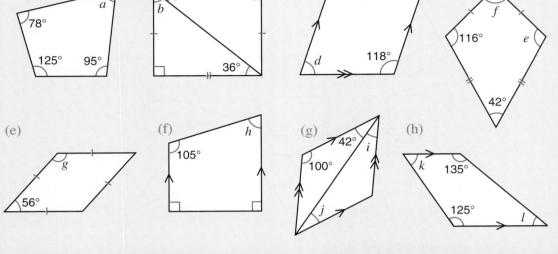

(a)

(b)

(c)

(d)

(e)

(f)

(g)

(h)

Symmetry of quadrilaterals

Remember:
A two-dimensional shape has line symmetry if the line divides the shape so that one side fits exactly over the other.
A two-dimensional shape has rotational symmetry if it fits into a copy of its own outline as it is rotated through 360°.

Parallelogram

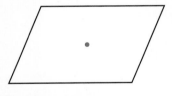

0 lines of symmetry.
Order of rotational symmetry 2.

Isosceles trapezium

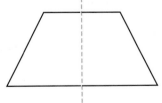

1 line of symmetry.

Rectangle

2 lines of symmetry.
Order of rotational symmetry 2.

Square

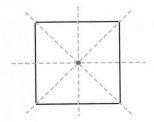

4 lines of symmetry.
Order of rotational symmetry 4.

Rhombus

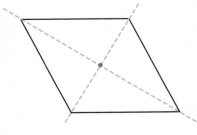

2 lines of symmetry.
Order of rotational symmetry 2.

Kite

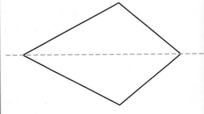

1 line of symmetry.

1 These quadrilaterals have been drawn on squared paper.

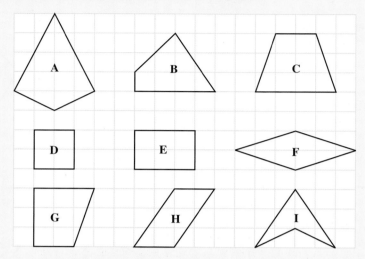

Copy and complete the table for each shape.

Shape	A	B	C	D	E	F	G	H	I
Number of lines of symmetry									
Order of rotational symmetry									

2 How many lines of symmetry has each of these quadrilaterals?

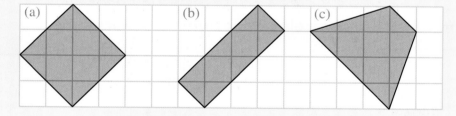

3 What is the order of rotational symmetry for each of these quadrilaterals?

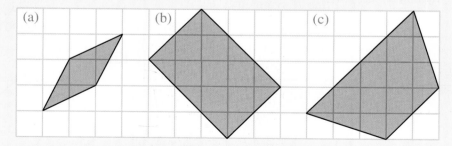

4 (a) Draw a rhombus of side 4 cm, with angles of 80° and 100°.
(b) Mark on your diagram any lines of symmetry.
(c) What order of rotational symmetry has the rhombus?

Perimeters of rectangles and squares

The **perimeter** is the distance round the outside of a shape.
The perimeter of a rectangle (or square) is the sum of the lengths of its four sides.

Measure the sides of this rectangle.
What is the perimeter of the rectangle?

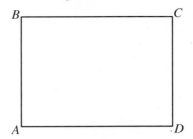

You should find:
$AB = 3\,cm, \quad BC = 4\,cm,$
$CD = 3\,cm, \quad DA = 4\,cm.$
Perimeter $= 3 + 4 + 3 + 4$
$\qquad\qquad = 14\,cm$

Area

Area is the amount of surface covered by a shape.
The standard unit for measuring area is the square centimetre, cm^2.
Small areas are measured using square millimetres, mm^2.
Large areas are measured using square metres, m^2, or square kilometres, km^2.

Activity

Finding areas by counting squares
The diagram shows two rectangles which have been drawn on centimetre-squared paper.

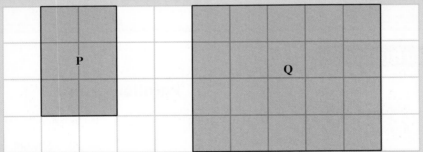

Rectangle **P** covers 6 squares.
The area of each square is $1\,cm^2$.
The area of rectangle **P** is $6\,cm^2$.

What is the area of rectangle **Q**?

This square has been drawn on
centimetre-squared paper.

What is the area of the square?

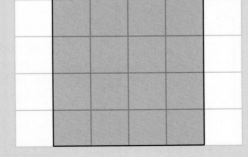

Can you find a rule to find the areas of rectangles and squares without having to count squares?

Quadrilaterals . . . Quadrilaterals . . . Quadrilaterals . . .

Activity

Look at the following diagram.
It shows a rectangle and a parallelogram drawn on centimetre-squared paper.

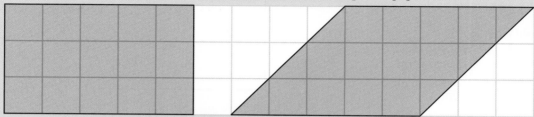

Find the area of the rectangle by counting squares.
Find the area of the parallelogram by counting squares.
What do you notice?

Can you find a rule to find the area of a parallelogram without having to count squares?
Use your rule to find the areas of these parallelograms.

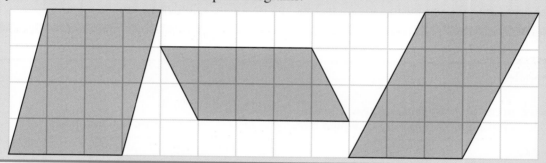

Area formulae

Rectangle

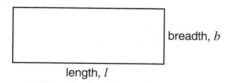

Area = length × breadth
$A = lb$

Square

Area = length × breadth
In a square length = breadth
Area = (length)²
$A = l^2$

Parallelogram

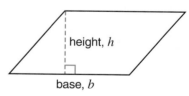

Area = base × height
$A = bh$

Base and perpendicular height
The **base** is the side of the shape from which the height is measured.
The base does not have to be at the bottom of the shape.
The height of a shape, measured at right angles to the base, is called the **perpendicular height**.

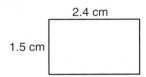

EXAMPLES

1 Find the perimeter and area of this rectangle.

2.4 cm

1.5 cm

Perimeter = 1.5 + 2.4 + 1.5 + 2.4
= 7.8 cm

Area = length × breadth
= 2.4 × 1.5
= 3.6 cm²

2 The area of a rectangular room is 17.5 m². The room is 5 m long. Find the width of the room.

Area = 17.5 m² b

5 m

$A = lb$

$17.5 = 5 \times b$

$b = \dfrac{17.5}{5}$

$b = 3.5$ m

Exercise **21.3**

You should be able to do questions 1 to 4 without using a calculator.

1 These rectangles have been drawn on 1 cm squared paper.
Find   (i)   the perimeter and   (ii)   the area of each rectangle.

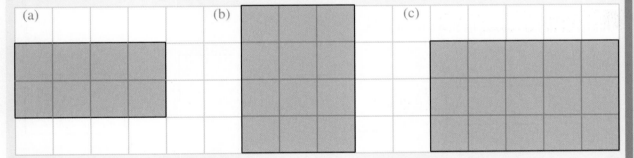

(a)

(b)

(c)

2 These squares have been drawn on 1 cm squared paper.
Find   (i)   the perimeter and   (ii)   the area of each square.

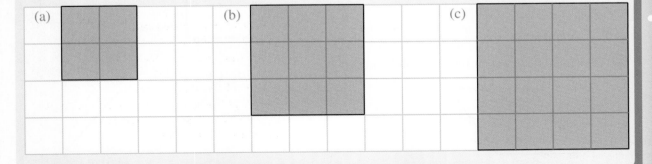

(a)

(b)

(c)

3 Four rectangles are shown.

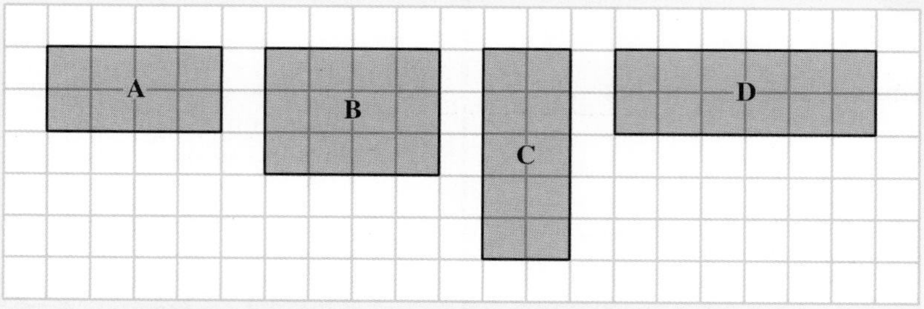

(a) Which of these rectangles have the same perimeter?
(b) Which of these rectangles have the same area?

4 These shapes have been drawn on 1 cm squared paper.
Find the area of each shape.

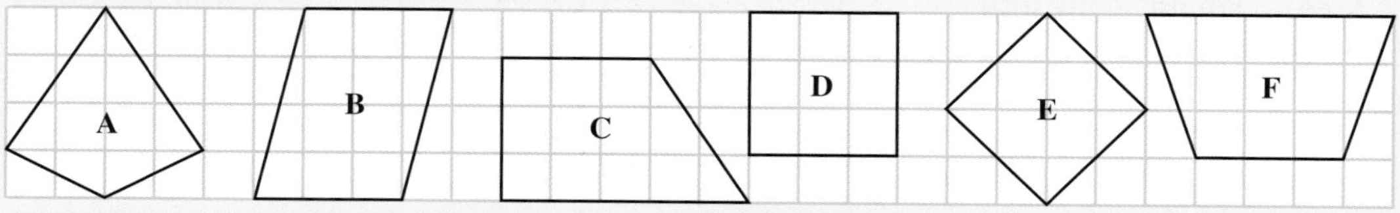

5 Calculate the perimeters of these rectangles and squares.

(a)
2.5 cm
1.5 cm

(b)
3.1 cm
0.9 cm

(c)
2.8 cm
2.8 cm

(d)
1.4 cm
1.4 cm

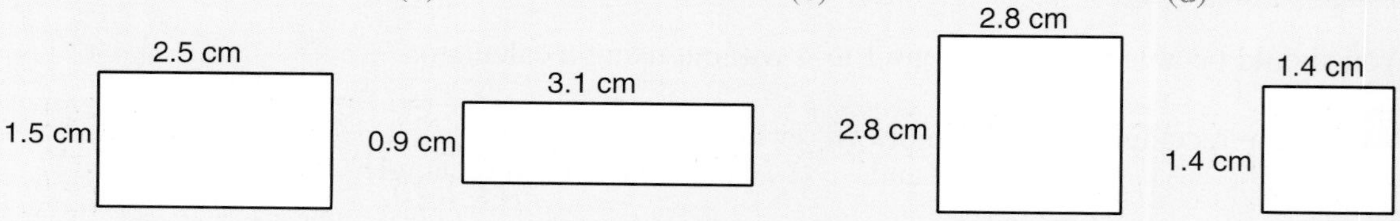

6 Calculate the areas of these rectangles.

(a)
4 cm
1.5 cm

(b)
3 cm
1.8 cm

(c)
2.5 cm
4.6 cm

(d)
3.6 cm
2.2 cm

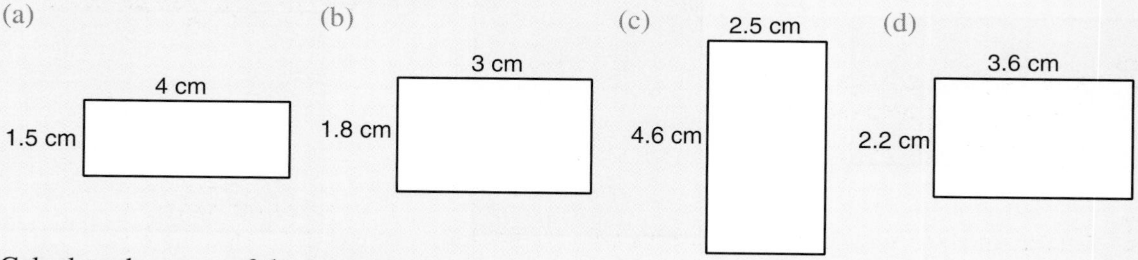

7 Calculate the areas of these squares.

(a)
7 cm

(b)
2.4 cm

(c)
4.3 cm

(d)
1.8 cm

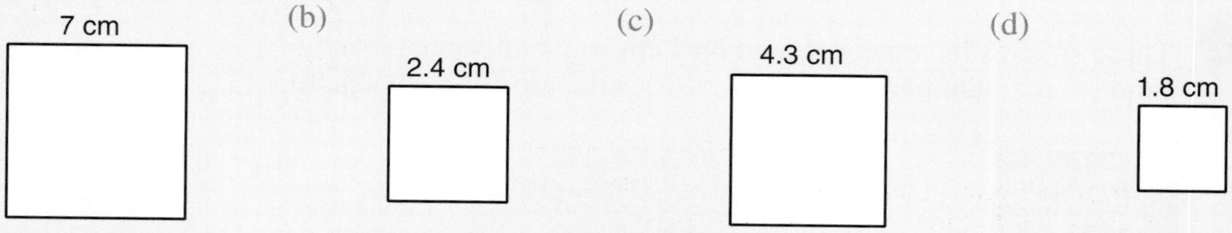

8 Calculate the areas of these parallelograms.

(a)
5 cm
6 cm

(b)
2.5 cm
4 cm

(c)
3 cm
4.5 cm

206

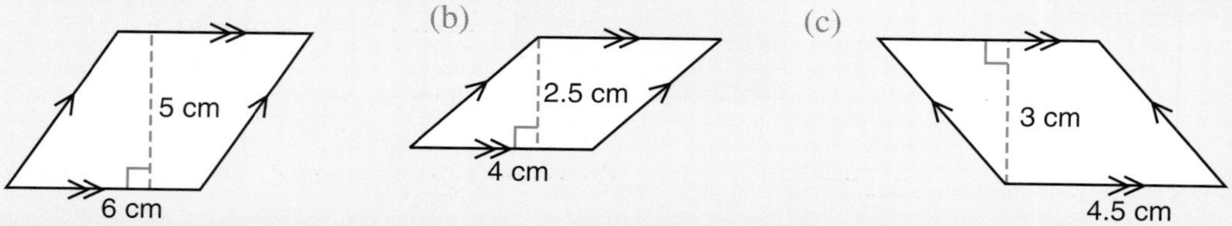

9 These rectangles each have an area of 24 cm².
Find the breadth, *b*, of each rectangle.

(a)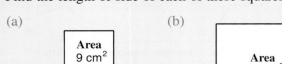
6 cm
b

(b)
8 cm
b

(c)
12 cm
b

10 Find the length of side of each of these squares.

(a)
Area
9 cm²

(b)
Area
36 cm²

(c)
Area
64 cm²

11 A carpet measuring 4 m by 4 m is placed on a rectangular floor measuring 5 m by 6 m.
What area of floor is not carpeted?

12 The diagram shows a picture in a frame.
The outer dimensions of the frame are 18 cm by 10 cm.
The frame is 2 cm wide.
What is the area of the picture?

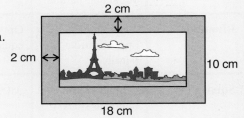
2 cm
2 cm
10 cm
18 cm

13 A rectangle has an area of 36 cm².
The length of the rectangle is 9 cm.
What is the breadth?

14 The diagram shows a square drawn inside a rectangle.
Calculate the shaded area.

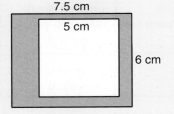
7.5 cm
5 cm
6 cm

15 The parallelogram has the same area as the square.
Calculate the height of the parallelogram.

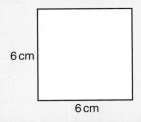
6 cm
6 cm

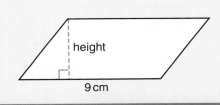
height
9 cm

- A **quadrilateral** is a shape made by four straight lines.
- The sum of the angles in a quadrilateral is 360°.

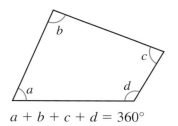

$$a + b + c + d = 360°$$

- Facts about these special quadrilaterals:

parallelogram   rectangle   square   rhombus   trapezium   isosceles trapezium   kite

Quadrilateral	Sides	Angles	Diagonals	Line symmetry	Order of rotational symmetry
Parallelogram	Opposite sides equal and parallel	Opposite angles equal	Bisect each other	0	2
Rectangle	Opposite sides equal and parallel	All 90°	Bisect each other	2	2
Rhombus	4 equal sides, opposite sides parallel	Opposite angles equal	Bisect each other at 90°	2	2
Square	4 equal sides, opposite sides parallel	All 90°	Bisect each other at 90°	4	4
Trapezium	1 pair of parallel sides				
Isosceles trapezium	1 pair of parallel sides, non-parallel sides equal	2 pairs of equal angles	Equal in length	1	1
Kite	2 pairs of adjacent sides equal	1 pair of opposite angles equal	One bisects the other at 90°	1	1

- **Area formulae**
  Rectangle

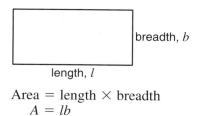

breadth, b

length, l

Area = length × breadth
$A = lb$

Square

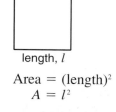

length, l

Area = (length)²
$A = l^2$

Parallelogram

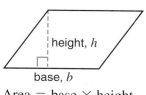

height, h

base, b

Area = base × height
$A = bh$

IDEAS FOR INVESTIGATION

1 **Area of a trapezium**

A trapezium has been drawn on centimetre-squared paper.

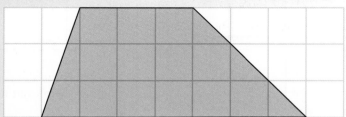

Find the area of the trapezium by counting squares.
Can you find a rule to find the area of the trapezium without having to count squares?
Investigate for other trapeziums.

2 Investigate the areas of kites.

Review Exercise   Do not use a calculator for questions 1 to 10.

1 (a) Which of these shapes is a square?

(b) What special name is given to shape **E**?

(c) How many lines of symmetry has shape **B**?

(d) Which shape has no lines of symmetry?

(e) What is the order of rotational symmetry
of shape **D**?

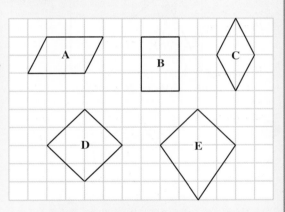

2 These shapes have been drawn on 1 cm squared paper.

(a) (i) What is the perimeter of shape **R**?
(ii) Which two shapes have the same perimeter?

(b) (i) What is the area of shape **Q**?
(ii) Which two shapes have the same area?

209

3

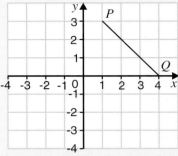

Copy the diagram.
(a) R is at $(1, -3)$.
   Mark the position of R on your diagram.
(b) $PQRS$ is a square.
   What are the coordinates of S?

4 $WXYZ$ is a rectangle.

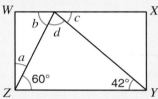

Calculate angles a, b, c and d.

5

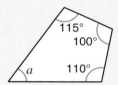

Work out the size of angle a.
Give a reason for your answer.

6 (a) How many lines of symmetry has a kite?
   (b) The diagram shows a kite.

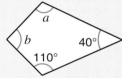

   (i) What is the size of angle a?
      Give a reason for your answer.
   (ii) What is the size of angle b?

7 The diagram shows a trapezium.
Find the size of angle a and angle b.

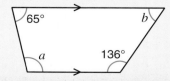

8 $ABCD$ is a rectangle.

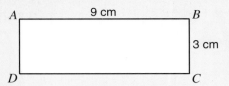

(a) Find the perimeter of $ABCD$.
(b) Work out the area of $ABCD$.

9 Three rectangles each have an area of 28 cm^2.
The lengths of all the sides are whole numbers of centimetres.
For each rectangle work out the lengths of the two sides.   Edexcel

10 A square has a perimeter of 20 cm.
Calculate the area of the square.

11 The area of a rectangle is 54 cm^2.
The length of the rectangle is 9 cm.
(a) What is the width of the rectangle?
(b) What is the perimeter of the rectangle?

12 The plan of a lounge floor is shown.
The lounge floor is a rectangle.

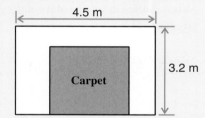

(a) What is the area of the lounge floor?

A rectangular carpet is placed on the floor.
(b) The carpet measures 2.8 m by 2.5 m.
   What area of the floor is **not** covered by the carpet?

13 $ABCD$ is a trapezium.

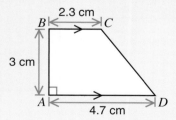

Calculate the area of the trapezium.

14 $WXYZ$ is a rhombus with sides of length 4 cm.
Angle WXY is $60°$.
Make an accurate drawing of the rhombus.

 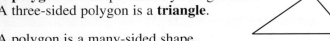

A **polygon** is a shape made by straight lines.
A three-sided polygon is a **triangle**.

A four-sided polygon is called a **quadrilateral**.

A polygon is a many-sided shape.
Look at these polygons.

Pentagon
5 sides

Hexagon
6 sides

Heptagon
7 sides

Octagon
8 sides

Interior and exterior angles of a polygon

Angles formed by sides inside a polygon are called **interior angles**.

When a side of a polygon is extended, as shown, the angle formed is called an **exterior angle**.

At each vertex of the polygon:
    interior angle + exterior angle = 180°

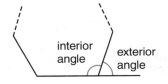

interior angle

exterior angle

Sum of the interior angles of a polygon

The diagram shows polygons with the diagonals from one vertex drawn.

 P
Q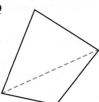
R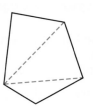
S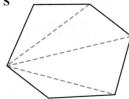

The diagonals divide the polygons into triangles.

Shape	Number of sides	Number of triangles	Sum of interior angles
P	3	1	$1 \times 180° = 180°$
Q	4	2	$2 \times 180° = 360°$
R	5	3	$3 \times 180° = 540°$
S	6	4	$4 \times 180° = 720°$

In general, for any n-sided polygon, the sum of the interior angles is $(n - 2) \times 180°$.

Sum of the exterior angles of a polygon

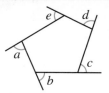

The sum of the exterior angles of **any** polygon is 360°.

$$a + b + c + d + e = 360°$$

EXAMPLES

1 Find the size of angle x.

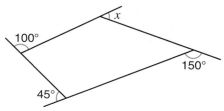

The sum of the exterior angles is 360°.
$x + 100° + 45° + 150° = 360°$
$x + 295° = 360°$
$\quad\quad x = 360° - 295°$
$\quad\quad x = 65°$

2 Find the sum of the interior angles of a pentagon.

To find the sum of the interior angles of a pentagon substitute $n = 5$ into $(n - 2) \times 180°$.
$(5 - 2) \times 180°$
$= 3 \times 180°$
$= 540°$

3 Find the size of the angles marked a and b.

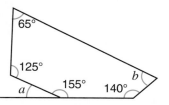

$155° + a = 180°$
(int. angle + ext. angle = 180°)
$a = 180° - 155°$
$a = 25°$

The sum of the interior angles of a pentagon is 540°.
$b + 140° + 155° + 125° + 65° = 540°$
$b + 485° = 540°$
$\quad\quad b = 540° - 485°$
$\quad\quad b = 55°$

Exercise 22.1

The diagrams in this exercise have not been drawn accurately.
You should be able to do this exercise without using a calculator.
Having completed the exercise you may use a calculator to check your working.

1 What special name is given to each of these polygons?

(a)　　　　(b)　　　　(c)　　　　(d)

2 Work out the size of the angles marked with letters.

(a) 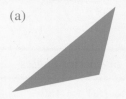　　(b)  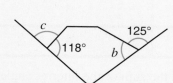　　(c)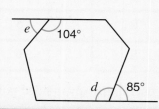

3 Work out the size of the angles marked with letters.

(a)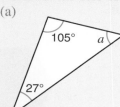

(b)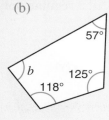

(c)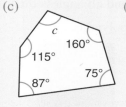

(d)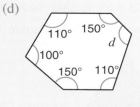

4 Work out the size of the angles marked with letters.

(a)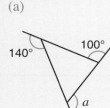

(b)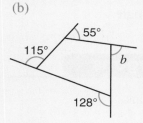

(c)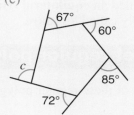

(d)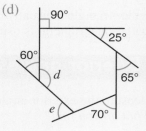

5 Work out the sum of the interior angles of these polygons.

(a)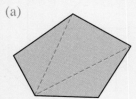

(b)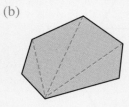

(c)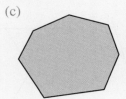

(d)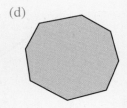

6 Work out the size of the angles marked with letters.

(a)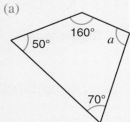

(b)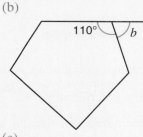

(c)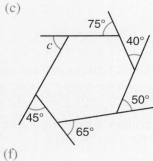

(d)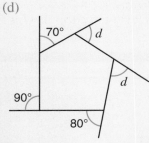

(e)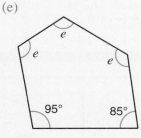

(f)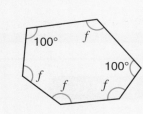

7 Work out the size of the angles marked with letters.

(a)

(b)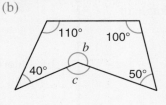

(c)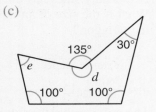

Regular polygons

A polygon with all sides equal and all angles equal is called a **regular polygon**.

These are the first four regular polygons.

Regular triangle

Regular quadrilateral

Regular pentagon

Regular hexagon

A regular triangle is usually called an **equilateral triangle**.
A regular quadrilateral is usually called a **square**.

Exterior angles of regular polygons

Measure the exterior angles of these regular polygons.
What do you find?

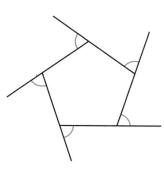

Regular pentagon

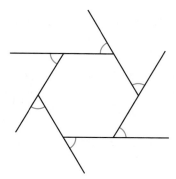

Regular hexagon

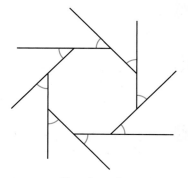

Regular octagon

You should find the exterior angles of a regular polygon are equal.

In general, for any regular n-sided polygon: exterior angle $= \dfrac{360°}{n}$

By rearranging the formula we can find the number of sides, n, of a regular polygon when we know the exterior angle. $n = \dfrac{360°}{\text{exterior angle}}$

EXAMPLE

A regular polygon has an exterior angle of 30°.
(a)   How many sides has the polygon?
(b)   What is the size of an interior angle of the polygon?

(a) $n = \dfrac{360°}{\text{exterior angle}}$

$n = \dfrac{360°}{30°} = 12$

The polygon has 12 sides.

Remember:
It is a good idea to write down the formula you are using.

(b)   interior angle + exterior angle $= 180°$
int. $\angle + 30° = 180°$
int. $\angle = 180° - 30°$
interior angle $= 150°$

214

Exercise 22.2

1 Calculate (a) the exterior angle and (b) the interior angle of these regular polygons.

(i)    (ii)    (iii)    (iv)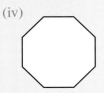

2 A regular polygon has an exterior angle of 18°.
How many sides has the polygon?

3 Calculate the number of sides of regular polygons with an exterior angle of:
(a) 9°   (b) 24°   (c) 40°   (d) 60°

4 A regular polygon has an interior angle of 135°.
How many sides has the polygon?

5 Calculate the number of sides of regular polygons with an interior angle of:
(a) 108°   (b) 162°   (c) 171°   (d) 90°

6 (a) Calculate the size of an exterior angle of a regular pentagon.
(b) What is the size of an interior angle of a regular pentagon?
(c) What is the sum of the interior angles of a pentagon?

7 The following diagrams are drawn using regular polygons.
Work out the values of the marked angles.

(a) 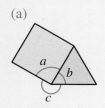   (b) 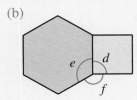   (c) 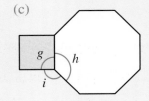   (d)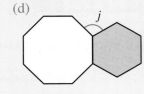

(e) 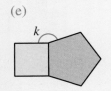   (f) 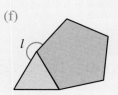   (g) 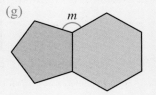   (h)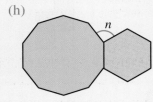

8 The following diagrams are drawn using regular polygons.
Work out the values of the marked angles.

(a) 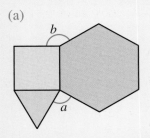   (b) 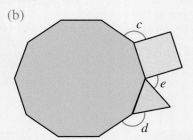   (c)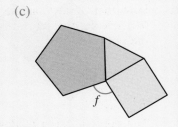

9 The following diagrams are drawn using regular polygons.
Work out the values of the marked angles.

(a)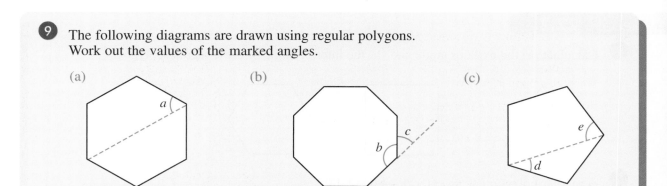

(b)

(c)

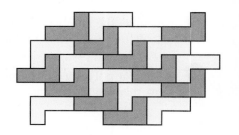

Tessellations

Covering a surface with identical shapes produces
a pattern called a **tessellation**.

To tessellate the shape must not overlap and there must be no gaps.

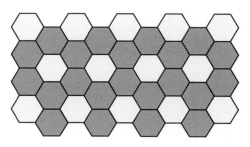

Regular tessellations

This pattern shows a tessellation of regular
hexagons.
This pattern is called a **regular tessellation** because
it is made by using a single regular polygon.

Exercise 22.3

1 Draw diagrams to show tessellations of these shapes.

(a)   (b)   (c)

2 Copy these regular tessellations.
Continue the tessellation by drawing four more shapes.

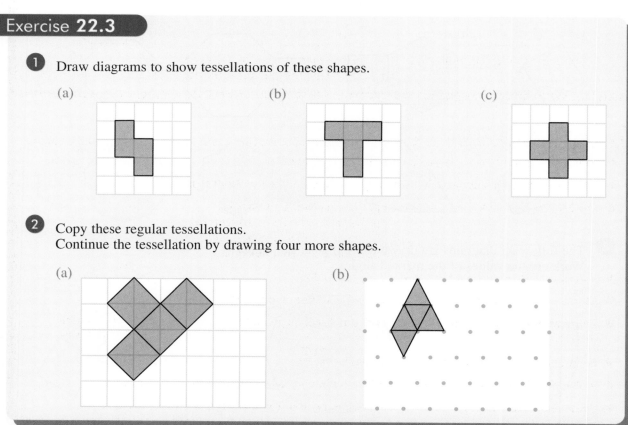

(a)   (b)

3 (a) The diagram shows part of a tessellation.
Copy the diagram.
Continue the tessellation by drawing
four more triangles.

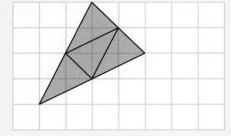

(b) All triangles tessellate.
Draw a triangle of your own, make copies,
and show that it will tessellate.

4 (a) The diagram shows part of a tessellation.
Copy the diagram.
Continue the tessellation by drawing
four more quadrilaterals.

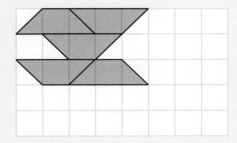

(b) All quadrilaterals tessellate.
Draw a quadrilateral of your own, make copies,
and show that it will tessellate.

5 (a) Draw a regular hexagon.
(b) (i) Draw all the lines of symmetry on your diagram.
(ii) How many lines of symmetry has a regular hexagon?
(c) What is the order of rotational symmetry of a regular hexagon?

6 The diagram shows three regular polygons.

(a) 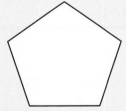 (b) 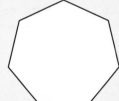 (c)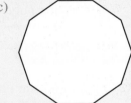

For each regular polygon find: (i) the number of lines of symmetry,
(ii) the order of rotational symmetry.

What you need to know

- A **polygon** is a many-sided shape made by straight lines.

- A polygon with all sides equal and all angles equal is called a **regular polygon**.

- Shapes you need to know: A 3-sided polygon is called a **triangle**.
  A 4-sided polygon is called a **quadrilateral**.
  A 5-sided polygon is called a **pentagon**.
  A 6-sided polygon is called a **hexagon**.

- The sum of the exterior angles of any polygon is 360°.

- At each vertex of a polygon: interior angle + exterior angle = 180°

- The sum of the interior angles of an n-sided polygon is given by:
  $(n - 2) \times 180°$

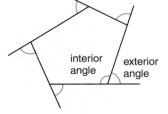

interior angle

exterior angle

- For a regular n-sided polygon: exterior angle = $\dfrac{360°}{n}$

- A shape will **tessellate** if it covers a surface without overlapping and leaves no gaps.

- Equilateral triangles, squares and hexagons can be used to make **regular tessellations**.

Inscribed regular polygons

Inscribed regular polygons can be constructed by equal divisions of a circle. To draw an inscribed regular polygon follow these steps.

Step 1 Find the exterior angle of the polygon.

$$\text{Exterior angle} = \frac{360°}{\text{number of sides}}$$

Step 2 Draw a circle.
Divide the circle into equal sectors, where the sector angles are equal to the exterior angle of the polygon.

Step 3 Join the divisions on the circumference of the circle to form the polygon.

Example Draw an inscribed regular hexagon.

Step 1

A hexagon has 6 sides.

$$\text{Exterior angle} = \frac{360°}{6}$$
$$= 60°$$

Step 2

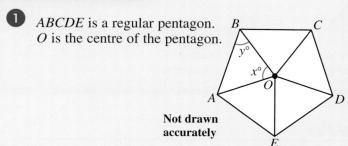

Step 3

(a) Draw an inscribed equilateral triangle.
(b) Draw an inscribed square.
(c) Draw other inscribed regular polygons.

Which regular polygons are difficult to draw accurately? Explain why.

Review Exercise

1 *ABCDE* is a regular pentagon. *O* is the centre of the pentagon.

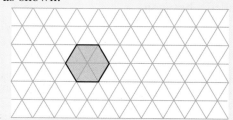

Not drawn accurately

(a) Write down the order of rotational symmetry of the regular pentagon.
(b) Work out the value of
    (i) *x*,   (ii) *y*.
(c) Draw a regular hexagon on isometric paper as shown.

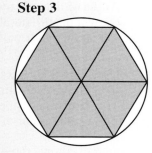

Show how regular hexagons tessellate.
(d) Explain why regular pentagons will not tessellate.

2 Part of a regular polygon is shown.

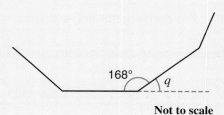

Not to scale

(a) What is the size of angle *q*?
(b) How many sides has the polygon?

3 Copy the following diagram onto squared paper and draw six more shapes to form a tessellation.

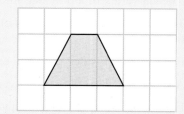

Edexcel

218

4 A square, an equilateral triangle and a regular pentagon are drawn as shown.

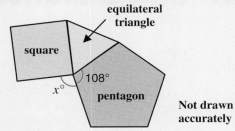

equilateral triangle

square

108°

$x°$

pentagon

Not drawn accurately

(a) Describe the symmetries of each of the shapes.
Mention both line and rotational symmetry.

(b) Work out the value of x in the diagram.
Explain your reasoning carefully.   Edexcel

5 *ABCDEF* is a regular polygon.

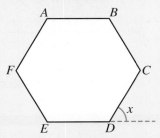

(a) What name is given to this polygon?
(b) What is the size of the exterior angle marked x?
(c) What is the sum of the interior angles?

6 Work out the size of angle x.

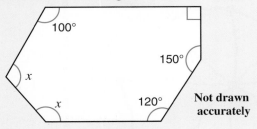

100°

150°

x

x

120°

Not drawn accurately

7 A regular octagon, drawn below, has eight sides. One side of the octagon has been extended to form angle p.

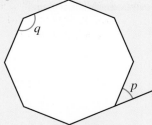

q

p

(a) Work out the size of angle p.
(b) Work out the size of angle q.

8 *ABCDE* is a regular pentagon.

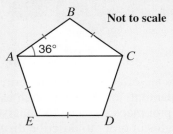

B   Not to scale

A   36°   C

E   D

Given that $\angle BAC = 36°$, explain why *AC* is parallel to *ED*.

9 The diagram shows a regular 9-sided polygon.

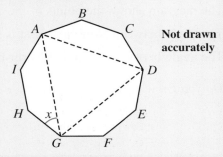

B

A   C   Not drawn accurately

I   D

H x E

G   F

(a) What type of triangle is *ADG*? Give a reason for your answer.
(b) What is the size of the angle marked x?

10 The diagram shows a regular decagon which has been divided into three parts.

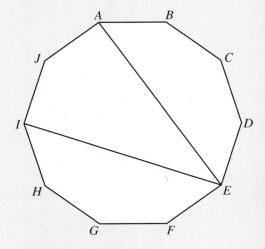

A   B

J   C

I   D

H   E

G   F

(a) What name is given to the quadrilateral *AEIJ*?
(b) What name is given to the shape *ABCDE*?
(c) Work out the size of angle *AED*.
(d) What is the size of angle *AEI*?

CHAPTER 23 · Direction and Distance

Journeys are often described in terms of **direction** and **distance**.
When planning journeys we often use **maps**.
To interpret maps we need to understand:
      angles in order to describe **direction**,
      scales in order to find **distances**.
Compass points and **three-figure bearings** are used to describe direction.

> In Chapter 18
> we looked at:
> measuring angles,
> drawing angles.

Compass points

The diagram shows the points of the compass.

The angle between North and East is 90°.

The angle between North and North-East is 45°.

Do you know the names of any other compass points?

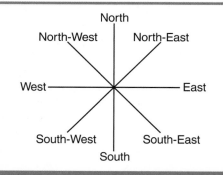

Exercise 23.1

1   A map of a cycle track is shown.

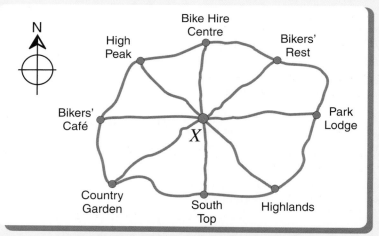

(a)   (i)   Which place is due North of South Top?
     (ii)   Which place is due West of Park Lodge?
    (iii) Which place is North-East of Country Garden?
    (iv) Which place is North-West of Highlands?

(b)   John is at the position marked *X* on the map.
     (i)   Which place is South-East of John?
     (ii)   In which direction does he need to cycle to reach Bikers' Rest?
    (iii) He cycles South-West. Which place will he reach?

2 The diagram shows a road junction.

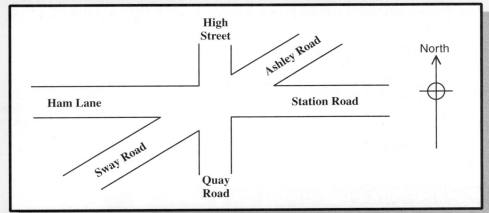

(a) A car travels from the junction along Quay Road.
In which direction is it travelling?

(b) A coach travels from the junction along Station Road.
In which direction is it travelling?

(c) A taxi drives along Station Road towards the junction.
In which direction is it travelling?

(d) Sway Road is directly opposite Ashley Road.
When traffic goes from the junction along Ashley Road it is travelling North-East.
In which direction is traffic travelling when it goes from the junction along Sway Road?

3 (a) What is the angle between North and North-West?
(b) What is the angle between South and North-West?
(c) What is the angle between South-West and South-East?
(d) What is the angle between North-West and South-West?
(e) What is the angle between South-East and North-West?

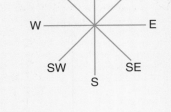

4 (a) Lyn is facing North.
She turns through an angle of 180°.
In which direction is she now facing?

(b) Tony is facing West.
He turns through an angle of 90° clockwise.
In which direction is he now facing?

5 (a) Claire is facing South. In which direction will she face after turning clockwise through an angle of 135°?

(b) Kevin turned anticlockwise through an angle of 270°. He is now facing South-East.
In which direction was he facing?

6 Copy and complete this table.
The first line has been done for you.

Start facing	Amount of turn	Finish facing
South	135° clockwise	North-West
North-East	90° clockwise	
West	135° anticlockwise	
	270° clockwise	East
	45° anticlockwise	West

Three-figure bearings

Bearings are used to describe the direction in which you must travel to get from one place to another.

A bearing is an angle measured from the North line in a clockwise direction.

The angle, which can be from 0° to 360°, is written as a three-figure number.

Bearings which are less than 100° include noughts to make up the three figures, e.g. 005°, 087°.

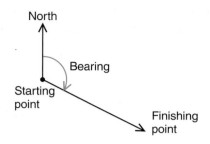

To show the direction given by a bearing

Example

The bearing of *C* from *D* is 153°. Draw a diagram to show this information.

The bearing of *C* **from** *D* tells you that *D* is the starting point.

1 Draw a North line. Mark and label point *D* on the North line.

2 Using your protractor, centred on point *D*, mark an angle of 153° measured in a clockwise direction from the North line.

3 Draw a line from *D* through the marked point.
An arrow is drawn on the line to show the direction in which you must travel to get to *C*.

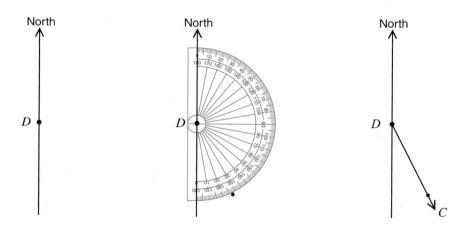

This diagram shows the positions of Bath and Poole.

The bearing of Poole from Bath is 162°.

If you are at Bath, facing North and turn through 162° in a clockwise direction you will be facing in the direction of Poole.

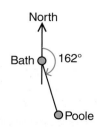

222

Back bearings

The return bearing of Bath from Poole is called a **back bearing**.
Back bearings can be found by using parallel lines and alternate angles.

The bearing of Poole from Bath is 162°.

$a = 162°$ (alternate angles)

Required angle = 180° + 162° = 342°.
The bearing of Bath from Poole (the back bearing) is 342°.

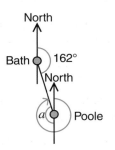

Exercise 23.2

In this exercise diagrams have been drawn accurately.
Use your protractor to measure angles.

1 Find the three-figure bearings of A from B in each of the following.

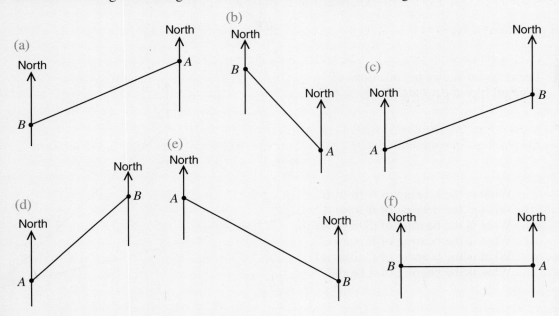

2 (a) Draw sketches to show the following information.
  (i)   The bearing of F from E is 050°.
  (ii) The bearing of C from H is 125°.
  (iii) The bearing of K from Q is 195°.
  (iv) The bearing of L from B is 260°.
  (v)   The bearing of A from J is 305°.
  (vi) The bearing of X from T is 175°.

  (b) Use your sketches to give the back bearings for each of the directions in part (a).

3 Copy the diagram.

R is on a bearing of 100° from P.
R is on a bearing of 060° from Q.
Mark the position of R on your diagram.

4 The diagram shows the positions of three towns.

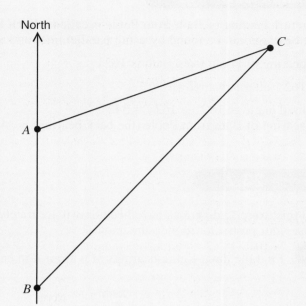

(a) What is the bearing of B from A?
(b) What is the bearing of C from A?
(c) What is the bearing of A from C?
(d) What is the bearing of C from B?
(e) What is the bearing of B from C?

5 The diagram shows the positions of three oil rigs at A, B and C.

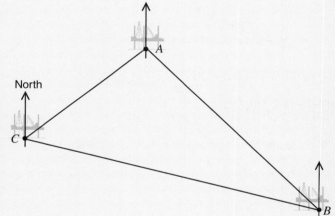

(a) What is the bearing of A from B?
(b) What is the bearing of B from A?
(c) What is the bearing of C from B?
(d) What is the bearing of B from C?
(e) What is the bearing of C from A?
(f) What is the bearing of A from C?

6 Copy the diagram.

Q is on a bearing of 070° from P.
Q is on a bearing of 320° from R.
Mark the position of Q on your diagram.

Scale drawing

Maps and plans are scaled down representations of real-life situations.
The **scale** used in drawing a map or plan determines the amount of detail that can be shown.

The distances between different points on a map are all drawn to the same scale.
There are two ways to describe a scale.

1 A scale of 1 cm to 10 km means that a distance of 1 cm on the map represents an actual distance of 10 km.

2 A scale of 1 : 10 000 means that all distances measured on the map have to be multiplied by 10 000 to find the real distance.

EXAMPLES

1 A road is 3.7 cm long on a map.
The scale given on the map is
'1 cm represents 10 km'.
What is the actual length of the road?

1 cm represents 10 km.
Scale up, so multiply.
3.7 cm represents 3.7 × 10 km
     = 37 km
The road is 37 km long.

2 A plan of a field is to be drawn using a scale of 1 : 500.
Two trees in the field are 350 metres apart.
How far apart will they be on the plan?

Scale down, so divide.
Distance on plan = 350 m ÷ 500
Change 350 m to centimetres.
     = 35 000 cm ÷ 500
     = 70 cm
The trees will be 70 cm apart on the plan.

Exercise 23.3

1 A forest walk measures 8.4 cm on a map.
The scale given on the map is "1 cm represents 2 km".
What is the actual length of the walk in kilometres?

2 A motor-racing circuit is 9.6 km in length.
A plan of the circuit has been drawn to a scale of 1 cm to 3 km.
What is the length of the circuit on the plan?

3 Here is a map of an island.

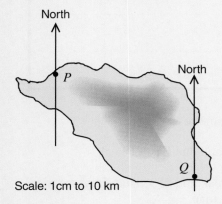

Scale: 1cm to 10 km

(a) Use your protractor to find:
   (i)   the bearing of Q from P,
   (ii) the bearing of P from Q.

(b) (i)   Measure the distance between
         P and Q on the map.
    (ii) What is the actual distance
         between P and Q?

4

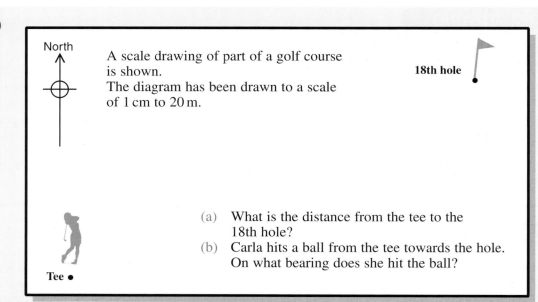

A scale drawing of part of a golf course is shown.
The diagram has been drawn to a scale of 1 cm to 20 m.

18th hole

North

Tee •

(a) What is the distance from the tee to the 18th hole?
(b) Carla hits a ball from the tee towards the hole. On what bearing does she hit the ball?

5 The diagram shows a group of islands.
The map has been drawn to a scale of 1 cm to 5 km.

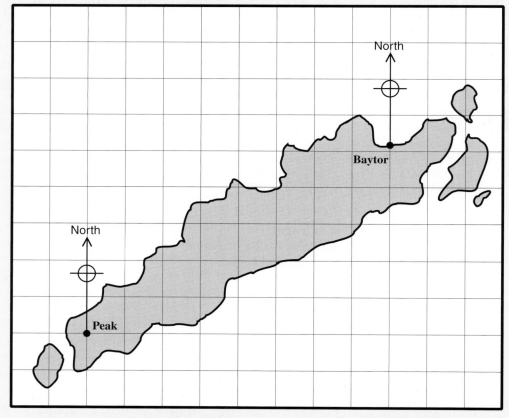

North

Baytor

North

Peak

(a) A straight road joins Baytor to Peak.
Use the map to find the length of this road in kilometres.
(b) Copy the map onto squared paper.
 (i) A ship is on a bearing of 200° from Baytor and due East of Peak.
 Show the position of the ship on your map.
 (ii) A lighthouse is on a bearing of 035° from Peak and 253° from Baytor.
 Show the position of the lighthouse on your map.

6 The plan of a house is drawn using a scale of 1 : 100.
The lounge is 4.6 m in length.
What is the length of the lounge on the plan?

7 The diagram shows the plan of a building plot.
The plan has been drawn to a scale of 1 : 1000.

AB is the width of the plot.
(a) Measure *AB*.
(b) What is the width of the plot in metres?

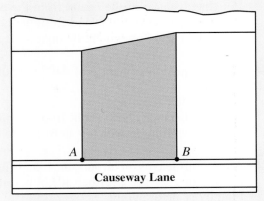

Causeway Lane

8 The diagram shows the flight path of a plane
between two airports.
The diagram has been drawn to a scale of
1 : 250 000.
Use the diagram to find:
(a) the actual distance between the airports,
in kilometres,
(b) the bearing of *B* from *A*,
(c) the bearing of *A* from *B*.

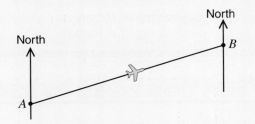

9 The diagram shows the plan of a cross-country course.
Runners have to go round markers at *A*, *B* and *C*.
(a) What is the bearing of *B* from *A*?
(b) What is the bearing of *A* from *C*?

The plan has been drawn to a scale of 1 : 20 000.
(c) What is the distance from *A* to *C* in metres?

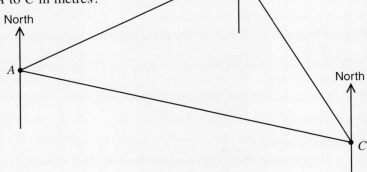

10 The sketch shows the positions of Ayton,
Boulder, Carey and Dole.

Carey is 12 km due West of Dole.
Carey is 8 km due North of Boulder.
Ayton is on a bearing 100° from Boulder
and 160° from Dole.
By using a scale of 1 cm to 2 km, find by scale
drawing the distance of Ayton from Carey.

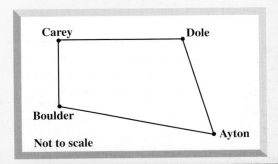

Not to scale

11 A boat leaves port and sails on a bearing of 144° for 4 km.
It then changes course and sails due East for 5 km to reach an island.
Find by scale drawing:
(a) the distance of the island from the port,
(b) the bearing of the island from the port,
(c) the bearing on which the boat must sail to return directly to the port.

12 A yacht sails on a bearing of 040° for 5000 m and then a further 3000 m on a bearing of 120°.
Find by scale drawing:
(a) the distance of the yacht from its starting position,
(b) the bearing on which it must sail to return directly to its starting position.

13 An aircraft leaves an airport, at A, and flies on a bearing of 035° for 50 km and then on a bearing of 280° for a further 40 km before landing at an airport, at B.
Find by scale drawing:
(a) the distance between the airports,
(b) the bearing of B from A,
(c) the bearing of A from B.

What you need to know

- Compass points

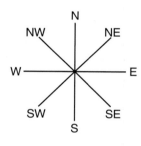

- **Bearings** are used to describe the direction in which you must travel to get from one place to another.
  A bearing is an angle measured from the North line in a clockwise direction.

- A bearing can be any angle from 0° to 360° and is written as a three-figure number.

- To find a bearing:
  measure angle a to find the bearing of Y from X,
  measure angle b to find the bearing of X from Y.

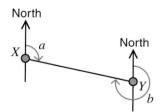

- **Scales**
  The distances between points on a map are all drawn to the same scale.
  There are two ways to describe a scale.
  1. A scale of 1 cm to 10 km means that a distance of 1 cm on the map represents an actual distance of 10 km.
  2. A scale of 1 : 10 000 means that all distances measured on the map have to be multiplied by 10 000 to find the real distance.

3-dimensional coordinates

One coordinate identifies a point on a line.
Two coordinates identify a point on a plane.
Three coordinates identify a point in space.

The diagram shows a cuboid drawn in 3-dimensions.

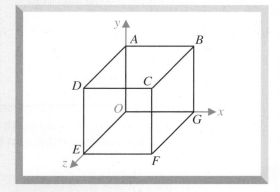

Using the axes x, y and z shown:

Point A is given as (0, 2, 0).

Point B is given as (2, 2, 0).

Point C is given as (2, 2, 3).

Give the 3-dimensional coordinates of points, D, E, F, and G.

Review Exercise

① Here is a map.
  (a) Name the town north of Manchester.
  (b) Name the town south-west of Birmingham.

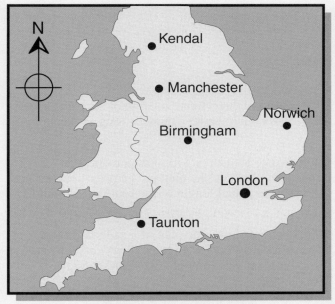

Edexcel

② Copy the diagram onto squared paper.
  (a) Draw a line at A pointing East.
  (b) Draw a line at B pointing North-East.
  (c) In which direction is A from B?

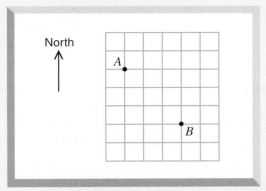

Edexcel

3

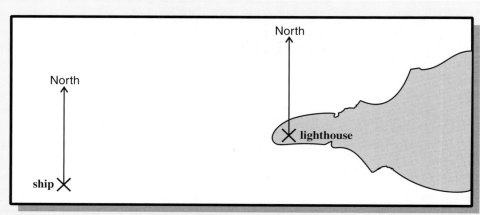

A ship and a lighthouse are marked (with an ✕) on the map.
Measure the 3-figure bearing of **the ship from the lighthouse**.

Edexcel

4 The diagram shows the positions of three villages.

The diagram has not been drawn accurately.

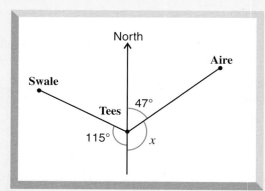

(a) Work out the size of angle x.
(b) Give the three-figure bearing of Aire from Tees.
(c) Work out the three-figure bearing of Swale from Tees.

5 A bus route measures 7.3 cm on a map.
The scale given on the map is "1 cm represents 2 km".
What is the actual length of the route in kilometres?

6 The diagram shows the plan of a sailboard race.
The sailboards have to go round buoys at A, B and C.
Buoy B is on a bearing of 050° from buoy A.
Angle ABC is 90°.

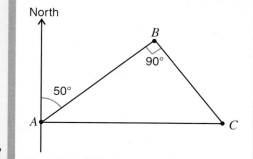

(a) What is the bearing of A from B?
(b) What is the bearing of C from B?

The plan has been drawn to a scale of 1 : 20 000.
(c) (i) Measure AB.
    (ii) What is the distance from A to B in metres?

7 Axford is 70 km from Moxley on a bearing of 065°.
Parley is 55 km from Moxley on a bearing of 125°.
(a) By using a scale of 1 cm to 10 km, draw an accurate diagram to show the positions of
Axford, Parley and Moxley.
(b) What is the bearing of Moxley from Axford?
(c) By taking measurements from your diagram work out
(i) the distance of Parley from Axford,
(ii) the bearing of Parley from Axford.

CHAPTER 24

**Circles** ●●●●●●●●●●●●●●●●●●●

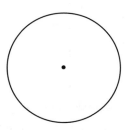

A **circle** is the shape drawn by keeping a pencil the same distance
from a fixed point on a piece of paper.
Compasses can be used to draw circles accurately.

It is important that you understand the meaning of the following words:

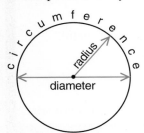

Circumference – special name used for the perimeter of a circle.

Radius – distance from the centre of the circle to any point on
the circumference. The plural of radius is **radii**.

Diameter – distance right across the circle, passing through the
centre point. Notice that the diameter is twice as long as the radius.

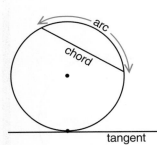

Chord – a line joining two points on the circumference.
The longest chord of a circle is the diameter.

Tangent – a line which touches the circumference of a circle at
one point only.

Arc – part of the circumference of a circle.

Activity

Draw a circle with radius 2 cm.
Use thread or the edge of a strip of paper to measure the circumference of your circle.
Draw circles with radii 3 cm, 4 cm and so on.
Measure the circumference of each circle and write your results in a table.

Radius (cm)	2	3	4	5	6	7	8
Diameter (cm)							
Circumference (cm)							

What do you notice?

The Greek letter π

The circumference of any circle is just a bit bigger than three times the diameter of the circle.
The Greek letter π is used to represent this number.

We use an approximate value for π, such as 3, $3\frac{1}{7}$, 3.14, or the π key on a calculator, depending on the
accuracy we require.

Circumference of a circle

The diagram shows a circle with radius r and diameter d.

The **circumference** of a circle can be found using the formulae:

$$C = \pi \times d$$

$$\text{or} \quad C = 2 \times \pi \times r$$

Remember: $\quad d = 2 \times r$

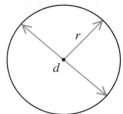

EXAMPLES

1 Estimate the circumference of a circle with radius 7 cm.
Take π to be 3.

$$C = 2 \times \pi \times r$$
$$= 2 \times 3 \times 7 \,\text{cm}$$
$$= 42 \,\text{cm}$$

Circumference is approximately 42 cm.

2 Find the circumference of a circle with diameter 80 cm.
Take π to be 3.14.
Give your answer to the nearest centimetre.

$$C = \pi \times d$$
$$= 3.14 \times 80 \,\text{cm}$$
$$= 251.2 \,\text{cm}$$

Circumference is 251 cm to the nearest centimetre.

Exercise 24.1

Do not use a calculator for questions 1 to 3.

1 Estimate the circumference of these circles.
Use the approximate rule: Circumference = 3 × diameter.

(a)
4 cm

(b)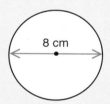
8 cm

(c)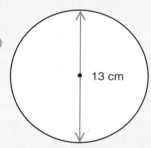
13 cm

2 Use the approximate rule to estimate the circumference of these circles.

Remember: diameter = 2 × radius.

(a)
2.5 cm

(b)
5 cm

(c)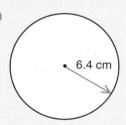
6.4 cm

3 The diagram shows the actual size of a 1p coin and a 2p coin.
(a) Find, by measurement, the diameter of each coin.
(b) Use the approximate rule:
Circumference = 3 × diameter
to estimate the circumference of each coin.

1p 2p

In questions 4 to 12, take π to be 3.14 or use the π key on your calculator.

4 Calculate the circumference of these circles.
Use the formula $C = \pi \times d$.

(a)

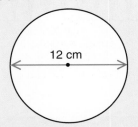

12 cm

(b)

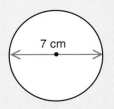

7 cm

(c)

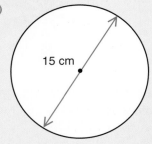

15 cm

5 Calculate the circumference of these circles.
Use the formula $C = 2 \times \pi \times r$.

(a)

4.5 cm

(b)

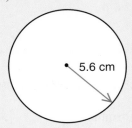

5.6 cm

(c)

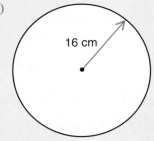

16 cm

6 A circle has a diameter of 9 cm.
Calculate the circumference of the circle.
Give your answer correct to the nearest whole number.

7 A circular biscuit tin has a diameter of 24 cm.
What is the circumference of the tin?

8 A dinner plate has a radius of 13 cm.
Calculate the circumference of the plate.
Give your answer to an appropriate degree of accuracy.

9 A circle has a radius of 6.5 cm.
Calculate the circumference of the circle.
Give your answer correct to one decimal place.

10 Stan marks the centre circle of a football pitch.
The circle has a radius of 9.15 m.
What is the circumference of the circle?

11 The radius of a tractor wheel is 0.8 m.
Calculate the circumference of the wheel.

12 Two cyclists go once round a circular track.
Eddy cycles on the inside of the track which has a radius of 20 m.
Reg cycles on the outside of the track which has a radius of 25 m.
How much further does Reg cycle?

Activity

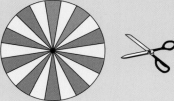

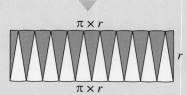

Cut out the 20 sectors.
Arrange them like this.

Draw a circle.
Divide it into 20 equal **sectors**.
Colour the sectors using two colours.

The circumference of a circle is given by $2 \times \pi \times r$.
Half of the circumference is $\pi \times r$.
So the length of the rectangle is $\pi \times r$.
The width of the rectangle is the same as the radius of the circle, r.

Using area of a rectangle = length $\times$ breadth
area of a circle = $\pi \times r \times r$
area of a circle = $\pi \times r^2$

Take the end sector and cut it in half.
Place one piece at each end of the pattern

Area of a circle

The area of a circle can be found using the formula:

$A = \pi \times r^2$

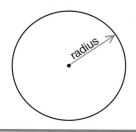

EXAMPLES

1 Estimate the area of a circle
with radius of 6 cm.
Take π to be 3.

$A = \pi \times r \times r$
$= 3 \times 6 \times 6$
$= 108 \text{ cm}^2$
Area is approximately 108 cm².

2 Calculate the area of a circle with diameter 9 cm.
Use the π key on your calculator.
Give your answer correct to the nearest whole number.

$A = \pi \times r \times r$
$= \pi \times 4.5 \times 4.5$
$= 63.617... \text{ cm}^2$
Area is 64 cm², to the nearest whole number.

> **Remember:** $r = \dfrac{d}{2}$

Exercise 24.2

Do not use a calculator for questions 1 and 2.

1 Estimate the areas of these circles.
Use the approximate rule: Area = $3 \times (\text{radius})^2$.

(a)

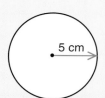

5 cm

(b)

7 cm

(c)

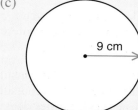

9 cm

② Estimate the areas of these circles.
Take π to be 3.

> **Remember:** Radius $= \dfrac{\text{diameter}}{2}$

(a)

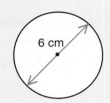
6 cm

(b)

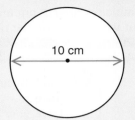
10 cm

(c)

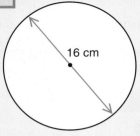
16 cm

In questions 3 to 11, take π to be 3.14 or use the π key on your calculator.

③ Calculate the areas of these circles.
Give your answers to the nearest whole number.

(a)

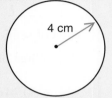
4 cm

(b)

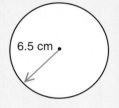
6.5 cm

(c)

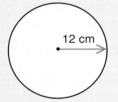
12 cm

④ Calculate the areas of these circles.
Give your answers correct to one decimal place.

(a)

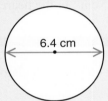
6.4 cm

(b)

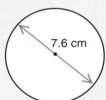
7.6 cm

(c)

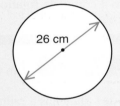
26 cm

⑤ The base of a paddling pool is a circle with radius 84 cm.
Find the area of the base.

⑥ The lid on a tin of paint is a circle of radius 72 mm.
Calculate the area of the lid.

⑦ The diameter of a bicycle wheel is 66 cm.
A plastic spoke cover is made for the wheel.
What is the area of the spoke cover?

66 cm

⑧ A dinner plate has a diameter of 25 cm.
Find the area of the plate.
Give your answer correct to the nearest whole number.

⑨ A circular table has a diameter of 1.2 m.
Calculate the area of the table.
Give your answer correct to one decimal place.

⑩ A circular rug has a radius of 0.5 m.
Calculate the area of the rug.
Give your answer correct to two decimal places.

⑪ A mug has a diameter of 8 cm.
Calculate the area of the base of the mug.
Give your answer to an appropriate degree of accuracy.

Mixed questions involving circumferences and areas of circles

Some questions will involve finding the area and some the circumference of a circle.

Remember: Choose the correct formula for area or circumference.
You need to think about whether to use the radius or the diameter.

EXAMPLES

1   Gina's bicycle wheel has a radius of 24 cm.
How many complete rotations of the wheel are needed to cycle 500 cm?
Take $\pi = 3.14$.

Find the circumference of the wheel.
$C = 2 \times \pi \times r$
$\quad = 2 \times 3.14 \times 24\,\text{cm}$
$\quad = 150.72\,\text{cm}$

Number of rotations
$\quad = 500\,\text{cm} \div \text{circumference}$
$\quad = 500\,\text{cm} \div 150.72\,\text{cm}$
$\quad = 3.317\ldots$

So 4 complete rotations of the wheel are needed.

2   Find the area of a semi-circle with radius 4 cm.
Take $\pi = 3.14$.
Give your answer to the nearest whole number.

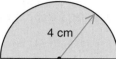

Begin by finding the area of a circle with radius 4 cm.

$A = \pi \times r^2$
$\quad = 3.14 \times 4 \times 4\,\text{cm}^2$
$\quad = 50.24\,\text{cm}^2$

Area of semi-circle
$\quad = \frac{1}{2} \times \text{area of circle}$
$\quad = \frac{1}{2} \times 50.24\,\text{cm}^2$
$\quad = 25.12\,\text{cm}^2$

Area of semi-circle is 25 cm², to the nearest whole number.

Exercise 24.3

In this exercise take π to be 3.14 or use the π key on your calculator.

1   A tea plate has a radius of 9 cm.
  (a)   What is the circumference of the plate?
  (b)   What is the area of the plate?

2   The top of a tin of cat food is a circle of diameter 8.4 cm.
  (a)   Calculate the circumference of the tin.
        Give your answer correct to the nearest whole number.
  (b)   Calculate the area of the top of the tin.
        Give your answer correct to one decimal place.

3   The front wheel on Nick's tricycle has a diameter of 18 cm.
  (a)   Calculate the circumference of the front wheel.
  (b)   How far does Nick have to cycle for the front wheel to make 20 complete turns?

4   The letter O is cut from card.
The inside radius of the letter is 3 cm.
The outside radius of the letter is 4 cm.
Calculate the area of the letter.

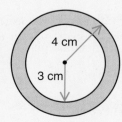

5   Which has the greater area:
       a circle with radius 4 cm, or a semi-circle with diameter 11 cm?
You must show all your working.

6 A circle is drawn inside a square, as shown.
The square has sides of length 10 cm.
Calculate the area of the shaded region.

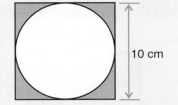

10 cm

7 Thirty students join hands to form a circle.
The diameter of the circle is 8.5 m.
   (a) Find the circumference of the circle.
        Give your answer to the nearest metre.
   (b) What area is enclosed by the circle?
        Give your answer to an appropriate degree of accuracy.

8 Find the perimeter of a semi-circle with radius 6 cm.
Give your answer to the nearest whole number.

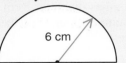

6 cm

9 A bicycle wheel has a diameter of 66 cm.
   (a) What is the circumference of the wheel?
   (b) Adrian cycles a distance of 1000 cm.
        How many complete rotations does the wheel make?

10 A cotton reel is a cylinder with radius 1.3 cm.
200 cm of cotton is wrapped round the reel.
How many times does it wrap round?

11 A circular flower bed has diameter 12 m.
   (a) How much edging is needed to go right round the bed?
   (b) The gardener needs one bag of fertiliser for each 7 m².
        How many bags of fertiliser are needed for this bed?

12 A pastry cutter is in the shape of a semi-circle.
The straight side of the semi-circle is 12 cm long.
How long is the curved side?

What you need to know

- A **circle** is the shape drawn by keeping a pencil the same distance
  from a fixed point on a piece of paper.
- Words associated with circles:
  Circumference – perimeter of a circle.
  Radius – distance from the centre of the circle to
  any point on the circumference.
  The plural of radius is **radii**.
  Diameter – distance right across the circle,
  passing through the centre point.
  Chord – a line joining two points on the circumference.
  Tangent – a line which touches the circumference of a
  circle at one point only.
  Arc – part of the circumference of a circle.

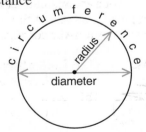

- Diameter = 2 × radius
- The **circumference** of a circle is given by:
  $C = \pi \times d$ or $C = 2 \times \pi \times r$
- The **area** of a circle is given by:
  $A = \pi \times r^2$

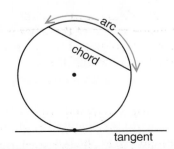

Take π to be 3.14 or use the π key on your calculator.

1 The diagram shows two pulleys.

The larger pulley has radius 5 cm.
(a) What is the area of the larger pulley?

The smaller pulley has diameter 8 cm.
(b) What is the circumference of the smaller pulley?

2 A new wire mesh fence is to be put round a **circular** training ring.

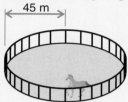

The radius of the ring is 45 m.

(a) Calculate, to the nearest metre, the length of fence needed.
(b) Calculate, to the nearest 10 square metres, the area of the ring.   Edexcel

3 The diagram represents a circular training track.

The diameter of the track, AB, is 70 metres.
Alisa and Bryony have a race.
Alisa runs along the diameter from A to B and back again.
Bryony starts at A and runs all the way round the track to A again.
Work out how much further Bryony runs than Alisa.   Edexcel

A |← 70 m →| B

4

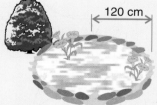

120 cm

The diagram shows a **circular** garden pond.
The radius of the pond is 120 cm.
Calculate, to the nearest 10 cm, the circumference of the pond.   Edexcel

5 The diagram shows a cardboard ring.
The inner radius is 9 cm.
The outer radius is 11 cm.

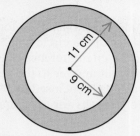

11 cm

9 cm

Calculate the area of the ring.

6 Susie has a new bike.
The radius of its wheels is 30 cm.
(a) Work out the circumference of one of the wheels.

Susie rides her bike to school which is 1 km from her home.
(b) How many times will one of the wheels of Susie's bike turn on the way to school?   Edexcel

7 A circular table top has radius 1.3 m.
(a) Calculate the circumference of the top of the table.
(b) The top of the table is varnished.
1 litre of varnish covers 5 m².
Find, correct to one decimal place, the number of litres of varnish needed to cover the top of the table.

8

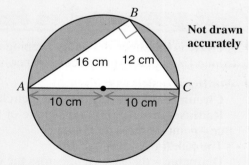

Not drawn accurately

B

16 cm   12 cm

A 10 cm   10 cm C

The diagram shows a right-angled triangle ABC and a circle.
A, B and C are points on the circumference of the circle.
AC is a diameter of the circle.
The radius of the circle is 10 cm.
$AB = 16$ cm and $BC = 12$ cm.

Work out the area of the shaded part of the circle.
Give your answer correct to the nearest cm².   Edexcel

CHAPTER 25

Area and Volume

3-dimensional shapes (or solids)

These are all examples of 3-dimensional shapes.

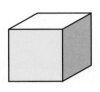

Cube

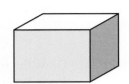

Cuboid

Cylinder

Sphere

Triangular prism

Pyramid with square base

Cone

What other 3-dimensional shapes do you know?

These 3-dimensional shapes are called **prisms**.

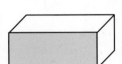

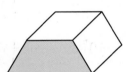

What do prisms have in common?
Draw a different 3-dimensional shape which is a prism.

Making and drawing 3-dimensional shapes

Nets

3-dimensional shapes can be made using **nets**.

This is the net of a cube.

The net can be folded to make a cube.

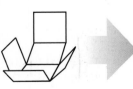

2-dimensional drawings of 3-dimensional shapes

Isometric drawings are used to draw 3-dimensional shapes.
Here are two isometric drawings of a cube of side 2 cm.

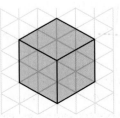

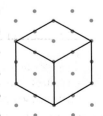

239

EXAMPLE

This prism is 6 cm long.
The ends are equilateral triangles with sides of 3 cm.
Draw an accurate net of the prism.

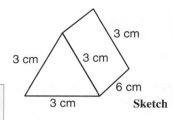

Sketch

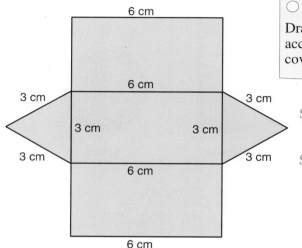

Drawing triangles accurately was covered in Chapter 19.

Step 1: Draw the rectangular faces of the prism. Each rectangle is 6 cm long and 3 cm wide.

Step 2: The ends of the prism are equilateral triangles.
The length of each side of the triangles is 3 cm.
Use your compasses to construct the equilateral triangles.

Naming parts of a solid shape

Each flat surface is called a **face**.
Two faces meet at an **edge**.
Edges of a shape meet at a corner, or point, called a **vertex**.
The plural of vertex is **vertices**.

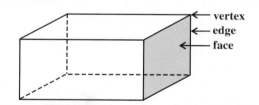

← vertex
← edge
← face

Exercise 25.1

1 This is a cuboid.

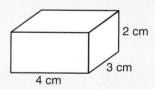

2 cm
3 cm
4 cm

Sarah has started to draw a net of the cuboid on squared paper.

(a) Copy the diagram.
(b) Complete the net of the cuboid.

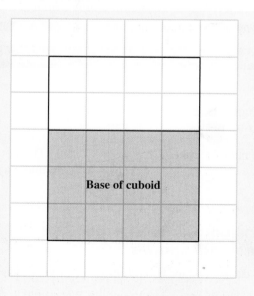

Base of cuboid

2 A cube has edges of length 3 cm.
Use squared paper to draw an accurate net of the cube.

3 Use squared paper to draw an accurate net of this cuboid.

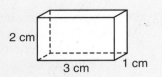

2 cm
3 cm
1 cm

4 Draw an accurate net for each of these 3-dimensional shapes.

(a)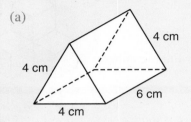

4 cm
4 cm
6 cm
4 cm

(b)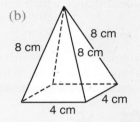

8 cm
8 cm
8 cm
4 cm
4 cm

(c)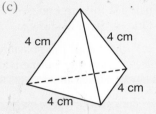

4 cm
4 cm
4 cm
4 cm

5 The diagram shows part of a net of a cube.

(a) In how many different ways can you complete the net? Draw each of your nets.

(b) Explain why the diagram above is **not** the net of a cube.

6 Look at these diagrams of 3-dimensional shapes.
Dotted lines are used to show the edges which cannot be seen when you look at the shape from one side.

(a)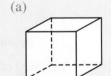

(b)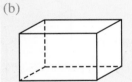

(c)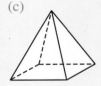

(d)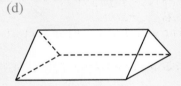

Copy and complete this table.

	Name of shape	Number of faces	Number of vertices	Number of edges
(a)				
(b)				
(c)				
(d)				

7 The diagram shows a pyramid.
A model of the pyramid is to be made using straws.
The straws are each 10 cm long and are joined using pipe cleaners.

(a) How many edges does the pyramid have?
(b) How many vertices does the pyramid have?
(c) How many straws are needed to make the pyramid?
(d) What is the total length of the edges of the pyramid?

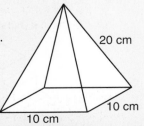

20 cm
10 cm
10 cm

8 (a) Draw these 3-dimensional shapes on isometric paper.
  (i) A cube of side 3 cm.
  (ii) A 3 cm by 2 cm by 1 cm cuboid.
  (iii) A cuboid measuring 3 cm by 4 cm by 5 cm.
 (b) Draw a net for each of the 3-dimensional shapes in (a).

9 There are 8 different 3-dimensional shapes which can be made using 4 linking cubes.
One of them is shown.

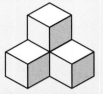

 (a) Make all the possible 3-dimensional shapes using four linking cubes.
 (b) Draw the 3-dimensional shapes on isometric paper.

Plans and Elevations

When an architect designs a building he has to draw diagrams to show what the building will look like from different directions.
These diagrams are called **plans and elevations**.

The view of a building looking from above is called the **plan**.
The views of a building from the front or sides are called **elevations**.

To show all the information about a 3-dimensional shape we often need to draw several diagrams.

> **EXAMPLE**
>
> The diagram shows a 3-dimensional shape.
> Draw the plan and the elevations **A**, **B** and **C**.
>
>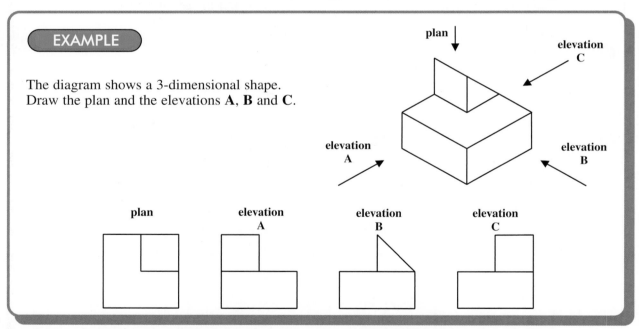

Exercise 25.2

1 Draw a sketch to show the plan view of each of these 3-dimensional shapes.

 (a) **a staircase** (b) **a pyramid** (c) **a cup**

2 Each of these 3-dimensional shapes has been made using 5 linking cubes of side 1 cm.
On squared paper, draw diagrams to show the plan and the elevations **A**, **B** and **C** of each shape.

(a)

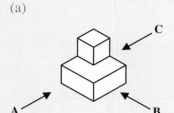

(b)

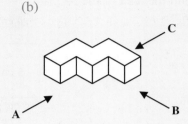

(c)

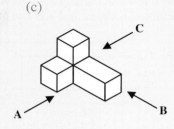

3 The diagram shows a plastic cylinder of height 3 cm and radius 2 cm
with a hole of radius 1 cm drilled through the centre.
Draw the plan and a side elevation of the cylinder.

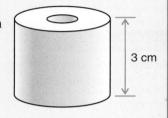

4 The diagram shows an open box
containing 3 balls of radius 2 cm.

(a) Draw a plan of the box.
(b) Draw an elevation of the box
from the direction marked **A**.

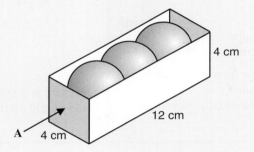

5 The plans and elevations of 3-dimensional shapes made from linking cubes of side 1 cm are
shown. Draw each of the 3-dimensional shapes on isometric paper.

(a)   **Plan**   **Left - side**   **Front**   **Right - side**
                           elevation   **elevation**   **elevation**

(b)   **Plan**   **Left - side**   **Front**   **Right - side**
                           elevation   **elevation**   **elevation**

(c)   **Plan**   **Left - side**   **Front**   **Right - side**
                           elevation   **elevation**   **elevation**

Area and Volume . . . . Area and Volume . . . .

Opposite faces of a cuboid are the same shape and size.

To find the surface area of a cuboid find the area of the six rectangular faces and add the answers.

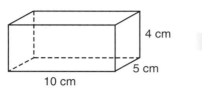

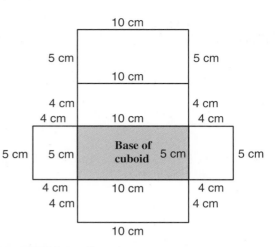

The surface area of a cuboid can also be found by finding the area of its net.

Volume

Volume is the amount of space occupied by a 3-dimensional shape.

This **cube** is 1 cm long, 1 cm wide and 1 cm high. It has a volume of **1 cubic centimetre**. The volume of this cube can be written as 1 cm³.

Volume = 1 cm³

Small volumes can be measured using cubic millimetres (mm³).
Large volumes can be measured using cubic metres (m³).

Volume of a cuboid

The formula for the volume of a cuboid is:
Volume = length × breadth × height
This formula can be written using letters as:
$$V = l \times b \times h$$

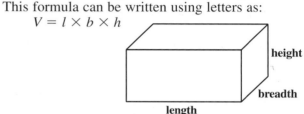

A **cube** is a special cuboid in which the length, breadth and height all have the same measurement.
$$V = l^3$$

EXAMPLE

A cuboid measures 30 cm by 15 cm by 12 cm.
(a) Find the surface area of the cuboid.
(b) Find the volume of the cuboid.

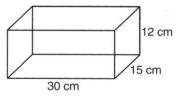

(a)

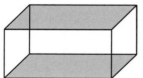

Top and bottom faces.
Each 30 cm × 15 cm.

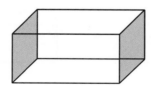

Two side faces.
Each 15 cm × 12 cm.

Remember
The area of a rectangle is given by the formula:
Area = length × breadth
$A = l \times b$

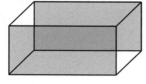

Front and back faces.
Each 30 cm × 12 cm.

Surface area = (2 × 30 × 15) + (2 × 15 × 12) + (2 × 30 × 12)
= 900 + 360 + 720
= 1980 cm²

(b) Volume = length × breadth × height
= 30 cm × 15 cm × 12 cm
= 5400 cm³

Exercise 25.3   Do not use a calculator for questions 1 to 5.

1   This is a cuboid.
(a)   Draw a net of the cuboid on one-centimetre squared paper.
(b)   Calculate the area of the net.
(c)   What is the surface area of the cuboid?

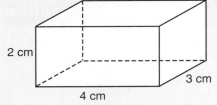

2 cm   3 cm   4 cm

2   These cuboids are made using one-centimetre cubes.
What is the volume of each cuboid?

(a)   (b) 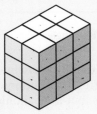   (c)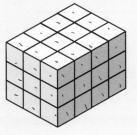

3   Large cubes are made from small cubes of edge 1 cm.
(a)   How many small cubes are in each of the large cubes?
(b)   What is the surface area of each large cube?

(i) 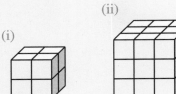   (ii)   (iii)   (iv)

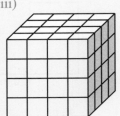 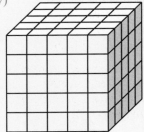

4   Calculate the volumes and surface areas of these cubes and cuboids.

(a)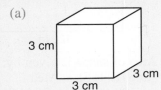
3 cm   3 cm   3 cm

(b)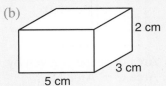
2 cm   3 cm   5 cm

(c)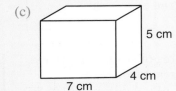
5 cm   4 cm   7 cm

5   Shapes are made using one-centimetre cubes.
Find the volume and surface area of each shape.

(a)   (b)    (c)   (d) 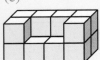   (e)   (f)

6   Calculate the volumes and surface areas of these cuboids.
Where necessary give your answer to an appropriate degree of accuracy.
(a)   3 cm by 5 cm by 10 cm.
(b)   2.4 cm by 3.6 cm by 6 cm.
(c)   18 cm by 24 cm by 45 cm.
(d)   3.2 cm by 4.8 cm by 6.3 cm.
(e)   5.8 cm by 10.6 cm by 14.9 cm.

Finding areas by splitting shapes up

In earlier chapters you found the areas of various shapes by counting squares and using formulae. Here is a reminder of some of those shapes.

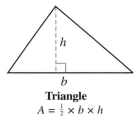

Triangle
$A = \frac{1}{2} \times b \times h$

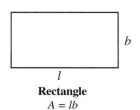

Rectangle
$A = lb$

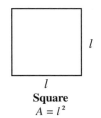

Square
$A = l^2$

We are going to look at shapes formed by combining rectangles, squares and triangles.
You can find the areas of such shapes by splitting them up into rectangles, squares and triangles.
There are several ways to split up most shapes, but they should all give the same answer.

EXAMPLES

Calculate the areas of these shapes.

1

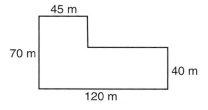

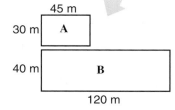

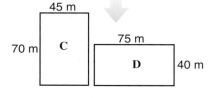

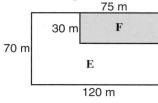

Area of shape is given by:
Area A + Area B
$= (45 \times 30) + (120 \times 40)$
$= 1350 + 4800$
$= 6150\,\text{m}^2$

Area of shape is given by:
Area C + Area D
$= (45 \times 70) + (75 \times 40)$
$= 3150 + 3000$
$= 6150\,\text{m}^2$

Area of shape is given by:
Area (E + F) − Area F
$= (120 \times 70) - (75 \times 30)$
$= 8400 - 2250$
$= 6150\,\text{m}^2$

All the methods give the same answer so use the method you find easiest.

2

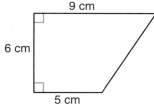

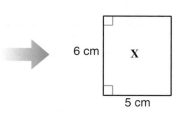

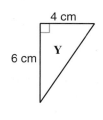

Area of shape is given by: Area X + Area Y
$= (6 \times 5) + \left(\frac{1}{2} \times 6 \times 4\right)$
$= 30 + 12$
$= 42\,\text{cm}^2$

Do not use a calculator for questions 1 to 3.

1   These letters have been drawn on centimetre-squared paper.

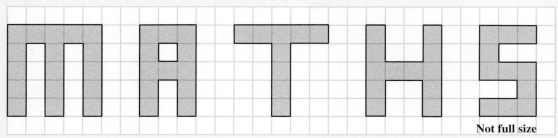

Not full size

(a)   Find the area of each letter.   (b)   Which letter has the largest area?

(c)   Which letter has the smallest area?   (d)   Which two letters have the same area?

2   A square has sides of length 5 cm.
A square with sides of 2 cm is cut from the corner
of the larger square.

(a)   What is the area of the larger square?

(b)   What is the area of the smaller square?

(c)   Find the shaded area in the diagram.

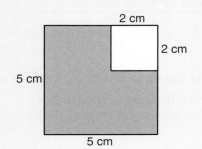

3   Find the areas of these shapes which are made up of rectangles and squares.

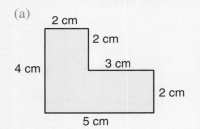
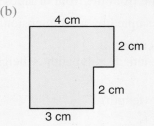
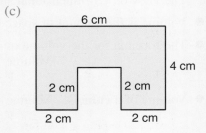

4   Find the areas of these shapes which are made up of rectangles.

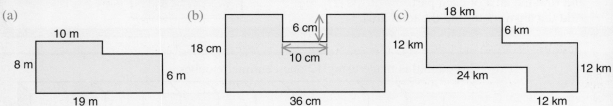

5   Find the areas of these shapes which are made up of rectangles and right-angled triangles.

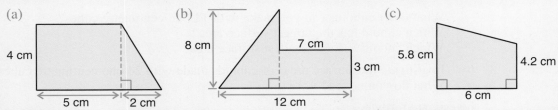

6 Find the area of the shaded shape.

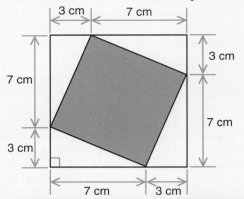

3 cm   7 cm

3 cm

7 cm

7 cm

3 cm

7 cm   3 cm

7 The diagram shows a car park.
Calculate the area of the car park.

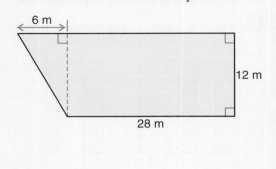

6 m

12 m

28 m

What you need to know

- **Faces**, **vertices** (corners) and **edges**.
  For example, a cube has 6 faces, 8 vertices and 12 edges.

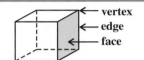

vertex
edge
face

- A **net** can be used to make a solid shape.

- **Isometric paper** is used to make
  2-dimensional drawings of 3-dimensional shapes.

- **Plans and Elevations**
  The view of a 3-dimensional shape looking from above is called a **plan**.
  The view of a 3-dimensional shape from the front or sides is called an **elevation**.

- Volume is the amount of space occupied by a 3-dimensional shape.

- The formula for the volume of a **cuboid** is:
  $$\text{Volume} = \text{length} \times \text{breadth} \times \text{height}$$
  $$V = l \times b \times h$$

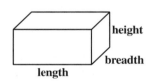

height
breadth
length

- Volume of a **cube** is: $\text{Volume} = (\text{length})^3$
  $$V = l^3$$

- To find the area of complex shapes:
  Split the shape into rectangles, squares and triangles
  and find the area of each part.
  Add the answers to find the total area.

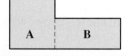

A   B

IDEAS FOR INVESTIGATION

(a) This cuboid is made using 12 one-centimetre cubes.

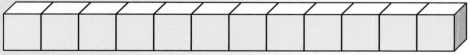

Find the surface area of the cuboid.

What other cuboids can you make with 12 one-centimetre cubes?
Which cuboid has the largest surface area?
Which cuboid has the smallest surface area?

(b) Investigate the surface areas of cuboids made with 24 one-centimetre cubes.
What do you notice?

Investigate further.

Review Exercise

Do not use a calculator for questions 1 to 8.

1 (a) Write down the mathematical name of each of these three dimensional shapes.

(i)

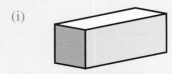

(ii)

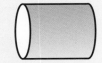

(iii)

(b) Here is the net of a three dimensional shape.

Write down the mathematical name of the three dimensional shape.

Edexcel

2 This shape is a triangular prism.

How many faces, edges and vertices has the triangular prism?

3 The diagram shows a cuboid.

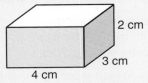

2 cm

3 cm

4 cm

(a) Draw an accurate net of the cuboid on one-centimetre square paper.

(b) Work out the total surface area of the cuboid.

4 (a) Copy and complete the table to show the areas and perimeters of the shapes **G**, **H** and **I**.

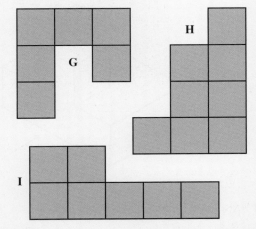

H

G

I

Shape	Area (centimetre squares)	Perimeter (centimetres)
G		
H		
I		

(b) Draw a shape that has the same area as shape **G**, but a different perimeter.

Edexcel

5 Which of these shapes is the net of a cube?

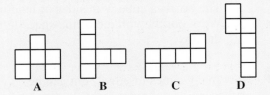

A   B   C   D

6 The diagram represents an L-shaped room whose corners are all right angles.

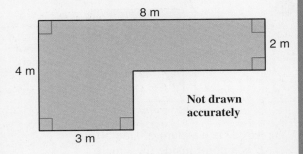

8 m

2 m

4 m

Not drawn accurately

3 m

(a) Work out the perimeter of the room.

(b) Work out the area of the room.

Edexcel

Area and Volume . . . Area and Volume . . . Area and Volume . . . .

25

7 This 3-dimensional shape has been made using linking cubes of side 1 cm.
On squared paper, draw diagrams to show the plan and the elevation from **X**.

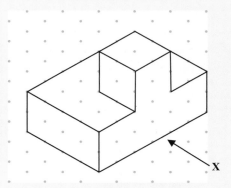

X

8 Two views of a model are shown.

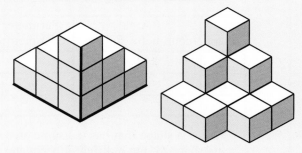

The model is made using one centimetre cubes.
(a) (i) What is the volume of the model?
    (ii) What is the surface area of the model?
(b) The model is put into a box.
The box is a cube with sides of length 3 cm.
Work out the volume of the space left in the box.

9 How many cubes of edge 2 cm can be packed into a cuboid which has dimensions 7 cm by 12 cm by 6 cm?

10

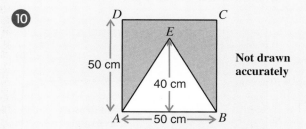

D   *C*
     E
50 cm   **Not drawn accurately**
    40 cm
A ← 50 cm → *B*

ABCD is a square of side 50 cm.
E is a point inside the square.
E is 40 cm from the line *AB*.
Work out the area of the shaded region.

Edexcel

11 The diagram shows a car park.
Calculate the area of the car park.

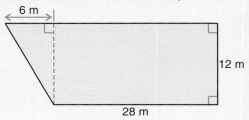

6 m
12 m
28 m

12 The diagram shows a cuboid.

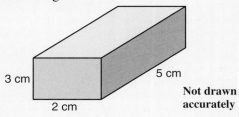

3 cm   5 cm
    2 cm   **Not drawn accurately**

(a) Work out the volume of the cuboid.
(b) On isometric paper, make an accurate full-size drawing of the cuboid.

Edexcel

13 A block of wood measures 15 cm by 8 cm by 3 cm.
A letter F is cut out of the block of wood, as shown.

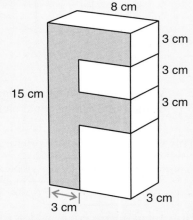

8 cm
3 cm
3 cm
15 cm   3 cm
     3 cm
3 cm

(a) Calculate the shaded area.
(b) Calculate the volume of the letter F.

14 Matt has two pieces of wood.

A cuboid which measures 6 cm by 5 cm by 4 cm.
A cube of edge 5 cm.

(a) Which piece of wood has the larger volume?
(b) Which piece of wood has the larger surface area?
Show working for each of your answers.

CHAPTER 26

Transformations

The movement of a shape from one position to another is called a **transformation**.
The change in position of the shape can be described in terms of a **reflection**, a **rotation** or a **translation**.
Later in the chapter you will meet another transformation, called an **enlargement**.

Reflection

Look at this diagram.
It shows a **reflection** of a shape in the line PQ.
The line PQ is sometimes called a **mirror line**.
Place a mirror on the line PQ and look at
the reflection.
You should see that the image of the
shape is the same distance from the
mirror as the original.

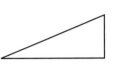
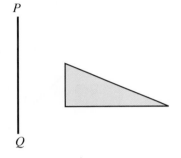

In this diagram the shape $WXYZ$ has been reflected in the line AB to $W_1X_1Y_1Z_1$.

If you join the points W and W_1:
    the distance from W to the mirror line is the same
    as the distance from the mirror line to W_1,
    the line WW_1 is at right angles to the mirror line.

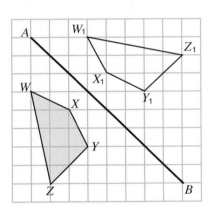

Notation
$W_1X_1Y_1Z_1$ is the **image** of $WXYZ$.

When a shape is reflected it stays the same shape and
size but it is turned over.

For a reflection we need:
    a mirror line.

EXAMPLE

Copy the shape P onto squared paper.
Draw the reflection of shape P in the y axis.

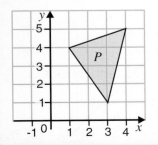

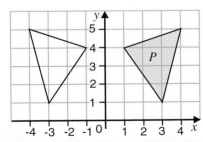

Notice that:
$(1, 4) \rightarrow (-1, 4)$
$(4, 5) \rightarrow (-4, 5)$
$(3, 1) \rightarrow (-3, 1)$
Can you see a pattern?

1 Copy each of the following shapes and draw the reflection of the shape in the line *AB*.

(a)

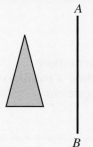

(b)

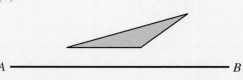

(c)

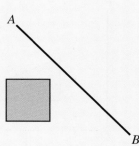

(d)

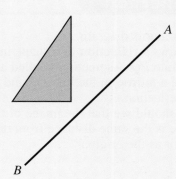

2 Copy each of the following shapes onto squared paper and draw the image of the shape after reflection in the line *AB*.

(a)

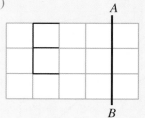

(b)

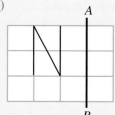

(c)

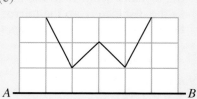

(d)

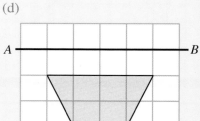

(e)

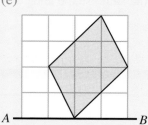

(f)

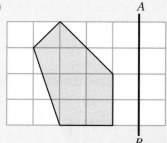

3 Copy each of the following shapes onto squared paper and draw the image of the shape after reflection in the line *AB*.

(a)

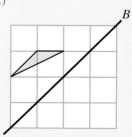

(b)

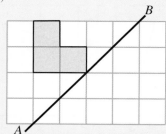

(c)

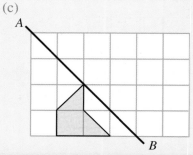

4 Copy each of the following diagrams onto squared paper and draw the reflection of each shape in the line given.

(a)

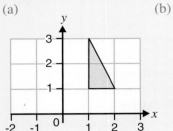

Reflect in the *y* axis.

(b)

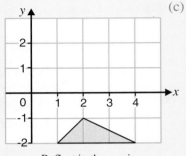

Reflect in the *x* axis.

(c)

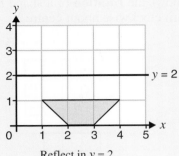

Reflect in *y* = 2.

(d)

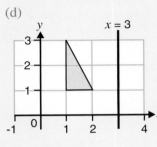

Reflect in *x* = 3.

(e)

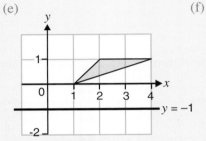

Reflect in *y* = −1.

(f)

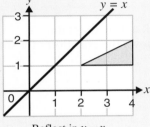

Reflect in *y* = *x*.

5 Copy the diagram onto squared paper.
Draw the image of the shape after:
(a) a reflection in the *x* axis,
(b) a reflection in the *y* axis,
(c) a reflection in the line *x* = 3,
(d) a reflection in the line *x* = −1,
(e) a reflection in the line *y* = *x*.

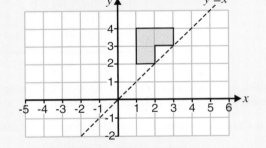

6 In the diagram, *P* is the point (2, 1).
Find the coordinates of the image of *P* under a reflection in:
(a) the *x* axis,
(b) the *y* axis,
(c) the line *x* = 1,
(d) the line *y* = −1.

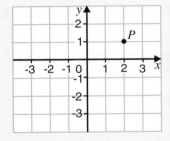

7 The diagram shows a quadrilateral *ABCD*.
Give the coordinates of *B* after:
(a) a reflection in the *x* axis,
(b) a reflection in the *y* axis,
(c) a reflection in the line *x* = 4,
(d) a reflection in the line *x* = −1.

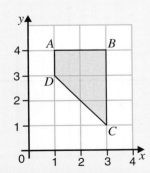

Rotation

Look at this diagram.
It shows the **rotation** of a shape P through a $\frac{1}{4}$ of a turn clockwise about centre X.

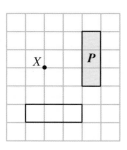

When describing rotations the direction of turn can be **clockwise** or **anticlockwise**.

Remember: clockwise

anticlockwise

Look at this diagram.
It shows the **rotation** of a shape P through 90° anticlockwise about O (the origin).

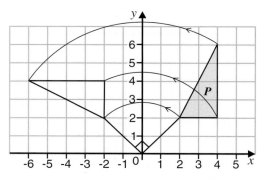

All points on shape P are turned through the same angle about the same point. This point is called the **centre of rotation**.

When a shape is rotated it stays the same shape and size but its **position** on the page changes.

For a rotation we need: a centre of rotation, an amount of turn, a direction of turn.

EXAMPLE

Copy triangle P onto squared paper.
Draw the new position of triangle P after it has been rotated 90° clockwise, about O.

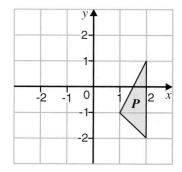 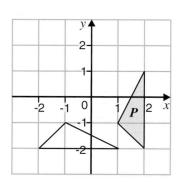

254

Exercise 26.2

1 Copy each of these shapes onto squared paper.
   Draw the new position of each shape after the rotation given.

(a)

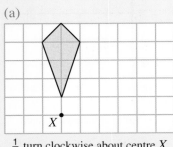

$\frac{1}{4}$ turn clockwise about centre X.

(b)

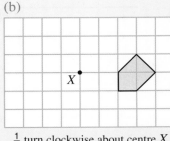

$\frac{1}{2}$ turn clockwise about centre X.

(c)

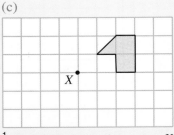

$\frac{1}{4}$ turn anticlockwise about centre X.

(d)

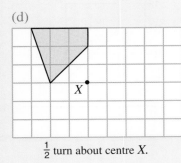

$\frac{1}{2}$ turn about centre X.

(e)

$\frac{3}{4}$ turn clockwise about centre X.

(f)

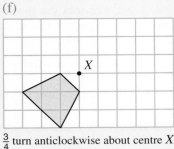

$\frac{3}{4}$ turn anticlockwise about centre X.

2 Copy each of the following shapes onto squared paper.
   Draw the new position of the shape after the rotation given.

(a)

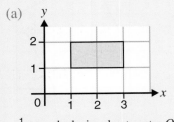

$\frac{1}{4}$ turn clockwise about centre O.

(b)

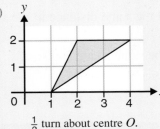

$\frac{1}{2}$ turn about centre O.

(c)

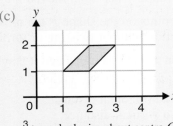

$\frac{3}{4}$ turn clockwise about centre O.

3 Copy each of the following shapes onto squared paper.
   Draw the new position of the shape after the rotation given.

(a)

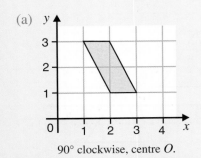

90° clockwise, centre O.

(b)

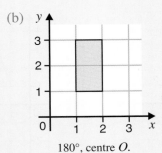

180°, centre O.

(c)

270° clockwise, centre O.

4 Copy each of the following shapes onto squared paper.
Draw the new position of the shape after the rotation given.

(a)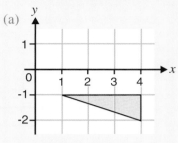

90° clockwise, centre *O*.

(b)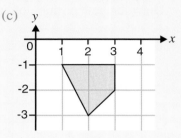

270° clockwise, centre *O*.

(c)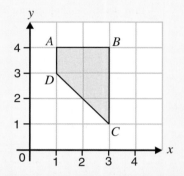

90° anticlockwise, centre *O*.

5 The diagram shows a quadrilateral *ABCD*.

(a) Give the coordinates of *B* after:
   (i)   a rotation through 90°, clockwise about (0, 0),
   (ii)   a rotation through 90°, anticlockwise about (0, 0),
   (iii) a rotation through 180°, about (0, 0).

(b) Give the coordinates of *C* after:
   (i)   a rotation through 270°, clockwise about (0, 0),
   (ii)   a rotation through 270°, anticlockwise about (0, 0).

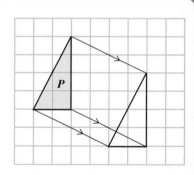

Translation

Look at this diagram.
It shows a **translation** of a shape *P*.

The shape *P* has been moved 4 units to the right and 2 units down.

All points on the shape *P* are moved the same distance in the same direction without twisting or turning.

When a shape is translated it stays the same shape and size.

For a translation we need:
    a horizontal distance,
    a vertical distance.

EXAMPLE

Copy shape *P* onto squared paper.
Draw the new position of shape *P* after it has been translated 4 units to the right and 3 units down.

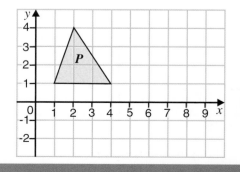

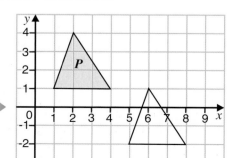

1 Copy the shape onto squared paper.

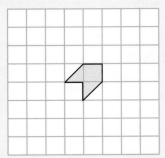

Draw the new position of the shape after each of the following translations:
(a)   2 units to the right and 3 units up,
(b)   1 unit to the right and 2 units down,
(c)   3 units to the left and 2 units up,
(d)   1 unit to the left and 3 units down.

2 Copy the shape onto squared paper.
Draw the new position of the shape after
each of the following translations:
(a)   3 units to the right and 2 units up,
(b)   2 units to the right and 3 units down,
(c)   2 units to the left and 3 units up,
(d)   2 units to the left and 3 units down.

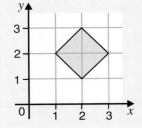

3 The diagram shows a quadrilateral $ABCD$.
Give the coordinates of B after the shape has been translated:
(a)   2 units to the right and 1 unit up,
(b)   2 units to the left and 2 units up,
(c)   1 unit to the right and 3 units down,
(d)   2 units to the left and 3 units down.

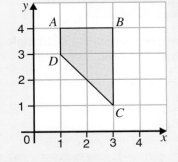

4 Describe the translation which moves:
(a) $X(1, 1)$ onto $P(3, 2)$,   (b) $X(1, 1)$ onto $Q(2, -1)$,
(c) $X(1, 1)$ onto $R(-2, 2)$,   (d) $X(1, 1)$ onto $S(-2, -1)$.

5 The diagram shows a quadrilateral S.

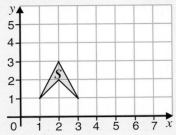

Copy S onto squared paper.
(a) S is translated 3 units to the right and 2 units up.
        Draw the new position of S on your diagram.
(b)   Describe the translation that would move S back to its original position.

Enlargement

This diagram shows another transformation, called an **enlargement**.
It shows an enlargement of a shape P with scale factor 2 and centre O.

When a shape is enlarged:
- **angles** remain unchanged,
- all **lengths** are multiplied by a **scale factor**.

Scale factor $= \dfrac{\text{new length}}{\text{original length}}$

For an enlargement we need:
- a centre of enlargement,
- a scale factor.

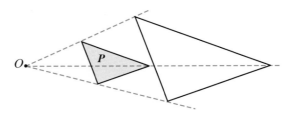

Similar figures

When one figure is an enlargement of another, the two figures are **similar**.

For example, figures **B** and **C** are enlargements of figure **A**.
Figures **A**, **B** and **C** are similar.

When two figures are **similar**:
- their **shapes** are the same,
- their **angles** are the same,
- corresponding **lengths** are in the same ratio,
- this ratio is the **scale factor** of the enlargement.

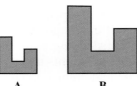

A   B   C

EXAMPLE

Draw an enlargement of triangle ABC,
with scale factor 3, centre O.

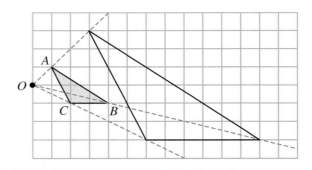

Exercise 26.4

1. The shapes in this question have been drawn accurately.
   (a) Explain why these two shapes are not similar to each other.

   (b) Which two of these shapes are similar to each other?

   P   Q

   R

2 Which of the following must be similar to each other?
(a) Two circles. (b) Two kites. (c) Two parallelograms. (d) Two squares. (e) Two rectangles.

3 Shape A is enlarged to make shape B.
What is the scale factor of the enlargement?

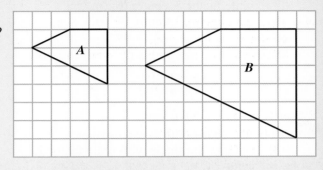

4 Copy each diagram onto squared paper and draw an enlargement with the given scale factor.

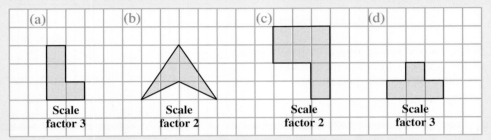

(a) Scale factor 3
(b) Scale factor 2
(c) Scale factor 2
(d) Scale factor 3

5 Copy the following shapes and draw the enlargement, with scale factor 2, centre O.

(a)

(b)
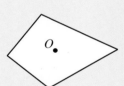

(c)
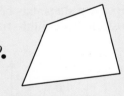

6 Copy the following shapes onto squared paper and draw the enlargement given.
(a) Scale factor 2, centre X.
(b) Scale factor 3, centre X.

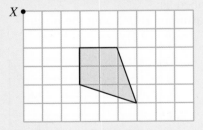

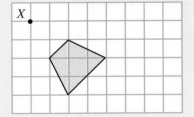

7 Copy the following shapes onto squared paper and draw the enlargements given.
(a) Scale factor 2, centre $(0, 0)$.
(b) Scale factor 3, centre $(0, 0)$.

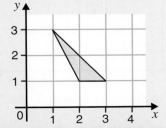

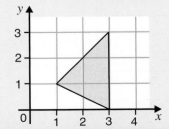

8 The diagram shows a quadrilateral *ABCD*.

Give the coordinates of *B* after an enlargement:
(a) scale factor 2, centre (0, 0),
(b) scale factor 3, centre (0, 0).

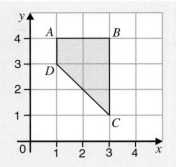

9 Copy the shape onto squared paper.
(a) Enlarge the shape with scale factor 2, centre *X*.
(b) Enlarge the shape with scale factor 2, centre *Y*.
(c) Enlarge the shape with scale factor 2, centre *Z*.
(d) What do you notice about the positions of the centres of enlargement and the positions of the enlarged shapes?

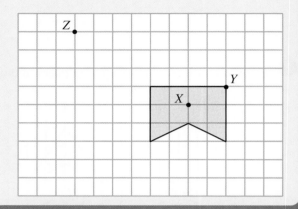

Describing transformations

Look at each of these diagrams.
In each case a shape has been moved to a new position by a **single transformation**.

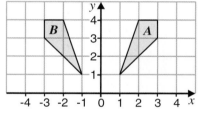

The transformation which takes *A* onto *B* is described as:
a **reflection** in the *y* axis.

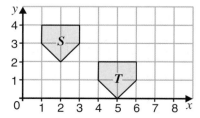

The transformation which takes *S* onto *T* is described as:
a **translation** 3 units to the right and 2 units down.

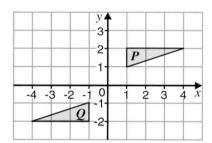

The transformation which takes *P* onto *Q* is described as:
a **rotation** of 180° about the origin.

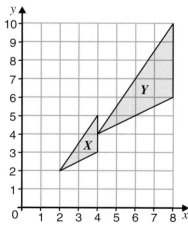

The transformation which takes *X* onto *Y* is described as:
an **enlargement** scale factor 2, centre (0, 0).

Exercise 26.5

1 Which of these transformations takes *X* onto *Y* in each diagram?
reflection   **rotation**   **translation**   **enlargement**

(a)

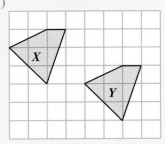

(b)

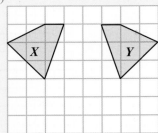

(c)

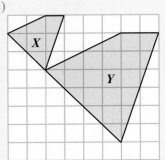

(d)

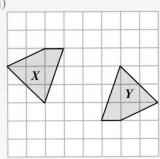

2 Describe fully the single transformation which takes *P* onto *Q* in each diagram.

(a)

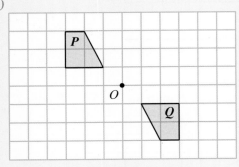

(b)

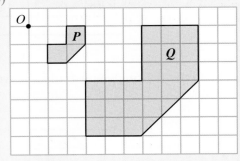

3 Describe fully the single
transformation which takes
(a) **L₁**, onto **L₂**,
(b) **L₁**, onto **L₃**,
(c) **L₁**, onto **L₄**,
(d) **L₁**, onto **L₅**,
(e) **L₁**, onto **L₆**.

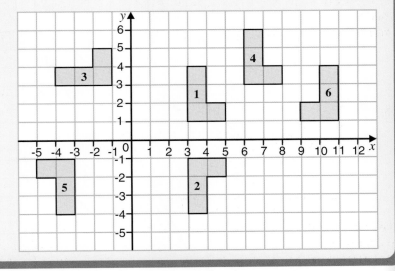

4 Describe fully the single transformation which takes
    (a)   *T* onto *U*,   (b)   *T* onto *V*,   (c)   *T* onto *W*.

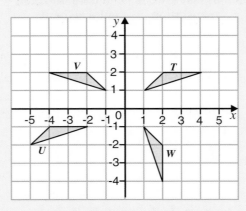

5 Describe fully the single transformation which takes
    (a)   *A* onto *B*,   (b)   *A* onto *C*,   (c)   *A* onto *D*.

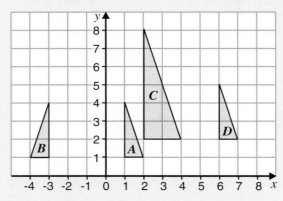

6 Describe fully the single transformation which takes
    (a)   *P* onto *Q*,   (b)   *P* onto *R*,   (c)   *P* onto *S*,   (d)   *P* onto *T*.

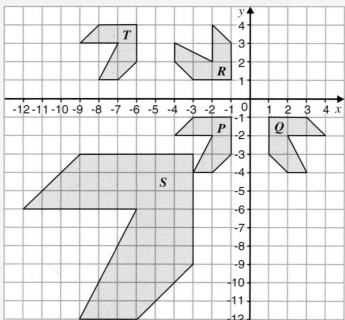

- The movement of a shape from one position to another is called a **transformation**.
- **Single transformations** can be described in terms of a reflection, a rotation, a translation or an enlargement.
- **Reflection**: The image of the shape is the same distance from the mirror line as the original.
- **Rotation**: All points are turned through the same angle about the same point, called a centre of rotation.
- **Translation**: All points are moved the same distance in the same direction without twisting or turning.
- **Enlargement**: All lengths are multiplied by a scale factor. Scale factor = $\frac{\text{new length}}{\text{original length}}$
- When two figures are **similar**:
  - their **shapes** are the same,
  - their **angles** are the same,
  - corresponding **lengths** are in the same ratio,
  - this ratio is the **scale factor** of the enlargement.

- All circles are similar to each other.
- All squares are similar to each other.

- How to fully describe a transformation.

Transformation	Image same shape and size?	Details needed to describe the transformation
Reflection	Yes	Mirror line, sometimes given as an equation.
Rotation	Yes	Centre of rotation, amount of turn, direction of turn.
Translation	Yes	Horizontal movement and vertical movement.
Enlargement	No	Centre of enlargement, scale factor.

IDEAS FOR INVESTIGATION

Enlargement and Perimeter

(a) These shapes are **similar** because shape B is an enlargement of shape A.

Shape A

Shape B

What is the scale factor of the enlargement?
What is the ratio,   perimeter of shape A : perimeter of shape B?
What do you notice?

(b) These shapes are **similar** because shape Q is an enlargement of shape P.

Shape P

Shape Q

What is the scale factor of the enlargement?
What is the ratio,   perimeter of shape P : perimeter of shape Q?
What do you notice?
Investigate for other shapes.

1 A wallpaper pattern is designed using rectangles as shown.

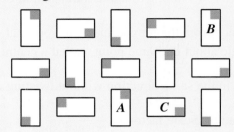

Using only one of the words reflection, rotation, translation or enlargement, describe a transformation which would
(a)   take *A* onto *B*,
(b)   take *A* onto *C*.

2 Copy the diagram.

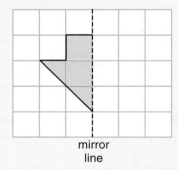

mirror
line

Draw the reflection of the shape in the mirror line.   Edexcel

3 Copy the diagram.

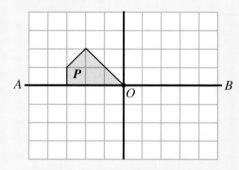

(a)   Reflect shape *P* in the line *AB*. Label the new position *Q*.

(b)   Rotate shape *P* through $\frac{1}{4}$ turn clockwise, about centre *O*. Label the new position *R*.

(c)   Rotate shape *P* through 180° about centre *O*. Label the new position *S*.

4 Copy the diagram.

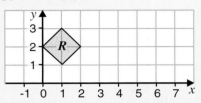

Shape *R* is reflected in the line $x = 3$. Draw the new position of *R* on your diagram.

5 Copy the diagram.

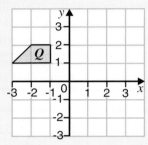

Shape *Q* is rotated 90° anticlockwise about centre (0, 0).
Draw the new position of *Q* on your diagram.

6 Copy the diagram.

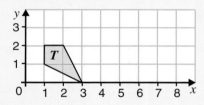

Shape *T* is translated 3 units to the right and 2 units up.
Draw the new position of *T* on your diagram.

7 A shaded shape is shown.

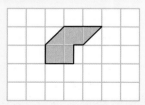

Copy the shape onto squared paper.
Draw an enlargement, scale factor 2, of the shaded shape.   Edexcel

8 Copy the diagram.

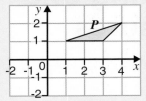

(a) Shape *P* is reflected in the line $y = -1$.
Draw the new position of *P* on your diagram.

(b) Draw an enlargement of shape *P*, scale factor 3, centre (0, 0).

9

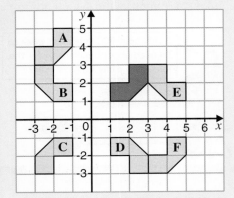

(a) Give the letter of the finishing position,
  (i) after the shaded shape is reflected in the *y* axis,
  (ii) after the shaded shape is rotated $\frac{1}{2}$ turn about (0, 0),
  (iii) after the shaded shape is translated 4 units left and 2 units up.

(b) Describe fully the single transformation which will map the shaded shape onto **E**.

10 Copy the diagram.

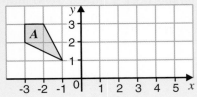

(a) *A* is translated 4 units to the right and 1 unit down.
Draw the new position of *A* on your diagram.

(b) Describe the translation that takes *A* back to its original position.

11 The shape **P** has been drawn on a grid, as shown.

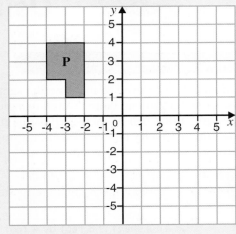

Copy the diagram.

(a) Reflect the shape **P** in the *y* axis. Label the image **Q**.

(b) Rotate the shape **Q** through 180° about (0, 0). Label this image **R**.

(c) Describe fully the single transformation which maps the shape **P** to the shape **R**.   Edexcel

12 The diagram shows the positions of triangles *A*, *B*, *C*, *D* and *E*.

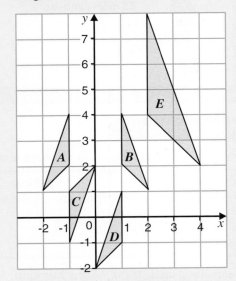

Describe fully the single transformation that takes

(a) *A* onto *B*,
(b) *C* onto *D*,
(c) *A* onto *D*,
(d) *D* onto *A*,
(e) *B* onto *E*.

Understanding and Using Measures

Units of measurement

Different units can be used to measure the same quantity. For example:

The same **length** can be measured using centimetres, kilometres, inches, miles, …

The same **mass** can be measured using grams, kilograms, pounds, ounces, …

The same **capacity** can be measured using litres, millilitres, gallons, pints, …

There are two sorts of units in common use − **metric** units and **imperial** units.

Activity   Which of the units mentioned in these statements are metric and which are imperial?

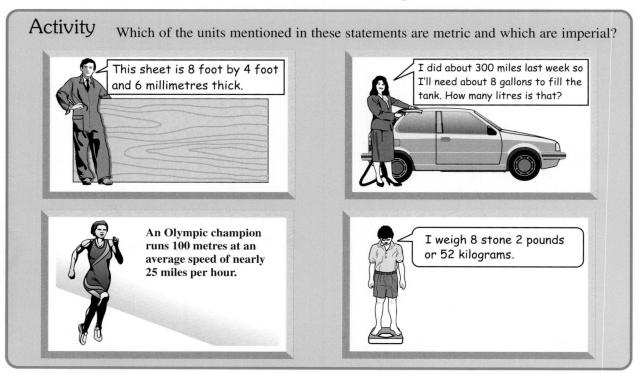

This sheet is 8 foot by 4 foot and 6 millimetres thick.

I did about 300 miles last week so I'll need about 8 gallons to fill the tank. How many litres is that?

An Olympic champion runs 100 metres at an average speed of nearly 25 miles per hour.

I weigh 8 stone 2 pounds or 52 kilograms.

Metric units

The common metric units used to measure length, mass (weight) and capacity (volume) are shown below.

Length	Mass	Capacity and volume
1 kilometre (km) = 1000 metres (m)	1 tonne (t) = 1000 kilograms (kg)	1 litre = 1000 millilitres (ml)
1 m = 100 centimetres (cm)	1 kg = 1000 grams (g)	1 cm³ = 1 ml
1 m = 1000 millimetres (mm)		
1 cm = 10 mm		

Kilo means thousand, 1000.   So, a **kilo**gram is one thousand grams.

For example: 3 kilograms = 3000 grams.

Centi means hundredth, $\frac{1}{100}$.   So, a **centi**metre is one hundredth of a metre.

For example: 2 centimetres = $\frac{2}{100}$ metre.

Milli means thousandth, $\frac{1}{1000}$.   So, a **milli**litre is one thousandth of a litre.

For example: 5 millilitres = $\frac{5}{1000}$ litre.

Changing from one metric unit to another

Changing from one metric unit to another involves multiplying, or dividing, by a power of 10 (10, 100 or 1000). Multiplying and dividing by powers of 10 was covered in Chapter 1.

EXAMPLES

 1

$$1 \text{ centimetre (cm)} = 10 \text{ millimetres (mm)}$$

(a) Change 6.3 cm into millimetres.

To change centimetres into millimetres, multiply by 10.
$6.3 \times 10 = 63$
$6.3 \text{ cm} = 63 \text{ mm}$

(b) Change 364 mm into centimetres.

To change millimetres into centimetres, divide by 10.
$364 \div 10 = 36.4$
$364 \text{ mm} = 36.4 \text{ cm}$

2

$$1 \text{ metre (m)} = 100 \text{ centimetres (cm)}$$

(a) Change 4.2 m into centimetres.

To change metres into centimetres, multiply by 100.
$4.2 \times 100 = 420$
$4.2 \text{ m} = 420 \text{ cm}$

(b) Change 850 cm into metres.

To change centimetres into metres, divide by 100.
$850 \div 100 = 8.5$
$850 \text{ cm} = 8.5 \text{ m}$

3

$$1 \text{ kilogram (kg)} = 1000 \text{ grams (g)}$$

(a) Change 19.4 kg into grams.

To change kilograms into grams, multiply by 1000.
$19.4 \times 1000 = 19\ 400$
$19.4 \text{ kg} = 19\ 400 \text{ g}$

(b) Change 245 g into kilograms.

To change grams into kilograms, divide by 1000.
$245 \div 1000 = 0.245$
$245 \text{ g} = 0.245 \text{ kg}$

Changing units - areas and volumes

$$1 \text{ m} = 100 \text{ cm}$$
$$1 \text{ m}^2 = 100 \times 100 \text{ cm}^2 = 10\ 000 \text{ cm}^2$$
$$1 \text{ m}^3 = 100 \times 100 \times 100 \text{ cm}^3 = 1\ 000\ 000 \text{ cm}^3$$

How many mm equal 1 cm?

How many mm² equal 1 cm²?

How many mm³ equal 1 cm³?

Exercise 27.1

Do not use a calculator.

1 Change each of the following lengths into millimetres.
(a) 6 cm   (b) 32 cm   (c) 632 cm   (d) 8.6 cm   (e) 0.8 cm   (f) 0.08 cm

2 Change each of the following lengths into centimetres.
(a) 90 mm   (b) 210 mm   (c) 3500 mm   (d) 73.5 mm   (e) 2 mm   (f) 3.5 mm

3 Change each of the following lengths into metres.
- (a) 200 cm
- (b) 320 cm
- (c) 4550 cm
- (d) 66 cm
- (e) 8 cm
- (f) 9.8 cm

4 Change each of the following lengths into centimetres.
- (a) 6 m
- (b) 56 m
- (c) 7.6 m
- (d) 23.5 m
- (e) 0.9 m
- (f) 0.07 m

5 Change each of the following lengths into kilometres.
- (a) 4000 m
- (b) 35 000 m
- (c) 6500 m
- (d) 455 m
- (e) 75 m
- (f) 7 m

6 Change each of the following lengths into metres.
- (a) 6 km
- (b) 32 km
- (c) 650 km
- (d) 3.31 km
- (e) 0.35 km
- (f) 0.085 km

7 Change each of the following areas into square centimetres (cm²).
- (a) 2 m²
- (b) 10 m²
- (c) 0.5 m²

8 Change each of the following volumes into cubic centimetres (cm³).
- (a) 3 m³
- (b) 20 m³
- (c) 0.4 m³

9 Change each of the following masses into grams.
- (a) 2 kg
- (b) 45 kg
- (c) 7.5 kg
- (d) 42.5 kg
- (e) 0.6 kg
- (f) 0.025 kg

10 Change each of the following masses into kilograms.
- (a) 3000 g
- (b) 32 000 g
- (c) 9300 g
- (d) 220 g
- (e) 83 g
- (f) 6 g

11 Copy and complete each of the following.
- (a) 320 000 ml = ... l
- (b) 0.32 t = ... kg = ... g
- (c) 3200 g = ... kg = ... t
- (d) 320 mm = ... cm = ... m
- (e) 32 000 cm = ... m = ... km
- (f) 3.2 km = ... m = ... cm

12 Find the number of kilograms in:
- (a) 6 t
- (b) 8000 g
- (c) 800 g
- (d) 0.65 t

13 Find the number of metres in:
- (a) 4 km
- (b) 8000 mm
- (c) 8.6 cm
- (d) 0.04 km

14 Find the number of millilitres in:
- (a) 2 l
- (b) $\frac{1}{2} l$
- (c) 0.85 l
- (d) 0.03 l

15 Which two lengths are the same?
2000 m   20 km   200 m   2 km   0.02 km

16 Which two weights are the same?
8 g   8 kg   8000 g   0.8 kg   80 kg

17 Which length is longest?
0.5 km   50 m   5000 mm   500 cm

18 Which weight is heaviest?
0.3 t   3000 g   3 kg   30 kg

19
- (a) How many metres are there in 3123 mm?
- (b) How many centimetres are there in 4.5 m?
- (c) How many metres are there in 3.24 km?
- (d) How many grams are there in 1 tonne?
- (e) How many litres are there in 400 ml?

20 Which area is larger?
0.5 m²   or   500 cm²
Give a reason for your answer.

21 Which volume is larger?
0.08 m³   or   800 000 cm³
Give a reason for your answer.

22 A can of coke contains 330 ml.
How many litres of coke are there in 6 cans?

23 One lap of a running track is 400 m.
How many laps are run in an 8 km race?

24 Twenty children at a party share equally 1 kg of fruit pastilles.
How many grams of pastilles does each child receive?

25 A recipe for a dozen biscuits uses 240 g of flour.
James has 1.2 kg of flour.
How many biscuits can he make?

26 Ben takes two 5 ml doses of medicine four times a day.
Ben stops taking the medicine after 5 days.
Originally, there was $\frac{1}{4}$ of a litre of medicine.
How much medicine is left?

Estimating length, mass and capacity

It is a useful skill to be able to estimate length, mass and capacity.
These facts might help you.

Length
Most maths exercise books are about 5 mm thick.
Most adults are between 1.5 m and 1.8 m tall.
The door to your classroom is about 2 m high.
Find some more facts which will help you to estimate length and distance.

Mass
A biro weighs about 5 g.
A standard bag of sugar weighs 1 kg.
A tall male adult weighs about 80 kg.
Find some more facts which will help you to estimate weight or mass.

Capacity
A teaspoon holds about 5 ml.
A can of pop holds about 330 ml.
The fuel tank of a small car holds about 30 *l*.
Find some more facts which will help you to estimate volume and capacity.

EXAMPLES

1 The diagram shows a house.
The door is approximately 2 m high.
Estimate the height of the house.

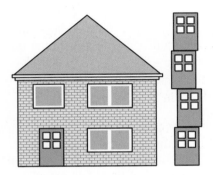

The height of the house is roughly the same as the height of four doors.
So the height of the house is about 4 × 2 = 8 m.

2 Complete each of the following statements by choosing one of the quantities given.
  (a) A cup holds about ...... of tea.
  (b) The height of a car is about ......
  (c) The weight of this book is about ......
  (d) The weight of an elephant is about ......
  (e) The distance from London to Newcastle is about ......

8 g	200 ml	7 *l*
8 kg	15 cm	700 kg
1.5 m	4 km	2 kg
400 km	0.07 *l*	15 mm

  (a) 200 ml   (b) 1.5 m   (c) 2 kg   (d) 700 kg   (e) 400 km

Choosing an appropriate unit

EXAMPLES

1 The Great Wall of China is the longest man-made structure in the world.
It is the only man-made structure that can be seen from space.
What unit should be used for its length?

For very long lengths use the **kilometre**.
The Great Wall of China is actually about 2350 km long.

2 The smallest known mammal is the Kitti's hog-nosed bat.
It is not much bigger than a pea.
  (a) What unit should be used for its mass?
  (b) What unit should be used for its length?

  (a) For very small masses use the **gram**.
   The Kitti's hog-nosed bat actually weighs about 1.5 g.
  (b) For very small lengths use the **millimetre**.
   The length of the Kitti's hog-nosed bat is about 10 mm.

1 Estimate, in metres, centimetres or millimetres, the following lengths in your classroom.
 (a) The length of the room.
 (b) The height of the room.
 (c) The height of your desk.
 (d) The thickness of a watch strap.
 (e) The width of the door.
 (f) The diameter of your pen (or pencil).
 (g) The length of your exercise book.
 (h) The length of a pencil sharpener.

2 Estimate, in grams or kilograms, the weights of the following.
 (a) A pea   (b) A chair
 (c) A cat   (d) A calculator
 (e) A pencil   (f) A dinner plate
 (g) A car   (h) Your desk

3 Estimate, in litres or millilitres, the following.
 (a) The volume of milk you would add to a cup of tea.
 (b) The volume of milk you would pour on a bowl of breakfast cereal.
 (c) The volume of water you drink in a day.

4 Which of the following is the best estimate for the mass of a banana?
 1 kg   5 g   250 g
 30 g   3 kg   750 g

5 Which of the following is the best estimate for the diameter of a football?
 2 m   50 mm   30 cm
 1.5 m   0.6 m   800 mm

6 Which of the following would be the best estimate for the capacity of a mug?
 15 ml   1200 ml   2 *l*
 0.5 *l*   200 ml   800 ml

7 Give a sensible estimate using an appropriate unit for the following measures:
 (a) the length of a matchstick,
 (b) the length of a football pitch,
 (c) the weight of a 30 cm ruler,
 (d) the weight of a double decker bus,
 (e) the volume of drink in a glass.

8 Give the most appropriate metric unit that you would use to measure the following.
 (a) The distance from London to York.
 (b) The distance across a road.
 (c) The length of your foot.
 (d) The length of your little finger nail.
 (e) The weight of a bag of potatoes.
 (f) The weight of an egg.
 (g) The capacity of a bucket.
 (h) The capacity of a medicine bottle.

9 The diagram, which is drawn to scale, shows a man standing next to a tree.

Using an appropriate metric unit estimate the height of the tree.
State the degree of accuracy that you have used in making your estimate.

10 "My teacher's height is about 1.7 mm."
This statement is incorrect.

It can be corrected by changing the unit:
"My teacher's height is about 1.7 m."
It can also be corrected by changing the quantity:
"My teacher's height is about 1700 mm."

Each of these statements is also incorrect.
"Tyrannosaurus, a large meat-eating dinosaur, is estimated to have been about 12 cm long."

"The tallest mammal is the giraffe which grows up to about 5.9 mm tall."

"My car used 5 ml of petrol on a journey of 35 miles."

"The area of the school hall is about 500 mm²."

Correct each statement:
 (a) by changing the unit,
 (b) by changing the quantity.

Imperial units

The following imperial units of measurement are in everyday use.

Length	**Mass**	**Capacity and volume**
1 foot = 12 inches	1 pound = 16 ounces	1 gallon = 8 pints
1 yard = 3 feet	14 pounds = 1 stone	

EXAMPLES

1 Jane is 5 feet 3 inches tall.
How many inches is this?

There are 12 inches in 1 foot.
5 feet = 5 × 12 = 60 inches.
60 + 3 = 63
Jane is 63 inches tall.

2 Jane weighs 89 pounds.
Give her weight in stones and pounds.

There are 14 pounds in 1 stone.
6 × 14 = 84
So 6 stones is the same as 84 pounds.
89 − 84 = 5
Jane weighs 6 stones 5 pounds.

Metric and imperial conversions

In order to convert to and from metric and imperial units you need to know these facts.

Length	**Mass**	**Capacity and volume**
5 miles is about 8 km	1 kg is about 2.2 pounds	1 litre is about 1.75 pints
1 inch is about 2.5 cm		1 gallon is about 4.5 litres
1 foot is about 30 cm		
1 m is about 39 inches		

EXAMPLES

1 Convert 40 cm to inches.

1 inch is about 2.5 cm.
40 cm is about 40 ÷ 2.5 inches.
40 cm is about 16 inches.

2 How many pints are there in a
4 litre carton of milk?

1 litre is about 1.75 pints.
4 litres is about 4 × 1.75 pints.
4 litres is about 7 pints.

3 Change 5 kg to pounds.

1 kg is about 2.2 pounds.
5 kg is about 5 × 2.2 pounds.
5 kg is about 11 pounds.

4 Tim is 6 feet 2 inches tall.
Estimate Tim's height in centimetres.

6 feet 2 inches = 6 × 12 + 2 = 74 inches.
74 inches is about 74 × 2.5 cm.
6 feet 2 inches is about 185 cm.

5 The capacity of a car's petrol tank is 12 gallons.
How much does the petrol tank hold in litres?

1 gallon is about 4.5 litres.
12 gallons is about 12 × 4.5 litres.
12 gallons is about 54 litres.

6 How long is 32 km in miles?

There are 32 ÷ 8 = 4 lots of 8 km in 32 km.
So there must be 4 lots of 5 miles in 32 km.
4 × 5 = 20.
There are 20 miles in 32 km.

1 Change the following lengths into centimetres.
   (a) 2 inches   (b) 10 inches
   (c) 2 feet   (d) 10 feet

2 Change the following lengths into inches.
   (a) 2 m   (b) 40 m
   (c) 2 cm   (d) 20 cm

3 Change the following lengths into kilometres.
   (a) 5 miles   (b) 45 miles
   (c) 100 miles   (d) 500 miles

4 Change the following lengths into miles.
   (a) 8 km   (b) 24 km
   (c) 40 km   (d) 800 km

5 Change the following weights into pounds.
   (a) 10 kg   (b) 50 kg
   (c) 1 t   (d) 5 t

6 Change the following masses into kilograms. Give your answers to the nearest kilogram.
   (a) 22 pounds   (b) 150 pounds
   (c) 14 stones   (d) 6 stones 11 pounds

7 Estimate the number of litres in each of the following.
   (a) 10 gallons   (b) 5 pints
   (c) 30 gallons   (d) 2 gallons 3 pints

8 Convert each quantity to the units given.
   (a) 10 kg to pounds.
   (b) 20 litres to pints.
   (c) 5 metres to inches.
   (d) 6 inches to millimetres.
   (e) 50 cm to inches.

9 A box contains 200 balls.
Each ball weighs 50 g.
Estimate the total weight of the balls in pounds.

10 James is 5 feet 8 inches tall.
Estimate James' height in centimetres.

11 James weighs 10 stones 6 pounds.
Estimate James' weight in kilograms.

12 Estimate:
   (a) the number of metres in 2000 feet,
   (b) the number of kilometres in 3 miles,
   (c) the number of feet in 170 centimetres,
   (d) the number of pounds in 1250 grams.

13 A sheet of card measures 12 inches by 20 inches.
What is the area of the card in square centimetres?

14 Lauren says 10 kg of potatoes weighs the same as 20 lb of sugar.
Is she correct?
Show all your working.

15 Alfie cycles 6 miles.
Jacob cycles 10 kilometres.
Alfie claims that he has cycled further than Jacob.
Is he correct?
Show all your working.

Reading scales

EXAMPLE

1 (a) Use an appropriate metric unit to measure accurately the length of each of lines **A**, **B** and **C**.

A ——————————————————

B ————————————————————————

C ——————————

(b) What is the total length of lines **A**, **B** and **C**?
(c) What is the difference in length between lines **B** and **C**?

(a) Line **A** is 7 cm (or 70 mm) long.   (b) $7 + 12.5 + 4.6 = 24.1$ cm (or 241 mm).
     Line **B** is 12.5 cm (or 125 mm) long. (c) $12.5 - 4.6 = 7.9$ cm (or 79 mm).
     Line **C** is 4.6 cm (or 46 mm) long.

EXAMPLE

2 Chandni, Jill and Susan measured their weights.
The diagram shows the readings on the scale.
What are each of their weights?

Chandni weighs 46 kg.
Jill weighs 55 kg.
Susan weighs 51 kg.

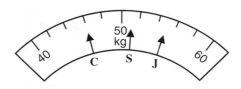

Exercise 27.4

1 Measure the lengths of these lines.

X ————————————————————

Y ————————

(a) What is the length of each line in centimetres?
(b) What is the length of each line in millimetres?

2 (a) Read each of the following scales at pointers **A**, **B** and **C**.

(i)

(ii)
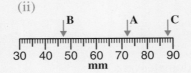

(iii)
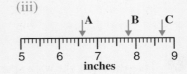

(iv)
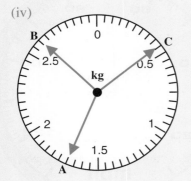

(v)
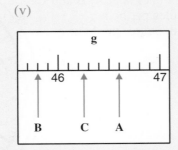

(vi)
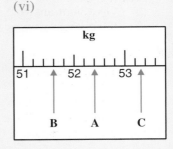

(vii)
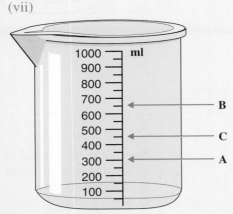

(viii)
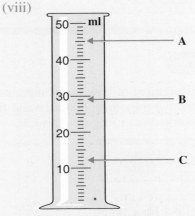

(b) For each of the above scales work out the difference between the highest and lowest readings.

3 What is the temperature shown by pointers **A**, **B** and **C**?

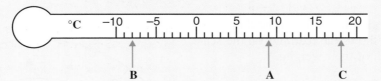

4 (a) The diagram shows the petrol gauge on a car.
The car's petrol tank holds 12 gallons when full.
  (i) How many gallons are in the petrol tank?
  (ii) How many litres are in the petrol tank?

(b) The diagram shows the petrol gauge on another car.
The car's petrol tank holds 60 litres when full.
  (i) Estimate how many litres are in the petrol tank.
  (ii) Estimate how many gallons are in the petrol tank.

5 This diagram shows a speedometer on a car.
What is the speed when the pointer is at **A**, **B** and **C**?
  (a) Give your answers in miles per hour.
  (b) Give your answers in kilometres per hour.

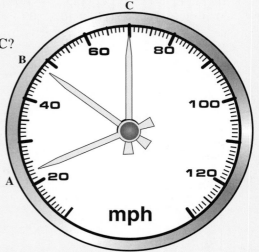

Speed

Speed is a measurement of how fast something is travelling.
It involves two other measures, **distance** and **time**.
Speed can be worked out using this formula.

$$\text{Speed} = \frac{\text{Distance}}{\text{Time}}$$

Speed can be measured in:
    kilometres per hour (km/h),
    metres per second (m/s),
    miles per hour (mph),
    and so on.

Speed can be thought of as the **distance** travelled in **one unit of time** (1 hour, 1 second, ...)

Average speed

When the speed of an object is **constant** it means that the object doesn't slow down or go faster.
However, in many situations, speed is not constant.
For example:

A sprinter needs time to start from the starting blocks and is well into the race before running at top speed.
A plane changes speed as it takes off and lands.

In situations like this the idea of **average speed** can be used.
The formula for average speed is:

$$\text{Average speed} = \frac{\text{Total distance travelled}}{\text{Total time taken}}$$

The formula linking speed, distance and time can be rearranged and remembered as:

(average) **speed** = (total) **distance** ÷ (total) **time**
(total) **distance** = (average) **speed** × (total) **time**
(total) **time** = (total) **distance** ÷ (average) **speed**

$$S = D ÷ T$$
$$D = S × T$$
$$T = D ÷ S$$

EXAMPLES

1 A cheetah takes 4 seconds to travel 100 m. What is the speed of the cheetah?

$$\text{Speed} = \frac{\text{Distance}}{\text{Time}} = \frac{100}{4} = 100 ÷ 4 = 25 \text{ m/s}$$

2 Robert drives a distance of 260 km. His journey takes 5 hours. What is his average speed on the journey?

$$\text{Speed} = \frac{\text{Distance}}{\text{Time}} = \frac{260}{5} = 260 ÷ 5 = 52 \text{ km/h}$$

3 Lisa drives at an average speed of 80 kilometres per hour on a journey that takes 3 hours. What distance has she travelled?

$$\begin{aligned} \text{Distance} &= \text{Speed} × \text{Time} \\ &= 80 × 3 \\ &= 240 \text{ km} \end{aligned}$$
So in 3 hours she travels 240 km.

4 Lucy cycles at an average speed of 7 km/h on a journey of 28 km. How long does she take?

$$\begin{aligned} \text{Time} &= \text{Distance} ÷ \text{Speed} \\ &= 28 ÷ 7 \\ &= 4 \end{aligned}$$
So her journey takes 4 hours.

Exercise **27.5** Do not use a calculator.

1 John cycles 16 miles in 2 hours. What is his average speed in miles per hour?

2 Sue runs 21 km in 3 hours. What is her average speed in kilometres per hour?

3 Joe swims 100 m in 4 minutes. What is his average speed in metres per minute?

4 Calculate the average speed for each of the following journeys in km/h.

	Total distance travelled	Total time taken
(a)	60 km	3 hours
(b)	100 km	2 hours
(c)	10 km	$2\frac{1}{2}$ hours

5 Beverley walks for 2 hours at an average speed of 4 kilometres per hour. How many kilometres does she walk?

6 Howard cycles for 5 hours at an average speed of 6 miles per hour. How far does he cycle?

7 Judy runs at 6 km/h for $\frac{1}{2}$ hour. How far does she run?

8 Calculate the total distance travelled on each of the following journeys.

	Total time taken	Average speed
(a)	3 hours	50 km/h
(b)	2 hours	45 km/h
(c)	$\frac{1}{2}$ hour	80 km/h

9 Ahmed drives 30 miles at an average speed of 60 miles per hour. How long does the journey take?

10 Lauren cycles 100 m at 5 metres per second. How long does she take?

11 A train travels 75 km at an average speed of 50 km/h. How long does the journey take?

12 Calculate the total time taken on each of the following journeys.

	Total distance travelled	Average speed
(a)	30 km	10 km/h
(b)	80 km	40 km/h
(c)	210 km	60 km/h

13 On the first part of a journey a car travels 140 km in 3 hours.
On the second part of the journey the car travels 160 km in 2 hours.
(a) What is the total distance travelled on the journey?
(b) What is the total time taken on the journey?
(c) What is the average speed of the car over the whole journey?

14 A car travels 120 km in 2 hours.
(a) What is its average speed in km/hour?
(b) How many hours would the car take to travel 120 km if it had gone twice as fast?

15 Liam drives for 60 km at an average speed of 40 km/h.
He starts his journey at 9.50 am.
At what time does his journey end?

What you need to know

- The common units — both **metric** and **imperial** — used to measure **length**, **mass** and **capacity**.
- How to convert from one unit to another. This includes knowing the connection between one metric unit and another and the approximate equivalents between metric and imperial units.

Metric Units	Imperial Units	Conversions
Length 1 kilometre (km) = 1000 metres (m) 1 m = 100 centimetres (cm) 1 m = 1000 millimetres (mm) 1 cm = 10 mm **Mass** 1 tonne (t) = 1000 kilograms (kg) 1 kg = 1000 grams (g) **Capacity and volume** 1 litre = 1000 millilitres (ml) 1 cm^3 = 1 ml	**Length** 1 foot = 12 inches 1 yard = 3 feet **Mass** 1 pound = 16 ounces 14 pounds = 1 stone **Capacity and volume** 1 gallon = 8 pints	**Length** 5 miles is about 8 km 1 inch is about 2.5 cm 1 foot is about 30 cm 1 m is about 39 inches **Mass** 1 kg is about 2.2 pounds **Capacity and volume** 1 litre is about 1.75 pints 1 gallon is about 4.5 litres

- How to change between units of area. For example 1 m^2 = 10 000 cm^2.
- How to change between units of volume. For example 1 m^3 = 1 000 000 cm^3.
- How to estimate length, mass and capacity using appropriate units.
- How to read scales accurately.
- **Speed** is a measure of how fast something is travelling.
  Speed involves two other measures, **distance** and **time**.
  It can be worked out using this formula.

$$\text{Speed} = \frac{\text{Distance}}{\text{Time}}$$

In most situations the idea of average speed is used.

$$\text{Average speed} = \frac{\text{Total distance travelled}}{\text{Total time taken}}$$

Do not use a calculator for questions 1 to 6.

1 Write down the readings shown on these scales.

(a)

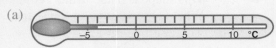

(b)

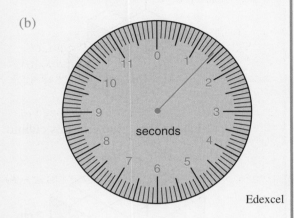

Edexcel

2 Write down the **metric** unit you would use to measure,
(a) the length of a person's hand,
(b) the weight of a mouse,
(c) the distance from Manchester to London,
(d) a teaspoon of medicine. Edexcel

3 A model of a ship weighs 1500 g. How many kilograms is this?

4 One glass of lemonade contains 300 ml. How many glasses of lemonade can be poured from a jug which contains 2.4 litres?

5

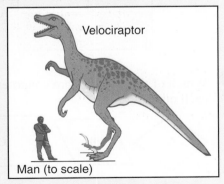

Velociraptor

Man (to scale)

The scale diagram shows a man and a dinosaur called a velociraptor.
The man is 6 feet tall.
Estimate the height of the velociraptor
(a) in feet, (b) in metres. Edexcel

6

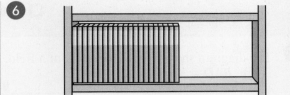

1.2 m

Not to scale

How many magazines, each 0.6 cm thick, will fit on a bookcase shelf which is exactly 1.2 m wide?

7 (a) How many metres are there in 2.65 kilometres?
(b) The distance from Calais to Paris is 280 km.
What is this distance in miles?

8 Tim is 5 feet 10 inches tall and weighs 72 kg. Sam is 165 cm tall and weighs 11 stone 7 pounds.
Who is taller? Who is heavier?

9 The chart shows the distances in kilometres between some towns.

London			
326	Manchester		
270	60	Sheffield	
129	376	334	Southampton

Mrs Hill drove from Manchester to Southampton.
She completed the journey in 4 hours.
What was her average speed for the journey in kilometres per hour?

10 Mr Mogg took 5 hours to drive from Cardiff to Leeds.
His average speed was 48 miles per hour.
What is the distance from Cardiff to Leeds?

11 A train travels 120 kilometres at an average speed of 80 kilometres per hour.
How long will the journey take?

12 On Monday, Gareth drove from Swindon to Newcastle.
The distance was 325 miles.
He left Swindon at 0800.
He arrived in Newcastle at 1430.
Work out Gareth's average speed. Edexcel

Understanding and Using Measures

Section Review - Shape, Space and Measures

1 The diagram shows a scale drawing of a field. Angle *BAD* = angle *ADC* = 90°.

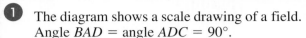
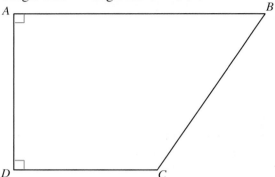

(a) Which two lines are parallel to each other?
(b) Which line is perpendicular to *DC*?
(c) Measure angle *ABC*.
(d) Measure the length of the line *CB*.

2 Copy the diagram and draw a reflection of the shape in the mirror line *AB*.

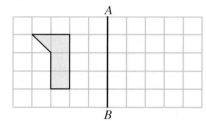

3 This shape has been drawn on 1 cm squared paper.

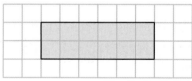

Not full size

(a) What is the area of the shape?
(b) What is the perimeter of the shape?

4 Copy the diagram and draw the line of symmetry.

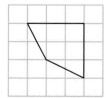

5 (a) This shape is made using 1 cm cubes. What is the volume of the shape?

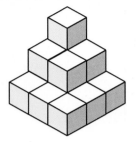

(b) Calculate the volume of this cuboid.

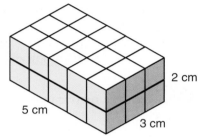

2 cm

5 cm

3 cm

(c) Which of these diagrams is the net of a cube?

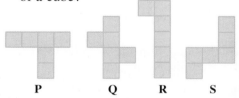

P   Q   R   S

6 Write down the length shown by the scale.

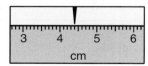

7 Which of these shapes are congruent to each other?

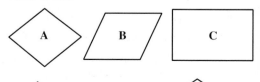
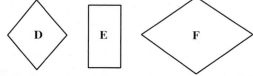

278

8 (a) Copy the diagram and
  (i) plot the points $B(4, 3)$ and $C(3, 6)$,
  (ii) join A, B and C to make a triangle.

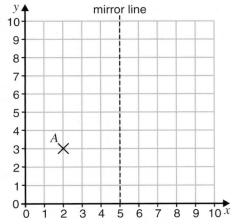

(b) Draw the reflection of triangle ABC in the mirror line.

(c) Choose three descriptions from the box to complete the sentence correctly.

scalene
isosceles
right-angled
equilateral
acute-angled
obtuse-angled
congruent

Triangle ABC and its reflection

are .... triangles,

and .... triangles,

and .... triangles.

Edexcel

9

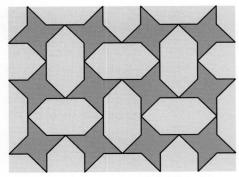

This pattern is from the tiled floor of the Taj Mahal in India.

The pattern is made from these 2 shapes.

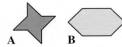

A   **B**

(a) (i) Write down the order of rotational symmetry of shape **A**.
  (ii) Write down the number of lines of symmetry of shape **B**.

(b) Show how shape **B** will tessellate. You should draw at least 5 shapes.

Edexcel

10 Find the size of the angles a, b and c.

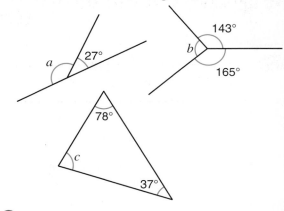

11 The diagram shows a pyramid with a square base of side 3 cm.
The length of each sloping edge is 4 cm.
Draw an accurate net of the pyramid.

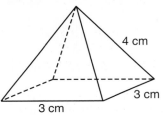

12 (a) Adrian is 6 feet 3 inches tall. Work out Adrian's height in centimetres.

(b) Adrian weighs 78 kg. Work out Adrian's weight in pounds.

13 The diagram shows the position of X and a shape.

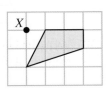

Copy the diagram onto square paper. Draw an enlargement of the shape, scale factor 3, centre X.

14 The diagram shows a parallelogram and a rectangle.

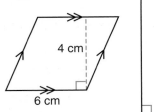

Both shapes have the same area. Calculate the length of the rectangle.

15 Here is a sketch of a triangle.
$PR = 6.4$ cm
$QR = 7.7$ cm
Angle $R = 35°$

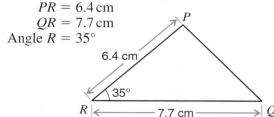

(a) Make an accurate drawing of the triangle.
(b) Measure the size of angle Q on your accurate drawing.
Edexcel

16 The diagram shows a cuboid.

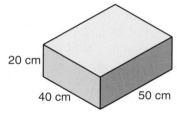

Work out the volume, in cm³, of the cuboid.
Edexcel

17 In triangle ABC, $AB = AC$ and angle $C = 50°$.

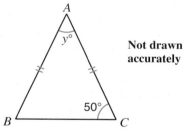

Not drawn accurately

(a) Write down the special name for triangle ABC.
(b) Work out the value of y. Edexcel

18 This 3-dimensional shape has been made using linking cubes of side 1 cm.
On squared paper, draw diagrams to show the plan and the elevation from **X**.

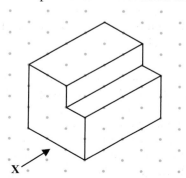

19 (a) The diagram shows a pair of parallel lines.
The lines marked with the arrows are parallel.
Work out the size of the angles marked $e°$, $f°$ and $g°$.

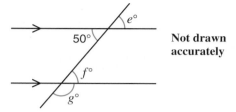

Not drawn accurately

(b) Work out the size of the angle marked $h°$.

Not drawn accurately

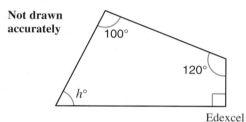

Edexcel

20

This signpost is on the road from Paris to Dijon.
(a) Work out the approximate distance, in miles, from the signpost to Paris.

Andrew drove to Dijon **starting at the signpost** at an average speed of 80 km an hour.
(b) How long did the journey take? Give your answer in hours and minutes. Edexcel

21 What is the area of this triangle?

6 cm

8 cm

22 Find the size of the angle marked a in this kite.
Explain how you found your answer.

a

$52°$ $118°$

23 A table top is a circle of radius 50 cm.
   (a) Calculate the circumference of the table top.
   (b) Calculate the area of the table top.

24 The diagram shows triangles **P**, **Q** and **R**.

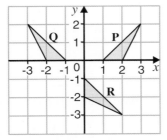

   (a) Describe the single transformation which takes **P** onto **Q**.
   (b) Describe the single transformation which takes **P** onto **R**.

Copy triangle **P** onto squared paper.
   (c) Draw an enlargement of triangle **P** with scale factor 2, centre (0, 0).

25 (a) Work out the area of Shape **A**.

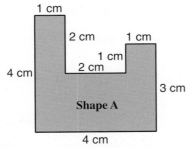

   (b) (i) Work out the perimeter of the semicircle.

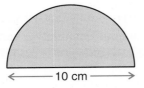

       (ii) Work out the area of the semicircle.   *Edexcel*

26 The diagram shows a cube.

The surface area of the cube is 24 cm².
   (a) What is the volume of the cube?
   (b) How many of these cubes will fit into a cuboid which measures 4 cm by 7 cm by 10 cm?

27 (a) The diagram shows a regular hexagon.

Not drawn accurately

Work out the size of the angle marked *a*.
   (b) The diagram shows a regular octagon.

Not drawn accurately

Work out the size of the angle marked *b*.
                               Edexcel

28 Calculate the area of this trapezium.

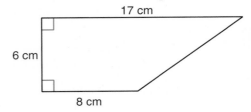

29 The front wheels of a tractor each have diameter 100 cm.
The tractor is driven 100 metres.
How many complete turns do each of the front wheels make?

30 The diagram represents the positions of Wigan and Manchester.

N ↑

Wigan ✕   N ↑

   (a) Measure and write down the bearing of Manchester from Wigan.   Manchester ✕
   (b) Find the bearing of Wigan from Manchester.   *Edexcel*

31 *Y* is 50 m from *X* on a bearing of 080°.
Z is 70 m from *Y* on a bearing of 110°.
   (a) Make a scale drawing to show the positions of *X*, *Y* and *Z*.
Use a scale of 1 cm to 10 m.
   (b) Find by measurement the distance and bearing of *X* from *Z*.

Collection and Organisation of Data

To answer questions such as:

Which is the most popular colour of car?

Is it going to rain tomorrow?

Which team won the World Cup in 1998?

we need to collect data.

Primary and secondary data

When data is collected by an individual or organisation to use for a particular purpose it is called **primary data**.
Primary data is obtained from experiments, investigations, surveys and by using questionnaires.

Data which is already available or has been collected by someone else for a different purpose is called **secondary data**.
Sources of secondary data include the Annual Abstract of Statistics, Social Trends and the Internet.

Data

Data is made up of a collection of **variables**.
Each variable can be described, numbered or measured.

Data which can only be **described** in words is **qualitative**.
Such data is often organised into categories, such as make of car, colour of hair, etc.

Data which is given **numerical** values, such as shoe size or height, is **quantitative**.
Quantitative data is either **discrete** or **continuous**.

Discrete data can only take certain values, usually whole numbers, but may include fractions (e.g. shoe sizes).

Continuous data can take any value within a range and is measurable (e.g. height, weight, temperature, etc.).

EXAMPLES

The taste of an orange is a qualitative variable.
The number of pips in an orange is a discrete quantitative variable.
The surface area of an orange is a continuous quantitative variable.

Exercise 28.1

State whether the following data is qualitative or quantitative.
If the data is quantitative state whether it is discrete or continuous.

1. The colours of cars in a car park.
2. The weights of eggs in a carton.
3. The numbers of desks in classrooms.
4. The names of students in a class.
5. The sizes of spanners in a toolbox.
6. The depths that fish swim in the sea.
7. The numbers of goals scored by football teams on a Saturday.
8. The brands of toothpaste on sale in supermarkets.
9. The sizes of ladies dresses in a store.
10. The heights of trees in a wood.

Collection of data

Data can be collected in a variety of ways; by observation, by interviewing people and by using questionnaires. The method of collection will often depend on the type of data to be collected.

Data collection sheets

Data collection sheets are used to record data.
To answer the question, "Which is the most popular colour of car?", we could draw up a simple data collection sheet and record the colours of passing cars by observation.

EXAMPLE

A **data collection sheet** for colour of car is shown, with some cars recorded.

Colour of car	Tally	Frequency
Black	||	2
Blue	︱︱︱︱ ︱︱︱︱ ︱︱︱	13
Green	︱︱︱︱	4
Red	︱︱︱︱ ︱︱︱︱ ︱	
Silver	︱︱︱︱ ︱︱	
White	︱︱︱︱ ︱︱︱︱ ︱︱︱︱	
	Total	

The colour of each car is recorded in the **tally** column by a single stroke.

To make counting easier, groups of 5 are recorded as ︱︱︱︱.

How many red cars are recorded?
How many cars are recorded altogether?

The total number of times each colour appears is called its **frequency**.
A table for data with the totals included is called a **frequency distribution**.

For large amounts of discrete data, or for continuous data, we organise the data into **groups** or **classes**. When data is collected in groups it is called a **grouped frequency distribution** and the groups you put the data into are called **class intervals**.

EXAMPLE

The weights of 20 boys are recorded in the grouped frequency table shown below.

Weight w kg	Tally	Frequency
$50 \leq w < 55$	|	1
$55 \leq w < 60$	|||	3
$60 \leq w < 65$	︱︱︱︱ ||||	9
$65 \leq w < 70$	︱︱︱︱ |	6
$70 \leq w < 75$	|	1
	Total	20

Weights are grouped into class intervals of equal width.

$55 \leq w < 60$ means 55 kg, or more, but less than 60 kg.

John weighs 54.9 kg. *In which class interval is he recorded?*
David weighs 55.0 kg. *In which class interval is he recorded?*

What is the width of each class interval?

1. The tally chart shows the number of glass bottles put into a bottle bank one day.

Colour of glass	Tally
Clear	〢〢〢 〢〢〢 〢〢〢 ||
Brown	〢〢〢 〢〢〢 〢〢〢 〢〢〢	
Green	〢〢〢 〢〢〢 〢〢〢

(a) How many green bottles were put into the bottle bank?

(b) How many brown bottles were put into the bottle bank?

2. John is doing a project about sport.
He asks people which sport they like best.
The data collection sheet shows his results.

Sport	Tally
Cricket	||
Football	〢〢〢 〢〢〢 〢〢〢 〢〢〢 〢〢〢	
Hockey	||||
Rugby	〢〢〢 |||
Tennis	〢〢〢

(a) How many people like rugby best?

(b) How many people did John ask?

3. Helen throws a dice 50 times.
The result of each throw is shown.

1	4	3	6	5	4	3	2	1	6
4	5	2	3	4	5	6	4	5	3
1	2	3	4	2	3	5	1	1	4
5	6	4	3	2	5	4	6	5	6
2	3	1	3	4	1	6	5	2	2

(a) Copy and complete this table to record her results.

Number on dice	Tally
1	
2	
3	
4	
5	
6	

(b) Which number occurred most frequently?

4 The colours of 40 cars in a car park are shown.

red	red	blue	green	white	grey
blue	red	red	grey	white	green
red	white	white	blue	red	white
blue	blue	green	black	white	blue
red	silver	silver	blue	red	red
silver	white	white	red	blue	green
red	blue	silver	white		

(a) Make a frequency table for the data.
(b) Which colour of car is most popular?

5 The days of the week on which some students were born are recorded.

Monday	Monday	Sunday	Wednesday	Thursday
Friday	Saturday	Tuesday	Monday	Friday
Thursday	Sunday	Monday	Friday	Tuesday
Thursday	Wednesday	Tuesday	Monday	Wednesday
Friday	Monday	Saturday	Friday	Thursday
Tuesday	Thursday	Monday	Sunday	Tuesday
Saturday	Wednesday	Friday	Thursday	Tuesday
Monday	Wednesday	Friday	Sunday	Thursday
Tuesday	Wednesday	Sunday		

(a) Make a frequency table for the data.
(b) How many students are included?
(c) On which day of the week did most births occur?

6 The ages of 40 people are shown below.

27	34	54	57	3	12
15	19	29	30	33	47
35	20	39	28	9	11
26	42	50	26	10	7
33	49	21	18	1	25
24	34	19	20	27	37
43	56	37	34		

(a) Copy and complete the grouped frequency table for the data given.

Age	Tally	Frequency
0 - 9		
10 - 19		
20 - 29		

(b) What is the width of each class interval?
(c) How many people are in the class interval 30 - 39?
(d) How many people are less than 20 years old?
(e) How many people are 40 or older?

7 The heights, in centimetres, of 36 girls are recorded as follows.

148	161	175	156	155	160	178	159	170
163	147	150	173	169	170	174	166	163
162	158	155	165	168	154	156	163	167
172	170	165	160	164	172	157	173	161

(a) Copy and complete the grouped frequency table for the data.

Height h cm	Tally	Frequency
$145 \leqslant h < 150$		
$150 \leqslant h < 155$		

(b) What is the width of each class interval?
(c) How many girls are in the class interval $155 \leqslant h < 160$?
(d) How many girls are less than 160 cm?
(e) How many girls are 155 cm or taller?

8 Draw up a data collection sheet to record the month in which people were born. Collect data from 50 people.
(a) Make a frequency table for the data.
(b) In which month did most births occur?

Databases

If we need to collect data for more than one type of information, for example; the make, colour, registration letter and mileage of cars; we will need to collect data in a different way.

We could create a **data collection card** for each car.

Car	1
Make	Vauxhall
Colour	Grey
Registration letter	T
Mileage	18 604

Alternatively, we could use a data collection sheet and record all the information about each car on a separate line.

This is an example of a simple **database**.

Car	Make	Colour	Registration letter	Mileage
1	Vauxhall	Grey	T	18 604
2	Ford	Blue	R	33 216
3	Ford	White	S	27 435
4	Nissan	Red	P	32 006

When all the data has been collected, separate frequency or grouped frequency tables can be drawn up.

1 The database gives information about the babies born at a maternity hospital one day.

Baby's name	Time of birth	Weight (kg)	Length (cm)
Alistair	0348	3.2	44
Francis	0819	3.5	48
Louisa	1401	3.7	47

(a)   Which baby is the longest?
(b)   Which baby is the heaviest?
(c)   Which baby was born first?

2 Part of a database on some students is shown.

Student	Gender	Day of birth	Month of birth
Alex	F	Tuesday	January
Brian	M	Thursday	June
Cody	F	Monday	October
David	M	Friday	May
Evelyn	F	Saturday	September
Fay	F	Monday	February
George	M	Tuesday	May
Harry	M	Wednesday	September
Irene	F	Monday	September
Jay	M	Thursday	April

(a)   How many students were born on a Tuesday?
(b)   How many female students were born in September?
(c)   Which student was born on a Monday in February?

3 The following database gives information about ski resorts for one day in January.

Resort	Temp °C	Depth of snow		Piste	Weather
		Lower (cm)	Upper (cm)		
Aspen	2	50	70	good	fair
Cervinia	−7	80	170	hard	windy
Cortina	−2	10	60	good	fine
Kitzbuhel	−2	40	90	good	cloudy
Klosters	0	45	136	good	cloudy
Meribel	1	55	150	fair	fine
Soldeu	−4	50	90	good	sunny
Val d'Isere	−9	100	130	good	sunny

(a)   Which resort was coldest?
(b)   Which resort was windy?
(c)   At which resort was the piste hard?
(d)   What was the depth of snow on the upper slopes at Klosters?
(e)   At which resort was the depth of snow between 50 cm and 90 cm?

4 The following database gives information about a group of 16 year old students.

Student	Gender	Height (cm)	Shoe size	Pulse rate (beats/min)
Mary	F	162	6	72
Alan	M	170	8	64
Jim	M	186	10	72
Tony	M	180	10	68
Laura	F	172	8	70
Jane	F	168	7	82
Wendy	F	155	5	72
Mark	M	180	9	68
Peter	M	168	8	62
Beryl	F	166	7	72

(a) Which student has the smallest shoe size?
(b) What is the gender of the student with the highest pulse rate?
(c) Which students are the same height?
(d) How many students are taller than Jane?
(e) Which students have a pulse rate of 72?
(f) What is the difference between the highest pulse rate and the lowest pulse rate?

5 A database of cars is shown.

Car	Make	Colour	Registration letter	Mileage
1	Vauxhall	Grey	T	18 604
2	Ford	Blue	R	33 216
3	Ford	White	S	27 435
4	Nissan	Red	P	32 006
5	Vauxhall	Blue	R	31 598
6	Ford	Green	P	37 685
7	Vauxhall	Red	T	21 640
8	Nissan	White	R	28 763
9	Ford	White	S	30 498
10	Vauxhall	White	T	9 865
11	Nissan	Red	X	7 520
12	Vauxhall	Grey	T	16 482

(a) (i)   Draw up separate frequency tables for make, colour and registration letter.
      (ii) Draw up a grouped frequency table for mileage.
            Use class intervals of 5000 miles, starting at $0 \leqslant m < 5000$, $5000 \leqslant m < 10\,000$, . . .

(b) (i)   Which make of car is the most popular?
      (ii) How many Ford cars are white?
      (iii) How many cars have a mileage of 30 000 or more?
      (iv) How many cars have a T registration letter?

6 (a) By using copies of the data collection card for cars or by using a copy of the data collection sheet, record information about the cars in your school car park.

(b) Draw up frequency tables for make, colour and registration letter and a grouped frequency table for mileage.

(c) (i) Which make of car is the most popular?
(ii) Which colour of car is the most popular?
(iii) How many cars have a mileage of 30 000 or more?
(iv) How many cars have a T registration letter?

7 Use data collection cards to collect information about students in your class.
Include gender, height, shoe size and pulse rate.
Compare your data with the data in question 4.
What differences do you find?

8 (a) Design a data collection card to collect information on the leisure time activities of students.
(b) Draw up frequency or grouped frequency tables for the data.
(c) Which leisure time activity is the most popular?
(d) What differences are there in the leisure time activities of male and female students?

Questionnaires

Questionnaires are frequently used to collect data.
In business they are used to get information about products or services and in politics they are frequently used to test opinion on a range of issues and personalities.
When constructing questions for a questionnaire you should:

(1) use simple language, so that everyone can understand the question;

(2) ask short questions which can be answered precisely, with a "yes" or "no" answer, a number, or a response from a choice of answers;

(3) provide tick boxes, so that questions can be answered easily;

(4) avoid open-ended questions, like:
"What do you think of education?" which might produce long rambling answers which would be difficult to collate or process;

(5) avoid leading questions, like:
"Don't you agree that there is too much bad language on television?" and ask instead:
"Do you think that there is too much bad language on television?"

Yes ☐   No ☐

(6) ask questions in a logical order.

Multiple-response questions

In many instances a choice of responses should be provided.
Instead of asking "How old are you?" which does not indicate the degree of accuracy required and many people might consider personal, we could ask instead:
Which is your age group?

under 18 ☐

18 to 40 ☐

41 to 65 ☐

over 65 ☐

Notice there are no gaps and only **one** response applies to each person.

Sometimes we invite **multiple responses** by asking questions, such as:

Which soaps do you watch?

Coronation Street ☐

EastEnders ☐

Emmerdale ☐

Brookside ☐

Hollyoaks ☐

Tick as many as you wish.

1 John wants to find out what students think about the library service at his college.
Part of the questionnaire he has written is shown.

Q1. What is your name? . . . .

Q2. How many times a week do you go to the library?

☐ Often   ☐ Sometimes   ☐ Never

(a) Why should Q1 not be asked?
(b) What is wrong with the choices offered in Q2.

2 Susan wants to find out what people think about the Health Service.
Part of the questionnaire she has written is shown.

Q4. What is your date of birth?

Q5. Don't you agree that waiting lists for operations are too long?

Q6. How many times did you visit your doctor last year?

☐ less than 5   ☐ 5 - 10   ☐ 10 or more

(a) Why should Q4 not be asked?
(b) Give a reason why Q5 is unsuitable.
(c) (i)   Explain why Q6 is unsuitable in its present form.
     (ii) Rewrite the question so that it could be included in the questionnaire.

3 In preparing the questions for a questionnaire on radio listening habits the following
questions were rejected.

(a) When do you listen to the radio?
(b) What do you like about radio programmes?
(c) Don't you agree that the radio gives the best news reports.

Explain why each question is unsuitable and rewrite the question so that it could be included
in the questionnaire.

4 In preparing questions for a survey on the use of a library the following questions were
considered. Explain why each question in its present form is unsuitable and rewrite the
question.

(a) How old are you?
(b) How many times have you used the library?
(c) Which books do you read?
(d) How could the library be improved?

5 A mobile phone company wants to carry out a survey.
It wants to find out the distribution of the age and sex of customers and the frequency with which they use the phone.
The company intends to use a questionnaire.
Write three questions and responses that will enable the company to carry out the survey.

6 A school is to conduct a homework survey.
Suggest five questions which could be included.

7 A survey of reading habits is to be conducted.
Suggest five questions which could be included.

8 A survey of eating habits is to be conducted.
Suggest five questions which could be included.

Hypothesis

A **hypothesis** is a statement that may or may not be true.
To test a hypothesis we can construct a questionnaire, carry out a survey and analyse the results.

EXAMPLE

A questionnaire to test the hypothesis, "People think it is better to give than to receive" could include questions like these.

1.	**Gender:** male ☐	female ☐
2.	**Age:** 11 - 16 ☐ 17 - 21 ☐ 22 - 59 ☐ 60 & over ☐	
3.	**Do you think it is better to give than to receive?**	
	Yes ☐	No ☐
4.	**To which of the following have you given in the last year?**	
	School ☐ Charities ☐ Church ☐	
	Hospital ☐ Special appeals ☐ Homeless ☐	

Other (please list) _____

Suggest another question which could be included.

Sampling

When information is required about a small group of people it is possible to survey everyone.
When information is required about a large group of people it is not always possible to survey everyone and only a **sample** may be asked. The sample chosen should be large enough to make the results meaningful and representative of the whole group or the results may be **biased**.
For example, to test the hypothesis, "Girls are more intelligent than boys", you would need to ask equal numbers of boys and girls from various age groups.

1 George is investigating the cost of return journeys by train.
He plans to ask ten passengers who are waiting at a station at midday the cost of their return journeys.
Give two reasons why he might get biased results.

2 Judy is investigating shopping habits.
She plans to interview 50 women at her local supermarket on a Tuesday morning.
Give three reasons why she might get biased results.

3 Sam is investigating the hypothesis:
"Men watch more football than women".
Describe a suitable sample you could use to test this hypothesis.

4 Design a questionnaire to test the hypothesis: "Children watch more television than adults".

5 Design a questionnaire to test the hypothesis:
"People think that everyone should take part in sport".
Describe the sample you could use to test this hypothesis.

6 Design a questionnaire to test the hypothesis:
"People think that animals should not be used to test drugs".
Describe the sample you could use to test this hypothesis.

7 Design a questionnaire to test the hypothesis:
"Children have too much homework".
Describe the sample you could use to test this hypothesis.

8 Explain how you could test the hypothesis: "Boys are better at estimating than girls".

9 State one advantage and one disadvantage of a postal survey.

Two-way tables

We have already seen that the results of a survey can be recorded on data collection sheets and then collated using frequency or grouped frequency tables. We can also illustrate data using **two-way tables**.

A two-way table is used to illustrate the data for two different features (variables) in a survey.

EXAMPLE   The following two-way table shows the results of a survey.

(a) How many boys wear glasses?
(b) How many children wear glasses?
(c) How many children were surveyed?

	Wear Glasses	
	Yes	No
Boys	4	14
Girls	3	9

(a) 4   (b) 7   (c) 30

Do the results of the survey prove or disprove the hypothesis, "More boys wear glasses than girls"? Explain your answer.

① The two-way table shows information about the ages of people in a retirement home.

Age

	60 - 64	65 - 69	70 - 74	75 - 79	80 and over
Men	0	2	5	8	1
Women	2	5	6	5	6

(a) How many men are aged 75 - 79?
(b) How many men are included?
(c) How many people are aged 75 or more?
(d) How many people are included?
(e) What percentage of these people are aged 75 or more?

② A group of 25 students were each asked how many brothers and sisters they had.
The table shows the results.

Number of sisters

		0	1	2	3
	0	5	1	2	0
Number	1	4	3	2	1
of	2	2	3	1	0
brothers	3	0	1	0	0

(a) How many students have no brothers or sisters?
(b) How many students have one sister?
(c) How many students have one brother and one sister?
(d) How many students have more brothers than sisters?

③ The two-way table shows information about a class of pupils.

	Can swim	Cannot swim
Boys	14	6
Girls	8	2

(a) How many boys can swim?
(b) How many boys are in the class?
(c) What percentage of the boys can swim?
(d) What percentage of the girls can swim?
(e) Do the results prove or disprove the hypothesis:
    "More boys can swim than girls?"
    Explain your answer.

④ The two-way table shows the results of a survey to test the
hypothesis: "More girls are left-handed than boys".
Do the results prove or disprove the hypothesis?
Explain your answer.

	Left-handed	
	Yes	No
Boys	3	18
Girls	2	12

5. The two-way table shows the results of a spelling test.

Number of spellings correct

	1 to 5	6 to 10	11 to 15	16 to 20
Male	1	3	6	5
Female	0	5	6	9

(a) How many females took the test?
(b) How many females got less than 11 spellings correct?
(c) John says, "Males are better at spelling because fewer males got less than 11 spellings correct".
   Is he right?
   Give a reason for your answer.

6. The two-way table shows the number of boys and girls in families taking part in a survey.

Number of girls					
4					
3	1		2		
2	1	2	3		
1	5	9		1	1
0		3		2	
	0	1	2	3	4

Number of boys

(a) (i) How many families have two children?
   (ii) Does the data support the hypothesis: "More families have less than 2 children than more than 2 children".
       Explain your answer.

(b) (i) How many girls are included in the survey?
   (ii) Does the data support the hypothesis: "More boys are born than girls"?
       Explain your answer.

7. The two-way table shows the age and gender of people taking part in a survey.

Age

	Under 18	18 to 25	26 to 40	41 to 64	65 and over
Female	0	2	7	9	7
Male	0	4	17	19	10

Give a reason why the data collected may not be representative of the whole population.

8. Suggest a hypothesis of your own.
   (a) Design a suitable questionnaire to test your hypothesis.
   (b) Choose a suitable sample and collect data.
   (c) Does the data prove your hypothesis?

- **Primary data** is data collected by an individual or organisation to use for a particular purpose. Primary data is obtained from experiments, investigations, surveys and by using questionnaires.

- **Secondary data** is data which is already available or has been collected by someone else for a different purpose. Sources of secondary data include the Annual Abstract of Statistics, Social Trends and the Internet.

- **Qualitative** data – Data which can only be described in words.

- **Quantitative** data – Data that has a numerical value. Quantitative data is either **discrete** or **continuous**. **Discrete** data can only take certain values. **Continuous** data has no exact value and is measurable.

- **Data Collection Sheets** – Used to record data during a survey.

- **Tally** – A way of recording each item of data on a data collection sheet.
  A group of five is recorded as ⦀⦀.

- **Frequency Table** – A way of collating the information recorded on a data collection sheet.

- **Grouped Frequency Table** – Used for continuous data or for discrete data when a lot of data has to be recorded.

- **Database** – A collection of data.

- **Class Interval** – The width of the groups used in a grouped frequency distribution.

- **Questionnaire** – A set of questions used to collect data for a survey. Questionnaires should:
  (1) use simple language,
  (2) ask short questions which can be answered precisely,
  (3) provide tick boxes,
  (4) avoid open-ended questions,
  (5) avoid leading questions,
  (6) ask questions in a logical order.

- **Hypothesis** – A hypothesis is a statement which may or may not be true.

- When information is required about a large group of people it is not always possible to survey everyone and only a **sample** may be asked.
  The sample chosen should be large enough to make the results meaningful and representative of the whole group (population) or the results may be **biased**.

- **Two-way Tables** – A way of illustrating two features of a survey.

Review Exercise

1 This table shows the marks for five pupils.

Name	Maths	English	Science
Senga	24	26	28
Omar	25	30	26
Samantha	28	15	20
Ihab	15	28	30
Morag	30	23	30

(a) Write down the name of the pupil who has the highest Maths mark.
(b) Write down the name of the pupil who has the lowest English mark.
(c) Write down the name of the pupil who has two marks of 30.

Edexcel

2 A gym club has 69 members.
38 of these members are boys.
There are 19 members who are girls under 15 years old
There are 23 members who are boys 15 years old or over.
(a)   Copy and complete the two-way table.

	Under 15 years old	15 years old or over	Totals
Boys		23	38
Girls	19		
Totals			69

(b)   Work out how many members of the gym club are girls 15 years old or over.   Edexcel

3 Karl's and Eleanor's school is near a busy main road.
They decide to carry out a survey of the different types of vehicles that travel on the main road.
Design a suitable data sheet so that they can collect their data easily.   Edexcel

4 The eye colour of a group of 12 students is shown.

blue	brown	green	blue	brown	brown
brown	blue	brown	green	brown	blue

(a)   Copy and complete the frequency table.

Eye colour	Tally	Frequency
blue		
brown		
green		

(b)   Which eye colour is the most frequent?

5 In a factory there are 79 male and 74 female managers.
Managers can be either junior or senior. There are 28 male senior managers.
There is a total of 93 junior managers.

(a)   Construct a two-way table to show the
number of male and female managers
in junior and senior management.
(b)   Comment on the proportion of women
in junior and senior management.

	Male	Female
Junior management		
Senior management		

Edexcel

6 Fred is conducting a survey into television viewing habits.
One of the questions in his survey is:
    "How much television do you watch?"

His friend Sheila tells him that it is not a very good question.
Write down two ways in which Fred could improve his question.   Edexcel

7 The table shows the age and gender of people taking part in a survey to test the hypothesis
"Children have too much homework".

	Age				
	Under 11	11 to 16	17 to 25	26 to 50	Over 50
Male	0	4	6	5	5
Female	0	0	0	0	0

Give three reasons why the sample is biased.

8 A set of 25 times in seconds in recorded.

12.9	10.0	4.2	16.0	5.6	18.1	8.3	14.0	11.5	21.7
22.2	6.0	13.6	3.1	11.5	10.8	15.7	3.7	9.4	8.0
6.4	17.0	7.3	12.8	13.5					

(a) Copy and complete the frequency table below, using intervals of 5 seconds.

Time (t seconds)	Tally	Frequency
$0 \leqslant t < 5$		

(b) Write down the modal class interval.

Edexcel

9 Alfie is writing a questionnaire to survey opinion on whether nightclubs should be allowed to stay open all night.

(a) Which one of the following points is important when he is writing his questionnaire?
   P Write questions for people who go to nightclubs only.
   Q Write questions that do not require long answers.
   R Write as many questions as he can think of.

(b) Which one of the following points is important when he is deciding which people to ask?
   X Ask older people only.
   Y Ask people outside a nightclub.
   Z Ask some men and some women.

(c) Alfie wants to know the age distribution of respondents.
   He considers the following questions.
   A What is your age?
   B Are you older than: ☐ 25 ☐ 45 ☐ 65?
   (i) Give a reason why Question **A** is unsuitable.
   (ii) Give a reason why Question **B** is unsuitable.

10 Terry is carrying out a survey on the shopping habits of people at a superstore.
He says, "People who travel further to the store will come less often and spend more money per visit."
Write three questions which would help him test his statement.

11 The two-way table shows the results of a survey to test the hypothesis
"A higher proportion of detached houses than semi-detached houses have garages"?
Do the results prove or disprove the hypothesis?
Explain your answer.

	Garage	No garage
Semi-detached houses	27	9
Detached houses	16	4

12 A travel agent says "More women prefer holidays abroad than men".
The table shows the results of a survey to test this statement.
Do these results support the statement made by the travel agent?
Explain your answer.

	Men	Women
Prefer holidays abroad	18	21
Prefer holidays in the UK	6	7

13 Sylvia asks a number of women how many boys and girls they each have.
Her findings are shown in the table.

(a) How many women have 2 girls and 1 boy?
(b) How many women have 3 children altogether?
(c) How many women were included in Sylvia's survey?
(d) How many children did these women have altogether?

Number of boys					
4		1			
3	2	1			
2	3	1			
1	1	3	2	1	
0	5	2	1		1
	0	1	2	3	4

Number of girls

Most people find numerical data easier to understand if it is presented in a pictorial or diagrammatical form. For this reason television reports, newspapers and advertisements frequently use graphs and diagrams to present data.

Pictograms

A **pictogram** uses symbols to represent information.
Each symbol can represent one or more items of data.

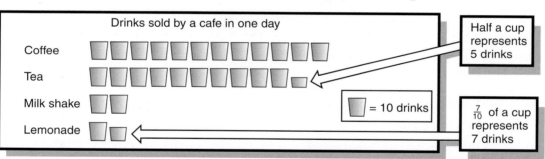

> **EXAMPLE** The table shows the number of drinks sold by a cafe in one day.
>
> | | |
> |---|---|
> | Coffee | 120 |
> | Tea | 105 |
> | Milk Shake | 20 |
> | Lemonade | 17 |
>
> To draw a pictogram of this information we can use one cup symbol to represent 10 drinks.
>
> **Drinks sold by a cafe in one day**
>
> Coffee
> Tea
> Milk shake
> Lemonade
>
> = 10 drinks
>
> Half a cup represents 5 drinks
>
> $\frac{7}{10}$ of a cup represents 7 drinks

Explain why some pictograms are difficult to read accurately.

Exercise 29.1

1 The pictogram shows the number of first class and second class stamps sold by a post office in one hour.

Number of stamps sold

First Class

Second Class

= 10 stamps

(a) How many first class stamps were sold?
(b) Estimate how many second class stamps were sold.

2 The pictogram shows the results of a survey of how students travel to college.
  (a) Fifteen students cycle to college. How many students walk?
  (b) How many students were included in the survey?

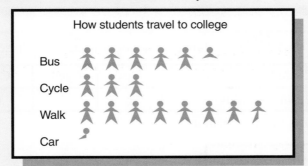

3 One hundred boys were asked which sport they preferred. The table shows the results.

Sport	Football	Cricket	Rugby	Hockey	Basketball
Number of boys	45	3	15	10	27

Draw a pictogram to represent this information.

Use = 5 boys.

4 The pictogram shows the colour of cars in a car park survey.

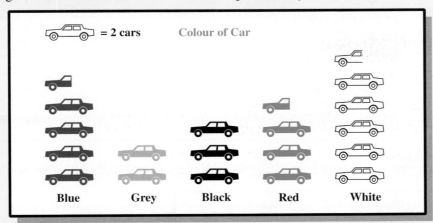

  (a) How many cars were blue?
  (b) How many cars were black?
  (c) Which colour is the most popular?
  (d) How many cars were included in the survey?

5 Fifty students were asked which european country they would visit next year.
The table shows the results.

Country	France	Germany	Spain	Italy
Number of students	23	15	7	5

Draw a pictogram to represent this information.

Use = 5 students.

Bar charts are a simple but effective way of displaying data.
Bars can be drawn either horizontally or vertically.

EXAMPLE

The table shows how a group of boys travelled to school one day.

Method of travel	Bus	Cycle	Car	Walk
Number of boys	2	7	1	5

The bar chart below shows this information.

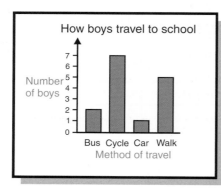

Notice that:
Bars are the same width.

There are gaps between the bars because data that can be counted is discrete.

The height of each bar gives the **frequency**.

The tallest bar represents the most frequent variable (category).

The most frequently occurring variable is called the **mode** or **modal** category.
Cycle is the modal category for these boys.

Bar-line graphs

Instead of drawing bars to show frequency we could draw vertical lines.
Such graphs are called **bar-line graphs** or **vertical line graphs**.
The lines can be drawn horizontally or vertically.

EXAMPLE

The graph shows the number of goals scored by a football team in 10 matches.

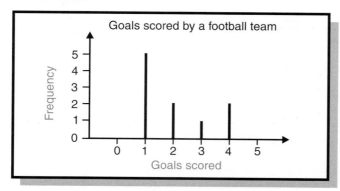

The frequency represents the number of matches played.

In how many matches was only one goal scored?

What is the difference between the largest number of goals scored in a match and the smallest number of goals scored?

The difference between the largest and smallest variable is called the **range**.
The range for the number of goals scored is $4 - 1 = 3$.

Exercise 29.2

① The hair colour of all the students in a class is recorded.
The bar graph shows the results.

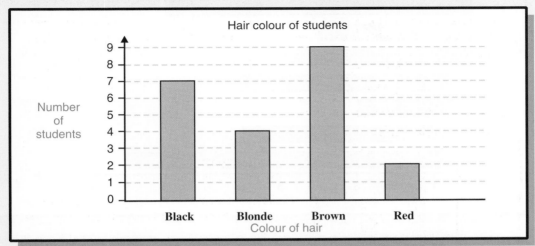

(a) How many students have black hair?
(b) Which hair colour is the mode?
(c) How many students are in the class?

② The bar-line graph shows the sales of shoes by a shoe shop on one day.

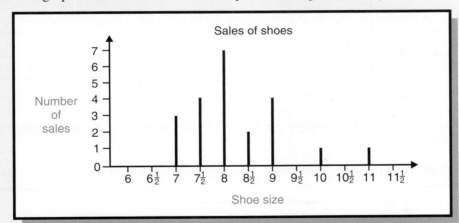

(a) Which shoe size is the mode?
(b) What is the range in the sizes of shoes sold?
(c) How many pairs of shoes were sold?

③ The result of throwing a dice 30 times is shown.

1	2	3	3	5	2	1	6	5	4
2	4	5	3	2	3	1	4	2	6
6	3	6	5	3	1	3	4	6	5

(a) Copy and complete the frequency table
for these scores.
(b) Draw a bar chart to show the data.
(c) Which score is the mode?

Score	Tally	Frequency
1		
2		
3		
4		
5		
6		

4 The bar chart shows the time Jim spent watching television each day last week.

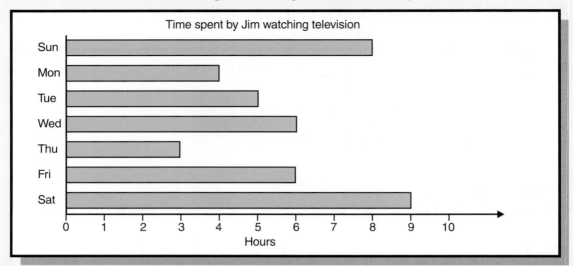

(a) On which day did Jim watch the most television?
(b) How many hours did Jim spend watching television on Tuesday?
(c) How many hours did Jim spend watching television last week?
(d) On which day did Jim spend a third of the day watching television?
(e) What fraction of the day did Jim spend watching television on Wednesday?
(f) What is the range of the number of hours per day Jim spent watching television?

5 The table shows the amount of pocket money given each week to 30 Year 11 girls.

Amount (£)	1	2	3	4	5	6	7	8	9	10
Number of girls	0	0	1	5	10	4	0	3	0	7

(a) Draw a bar-line graph of the data.
(b) What is the modal amount of pocket money?
(c) What is the range of the amount of pocket money given each week?
(d) What percentage of the girls got less than £5?

6 The bar-line graph illustrates the number of goals scored per match by a hockey team.

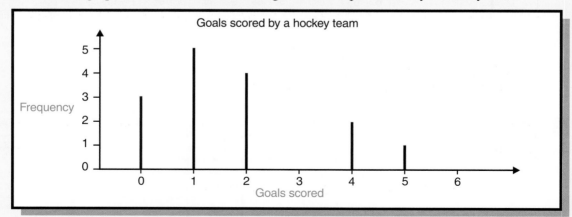

(a) How many matches have the team played?
(b) Which number of goals scored is the mode?
(c) What is the range of the number of goals scored?
(d) In what percentage of games were no goals scored?

7 A group of senior citizens were asked how many children were in their families. The table shows the results.

Number of children	1	2	3	4	5	6	7
Number of families	3	6	11	8	4	1	2

(a) Draw a bar chart of this information.
(b) What is the modal number of children per family?
(c) What is the range in the number of children per family?

8 Collect information about the number of children per family for students in your class. Draw a bar chart of the information and compare it with the information in question 7.

9 The bar chart shows the day of birth for a group of children.

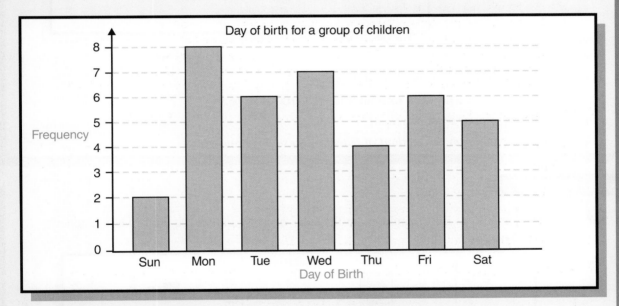

(a) How many children are in the group?
(b) Which day of birth is the mode?
The table shows the day of birth for the girls.

Day of birth	Sun	Mon	Tue	Wed	Thu	Fri	Sat
Number of girls	1	5	2	3	3	1	4

(c) Draw up a table to show the day of birth for the boys.

10 Record the day of birth for all the students in your class. Draw a bar chart of the data. Compare your data with the data given in question 9.

Comparing data

Bar charts can also be used to compare data.

The table shows how a class of children travelled to school one day.

Method of travel	Bus	Cycle	Car	Walk
Boys	2	7	1	5
Girls	3	1	5	6

To make it easier to compare information for boys and girls we can draw both bars on the same diagram, as shown.

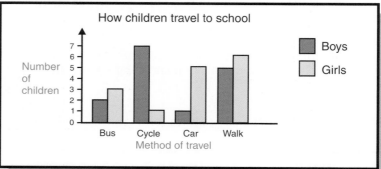

Seven boys cycle to school.
How many girls cycle to school?

There are 15 girls in the class and 6 walk to school.

The percentage of girls who walk to school is $\frac{6}{15} \times 100 = 40\%$.

What percentage of boys walk to school?

Compare and comment on the method of travel of these boys and girls.

Exercise 29.3

1 The bar chart shows information about the sales of fresh and frozen poultry at a butcher's one Saturday.

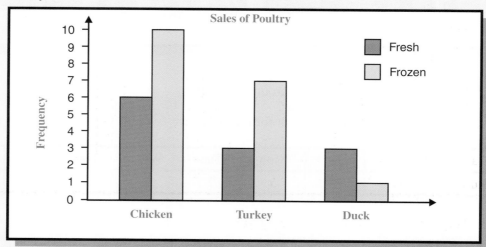

(a) How many frozen chickens were sold?
(b) How many fresh turkeys were sold?
(c) How many ducks were sold altogether?
(d) What fraction of the turkeys sold were frozen?
(e) What percentage of the ducks sold were fresh?

2 The bar chart shows the reason given by students for being absent from school one day.

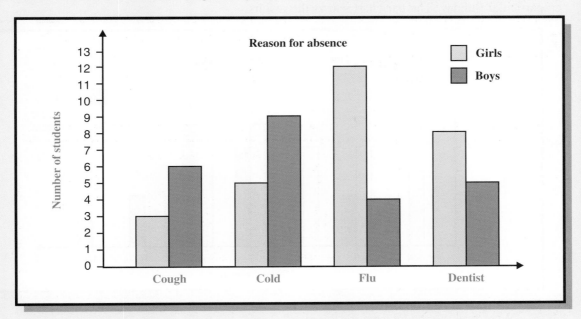

(a) How many girls were absent with flu?
(b) How many boys were absent with a cough?
(c) Which reason for absence was the mode?
(d) Compare and comment on the reasons for absence given by girls and boys.

3 The bar chart shows the marks scored by four different boys in both a numeracy test and an IQ test.

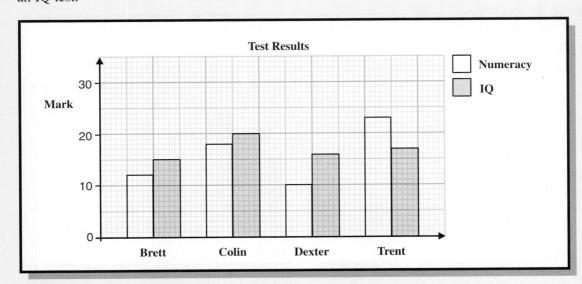

(a) Which boy scored the lowest IQ mark?
(b) Which boy scored the highest mark in numeracy?
(c) What is the range in the IQ marks?
(d) What is the range in the numeracy marks?
(e) The marks are added together to give each boy a total score.
   (i) Which boy had the highest score?
   (ii) Which boy had the lowest score?

4 A group of children were asked how many hours they had spent watching television on a particular Sunday. The bar chart shows the results.

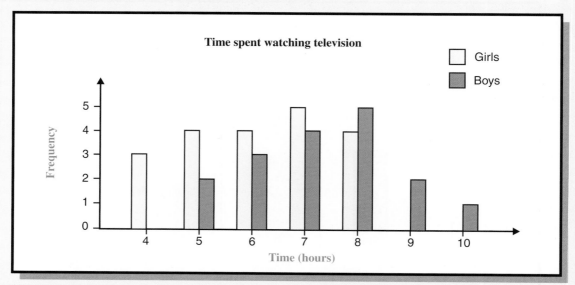

(a) What was the modal time for the girls?
(b) What was the range in time for the boys?
(c) How many boys watched television for more than 8 hours?
(d) (i) How many girls were included in the survey?
    (ii) What percentage of the girls watched television for 6 hours?
(e) Compare and comment on the time spent watching television for these boys and girls.

5 The bar chart shows the results of a survey of the shoe sizes of pupils in a Year 9 class.

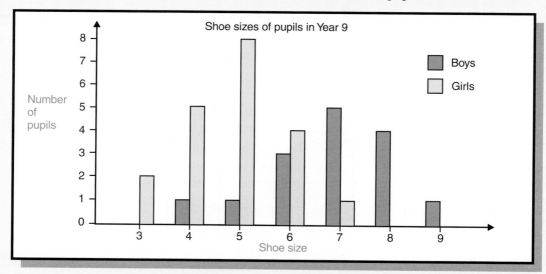

(a) Which size of shoe is the mode for the girls?
(b) Which size of shoe is the mode for the boys?
(c) (i) How many boys took part in the survey?
    (ii) What fraction of boys wear shoe size 8 or 9?
(d) What is the range of shoe size for girls?
(e) What is the range of shoe size for boys?
(f) Compare and comment on the shoe sizes of boys and girls.

Pie charts

Bar charts are useful for comparing the various types of data (categories) with each other.
To compare each category with **all** the data collected we use a **pie chart**.

A pie chart is a circle which is divided up into sectors.
The whole circle represents the total frequency and each sector represents the frequency of one part (category) of the data.

Drawing pie charts

The table shows the ways in which some children like to eat eggs.

Method of cooking	Poached	Boiled	Scrambled	Fried
Number of children	5	8	6	11

To show this information in a pie chart we must find the angles of the sectors which represent each category. First calculate the angle which represents each child.
30 children are represented by 360°.
1 child is represented by $360° \div 30 = 12°$.
Sector angle = Number of children in category $\times 12°$

Method of cooking	Poached	Boiled	Scrambled	Fried	**Total**
Number of children	5	8	6	11	**30**
Sector angle	60°	96°	72°	132°	**360°**

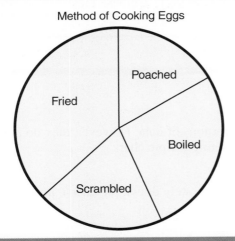

Method of Cooking Eggs

○○○○○○○○○○○○○○○○○
Using a table allows you to keep your work tidy and to make checks.

○○○○○○○○○○○○○○○○○
The whole circle represents the total frequency of 30.

Each sector represents the frequency of one category (method of cooking).

Exercise 29.4

1. The table shows information about the trees in a wood.

Type of tree	Ash	Beech	Maple
Number of trees	20	25	15

Draw a pie chart for this data.

2. The colour of eyes of 90 people were recorded.
   The table shows the results.

Colour of eyes	Brown	Blue	Green	Other
Number of people	40	25	15	10

Draw a pie chart for this data.

3 The table shows information about the cars owned by a company.

Make of car	Ford	Rover	Vauxhall	BMW
Frequency	10	9	15	6

Draw a pie chart for this data.

4 The breakfast cereal preferred by some adults is shown.

Breakfast cereal	Cornflakes	Muesli	Porridge	Branflakes
Number of adults	25	20	12	15

Show the information in a pie chart.

5 The table shows the sales of ice-cream cornets at a kiosk one day.

Ice-cream cornet	Vanilla	Strawberry	99	Raspberry Ripple
Frequency	40	20	25	15

Draw a pie chart for this data.

6 The table shows the results of a survey to find the most popular takeaway food.

Type of takeaway	Fish & chips	Chicken & chips	Chinese meal	Pizza
Number of people	165	204	78	93

Draw a pie chart for this data.

Interpreting pie charts

Pie charts are useful for showing and comparing proportions of data. However, they do not show frequencies. Such information can be found by interpreting the pie chart.

To interpret a pie chart we need to know:
- the sector angles (which can be measured from an accurately drawn pie chart), **and**
- the total frequency represented by the pie chart, **or**
  the frequency represented by one of the sectors.

EXAMPLE

The pie chart shows the makes of 120 cars.
(a) Which make of car is the mode?
(b) How many of the cars are Ford?

(a) The sector representing Vauxhall is the largest.
    Therefore, Vauxhall is the mode.

(b) The angle of the sector representing Ford is 72°.

    The number of Ford cars $= \frac{72}{360} \times 120 = 24$.

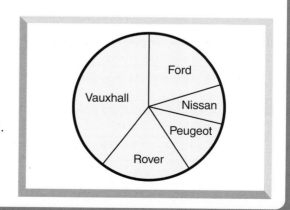

1 The pie chart shows the type of holiday chosen by 36 people.

(a) How many people chose a camping holiday?

(b) How many people chose a self-catering holiday?

(c) What type of holiday is the mode?

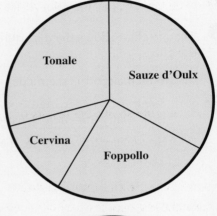

2 The pie chart shows the resorts chosen in Italy by 60 skiers.

(a) How many skiers chose Sauze d'Oulx?

(b) How many skiers chose Foppollo?

(c) Which resort is the mode?

3 The pie chart shows the holiday destinations of 180 people.

(a) Which holiday destination is the mode?

(b) How many people went to Italy?

(c) How many people went to Germany?

(d) How many people went to Austria?

4 The pie chart shows the membership of an international committee.
The USA has 7 committee members.

(a) How many committee members has the EU?

(b) How many committee members has Canada?

(c) How many committee members are there altogether?

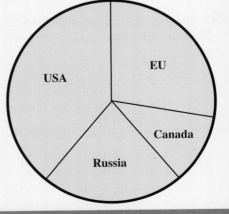

5 The pie chart shows the five types of fruit tree sold by a garden centre.

21 apple trees were sold.

(a) How many plum trees were sold?

(b) How many fruit trees were sold altogether?

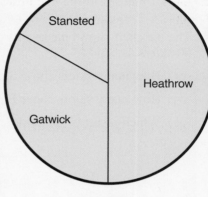

6 The pie chart shows the departure airports of some travellers.

(a) Which airport is the mode?

(b) 360 travellers departed from Gatwick.
How many travellers departed from Heathrow?

(c) How many travellers are there altogether?

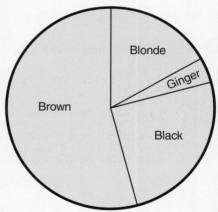

7 The pie chart illustrates the results of a survey of the colour of hair of 48 boys.

(a) Which colour of hair is the mode?

(b) How many boys have brown hair?

(c) What percentage of the boys have black hair?

8 The pie chart shows the different types of tree in a forest.

There are 54 oak trees and these are represented by a sector with an angle of 27°.

(a) The pine trees are represented by an angle of 144°.
How many pine trees are there?

(b) There are 348 silver birch trees.
Calculate the angle of the sector representing silver birch trees.

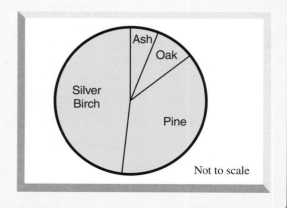

Not to scale

Stem and leaf diagrams

Data can also be represented using a **stem and leaf diagram**.

EXAMPLE

The times, in seconds, taken by 20 students to complete a puzzle are shown.

15	9	23	32	17	12	27	19	26	15
20	11	24	31	10	17	15	28	33	18

Construct a stem and leaf diagram to represent this information.

A stem and leaf diagram is made by splitting each number into two parts.
As the data uses 'tens' and 'units', the stem will represent the 'tens' and the leaf will represent the 'units'.
To draw the stem and leaf diagram begin by drawing a vertical line.
The digits to the left of the line make the **stem**.
The digits to the right of the line are the **leaves**.

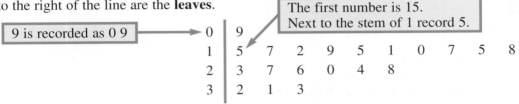

9 is recorded as 0 9

The first number is 15.
Next to the stem of 1 record 5.

```
0 | 9
1 | 5  7  2  9  5  1  0  7  5  8
2 | 3  7  6  0  4  8
3 | 2  1  3
```

Once the data has been recorded, it is usual to redraw the diagram so that the leaves are in numerical order.

```
                                1 | 5  means 15 seconds
0 | 9
1 | 0  1  2  5  5  5  7  7  8  9
2 | 0  3  4  6  7  8
3 | 1  2  3
```

Stem and leaf diagrams are often drawn without column headings in which case a key is necessary.
e.g. 1|5   means 15 seconds

Exercise 29.6

1   The amount of petrol, in litres, bought by 20 motorists is shown.

16	23	27	10	35	42	26	25	24	17
23	41	33	35	25	19	16	31	12	29

Construct a stem and leaf diagram to represent this information.

2   The times, in seconds, taken to answer 24 telephone calls are shown.

3.2	5.6	2.4	3.5	4.3	3.6	2.8	5.8	3.3	2.6	3.2	2.8
5.6	3.5	4.2	1.5	2.7	2.5	3.7	3.1	2.9	4.2	2.4	3.0

Copy and complete the stem and leaf diagram to represent this information.

```
          3 | 2  means 3.2 seconds
1 |
2 |
3 | 2
4 |
5 |
```

For this data
the stem represents 'units',
the leaf represents 'tenths'.

3 The number of press-ups completed by 18 students in one minute is shown.

$$21 \quad 36 \quad 41 \quad 25 \quad 18 \quad 32 \quad 40 \quad 36 \quad 22$$
$$9 \quad 16 \quad 24 \quad 33 \quad 36 \quad 27 \quad 32 \quad 20 \quad 28$$

Draw a stem and leaf diagram to represent this information.

4 The heights, in centimetres, of the heels on 20 different pairs of shoes are shown.

$$2.7 \quad 3.4 \quad 2.0 \quad 6.0 \quad 4.5 \quad 3.6 \quad 3.1 \quad 2.4 \quad 4.2 \quad 1.8$$
$$3.5 \quad 2.5 \quad 2.6 \quad 2.1 \quad 4.0 \quad 3.5 \quad 4.2 \quad 2.6 \quad 3.9 \quad 5.4$$

Construct a stem and leaf diagram to represent this information.

5 David did a survey to find the cost, in pence, of a loaf of bread.
The stem and leaf diagram shows the results of his survey.

```
                              2 | 7   means 27 pence
        2 | 7  9
        3 | 1  1  2  9  9  9
        4 | 2  5  9
        5 | 0
```

(a) How many loaves of bread are included in the survey?
(b) What is the range of the prices?
(c) Which price is the mode?

Back to back stem and leaf diagrams

Back to back stem and leaf diagrams can be used to compare two sets of data.

EXAMPLE

The results for examinations in Mathematics and English for a group of students are shown. The marks are given as percentages.

Mathematics: 91   27   55   69   83   25   45   53   67   71
                  30   52   45   59   86   73   65   47   54   38

English: 45   40   48   65   75   55   36   85   76   69
                64   58   47   64   67   72   83   74   62   51

(a) Construct a back to back stem and leaf diagram for this data.
(b) Compare and comment on the results in Mathematics and English.

(a)

```
        Mathematics                    English          3 | 6  means 36%
                    7  5 | 2 |
                    8  0 | 3 | 6
                 7  5  5 | 4 | 0  5  7  8
        9  5  4  3  2 | 5 | 1  5  8
                 9  7  5 | 6 | 2  4  4  5  7  9          For Mathematics:
                    3  1 | 7 | 2  4  5  6               5 | 2 means 25%
                    6  3 | 8 | 3  5
                       1 | 9 |
```

(b) The range of marks in Mathematics is larger than in English.
The modal group in English is 60 to 69, in Mathematics it is 50 to 59.

312

Exercise 29.7

1 The stem and leaf diagram shows the distribution of marks for a test marked out of 50.

			Boys						Girls						1	7 means 17 marks

```
        Boys              |   |      Girls            1 | 7  means 17 marks
                       0  | 9
              6    2   1  | 0   1   2   7
     7   6   4    3   2  | 1   3   5   5   6   7   8
9   5   3   2    0   3  | 2   5   9
              5    1   4  | 1
                      0   5  |
```

(a) What is the lowest mark for the girls?
(b) What is the highest mark for the boys?
(c) How many pupils scored more than 25 marks?
(d) Compare and comment on the marks for boys and girls.

2 The time taken to complete a computer game is recorded to the nearest tenth of a minute.
The times for a group of 20 adults and 20 children are shown.

Adults						Children			
7.9	8.2	7.3	9.2	6.4	6.4	5.4	4.9	6.6	7.1
6.5	6.1	8.2	7.8	7.0	5.1	6.5	6.3	7.4	6.5
9.4	8.0	7.3	5.4	7.7	8.2	7.7	5.9	6.8	7.6
10.1	5.9	6.7	7.3	6.0	5.3	6.2	8.0	4.7	7.9

(a) Construct a back to back stem and leaf diagram for this data.
(b) Compare and comment on the times for adults and children.

What you need to know

- **Bar chart**. Used for data which can be counted.
  Often used to compare quantities of data in a distribution.
  Bars can be drawn horizontally or vertically.
  Bars are the same width and there are gaps between bars.
  The length of each bar represents frequency.
  The longest bar represents the **mode**.
  The difference between the largest and smallest variable is called the **range**.

- **Bar-line graph**. Instead of drawing bars, horizontal or vertical lines are drawn to show frequency.

- **Pie chart**. Used for data which can be counted.
  Often used to compare proportions of data, usually with the total.
  The whole circle represents all the data.
  The size of each sector represents the frequency of data in that sector.
  The largest sector represents the **mode**.

- **Stem and leaf diagrams**. Used to represent data in its original form.
  Data is split into two parts. The part with the higher place value is the stem,
  e.g.   15   stem 1 leaf 5.
  The data is shown in numerical order on the diagram.
  e.g. 2|3 5 9 represents 23, 25, 29. A key is given to show the value of the data.
  e.g. 3|4 means 34 cm   or   3|4 means 3.4 cm etc.
  Back to back stem and leaf diagrams can be used to compare two sets of data.

1

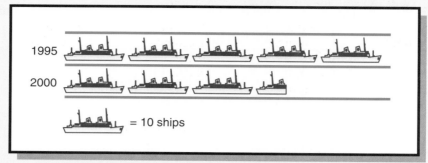

The diagram shows how many ships were in Mathsland's navy in 1995 and 2000.
Use the diagram to answer these questions.
(a)   How many ships were there in Mathsland's navy in 1995?
(b)   How many ships were there in Mathsland's navy in 2000?

Edexcel

2

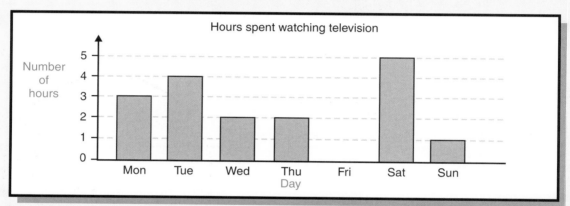

The bar chart shows the number of hours Jason spent watching television in one week.
(a)   Write down the day on which he watched most television.
(b)   Work out the total number of hours he spent watching television during the week.

Edexcel

3   A farmer has 40 hens.
The table shows the number of eggs laid
by the hens last week.

(a)   Draw a bar chart to show this information.
(b)   Work out the number of hens which
      laid 3 eggs or more.
(c)   Write down the mode.

Number of eggs	Frequency
0	2
1	8
2	9
3	11
4	6
5	4

Edexcel

4   Some families on holiday at a seaside resort were questioned about their holiday
accommodation.

Type of accommodation	Hotel	Bed & Breakfast	Self-catering	Caravan	Camping	Other
Number of families	9	17	11	8	2	3

(a)   Draw a bar chart to show this information.
(b)   What type of accommodation is the mode?
(c)   How many families were questioned?
(d)   What percentage of these families had Bed & Breakfast?

5 30 people used a Sports Centre one evening.
Here is a list of the activities in which they took part.

Gym	Swimming	Squash	Swimming	Aerobics
Swimming	Aerobics	Aerobics	Aerobics	Gym
Aerobics	Gym	Gym	Gym	Squash
Squash	Gym	Squash	Gym	Gym
Gym	Aerobics	Aerobics	Squash	Gym
Gym	Aerobics	Squash	Gym	Aerobics

(a) Copy and complete the table to show this information.

Activity	Tally	Frequency
Gym		
Swimming		
Squash		
Aerobics		
Total		30

(b) Draw a pie chart to show this information.

Edexcel

6 720 students were asked how they travelled to school.
The pie chart shows the results of this survey.

Work out how many of the students travelled to
school by bus.

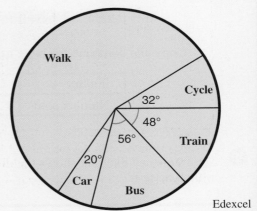

Edexcel

7 The pie chart shows the types of potato sold by a farmer.
(a) Which type of potato is the mode?

The farmer sold 24 tonnes of Estima potatoes.
(b) How many tonnes of King Edward's did he sell?

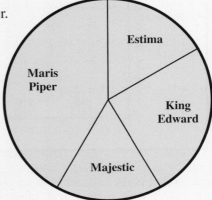

8 The weights in grams of 20 cherry tomatoes are shown.

| 5.4 | 4.6 | 6.7 | 3.9 | 4.2 | 5.0 | 6.3 | 5.4 | 4.8 | 3.5 |
| 4.6 | 5.6 | 5.8 | 6.0 | 2.8 | 4.4 | 4.7 | 5.6 | 5.1 | 4.8 |

(a) Draw a stem and leaf diagram to represent this information.
(b) What is the range in the weights of the tomatoes?

9 A butcher keeps a record of the fresh and frozen poultry he sells each day.
Of the poultry sold one Saturday he finds:
$\frac{7}{12}$ were chickens, $\frac{1}{3}$ were turkeys and the rest were ducks.

(a) Draw a pie chart to represent this information.

(b) He sold 21 chickens.
How much poultry did he sell altogether?

(c) The bar chart shows the frozen poultry he sold.

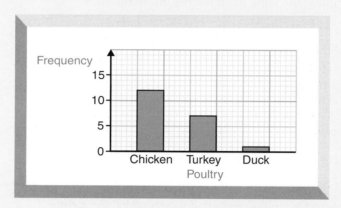

Copy and complete the table to show the fresh poultry he sold.

Poultry	Chicken	Turkey	Duck
Number sold			

10 The frequency diagram shows the distribution of marks for a class of 30 pupils in a mental arithmetic test.

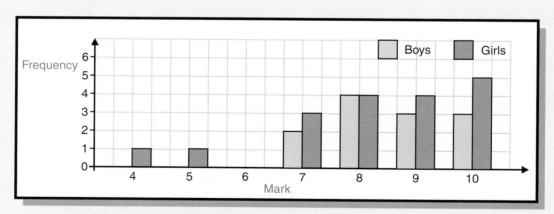

(a) What is the ratio of boys to girls in the class?
Give your answer in its simplest form.

(b) The test is marked out of 10.
What percentage of the class scored full marks?
Give your answer to a suitable degree of accuracy.

(c) By comparing the mode and range for the girls with the mode and range for the boys, comment on the marks scored.

CHAPTER 30

Averages and Range

Activity

Some friends went on a school trip. They each brought different amounts of spending money, as follows:

Penny £15   Keith £35   Nishpal £40   Jayne £10   Stephen £50   Ben £60
Charlotte £35   Suzie £50   Dan £55   Vicki £35   Jack £55

Ben brought the most and Jayne the least.
What was the difference in the amounts of spending money Ben and Jayne brought?
Which was the most common amount of money?
Who brought the middle amount of money? How much was this?
If the friends shared out their money equally, how much would each person get?

Range

The difference between the highest and lowest amounts is called the **range**.
Range = highest amount − lowest amount

Types of average

The most common amount is called the **mode**.
When the amounts are arranged in order of size, the middle one is called the **median**.
When the money is shared out equally, the amount each person gets is called the **mean**.

EXAMPLE

The price, in pence, of a can of cola in different shops is shown.
$$33, \quad 34, \quad 31, \quad 32, \quad 30, \quad 31, \quad 31, \quad 35.$$
Find   (a)   the mode,   (b)   the median,   (c)   the mean price.

(a)   The **mode** is the most common amount.
The most common price is 31.
The mode is 31 pence.
We sometimes say the modal price is 31p.

(b)   The **median** is found by arranging the data in order of size and taking the middle amount.
Arrange the data in order of size.
$$30, \quad 31, \quad 31, \quad 31, \quad 32, \quad 33, \quad 34, \quad 35.$$

The middle amount is $\dfrac{31 + 32}{2} = 31.5$

Where there are an even number of values the median is the average of the middle two.

The median is 31.5 pence.

(c)   The **mean** is found by finding the total of all the data and dividing the total by the number of data values.
Add the data.
$$33 + 34 + 31 + 32 + 30 + 31 + 31 + 35 = 257$$

The mean $= \dfrac{257}{8} = 32.125$

The mean is 32.125 pence.

Questions 1 to 6.

Do not use a calculator. Show your working clearly.

1 Tony recorded the number of birthday cards sold each day.

3   4   8   1   4

(a) Work out the range of the number of cards sold each day.

(b) Write down the mode.

(c) Find the median number of cards sold each day.

2 Four students had the following number of books in their bags.

3   4   1   4

(a) What is the range of the number of books?

(b) What is the mean number of books?

3 Claire recorded the number of e-mail messages she received each day.

2   1   7   4   1

(a) Write down the mode.

(b) Find the median number of messages received each day.

(c) Calculate the mean number of messages received each day.

4 A postman delivers letters to a block of flats.

There are 8 flats in the block.

The number of letters he delivers to each flat is shown below.

1   3   4   4   2   2   6   2

(a) What is the range of the number of letters delivered?

(b) Write down the mode.

(c) Calculate the mean number of letters delivered to each flat.

5 The price, in pence, of a bar of chocolate in four different shops is shown.

20   17   22   25

Find the median of these prices.

6 Gail noted the number of stamps on 6 parcels delivered to her office.

3   2   4   5   7   3

(a) Write down the mode.

(b) Find the range of the number of stamps on a parcel.

(c) Find the median number of stamps on a parcel.

(d) Calculate the mean number of stamps on a parcel.

Questions 7 to 13.

You may use a calculator.

7 Here is a list of the weights of some people, in kilograms.

68   74   63   81   76

(a) What is the range of the weights of the five people?

(b) Find the median weight.

(c) Calculate the mean weight.

8 Sanjay played a computer game 8 times and recorded his scores.

140   135   125   125   130   135   140   135

(a) Which score is the mode?

(b) Calculate the median of his scores.

(c) Find the mean score. Give your answer to the nearest whole number.

9 Frank counted the number of books on different shelves in a library.
He recorded the following numbers.

   38   40   26   49   37   43

(a) Find the median number of books on a shelf.
(b) What is the range of the number of books on a shelf?
(c) Calculate the mean number of books on a shelf.
      Give your answer correct to one decimal place.

10 Seven people have an average of 9 computer games each.
How many computer games do they have altogether?

11 The mean of six numbers is 5.
Five of the numbers are 2, 3, 7, 8 and 6.
What is the other number?

12 The mean of seven numbers is 6.
Six of the numbers are 2, 5, 7, 3, 7 and 10.
What is the other number?

13 The mean length of 8 rods is 75 cm.
An extra rod is added.
The total length of the 9 rods is 729 cm.
What is the length of the extra rod?

Using the range and mean to compare data

In statistics we frequently need to compare two sets of data.
A simple comparison can be made by using the range to compare **spread** and the mean to compare **average**.

EXAMPLE

The weights of a sample of Cherry tomatoes have a range of 30 g and a mean of 45 g.
The weights of a sample of Moneymaker tomatoes have a range of 90 g and a mean of 105 g.
Compare and comment on the weights of Cherry and Moneymaker tomatoes.

Range: Cherry tomatoes 30 g, Moneymaker tomatoes 90 g.
         The smaller range for Cherry tomatoes shows they are more consistent in weight.
Mean: Cherry tomatoes 45 g, Moneymaker tomatoes 105 g.
         The smaller mean for Cherry tomatoes shows they have a lower average weight.

Comment: The average weight of Cherry tomatoes is lower but they are more consistent in weight.

Exercise 30.2

1 The weights, in grams, of a sample of 10 economy potatoes are shown.

   70   76   83   86   95   98   113   117   122   130

(a) (i)   What is the range of these weights?
    (ii) Calculate the mean of these weights.

For a sample of 10 premium potatoes the range of their weights is 240 grams and the mean of their weights is 250 grams.
(b) Compare and comment on the weights of economy and premium potatoes.

2 The lateness of 12 buses is recorded.
The results, in minutes, are shown.

| 5 | 6 | 7 | 8 | 8 | 10 | 10 | 10 | 11 | 12 | 13 | 14 |

(a) (i) What is the range of lateness for these buses?
    (ii) Calculate the mean lateness for these buses.

The lateness of 12 trains is also recorded.
The range in lateness for these trains is 14 minutes and the mean lateness is 5 minutes.
(b) Compare and comment on the lateness for these buses and trains.

3 The numbers of words typed per minute by a group of students are shown.

| 45 | 51 | 58 | 59 | 63 | 87 | 64 | 59 | 58 | 63 | 53 |

(a) (i) What is the range of their typing speeds?
    (ii) Calculate the mean typing speed for these students.

For another group of students the mean of their typing speeds is 42 words per minute and the range is 67.
(b) Comment on the typing speeds of these two groups of students.

4 The numbers of goals scored in matches played by some first division football teams are shown.

| 1 | 5 | 0 | 2 | 2 | 3 | 0 | 4 | 2 | 0 | 1 |

(a) (i) What is the range of the number of goals scored?
    (ii) Calculate the mean number of goals scored.

The numbers of goals scored in matches played by some third division football teams are shown.

| 3 | 2 | 4 | 1 | 1 | 3 | 2 | 1 | 7 |

(b) Compare the numbers of goals scored by these first and third division football teams.

5 The times, in minutes, taken by 8 boys to swim 50 metres are shown.

| 1.8 | 2.0 | 1.7 | 2.2 | 2.1 | 1.9 | 1.8 | 2.1 |

(a) (i) What is the range of these times?
    (ii) Calculate the mean time.

The times, in minutes, taken by 8 girls to swim 50 m are shown.

| 2.1 | 1.9 | 1.8 | 2.3 | 1.6 | 2.0 | 2.6 | 1.9 |

(b) Comment on the times taken by these boys and girls to swim 50 m.

6 The table shows the percentage silver content of twenty ancient coins.

	Percentage silver content				
Roman coins	5.6	6.7	6.6	7.2	6.3
Chinese coins	6.8	6.7	6.2	5.4	7.3
Egyptian coins	5.1	7.0	5.8	6.9	7.6
Greek coins	5.6	7.2	6.6	6.8	5.7

For each type of coin
(a) calculate the range of the percentage silver content,
(b) calculate the mean of the percentage silver content.

(c) Comment on your answers to (a) and (b).

7 Pupils in Year 7 are arranged in nine classes.
The class sizes are:

| 30 | 27 | 28 | 29 | 27 | 29 | 29 | 28 | 28 |

(a) Calculate the mean class size.
(b) The range of the class sizes for Year 11 is 12.
What does this tell you about the class sizes in Year 11 compared with those in Year 7?

Frequency distributions

A **frequency distribution table** is used to present data.

Johti measured the lengths of some twigs. He recorded the following results.

2	3	2	6	3	6	2
3	5	4	3	2	2	3
5	6	2	6	5	6	2

His results are shown in this frequency distribution table.

Length (cm)	2	3	4	5	6
Number of twigs (frequency)	7	5	1	3	5

EXAMPLE

Find the mode, median, mean and range of the lengths of the twigs that Johti measured.

To find the mode: The mode is the amount with the greatest frequency.
There were 7 twigs of length 2 cm.
This is more than any other length of twigs.
The mode of the lengths is 2 cm.

To find the median: The median is the middle amount.
We could list the 21 twigs in order of length and split them up like this:

10 shortest twigs	middle twig	10 longest twigs

This shows that the median length is the length of the 11th twig.
From the table we can see that:
    the first 7 twigs are each 2 cm long,
    and the next 5 twigs are each 3 cm long.
So the 11th twig is 3 cm long.
The median length is 3 cm.

To find the mean: $\text{Mean} = \dfrac{\text{Total of all lengths}}{\text{Number of lengths}}$

The best way to do this is to use a table.

Length (cm) x	Number of twigs (frequency) f	Frequency $\times$ Number of twigs $f \times x$
2	7	14
3	5	15
4	1	4
5	3	15
6	5	30
Totals	Total $f = 21$	Total $fx = 78$

$\text{Mean} = \dfrac{\text{Total of all lengths}}{\text{Number of lengths}} = \dfrac{\text{Total } fx}{\text{Total } f}$

$\text{Mean} = \dfrac{78}{21} = 3.714\ldots$

Mean length = 3.7 cm, correct to 1 decimal place.

To find the range: Range = longest length − shortest length
$= 6 - 2$
$= 4 \text{ cm}$

Do not use a calculator for questions 1 and 2.

1 A milkman delivers bottles of milk to 30 houses in a street.
The number of bottles of milk he delivers to each house is shown below.

1	4	2	1	2	1	2	1	1	2
2	2	1	3	1	2	1	2	2	1
3	2	3	1	3	1	4	3	1	4

(a) Copy and complete this frequency distribution table.

Number of bottles	1	2	3	4
Number of houses				

(b) What is the mode of the number of bottles delivered?
(c) What is the median number of bottles delivered?
(d) Calculate the mean number of bottles of milk delivered to each house.

2 Mark asked some students, "How many keys do you have on your key ring?"
The data collection sheet shows the responses he recorded.

Number of keys	Tally
2	||
3	|||
4	卌 |||
5	卌
6	||

(a) Use Mark's data to make a frequency distribution table.
(b) How many students did Mark ask?
(c) Write down the mode of the number of keys on a key ring.
(d) Find the median number of keys.
(e) Calculate the mean number of keys on a key ring.

3 Pat recorded the weekly earnings of a group of students. Her results were as follows:

£15	£30	£20	£35	£15	£15	£20
£25	£35	£15	£25	£20	£25	£25
£25	£20	£25	£15	£35		

(a) Show the data in a frequency distribution table.
(b) Find the range of the weekly earnings.
(c) What is the modal weekly earnings?
(d) How many people were in the group?
(e) What is the median weekly earnings?
(f) Calculate the total weekly earnings of the group.
(g) Calculate the mean weekly earnings. Give your answer to the nearest penny.

4 Find the mode, median and mean for the following data.

(a)

Number of letters delivered	1	2	3	4	5	6
Number of days	6	9	6	6	2	1

(b)

Number of books read last month	0	1	2	3	4	5
Number of students	1	4	10	4	1	1

(c)

Number of days absent in a year	0	1	2	3	4	5	6	7	8	9	10	11
Number of students	56	0	0	4	14	10	24	11	21	15	8	2

Find the range, mode, median and mean of the ages for the data shown in the bar chart.

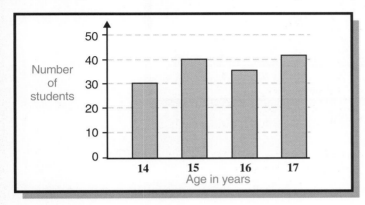

The range is the difference between the highest and lowest ages.
Range = 17 - 14
      = 3 years

The most common age is shown by the tallest bar.
So the modal age is 17 years.

Use a table to find the median and the mean.

Age x	Frequency f	Frequency × Age $f \times x$
14	30	420
15	40	600
16	36	576
17	41	697
Totals	Total f = 147	Total fx = 2293

The middle student is given by: $\dfrac{147 + 1}{2} = 74$

The 74th student in the list has the median age.
The first 70 students are aged 14 or 15 years.
The 74th student has age 16 years.
Median age is 16 years.

$$\text{Mean} = \frac{\text{Total of all ages}}{\text{Number of students}} = \frac{\text{Total } fx}{\text{Total } f}$$

$$\text{Mean} = \frac{2293}{147} = 15.598\ldots$$

Mean age is 15.6 years, correct to 1 d.p.

Exercise 30.4

Try to do questions 1 and 2 without using a calculator.

1   Hilary observed customers using the express checkout at a supermarket.

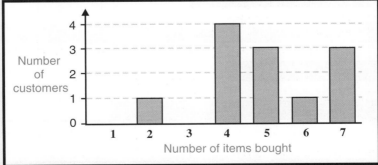

  (a)   Find the range of the number of items bought.
  (b)   What is the mode of the number of items bought?
  (c)   Work out the median number of items bought.
  (d)   Calculate the mean number of items bought.

2 During one week, the following numbers of various sizes of a particular style of shoe were sold.

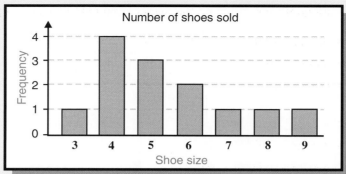

(a) Find the range of the shoe sizes sold.
(b) Which size is the median?
(c) Which size is the mode?
(d) Calculate the mean size.
    Comment on your answer.

3 (a) Find the range and mode of these prices.
(b) Calculate the median and mean price of a bottle of milk.

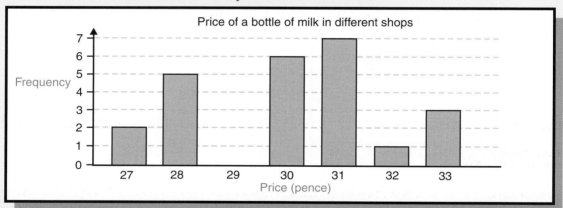

4 A group of students took part in a quiz on the Highway Code.
The bar chart shows their scores.

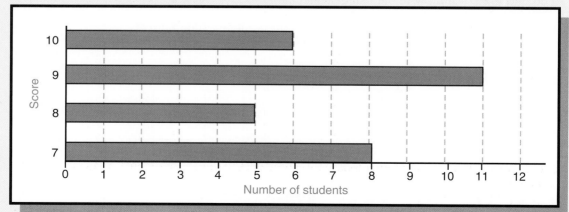

(a) Which score is the mode?
(b) What is the median score?
(c) How many students took part in the quiz?
(d) Calculate the mean score.

Comparing distributions

By answering the following questions, compare the marks obtained by boys and girls in a test.

Mark (out of 10)	7	8	9	10
Number of boys	2	5	3	0
Number of girls	4	0	2	1

(a) What was the highest mark?

A girl got the highest mark of 10.

(b) Which set of marks was more spread out?

Range = highest mark − lowest mark
Boys: Range = 9 − 7 = 2
Girls: Range = 10 − 7 = 3

The girls' marks were more spread out.

Note:
To compare the overall standard, the median could be used instead of the mean.

(c) Were the marks for the boys or the girls better overall?

Calculate the mean for each set of marks.

Boys: Mean = $\frac{2 \times 7 + 5 \times 8 + 3 \times 9 + 0 \times 10}{10} = \frac{81}{10} = 8.1$

Girls: Mean = $\frac{4 \times 7 + 0 \times 8 + 2 \times 9 + 1 \times 10}{7} = \frac{56}{7} = 8$

The boys did better overall.

Exercise 30.5

1 Use the mean and the range to compare the number of goals scored per match by these teams.

Jays

Number of goals scored per hockey match	Number of matches
0	3
1	5
2	2
3	2
4	1
5	2

Wasps

Number of goals scored per hockey match	Number of matches
0	0
1	2
2	3
3	1
4	2
5	0

2 Use the mean and the range to compare the number of visits to the cinema by these women and men.

Number of visits to the cinema last month	0	1	2	3	4	5	6	More than 6
Number of women	8	9	7	3	2	1	1	0
Number of men	0	12	7	1	0	0	0	0

3 For each of the following, calculate the medians and the ranges.
Use your results to compare 'Before' with 'After'.

(a) Monthly sales of bicycles, before and after a marketing campaign.

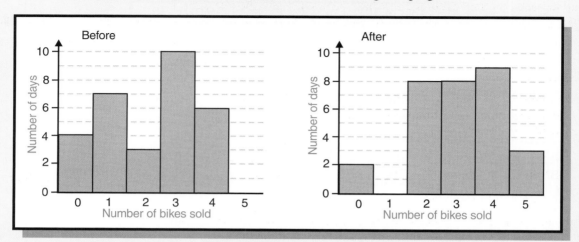

(b) Numbers of faults per machine, before and after servicing.

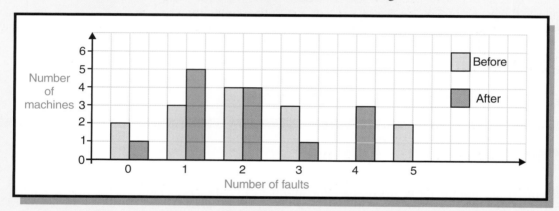

4 Deepak thought that the girls in his class wore smaller shoes than the boys on average, but that the boys' shoe sizes were less varied than the girls'.
He did a survey to test his ideas.
The table shows his results.
Was he correct?

Shoe size	$4\frac{1}{2}$	5	$5\frac{1}{2}$	6	$6\frac{1}{2}$	7	$7\frac{1}{2}$	8	$8\frac{1}{2}$	9	$9\frac{1}{2}$
Number of boys	1	0	5	4	4	2	1	0	1	0	0
Number of girls	0	2	0	2	3	0	2	0	3	1	1

5 (a) Find the modal class for the ages of customers in each of these two restaurants.
(b) Which restaurant attracts more younger people?
(c) Explain why it is only possible to find an approximate value for the range.

Age range	0 - 9	10 - 19	20 - 29	30 - 39	40 - 49	50 - 59	60 - 69	70 - 79	80 - 89
MacQuick	8	9	10	7	1	1	3	1	0
Pizza Pit	2	4	12	15	5	3	3	2	1

Which is the best average to use?

Many questions in mathematics have definite answers. This one does not.
Sometimes the mean is best, sometimes the median and sometimes the mode.
It all depends on the situation and what you want to use the average for.

EXAMPLE

A youth club leader gets a discount on cans of drinks if she buys all one size.
She took a vote on which size people wanted.
The results were as follows:

Size of can (ml)	100	200	330	500
Number of votes	9	12	19	1

Mode = 330 ml
Median = 200 ml
Mean = 245.6 ml, correct to one decimal place.

Which size should she buy?

The mean is no use at all because she can't buy cans of size 245.6 ml.
Even if the answer is rounded to the nearest whole number (246 ml), it's still no use.
The median is possible because there is an actual 200 ml can.
However, only 12 out of 41 people want this size.
In this case the **mode** is the best average to use, as it is the most popular size.

Exercise 30.6

In questions 1 to 3 find all the averages possible. State which is the most sensible and why.

1 On a bus: 23 people are wearing trainers,
   10 people are wearing boots,
   8 people are wearing lace-up shoes.

2 20 people complete a simple jigsaw. Their times, in seconds, are recorded.
   5, 6, 8, 8, 9, 10, 11, 11, 12, 12, 12, 15, 15, 15, 15, 18, 19, 20, 22, 200.

3 Here are the marks obtained by a group of 11 students in a mock exam.
   The exam was marked out of 100.
   5, 6, 81, 81, 82, 83, 84, 85, 86, 87, 88.

4 The times for two swimmers to complete each of ten 25 m lengths are shown below.

Swimmer A	30.1	30.1	30.1	30.6	30.7	31.1	31.1	31.5	31.7	31.8
Swimmer B	29.6	29.7	29.7	29.9	30.0	30.0	30.1	30.1	30.1	44.6

Which is the better swimmer? Explain why.

5 The table shows the number of runs scored by two batsmen in several innings.

Batsman A	0	0	10	12	20	22	50	51	81	104		
Batsman B	0	24	25	27	28	30	33	34	44	45	46	96

Which is the better batsman? Explain why.

6 A teacher sets a test.
   He wants to choose a minimum mark for a distinction so that 50% of his students get this result.
   Should he use the modal mark, the median mark or the mean mark?
   Give a reason for your answer.

What you need to know

- There are three types of **average**: the **mode**, the **median** and the **mean**.

- The **mode** is the most common amount.

- To find the **median**, first arrange the amounts in order of size.
  The median is the middle amount (or the mean of the two middle amounts).

- To find the **mean**, find the total of the amounts. Divide the total by the number of amounts.

  $$\text{Mean} = \frac{\text{Total of all amounts}}{\text{Number of amounts}}$$

- The **range** is a measure of **spread**.
  Range = highest amount − lowest amount

- To find the mean of a **frequency distribution** use:

  $$\text{Mean} = \frac{\text{Total of all amounts}}{\text{Number of amounts}} = \frac{\text{Total } fx}{\text{Total } f}$$

- Choosing the best average to use:
  When the most **popular** value is wanted use the **mode**.
  When **half** of the values have to be above the average use the **median**.
  When a **typical** value is wanted use either the **mode** or the **median**.
  When all the **actual** values have to be taken into account use the **mean**.
  When the average should not be distorted by a few very small or very large values do **not** use the mean.

Review Exercise

1 Here are the number of goals scored by a school football team in their matches this term.

3, 2, 0, 1, 2, 0, 3, 4, 3, 2.

(a) Work out the mean number of goals.
(b) Work out the range of the number of goals scored.

Edexcel

2 The cost of Bed and Breakfast at 11 different hotels is given.

£35   £26   £45   £20   £29   £28   £22   £27   £25   £22   £40

(a) Which cost is the mode?
(b) Work out the median cost.
(c) Give a reason why the mode would not be a sensible average for these data.

3 The list below gives the ages, in years, of the Mathematics teachers in a school.

34, 25, 37, 33, 26.

(a) Work out   (i) the mean age,
                (ii) the range.

In the same school, there are six English teachers.
The range of their ages is 20 years.
(b) What do the ranges tell you about the ages of the Mathematics teachers and the English teachers?

Edexcel

4 Some students took a mental arithmetic test.
Information about their marks is shown in the frequency table.

Mark	Frequency
4	2
5	1
6	2
7	4
8	7
9	10
10	3

(a) Work out how many students took the test.
(b) Write down the modal mark.

24 students had a higher mark than Caroline.
(c) Work out Caroline's mark.
(d) Find the median mark.
(e) Work out the range of the marks.

Edexcel

5 The graph shows the results of a survey of the number of faults in cars before and after servicing.

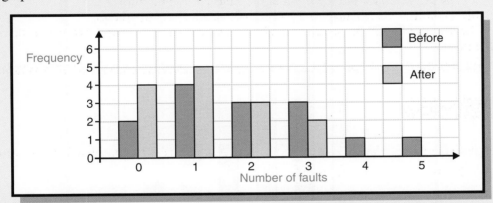

(a) A mechanic says, "The survey shows all cars have fewer faults after servicing."
Is this true? Explain your answer.
(b) A customer says, "The survey shows the average number of faults in cars before and after servicing is the same." Which average is being used?
(c) A report on the survey says, "The average number of faults per car before servicing is 2."
Which average is being used?
Use the same average to find the average number of faults per car after servicing.

6 Mrs Chowdery gives her class a maths test.
Here are the test marks for the girls.

7, 5, 8, 5, 2, 8, 7, 4, 7, 10, 3, 7, 4, 3, 6

(a) Work out the mode.
(b) Work out the median.

The median mark for the boys was 7 and the range of the marks of the boys was 4.
The range of the girls' marks was 8.
(c) By comparing the results explain whether the boys or the girls did better in the test.

Edexcel

7 Phillip and Elizabeth collected information about the heights and weights of their friends. They calculated the mean, median and mode of their results.

	Mean	Median	Mode
Phillip's friends	Height 180 cm	Height 175 cm	Height 177 cm
	Weight 50 kg	Weight 45 kg	Weight 40 kg
Elizabeth's friends	Height 175 cm	Height 175 cm	Height 172 cm
	Weight 45 kg	Weight 50 kg	Weight 50 kg

Philip says that most of his friends do not weigh as much as most of Elizabeth's friends.
(a)   Explain why this may not be true.

Elizabeth says that all Phillip's friends are taller than her friends.
(b)   Explain why this may not be true.

Edexcel

8 Ros asks a group of students,
"How many children are there in your family?"
The graph shows her findings.

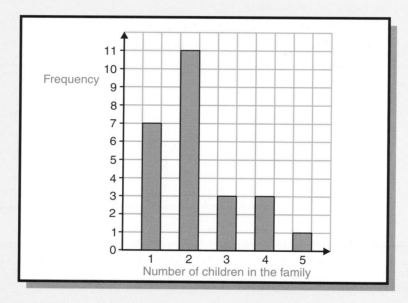

(a)   How many students are in the group?
(b)   What is the range in the number of children in the family for these students?
(c)   What is the most common number of children in the family for these students?
(d)   Calculate the mean number of children in the family for these students.
Give your answer to one decimal place.

9 The temperatures at midnight in January 1995 in Shiverton were measured and recorded.
The results were used to construct the frequency table.

Temperature in °C	0	1	2	3	4	5	6	7	8
Number of nights	4	5	5	3	3	7	3	0	1

(a)   Work out the range of the temperatures.
(b)   Work out the mean temperature.
Give your answer correct to one decimal place.

Edexcel

CHAPTER 31

Presentation of Data 2

Time series

The money spent on shopping **each day**, the gas used **each quarter** and the rainfall **each month** are all examples of **time series**.
A time series is a set of readings taken at time intervals.

A time series is often used to monitor progress and to show the **trend** (increases and decreases) so that future performance can be predicted.
The type of graph used in this situation is called a **line graph**.

EXAMPLE

The table shows the temperature of a patient taken every half-hour.

Time	0930	1000	1030	1100	1130	1200
Temperature °C	36.9	37.1	37.6	37.2	36.5	37.0

Draw a line graph to illustrate the data.

To draw a line graph of this information, the given values are plotted and then joined to show the trend.

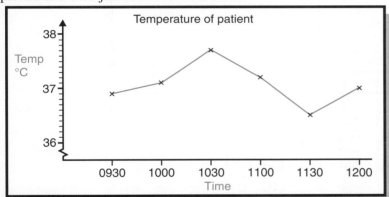

Only the plotted points show **known values**.

Lines are drawn to show the **trend**.

What is the highest temperature recorded?

*Explain why the graph can only be used to give an **estimate** of the patient's temperature at 1115.*

Exercise **31.1**

 The midday temperature at a seaside resort was recorded each day for one week.
The line graph shows the results.

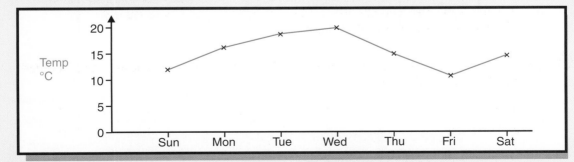

(a)   What was the midday temperature on Thursday?
(b)   Explain why you cannot use this line graph to estimate the temperature at midnight on Monday.

2 The number of cars sold by a car dealer is recorded each month.
The line graph shows the results for the first six months of a year.

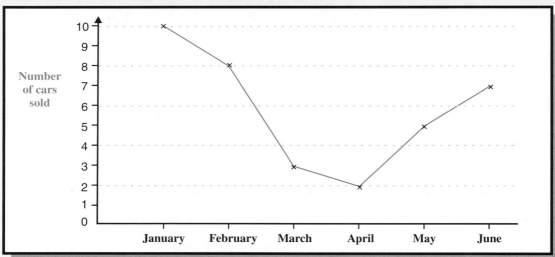

(a) How many cars were sold in February?
(b) In which months were more than 5 cars sold?
(c) Explain why you cannot estimate how many cars were sold halfway through April.

3 Each year, on his birthday, a teenager records his height.
The table shows the results.

Age (years)	13	14	15	16	17	18	19
Height (cm)	145	151	157	165	174	179	180

(a) Draw a line graph to represent this information.
(b) Use your graph to estimate:

   (i) the height of the teenager when he was $14\frac{1}{2}$ years of age,

   (ii) the age of the teenager when he reached 160 cm in height.

4 Joan is a member of Weight Watchers.
She records her weight at the beginning of each week.
The line graph shows a record of her weight for six weeks.

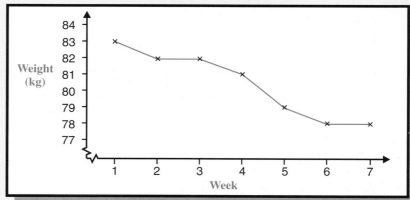

(a) What was Joan's weight at the beginning of Week 2?
(b) What was Joan's weight at the end of Week 2?
(c) How much weight did Joan lose in 6 weeks?
(d) In which week did Joan's weight first fall below 80 kg?

⑤ The table shows the amount of money in Jayne's savings account at the end of each month, for six months.

Month	January	February	March	April	May	June
Amount (£)	106	131	155	95	119	132

(a) Draw a line graph to represent this information.
(b) Use your graph to estimate the amount in her account in the middle of February.
(c) Explain what happened to the account between March and April.

Frequency diagrams

We use **bar charts** when data can be counted and there are only a few different items of data.
If there is a lot of data, or the data is continuous, we draw a **histogram** or **frequency polygon**.

Histograms

Histograms are used to present information contained in **grouped frequency distributions**. In this section we will only be drawing histograms for grouped frequency distributions that have equal class width intervals.

> Histograms with equal class width intervals look like bar charts with no gaps.

EXAMPLE **❶** A supermarket opens at 0800. The frequency diagram shows the distribution of the times employees arrive for work.

(a) How many employees arrive before 0730?
(b) How many employees arrive between 0730 and 0800?
(c) How many employees arrive after 0800?
(d) What is the modal class?

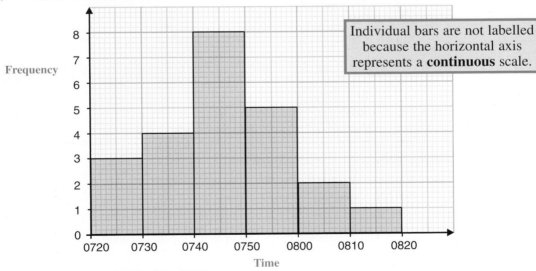

> Individual bars are not labelled because the horizontal axis represents a **continuous** scale.

(a) 3 employees arrive before 0730.
(b) Between 0730 and 0740, 4 employees arrive.
Between 0740 and 0750, 8 employees arrive.
Between 0750 and 0800, 5 employees arrive.
Employees arriving between 0730 and 0800 = 4 + 8 + 5 = 17.
(c) 3 employees arrive after 0800.
(d) The modal class is the time interval with the highest frequency.
The class interval 0740 to 0750 has the highest frequency.
The modal class is therefore, "0740 and less than 0750".

2 The frequency distribution of the heights of some boys is shown.

Height (h cm)	$130 \leqslant h < 140$	$140 \leqslant h < 150$	$150 \leqslant h < 160$	$160 \leqslant h < 170$	$170 \leqslant h < 180$
Frequency	1	7	12	9	3

Draw a histogram to illustrate the data.

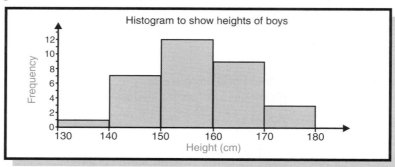

Exercise 31.2

1 The frequency diagram shows information about the weights of 100 people.

(a) How many people weigh between 60 kg and 70 kg?

(b) How many people weigh less than 60 kg?

(c) How many people weigh 70 kg or more?

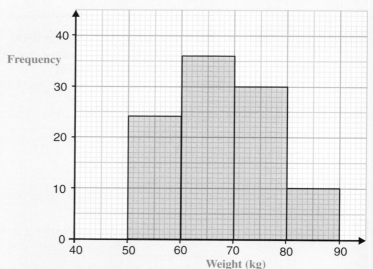

2 Here are the mileages of cars in a roadside survey.

5442	2345	18561	16080	12500	10000	35001	34056	5156	37584
21243	36573	25057	18656	15209	29067	39893	6368	15987	24891
9999	3089	16724	25598	37151	436	4080	39949	27950	6543

(a) Copy and complete the frequency distribution table for these results.

Distance (m miles)	Tally	Frequency
$0 \leqslant m < 10\,000$		
$10\,000 \leqslant m < 20\,000$		
$20\,000 \leqslant m < 30\,000$		
$30\,000 \leqslant m < 40\,000$		

(b) How many cars are included in the survey?
(c) Draw a frequency diagram to illustrate the data.
(d) Which is the modal class?

3 The distances, in metres, recorded in a long jump competition are shown.

5.46	5.80	5.97	5.43	6.72	5.93	6.26	6.64
5.13	6.05	6.36	6.88	6.11	5.50	6.38	5.71
6.55	6.10	5.84	5.49	6.20	5.67	6.34	6.00

(a) Copy and complete the following frequency distribution table.

Distance (m metres)	$5.00 \leqslant m < 5.50$	$5.50 \leqslant m < 6.00$	$6.00 \leqslant m < 6.50$	$6.50 \leqslant m < 7.00$
Frequency				

(b) Draw a histogram to illustrate the data.
(c) Which is the modal class?

4 Aimee does a survey of the distances people travel to work.
The frequency diagram shows the results.

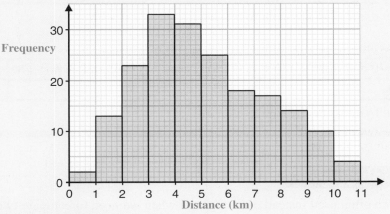

(a) Which is the modal class?
(b) How many people travel between 4 km and 5 km?
(c) How many people travel less than 2 km?
(d) How many people travel more than 10 km?
(e) How many people were included in the survey?

5 The frequency diagram illustrates the cost of holidays sold by a travel agent.

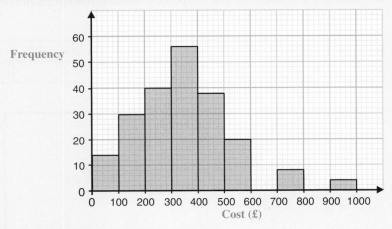

(a) How many holidays cost less than £100?
(b) How many holidays cost £400 or more?
(c) Which is the modal class?
(d) How many holidays were sold?

6 The table shows the distribution of the ages of people in a nursing home.

Age (years)	Number of people
60 and less than 70	3
70 and less than 80	13
80 and less than 90	7
90 and less than 100	6

Draw a histogram to show this information.

7 The table shows the grouped frequency distribution of the marks of 200 students.

Mark (%)	1 - 10	11 - 20	21 - 30	31 - 40	41 - 50	51 - 60	61 - 70	71 - 80	81 - 90	91 - 100
Number of Students	0	2	16	24	44	50	35	20	8	1

Draw a frequency diagram to show these results.

8 A frequency distribution of the heights of some girls is shown.

Height (h cm)	$130 \leqslant h < 140$	$140 \leqslant h < 150$	$150 \leqslant h < 160$	$160 \leqslant h < 170$	$170 \leqslant h < 180$
Frequency	3	5	12	4	1

Draw a histogram to illustrate the data.

Frequency polygons

Frequency polygons are often used instead of histograms when we need to compare two, or more, groups of data.

To draw a frequency polygon:

- plot the frequencies at the midpoint of each class interval,
- join successive points with straight lines.

To compare data, frequency polygons for different groups of data can be drawn on the same diagram.

In the last section we drew a histogram to illustrate the frequency distribution of the heights of some boys. The same data can be illustrated using a **frequency polygon**.

Height (h cm)	$130 \leqslant h < 140$	$140 \leqslant h < 150$	$150 \leqslant h < 160$	$160 \leqslant h < 170$	$170 \leqslant h < 180$
Frequency	1	7	12	9	3

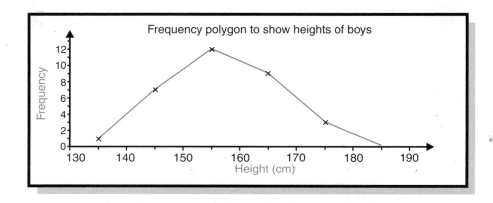

⑤ The table shows the results of students in tests in English and Mathematics.

Marks	English	Mathematics
0 and less than 10	0	1
10 and less than 20	4	4
20 and less than 30	9	9
30 and less than 40	12	7
40 and less than 50	0	4

(a) Draw a frequency polygon for the English marks.
(b) On the same diagram draw a frequency polygon for the Mathematics marks.
(c) Compare and comment on the marks of the students in these two tests.

⑥ The table shows the results for competitors in the 1999 and 2000 Schools' Javelin Championship.
Only the best distance thrown by each competitor is shown.

Distance thrown (m metres)	Number of competitors 1999	Number of competitors 2000
$10 \leqslant m < 20$	0	1
$20 \leqslant m < 30$	3	4
$30 \leqslant m < 40$	14	19
$40 \leqslant m < 50$	21	13
$50 \leqslant m < 60$	7	11
$60 \leqslant m < 70$	0	2

(a) On the same diagram draw a frequency polygon for the 1999 results and then a frequency polygon for the 2000 results.
(b) Compare and comment on the results.

Misleading graphs

Television programmes, newspapers and advertisements frequently use graphs and diagrams to present information.
Many of the graphs and diagrams they use are well presented and give a fair interpretation of the facts, others are deliberately drawn to mislead.

Look at the graph below.
Why is it misleading?

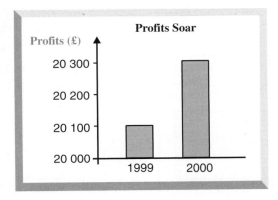

You should notice that the vertical scale does not begin at zero.
The actual increase in profits is only £200 but the graph makes it appear much more.

1 The following graph is misleading. Explain why.

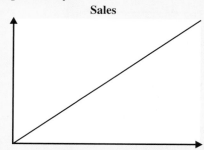

Sales

2 This graph is drawn to compare the money raised for charity by two schools.

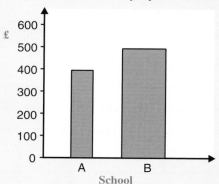

School A has raised £400.
School B has raised £500.
Why is the graph misleading?

3 This graph shows how the price of a litre of petrol has increased.

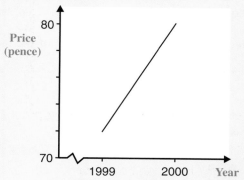

Why is the graph misleading?

4

> **PASS WITH US**
> Our learners only need an average of 8 lessons before they can take the driving test.

Give a reason why this advertisement may be misleading.

5 This diagram is used to compare the average price of a house in two different years.

Big growth in house prices

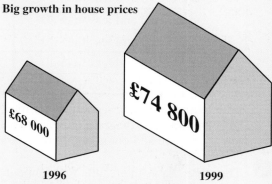

Why is the diagram misleading?

6 The graph shows the number of "Home" supporters and the number of "Away" supporters at a football match.
Why is the graph misleading?

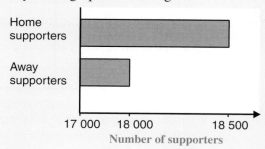

7 Why is this diagram misleading?

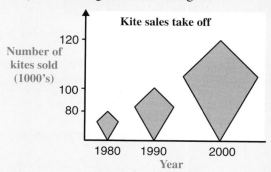

8 The graph shows the votes cast for a political party in five elections.

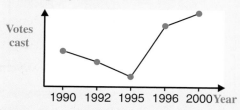

Why is the graph misleading?

What you need to know

- **Line graph**. Used to show **trend**.
  Only the plotted points represent actual values.
  Points are joined by lines to show the trend.

- **Histogram**. Used to illustrate **grouped frequency distributions.**
  The horizontal axis is a continuous scale.

- **Frequency polygon**. Used to illustrate grouped frequency distributions.
  Often used to compare two or more distributions on the same diagram.
  Frequencies are plotted at the midpoints of the class intervals and joined with straight lines.
  The horizontal axis is a continuous scale.

- **Misleading graphs**
  Graphs may be misleading if:
  the scales are not labelled,
  the scales are not uniform,
  the frequency does not begin at zero.

Review Exercise

1 The line graph shows the monthly advertising costs for Radical Records.

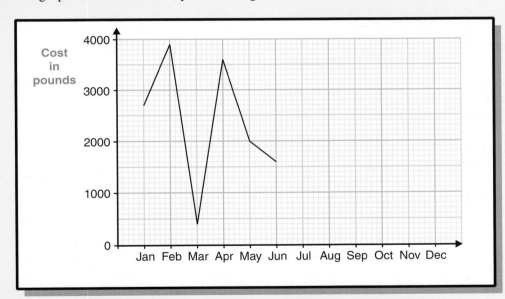

(a) How much was spent on advertising in March?

The company spent the following amounts on advertising in the next 3 months:

> July . . . . £ 700
>
> August £3600
>
> September £3000

(b) Copy and continue the line graph to show this information.

Edexcel

2 Jim bought his house in 1985.
The table shows the value of Jim's house on January 1st at 5-yearly intervals.

Year	1985	1990	1995	2000
Value of house (£)	60 000	95 000	68 000	84 000

(a) Draw a line graph to show this information.
(b) Estimate the value of Jim's house on July 1st 1988.
(c) Jim uses the graph to estimate the value of his house on January 1st 2005.
Give a reason why his estimate may not be very accurate.

3

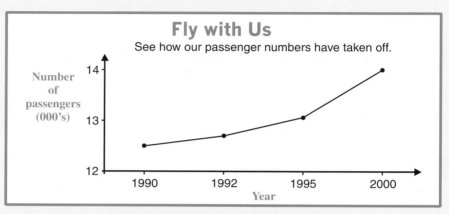

Write down two ways in which the graph is misleading.

4 Aimee does a survey of the distances people travel to work.
The frequency diagram shows the results.

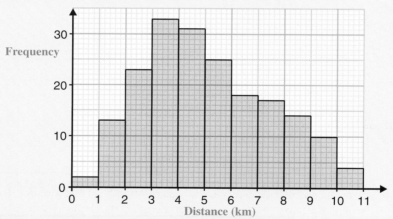

(a) Which is the modal class?
(b) How many people travel between 4 km and 5 km?
(c) How many people were included in the survey?

5 The grouped frequency table shows the results of a survey of the number of fish caught by some anglers last month.

Number of fish (f)	$0 \leqslant f < 4$	$4 \leqslant f < 8$	$8 \leqslant f < 12$	$12 \leqslant f < 16$	$16 \leqslant f < 20$
Frequency	15	24	36	10	5

(a) How many anglers caught less than 8 fish?
(b) Which is the modal class?
(c) Draw a frequency diagram to illustrate the data.

6 The frequency polygon illustrates the time taken by students to complete a puzzle.
Copy and complete the table for the data.

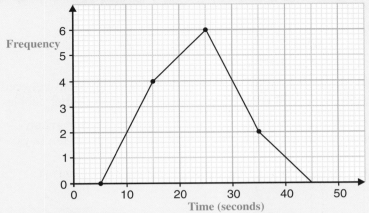

Time (seconds)	Frequency
10 and less than 20	
20 and less than 30	
30 and less than 40	

7 The following is a record of the heights, in centimetres, of 40 guinea pigs.

21	22	11	16	22	13	11	25	9	17
21	24	27	25	12	14	8	12	6	17
23	7	12	26	14	8	12	26	17	19
23	29	21	19	26	26	18	21	13	9

(a) Copy and complete the frequency table, using intervals of 5 cm.

Height (h cm)	Tally	Frequency
$5 \leqslant h < 10$		
$10 \leqslant h < 15$		

(b) Draw a frequency diagram for this information.
(c) How many guinea pigs were under 15 cm in height?
(d) Write down the modal class interval of the heights.   Edexcel

8 As part of his Geography fieldwork, Tony took measurements of the steepness of slopes.
The steepness was measured as the angle the slope made with the horizontal.

Tony's results are shown below.

15°, 16°, 9°, 21°, 32°, 37°, 25°, 36°, 40°, 8°,
13°, 21°, 32°, 29°, 32°, 7°, 4°, 18°, 17°, 32°

Tony decided to group the data into 4 equal class intervals on an observation sheet.
(a) Copy and complete the observation sheet below, using 4 equal class intervals.

Class interval (Steepness°)	Tally	Frequency
1 - 10		

(b) Use the completed observation sheet to draw a frequency diagram of the data.   Edexcel

CHAPTER 32

Scatter Graphs

When we investigate statistical information we often find there are connections between sets of data, for example height and weight. In general taller people weigh more than shorter people.

To see if there is a connection between two sets of data we can plot a **scatter graph**.
The scatter graph below shows information about the heights and weights of ten boys.

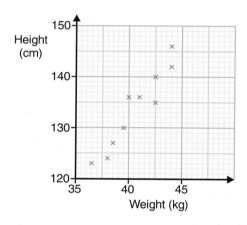

Each cross plotted on the graph represents the weight and height of one boy.

The diagram shows that taller boys generally weigh more than shorter boys.

Exercise **32.1**

1   The scatter graph shows the shoe sizes and heights of a group of girls.

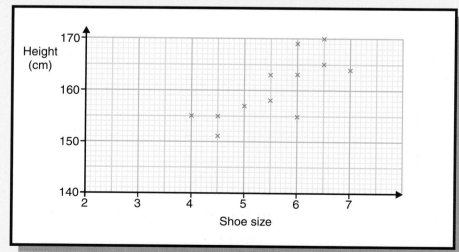

(a)   How many girls wear size $6\frac{1}{2}$ shoes?

(b)   How tall is the girl with the largest shoe size?

(c)   Does the shortest girl wear the smallest shoes?

(d)   What do you notice about the shoe sizes of taller girls compared to shorter girls?

2 The scatter graph shows the marks obtained by a group of students in a test in English and a test in French.

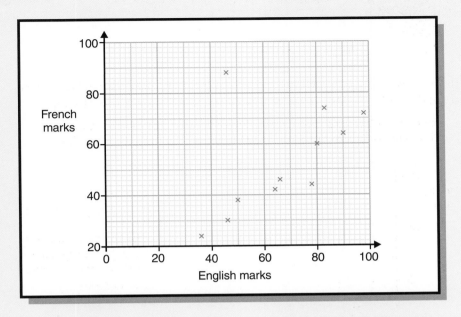

(a) Janice got the top mark in English. What mark did she get in French?
(b) The results of one student look out of place.
  (i) What marks did the student get in English and in French?
  (ii) Give a possible reason why this student has different results from the rest of the group.

3 The scatter graph shows the pulse rates of a group of women after doing aerobics for one minute and their weight.

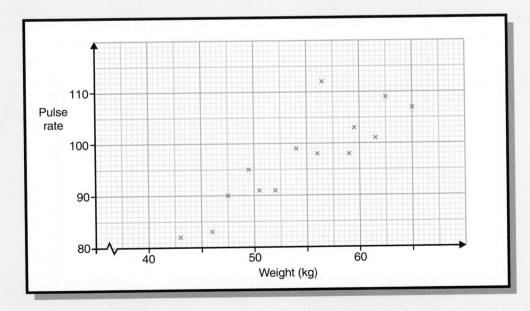

(a) How many of these women weigh less than 50 kg?
(b) What is the weight of the woman with the lowest pulse rate?
(c) What do you notice about the pulse rates of heavier women compared to lighter women?

4 The scatter graph shows the age and mileage of a number of cars.

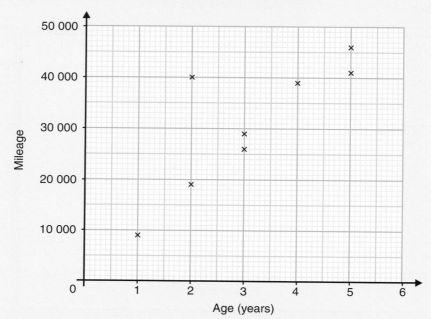

(a) One of these cars is 4 years old.
What is the mileage of this car?

(b) Describe the relationship shown by the scatter graph.

(c) The age and mileage of one of these cars looks out of place.
  (i) What is the age and mileage of this car?
  (ii) Give a possible reason why the results for this car are different from the rest of the group.

5 The scatter graph shows the number of books read by some children and the reading ages of these children.

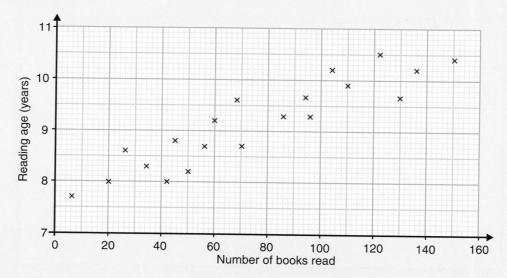

(a) How many children have read more than 100 books?

(b) One of these children has read 50 books.
What is the reading age of this child?

(c) Describe the relationship shown by the scatter graph.

Correlation

The relationship between two sets of data is called **correlation**.

In general the scatter graph of the heights and weights shows that as height increases, weight increases. This type of relationship shows there is a **positive correlation** between height and weight.

But if as the value of one variable increases the value of the other variable decreases, then there is a **negative correlation** between the variables.

The following graphs show types of correlation.

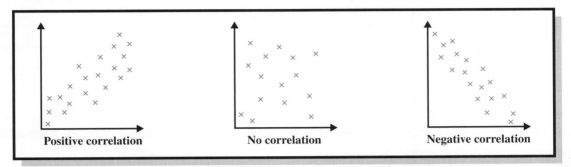

As points get closer to a straight line the stronger the correlation.

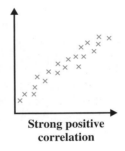

Exercise 32.2

1   (a)   Which of these graphs shows the strongest positive correlation?
    (b)   Which of these graphs shows negative correlation?
    (c)   Which of these graphs shows the weakest correlation?

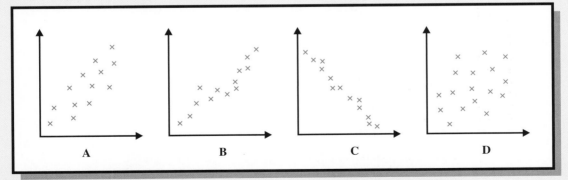

2   Describe the type of correlation you would expect between:
    (a)   the age of a car and its secondhand selling price,
    (b)   the heights of children and their ages,
    (c)   the shoe sizes of children and the distances they travel to school,
    (d)   the number of cars on the road and the number of road accidents,
    (e)   the engine size of a car and the number of kilometres it can travel on one litre of fuel.

3 The table shows the distance travelled and time taken by motorists on different journeys.

Distance travelled (km)	30	45	48	80	90	100	125
Time taken (hours)	0.6	0.9	1.2	1.2	1.3	2.0	1.5

(a) Draw a scatter graph for the data.
(b) What do you notice about distance travelled and time taken?

4 Tyres were collected from a number of different cars.
The table shows the distance travelled and depth of tread for each tyre.

Distance travelled (1000 km)	4	5	9	10	12	15	18	25	30
Depth of tread (mm)	9.2	8.4	7.6	8	6.5	7.4	7	6.2	5

(a) Draw a scatter graph for the data.
(b) What do you notice about the distance travelled and the depth of tread?
(c) Explain how you can tell that the relationship is quite strong.

Line of best fit

We have seen that **scatter graphs** can be used to illustrate two sets of data and from the distribution of points plotted an indication of the relationship which exists between the data can be seen.

The scatter graph of heights and weights has been redrawn below and a **line of best fit** has been drawn, by eye, to show the relationship between height and weight.

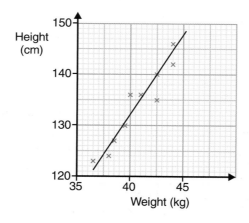

Lines of best fit

● The slope of the line shows the trend of the points.

● A line is only drawn if the correlation (positive or negative) is strong.

● The line does not have to go through the origin of the graph.

Where there is a relationship between the two sets of data the line of best fit can be used to estimate other values.

A boy is 132 cm tall.
Using the line of best fit an estimate of his weight is 40 kg.

In a similar way we can use the line to estimate the height of a boy when we know his weight.
A boy weighs 43 kg. Estimate his height.

Exercise **32.3**

1 The following table gives the marks obtained by some candidates taking examinations in French and German.

Mark in French	35	36	39	43	50	53	56	59
Mark in German	37	40	44	48	60	64	70	72

(a) Use this information to draw a scatter graph.
(b) Describe the relationship shown in the scatter graph.
(c) Draw the line of best fit by eye.
(d) Explain how you can tell that the relationship is quite strong.

2 The table shows the temperature of water as it cools in a freezer.

Time (minutes)	5	10	15	20	25	30
Temperature (°C)	36	29	25	20	15	8

(a) Use this information to draw a scatter graph.
(b) What type of correlation is shown?
(c) Draw a line of best fit.
(d) Use your scatter graph to estimate the time when the temperature of the water reaches 0°C.

3 The table shows the ages and weights of ten babies.

Age (weeks)	2	4	9	7	13	5	6	1	10	12
Weight (kg)	3.5	3.3	4.2	4.7	5	3.8	4	3	5	5.5

(a) Use this information to draw a scatter graph.
(b) What type of correlation is shown on the scatter graph?
(c) Draw a line of best fit.
(d) Mrs Wilson's baby is 11 weeks old.
Use your scatter graph to estimate the weight of her baby.

4 The table shows the weights and fitness factors for a number of women.
The higher the fitness factor the fitter a person is.

Weight (kg)	45	48	50	54	56	60	64	72	99	112
Fitness Factor	41	48	40	40	35	40	34	30	17	15

(a) Use this information to draw a scatter graph.
(b) What type of correlation is shown on the scatter graph?
(c) Draw a line of best fit.

What you need to know

- A **scatter graph** can be used to show the relationship between two sets of data.
- The relationship between two sets of data is referred to as **correlation**.
- You should be able to recognise **positive** and **negative** correlation.
  The correlation is stronger as points get closer to a straight line.

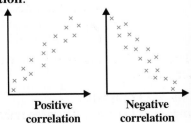

Positive correlation   Negative correlation

- When there is a relationship between two sets of data a **line of best fit** can be drawn on the scatter graph.
- The line of best fit can be used to **estimate** the value from one set of the data when the corresponding value of the other set is known.

1 The scatter graph shows the number of books read by some children and the reading ages of these children.

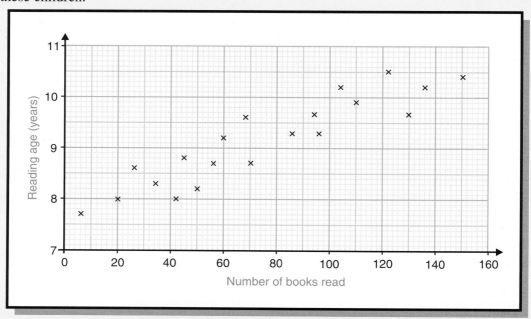

(a) How many children have read more than 100 books?
(b) One of these children has read 50 books.
     What is the reading age of this child?
(c) Describe the relationship shown by the scatter graph.
(d) A child has read 80 books.
     Use the scatter graph to estimate the reading age of this child.

2 The table gives information about the age and value of a number of cars of the same type.

Age (years)	Value (£)
1	8200
$4\frac{1}{2}$	4900
6	3800
3	6200
7	2800
2	7600
4	5200

(a) Use the information to draw a scatter graph.
     Label the horizontal axis **Age (years)** from 0 to 7.
     Label the vertical axis **Value (£)** from 0 to 9000.
(b) Describe the correlation shown between the age and value of these cars.
(c) Jo has a car of this type which is 5 years old.
     Use your scatter graph to estimate its value.
(d) Draw a line of best fit on your scatter graph.
(e) Explain how you can tell that the relationship is quite strong.

3

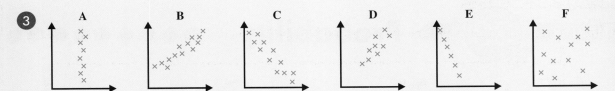

A   B   C   D   E   F

Sketches of six scatter graphs **A** to **F** are shown.

(a)   Which scatter graphs show
   (i)   positive correlation,   (ii)   negative correlation,   (iii)   no correlation?

The table gives information on underground railway ('tube') systems in 7 cities.

City	Kilometres of route (x)	Passenger journeys per year (millions) (y)
London	395	780
New York	390	1060
Paris	200	1190
Tokyo	155	1930
San Francisco	115	70
Washington DC	125	140
Kyoto	10	45

(b)   Plot a scatter graph to show this information.
   Label the horizontal axis **Kilometres of route** from 0 to 400.
   Label the vertical axis **Passenger journeys per year (millions)** from 0 to 2000.

Los Angeles hopes to open an underground railway. There will be 28 km of route.

(c)   Can you use your scatter graph to estimate the number of passenger journeys per year?
   Explain your answer.
   Edexcel

4

The table shows the number of units of electricity used in heating a house on ten different days and the average temperature for each day.

Average temperature (°C)	Units of electricity used
6	28
2	38
0	41
6	34
3	31
5	31
10	22
8	25
9	23
12	22

(a)   Draw a scatter graph to show the information in the table.
(b)   Describe the **correlation** between the number of units of electricity used and the average temperature.
(c)   Draw a line of best fit on your scatter graph.
(d)   Use your scatter graph to estimate the number of units of electricity used if the average temperature is 7°C.
   Edexcel

Probability

What is probability?

Probability, or **chance**, involves describing how likely something is to happen.
For example:
How likely is it to rain tomorrow?

We often make forecasts, or judgements, about how likely things are to happen.
When trying to forecast tomorrow's weather the following **outcomes** are possible:

sun, cloud, wind, rain, snow, …

We are interested in the particular **event**, rain tomorrow.

> The chance of an event happening can be described using these words:
> **Impossible   Unlikely   Evens   Likely   Certain**

> **Probability words**
> In any situation, the possible things that can happen are called **outcomes**.
> An outcome of particular interest is called an **event**.

Use one of the words in the box to describe the chance of rain tomorrow.

EXAMPLE

Describe the chance of each of the following events happening as:

Impossible   Unlikely   Evens   Likely   Certain

(a)   The next person who enters your classroom has green hair.
(b)   The next person who enters the classroom is male.
(c)   A number less than 5 is scored when a normal dice is rolled.

(a)   Very few people have green hair.
      So the chance of the event happening is nearly **impossible**.
(b)   Nearly impossible in an all girls school.
      Nearly certain in an all boys school.
      The probability is close to **evens** in a mixed school.
(c)   The outcomes in the event 'less than 5' are 1, 2, 3 and 4.
      The outcomes **not** in the event 'less than 5' are 5 and 6.
      There are more outcomes in the event than not in the event.
      So the chance of the event happening is **likely**.

Exercise 33.1

1   Describe each of the following events as: Impossible,   Evens,   Certain.

(a)   Christmas Day will be on 25th December next year.
(b)   You will be 5 centimetres shorter on your next birthday.
(c)   The next coin you drop will land 'tails' up.
(d)   A fairy lives at the bottom of your garden.
(e)   The next baby to be born will be a girl.

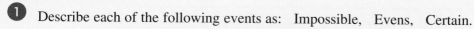

2 Describe each of the following events as:
   Unlikely   Likely
   (a) A 6 is scored at least 500 times when a normal dice is rolled 600 times.
   (b) A 6 is scored at least 80 times when a normal dice is rolled 600 times.
   (c) It will rain on three days running in April.
   (d) It will rain on three days running in August.
   (e) A coin is tossed five times and lands heads up on each occasion.
   (f) A coin is tossed five times and lands heads up at least once.

3 Describe each of the following events as:
   Impossible   Unlikely   Evens   Likely   Certain
   (a) Somewhere in the world it is raining today.
   (b) You roll a normal dice and get a 7.
   (c) You roll a normal dice and get an odd number.
   (d) A coin is tossed and it lands heads.
   (e) An apple will grow on a banana tree.
   (f) You win the next time you enter the lottery.

Probability and the probability scale

Estimates of probabilities can be shown on a **probability scale**. The scale goes from 0 to 1.
A **probability of 0** means that an event is **impossible**.
A **probability of 1** means that an event is **certain**.
Probabilities are written either as a fraction, a decimal or a percentage.

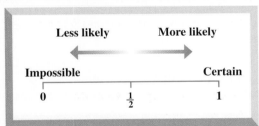

Describe the likelihood that an event will occur if it has a probability of $\frac{1}{2}$.

EXAMPLES Estimate the probability of each of the following events happening.
Show your estimate on a probability scale.

1 It will snow in London next July.

This is possible but very unlikely.
So the probability is very close to 0.

2 You will be given some homework today.

This is very likely (in most schools).
So the probability is close to 1.

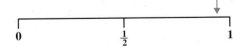

3 A coin lands heads when it is tossed.

There is one outcome in the event (Heads) and one outcome not in the event (Tails).
So there is an even chance that the coin lands heads.
So probability = $\frac{1}{2}$.

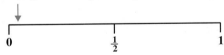

4 The next person to enter the classroom will be left-handed.

There are a lot less left-handed people than right-handed people.
The probability is between 0 and $\frac{1}{4}$.

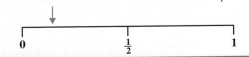

1 Look at the events **A**, **B**, **C**, **D** and **E** listed below.
  A The next person you see will be less than 10 cm tall.
  B 1, 2 or 3 is scored when an ordinary dice is rolled.
  C A day of the week ends with the letter Y.
  D It will snow on Christmas Day in London.
  E The school bus will be late tomorrow.

  (a) Which event has a probability of 0?

  (b) Which event has a probability of 1?

  (c) Which event has a probability of $\frac{1}{2}$?

2 The probability scale shows the probabilities of events **P**, **Q**, **R**, **S** and **T**.

Which of the five events
  (a) is certain to happen,
  (b) is impossible,
  (c) has an evens chance of happening,
  (d) is more likely to happen than to not happen, but is not certain to happen?

3 The probabilities of five events have been marked on a probability scale.

Copy the probability scale.

  Event V A coin lands 'heads' up.
  Event W A person is over 3 metres tall.
  Event X Picking a yellow sweet from a bag containing 7 yellow and 3 red sweets.
  Event Y Rolling an ordinary dice and getting a score less than 7.
  Event Z There is a 35% chance that it will rain tomorrow.

Label the arrows on your diagram to show which event they represent.

Calculating probabilities using equally likely outcomes

Probabilities can be **calculated** where all outcomes are **equally likely**.

> The probability of an event happening is given by:
>
> $$\text{Probability} = \frac{\text{Number of possible outcomes in the event}}{\text{Total number of possible outcomes}}$$

Probabilities can only be calculated using this method where there are **equally likely outcomes**.

Remember
Probabilities have values which lie between 0 and 1.
You must write them as a fraction, a decimal or a percentage.

Probability words
In many probability questions words such as '**random**' and '**fair**' are used. These are ways of saying that all outcomes are equally likely.
For example:
A card is taken at **random** from a pack of cards.
This means that each card has an equal chance of being taken.
A **fair** dice is rolled.
This means that the outcomes 1, 2, 3, 4, 5 and 6 are equally likely.
Another word for fair is **unbiased**.
If a dice is **not** fair it is **biased**.

EXAMPLES

1 A fair dice is rolled.
What is the probability of getting
(a) a 6,
(b) an odd number,
(c) a 2 or a 3?

Total number of possible outcomes is 6
(1, 2, 3, 4, 5 and 6).
The dice is fair so each of these
outcomes is equally likely.
(a) The number of outcomes in the
event getting a 6 is 1.

$$P(6) = \frac{1}{6}$$

(b) The total number of outcomes in
the event is 3 (1, 3, 5).

$$P(\text{an odd number}) = \frac{3}{6} = \frac{1}{2}$$

(c) The total number of outcomes in
the event is 2 (2, 3).

$$P(2 \text{ or } 3) = \frac{2}{6} = \frac{1}{3}$$

2 This table shows how 100 counters are
coloured red or blue and numbered 1 or 2.

	Red	Blue
1	23	19
2	32	26

The 100 counters are put in a bag and a
counter is taken from the bag at random.
(a) Calculate the probability that the
counter is red.
(b) Calculate the probability that the
counter is blue and numbered 1.

Total number of possible outcomes = 100
(a) Red counters = 23 + 32 = 55

$$P(\text{red}) = \frac{55}{100} = \frac{11}{20}$$

This could be written as 0.55 or 55%.
(b) There are 19 counters that are blue
and numbered 1.

$$P(\text{blue and 1}) = \frac{19}{100}$$

This could be written as 0.19 or 19%.

Exercise 33.3

1 A fair dice is rolled.
What is the probability of getting:
(a) a two,
(b) an even number,
(c) a number less than five,
(d) a 3 or a 6?

2 A bag contains a red counter,
a blue counter and a green counter.
A counter is taken from the bag at random.
What is the probability of taking:
(a) a red counter,
(b) a red or a green counter,
(c) a counter that is not blue?

3 A bag contains 3 red sweets and
7 black sweets.
A sweet is taken from the bag at random.
What is the probability of taking:
(a) a red sweet
(b) a black sweet?

4 You toss a fair coin.
What is the probability of getting:
(a) a head,
(b) a tail?

5 This fair spinner is used in a game.

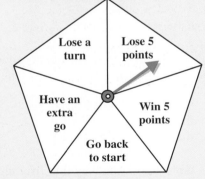

In the game a player spins the arrow.
What is the probability that the player:
(a) loses a turn,
(b) has an extra go,
(c) wins 5 points or loses 5 points?

6 The eleven letters of the word MISSISSIPPI
are written on separate tiles.
The tiles are placed in a bag and mixed up.
One tile is selected at random.
What is the probability that the tile selected
shows:
(a) the letter M,
(b) the letter I,
(c) the letter P?

7 The letters of the word TRIGONOMETRY are written on separate cards.
The cards are shuffled and dealt, face down, onto a table.
A card is selected at random.
What is the probability that the card shows:
(a) the letter Y, (b) the letter R?
Write your answers in their simplest form.

8 A card is taken at random from a full pack of playing cards with no jokers.
What is the probability that the card:
(a) is red, (b) is a heart,
(c) is the ace of hearts?

9 A bag contains 4 red counters, 3 white counters and 3 blue counters.
A counter is taken from the bag at random.
What is the probability that the counter is:
(a) red, (b) white or blue,
(c) red, white or blue, (d) green?

10 In a hat there are twelve numbered discs.

Nina takes a disc from the hat at random.
What is the probability that Nina takes a disc:
(a) with at least one 4 on it,
(b) that has not got a 4 on it,
(c) that has a 3 or a 4 on it?

11 This table shows the way that fifty red and blue counters are numbered either 1 or 2.

	Red	Blue
1	12	8
2	8	22

One of the counters is chosen at random.
What is the probability that the counter is:
(a) a 1, (b) blue, (c) blue and a 1?

A blue counter is chosen at random.
(d) What is the probability that it is a 1?

A counter numbered 1 is chosen at random.
(e) What is the probability that it is blue?

12 The table shows the way that 120 pupils from Year 7 travel to Linfield School.

	Boys	Girls
Walk	23	17
Bus	15	20
Car	12	8
Bike	20	5

A pupil from Year 7 is chosen at random.
What is the probability that the pupil:
(a) walks to school,
(b) is a girl who travels by car,
(c) is a boy who does not travel by bus?

A girl from Year 7 is chosen at random.
What is the probability that:
(d) she walks to school,
(e) she does not travel by car?

A Year 7 pupil who travels by bike is chosen at random.
(f) What is the probability that the pupil is a boy?

13 Tim plays a friend at Noughts and Crosses.
He says: 'I can either win, draw or lose, so the probability that I will win must be $\frac{1}{3}$'.
Explain why Tim is wrong.

14 The table shows the number of boys and girls in a class of 30 pupils who wear glasses.

	Boy	Girl
Wears glasses	3	1
Does not wear glasses	11	15

A pupil from the class is picked at random.
(a) What is the probability that it is a boy?
(b) What is the probability that it is a girl who does not wear glasses?

A girl from the class is picked at random.
(c) What is the probability that she wears glasses?

A pupil who wears glasses is picked at random.
(d) What is the probability that it is a boy?

Estimating probabilities

In question 13 in Exercise 33.3, probabilities **cannot** be calculated using equally likely outcomes.
In such situations probabilities can be estimated by carrying out **experiments** or by making **observations**.

Jamie does the following experiment with a bag containing 2 red and 8 blue counters.

> Take a counter from the bag at random.
> Record the colour then put the counter back in the bag.
> Repeat this for 100 trials.

Using the results from his experiment, Jamie calculated the probability of getting a red counter after every 10 trials. He then drew this graph.

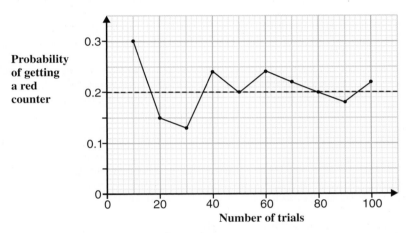

The dotted line on the diagram shows the probability of getting a red counter for equally likely results.

$$\text{Probability of red counter} = \frac{\text{number of red counters in the bag}}{\text{total number of counters in the bag}} = \frac{2}{10} = 0.2$$

Explain what happens to Jamie's graph as the number of trials increases.
Try the experiment yourself and draw a graph of your results.

EXAMPLES

1 In an experiment a drawing pin is dropped 100 times.
The drawing pin lands "point up" 37 times.
Use these results to estimate the probability that the next drawing pin lands "point up".

$$\text{Probability} = \frac{37}{100}$$
$$= 0.37$$

2 In an experiment a counter is taken from a bag of counters and then replaced.
The probability of getting a blue counter is found to be 0.4.
There are 200 counters in the bag.
How many of the counters are blue?

The probability of taking a blue counter is 0.4.
Total number of counters in the bag = 200
Number of blue counters = 200 × 0.4 = 80
There are 80 blue counters in the bag.

1 50 cars are observed passing the school gate.
14 of these cars are red.
Use these results to estimate the probability that the next car to pass the school gate will be red.

2 In an experiment a gardener plants 40 daffodil bulbs of which 36 grow to produce flowers.
Use these results to estimate the probability that a daffodil bulb will grow to produce a flower.

3 The results from 40 spins of a numbered spinner are:

2 1 4 3 2 1 3 4 5 2 1 2 2 3 2 1 2 4 5 2
1 5 3 4 2 3 3 3 2 4 2 3 4 2 1 5 3 3 5 3

Use these results to estimate the probability of getting a 2 with the next spin.

4 A counter is taken from a bag at random.
Its colour is recorded and the counter is then put back in the bag.
This is repeated 300 times.
The number of red counters taken from the bag after every 100 trials is shown in the table.

Number of trials	Number of red counters
100	52
200	102
300	141

(a) Estimate the probability of taking a red counter after each 100 trials.
(b) Which is the best estimate of taking a red counter from the bag?

5 Gemma keeps a record of her chess games with Helen.
Out of the first 10 games, Gemma wins 6. Out of the first 30 games Gemma wins 21.
Based on these results, estimate the probability that Gemma will win her next game of chess with Helen.

6 Rachel selects 40 holiday brochures at random.
The probability of a brochure being for a holiday in Italy is found to be 0.2.
How many brochures did Rachel select for holidays in Italy?

7 A counter is taken from a bag of counters and then replaced.
The probability of getting a red counter is found to be 0.3.
There are 60 counters in the bag.
How many red counters are in the bag?

8 500 tickets are sold for a prize draw.
Greg buys some tickets.
The probability that Greg wins first prize is $\frac{1}{20}$.
How many tickets did he buy?

9 A bypass is to be built to avoid a town.
There are three possible routes that the road can take.
A survey was carried out in the town and the table shows the percentages of people voting for each route.

Route	A	B	C
Percentage	40%	50%	10%

30 people voted for Route C.
(a) How many people were surveyed altogether?
(b) How many people voted for Route A?
(c) How many people voted for Route B?

Mutually exclusive events

Events which **cannot happen at the same time** are called **mutually exclusive events**.
For example, the event 'Heads' cannot occur at the same time as the event 'Tails'.

> When A and B are events which cannot happen at the same time:
> P(A or B) = P(A) + P(B)

In this book P(X) stands
for the probability of X.

The probability of an event not happening

> The events A and not A cannot happen at the same time.
> Because the events A and not A are certain to happen:
> P(not A) = 1 − P(A)

EXAMPLES

1 A bag contains 3 red (R) counters, 2 blue (B) counters and 5 green (G) counters.
A counter is taken from the bag at random.
What is the probability that the counter is:
(a) red,   (b) green,   (c) red or green?

Find the total number of counters in the bag.
$5 + 2 + 3 = 10$
Total number of possible outcomes $= 10$.

(a) Number of possible outcomes $= 3$.

$$P(R) = \frac{3}{10}$$

(b) Number of possible outcomes $= 5$.

$$P(G) = \frac{5}{10} = \frac{1}{2}$$

(c) Events R and G cannot happen at the same time.

$$P(R \text{ or } G) = P(R) + P(G) = \frac{3}{10} + \frac{5}{10} = \frac{8}{10} = \frac{4}{5}$$

2 A bag contains 10 counters.
3 of the counters are red (R).
A counter is taken from the bag at random.
What is the probability that the counter is:
(a) red,   (b) not red?

Total number of possible outcomes $= 10$.

(a) Number of possible outcomes $= 3$.

$$P(R) = \frac{3}{10}$$

(b) $P(\text{not } R) = 1 - P(R) = 1 - \frac{3}{10} = \frac{7}{10}$

1 A fish is taken at random from a tank.

The probability that the fish is black is $\frac{2}{5}$.

What is the probability that the fish is not black?

2 Tina has a bag of beads.
She takes a bead from the bag at random.
The probability that the bead is white is 0.6.
What is the probability that the bead is not white?

3 The probability of a switch working is 0.96.
What is the probability of a switch not working?

4 Six out of every 100 men are taller than 1.85 m.
A man is picked at random.
What is the probability that he is not taller than 1.85 m?

5 A bag contains red, white and blue balls.
A ball is taken from the bag at random.
The probability of taking a red ball is 0.4.
The probability of taking a white ball is 0.35.
What is the probability of taking a white ball or a blue ball?

6 Tom and Sam buy some tickets in a raffle.
The probability that Tom wins 1st prize is 0.03.
The probability that Sam wins 1st prize is 0.01.
(a)   What is the probability that Tom or Sam win 1st prize?
(b)   What is the probability that Tom does not win 1st prize?

7 A spinner can land on red, white or blue.
The probability of the spinner landing on red is 0.2.
The probability of the spinner landing on red or on blue is 0.7.
The spinner is spun once.
What is the probability that the spinner lands:
(a)   on blue,
(b)   on white?

8 A bag contains red, green, blue, yellow and white counters.
The table shows the probabilities of obtaining each colour when a counter is taken from the bag at random.

Red	Green	Blue	Yellow	White
30%	25%	20%	20%	10%

(a)   (i)   How can you tell that there is a mistake in the table?
      (ii) The probability of getting a white counter is wrong. What should it be?

A counter is taken from the bag at random.
(b)   (i)   What is the probability that it is either green or blue?
      (ii) What is the probability that it is either red, green or blue?
      (iii) What is the probability that it is not yellow?

9 Some red, white and blue cubes are numbered 1 or 2.
The table shows the probabilities of obtaining each
colour and number when a cube is taken at random.
A cube is taken at random.

	Red	White	Blue
1	0.1	0.3	0
2	0.3	0.1	0.2

(a) What is the probability of taking a red cube?
(b) What is the probability of taking a cube numbered 2?
(c) State whether or not the following pairs of events are mutually exclusive.
Give a reason for each answer.
    (i) Taking a cube numbered 1 and taking a blue cube.
    (ii) Taking a cube numbered 2 and taking a blue cube.
(d) (i) What is the probability of taking either a blue cube or a cube numbered 1 (or both)?
    (ii) What is the probability of taking either a blue cube or a cube numbered 2 (or both)?

Combining two events

EXAMPLES

1 A fair coin is thrown twice.
Identify all of the possible outcomes and write down their probabilities.

Method 1
List the outcomes systematically.

1st throw	2nd throw
Head (H)	Head (H)
Head (H)	Tail (T)
Tail (T)	Head (H)
Tail (T)	Tail (T)

Method 2
Use a **possibility space diagram**.

2nd throw

T	H & T	T & T
H	H & H	T & H
	H	T

1st throw

When a fair coin is tossed twice, there are four possible outcomes.

Because the coin is fair all the possible outcomes are **equally likely**.
Because all the outcomes are equally likely their probabilities can be worked out.

P(H and H) = P(H and T) = P(T and H) = P(T and T) = $\frac{1}{4}$.

2 A fair dice is rolled twice.
Use a possibility space diagram to show all the possible outcomes.
What is the probability of getting a 'double six'?
What is the probability of getting any 'double'?
What is the probability that exactly one 'six' is obtained?

2nd roll

6	1 and 6	2 and 6	3 and 6	4 and 6	5 and 6	6 and 6
5	1 and 5	2 and 5	3 and 5	4 and 5	5 and 5	6 and 5
4	1 and 4	2 and 4	3 and 4	4 and 4	5 and 4	6 and 4
3	1 and 3	2 and 3	3 and 3	4 and 3	5 and 3	6 and 3
2	1 and 2	2 and 2	3 and 2	4 and 2	5 and 2	6 and 2
1	1 and 1	2 and 1	3 and 1	4 and 1	5 and 1	6 and 1
	1	2	3	4	5	6

1st roll

The dice is fair so there are 36 equally likely outcomes.

P(double 6)
There is one outcome in the event (6 and 6).

P(double 6) = $\frac{1}{36}$

P(any double)
The 6 outcomes in the event are shaded blue.

P(any double) = $\frac{6}{36} = \frac{1}{6}$

P(exactly one six)
The 10 outcomes in the event are shaded grey.

P(exactly one six) = $\frac{10}{36} = \frac{5}{18}$

Probability • • • • Probability • • • • Probability • • • •

1 A red car (R), a blue car (B) and a green car (G) are parked on a narrow drive, one behind the other.
(a) List all the possible orders in which the three cars could be parked.

The cars are parked on the drive at random.
(b) What is the probability that the blue car is the first on the drive?

2 Two fair dice are rolled and the numbers obtained are added.
(a) Draw a possibility space diagram to show all of the possible outcomes.
(b) Use your diagram to work out:
   (i) the probability of obtaining a total of 10,
   (ii) the probability of obtaining a total greater than 10,
   (iii) the probability of obtaining a total less than 10.
(c) Explain why the probabilities you worked out in (b) should add up to 1.

3 A fair coin is tossed and a fair dice is rolled.
Copy and complete the table to show all the possible outcomes.

Dice

		1	2	3	4	5	6
Coin	H		H2				
	T						

What is the probability of obtaining:
(a) a head and a 5,   (b) a tail and an even number,
(c) a tail and a 6,   (d) a tail and an odd number,
(e) a head and a number more than 4,   (f) an odd number?

4 Sanjay has to travel to school in two stages.
Stage 1: he can go by bus or train or he can get a lift.
Stage 2: he can go by bus or he can walk.

(a) List all the different ways that Sanjay can travel to school.

Sanjay decides the way that he travels on each stage at random.
(b) What is the probability that he goes by bus in both stages?

5 The diagram shows an unbiased spinner.
It is divided into four equal sections numbered as shown.
The spinner is spun twice and the numbers the arrow lands on each time are added to obtain a score.
(a) Copy and complete this table to show all the possible scores.

2nd spin

		1	2	3	4
1st spin	1	2	3		
	2	3			
	3				
	4				

(b) Calculate the probability of getting a score of:
   (i) 2,   (ii) 3,   (iii) 6.

6 Bag A contains 2 red balls and 1 white ball.
Bag B contains 2 white balls and 1 red ball.
A ball is drawn at random from each bag.

(a) Copy and complete the table to show all possible
pairs of colours.

(b) Explain why the probability of each outcome is $\frac{1}{9}$.

(c) Calculate the probability that the two balls are the same colour.

Bag A

Bag B	R	R	W
W	RW		
W			
R			

7 The diagram shows two sets of cards A and B.

One card is taken at random from set A. One card is taken at random from set B.
(a) List all the possible outcomes.

The two numbers are added together.
(b) (i) What is the probability of getting a total of 5?
(ii) What is the probability of getting a total that is not 5?

All the cards are put together and one of them is taken at random.
(c) What is the probability that it is labelled A or 2 (or both)?

8 Students at a college must choose to study two subjects from the list:

Maths   English   Science   Art

(a) Write down all the possible pairs of subjects that the students can choose.

David chooses both subjects at random.
(b) What is the probability that one of the subjects he chooses is Maths?

James chooses Maths and one other subject at random.
(c) What is the probability that he chooses Maths and Science?

9 A spinner has an equal probability of landing on either red, green, blue, yellow or white.
The spinner is spun twice.
(a) List all the possible outcomes.
(b) (i) What is the probability that, on both spins, the spinner lands on white?
(ii) What is the probability that, on both spins, the spinner lands on white at least once?
(iii) What is the probability that, on both spins, the spinner lands on the same colour?

10 The diagram shows two unbiased spinners.
Each spinner is divided into equal sections and numbered as shown.
Each spinner is spun and the numbers that each arrow lands on are added together.

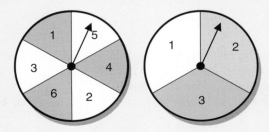

(a) Draw a possibility space diagram to show all the possible outcomes.
(b) Calculate the probability of getting a total of 2.
(c) Calculate the probability of getting a total of 6.

What you need to know

- You need to know the meaning of these terms:

  impossible, unlikely, evens, likely, certain

  outcome, event   fair, unbiased, biased, taken at random

  equally likely outcomes   trial

- **Probability** describes how likely or unlikely it is that an event will occur.
  Probabilities can be shown on a probability scale.
  Probability **must** be written as a fraction, a decimal or a percentage.

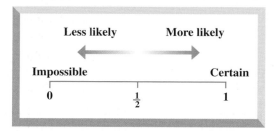

- How to work out probabilities using **equally likely outcomes**.
  The probability of an event is given by:

$$\text{Probability} = \frac{\text{Number of outcomes in the event}}{\text{Total number of possible outcomes}}$$

- How to decide the most appropriate way of determining probabilities from:
  - A calculation using **equally likely outcomes**.
  - A calculation using the **results of a survey**.
  - A calculation using the **results of an experiment**.
  - A calculation using **results from past records**.

- When A and B are events which cannot occur at the same time:

$$P(A \text{ or } B) = P(A) + P(B)$$

  A general rule for working out the probability of an event, A, not happening is:

$$P(\text{not } A) = 1 - P(A)$$

- How to find all the possible outcomes when two events are combined.
  - By **listing** the outcomes systematically.
  - By using a **possibility space diagram**.

Review Exercise

1. Copy the probability line below and mark the following probabilities.
   - (a) It will snow in London in June. Use the letter **S**.
   - (b) The sun will rise tomorrow. Use the letter **R**.
   - (c) A fair coin when tossed will come down heads. Use the letter **H**.

Edexcel

2 To play a game you spin the pointer. You win the prize on which the pointer stops.

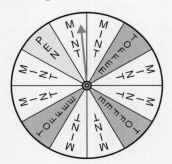

Richard has one spin.
(a) Which prize is Richard most likely to win?
(b) Explain your answer to part (a).

Copy the probability line below.

Donna has one spin.
(c) On your line mark with a P the probability that Donna will win a pen.
(d) On your line mark with a W the probability that Donna will win a watch.
    Edexcel

3 In a fish tank there are four white fish and one black fish.

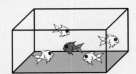

One fish is to be taken out at random. Write down the probability that the fish taken from the tank will be
(a) black,
(b) white.   Edexcel

4 A box contains only blue pencils and red pencils.
6 of the pencils are blue and 5 are red. A pencil is to be taken at random from the box.

Write down the probability that
(a) a blue pencil will be taken,
(b) a blue pencil will **not** be taken.
    Edexcel

5 A game is played with two spinners. They are spun at the same time. The result shown in the diagram is Blue 3.

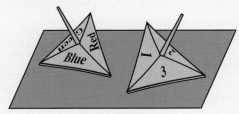

(a) List all the possible results when the spinners are spun.

Spinner A is a fair spinner.
(b) What is the probability of not getting green with spinner A?

Spinner B is weighted (biased). The probability of getting a 3 is 0.2 and the probability of getting a 1 is 0.3.
(c) What is the probability of getting a 2 with spinner B?   Edexcel

6 A machine makes compact discs. The probability that a perfect compact disc will be made by this machine is 0.85. Work out the probability that a compact disc made by this machine will not be perfect.   Edexcel

7 A game is played with two fair spinners.

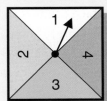 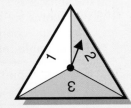

In each turn of the game both spinners are spun and the numbers are added to get a score.
(a) Copy and complete the following table to show each possible score.

	1	2	3	4
1				
2				
3				

(b) What is the probability of:
(i) scoring 6,
(ii) not scoring 6?
(c) To start the game a player needs to score either 2 or 5.
What is the probability that the game starts on the first throw?

8 Martin bought a packet of mixed flower seeds.
The seeds produce flowers that are Red or
Blue or White or Yellow.
The probability of a flower seed producing a
flower of a particular colour is:

Colour	Red	Blue	White	Yellow
Probability	0.6	0.15		0.15

(a) Write down the most common colour of
a flower.

Martin chooses a flower seed at random from
the packet.

(b) (i) Work out the probability that the
flower produced will be White.

(ii) Write down the probability that the
flower produced will be Orange.

Edexcel

9 A fair dice has the
numbers 1 to 6 on it.

(a) When the dice is rolled,
what is the probability
that a 4 will be scored?

A fair spinner has the
numbers 1, 2 and 3 on it.

(b) When the spinner is spun,
what is the probability
that a 3 will be scored?

In a game, the dice is rolled
and the spinner is spun.
The two scores are added.

(c) Copy and complete the table to show all
the possible **totals**.

Spinner / Dice	1	2	3
1			
2			
3			
4			
5			
6			

(d) What is the probability that a total of 4
will be scored?

A fair spinner with the numbers 1, 2, 3 and 4
on it is used in the game instead of the
3-sided spinner.

(e) Will there be an increase or decrease in
the probability that a total of 4 will be
scored?
Explain your answer.

Edexcel

10 Patrick has 20 marbles in a bag.
8 of the marbles are red.
7 of the marbles are blue.
The rest of the marbles are yellow.

(a) He takes one marble out of the bag
at random.
(i) What is the probability that it
is blue?
(ii) What is the probability that it
is red or blue?
(iii) What is the probability that it
is not blue?
Give your answers as fractions in
their simplest form.

(b) He takes two marbles out of the bag
at random.
List all the possible colour
combinations.

Edexcel

11 Georgina is watching a football match.
She says, "The probability that the team

I support will win is $\frac{1}{3}$ because there

are only three possible results: win, lose
or draw."
Explain why her statement may be
wrong.

12 The Orange Party, the Yellow Party and
the Purple Party stand in a school
election.
The table shows the voting intentions of
a sample of students before the election.

Voting intentions

	Orange Party	Yellow Party	Purple Party
Boys	4	5	6
Girls	5	7	3

(a) A student in the sample is chosen
at random.
What is the probability that the
person chosen intends to vote for
the Orange Party?

(b) A girl in the sample is chosen at
random.
What is the probability that she
intends to vote for the Purple Party?

(c) There are 960 students in the
school.
Use the results of the sample to
estimate the number of students in
the school who intend to vote for
the Yellow Party.

Section Review - Handling Data

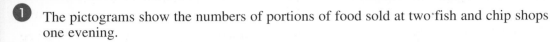

1 The pictograms show the numbers of portions of food sold at two fish and chip shops one evening.

The Pleasant Plaice

Type of food	Portions
Cod	🐟🐟🐟🐟
Plaice	🐟🐟
Chicken	🐟
Sausages	🐟🐟
Spring rolls	🐟

The Kettle O'Fish

Type of food	Portions
Cod	🐟🐟🐟🐟🐟
Plaice	🐟🐟
Chicken	🐟
Sausages	🐟
Spring rolls	🐟

Key: 🐟 10 portions   5 portions

(a) How many portions of plaice were sold at The Pleasant Plaice?
(b) How many portions of cod were sold at The Kettle O'Fish?
(c) What was the **total** number of portions of food sold at The Pleasant Plaice?
(d) For what type of food was there the greatest difference between the numbers of portions sold in the two shops?

Edexcel

2 A group of students were asked which sport they did most.
The bar chart shows the results.

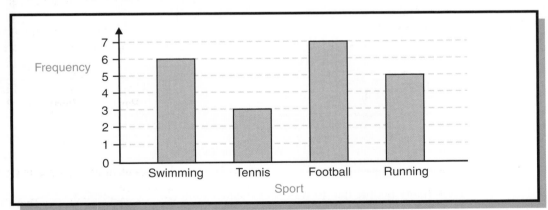

(a) How many students swim?
(b) How many students were asked?
(c) Which sport is the mode?

3 Edwina had 5 boxes of matches.
She counted the number of matches in each box.
Here are the numbers:

   28, 30, 31, 28, 27.

(a) Work out the mean number of matches per box.
(b) Work out the range of Edwina's numbers.

Edexcel

367

4 Zaheda conducted a probability experiment using a packet of 20 sweets.
She counted the number of sweets of each colour.
Her results are shown in the table.

Red	Green	Orange
12	3	5

(a) Draw a pictogram to represent this information.

Use the symbol ▷◯◁ to represent 2 sweets.

(b) Copy the line below and mark with an X the probability that Zaheda takes an orange sweet.

$$0 \qquad\qquad \tfrac{1}{2} \qquad\qquad 1$$

(c) Write down the probability
   (i) that Zaheda will take a green sweet from the packet,
   (ii) that the sweet Zaheda takes will **not** be red.

Edexcel

5 (a) The graph shows the results of a survey of the times people had to wait at airports for their flights.

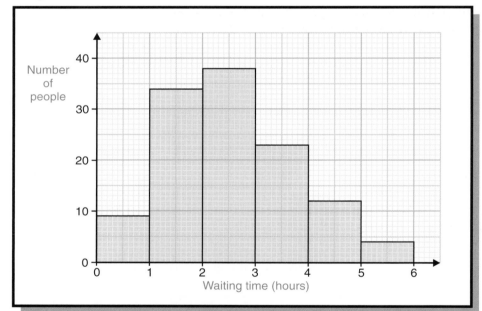

   (i) How many people had to wait more than 4 hours?
   (ii) How many people had to wait between 2 and 3 hours?

(b) The pie chart shows the departure airports of these people.
   (i) Which airport is the mode?
   (ii) 60 people departed from Heathrow. How many people departed from Gatwick?

(c) How many people were included in the survey?

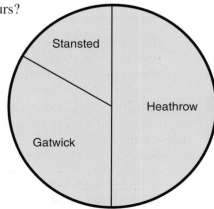

6 The marks, out of 100, obtained by 30 pupils in a mathematics test were:

| 51 | 53 | 54 | 90 | 91 | 49 | 64 | 63 | 62 | 39 | 77 | 45 | 62 | 66 | 51 |
| 36 | 28 | 47 | 82 | 47 | 76 | 64 | 66 | 56 | 48 | 54 | 63 | 72 | 53 | 39 |

(a) Copy and complete the frequency table, using class intervals 0 - 9, 10 - 19, 20 - 29, etc.

Class interval	Tally	Frequency
0 - 9		0
10 - 19		0
20 - 29		

Find the frequency in each class interval.

(b) Draw a bar chart for this frequency table.

Last time this class had a test, nobody scored more than 65 marks.
The median mark was in the 30s.
The mode was in the 20s.

(c) Explain briefly how the results of this test differ from the results of the last test.

Edexcel

7 A group of students was given a choice of four games to play.
The table shows the numbers choosing each game.

Game	Number of students
Badminton	8
Basketball	15
Squash	6
Volleyball	16

Draw a pie chart to show this information.

8 Jo measures the lengths, in centimetres, of a sample of runner beans.
The stem and leaf diagram shows the results.

```
                              1 | 3  means  13 cm
      ─────────────────────
      1 | 3   5   7   9

      2 | 0   3   4   6   6   6   7   8

      3 | 0   1   1
```

(a) How many runner beans are included in the sample?
(b) What is the range of their lengths?
(c) Which length is the median?
(d) Calculate the mean length.

9 A box contains 20 plastic ducks.
3 of the ducks are green, 10 are blue and the rest are yellow.
A duck is taken from the box at random.
(a) What is the probability that it is green?
(b) What is the probability that it is yellow?

10 Helen has a set of blue cards and a set of red cards, as shown.

Red cards   **Blue cards**

(a) A card is chosen at random from each set.
List all the possible combinations.
(b) What is the probability that both cards are 2's?

11 A class survey found the probability of having brown eyes is 0.6.
(a) What is the probability of not having brown eyes?
(b) There are 30 children in the class.
Estimate the number with brown eyes.

12 A group of students were each asked how many books they had read last month.
The frequency diagram shows the results.

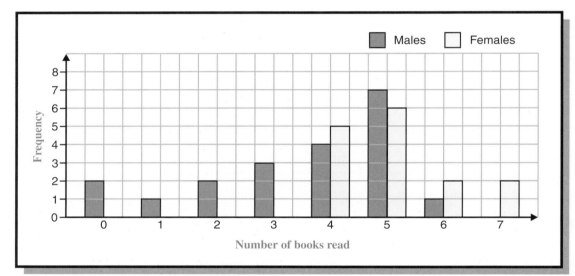

(a) How many students were included?
(b) What is the range in the number of books read by females?
(c) Calculate the mean number of books read by females.
(d) Compare and comment on the number of books read by males and the number of books
read by females.

13 A spinner is labelled as shown.
The results of the first 30 spins are given below.

| 1 | 2 | 3 | 3 | 5 | 1 | 3 | 2 | 2 | 4 | 5 | 3 | 2 | 1 | 2 |
| 5 | 2 | 4 | 1 | 5 | 1 | 5 | 2 | 2 | 4 | 2 | 5 | 4 | 2 | 3 |

Is the spinner fair?
Give a reason for your answer.

14 The table shows information about a group of children.

	Can swim	Cannot swim
Boys	16	4
Girls	19	6

(a) One of these children is chosen at random.
What is the probability that the child can swim?

(b) A girl in the group is chosen at random.
What is the probability that she cannot swim?

(c) Tony says, "These results show a higher proportion of girls can swim."
Is he correct?
Give reasons for your answer.

15 Laurie is designing a survey to find out about people who use a superstore near her home.
One of the things Laurie wants to find out is how far people have travelled to get to the superstore.

(a) Decide which question below is best to ask.
Give **two** reasons for your decision.

> [A] How far have you travelled to get here today?
>
> [B] Where do you live?
>
> [C] Do you live far from here?
>
> [D] Please show me on this map where you have travelled from.

Laurie decides to do her survey one Friday evening outside the superstore.
(b) Give **one** reason why this would give a biased sample.   Edexcel

16 The table gives you the marks scored by pupils in a French and in a German test.

French	15	35	34	23	35	27	36	34	23	24	30	40	25	35	20
German	20	37	35	25	33	30	39	36	27	20	33	35	27	32	28

(a) Draw a scatter graph of the marks scored in the French and German tests.
(b) Describe the correlation between the marks scored in the two tests.

Abigail scored 32 in the French test.
(c) Use the scatter graph to estimate the mark she scored in the German test.   Edexcel

17 Asif's bus could be on time or late or early.

> The probability that his bus will be on time is 0.9.
> The probability that his bus will be late is 0.03.

Work out the probability that Asif's bus will be early.   Edexcel

18 A shop employs 8 men and 2 women.
The mean weekly wage of the 10 employees is £396.
The mean weekly wage of the 8 men is £400.
Calculate the mean weekly wage of the 2 women.   Edexcel

Exam Practice - Non-calculator Paper

Do not use a calculator for this exercise.

1

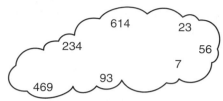

(a) Put the numbers in the cloud into order. Start with the **smallest** number.

(b) Write the number 469 in words. *Edexcel*

2

(a) Write the number two thousand one hundred and thirty-nine in figures.

(b) Write 573 to the nearest 10.

(c) Work out 1542 + 468.

3

> 11, 12, 13, 14, 15, 16, 17,
> 18, 19, 20, 21, 22, 23.

(a) From the list above, write down a number which can be divided exactly by 5.

(b) From the list above, write down the number which can be divided exactly by 5 and 2. *Edexcel*

4

(a) The number 8432 is multiplied by 100. What is the value of 3 in the answer?

(b) The number 8432 is divided by 10. What is the value of 4 in the answer?

5

Copy and draw in all the lines of symmetry on each of the following flags.

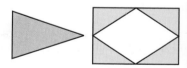

Edexcel

6

Dave buys these items.

JAM	BREAD	BUTTER
75 pence	**49 pence**	**62 pence**

(a) How much does he have to pay altogether?

(b) He pays with a £5 note. How much change is he given?

7

(a) What is the next number in this sequence?

1, 5, 9, 13, …

(b) Explain how you found your answer.

(c) Is 100 in the sequence? Give a reason for your answer.

8

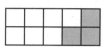

(a) What fraction of the shape is shaded?

(b) What percentage of the shape is shaded?

(c) Copy the shape and shade in more squares so that $\frac{4}{5}$ of the shape will be shaded. *Edexcel*

9

(a) Write $\frac{1}{2}$ as a percentage.

(b) Write $\frac{2}{5}$ as a decimal.

(c) Put these fractions in order, smallest first.

$$\frac{1}{2} \quad \frac{2}{3} \quad \frac{3}{4} \quad \frac{2}{5}$$

10

(a) Work out $236 - 149$.

(b) Work out $23.6 \div 10$.

(c) Work out 16×27.

11

What number must be put in the box to make each of these statements true?

(a) $\boxed{} \times 3 = 15$

(b) $3 + \boxed{} = 11$

(c) $\boxed{} - 3 = 7$

12

This shape has been drawn on 1 cm squared paper.

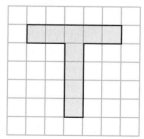

Not full size

Find the area and perimeter of this shape?

Edexcel

13 (a) The diagram shows four discs with numbers on.

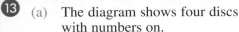

The number shown here is 1743. Using all these four discs only, write down
- (i) the **largest** number you could make,
- (ii) the **smallest** number you could make,
- (iii) the missing numbers in this problem.

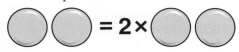

(b) Here is another disc. The number on this disc is doubled. Then 3 is added. The answer is then 15. What is the number on this disc?

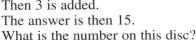

Edexcel

14 Kath said, "My new baby weighs 4.5 milligrams."
- (a) Which part of her statement is wrong?
- (b) What should she have said?

Edexcel

15 (a) Work out $32.4 - 14.9$.
- (b) Work out $23.6 \div 8$.
- (c) Work out 4×0.4.

16 Work out the size of the angles marked with letters.
Give a reason for each of your answers.

(a) 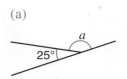   (b)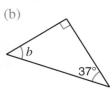

17 (a) Simplify $b \times b \times b$.
- (b) Drinks cost 35 pence each. How much will d drinks cost?
- (c) What is the value of $ab - 2c$ when $a = 4$, $b = 5$ and $c = 6$?

18 Steven pays 96 pence for 3 oranges and 2 grapefruit.
A grapefruit costs 27 pence.
How much is an orange?

19 A vase contains 5 red tulips and 4 yellow tulips. A tulip is taken from the vase at random. What is the probability that it is red?

20 These are the numbers of goals let in by a goalkeeper, Murray, in the first 10 matches of the season.

0   3   1   2   4   0   1   1   6   4

- (a) Calculate the mean number of goals per match.
- (b) What was the range for the number of goals?

Murray was injured for the next four matches and the reserve goalkeeper, Kent, played. The number of goals let in by Kent had a mean of 3 with a range of 2.
- (c) How many goals did Kent let in altogether in these four matches?

Both Murray and Kent are fit for the 15th match.
- (d) Write down **two** statements which might help the manager to decide which goalkeeper to choose.

Edexcel

21 Jim says, "I've driven 240 kilometres today." Estimate the distance he has driven in miles if one kilometre is approximately five eighths of a mile.

22 The diagram represents a cuboid. Draw accurately, on one-centimetre squared paper, a net of this cuboid.

Edexcel

23 (a) Solve the equations.
- (i) $x - 3 = 7$ (ii) $6x = 42$
- (b) Multiply out $2(a - 3)$.

24 A packet of crisps costs 26 pence.
- (a) Work out the total cost of 48 packets of crisps.

There are 48 packets of crisps in a box. The tuck shop sells approximately 2000 packets of crisps each week. Five pupils estimate how many boxes of crisps are needed.
Here are their answers:

Anna … 4   John … 40   Karl … 400
Frank … 50   Susan … 5

- (b) (i) Write down the name of the pupil who gave the most sensible answer.
  - (ii) Explain your answer to (i). *Edexcel*

25 Chippy the carpenter marks a
3 metre length of wood into three pieces.
One piece is 1.40 metres long.
Another piece is 84 centimetres long.
How long is the third piece of wood?

26 The diagram shows a target.

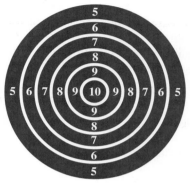

Billy fires at the target ten times.
The frequency table gives information
about his scores.

Score	Frequency
5	2
6	1
7	3
8	1
9	2
10	1

(a)   Write down his modal score.
(b)   Work out his total score.

27 Jane makes chocolates.

Each box she puts them in has
   Volume = 1000 cm³
   Length = 20 cm
   Width   = 10 cm

(a)   Work out the height of a box.

Jane makes 350 chocolates.
Each box will hold 18 chocolates.
(b)   Work out
   (i)   how many boxes Jane can fill
         completely,
   (ii)   how many chocolates will be
         left over.

28 (a) $p = -8$ and $q = 3$.
         Work out the value of $p - 2q$.

   (b)   Work out $\dfrac{-14 + 2}{3}$.

29 A sequence begins   15,   7,   3,   …
The rule for continuing the sequence is shown.

> Subtract 1 from the last number and then
> divide by 2.

Write down the next three numbers in the
sequence.

30 (a)   Write down the value of 7^3.
   (b)   What is the value of $\sqrt{81}$?
   (c)   What is the reciprocal of 2?

31 Joyce wants to calculate $\dfrac{59.6}{20.2 - 4.9}$.
By writing each of the numbers in Joyce's
calculation to the nearest whole number
estimate the answer.

32 In the diagram, PQR is an isosceles triangle.
The lines PQ and
RS are parallel.

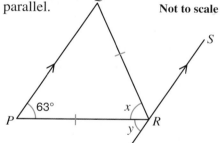

Not to scale

(a)   Work out the size of angle x.
(b)   (i)   What is the size of angle y?
      (ii)   Give a reason for your answer.

33 **A** and **B** are
two fair spinners.

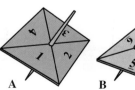

Jane spins the two spinners together once.
(a)   Copy and complete the table below to
      show **all** the possible results **and** the
      total scores.

Spinner **A**	Spinner **B**	Total score

(b)   Use your table to find the probability that
      Jane will get a total score of 7.

34   (a)   What is the value of $2x^2$ when $x = 3$?

      (b)   Simplify $3t - t - 3$.

      (c)   Solve $2(x - 3) = 8$.

35

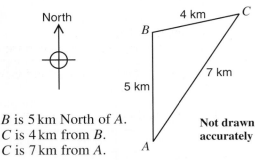

B is 5 km North of A.

C is 4 km from B.   **Not drawn accurately**

C is 7 km from A.

   (a)   Make an accurate scale drawing of triangle ABC.

        Use a scale of 1 cm to 1 km.

   (b)   From your accurate scale drawing, measure the bearing of C from A.

   (c)   Find the bearing of A from C.   Edexcel

36   (a)   A tin contains 60 toffees.

        Jacob eats 15% of the toffees.

        What fraction of the toffees are left?

        Give your answer in its simplest form.

   (b)   A box contains milk and plain chocolates in the ratio 2 : 1.

        The box contains 24 chocolates.

        How many are plain?

37   The diagram shows the positions of shapes T, M and N.

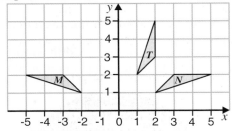

   (a)   Describe fully the single transformation which maps M onto N.

   (b)   Describe fully the single transformation which maps T onto M.

38   Work out.   (a) $\dfrac{5}{6} - \dfrac{2}{3}$ (b) $\dfrac{4}{5} + \dfrac{3}{4}$

39   Factorise   (a) $2m - 4n$,   (b) $t^2 - 2t$.

40   Solve the equations.

   (a) $4x + 2 = 26$ (b) $19 + 4y = 9 - y$

                                          Edexcel

41   An examination in history is marked out of 60 marks.

   (a)   Alex gets 80% of the marks.

        How many marks does she get?

   (b)   Reg gets 54 marks.

        What percentage of the marks does he get?

42

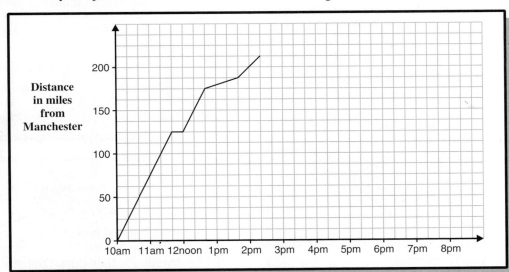

The graph represents part of Mrs. Hinton's journey from Manchester to London.

Mrs. Hinton stopped for a rest at a service station.

(a)   (i)   Write down the time at which she stopped.   (ii)   For how long did she stop?

For part of her journey Mrs. Hinton had to slow down because of a traffic queue.

(b)   For how many miles did she travel at a slower speed?

Mrs. Hinton spent an hour at a meeting in London.

She then returned home to Manchester, travelling at a steady speed of 50 miles per hour.

(c)   Copy and complete the graph of her journey.   Edexcel

Exam Practice - Calculator Paper ● ● ● ● ●

You may use a calculator for this exercise.

1 (a) Write the number 5624 in words.
(b) Write these numbers in order, starting with the smallest.

39   −4   3   120   −15

2 The diagram shows a quadrilateral *PQRS*.

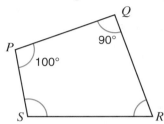

(a) Which line is perpendicular to *PQ*?
(b) Find by measuring the size of angle *PSR* and angle *QRS*.
(c) Which angle is an acute angle?
(d) Measure the length of *SR*.

3 Les writes down six numbers.

2   3   6   7   9   24

(a) Which of these numbers are odd numbers?
(b) Which of these numbers are factors of 12?
(c) Which of these numbers is a multiple of 12?
(d) Which of these numbers is a square number?

4 (a) Which of these shapes is a rhombus?

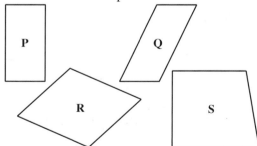

(b) Which two of these shapes are congruent to each other?

5 Rosie gets on a bus at 1745 and gets off the bus at 1806.
(a) How long was she on the bus?
(b) What time did she get off the bus using the 12-hour clock?

6 The results from 40 spins of a numbered spinner are:

2 1 4 3 2 1 3 4 5 2
1 5 3 4 2 3 3 3 2 4
1 2 ¯2 3 2 1 2 4 5 2
2 3 4 2 1 5 3 3 5 3

(a) Copy and complete the frequency table for these results.

Result	Tally	Frequency
1		
2		

(b) Draw a bar chart to show the results.
(c) Which result is the mode?

7 A theatre has 42 rows of seats.
Each row has 28 seats.
Everyone has to pay £4.75 to go to the theatre.
(a) Calculate the amount of money taken when every seat is filled.
(b) Give your answer to part (a) to the nearest thousand pounds.

8 Ivan builds fences in different lengths using pieces of wood.

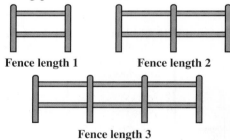

Fence length 1   Fence length 2

Fence length 3

(a) Sketch fence length 5.

Ivan counted how many pieces of wood he needed to make each fence length. He then drew the table below.

Fence length	1	2	3	4	5	6
Number of pieces	4	7	10			

(b) Complete the table to show how many pieces of wood he would use for fence lengths 4, 5, and 6.
(c) Explain how you would work out the number of pieces needed for fence length 25.

Edexcel

9 The diagram shows the positions of points A, B and C.

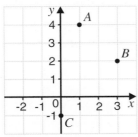

(a) What are the coordinates of A?

(b) (i) Copy the diagram and mark the position of D so that $ABCD$ is a rectangle.

(ii) What are the coordinates of D?

10 (a) A fence is 2.3 metres high. What is the height of the fence in centimetres?

(b) A cycle race is 26 miles. How many kilometres is this?

(c) A rule for changing litres into gallons is:

> **Divide by 4.5**

A lorry's fuel tank holds 180 litres. Use this rule to work out how many gallons the lorry's fuel tank holds.

11 (a) Write down the order of rotational symmetry for these shapes.

(i) 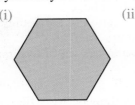 (ii)

(b) On squared paper, draw a shape with 2 lines of symmetry **and** rotational symmetry of order 2. *Edexcel*

12 This rule is used to work out take home pay.

$$\text{Take home pay} = \text{hours worked} \times \text{hourly rate} - \text{deductions}$$

(a) Kirsty worked 17 hours. Her hourly rate was £4.50. Her deductions were £8.25. Work out her take home pay.

(b) Mary's hourly rate was £5. Her deductions were £7. Her take home pay was £68. Work out the number of hours she worked. *Edexcel*

13
[thermometer diagram: °C scale from −10 to 10]

(a) Write down the temperature shown on the thermometer.

At 6 a.m., the temperature in Fred's garden was $-3°C$.
By noon, the temperature had risen by $12°C$.

(b) Work out the temperature at noon.

By midnight, the temperature in Fred's garden had fallen to $-7°C$.

(c) Work out the fall in temperature from noon to midnight. *Edexcel*

14 (a) Simplify $t + 2t + 3t$.

(b) Solve the equations
(i) $2w = 6$, (ii) $x + 3 = 5$.

(c) What number must go in the box to make this statement true?

$$\boxed{} \times 3 + 2 = 17$$

15 A school buys a trampoline. The school is given a discount of $\frac{1}{8}$ of the price.

(a) Write $\frac{1}{8}$ as (i) a decimal,
(ii) a percentage.

The price of the trampoline is £3218.

(b) Work out the amount the school actually has to pay. *Edexcel*

16 This shape has been made using 1 cm cubes.

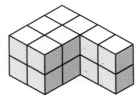

Not to scale

What is the volume of the shape?

17 (a) Calculate $\sqrt{6}$. Give your answer correct to one decimal place.

(b) Calculate $3.5(2.3 + 3.7)$.

18 Laura buys 18 cartons of juice. She pays with a £10 note. She gets £2.98 change. How much is each carton of juice?

19 (a) Copy and complete this table of values
for $y = x + 2$.

x	-3	-2	-1	0	1	2	3
y			1		3	4	

(b) Plot the points given by the values in
your table.
Join the points.

(c) Work out the value of x when $y = 2.5$

Edexcel

20 There are 27 wall tiles
in a pack.
Only full packs of
tiles are sold.

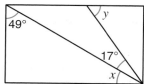

Barry needs 200 tiles.

(a) How many full packs
of tiles must he buy?

Each tile is a rectangle 20 cm by 15 cm.

(b) Work out the area of one tile.

Navdeep wants to tile a wall.
The wall is a rectangle 3 metres by 2.4 metres.

(c) Work out the number of tiles she needs
to cover the wall completely. Edexcel

21 A caretaker is paid at a basic rate of
£7.76 per hour for 36 hours a week.
Overtime is paid at one and a half times
the basic rate.
One week the caretaker works 42 hours.
How much is the caretaker paid that week?

22 The diagram shows a rectangle.

Work out the size of angles x and y.

23 A candle weighs x grams.

(a) Write an expression, in terms of x, for
the weight of 20 candles.

(b) A box of 20 candles weighs 3800 grams.
The box weighs 200 grams.
What is the weight of a candle?

24 30 girls and 20 boys applied to go on a
skiing course.
$\frac{3}{5}$ of the girls and $\frac{7}{10}$ of the boys went on
the course.
What percentage of the 50 students who
applied went on the course?

25 (a) Work out 20% of £25.

(b) Work out $\frac{3}{8}$ of 6 metres. Edexcel

26

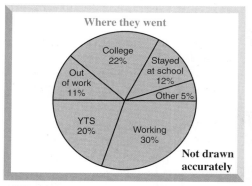

300 young people were asked what they
did after completing Year 11 at school.
The pie chart shows the results of the
survey.

(a) How many of the young people
were working?

Gwen made an accurate drawing of the
pie chart.
She first drew the sector representing the
young people out of work.

(b) Calculate the size of the angle of
this sector.
Give your answer correct to the
nearest degree.

(c) Change to a decimal the percentage
going to college.

(d) What fraction of the young people
stayed at school?
Give your answer in its simplest
form. Edexcel

27 A shop sells flour in two sizes.
Size 1: weight 500 g, cost 39 pence.
Size 2: weight 800 g, cost 59 pence.
Which size gives better value for money?
You **must** show all your working.

28 The stem and leaf diagram shows the
results of measuring the lengths of
some leaves.

						4	3	means 4.3 cm
4	7	9						
5	0	3	6	8				
6	1	4	5	5	7			
7	2							

(a) How many leaves were measured?
(b) What is the range in the lengths?
(c) Calculate the mean length.

29 (a) Calculate $\dfrac{81.2 \times 9.8}{10.1 + 29.3}$

(b) By using approximations show that your answer to (a) is about right. You must show all your working.

30 Mr Habib receives a gas bill for £124 + VAT.
The rate of VAT is 5%.
How much is the gas bill altogether?

31 $AB = BC$.
Angle $ACB = 63°$.
ACE and BCD are straight lines.

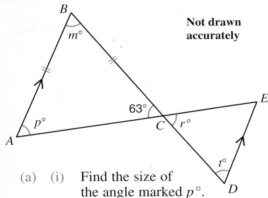

Not drawn accurately

(a) (i) Find the size of the angle marked $p°$.
(ii) Give a reason for your answer.
(b) Work out the size of
(i) the angle marked $m°$,
(ii) the angle marked $r°$.

AB is parallel to DE.
(c) (i) Find the size of the angle marked $t°$.
(ii) Explain how you worked out your answer. *Edexcel*

32

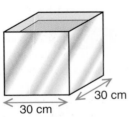

Water is stored in a tank in the shape of a cuboid with a square base.
The sides of the base are 30 cm long.
The depth of the water is 20 cm.
(a) Work out the volume of the water.

More water is put in the tank.
The depth of the water rises to 21.6 cm.
(b) Calculate the percentage increase in the volume of the water in the tank. *Edexcel*

33 Ben has some coloured cubes in a bag.
The table shows the number of cubes of each colour.

Red	Blue	Yellow	Brown
7	4	8	6

Ben is going to take one cube at random from the bag.
Write down the probability that Ben
(a) will take a yellow cube,
(b) will **not** take a brown cube. *Edexcel*

34 Justin is making a circular hoop for his brother.
The diameter of the hoop is 60 cm.
Work out the circumference of the hoop.
Edexcel

35 A garden is a rectangle measuring 26 m by 11.5 m.
Grass covers 67% of the area of the garden.
Calculate the area of grass.
Give your answer to a suitable degree of accuracy.

36 Aisha is carrying out a survey into radio listening habits.
One of the questions she writes is:
"How often do you listen to the radio?"

A friend tells her that this question is unsuitable.
Write down two ways in which this question could be improved.

37 (a) A kilogram of strawberries costs £1.70.
Estimate, to the nearest £, the cost of 5 lbs of strawberries.
(b) A bowl of strawberries and cream weighs 210 grams.
The ratio, by weight, of strawberries to cream is 5 : 1.
What is the weight of the cream?

38 (a) Calculate $\sqrt{8} \times 3.6^2$.
Give your answer correct to 2 decimal places.
(b) Work out 8^3.
(c) Find the value of $\dfrac{1}{x} + y^3$
when $x = 5$ and $y = 0.5$.

39 (a) Solve $3x - 9 = 7 - 2x$.
(b) Factorise $3a - 6b$.
(c) Simplify $5x + 2(x + 3)$.

Answers

CHAPTER 1

Exercise 1.1   Page 1

1. (a) $923 = 900 + 20 + 3$
   $= 9 \times 100 + 2 \times 10 + 3$
   (b) $456 = 400 + 50 + 6$
   $= 4 \times 100 + 5 \times 10 + 6$
   (c) $54 = 50 + 4$
   $= 5 \times 10 + 4$
   (d) $765 = 700 + 60 + 5$
   $= 7 \times 100 + 6 \times 10 + 5$
   (e) $492 = 400 + 90 + 2$
   $= 4 \times 100 + 9 \times 10 + 2$
   (f) $1872 = 1000 + 800 + 70 + 2$
   $= 1 \times 1000 + 8 \times 100 + 7 \times 10 + 2$
   (g) $1023 = 1000 + 20 + 3$
   $= 1 \times 1000 + 2 \times 10 + 3$
   (h) $3405 = 3000 + 400 + 5$
   $= 3 \times 1000 + 4 \times 100 + 5$

2. (a) 50, 3   (b) 300, 40, 1
   (c) 600, 70, 3   (d) 900, 80, 7
   (e) 300, 30, 3   (f) 1000, 800, 90, 7
   (g) 1000, 50, 2   (h) 1000, 500, 20

3. (a) 30   (b) 2000
   (c) 600   (d) 6

4. (a) 1 in 512   (b) 7 in 745
   (c) 5 in 599

5. (a) 302   (b) 23

6. (a) 39, 74, 168, 421
   (b) 544, 545, 554, 555
   (c) 3801, 3842, 3874, 4765, 5814

7. (a) 429, 425, 399, 103, 84
   (b) 349, 324, 239, 234
   (c) 9951, 9653, 9646, 9434

8. 732, 723, 372, 327, 273, 237

9. 3458   4358   5348   8345
   3485   4385   5384   8354
   3548   4538   5438   8435
   3584   4583   5483   8453
   3845   4835   5834   8534
   3854   4853   5843   8543
   6 numbers beginning with 8

10. (a) 754 Put digits in order, largest to smallest.
    (b) 457 Put digits in order, smallest to largest.

11. (a) 6521   (b) 1256

12. (a) 76 541   (b) 14 567

Exercise 1.2   Page 2

1. (a) Seventeen
   (b) Eighty-eight
   (c) One hundred and eighty-seven
   (d) Two thousand and forty-five
   (e) Five thousand six hundred and twelve
   (f) Seven thousand eight hundred and two
   (g) Eight thousand eight hundred and eighty-eight
   (h) Ninety-two thousand
   (i) One hundred and thirty-two thousand and forty-five
   (j) One million five hundred thousand

2. (a) (i) 1   (ii) 10   (iii) 100
   (iv) 1000   (v) 10 000
   (b) Previous number multiplied by ten, nought added
   (c) 100 000, one hundred thousand, 1 000 000, one million

3. (a) 546   (b) 607
   (c) 1010   (d) 70 200
   (e) 1 200 052

4. (a) 2 000 000   (b) 10 000 000
   (c) 500 000   (d) 1 500 000

5. The attendance at a football match was 48 000.
   The pitch measured 119 yards by 62 yards.
   After 25 minutes the centre forward (who cost £15 000 000) scored from 18 yards.

6. (a) 7030   (b) 463
   (c) 11 000

Exercise 1.3   Page 3

1. (a) 28   (b) 33

2. (a) 29   (b) 43   (c) 43
   (d) 53

3. (a) 12   (b) 15   (c) 27
   (d) 56   (e) 35   (f) 74
   (g) 70   (h) 112

4. (a) 91   (b) 4   (c) 55
   (d) 63   (e) 38   (f) 17
   (g) 76   (h) 23

5. 112 miles   6. £276

7. (a) 62p   (b) 54p   (c) 81p

8. £539

9. (a) 83   (b) 82   (c) 78
    (d) 243

10. (a) 788   (b) 83   (c) 174
    (d) 952   (e) 2002   (f) 12 203
    (g) 201   (h) 1541

11. 1030 grams   13. 81 030

12. 1378   14. £670   15. 520 km

Exercise 1.4   Page 6

1. (a) 33   (b) 27

2. (a) 32   (b) 27   (c) 18
    (d) 26

3. (a) 5   (b) 92   (c) 43
    (d) 68   (e) 76   (f) 17
    (g) 59   (h) 21

4. £87

5. (a) 4   (b) 16   (c) 17
    (d) 50   (e) 49   (f) 90
    (g) 105   (h) 150   (i) 301
    (j) 4

6. £26   7. £615

8. (a) 354   (b) 428   (c) 1284
    (d) 158   (e) 2224   (f) 469
    (g) 6268   (h) 3277

9. 48   10. 89   11. 384

12. (a) 23p   (b) 31p

13. (a) Tomato 39, Oxtail 18, Chicken 55
    (b) 112

14. (a) £74   (b) £60

Exercise 1.5   Page 8

1. 40   2. 72   3. 144   4. £5.52

5. (a) 40p   (b) 72p   (c) £1.32
    (d) £2.01   (e) 62p

6. (a) 84   (b) 136   (c) 85
    (d) 378   (e) 252   (f) 549
    (g) 2112   (h) 15 895   (i) 24 072
    (j) 42 084

7. (a) 68   (b) 275   (c) 666
    (d) 46

8. 29

Exercise 1.6   Page 9

1. (a) 1320   (b) 12 300   (c) 47 000
    (d) 38 400

2. (a) 2310   (b) 514   (c) 100

3. (a) £1200   (b) £5900   (c) £71 000

4. (a) 240   (b) £3.90

5. 250

6. (a) £120   (b) £700   (c) £8200

7. (a) 210   (b) 140

8. (a) 300   (b) 540

9. 1600 kg

10. (a) 7140   (b) 18 960   (c) 21 480
    (d) 13 000   (e) 13 020   (f) 21 510

11. (a) E.g. To multiply by 200, multiply by 2
      and then by 100.
    (b) (i) 13 400   (ii) 10 500

12. 10 000

Exercise 1.7   Page 10

1. (a) 16   (b) 20   (c) 8

2. 15

3. (a) 17   (b) 157
    (c) 136   (d) 75 remainder 5
    (e) 393 remainder 2   (f) 206
    (g) 1098   (h) 20 140

4. (a) 10   (b) 3 pence

5. (a) 13   (b) 4 pence

Exercise 1.8   Page 11

1. (a) 456   (b) 465   (c) 64
    (d) 654

2. (a) 100   (b) 702 000   (c) 10

3. 12   4. 7   5. 25   6. 7

7. (a) 253   (b) 79   (c) 537
    (d) 126   (e) 45   (f) 613

8. (a) E.g. To divide by 200, divide by 100
      then by 2.
    (b) (i) 26   (ii) 412

Exercise 1.9

Page 13

1. (a) 204   (b) 345   (c) 1344
   (d) 2432   (e) 4862   (f) 38 772

2. 216   4. £966   6. £1392

3. 255   5. 1316   7. £5191

8. (a) 43   (b) 32   (c) 27
   (d) 32   (e) 48   (f) 41
   (g) 21   (h) 29

9. (a) 16 remainder 10   (b) 25 remainder 7
   (c) 17 remainder 35   (d) 13 remainder 13

10. 17 pints, 7p change

11. (a) 41   (b) 16

12. (a) 20   (b) 35, 10p change
    (c) 14, 10p change

Review Exercise 1

Page 14

1. (a) Eight hundred and seven
   (b) 100 057
   (c) 483, 712, 2104, 2901, 5342

2. 5 hundreds, 500

3. (a) 67
   (b) (i) 83   (ii) 45   (iii) 71
   (c) (i) 500   (ii) 25

4. (a) Three thousand   (b) 7 000 000

5. (a) $66 + 20 = 86$
   $86 + 20 = 106$
   (b) True, because $5 \times 20 = 100$
   and $100 + ?$ is greater than 100.

6. (a) 8752   (b) 2587

7. (a) 108   (b) 491   (c) 2059   (d) 587

8. 298 miles

9. (a) 97, 404   (b) 114, 306
   (c) 92, 209

10. (a) 234   (b) 26   (c) 6462   (d) 241

11. (a) 73 500   (b) 6420
    (c) 3020   (d) 462

12. £2175

13. 14 664

14. 120

15. (a) 166
    (b) 4

16. £16 297

17. (a) 163
    (b) £3 200 000

18. £17

19. 136

20. (a) 1375 kg
    (b) 65

CHAPTER 2

Exercise 2.1

Page 16

1. (a) 37   (b) 3   (c) 9
   (d) 58   (e) 6   (f) 30
   (g) 5   (h) 19   (i) 14
   (j) 20   (k) 24   (l) 4
   (m) 0   (n) 5   (o) 6

2. (a) $5 \times 6 + 7 = 37$
   (b) $5 + 6 \times 7 = 47$
   (c) $15 + 8 \times 9 = 87$
   (d) $15 \times 8 + 9 = 129$
   (e) $15 \times 8 - 9 = 111$
   (f) $15 \div 5 + 3 = 6$
   (g) $5 - 24 \div 6 = 1$
   (h) $19 \div 19 + 7 = 8$
   (i) $4 \times 4 + 7 \times 2 = 30$

3. Many answers, for example:
   $6 - 3 \times 2 + 1 = 1$ $6 - 3 - 2 + 1 = 2$
   $6 \div 3 + 2 - 1 = 3$ $6 \div 3 + 2 \times 1 = 4$
   $6 - 3 + 2 \times 1 = 5$ $6 - 3 + 2 + 1 = 6$
   $6 + 3 - 2 \times 1 = 7$ $6 \times 3 \div 2 - 1 = 8$
   $6 \times 3 \div 2 \times 1 = 9$ $6 + 3 + 2 - 1 = 10$

Exercise 2.2

Page 17

1. 148 cm

2. (a) 58p   (b) 2p   (c) 15p

3. 25

4. 75 g

5. 35 cm

6. 155 cm

7. 15 g

8. (a) 63   (b) 75

Exercise 2.3

Page 19

1. (a) 4870   (b) 4900   (c) 5000

2. (a) 7430   (b) 7400   (c) 7000

3. (a) 40   (b) 80   (c) 90
   (d) 130   (e) 740   (f) 1840

4. (a) 400   (b) 600   (c) 400
   (d) 1400   (e) 100   (f) 2600

5.

Number	Nearest 10	Nearest 100	Nearest 1000
7613	7610	7600	8000
977	980	1000	1000
61 115	61 120	61 100	61 000
9714	9710	9700	10 000
623	620	600	1000
9949	9950	9900	10 000
5762	5760	5800	6000
7501	7500	7500	8000
7499	7500	7500	7000

6. (a) 7000   (b) 4000   (c) 19 000
    (d) 21 000   (e) 50 000   (f) 132 000

7. (a) 19 000 (nearest thousand)
    (b) 260 (nearest ten)
    (c) 140 (nearest ten)
    (d) £50 (nearest pound)
    (e) 130 (nearest ten)
    (f) 24 100 (nearest hundred)
    (g) 309 000 km^2 (nearest thousand km^2)
    (h) 190 km (nearest ten kilometres)
    (i) £51 (nearest pound)
    (j) 700 (nearest hundred)

8. (a) 745, 746, 747, 748, 749
    (b) 750, 751, 752, 753, 754
    (c) Any number from 8450 to 8499
    (d) Any number from 8500 to 8549

9. 42 500   **10.** 135, 144   **11.** 2749

Exercise 2.4   Page 20

1. 4   **4.** 5   **7.** 29
2. 5   **5.** 9   **8.** 19   **10.** 7
3. 10   **6.** 24   **9.** 5   **11.** 5

Exercise 2.5   Page 22

1.

Number	Rounded to 1 sig. fig.
17	20
32	30
467	500
523	500
350	400
2400	2000
620	600
99	100

2. £6000 + £2000 = £8000

3. (a) (i)   40 × 20 = 800
       (ii)   100 × 20 = 2000
       (iii) 800 × 50 = 40 000
       (iv) 900 × 60 = 54 000
    (b) (i)   80 ÷ 20 = 4
       (ii)   600 ÷ 30 = 20
       (iii) 900 ÷ 60 = 15
       (iv) 4000 ÷ 80 = 50

4. 20 × 30 = 600

5. 600 ÷ 30 = 20

6. (a) 30 is bigger than 29 and 50 is bigger
      than 48.
      So, 30 × 50 is bigger than 29 × 48.
    (b) 200 ÷ 10 = 20, 14, estimate is bigger

Exercise 2.6   Page 23

1. (a) 5   (b) 2   (c) 2
    (d) 3   (e) 2   (f) 5

2. (a) 200 × 300   (b) 60 000   (c) 956

3. (a) 30 × 40 = 1200,   1312
    (b) 10 × 70 = 700,   792
    (c) 60 × 30 = 1800,   1972
    (d) 70 × 50 = 3500,   3240
    (e) 30 × 80 = 2400,   2652
    (f) 20 × 200 = 4000,   3723
    (g) 300 × 60 = 18 000,   16 296
    (h) 300 × 20 = 6000,   7176

4. (a) 600 ÷ 20 = 30,   33
    (b) 600 ÷ 20 = 30,   29
    (c) 300 ÷ 20 = 15,   16
    (d) 800 ÷ 40 = 20,   24

5. (a) $\dfrac{50 \times 200}{20} = 500, \quad 461.3\ldots$

    (b) $\dfrac{600}{10 \times 30} = 2, \quad 1.6695\ldots$

    (c) $\dfrac{20 \times 60}{40 \div 4} = 120, \quad 108$

    (d) $\dfrac{60}{90 \div 9} + 50 = 56, \quad 54.48\ldots$

Review Exercise 2   Page 24

1. (a) 8480   (b) 8500   (c) 8000

2. (a) 3 967 000   (b) 4 000 000

3. (a) £879   (b) £900

4. (a) 5500   (b) (i)   40 000
              (ii) 10 000

5. No. Second most significant figure (4) is less than 5, so round down, i.e. £9000

6. (a) 50   (b) 14
    (c) 10   (d) 50

7. No. $84 + 16 \times 5 = 84 + 80 = 164$

8. 45 pence

9. 184 cm

10. 7

11. 39

12. (a) 70   (b) 100
    (c) 800   (d) 700
    (e) 80   (f) 1000

13. (a) 20×70 (b) 1400
    (c) 118

14. (a) 600×300 (b) 180 000
    (c) 5016

15. (a) $700 - 40 + 400 = 1060$
    (b) 1043

16. $\dfrac{500 + 100}{30} = 20$ Answer is wrong.

CHAPTER 3

1. (a) $4.7 = 4 + 0.7$
    (b) $5.55 = 5 + 0.5 + 0.05$
    (c) $7.62 = 7 + 0.6 + 0.02$
    (d) $37.928 = 30 + 7 + 0.9 + 0.02 + 0.008$
    (e) $7.541 = 7 + 0.5 + 0.04 + 0.001$

2. (a) 0.7   (b) 0.02   (c) 0.4
    (d) 0.009   (e) 80

3. (a) 1.68   (b) 1.09

4.

5. (a) A 3.2, B 3.5, C 3.9
    (b) D 5.6, E 6.3
    (c) F 7.2, G 7.6
    (d) H 10.5, I 11
    (e) J 0.52, K 0.54, L 0.59
    (f) M 0.751, N 0.755, P 0.757

6.

---

7. (a) 0.07   (b) 0.6

8. 93.07   **9.** 47.5074

10. (a) 3.001, 3.01, 3.1, 3.15, 3.2
     (b) 3.567, 3.576, 3.657, 3.675
     (c) 0.1, 0.15, 0.45, 0.5, 0.55

11. (a) 9.87, 9.78, 8.97, 8.79
     (b) 1.5, 0.15, 0.015, 0.00015
     (c) 2.701, 2.7, 2.67, 2.599

1. (a) 18.8   (b) 6.4   (c) 18.3
    (d) 33.1   (e) 8.86   (f) 13.1
    (g) 12.38   (h) 17.49   (i) 12.449
    (j) 26.02   (k) 32.36   (l) 18.163

2. (a) 3.2, 4.1   (b) 1.6, 0.8   (c) 4.1, 2.5
    (d) 4.1, 0.8

3. (a) 6.84   (b) 3.07   (c) 86.33
    (d) 15.781   (e) 16.033   (f) 24.88

4. 39.99 seconds   **5.** 4.35 kg

6. (a) Team A 148.93s,   Team B 149.53s,
      Team C 149.08s
    (b) Team A, Team C, Team B

1. (a) (i) 4.4   (ii) 6.23   (iii) 4.6
      (iv) 14.8   (v) 4.96   (vi) 20.8
      (vii) 11.08   (viii) 24.68

2. (a) 2.14   (b) 5.22   (c) 5.003
    (d) 1.24   (e) 8.28   (f) 6.273
    (g) 9.04   (h) 1.896

3. (a) (i) £3.30   (ii) £1.70
    (b) (i) £11.24   (ii) £3.76
    (c) (i) 83p   (ii) £9.17
    (d) (i) £16.24   (ii) £33.76

4. 4.88 m   **5.** 1.55 m   **6.** 0.719 seconds

1. 1.3   **5.** 11   **9.** 1.7

2. 10.9   **6.** 17.78   **10.** 0.32

3. 1.65   **7.** 1.2   **11.** 9.44

4. 0.9   **8.** 0.6   **12.** 3.2

Exercise **3.5** — Page 32

1.
(a) 250.6 (b) 2506 (c) 25 060
(d) 9.3 (e) 93 (f) 930
(g) 0.623 (h) 6.23 (i) 62.3
(j) 94.51 (k) 945.1 (l) 9451

2.
(a) 3.77 (b) 0.377 (c) 0.0377
(d) 0.027 (e) 0.0027 (f) 0.00027
(g) 18.902 (h) 1.8902 (i) 0.18902
(j) 0.9 (k) 0.09 (l) 0.009

3.
(a) (i) 0.64 (ii) 6.4 (iii) 64
(b) (i) 0.64 (ii) 0.064 (iii) 0.0064

4. (a) £2.50 (b) £25 (c) £250

5. (a) 5.04 km (b) 50.4 km (c) 504 km

6. (a) £7.95 (b) £0.12 (c) 66.9p

7. 12.3 × 1000 and 12.3 ÷ 0.001
12.3 ÷ 100 and 12.3 × 0.01
12.3 × 0.1 and 12.3 ÷ 10
12.3 ÷ 0.01 and 12.3 × 100
12.3 × 10 and 12.3 ÷ 0.1
12.3 × 0.001 and 12.3 ÷ 1000

Exercise **3.6** — Page 34

1.
(a) 1.2 (b) 8.5 (c) 12.8
(d) 3.6 (e) 13 (f) 17.6
(g) 10.8 (h) 30.1 (i) 28.8
(j) 34.8

2. £7.60 **3.** £8.05

4. (a) £9.95 (b) 5 pence

5. (a) £7.25 (b) £20.65 (c) £1.65

6.
(a) 0.42 (b) 0.06 (c) 8.75
(d) 16.53 (e) 19.44 (f) 1.025
(g) 3.888 (h) 9.38 (i) 3.78
(j) 0.0432 (k) 0.028 (l) 0.0014

7.
(a) (i) 3 (ii) 1.5 (iii) 0.24 (iv) 15
(b) Each answer is less than the original number.

8. (a) 21p (b) £1.84 (c) 78p

9. (a) £13.93 (b) £10.08 (c) £54.21
(d) £26.24

10. (a) £4.34 (b) £5.12 (c) £2.60
(d) £2.34

Exercise **3.7** — Page 35

1.
(a) 0.3 (b) 1.5 (c) 1.7
(d) 3.2 (e) 4.4

2.
(a) 1.75 (b) 1.6 (c) 0.15
(d) 2.6 (e) 1.75

3. (a) 5 (b) 12 (c) 350

4.
(a) 4 (b) 15 (c) 15
(d) 4 (e) 50

5.
(a) 12.3 (b) 2.92 (c) 6.05
(d) 1430 (e) 0.05 (f) 12.5
(g) 6.54 (h) 37.5

6.
(a) 37 (b) 5.6 (c) 43.75
(d) 46.9 (e) 1.062

7.
(a) (i) 10 (ii) 6 (iii) 0.3
(b) Each answer is greater than the original number.

8. 47p **11.** 9p

9. £1.35 **12.** 66.8p **14.** 67

10. 11p **13.** 120 **15.** 45

Exercise **3.8** — Page 37

1.
(a) $\frac{1}{4}$ (b) $\frac{1}{2}$ (c) $\frac{3}{4}$
(d) $\frac{1}{10}$

2.
(a) $\frac{7}{10}$ (b) $\frac{2}{5}$ (c) $\frac{1}{100}$
(d) $\frac{1}{5}$ (e) $\frac{1}{20}$ (f) $\frac{3}{20}$
(g) $\frac{13}{25}$ (h) $\frac{7}{100}$ (i) $\frac{1}{8}$
(j) $\frac{13}{20}$ (k) $\frac{3}{5}$ (l) $\frac{19}{20}$

3.
(a) $1\frac{7}{10}$ (b) $2\frac{3}{10}$ (c) $1\frac{2}{5}$
(d) $3\frac{1}{4}$ (e) $4\frac{4}{5}$ (f) $12\frac{1}{10}$
(g) $16\frac{3}{4}$ (h) $5\frac{1}{20}$

Exercise **3.9** — Page 38

1. (a) 3.962 (b) 3.96 (c) 4.0

2. (a) 567.65 (b) 567.7 (c) 568

3. Missing entries:
0.96, 0.97, 15.281, 0.06, 4.99, 5.00

4. 4.86

5. (a) (i) 46.1   (ii) 59.7
      (iii) 569.4   (iv) 17.1   (v) 0.7
   (b) (i) 46.14   (ii) 59.70
      (iii) 569.43   (iv) 17.06   (v) 0.66
   (c) (i) 46.145   (ii) 59.697
      (iii) 569.434   (iv) 17.059   (v) 0.662

6. (a) £12.16, nearest penny
   (b) £3.57, nearest penny
   (c) £2.37, nearest penny
   (d) 35.7 cm, nearest millimetre
   (e) £1.33, nearest penny
   (f) £12.70, nearest penny

7. (a) $4 \times 2 = 8$,   7.56
   (b) $9 \times 3 = 27$,   27.59
   (c) $50 \times 4 = 200$,   202.02
   (d) $100 \times 3 = 300$,   299.86

8. (a) $10 \div 5 = 2$,   2.2
   (b) $20 \div 4 = 5$,   4.8
   (c) $30 \div 3 = 10$,   9.5
   (d) $200 \div 5 = 40$,   39.9

9. (a) $10 \times 4 \div 5 = 8$,   8.45625
   (b) $(10 + 50) \div 6 = 10$,   9.774…
   (c) $400 \times 0.3 \div 6 = 20$,   18.709…
   (d) $(80 \times 5) \div (2 \times 10) = 20$,   20.456…

Review Exercise 3   Page 39

1. 0.5, 0.55, 0.7, 0.8, 0.85

2. $\dfrac{9}{20}$

3. (a) 12.41   (b) 4.33
   (c) $4.33 + 5.67 = 10$

4. (a) 14.4   (b) 4.2
   (c) 1.3   (d) 20

5. 4.2 kg

6. 2.37 m

7. (a) 2619   (b) 2.91

8. (a) £247.50   (b) £7.99

9. 17.8 is less than 18 **and**
0.97 is less than 1,
so answer is less than 18.

10. (a) 25.57   (b) 25.6

11. £5.43

12. (a) £46.62   (b) 70p

13. 49.72

14. 400.50 dollars

CHAPTER 4

Exercise 4.1   Page 40

1. (a) 10, 20, 30, 40, 50
   (b) 3, 6, 9, 12, 15
   (c) 7, 14, 21, 28, 35
   (d) 6, 12, 18, 24, 30
   (e) 9, 18, 27, 36, 45
   (f) 20, 40, 60, 80, 100

2. (a) 20   (b) 42   (c) third
   (d) seventh   (e) 10   (f) 9

3. (a) second   (b) second   (c) fifth
   (d) eighth   (e) third

4. (a) 35   (b) 48

5. (a) (i) Answers are even numbers.
      (ii) Answers are even numbers.
      (iii) Answers are even numbers.
      (iv) Answers are odd numbers.

   (b) (i)

×	2	3	6	7	9
2	E	E	E	E	E
3	E	O	E	O	O
6	E	E	E	E	E
7	E	O	E	O	O
9	E	O	E	O	O

      (ii)

×	O	E
O	O	E
E	E	E

   (c) Only **O** × **O** gives an odd number.

Exercise 4.2   Page 42

1. (a) 1, 2, 3, 4, 6, 12
   (b) $12 \div 8 = 1.5$
     To be a factor, 8 would need to divide
     into 12 a whole number of times.

2. (a) $1 \times 18, 2 \times 9, 3 \times 6$
   (b) 1, 2, 3, 6, 9, 18

3. (a) $1 \times 20, 2 \times 10, 4 \times 5$
   (b) 1, 2, 4, 5, 10, 20

4. (a) 1, 2, 4, 8, 16
   (b) 1, 2, 4, 7, 14, 28
   (c) 1, 2, 3, 4, 6, 9, 12, 18, 36
   (d) 1, 3, 5, 9, 15, 45
   (e) 1, 2, 3, 4, 6, 8, 12, 16, 24, 48
   (f) 1, 2, 5, 10, 25, 50
   (g) 1, 2, 3, 4, 5, 6, 10, 12, 15, 20, 30, 60
   (h) 1, 2, 4, 5, 8, 10, 16, 20, 40, 80

5. (a) (i) 1, 2   (ii) 1, 3   (iii) 1, 5
     (iv) 1, 7   (v) 1, 11   (vi) 1, 13
   (b) 17, 19, 23, 29, 31, …

6. (a) (i) 1, 2, 4   (ii) 1, 3, 9
     (iii) 1, 5, 25   (iv) 1, 7, 49
   (b) 121, 169, 289, 361, …

7. (a) (i) 1, 2, 3, 6   (ii) 1, 2, 5, 10
     (iii) 1, 2, 7, 14   (iv) 1, 2, 13, 26
     (v) 1, 5, 11, 55   (vi) 1, 2, 19, 38
   (b) 15, 21, 22, 33, 35, …

8. 6, 36

9. (a) 1, 5   (b) 1, 2, 4
   (c) 1, 2   (d) 1, 2, 3, 4, 6, 12
   (e) 1, 2, 3, 6

10. (a) 5   (b) 27   (c) 3, 5

11. (a) 4 (6, 12, 18, 36)
   (b) 8 (5, 10, 15, 20, 30, 40, 60, 120)
   (c) 6 (2, 4, 10, 20, 50, 100)
   (d) 8 (4, 8, 12, 16, 24, 32, 48, 96)

12. (i) 2, 3, 5, 7, 11, 13, 17, 19, 23, 29, 31, 37, 41, 43, 47
     Each number has 2 factors.

Exercise 4.3   Page 44

1. (a) $5^2 = 5 \times 5$
   (b) $2^3 = 2 \times 2 \times 2$
   (c) $10^5 = 10 \times 10 \times 10 \times 10 \times 10$
   (d) $2.8^3 = 2.8 \times 2.8 \times 2.8$
   (e) $0.4^2 = 0.4 \times 0.4$

2. (a) 4^3 (b) 8^2 (c) 0.3^3
   (d) 1.6^2 (e) 10^3 (f) 10^7

3.

Expression	Index form	Value
$10 \times 10 \times 10 \times 10 \times 10 \times 10$	10^6	1 000 000
$10 \times 10 \times 10 \times 10 \times 10$	10^5	100 000
$10 \times 10 \times 10 \times 10$	10^4	10 000
$10 \times 10 \times 10$	10^3	1000
10×10	10^2	100
10	10^1	10

4. (a) 8   (b) 36   (c) 27
   (d) 144   (e) 125   (f) 10 000 000

5. (a) 1, 4, 9, 16, 25, 36, 49, 64, 81, 100, 121, 144, 169, 196, 225, 256, 289, 324, 361, 400
   (c) $21^2 = 400 + 41 = 441$

6. 1, 8, 27, 64, 125, 216, 343, 512, 729, 1000

7. (a) 1.69   (b) 4.913   (c) 29.16
   (d) 110.592

8. (a) 7.464   (b) 382.2025   (c) 8.1

Exercise 4.4   Page 46

1. (a) 5   (b) 10   (c) 8   (d) 7

2. (a) 2   (b) 4   (c) 5   (d) 3

3. (a) 5   (b) 3

4. (a) (i) 4.5   (ii) 10.4   (iii) 2.8

5. (a) 3.6   (b) 5.8   (c) 1.7

6. 7.4 m   **7.** 16.51 mm

Exercise 4.5   Page 47

1. (a) (i) 169   (ii) 289   (iii) 6.25
     (iv) 0.64   (v) 94.09
   (b) (i) 216   (ii) 3375   (iii) 13.824
     (iv) 0.343   (v) 175.616

2. (a) (i) 0.5   (ii) 0.2   (iii) 0.1
     (iv) 2   (v) 10   (vi) 5
   (b) (i) 0.25   (ii) 0.05   (iii) 0.04
     (iv) 4   (v) 2.5   (vi) 6.25

3. (a) 9943.75   (b) 5.976
   (c) 1 562 500   (d) 3.333…

4. 8

5. (a) 10.46   (b) 0.23   (c) 2.22
   (d) 114.20   (e) 2.50   (f) 0.14
   (g) 15.07   (h) 0.60

Review Exercise 4   Page 48

1. 1, 2, 3, 4, 6, 12

2. 7, 14, 21

3. (a) 2, 4, 6, 8   (b) 3, 6, 9
   (c) 2, 3, 6

4. 36

5. (a) multiple   (b) square
   (c) factor

6. (a) (i) 68, 390, 764, 9010
     (ii) 85, 105, 390, 9010
     (iii) 390, 9010
   (b) (i) even
     (ii) end in 5 or 0
     (iii) end in 0

7. (a) square numbers: 4, 16, 64
square roots: 2, 4, 8
(b) cube numbers: 8, 64
cube roots: 2, 4

8. 3   **9.** 70 seconds

10. (a) 125   (b) 6   (c) 72

11. $\sqrt{400}$. $\sqrt{400} = 20,\ 4^3 = 64$

12. 7.07   **13.** 5.8

14. (a) 3.375   (b) 0.167

15. (a) (i) 10^2 (ii) 10^6 (b) 10^4

16. 2.8   **17.** 46.8

CHAPTER 5

Exercise 5.1   Page 50

1. (a) Warmer   (b) Colder
(c) Warmer   (d) Colder

2. (a) Less   (b) More
(c) Less   (d) More

3. (a) Colombo   (b) Moscow
(c) $-22°C, -17°C, -7°C, 0°C, 3°C, 15°C, 21°C.$

4. (a) $-28°C, -13°C, -3°C, 19°C, 23°C.$
(b) $-11°C, -9°C, -7°C, 0°C, 10°C, 12°C.$
(c) $-29°C, -15°C, 2°C, 18°C, 27°C.$
(d) $-20°C, -15°C, -5°C, 0°C, 10°C, 20°C.$

5. (a) $-78, -39, -16, -9, 11, 31, 51.$
(b) $-5, -3, -2, -1, 0, 1, 2, 4, 5.$
(c) $-103, -63, -19, -3, 5, 52, 99, 104.$
(d) $-50, -30, -20, 0, 10, 30, 40.$
(e) $-30, -15, -10, 0, 8, 17, 27.$

Exercise 5.2   Page 51

1. (a) 1   (b) -2 (c) -2
(d) -4 (e) -3

3. (a) -3 (b) -2 (c) -3
(d) -2 (e) -3 (f) -4
(g) -7 (h) -12 (i) -10
(j) -7 (k) -21 (l) -1

4. (a) 9   (b) 1   (c) 12
(d) -10 (e) 30   (f) 15

5. $-£75$ (£75 overdrawn)

6. 11°C   **7.** 5°C   **8.** 17 cm   **9.** 8 kg

10. (a) -80 m   (b) -200 m
(c) 60 m   (d) 60 m
(e) 120 m   (f) 70 m
(g) 300 m   (h) 50 m
(i) 130 m   (j) 240 m
(k) 250 m

Exercise 5.3   Page 52

1. (a) 2   (b) 1   (c) -9
(d) 8   (e) 4   (f) -5
(g) -7 (h) 7   (i) 1
(j) -15 (k) -3 (l) -6

2. (a) 13   (b) 6   (c) 7
(d) 7   (e) 5   (f) -12
(g) -1 (h) 13   (i) -11
(j) 11   (k) 9   (l) 0

3. (a) 5   (b) 3   (c) 3
(d) -7 (e) -6 (f) -1

4. (a) 6   (b) -8 (c) -28
(d) 0   (e) -35 (f) 19

5. (a) 3°C   (b) 10°C   (c) 5°C
(d) 6°C   (e) 37°C

6. $-15°C$ **7.** $-22°C$ **8.** 2°C

Exercise 5.4   Page 54

1. 35   **11.** 64   **21.** -4

2. -35 **12.** -42 **22.** 4

3. 35   **13.** 42   **23.** 5

4. 10   **14.** -80 **24.** -5

5. -10 **15.** -80 **25.** -5

6. 10   **16.** -20 **26.** 5

7. 1   **17.** 60   **27.** 6

8. -24 **18.** -30 **28.** -6

9. -24 **19.** 60   **29.** 4

10. -45 **20.** -60 **30.** -8

31. (a) Ahmed 26,   Bridget 21,
Chris -21,   Dileep -19,
Evan -3
(b) Ahmed, Bridget, Evan, Dileep, Chris

1. $-20, -5, 0, 15, 25.$

2. (a) Poole   (b) Selby

3. (a) -18 (b) 4   (c) 4

4. 4191 m

5. (a) $-6°C$ (b) 9 degrees   (c) $-2°C$

6. $-£33.55$ ($£33.55$ overdrawn)

7. (a) $8°C$ (b) $18°C$ (c) $26°C$

8. (a) -30 (b) 12   (c) -6
    (d) 6

9. (a) (i) -1 (ii) 6   (b) (i) 6   (ii) 2

10. (a) -20
    (b) Naomi
       Tim: $10 \times 2 + 10 \times (-1) = 10$
       Naomi: $8 \times 2 + 5 \times (-1) = 11$

CHAPTER   6

1. **W**: $\frac{1}{3}$ **X**: $\frac{5}{6}$ **Y**: $\frac{7}{15}$ **Z**: $\frac{6}{25}$

3. (a) $\frac{1}{4}$ (b) $\frac{1}{2}$ (c) $\frac{1}{2}$

4. (a) $\frac{1}{3}$ (b) $\frac{1}{3}$ (c) $\frac{1}{3}$
    (d) $\frac{1}{3}$ (e) $\frac{1}{2}$

5. (a) **P**   (b) **P**   (c) **R**
    (d) **R**   (e) **Q**   (f) **S**

6. (a) (ii) $\frac{1}{6}$ (b) (ii) $\frac{1}{12}$

1. E.g. $\frac{40}{50}, \frac{20}{25}, \frac{4}{5}$

    $\frac{4}{5}$ is the simplest form.

2. E.g. $\frac{15}{24}, \frac{30}{48}, \frac{45}{72}, \ldots, \frac{10}{16}, \frac{20}{32}, \ldots$

    simplest form $\frac{5}{8}$

5. (a) 1   (b) 2   (c) 8

6. (a) E.g. $\frac{2}{6} = \frac{3}{9} = \frac{4}{12}$

    (b) E.g. $\frac{4}{18} = \frac{6}{27} = \frac{8}{36}$

    (c) E.g. $\frac{10}{16} = \frac{15}{24} = \frac{20}{32}$

    (d) E.g. $\frac{8}{10} = \frac{12}{15} = \frac{16}{20}$

    (e) E.g. $\frac{6}{20} = \frac{9}{30} = \frac{12}{40}$

    (f) E.g. $\frac{14}{24} = \frac{21}{36} = \frac{28}{48}$

7. (a) 2   (b) 3   (c) 3

8. (a) 6   (b) 8   (c) 12

9. $\frac{7}{16}, \frac{5}{8}, \frac{3}{4}$

10. $\frac{7}{10}, \frac{2}{3}, \frac{3}{5}, \frac{8}{15}$

11. $\frac{4}{5}$

12. (a) $\frac{3}{4}$ (b) $\frac{4}{5}$ (c) $\frac{2}{3}$
    (d) $\frac{2}{9}$ (e) $\frac{2}{3}$ (f) $\frac{2}{5}$
    (g) $\frac{6}{25}$ (h) $\frac{4}{5}$

13. (a) $\frac{4}{20} = \frac{1}{5}$ (b) $\frac{3}{12} = \frac{1}{4}$ (c) $\frac{8}{12} = \frac{2}{3}$
    (d) $\frac{24}{60} = \frac{2}{5}$ (e) $\frac{60}{105} = \frac{4}{7}$

14. $\frac{4}{32} = \frac{1}{8}$ **16.** (a) $\frac{48}{60} = \frac{4}{5}$ (b) $\frac{12}{60} = \frac{1}{5}$

15. $\frac{30}{50} = \frac{3}{5}$ **17.** (a) $\frac{7}{10}$ (b) $\frac{1}{5}$

18. (a) 24   (b) $\frac{1}{6}$

1. (a) $1\frac{3}{10}$ (b) $1\frac{1}{2}$ (c) $2\frac{1}{8}$
    (d) $3\frac{3}{4}$ (e) $4\frac{3}{5}$ (f) $4\frac{6}{7}$
    (g) $3\frac{1}{2}$ (h) $3\frac{2}{3}$ (i) $1\frac{7}{9}$

2. (a) $\dfrac{27}{10}$ (b) $\dfrac{8}{5}$ (c) $\dfrac{35}{6}$

    (d) $\dfrac{63}{20}$ (e) $\dfrac{41}{9}$ (f) $\dfrac{53}{7}$

    (g) $\dfrac{13}{4}$ (h) $\dfrac{14}{3}$ (i) $\dfrac{19}{8}$

3. (a) 3   (b) 4   (c) 3
    (d) 8   (e) 8   (f) 9
    (g) 12   (h) 20   (i) 40
    (j) 12

4. (a) 6   (b) 24   **7.** £5

5. 56   **8.** £7.70

6. 28   **9.** £148.40

10. (a) 9   (b) 10   (c) $\dfrac{5}{24}$

Exercise **6.4**   Page 64

1. (a) $\dfrac{3}{8}$ (b) $\dfrac{7}{12}$ (c) $\dfrac{7}{10}$

    (d) $\dfrac{8}{15}$ (e) $\dfrac{9}{14}$ (f) $\dfrac{9}{20}$

2. (a) $\dfrac{1}{8}$ (b) $\dfrac{1}{12}$ (c) $\dfrac{3}{10}$

    (d) $\dfrac{2}{15}$ (e) $\dfrac{5}{14}$ (f) $\dfrac{1}{20}$

3. (a) $1\dfrac{1}{4}$ (b) $1\dfrac{1}{2}$ (c) $1\dfrac{11}{20}$

    (d) $1\dfrac{8}{21}$ (e) $1\dfrac{5}{24}$ (f) $1\dfrac{3}{20}$

4. (a) $\dfrac{1}{8}$ (b) $\dfrac{8}{15}$ (c) $\dfrac{5}{8}$

    (d) $\dfrac{1}{15}$ (e) $\dfrac{1}{3}$ (f) $\dfrac{5}{24}$

5. (a) $4\dfrac{1}{4}$ (b) $3\dfrac{5}{6}$ (c) $4\dfrac{3}{8}$

    (d) $5\dfrac{17}{20}$ (e) $6\dfrac{13}{30}$ (f) $5\dfrac{9}{20}$

6. (a) $1\dfrac{1}{10}$ (b) $\dfrac{5}{12}$ (c) $1\dfrac{3}{8}$

    (d) $3\dfrac{3}{10}$ (e) $2\dfrac{1}{4}$ (f) $1\dfrac{1}{16}$

7. (a) $\dfrac{5}{6}$ (b) $\dfrac{1}{6}$

8. $\dfrac{11}{20}$ **9.** (a) $\dfrac{5}{12}$ (b) $\dfrac{11}{12}$

10. (a) $\dfrac{1}{4}$ (b) Billy

Exercise **6.5**   Page 66

1. (a) $3\dfrac{1}{2}$ (b) $2\dfrac{2}{3}$ (c) $1\dfrac{4}{5}$

    (d) $6\dfrac{1}{4}$ (e) $6\dfrac{6}{7}$

2. (a) $\dfrac{1}{10}$ (b) $\dfrac{3}{8}$ (c) $\dfrac{1}{3}$

    (d) $\dfrac{1}{10}$ (e) $\dfrac{2}{7}$

3. (a) $\dfrac{1}{6}$ (b) $\dfrac{1}{20}$ (c) $\dfrac{1}{10}$

    (d) $\dfrac{5}{21}$ (e) $\dfrac{1}{6}$

4. (a) $\dfrac{3}{8}$ (b) $\dfrac{3}{10}$ (c) $\dfrac{1}{3}$

    (d) $\dfrac{1}{3}$ (e) $\dfrac{3}{16}$ (f) $\dfrac{2}{35}$

    (g) $\dfrac{1}{2}$ (h) $\dfrac{1}{4}$

5. $1\dfrac{1}{2}$ kg   **6.** $\dfrac{1}{10}$

7. (a) $\dfrac{1}{8}$ (b) $\dfrac{1}{8}$

8. (a) $\dfrac{4}{15}$ (b) $\dfrac{2}{5}$

9. (a) $\dfrac{4}{15}$ (b) 15

Exercise **6.6**   Page 68

1. (a) $\dfrac{3}{25}$ (b) $\dfrac{3}{5}$ (c) $\dfrac{8}{25}$

    (d) $\dfrac{7}{40}$ (e) $\dfrac{9}{20}$ (f) $\dfrac{13}{20}$

    (g) $\dfrac{11}{50}$ (h) $\dfrac{101}{500}$ (i) $\dfrac{7}{25}$

    (j) $\dfrac{111}{200}$ (k) $\dfrac{5}{8}$ (l) $\dfrac{21}{25}$

2. (a) (i) 0.25   (ii) 0.5   (iii) 0.75
    (b) (i) 0.1   (ii) 0.3   (iii) 0.7
    (c) (i) 0.4   (ii) 0.6   (iii) 0.8

3. (a) (i) 0.15   (ii) 0.35   (iii) 0.95
    (b) (i) 0.16   (ii) 0.36   (iii) 0.92
    (c) (i) 0.07   (ii) 0.23   (iii) 0.53

4. (a) 0.125   (b) 0.625   (c) 0.225
    (d) 0.725

5. (a) 0.33   (b) 0.67   (c) 0.43
    (d) 0.45   (e) 0.78

1. (a) $\dfrac{4}{12} = \dfrac{1}{3}$ (b) Shade any 8 squares

2. $\dfrac{8}{20}$ **3.** $a = 4,\ b = 12$

4. (a) 3   (b) $\dfrac{1}{3}$ (c) $\dfrac{7}{15}$

5. 15   **6.** $4\dfrac{3}{8}$ **7.** E.g. $\dfrac{3}{8},\ \dfrac{5}{16}$

8. (a) 0.17   (b) $\dfrac{2}{5}$

9. (a) 64   (b) $\dfrac{7}{16}$

10. (a) £3.50   (b) £18   **13.** $\dfrac{1}{4}$

11. £25.80   **14.** $\dfrac{1}{10}$

12. (a) $\dfrac{11}{12}$ (b) $\dfrac{11}{40}$ **15.** $\dfrac{7}{10}$

CHAPTER 7

1. (a) 35%   (b) 54%   (c) 24%
    (d) 16%   (e) 84%   (f) 42%
    (g) 5%   (h) 46%

2. (a) (i) 40   (ii) 40%
    (b) (i) 60, 60%   (ii) 70, 70%
        (iii) 45, 45%   (iv) 24, 24%
        (v) 46, 46%   (vi) 68, 68%

3. (a) Missing entries: $\dfrac{1}{5},\ \dfrac{1}{4},\ \dfrac{1}{2},\ \dfrac{3}{4},\ \dfrac{4}{5}$

   (b) Missing entries: 0.2, 0.25, 0.5, 0.75, 0.8

4. (a) $\dfrac{3}{20}$ (b) $\dfrac{1}{20}$ (c) $\dfrac{9}{50}$

    (d) $\dfrac{13}{25}$ (e) $\dfrac{23}{100}$ (f) $\dfrac{1}{8}$

5. (a) 0.15   (b) 0.05   (c) 0.47
    (d) 0.72   (e) 0.875   (f) 1.5

1. Missing entries: 30%, 40%, 12%, 35%

2. Missing entries: 70%, 45%, 5%, 120%

3. $33\dfrac{1}{3}\%$

4. (a) 34%   (b) 48%   (c) 15%   (d) 80%

    (e) 27%   (f) 65%   (g) $66\dfrac{2}{3}\%$ (h) $22\dfrac{2}{9}\%$

5. (a) 15%   (b) 32%   (c) 12.5%
    (d) 7%   (e) 112%   (f) 1.5%

6. (a) $\dfrac{2}{5},\ \dfrac{1}{2},\ 0.55,\ 60\%$

   (b) $0.42,\ 43\%,\ \dfrac{11}{25},\ \dfrac{9}{20}$

   (c) $28\%,\ 0.2805,\ \dfrac{57}{200},\ \dfrac{23}{80}$

7. 80%

8. (a) 90%   (b) 85%   (c) 88%   (d) 80%

9. B   **10.** Team A

1. (a) 60%   (b) 16%   (c) 70%
    (d) 21%   (e) 21%

2. (a) 32%   (b) 10%   (c) 60%
    (d) 15%   (e) 30%

3. 32%   **6.** 12.5%

4. 30%   **7.** 37.5%

5. (a) 40%   (b) 60%   **8.** 6%

9. (a) $33\dfrac{1}{3}\%$ (b) $66\dfrac{2}{3}\%$ (c) $12\dfrac{1}{2}\%$

    (d) $42\dfrac{1}{2}\%$ (e) $56\dfrac{1}{2}\%$

10. 9.5%   **11.** 25%

1. (a) 50   (b) 40   (c) 140
    (d) 60   (e) 240   (f) 110
    (g) 2.5   (h) 12   (i) 19.5
    (j) 17   (k) 60   (l) 64

2. (a) £16   (b) £15   (c) £66
    (d) £52.50   (e) £25   (f) £30
    (g) £27   (h) 4 m   (i) 24 kg
    (j) 280 m   (k) £11.25   (l) 12p

3. (a) 60   (b) 105   (c) 45%

4. £20   **7.** £2.70

5. 270   **8.** £4.50

6. £42   **9.** (a) 660 (b) 198   **10.** 24 g

1. (a) £480   (b) £420   (c) £2800
    (d) £1080   (e) £3450   (f) £1260
    (g) £80   (h) £13   (i) £16.50
    (j) £57.50

2. (a) £420 (b) £600 (c) £2000
(d) £150 (e) £10 200 (f) £4550
(g) £510 (h) £5.50 (i) £33.60
(j) £40.95

3. 40p per minute

4. £215

5. 759 g

6. £18.45

7. £244.64

8. £4706

9. £2372.50

10. £14 560

11. £10 530

12. £492

Exercise 7.6 — Page 76

1. 20%

2. 10%

3. 20%

4. 12.5%

5. 28%

6. (a) $12\frac{1}{2}\%$ (b) 12%
Rent went up by a greater percentage.

Review Exercise 7 — Page 77

1. (a) 25% (b) $\frac{7}{10}$ (c) 0.4

2. 50%

3. 10% of £20 → £2
50% of £10 → £5
25% of £40 → £10

4. 39%, $\frac{2}{5}$, 0.41, $\frac{21}{50}$

5. (a) 4 (b) 45%

6. (a) 26 (b) 45%

7. (a) 40% (b) $\frac{3}{10}$ (c) 0.06

8. 180

9. £32.50

10. 90%

11. £3375

12. 62.5%

13. £8.82

14. 25%

15. (a) 159 cm (b) 10%

CHAPTER 8

Exercise 8.1 — Page 79

1. (a) 1030 (b) 2230 (c) 0145
(d) 1345 (e) 2350

2. (a) 2.15 pm (b) 5.25 am (c) 11.20 pm
(d) 10.05 am (e) 5.05 pm

3. (a) 7 am (b) 0700

4. (a) Start 9 am, Finish 3.30 pm
(b) Start 0900, Finish 1530
(c) 6 hours 30 minutes

5. (a) Start 11.54 am, Finish 1.35 pm
(b) 1 hour 41 minutes

6. (a) 1835, 1920, 2000, 2050
(b) 40 minutes (c) 45 minutes

7. (a) 1230, 1255, 1320, 1325
(b) 25 minutes

8. (a) 2.28 pm (b) 48 minutes

9. (a) 1.15 pm (b) 2 hours 50 minutes

10. (a) 1325 (b) 4 hours 15 minutes

11. (a) 1318 (b) 53 minutes

12. (a) 1.30 pm (b) 1330

13. (a) 3.25 pm (b) 1525

14. (a) 1343 (b) 1.43 pm

15. (a) 1441 (b) 2.41 pm

Exercise 8.2 — Page 80

1. (a) (i) 35 minutes (ii) 2.50 pm
(b) (i) 24 minutes (ii) 3.08 pm

2. (a) (i) 5 minutes (ii) 1.03 pm
(b) 1233

3. (a) 36 minutes (b) 1503 (c) 1713

4. (a) 49 minutes (b) 1 hour 35 minutes
(c) 1.42 pm (d) 0815

5. (a) (i) 4.03 pm (ii) 25 minutes
(b) 1540

Exercise 8.3 — Page 82

1. £15.99

2. 29p

3. 50p

4. 86p

5. 96p

6. 85p

7. £1.60

8. 90p

9. £4.80

10. (a) £47 (b) 10 days

11. (a) £13 (b) 7 days

12. (a) £39 (b) 120 miles

13. £26 **14.** £638 **15.** £165 **16.** £40.50

Exercise 8.4 — Page 84

1. (a) 0.5p (b) 5.25p

2. Small: 5.2 g per penny.
Large: 5.1 g per penny.
Small tin is better buy.

3. Small pot   **5.** Large pot

4. 700 g   **6.** Medium

7. (a) Daisy's £448, Alfie's £438
     (b) Alfie's

8. 1 kg   **9.** Medium   **10.** 1.5 litre bottle

Exercise 8.5   **Page 85**

1. £6

2. (a) £3.50   (b) £73.50

3. (a) £59.50   (b) £399.50

4. (a) £15.75   (b) £105.75

5. (a) £8.97   (b) £188.50

6. £291.40   **9.** £44.13

7. £170.37   **10.** £428.87

8. £216.20   **11.** £69.32

Exercise 8.6   **Page 86**

1. (a) 310 euros   (b) 34 600 yen
     (c) 126 liri   (d) 2496 krone
     (e) 460 francs   (f) 284 dollars

2. (a) £39.13   (b) £28.90
     (c) £48.39   (d) £18.03
     (e) £24.65

3. (a) 38.75 euros   (b) £15

4. (a) 276 francs   (b) £10.65

5. (a) £387.10   (b) 46.50 euros

6. (a) £240.38   (b) 561.60 krone

7. (a) 710 dollars   (b) £18.13

8. £131.92

9. France: £5806.45, Japan: £5780.35
     Cheaper in Japan by £26.10

Review Exercise 8   **Page 87**

1. 187 minutes

2. (a) 1215   (b) 5.42 pm

3. 19p   **4.** 68 pence   **5.** £91.20

6. (a) 320 euros   (b) £3

7. (a) £1053.93   (b) £645.05

8. (a) £41.85   (b) 231 miles

9. £77

10. 400 g: 0.54 g per penny
     125 g: 0.51 g per penny
     400 g jar is better value

11. Calculators are Us: £8.81
     Top Calculators: £8.75
     Difference 6 pence

12. 350 dollars

CHAPTER 9

Exercise 9.1   **Page 89**

1. £84   **8.** £272

2. £4.50   **9.** £203.40

3. 38 hours   **10.** £10.20

4. £10.80   **11.** £15 600

5. £9.60   **12.** £23 220

6. £6.60   **13.** £1100

7. £313.60   **14.** £15 000

Exercise 9.2   **Page 91**

1. £8015   **2.** £8153

3. (a) £1215   (b) £121.50

4. (a) £1363   (b) £136.30
     (c) £11.36

5. £4069.30   **6.** £94.91   **7.** £18.91

Exercise 9.3   **Page 92**

1. (a) £300   (b) £25

2. £168.41   **6.** £6.30

3. £74.84   **7.** £971.65

4. £25.75   **8.** £112

5. 810   **9.** £46.76

10. (a) £231   (b) £84 000
     (c) £95   (d) £108

11. £334.90   **12.** £12 400

13. (a) £8.59   (b) £1892.80

Review Exercise 9 **Page 94**

1. £168

2. £16

3. (a) £1289 (b) £128.90

4. £39.27

5. £324

6. (a) 8 hours (b) £260

7. £252.74

CHAPTER **10**

Exercise 10.1 **Page 95**

1. (a) 2 GLUMS (b) 5 : 2

2. (a) 3 SMILERS (b) 3 : 1

3. (a) 3 GLUMS (b) 5 : 3

4. 7 : 3

5. (a) 8 SMILERS and 2 GLUMS
   (b) 3 SMILERS and 9 GLUMS

6. (a) 75 (b) 12 (c) (i) 56 (ii) 140

7. (a) 16 (b) 9 (c) (i) 84 (ii) 112

8. (a) 14 SMILERS and 6 GLUMS
   (b) 9 SMILERS and 6 GLUMS

9. (a) (i) $\frac{1}{5}$ (ii) $\frac{4}{5}$ (iii) 1 : 4 (b) 3 : 1

10. (a) (i) 30% (ii) 70% (b) 3 : 2

11. $\frac{2}{5}$

12. 75%

Exercise 10.2 **Page 98**

1. (a) E.g. 12 : 2, 18 : 3, 24 : 4.
   (b) E.g. 14 : 4, 21 : 6, 28 : 8.
   (c) E.g. 6 : 10, 9 : 15, 12 : 20.

2. (a) 1 : 2 (b) 1 : 3 (c) 3 : 4
   (d) 2 : 5 (e) 3 : 4 (f) 2 : 5
   (g) 3 : 7 (h) 9 : 4 (i) 4 : 9
   (j) 7 : 3

3. (a) 12 (b) 28 (c) 100
   (d) 20

4. 198 cm

5. 400 g

6. 64

7. 18 years old

8. 2 : 3

9. 5 : 2

10. 1 : 250

11. 1 : 1500

12. (a) 4 : 1 (b) 2 : 25 (c) 11 : 2
    (d) 5 : 2 (e) 4 : 1 (f) 40 : 17
    (g) 9 : 20 (h) 25 : 1 (i) 1 : 15
    (j) 2 : 1

13. 40 : 9 15. 2 : 3

14. 1 : 3 16. 1 : 2 17. 3 : 2

Exercise 10.3 **Page 99**

1. (a) 6, 3 (b) 15, 5 (c) 7, 28
   (d) 90, 10 (e) 60, 40

2. 18

3. Sunny £36, Chandni £12

4.

	4 : 1	3 : 2
(a)	32, 8	24, 16
(b)	16, 4	12, 8
(c)	64 kg, 16 kg	48 kg, 32 kg
(d)	160 g, 40 g	120 g, 80 g
(e)	£960, £240	£720, £480

5. (a) £14, £21 (b) £32, £24
   (c) £3.50, £2

6. 45

7. £192

8. 2 033 000

9. $\frac{1}{4}$

10. 80%

11. $\frac{5}{8}$

12. 60%

13. 48%

14. 168 000 km^2

15. (a) Jenny 50, Tim 30 (b) 10

16. (a) 5 : 2 (b) 6 (c) 55
    (d) 32 is not a multiple of 5 + 2 = 7

Exercise 10.4 **Page 100**

1. (a) 16p (b) £1.28

2. (a) £6 (b) £60

3. (a) 30p (b) £2.40

4. (a) £4.50 (b) £90

5. £2.85

6. (a) 120 cm (b) 2 kg

7. £201.60

8. £36

9. £2.85

10. £14.76

11. (a) 50 g (b) 720 g

12. £44.64   **13.** £32

14. (a) £1.54   (b) 12 minutes

15. (a) 180 g   (b) 675 ml
     (c) 210 g

16. (a) 12 minutes   (b) 16 miles

17. (a) 12 m²   (b) 12 litres

18. (a) £130   (b) 32

Review Exercise 10   Page 102

1. 1 : 3   **4.** 12

2. 3 : 4   **5.** 8

3. 9   **6.** 200 g flour, 25 g sugar

7. 7000 kg

8. (a) 6 oz flour, 4 oz sugar, 4 oz margarine,
       5.3 oz dried fruit, 2 eggs   (b) 27

9. Tracey £4000, Wayne £3200   **11.** £4.80

10. 1 : 500   **12.** £1.54

Section Review   Page 103

1. 7, 23, 36, 39, 46, 49.

2. (a) (i) 52 406   (ii) 52 000
     (b) (i) Ten thousand two hundred and
          ninety-two
        (ii) 10 300

3. (a) (i) 87   (ii) 56   (iii) 61
     (b) (i) 7000   (ii) 9.5

4. 6

5. (a) 300 miles   (b) 286 miles

6. (a) 801   (b) 183
     (c) 4   (d) 5

7. 3, 10, 17, 24, 31.

8. −3, −1, 0.9, 2, 2.5

9. (a) 2.25 pm   (b) 32 minutes

10. 511   **11.** £19.50

12. (a) 6 thousand, 6000
     (b) (i) 2   (ii) 8   (iii) 9   (iv) 2598

13. (a) 11 degrees Celsius   (b) −2°C

14. (a) 550   (b) 29

15. £5.85

16. (a) £5.15   (b) £4.85

17. (a) $\frac{1}{3}$ (b) Shade any 4 squares

18. (a) 5   (b) $\frac{1}{2}$ (c) 6

19. (a) 15, 40   (b) 42   (c) 36

20. (a) 49   (b) 9

21. (a) 10%, $\frac{1}{4}$, 0.3   (b) £5   (c) 30%

22. (a) 60 × 30   (b) 1800   (c) 88

23. £3978

24. (a) 120   (b) 250

25. (a) 125   (b) 350

26. (a) 3040   (b) 2736

27. (a) £1.92   (b) £1.80

28. (a) 18   (b) 20%

29. (a) 18
     (b) 5² is smaller. 3³ = 27, 5² = 25

30. 62p

31. (a) £4   (b) $\frac{1}{2}$

32. (a) 36   (b) (i) $1\frac{5}{12}$ (ii) $\frac{1}{10}$

33. (a) 2, 4, 6   (b) 432

34. (a) $\frac{80}{10-2}$ (b) 10

35. (a) $\frac{1}{4}$, $\frac{1}{3}$, $\frac{2}{5}$, $\frac{1}{2}$, $\frac{2}{3}$, $\frac{3}{4}$
     (b) Any decimal between 0.25 and 0.33…
     (c) $\frac{3}{10}$

36. 2500

37. (a) (i) 14   (ii) $\frac{9}{25}$ (b) 2490

38. (a) 0.625   (b) $\frac{3}{5}$

39. (a) £2.76   (b) 64p
     (c) £34.27   (d) 35p
     (e) 42p per kilogram

40. 11.20 am   **41.** £5.62

42. (a) 11   (b) £5265
     (c) £265   (d) 5.3%

43. (a) 3.21   (b) 6.5

44. (a) 240 euros   (b) £9.38

45. 80 kg, nearest kilogram   **46.** 4.7

47. (a) 1728   (b) 0.143

48. (a) £3 (b) 5% **49.** 20

50. (a) £8.60
    (b) 250 g pot.
       145 g pot: 3.71 g/p, 250 g pot: 3.79 g/p

51. (a) £9.40 (b) 75 (c) 37.5%

52. £1660   **53.** £107.50   **54.** 9.8

55. (a) flour 345 g, butter 225 g, sugar 150 g,
      eggs 3.
    (b) 177°C (c) 130

56. (a) £284.24 (b) 5 hours

57. 1183 euros

58. 31.6%

CHAPTER 11

Exercise 11.1   Page 108

1. $n + 4$

2. $n - 3$ **9.** $25p$

3. $3n$ **10.** $6k$

4. $m + 6$ **11.** $5b$ pence

5. $m - 12$ **12.** $\frac{c}{3}$ pence

6. $8m$ **13.** $\frac{a}{5}$ pence

7. $p - 1$ **14.** $\frac{36}{g}$

8. $p + 5$ **15.** (a) $2t$ (b) $10t$

Exercise 11.2   Page 110

1. (a) $2y$ (b) $3c$ (c) $5x$
    (d) $7p$ (e) $2t$ (f) $3d$
    (g) $3n$ (h) $5y$ (i) $10g$
    (j) $8m$ (k) $13z$ (l) $2r$
    (m) $5t$ (n) $4y$ (o) $3j$
    (p) $4c$ (q) $7x$ (r) w
    (s) 0 (t) $-5y$ (u) $-5x$
    (v) $-14a$ (w) $6b$ (x) $2m$

2. (a) $4x$ (b) $6a$ (c) $9y$
    (d) $6u$

3. (a) Can be simplified, $2v$.
    (b) Cannot be simplified, different terms.
    (c) Can be simplified to $3v + 4$.
    (d) Cannot be simplified, different terms.

4. (a) $8x + y$ (b) $w + 2v$
    (c) $2a - 2b$ (d) $5x + 3y$
    (e) $3 + 7u$ (f) $p + 4q$
    (g) $3d - 7c$ (h) $2y + 1$
    (i) $a + b$ (j) $4m + n$
    (k) $9c - d$ (l) $x + y$
    (m) $6p$ (n) $5 - 5k$
    (o) $a + 3$

5. (a) $8a + 3b$ (b) $3p + 3q$
    (c) $3m + 2n$ (d) $x - 2y$
    (e) $2x + 3y$ (f) $d + 3$
    (g) $3b - 2a$ (h) 7
    (i) $a + 2b$ (j) $-2f$
    (k) $v - 4w$ (l) $-2 - 5t$
    (m) $4q - 4p$ (n) $1 - 7k$
    (o) $c - d + 11$

6. (a) $4x + 2$ (b) $4a + 6b$
    (c) $3x$ (d) $6y + 9$
    (e) $10a$ (f) $12a + 15$

Exercise 11.3   Page 111

1. (a) $3a$ (b) $7b$ (c) $8c$
    (d) $9d$ (e) $4e$ (f) $8f$
    (g) $6p$ (h) $15q$ (i) r^2
    (j) g^2 (k) $2g^2$ (l) $6g^2$
    (m) t^2 (n) $4t^2$ (o) $12t^2$
    (p) $15u^2$ (q) $10m^2$ (r) $9d^2$
    (s) $15x^2$ (t) $12y^2$ (u) $6k^2$

2. (a) $5a$ (b) $4b$ (c) $4x$
    (d) $4y$ (e) 10 (f) 16
    (g) 12 (h) 20 (i) $2y$
    (j) 8 (k) $3p$ (l) 18

3. (a) ab (b) xy (c) y^2
    (d) $2pq$ (e) $2a^2$ (f) $3xy$
    (g) $6ab$ (h) $12gh$ (i) $6d^2$
    (j) $3g^2$ (k) $5ab$ (l) $6gh$
    (m) abc (n) m^3 (o) $2d^3$
    (p) $3g^3$ (q) $6x^3$ (r) m^2n
    (s) $3abc$ (t) $6pqr$ (u) $10xy^2$

4. (a) a^2 (b) $4x^2$ (c) $6g^2$
    (d) $10y^2$

Exercise 11.4   Page 112

1. (a) $2x + 10$ (b) $3a + 18$
    (c) $4y + 12$ (d) $4a + 2$
    (e) $6y + 4$ (f) $3a + 3b$

2. (a) $3x + 6$ (b) $2y + 10$
    (c) $4x + 2$ (d) $3p + 3q$

3. $2(q + 2)$ and $2q + 4$ $2(q - 1)$ and $2q - 2$
    $2(q + 1)$ and $4q + 2$ $2(2 - q)$ and $4 - 2q$

4. (a) $2x + 8$ (b) $4b + 4$
(c) $3p + 18$ (d) $5a + 35$
(e) $8x + 4$ (f) $6a + 2b$
(g) $3t - 6$ (h) $20 - 4a$
(i) $6 - 12p$ (j) $6b + 12c$
(k) $6m - 15n$ (l) $7a + 7b + 7c$

5. (a) $a^2 + a$ (b) $2d + d^2$
(c) $2x^2 + x$

6. (a) $x^2 + 3x$ (b) $2y + y^2$
(c) $t^2 - 5t$ (d) $2g^2 + 3g$
(e) $2m - 3m^2$ (f) $3a^2 + 4a$
(g) $2p^2 + 6p$ (h) $2d - 3d^2$

7. (a) $2x + 5$ (b) $3a + 11$
(c) $6w - 17$ (d) $10 + 2p$
(e) $3q$ (f) $7 - 3t$
(g) $5z + 8$ (h) $8t + 15$
(i) $2c - 6$ (j) $5a - 9$
(k) $3y - 10$ (l) $2x + 6$
(m) $8a + 23$ (n) $10x - 12$
(o) $2p - 11$ (p) $5a + 2b$
(q) $3x + y$ (r) $2p - 5q$

8. (a) $5x + 8$ (b) $5a + 13$
(c) $9y + 23$ (d) $9a + 5$
(e) $26t + 30$ (f) $5z + 13$
(g) $8q + 24$ (h) $7x + 9$
(i) $10e - 11$ (j) $13d + 5$

Exercise 11.5   Page 114

1. (a) $2(x + y)$ (b) $3(a - 2b)$
(c) $2(3m + 4n)$ (d) $x(x - 2)$
(e) $a(b + 1)$ (f) $x(2 - y)$
(g) $2(b - 2a)$ (h) $x(2x + 3)$
(i) $g(1 - g)$

2. (a) $2(a + b)$ (b) $5(x - y)$
(c) $3(d + 2e)$ (d) $2(2m - n)$
(e) $3(2a + 3b)$ (f) $2(3a - 4b)$
(g) $4(2t + 3)$ (h) $5(a - 2)$
(i) $2(2d - 1)$ (j) $3(1 - 3g)$
(k) $5(1 - 4m)$ (l) $4(k + 1)$

3. (a) $x(y - z)$ (b) $g(f + h)$
(c) $b(a - 2)$ (d) $q(3 + p)$
(e) $a(1 + b)$ (f) $g(h - 1)$
(g) $a(a + 3)$ (h) $t(5 - t)$
(i) $d(1 - d)$ (j) $m(m + 1)$
(k) $r(5r - 3)$ (l) $x(3x + 2)$

Review Exercise 11   Page 115

1. $6t$ pence   **2.** $x + 3$ years old

3. (a) $2x$ cm   (b) $x + 3$ cm

4. (a) $x + y$ (b) £$5(x + y)$

5. $18n + 5g$ pence

6. (a) $3w$ (b) $w + 2$
(c) w^2

7. (a) (i) $4q$ (ii) c^3 (iii) $12xy$
(b) $15h + 10$

8. (a) (i) $2n + 3$ (ii) $6n^2$
(b) $2x + 6$ (c) $2x + 1$
(d) $3(x - 2)$

9. (a) $3ab$ (b) $a^2 + 2a$
(c) $2x - 6$

10. mp pence   **11.** $7d + 3$

12. (a) $5n$ pence   (b) $n - 15$ pence
(c) $5n - 45$ pence

13. (a) $4a$ (b) $2a + 2b$
(c) $8a + 1$ (d) $15a - 15$

14. (a) $3n - 5$ (b) $9a - 1$
(c) $x(2x + y)$

15. $x^2 + 3x$

16. (a) $3(2x - 5)$ (b) $y(y + 7)$

CHAPTER 12

Exercise 12.1   Page 116

1. (a) 3   (b) 4   (c) 9   (d) 16

2. (a) $x = 4$ (b) $a = 3$ (c) $y = 8$
(d) $t = 6$ (e) $h = 22$ (f) $d = 1$
(g) $z = 30$ (h) $p = 0$ (i) $c = 99$

3. (a) 5   (b) 5   (c) 9   (d) 3

4. (a) $a = 4$ (b) $b = 9$ (c) $c = 5$
(d) $e = 6$ (e) $f = 7$ (f) $g = 8$
(g) $p = 4$ (h) $r = 3$ (i) $x = 6$

5. (a) 1   (b) 4   (c) 4
(d) 2   (e) 3   (f) 5

Exercise 12.2   Page 117

1. 3   **5.** 11

2. 14   **6.** 5

3. 5   **7.** 4   **9.** 4

4. 6   **8.** 3   **10.** 7

11. (a) 2   (b) $2(x + 3) = 2x + 6$

12. (a) 9   (b) $3(x - 2) = 3x - 6$

13. (a) 6   (b) $2x + 3$

Exercise **12.3** — Page 119

1. (a) $y = 3$ (b) $x = 6$ (c) $a = 10$
   (d) $e = 15$ (e) $d = 11$ (f) $c = 20$
   (g) $x = 2$ (h) $y = 19$ (i) $m = 7$

2. (a) $q = 7$ (b) $m = 10$ (c) $n = 16$
   (d) $p = 18$ (e) $x = 31$ (f) $y = 17$
   (g) $a = 2$ (h) $k = 4$ (i) $h = 12$

3. (a) $x = 14$ (b) $t = 28$ (c) $f = 18$
   (d) $y = 19$ (e) $b = 7$ (f) $x = 29$
   (g) $m = 4$ (h) $k = 5$ (i) $y = 7$

4. (a) $c = 4$ (b) $a = 4$ (c) $f = 3$
   (d) $p = 3$ (e) $h = 5$ (f) $u = 2$
   (g) $d = 10$ (h) $e = 7$ (i) $f = 9$

5. (a) $p = 4$ (b) $t = 3$ (c) $h = 7$
   (d) $b = 2$ (e) $d = 10$ (f) $x = 6$
   (g) $c = 5$ (h) $n = 3$ (i) $x = 2$

6. (a) $c = 7$ (b) $x = 4$ (c) $y = 4$
   (d) $x = 2$ (e) $b = 6$ (f) $x = 4$
   (g) $k = 2$ (h) $b = 3$ (i) $c = 2$

7. (a) $a = 3$ (b) $x = 9$ (c) $a = 0$
   (d) $p = 1$ (e) $y = 5$ (f) $p = 4$
   (g) $x = 9$ (h) $k = 4$ (i) $m = 3$

Exercise **12.4** — Page 120

1. (a) $k = \frac{1}{2}$ (b) $a = -3$ (c) $d = -4$
   (d) $n = -\frac{1}{2}$ (e) $t = -5$ (f) $n = 1$
   (g) $m = 1\frac{1}{2}$ (h) $x = 2\frac{1}{3}$ (i) $y = -\frac{1}{2}$

2. (a) $x = -2$ (b) $y = -3$ (c) $t = -2$
   (d) $a = -2$ (e) $d = -3$ (f) $g = -3$
   (g) $t = \frac{1}{2}$ (h) $x = 7\frac{1}{2}$ (i) $d = 1\frac{2}{5}$
   (j) $a = 1\frac{1}{2}$ (k) $g = \frac{1}{5}$ (l) $b = 4\frac{1}{2}$

3. (a) $x = -2$ (b) $n = -\frac{1}{2}$ (c) $x = -1$
   (d) $y = -3$ (e) $x = -1$ (f) $x = -3$
   (g) $x = -1\frac{1}{2}$ (h) $x = -4$ (i) $x = -1\frac{1}{2}$

Review Exercise **12** — Page 121

1. (a) 4 (b) 3 (c) 6 (d) 4
2. 12
3. (a) $a = 10$ (b) $a = 5$ (c) $a = 7$
4. 11
5. (a) $x = 4$ (b) $n = 2$

6. (a) $3x - 5$ (b) -8 (c) 7
7. (a) $y = 2$ (b) $t = -3$
   (c) $g = \frac{1}{2}$ (d) $x = \frac{3}{5}$
8. $x = 12$
9. (a) $x = -4$ (b) $y = \frac{1}{2}$
10. (a) $x = -\frac{4}{5}$ (b) $y = -\frac{1}{2}$

CHAPTER 13

Exercise **13.1** — Page 122

1. $a = 3$ 6. $k = -2$ 11. $g = -1\frac{1}{2}$
2. $x = 2$ 7. $x = 3$ 12. $p = 4\frac{1}{2}$
3. $m = -3$ 8. $w = \frac{1}{2}$ 13. $n = -5$
4. $y = \frac{1}{2}$ 9. $n = -\frac{4}{5}$ 14. $y = 1\frac{1}{2}$
5. $y = -5$ 10. $m = -2$ 15. $d = -2\frac{1}{2}$

Exercise **13.2** — Page 123

1. (a) $x = 3$ (b) $a = 2$ (c) $t = 2$
   (d) $y = 0$ (e) $e = 5$ (f) $x = 2$

2. (a) $p = 5$ (b) $c = 6$ (c) $x = 3$
   (d) $y = 9$ (e) $g = 11$ (f) $q = 8$

3. (a) $a = 4$ (b) $b = 6$ (c) $c = 1$
   (d) $d = 9$ (e) $e = 5$ (f) $f = 4$

4. (a) $w = 2$ (b) $s = 3$ (c) $x = 2$
   (d) $g = 3$ (e) $q = 4$ (f) $t = 3$
   (g) $w = 4$ (h) $x = 3$ (i) $y = 5$

5. (a) $p = -1$ (b) $d = -2$ (c) $g = -2$
   (d) $x = 8\frac{1}{2}$ (e) $y = \frac{2}{5}$ (f) $t = \frac{1}{2}$
   (g) $t = 1\frac{3}{4}$ (h) $a = 2\frac{1}{2}$ (i) $m = 2\frac{3}{5}$

Exercise **13.3** — Page 123

1. (a) $x = 5$ (b) $q = 2$ (c) $t = 3$
   (d) $e = 3$ (e) $g = 4$ (f) $y = 1$
   (g) $x = 2$ (h) $k = 1$ (i) $a = 4$
   (j) $p = 6$ (k) $m = 2$ (l) $d = 5$
   (m) $y = 5$ (n) $u = 3$ (o) $q = 0$

2. (a) $d = 8$ (b) $q = 3$ (c) $c = 2$
   (d) $t = 3$ (e) $w = 2$ (f) $e = 3$
   (g) $g = 5$ (h) $z = 4$ (i) $m = 6$
   (j) $a = 5$ (k) $x = 4$ (l) $y = 3$

3. (a) $m = -4$ (b) $t = -2$

    (c) $p = -2$ (d) $x = 3\frac{1}{2}$

    (e) $a = \frac{1}{2}$ (f) $b = \frac{4}{5}$

    (g) $y = \frac{4}{5}$ (h) $d = \frac{3}{4}$

    (i) $f = -3\frac{1}{2}$

Exercise 13.4   Page 124

1. (a) $12x$ (b) $x = 15$

2. (a) $6k\,\text{kg}$ (b) $2\frac{1}{2}\,\text{kg}$

3. (a) $2x$ pence   (b) 64 pence

4. (a) $3y + 15\,\text{cm}$ (b) $y = 8$

5. (a) $6a + 3$ (b) 7

6. (a) $n - 7$ years old
    (b) Dominic is 25 years old,
      Marcie is 18 years old.

7. (a) $4y - 2\,\text{cm}$ (b) $19\,\text{cm}$

8. (a) (i) £$(p + 4)$ (ii) £$(p - 3)$
      (iii) £$(3p + 1)$
    (b) Aimee £12, Grace £8, Lydia £5

9. (a) $x + 10$ pence   (b) $3x + 10$ pence
    (c) 15 pence

Review Exercise 13   Page 126

1. (a) $y = 4$ (b) $y = 3$
    (c) $y = -1$

2. (a) $m = 7$ (b) $t = 5$

3. (a) $a = 2$ (b) $b = 4$
    (c) $c = -5$

4. (a) $x = 5$ (b) $x = -1$

5. (a) $p = 9$ (b) $q = 8\frac{1}{2}$
    (c) $r = -7$

6. (a) $a = -5$ (b) $x = \frac{4}{5}$

7. $x = 3$

8. (a) 34 years old   (b) 19 years old

9. $x = 9\frac{1}{2}$

10. (a) $9x + 4\,\text{cm}$ (b) $x = 6$
    (c) $24\,\text{cm}$

11. (a) (i) $x + 7$ pence   (ii) $3x + 7$ pence
    (b) $x = 30$, cake costs 37p

12. $2\frac{1}{2}$ litres

CHAPTER (14)

Exercise 14.1   Page 127

1. (a) 5   (b) 2   (c) 12
    (d) 9

2. (a) 10   (b) -2 (c) 10
    (d) 25

3. (a) 8   (b) 0   (c) 12
    (d) 32

4. (a) 24   (b) -3 (c) 2
    (d) 18   (e) 18

5. (a) 15   (b) 0   (c) 2
    (d) 50   (e) 15

6. (a) 27   (b) -3 (c) $2\frac{1}{2}$
    (d) 90   (e) 54

Exercise 14.2   Page 128

1. (a) -1 (b) -4 (c) -12
    (d) 3

2. (a) 0   (b) -8 (c) -10
    (d) -16

3. (a) -8 (b) -8 (c) -12
    (d) 2

4. (a) 12   (b) -9 (c) -2
    (d) -18 (e) 6

5. (a) -5 (b) -20 (c) -2
    (d) -50 (e) -45

6. (a) 3   (b) -21 (c) $-2\frac{1}{2}$
    (d) -90 (e) 54

Exercise 14.3   Page 129

1. (a) $5y$ pence   (b) $y + 8$ pence

2. $12e$

3. (a) $a + 1$ years old   (b) $a - 4$ years old
    (c) $a + n$ years old

4. $b - 3$ **5.** $h + 12\,\text{cm}$

6. (a) $2d$ (b) $2d + 5$

7. (a) $P = y + 5$ (b) $P = y - 2$
    (c) $P = 2y$

8. Ben: $A = d - 2$ Charlotte: $A = 2d$

    Erica: $A = \dfrac{d}{2}$

9. (a) $P = 4g$ (b) $P = 4y + 4$
(c) $P = 3x - 1$ (d) $P = 2a + 2b$

10. $C = 25d$

11. (a) £44 (b) £80
(c) $C = 12x + 8$

12. (a) 115 (b) 175 (c) 45

(d)

n	$n + 1$	$n + 2$
	$n + 11$	
	$n + 21$	

(e) $S_n = 5n + 35$

Exercise 14.4　　　Page 131

1. £48 **2.** 17 points

3. (a) $A = 8$ (b) $A = 12$
(c) $A = -2$

4. (a) $C = 3$ (b) $C = 0$
(c) $C = -8$

5. (a) $P = 2$ (b) $P = 1$
(c) $P = \frac{1}{2}$

6. (a) $S = 1$ (b) $S = 1.5$
(c) $S = 2$

7. (a) $M = 7$ (b) $M = 1$
(c) $M = 0$

8. (a) $H = -8$ (b) $H = 2.5$
(c) $H = -3$

9. (a) $F = 35$ (b) $F = 75$
(c) $F = -15$

10. (a) $V = 26$ (b) $V = 2$
(c) $V = 16$

11. (a) $P = 3$ (b) $P = -9$
(c) $P = 12$

12. (a) $C = 104$ (b) $C = 32$
(c) $C = -24$

13. (a) $S = 40$ (b) $S = -2$
(c) $S = 6$

14. (a) $T = 35$ (b) $T = -2$
(c) $T = -18$

15. (a) $K = 11$ (b) $K = 13$

16. (a) $L = 2$ (b) $L = -11$

17. (a) $S = 9$ (b) $S = 16$
(c) $S = 100$

18. (a) $S = 18$ (b) $S = 32$
(c) $S = 200$

19. (a) $T = -2$ (b) $T = 12$
(c) $T = 180$

20. (a) $A = 8$ (b) $A = 27$
(c) $A = 64$

21. (a) $S = 16$ (b) $S = 54$
(c) $S = 128$

22. 33

23. (a) 96 m (b) 720 m
(c) 36 m

24. (a) 10°C (b) −20°C
(c) 25°C (d) −40°C

25. (a) 50°F (b) 14°F
(c) 86°F (d) −40°F

26. 138 minutes

27. 240 volts

Exercise 14.5　　　Page 133

1. (a) £13 (b) $C = 2k + 3$
(c) 2 km

2. (a) 140 minutes (b) $C = 40k + 20$
(c) 2 kg

3. (a) $F = 42$ (b) $F = 2C + 30$
(c) $C = 14$

4. (a) 410 (b) $b = 3n + 50$
(c) 140

5. (a) £51 (b) $T = 15d + 6$
(c) 6 days

6. (a) £295 (b) $C = 45n + 70$
(c) 9 days

Review Exercise 14　　　Page 134

1. 16 **5.** $S = -14$

2. (a) 7 (b) −1 (c) 12 **6.** $P = 7.5$

3. $V = 17$ **7.** 108

4. 4 **8.** 6

9. (a) £35 (b) 4 hours

10. $C = 4w$

11. $C = 20 - 4n$

12. (a) £74 (b) 6 drawers

13. (a) $y = 3k - 1$ (b) $k = 5$

14. (a) £90   (b) $C = 15d + 45$

15. (a) $T = hx + 20$ (b) £6

16. (a) £17   (b) $C = 0.15n + 5$
     (c) 480

CHAPTER 15

Exercise 15.1   Page 135

1. (a) 17, 21, 25   (b) 14, 16, 18
    (c) 16, 13, 10   (d) 28, 33, 38
    (e) 48, 96, 192   (f) 2, 1, $\frac{1}{2}$
    (g) 2, 0, −2   (h) 5, 2.5, 1.25
    (i) 21, 28, 36   (j) 29, 47, 76

2. (a) 8, 14   (b) 10, 22
    (c) 8, 32   (d) 16, −2
    (e) 16, 36   (f) 8, 21
    (g) 2, 20, 26

3. (a) Add 7; 37, 44
    (b) Add 2; 13, 15
    (c) Add 4; 21, 25
    (d) Subtract 5; 11, 6
    (e) Divide by 2; 2, 1
    (f) Multiply by 3; 81, 243
    (g) Subtract 2; −10, −12
    (h) Subtract 3; −5, −8

4. (a) 28
    (b) Keep on adding 3 to the last term until you get to the 10th term, 28.

5. (a) David multiplies the last term by 2, $4 \times 2 = 8$.
      Tony adds the next counting number, $4 + 3 = 7$.
    (b) 512   (c) 46

6. No.
    To find the next number, add 6 to the last term. All numbers in the sequence will be odd.

Exercise 15.2   Page 137

1. (a) 1, 5, 9, 13, 17   (b) 1, 2, 4, 8, 16
    (c) 40, 35, 30, 25, 20   (d) 4, 5, 7, 11, 19
    (e) 47, 23, 11, 5, 2   (f) 2, 6, 4, 5, 4.5

2. (a) 2, 4, 8   (b) 6, 12, 24
    (c) −2, −4, −8

3. (a) 4, 10, 22   (b) 8, 18, 38
    (c) −4, −6, −10

4. (a) (i) 21 (ii) 3   (b) 37

5. (a) (i) 36 (ii) 123   (b) 10

6. −6, −27

7. (a) 49, 97   (b) 1537

Exercise 15.3   Page 140

1. (a) 10   (b) 27 is an odd number
    (c) 14   (d) 24

2. (a) 17   (b) 4   (c) 33
    (d) 81

3. (a) 15   (b) 30   (c) 300

4. (a) (i) 18 (ii) 82
    (b) Pattern 7

5. (a) 51   (b) 100

6. (a) 22 cm²   (b) 42 cm²   (c) 9

7. (a) 27   (b) 52   (c) 252
    (d) Pattern 15

8. (a) 11   (b) Pattern 7
    (c) Pattern 18

Review Exercise 15   Page 142

1. (a) 18   (b) 32   (c) −6

2. (a) 35, 42   (b) Add 7

3. (a) 16
    (b) No. Not (multiple of 3) + 1.
    (c) 103

4. (a) 9   (b) 12   (c) 10

5. (a) 14, 7, 12
    (b) Repeats 6, 3, 8, 4, 2, 1

6. (a) 8, 13
    (b) Add the next odd number.

7. (a)

          Shape 4
    (b) Missing entry: 14   (c) 185

8. (a) 17   (b) 43

9. (a) 2, −1
    (b) Subtract 3 from last number.

10. (a) 7   (b) −5, −13

CHAPTER 16

Exercise 16.1   Page 143

1. $A(1, 2)$, $B(3, 1)$, $C(1, -2)$, $D(4, -4)$,
    $E(-4, -3)$, $F(-2, -2)$, $G(-2, 1)$,
    $H(-4, 3)$, $I(0, 4)$, $J(4, 0)$, $K(0, -3)$,
    $L(-4, 0)$

3. (b) (2, 4) **4.** (c) $D(-1, 2)$

5. (a) $A(3, 3)$, $B(3, 2)$, $C(3, 1)$, $D(3, 0)$,
$E(3, -1)$, $F(3, -2)$, $G(3, -3)$
(b) $P(-2, 3)$, $Q(-2, 2)$, $R(-2, 1)$,
$S(-2, 0)$, $T(-2, -1)$, $U(-2, -2)$,
$V(-2, -3)$
(c) In part (a) x coordinates $= 3$.
In part (b) x coordinates $= -2$.

6. (a) $A(-3, 3)$, $B(-2, 3)$, $C(-1, 3)$,
$D(0, 3)$, $E(1, 3)$, $F(2, 3)$, $G(3, 3)$
(b) $P(-3, -2)$, $Q(-2, -2)$, $R(-1, -2)$,
$S(0, -2)$, $T(1, -2)$, $U(2, -2)$,
$V(3, -2)$
(c) In part (a) y coordinates $= 3$.
In part (b) y coordinates $= -2$.

7. (a) $A(-3, -3)$, $B(-2, -2)$, $C(-1, -1)$,
$D(0, 0)$, $E(1, 1)$, $F(2, 2)$, $G(3, 3)$
(b) x coordinate $= y$ coordinate

8. (a) C (b) G (c) F (d) E
(e) D (f) B (g) G

Exercise 16.2   Page 146

1. (1) $x = 1$ **2.**
(2) $x = -3$
(3) $y = 4$
(4) $y = -1$
(5) $y = x$

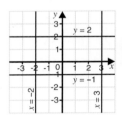

3.

	x	1	2	3
(a)	y	3	4	5
(b)	y	2	4	6
(c)	y	3	5	7
(d)	y	2	1	0

4. (a)   (b)

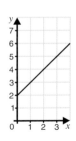

(c)   (d)

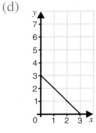

5.

x	-2	-1	0	1	2	3
(a) y	-3	-2	-1	0	1	2
(b) y		-2	1	4	7	10

6. (b) Same slope, parallel
y-intercept is different

7. (b) Same slope, parallel
y-intercept is different

8. (b) Same y-intercept, 3
Different slope

10. (a) Missing entries: 6, 4, 3
(b) (i) $y = 2.5$ (ii) $y = 4.5$

11. (b) (i) $y = -2$ (ii) $x = 0.5$

12. (b) $x = 0.5$

13. (b) (2.5, 8.5)

14.

x	1	2	3
$y = x + 2$	3	4	5
$y = 5 - x$	4	3	2

(a) (above) (c) (1.5, 3.5)

Exercise 16.3   Page 149

1. (a) (0, 7) (c)
(b) (7, 0)

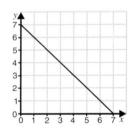

2. (a)

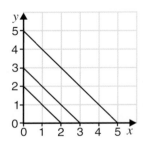

(b) Parallel lines, same gradient.

3. (a) (0, 6) (c)
(b) (2, 0)

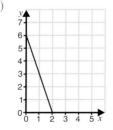

402

4. (a) 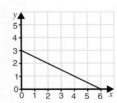 (b)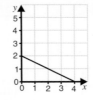

(c)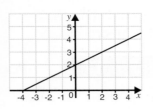

5. (a) $(0, 5)$
(b) $(3, 0)$
(c)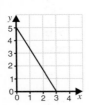

6. (a) 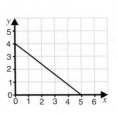 (b)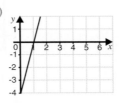

(c)

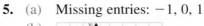
Review Exercise 16   Page 150

1. (a) $P(3, 2)$ (b) $Q(-1, 3)$

2. (a) $A(0, 2)$ (b) $D(-2, 0)$

3. (a) $M(1, -1)$ (b) $N(-3, -1)$

4. (a)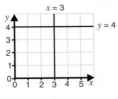

(b) $(3, 4)$

5. (a) Missing entries: $-1, 0, 1$
(b)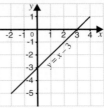

6. (a)

x	-2	0	2
y	0	2	4

(b)   (c) $a = 2, \quad b = 1$

7.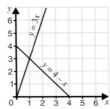

8. (a)

x	-3	-2	-1	0	1	2
y	-3	-1	1	3	5	7

(b) 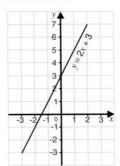   (c) (i) $y = 6$
(ii) $x = -1.75$

9. (a)

x	-2	-1	0	1	2	3
y	-5	-3	-1	1	3	5

(c) (i) $y = -3.8$
(ii) $x = 2.4$

10. (b) $(2, 3)$

11. (a)

x	-2	0	2	4
y	3	2	1	0

(b)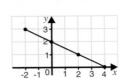

CHAPTER 17

Exercise **17.1**　　Page 151

1. (a) 4 inches　　(b) 25 centimetres
   (c) 40 centimetres

2. (a) 12.80 dollars　　(b) £6.25

3. (a) 5.6 km　　(b) 3.1 miles

4. (a) 8.8 pounds　　(b) 6.8 kg

5. (a) 10°C　　(b) 167°F

Exercise **17.2**　　Page 153

1. (a) 1005　　(b) 24 miles
   (c) 3

2. (a) 1042　　(b) 28 km
   (c) (i) 1115　　(ii) 8 km

3. (a) 125 km　　(b) 1 hour
   (c) Faster going to Leeds - graph steeper.

4. (a) 50 km/h　　(b) 20 m/s
   (c) 9 miles/hour

5. (a) 0930　　(b) 2 hours
   (c) 30 miles/hour

6. 18 km/h

7. (a) 10 km/h　　(b) 6.7 km/h
   (c) 8 km/h

8. (a)　　(b) 1130
   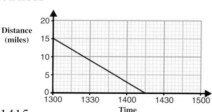

9. (a) 9 miles/hour
   (b) (i)

   (ii) 1415

10. (a) (b) (i)

    (b) (ii) 1110

Exercise **17.3**　　Page 156

1. (a) 80　　(b) 40　　(c) 1200, 1400
   (d) 1315 and 1400　　(e) 140

2. (a) 4 kg　　(b) 6.5 cm

3. (a) 14 mm　　(b) 150 g　　(c) 8 mm

4. (a) £140　　(b) 35 km　　(c) £60

5. (a) 25 m　　(b) 100 m
   (c) 2 minutes 20 seconds

Review Exercise **17**　　Page 158

1. (a) (i) £5　　(ii) 20 dollars
   (b) £10 = 16 dollars
   £300 = 30 × 16 = 480 dollars

2. (b) 72 hectares

3. (a) £70　　(b) £25

4. (a) 2 hours　　(b) 15 miles/hour
   (c)
   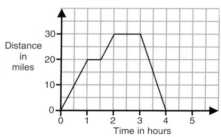

5. (a) (i) 1300　　(ii) 20 km/h
   (b)
   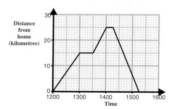

6. (a)
   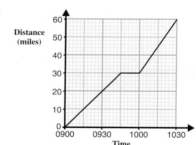
   (b) 40 miles/hour

Section Review　　Page 160

1. (a) (1, 2)　　**2.** (a) 20　　(b) 8, 23

3. £42

4. (a) (i) 13, 17　　(ii) 37
   (iii) No. Not an odd number.
   (b) (i) 14
   (ii) Subtract 4 from last number.

5.

Input	Output
7	21
8	24

6. (a) (i)

      Pattern 4   Pattern 5

    (b)

Pattern	1	2	3	4	5	6	7
Number of dots	5	8	11	14	17	20	23

    (c) Multiply the Pattern number by 3 then add 2. $3 \times 12 + 2 = 38$

7. (a) 7   (b) 9

8. (a) 24, 30   (b) Add 6 to last number.

9. (a) 81, 243   (b) Multiply last number by 3.

10. (b) $M(-1, 1)$

11. £210

12. (a) 11, 19   (b) $-1, -5$

13. (a) 90 minutes   (b) 1830

14. (a)

    (b)

Black tiles	1	2	3	4	5	6
White tiles	0	1	2	3	4	5
Total tiles	1	3	5	7	9	11

    (c) (i) Odd numbers for total tiles.
           Numbers of black and white tiles increase by 1 each time.
           White tiles one less than black tiles.
       (ii) 20 black + 19 white = 39 tiles

15. (a) $3g$ (b) $12m$ (c) n^2

16. (a) $3x$ pence   (b) $x + 7$ pence

17. (a) $y = 8$ (b) $a = 8$

18. (a) 4   (b) 14

19. (a) Odd number   (b) Even number
    (c) Could be even or odd.

20. (a) 3   (b) 5

21. (a) (i) $4a$ (ii) $5a - b$ (iii) $3a^2$
    (b) $x = 6$ (c) $d = 29$

22. (a) $5t$ pence   (b) $t - 10$ pence
    (c) $2t$ pence

23. (a) (i) 68°F   (ii) 54°F
    (b) (i) 16°C   (ii) 2°C

24. **A** and **R**, **B** and **Q**, **C** and **P**, **D** and **S**

25. (a) (i) 40 miles.
       (ii) The cyclist was not moving.
      (iii) 10 miles per hour.
    (b) $2\frac{1}{2}$ hours.

26. (a) £19   (b) 12 hooks

27. (a) 24   (b) -1 (c) -5

28. (a) $x = 5$ (b) $v = 24$ (c) 6

29. (a) $x = 2$ (b) $x = 4$

30. (a) $x = 5$ (b) $y = 5$
    (c) $z = 14$

31. (a) 18   (b) $2x - 1$
    (c) $y = 4$

32. (a) $y = 4$ (b) $x = -1$
    (c) No. $3 \times 10 - 2 \neq 27$

33. (a)

    (b) $(3, 3)$

34. (a) $y = -3$ (b) $x = 3$

35. (a) $g = 4.5$ (b) $g = 4$
    (c) $g = 3.5$

36. (a) $5a + 3$ cm   (b) $5a + 3 = 23$, $a = 4$

37. (a) $2x$ pence   (b) $3(x + 5)$ pence
    (c) 16 pence

38. (a) $x = 5$ (b) $y = 4$ (c) $p = 3.2$

39. (a)

x	-2	-1	0	1	2	3
y	-7	-4	-1	2	5	8

    (b)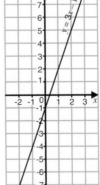

    (c) (i) $x = 1.5$
       (ii) $y = -5.5$

40. (a) (i) $2(2a + b)$ (ii) $t(3 - t)$
    (b) $x^2 - 2x$

CHAPTER 18

Exercise 18.1   Page 164

1. (a) 180°   (b) 90°   (c) 270°
    (d) 90°   (e) 120°   (f) 6°
    (g) 42°   (h) 720°   (i) 540°
    (j) 810°

2. (a) 45°   (b) 315°

3. (a) 45°   (b) 360°

4. Acute: **A**, **G**   Obtuse: **B**, **C**, **F**, **H**
Reflex: **D**, **I**   Right: **E**

Exercise **18.2**   Page 165

1. (a) 39°   (b) 118°   (c) 42°

2. (a) 217°   (b) 234°

Exercise **18.3**   Page 167

1. (a) $p = 65°$ (b) $p = 73°$
    (c) $p = 36°$

2. (a) $q = 35°$ (b) $q = 144°$
    (c) $q = 62°$

3. (a) $x = 110°$ (b) $x = 135°$
    (c) $x = 30°$

4. (a) $y = 120°$ (b) $y = 150°$
    (c) $y = 165°$

5. (a) $a = 35°$ (b) $b = 26°$
    (c) $c = 105°$

6. (a) $a = 30°$ (b) $b = 150°$
    (c) $c = 42°$ (d) $d = 20°$
    (e) $e = 126°$ (f) $f = 203°$
    (g) $g = 133°$, $h = 47°$
    (h) $i = 112°$
    (i) $j = 127°$, $k = 53°$, $l = 37°$
    (j) $m = 96°$
    (k) $n = 47°$, $p = 43°$

7. (a) $x = 45°$ (b) $x = 30°$
    (c) $x = 60°$ (d) $x = 36°$
    (e) $x = 40°$ (f) $x = 80°$
    (g) $x = 20°$ (h) $x = 30°$

Exercise **18.4**   Page 171

1. (a) $a = 65°$ (b) $b = 115°$
    (c) $c = 105°$ (d) $d = 100°$

2. (a) $a = 130°$, $b = 130°$
    (b) $c = 60°$, $d = 120°$
    (c) $e = 40°$, $f = 40°$
    (d) $g = 65°$, $h = 65°$

3. (a) $a = 63°$ (b) $b = 68°$, $c = 112°$
    (c) $d = 87°$ (d) $e = 124°$
    (e) $f = 65°$ (f) $g = 54°$
    (g) $h = 113°$ (h) $i = 124°$

4. (a) $a = 125°$, $b = 125°$
    (b) $c = 62°$, $d = 118°$, $e = 62°$
    (c) $f = 74°$, $g = 106°$
    (d) $h = 52°$, $i = 128°$

5. (a) $a = 84°$, $b = 116°$
    (b) $c = 56°$, $d = 116°$
    (c) $e = 61°$
    (d) $f = 270°$

Exercise **18.5**   Page 172

1. (a) $\angle BAC$ (b) $\angle RQS$ (c) $\angle XZY$

2. $a = \angle QPS$, $b = \angle PQS$, $c = \angle RQS$,
   $d = \angle QRS$, $e = \angle QSR$, $f = \angle PSQ$

3. (a) 93°   (b) 108°   (c) 52°
    (d) 110°   (e) 65°   (f) 295°
    (g) 283°   (h) 326°

4. (a) (i) 43°   (ii) supplementary angles
    (b) (i) 125°   (ii) vertically opposite angles
    (c) (i) 63°   (ii) corresponding angles

5. (a) 132°   (b) 126°   (c) 141°
    (d) 85°   (e) 65°
    (f) $\angle QSP = 105°$, $\angle STU = 105°$

6. (a) $\angle AOB = 153°$, $\angle COD = 37°$
    (b) $\angle QTU = 48°$, $\angle QTS = 132°$
    (c) reflex $\angle TUV = 280°$

Review Exercise **18**   Page 174

1. (a) (i) d (ii) a, c (iii) b (iv) e, f
    (b) $a = 106°$, $b = 90°$, $c = 111°$,
      $d = 53°$, $e = 307°$, $f = 254°$

2. (a)   (b)

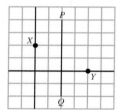

3. (a) $a = 57°$, supplementary angles
    (b) $b = 97°$, angles at a point $= 360°$
    (c) $x = 30°$

4. (a) (i) $x = 59°$
      (ii) vertically opposite angles
    (b) (i) $y = 121°$
      (ii) allied angles

5. (a) Corresponding angles
    (b) $r = 80°$
    (c) (i) $x = 80°$ (ii) alternate angles

6. (a) 78°   (b) 75°

7. (a) $a = 51°$ (b) $b = 51°$ (c) $c = 129°$

8. $x = 30°$

9. (a) $p = 135°$ (b) $q = 45°$ (c) $r = 55°$

CHAPTER 19

Exercise **19.1**   Page 177

1. (a) Yes   (b) Yes   (c) No
    (d) No   (e) Yes   (f) No

2. (a) Yes, obtuse-angled   (b) No
    (c) Yes, acute-angled
    (d) Yes, right-angled
    (e) Yes, obtuse-angled   (f) No

3. (a) $a = 70°$ (b) $b = 37°$
    (c) $c = 114°$ (d) $d = 43°$
    (e) $e = 63°$ (f) $f = 13°$

Exercise 19.2   Page 178

1. (a) $a = 120°$ (b) $b = 110°$
    (c) $c = 50°$ (d) $d = 80°$
    (e) $e = 88°$ (f) $f = 55°$

2. (a) $a = 32°$, $b = 148°$ (b) $c = 63°$
    (c) $d = 52°$, $e = 64°$

Exercise 19.3   Page 180

1. ΔPQT, ΔQRT, ΔRST

2. (a) Isosceles   (b) Equilateral
    (c) ΔBCE

3. (b) (i) Acute-angled, scalene
      (ii) Right-angled, scalene
      (iii) Acute-angled, isosceles
      (iv) Obtuse-angled, isosceles

4. $AC = BC$ $\angle BAC = \angle ABC$

5. (6, 2), (6, 8)

6. (a) $a = 60°$ (b) $a = 85°$
    (c) $a = 75°$ (d) $a = 50°$

7. $a = 40°$, $b = 120°$, $c = 62°$, $d = 128°$,
$e = 18°$, $f = 144°$, $g = 85°$, $h = 116°$,
$i = 26.5°$, $j = 153.5°$

8. (a) Equilateral   (b) 60°   (c) 78°

9. (a) Isosceles   (b) 74°   (c) 46°

10. (a) $\angle BCD = 120°$
    (b) $\angle PRQ = 80°$, $\angle QRS = 160°$
    (c) $\angle MNX = 50°$

Exercise 19.4   Page 183

5. (b) 9.3 cm   (c) 39°

6. (b) 5.9 cm   (c) 34°

Exercise 19.5   Page 185

1. (a) 13 cm   (b) 13.3 cm   (c) 19.9 cm

2. $\Delta PQR = 33$ cm, $\Delta QRS = 32$ cm,
$\Delta RST = 35$ cm. ΔRST has greatest perimeter

3. (a) $a = 7$ cm   (b) $b = 3.8$ cm   (c) $c = 3$ cm

4. (a) 4.5 cm²   (b) 10 cm²   (c) 6 cm²

5. (a) 9 cm²   (b) 6 cm²
    (c) 3.6 cm²

6. (a) 7.2 cm²   (b) 4.16 cm²
    (c) 11.52 cm²

7. (a) 3.8 cm²   (b) 8 cm²
    (c) 3.24 cm²

8. (a) $h = 6$ cm   (b) $h = 12$ cm
    (c) $h = 4$ cm

9. (a) $a = 8$ cm   (b) $b = 4$ cm
    (c) $c = 16$ cm

10. 67.5 cm²   **11.** 60 cm

Review Exercise 19   Page 188

1. (b) (i) Isosceles   (ii) 8 cm²
    (c) Point S on line $y = 5$.

2. (a) $x = 70°$ (b) $y = 110°$

3. (a) $\angle DCA = 53°$
    (b) $\angle BAC = 50°$
      $\angle ABC = \angle BCA$ (ΔABC is isosceles)
      $\angle BAC = 180° - (2 \times 65°)$

4. (b) (i) $\angle BAC = 50°$ (ii) acute angle

5. (a) 28 cm²   (b) 7 cm²   (c) 21 cm²

6. 9.6 cm²   **7.** (b) 16 cm²

8. (a) 45 cm   (b) 75 cm²   (c) 10 cm

CHAPTER   20

Exercise 20.1   Page 190

3. (a) 5   (b) 2   (c) 0

4. 1, 1, 1, 2, 0

5. (a) 2   (b) 3   (c) 4
    (d) 2   (e) 6   (f) 8

6. 1, 1, 3

7. (a) MY   (b) NZ   (c) JP

8. (a) 1   (b) (i) (ii)

9. (a)   (b) 3

10. (a) (i) 0 (ii) 2   (b) (i) 1 (ii) 1
    (c) (i) 2 (ii) 2   (d) (i) 0 (ii) 4
    (e) (i) 1 (ii) 1

Exercise **20.2**
Page 192

1. 9

2. (a) 4   (b) 4   (c) 2   (d) Infinite

3. (a) 2   (b) 2   (c) 4

4. (a) 4   (b) 1, 4

5. (a) 4   (b) 4

Exercise **20.3**
Page 193

1. A, O;   F, L;   C, G;   H, J;   D, P

2. **D**, **E**

3. (a) ΔCED (b) $CBFE$

4. (a) ΔAXZ and ΔZYC, ΔBXZ and ΔZYB

Exercise **20.4**
Page 195

1. **A**, **D** (SSS)   **2.** **A**, **D** (ASA)

3. (a) Yes, ASA   (b) No
    (c) Yes, SAS   (d) Yes, SSS
    (e) No   (f) Yes, RHS

4. (a) No   (b) No
    (c) Yes, RHS   (d) No
    (e) Yes, ASA   (f) Yes, ASA

5. **A** and **H**, ASA   **B** and **F**, SSS
    D and **G**, RHS   **E** and **I**, SAS

Review Exercise **20**
Page 196

1.

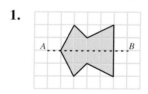

2. (a) **X**, **Y**   (b) **X**, **Z**

3.

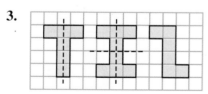

4. (a) 16   (b) 2

5. (a) **Y**   (b) **Z**   (c) **X**

6. (a)   (b)

7. (a) 4   (b) 2

---

8. (a) E.g.   (b) E.g.

9. **A** and **B**, **D** and **H**

10. (a) ΔCDE (b) ΔCEF (c) $CDEF$

Exercise **21.1**
Page 199

1. (b) (i)   Isosceles trapezium
      (ii)   Parallelogram
      (iii)   Rhombus
      (iv)   Kite
      (v)   Square

2. $M(1, 4)$ **5.** $Y(6, 4)$

3. $S(3, 1)$ **6.** $A(1, 3)$

4. $C(5, 4)$ **7.** $(3, 1), (3, 5)$

8. (a) $a = 90°$ (b) $a = 35°$
    (c) $a = 140°$ (d) $a = 114°$

9. (a) $a = 90°$, $b = 53°$, $c = 37°$
    (b) $d = 42°$, $e = 48°$
    (c) $f = 27°$, $g = 117°$
    (d) $h = 16°$, $i = 99°$, $j = 65°$

10. (a) $a = 36°$, $b = 144°$
    (b) $c = 124°$, $d = 56°$
    (c) $e = 130°$, $f = 23°$, $g = 23°$
    (d) $h = 42°$, $i = 84°$

11. (a) $a = 110°$, $b = 100°$ (b) $c = 95°$
    (c) $d = 46°$ (d) $e = 96°$

12. (a) $a = 115°$, $b = 44°$

13. $\angle WXY = 72°$, $\angle XYZ = 108°$

14. (a) $a = 62°$ (b) $b = 54°$, $c = 36°$
    (c) $d = 62°$ (d) $e = 116°$, $f = 86°$
    (e) $g = 124°$ (f) $h = 75°$
    (g) $i = 38°$, $j = 42°$
    (h) $k = 55°$, $l = 45°$

Exercise **21.2**
Page 202

1.

A	B	C	D	E	F	G	H	I
1	0	1	4	2	2	0	0	1
1	1	1	4	2	2	1	2	1

2. (a) 4   (b) 2   (c) 1

3. (a) 2   (b) 2   (c) 1

4. (b) 2   (c) 2

1. (a) (i) 12 cm   (ii) 8 cm²
   (b) (i) 14 cm   (ii) 12 cm²
   (c) (i) 16 cm   (ii) 15 cm²

2. (a) (i) 8 cm   (ii) 4 cm²
   (b) (i) 12 cm   (ii) 9 cm²
   (c) (i) 16 cm   (ii) 16 cm²

3. (a) **B** and **C**   (b) **B** and **D**

4. **A** 8 cm²   **B** 12 cm²   **C** 12 cm²
   D 9 cm²   **E** 8 cm²   **F** 12 cm²

5. (a) 8 cm   (b) 8 cm
   (c) 11.2 cm   (d) 5.6 cm

6. (a) 6 cm²   (b) 5.4 cm²
   (c) 11.5 cm²   (d) 7.92 cm²

7. (a) 49 cm²   (b) 5.76 cm²
   (c) 18.49 cm²   (d) 3.24 cm²

8. (a) 30 cm²   (b) 10 cm²
   (c) 13.5 cm²

9. (a) $b = 4$ cm   (b) $b = 3$ cm
   (c) $b = 2$ cm

10. (a) 3 cm   (b) 6 cm   (c) 8 cm

11. 14 m²   13. 4 cm

12. 84 cm²   14. 20 cm²   15. 4 cm

1. (a) **D**   (b) Kite   (c) 2
   (d) **A**   (e) 4

2. (a) (i) 12 cm   (ii) **Q** and **S**
   (b) (i) 12 cm²   (ii) **P** and **S**

3. (b) $S(-2, 0)$

4. $a = 30°$, $b = 60°$, $c = 42°$, $d = 78°$

5. $a = 35°$. Sum of angles is $360°$.

6. (a) 1
   (b) (i) $a = 110°$,
          opposite angles of line of symmetry
       (ii) $b = 100°$

7. $a = 115°$, $b = 44°$

8. (a) 24 cm   (b) 27 cm²

9. 1 cm by 28 cm,   2 cm by 14 cm,   4 cm by 7 cm

10. 25 cm²

11. (a) 6 cm   (b) 30 cm

12. (a) 14.4 m²   (b) 7.4 m²

13. 10.5 cm²

CHAPTER 22

1. (a) triangle   (b) quadrilateral
   (c) pentagon   (d) hexagon

2. (a) $a = 63°$ (b) $b = 55°$, $c = 62°$
   (c) $d = 95°$, $e = 76°$

3. (a) $a = 48°$ (b) $b = 60°$
   (c) $c = 103°$ (d) $d = 100°$

4. (a) $a = 120°$ (b) $b = 62°$
   (c) $c = 76°$ (d) $d = 120°$, $e = 50°$

5. (a) 540°   (b) 720°
   (c) 900°   (d) 1080°

6. (a) $a = 80°$ (b) $b = 70°$
   (c) $c = 85°$ (d) $d = 60°$
   (e) $e = 120°$ (f) $f = 130°$

7. (a) $a = 199°$ (b) $b = 240°$, $c = 120°$
   (c) $d = 225°$, $e = 85°$

1. (a) (i) 120°   (ii) 90°
       (iii) 60°   (iv) 45°
   (b) (i) 60°   (ii) 90°
       (iii) 120°   (iv) 135°

2. 20

3. (a) 40   (b) 15   (c) 9
   (d) 6

4. 8

5. (a) 5   (b) 20   (c) 40
   (d) 4

6. (a) 72°   (b) 108°   (c) 540°

7. (a) $a = 90°$, $b = 60°$, $c = 210°$
   (b) $d = 90°$, $e = 120°$, $f = 150°$
   (c) $g = 90°$, $h = 135°$, $i = 135°$
   (d) $j = 105°$
   (e) $k = 162°$
   (f) $l = 192°$
   (g) $m = 132°$
   (h) $n = 96°$

8. (a) $a = 90°$, $b = 150°$
   (b) $c = 126°$, $d = 156°$, $e = 66°$
   (c) $f = 102°$

9. (a) $a = 60°$
   (b) $b = 135°$, $c = 45°$
   (c) $d = 36°$, $e = 72°$

5. (b) (ii) 6　　(c) 6

6. (a) (i) 5　　(ii) 5
   (b) (i) 7　　(ii) 7
   (c) (i) 10　　(ii) 10

Review Exercise 22　　**Page 218**

1. (a) 5
   (b) (i) $x = 72°$
       (ii) $y = 54°$

   (c) E.g.

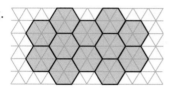

   (d) At any vertex, sum of angles cannot equal 360°.

2. (a) $q = 12°$　　(b) 30 sides

3. E.g.

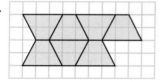

4. (a) Square: line 4, rotation 4.
       Equilateral triangle: line 3, rotation 3.
       Pentagon: line 5, rotation 5.
   (b) $x = 102°$
       $x = 360° - (108° + 60° + 90°) = 102°$

5. (a) Hexagon
   (b) $x = 60°$
   (c) 720°

6. $x = 130°$

7. (a) $p = 45°$
   (b) $q = 135°$

8. $\angle AED = 108°$ (int. $\angle$ of a pentagon)
   $\angle CAE = 108° - 36° = 72°$
   $\angle CAE + \angle AED = 180°$ (allied angles)
   So AC is parallel to ED.

9. (a) Equilateral. Three sides equal.
   (b) $x = 40°$

10. (a) Kite
    (b) Pentagon
    (c) $\angle AED = 54°$
    (d) $\angle AEI = 36°$

CHAPTER ㉓

Exercise 23.1　　**Page 220**

1. (a) (i) Bike Hire Centre
       (ii) Bikers' Cafe
       (iii) Bikers' Rest
       (iv) High Peak
   (b) (i) Highlands
       (ii) North-east
       (iii) Country Garden

2. (a) South　　(b) East　　(c) West
   (d) South-west

3. (a) 45°　　(b) 135°　　(c) 90°
   (d) 90°　　(e) 180°

4. (a) South　　(b) North

5. (a) North-west　　(b) North-east

6. Entries are: south-east, south-east, south, north-west

Exercise 23.2　　**Page 223**

1. (a) 065°　　(b) 140°　　(c) 249°
   (d) 228°　　(e) 300°　　(f) 090°

2. (b) (i) 230°　　(ii) 305°　　(iii) 015°
       (iv) 080°　　(v) 125°　　(vi) 355°

3.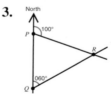
   4. (a) 180°
      (b) 070°
      (c) 250°
      (d) 043°
      (e) 223°

5. (a) 315°　　(b) 135°　　(c) 285°
   (d) 105°　　(e) 230°　　(f) 050°

6.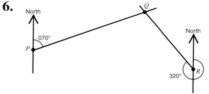

Exercise 23.3　　**Page 225**

1. 16.8 km　　2. 3.2 cm

3. (a) (i) 128°　　(ii) 308°
   (b) (i) 4.7 cm　　(ii) 47 km

4. (a) 240 m　　(b) 063°

5. (a) 48 km

(b)

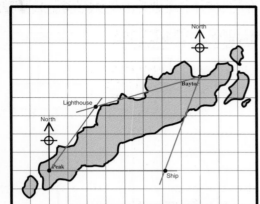

6. 4.6 cm

7. (a) 2.5 cm (b) 25 m

8. (a) 13.5 km (b) 072°
(c) 252°

9. (a) 065° (b) 282°
(c) 1800 m

10. 19.8 km

11. (a) 8 km (b) 114°
(c) 294°

12. (a) 6300 km (b) 248°

13. (a) 50 km (b) 347°
(c) 167°

Review Exercise 23   **Page 229**

1. (a) Kendal (b) Taunton

2. (a) (b)

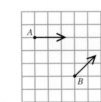

(c) North-West

3. 257°

4. (a) $x = 133°$ (b) 047°
(c) 295°

5. 14.6 km

6. (a) 230° (b) 140°
(c) (i) 3.7 cm (ii) 740 m

7. (b) 245°
(c) (i) 64 km (ii) 197°

CHAPTER 24

Exercise 24.1   **Page 232**

1. (a) 12 cm (b) 24 cm (c) 39 cm

2. (a) 15 cm (b) 30 cm (c) 38.4 cm

3. (a) 1p: 2 cm, 2p: 2.6 cm
(b) 1p: 6 cm, 2p: 7.8 cm

4. (a) 37.68 cm   **5.** (a) 28.26 cm
(b) 21.98 cm   (b) 35.168 cm
(c) 47.1 cm   (c) 100.48 cm

6. 28 cm   **8.** 82 cm   **10.** 57.5 m

7. 75.4 cm   **9.** 40.8 cm   **11.** 5.03 m

12. Eddy: 125.7 m, Reg: 157.1 m
Reg cycles 31.4 m further.

Exercise 24.2   **Page 234**

1. (a) 75 cm² (b) 147 cm² (c) 243 cm²

2. (a) 27 cm² (b) 75 cm² (c) 192 cm²

3. (a) 50 cm² (b) 133 cm² (c) 452 cm²

4. (a) 32.2 cm² (b) 45.4 cm² (c) 531 cm²

5. 22 167 cm²

6. 16 286 mm²   **8.** 491 cm²   **10.** 0.79 m²

7. 3421 cm²   **9.** 1.13 m²   **11.** 50.3 cm²

Exercise 24.3   **Page 236**

1. (a) 56.5 cm (b) 254.5 cm²

2. (a) 26 cm (b) 55.4 cm²

3. (a) 56.5 cm (b) 11.3 m

4. 22.0 cm²

5. Circle: 50.3 cm²   Semi-circle: 47.5 cm²
The circle is bigger.

6. 21.5 cm²   **7.** (a) 27 m (b) 56.7 m²

8. 31 cm   **9.** (a) 207 cm (b) 4

10. 24.5   **11.** (a) 37.7 m (b) 17

12. 18.8 cm

Review Exercise 24

Page 238

1. (a) 78.5 cm²   (b) 25.1 cm

2. (a) 283 m   (b) 6360 m²

3. 80 m   **4.** 750 cm   **5.** 126 cm²

6. (a) 188.5 m   (b) 530

7. (a) 8.2 m   (b) 1.1 litres

8. 218 cm²

CHAPTER 25

Exercise 25.1

Page 240

5. (a) 4   (b) 2 faces overlap

6. (a) Cube, 6, 8, 12
  (b) Cuboid, 6, 8, 12
  (c) Pyramid, 5, 5, 8
  (d) Triangular prism, 5, 6, 9

7. (a) 8   (b) 5   (c) 12   (d) 120 cm

Exercise 25.2

Page 242

1. (a)    (b)

(c)

2. (a)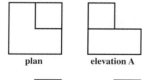

(b)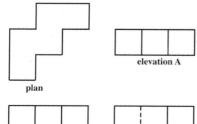

(c)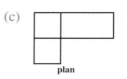

plan   elevation A

elevation B   elevation C

3.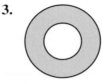

plan   elevation A

4. (a)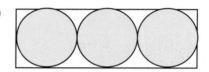

(b)

5. (a) 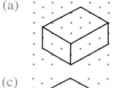   (b)

(c)

Exercise 25.3

Page 245

1. (b) 52 cm²   (c) 52 cm²

2. (a) 6 cm³   (b) 18 cm³   (c) 36 cm³

3. (a) (i) 8   (ii) 27
    (iii) 64   (iv) 125
  (b) (i) 24 cm²   (ii) 54 cm²
    (iii) 96 cm²   (iv) 150 cm²

4. (a) 27 cm³, 54 cm²
  (b) 30 cm³, 62 cm²
  (c) 140 cm³, 166 cm²

5. (a) 4 cm³, 18 cm²   (b) 5 cm³, 20 cm²
  (c) 8 cm³, 28 cm²   (d) 7 cm³, 24 cm²
  (e) 14 cm³, 40 cm²   (f) 10 cm³, 32 cm²

6. (a) 150 cm³,   190 cm²
    (b) 51.84 cm³,   89.28 cm²
    (c) 19 440 cm³,   4644 cm²
    (d) 96.8 cm³,   131.5 cm²
    (e) 916.1 cm³,   611.7 cm²

Exercise 25.4   Page 247

1. (a) **M** 17 cm², **A** 12 cm², **T** 9 cm²,
    H 12 cm², **S** 11 cm²
    (b) **M**   (c) **T**   (d) **A** and **H**

2. (a) 25 cm²   (b) 4 cm²   (c) 21 cm²

3. (a) 14 cm²   (b) 14 cm²   (c) 20 cm²

4. (a) 134 m²   (b) 588 cm²   (c) 396 km²

5. (a) 24 cm²   (b) 41 cm²   (c) 30 cm²

6. 58 cm²   **7.** 372 m²

Review Exercise 25   Page 249

1. (a) (i) cuboid (ii) cylinder (iii) cone
    (b) square based pyramid

2. 5 faces, 9 edges, 6 vertices

3. (a) 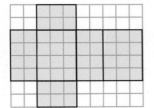   (b) 52 cm²

4. (a)

Shape	Area (centimetre squares)	Perimeter (centimetres)
G	6 cm²	14 cm
H	8 cm²	14 cm
I	7 cm²	14 cm

    (b) E.g.
    Not full size

5. **C**

6. (a) 24 cm   (b) 22 cm²

7.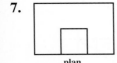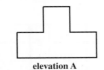
    plan   elevation A

8. (a) (i) 12 cm³   (ii) 40 cm²
    (b) 15 cm³

9. 54   **10.** 1500 cm²   **11.** 372 m²

12. (a) 30 cm³   (b)
    Not full size

13. (a) 75 cm²   (b) 225 cm³

14. (a) Cube. Cuboid: 120 cm³, cube: 125 cm³.
    (b) Cube. Cuboid: 148 cm², cube: 150 cm².

CHAPTER 26

Exercise 26.1   Page 252

1. (a) 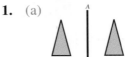   (b)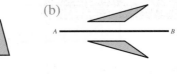

    (c) 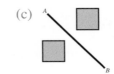   (d)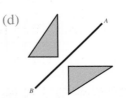

2. (a) (b)

    (c) (d)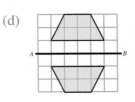

    (e) (f)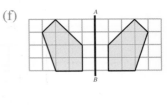

3. (a) (b)
    (c)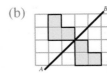

413

4. (a)

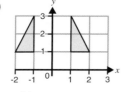

(b)

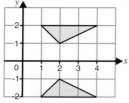

(c)

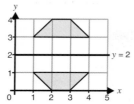

(d)

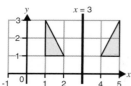

(e)

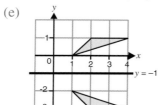

(f)

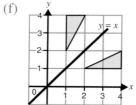

5.

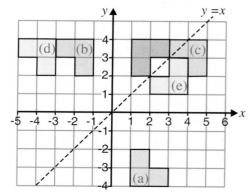

6. (a) $(2, -1)$ (b) $(-2, 1)$
    (c) $(0, 1)$ (d) $(2, -3)$

7. (a) $(3, -4)$ (b) $(-3, 4)$
    (c) $(5, 4)$ (d) $(-5, 4)$

414

1. (a)

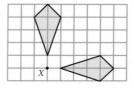

(b)

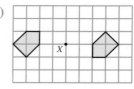

(c)

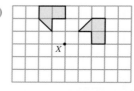

(d)

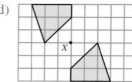

(e)

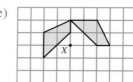

(f)

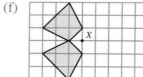

2. (a)

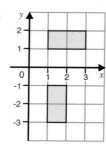

(b)

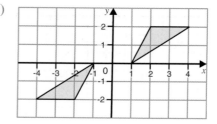

(c)
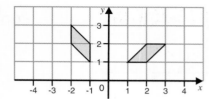

3. (a)
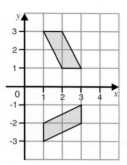

(b)
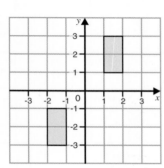

(c)
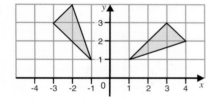

4. (a)
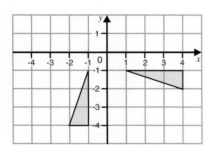

(b)
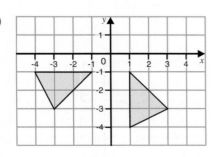

(c)
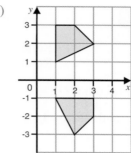

5. (a) (i) $(4, -3)$ (ii) $(-4, 3)$
   (iii) $(-3, -4)$
   (b) (i) $(-1, 3)$ (ii) $(1, -3)$

Exercise **26.3**

Page 257

1.
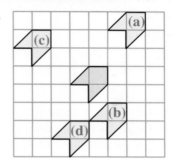

2.
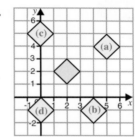

3. (a) (5, 5)   (b) (1, 6)
   (c) (4, 1)   (d) (1, 1)

4. (a) 2 units right and 1 unit up
   (b) 1 unit right and 2 units down
   (c) 3 units left and 1 unit up
   (d) 3 units left and 2 units down

5. (b) 3 units left and 2 units down

Exercise **26.4**

Page 258

1. (a) Corresponding lengths not in same ratio.
   (b) **P** and **R**

2. (a) Two circles   (d) Two squares

3. 2

7. (a) Enlarged shape: (4, 2), (6, 2), (2, 6)
   (b) Enlarged shape: (3, 3), (9, 0), (9, 9)

8. (a) (6, 8)   (b) (9, 12)

415

1. (a) Translation   (b) Reflection
    (c) Enlargement   (d) Rotation

2. (a) Rotation, $\frac{1}{2}$ turn about O

    (b) Enlargement, scale factor 3, centre O

3. (a) Reflection in x axis
    (b) Rotation, 90° anticlockwise, about (0, 0)
    (c) Translation, 3 units right and 2 units up
    (d) Rotation, 180°, about (0, 0)
    (e) Reflection in $x = 7$

4. (a) Translation, 6 units left and 3 units down
    (b) Reflection in y axis
    (c) Rotation, 90° clockwise, about (0, 0)

5. (a) Reflection in $x = -1$
    (b) Enlargement, scale factor 2, centre (0, 0)
    (c) Translation, 5 units right and 1 unit up

6. (a) Reflection in y axis
    (b) Rotation, 90° clockwise, about (0, 0)
    (c) Enlargement, scale factor 3, centre (0, 0)
    (d) Translation, 5 units left and 5 units up

1. (a) Translation   (b) Rotation

2.

3. (a) (b) (c)
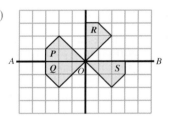

4.
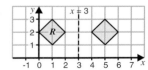

5.
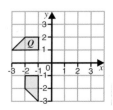

6.
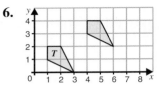

7.
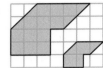

8.
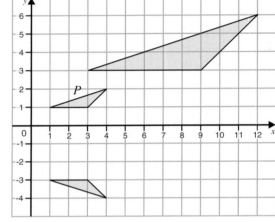

9. (a) (i) **B**   (ii) **C**   (iii) **A**
    (b) Reflection in $x = 3$

10. (a)
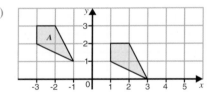

    (b) 4 units left and 1 unit up

11. (a) (b)
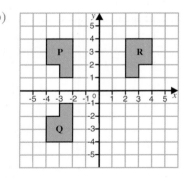

    (c) Reflection in the x axis

12. (a) Reflection in the y axis
    (b) Rotation, 180°, about (0, 0)
    (c) Translation, 2 units right and 3 units down
    (d) Translation, 2 units left and 3 units up
    (e) Enlargement, scale factor 2, centre (0, 0)

CHAPTER 27

Exercise **27.1**   **Page 267**

1. (a) 60 mm   (b) 320 mm
   (c) 6320 mm   (d) 86 mm
   (e) 8 mm   (f) 0.8 mm

2. (a) 9 cm   (b) 21 cm
   (c) 350 cm   (d) 7.35 cm
   (e) 0.2 cm   (f) 0.35 cm

3. (a) 2 m   (b) 3.2 m
   (c) 45.5 m   (d) 0.66 m
   (e) 0.08 m   (f) 0.098 m

4. (a) 600 cm   (b) 5600 cm
   (c) 760 cm   (d) 2350 cm
   (e) 90 cm   (f) 7 cm

5. (a) 4 km   (b) 35 km
   (c) 6.5 km   (d) 0.455 km
   (e) 0.075 km   (f) 0.007 km

6. (a) 6000 m   (b) 32 000 m
   (c) 650 000 m   (d) 3310 m
   (e) 350 m   (f) 85 m

7. (a) 20 000 cm^2 (b) 100 000 cm^2
   (c) 5000 cm^2

8. (a) 3 000 000 cm^3 (b) 20 000 000 cm^3
   (c) 400 000 cm^3

9. (a) 2000 g   (b) 45 000 g
   (c) 7500 g   (d) 42 500 g
   (e) 600 g   (f) 25 g

10. (a) 3 kg   (b) 32 kg
    (c) 9.3 kg   (d) 0.22 kg
    (e) 0.083 kg   (f) 0.006 kg

11. (a) 320 000 ml = 320l
    (b) 0.32t = 320 kg = 320 000 g
    (c) 3200 g = 3.2 kg = 0.0032t
    (d) 320 mm = 32 cm = 0.32 m
    (e) 32 000 cm = 320 m = 0.32 km
    (f) 3.2 km = 3200 m = 320 000 cm

12. (a) 6000 kg   (b) 8 kg
    (c) 0.8 kg   (d) 650 kg

13. (a) 4000 m   (b) 8 m
    (c) 0.086 m   (d) 40 m

14. (a) 2000 ml   (b) 500 ml
    (c) 850 ml   (d) 30 ml

15. 2000 m and 2 km   17. 0.5 km

16. 8 kg and 8000 g   18. 0.3 t

19. (a) 3.123 m   (b) 450 cm
    (c) 3240 km   (d) 1 000 000 g
    (e) 0.4 l

20. 0.5 m^2 is larger than 500 cm^2.
    0.5 m^2 = 5000 cm^2

21. 800 000 cm^3 is larger than 0.08 m^3.
    0.08 m^3 = 80 000 cm^3

22. 1.98 l 24. 50 g

23. 20   25. 60   26. 50 ml

Exercise **27.2**   **Page 270**

4. 250 g   5. 30 cm   6. 200 ml

8. (a) kilometres   (b) metres
   (c) centimetres   (d) millimetres
   (e) kilograms   (f) grams
   (g) litres   (h) millilitres

9. 6.4 m, nearest 0.1 m

10. (a) 12 m, nearest metre
        5.9 m, nearest 100 cm
        5 l, nearest litre
        500 m^2, nearest 50 m^2
    (b) 1200 cm, nearest 100 cm
        5900 mm, nearest 100 mm
        5000 ml, nearest 1000 ml
        500 000 000 mm^2, nearest 50 000 000 mm^2

Exercise **27.3**   **Page 272**

1. (a) 5 cm   (b) 25 cm
   (c) 60 cm   (d) 300 cm

2. (a) 78 inches   (b) 1560 inches
   (c) 0.8 inches   (d) 8 inches

3. (a) 8 km   (b) 72 km
   (c) 160 km   (d) 800 km

4. (a) 5 miles   (b) 15 miles
   (c) 25 miles   (d) 500 miles

5. (a) 22 pounds   (b) 110 pounds
   (c) 2200 pounds   (d) 11 000 pounds

6. (a) 10 kg   (b) 68 kg
   (c) 89 kg   (d) 43 kg

7. (a) 45 litres   (b) 3 litres
   (c) 135 litres   (d) 11 litres

8. (a) 22 pounds   (b) 35 pints
   (c) 195 inches   (d) 150 mm
   (e) 20 inches

9. 22 pounds   10. 170 cm   11. 66.4 kg

12. (a) 610 m   (b) 4.8 km
    (c) 5.57 feet   (d) 2.75 pounds

13. 1500 cm^2

14. No. 10 kg is about 22 pounds.

15. No. 6 miles is about 9.6 km.

1. (a) **X**: 8.5 cm   **Y**: 3.2 cm
    (b) **X**: 85 mm   **Y**: 32 mm

2. (a) (i)   **A**: 8.5 cm,   **B**: 4.5 cm,
                C: 0.5 cm
         (ii)   **A**: 72 mm,   **B**: 47 mm,
                C: 88 mm
         (iii) **A**: 6.6 inches, **B**: 7.8 inches,
                C: 8.7 inches
         (iv)   **A**: 1.7 kg,   **B**: 2.6 kg,
                C: 0.45 kg
         (v)   **A**: 46.6 g,   **B**: 45.8 g,
                C: 46.25 g
         (vi)   **A**: 52.4 kg,   **B**: 51.6 kg,
                C: 53.3 kg
         (vii) **A**: 300 ml,   **B**: 650 ml,
                C: 450 ml
         (viii) **A**: 45 ml,   **B**: 29 ml,
                C: 12 ml
    (b) (i)   8 cm   (ii)   41 mm
         (iii) 2.1 inches   (iv)   2.15 kg
         (v)   0.8 kg   (vi)   1.7 kg
         (vii) 350 ml   (viii) 33 ml

3. **A**: 9°C,   **B**: − 8°C,   **C**: 18°C

4. (a) (i) 9 gallons   (ii) 40.5 litres
    (b) (i) 22.5 litres (ii) 5 gallons

5. (a) **A**: 23 mph,   **B**: 48 mph,
         C: 70 mph
    (b) **A**: 37 km/h,   **B**: 77 km/h,
         C: 112 km/h

1. 8 miles per hour

2. 7 km/h

3. 25 metres per second

4. (a) 20 km/h   (b) 50 km/h
    (c) 4 km/h

5. 8 km   **6.** 30 miles   **7.** 3 km

8. (a) 150 km   (b) 90 km
    (c) 40 km

9. $\frac{1}{2}$ hour

10. 20 seconds

11. $1\frac{1}{2}$ hours

12. (a) 3 hours   (b) 2 hours

    (c) $3\frac{1}{2}$ hours

13. (a) 300 km   (b) 5 hours
    (c) 60 km/h

14. (a) 60 km/h   (b) 1 hour

15. 11.20 am

1. (a) −4°C   (b) 1.45 seconds

2. (a) centimetres   (b) grams
    (c) kilometres   (d) millilitres

3. 1.5 kg   **4.** 8 full glasses

5. (a) 20 feet   (b) 6 m

6. 200

7. (a) 2650 m   (b) 175 miles

8. Taller: Tim by about 10 cm,
    heavier: Sam by about 1 kg

9. 94 km/h   **11.** $1\frac{1}{2}$ hours

10. 240 miles   **12.** 50 miles/hour

1. (a) *AB* and *DC*   (b) *AD*
    (c) 56°   (d) 5.2 cm

2.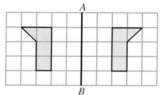

3. (a) 12 cm²   (b) 16 cm

4.

5. (a) 14 cm³   (b) 30 cm³   (c) **Q**

6. 4.4 cm   **7.** **A** and **D**

8. (a) (b)

    (c) isosceles, acute-angled, congruent

9. (a) (i) 4 (ii) 2 (b)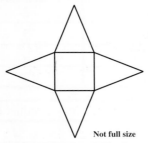

10. $a = 153°$, $b = 52°$, $c = 65°$

11.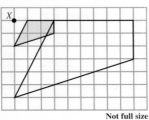

Not full size

12. (a) 187.5 cm
(b) 172 pounds

13.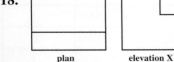

Not full size

14. 8 cm

15. (b) 55°

16. 40 000 cm³

17. (a) Isosceles
(b) $y = 80°$

18.

plan   elevation X

19. (a) $e = 50°$, $f = 50°$, $g = 130°$
(b) $h = 50°$

20. (a) 85 miles (b) 2 hours 15 minutes

21. 24 cm²

22. $a = 95°$
Sum of angles $= 360°$.
One pair of opposite angles are equal, so
$52° + 2a + 118° = 360°$.

23. (a) 314 cm (b) 7854 cm²

24. (a) Reflection in the y axis
(b) Rotation, 90° clockwise, about (0, 0)

25. (a) 11 cm²
(b) (i) 25.7 cm (ii) 39.2 cm²

26. (a) 8 cm³ (b) 30

27. (a) $a = 60°$ (b) $b = 135°$

28. 75 cm² **30.** (a) 121° (b) 301°

29. 31 **31.** (b) 116 m, 276°

CHAPTER 28

Exercise 28.1 **Page 282**

1. qualitative
2. quantitative, continuous

3. quantitative, discrete
4. qualitative
5. quantitative, discrete
6. quantitative, continuous
7. quantitative, discrete
8. qualitative
9. quantitative, discrete
10. quantitative, continuous

Exercise 28.2 **Page 284**

1. (a) 15 (b) 21 **2.** (a) 8 (b) 45

3. (a)

Number on dice	Tally
1	ⵌ‖‖
2	ⵌ‖‖‖
3	ⵌ‖‖‖‖
4	ⵌ ⵌ
5	ⵌ‖‖‖‖
6	ⵌ‖‖

(b) 4

4. (a)

Colour of car	Frequency
Black	1
Blue	9
Green	4
Grey	2
Red	11
Silver	4
White	9
Total	40

(b) red

5. (a)

Day	Frequency
Monday	8
Tuesday	7
Wednesday	6
Thursday	7
Friday	7
Saturday	3
Sunday	5
Total	43

(b) 43 (c) Monday

6. (a)

Age	Tally	Frequency
0 - 9	IIII	4
10 - 19	HHT II	7
20 - 29	HHT HHT I	11
30 - 39	HHT HHT	10
40 - 49	IIII	4
50 - 59	IIII	4

(b) 10 years   (c) 10
(d) 11   (e) 8

7. (a)

Height h cm	Frequency
$145 \leqslant h < 150$	2
$150 \leqslant h < 155$	2
$155 \leqslant h < 160$	7
$160 \leqslant h < 165$	9
$165 \leqslant h < 170$	6
$170 \leqslant h < 175$	8
$175 \leqslant h < 180$	2
Total	36

(b) 5 cm   (c) 7
(d) 11   (e) 32

Exercise 28.3   Page 287

1. (a) Francis   (b) Louisa
   (c) Alistair

2. (a) 2   (b) 2   (c) Fay

3. (a) Val d'Isere   (b) Cervinia
   (c) Cervinia   (d) 136 cm
   (e) Soldeu

4. (a) Wendy
   (b) Female
   (c) Tony and Mark 180 cm,
      Peter and Jane 168 cm
   (d) 5
   (e) Mary, Jim, Wendy, Beryl
   (f) 20 beats per minute

5. (a) (i)

Make	Frequency
Ford	4
Nissan	3
Vauxhall	5
Total	12

Colour	Frequency
Blue	2
Green	1
Grey	2
Red	3
White	4
Total	12

Registration letter	Frequency
P	2
R	3
S	2
T	4
X	1
Total	12

(ii)

Mileage (m)	Frequency
$0 \leqslant m < 5000$	0
$5000 \leqslant m < 10\,000$	2
$10\,000 \leqslant m < 15\,000$	0
$15\,000 \leqslant m < 20\,000$	2
$20\,000 \leqslant m < 25\,000$	1
$25\,000 \leqslant m < 30\,000$	2
$30\,000 \leqslant m < 35\,000$	4
$35\,000 \leqslant m < 40\,000$	1
Total	12

(b) (i) Vauxhall   (ii) 2   (iii) 5   (iv) 4

Exercise 28.4   Page 290

1. (a) Replies should be anonymous
   (b) Not specific

2. (a) Too personal   (b) Leading
   (c) (i) Groups overlap
      (ii) ☐ less than 5   ☐ 5 to 9
         ☐ 10 or more

3. (a) Too open   (b) Too open   (c) Leading

4. (a) Too personal   (b) Too open
   (c) Too open   (d) Too open

Exercise 28.5   Page 292

1. Small sample.   One data collection time.

2. Women only.   One location.
   One data collection time.

3. Equal numbers of men and women from various age groups, chosen at different locations, at different times.

9. Advantage: confidential, wider circulation, etc
Disadvantage: slow, non-response, etc

Exercise **28.6**   Page 293

1. (a) 8 (b) 16 (c) 20 (d) 40 (e) 50%

2. (a) 5 (b) 8 (c) 3 (d) 10

3. (a) 14 (b) 20 (c) 70% (d) 80%
(e) Disprove. 80% is greater than 70%.

4. Disprove, Boys $\frac{3}{21} = \frac{1}{7}$, Girls $\frac{2}{14} = \frac{1}{7}$, same proportion

5. (a) 20   (b) 5
(c) No. Smaller proportion of females got less than 11 spellings correct.
Males: $\frac{4}{15} = 26.7\%$ Females: $\frac{5}{20} = 25\%$

6. (a) (i) 10 (ii) No. Less 8, More 12
(b) (i) 37 (ii) No. Girls 37, Boys 37, same

7. Fewer females than males, no-one under 18.

Review Exercise **28**   Page 295

1. (a) Morag (b) Samantha (c) Morag

2. (a)

	Under 15 years old	15 years old or over	Totals
Boys	15	23	38
Girls	19	12	31
Totals	34	35	69

(b) 35

3. For example:

Type of vehicle	Tally	Frequency
Car		
Lorry		
Bus		

4. (a)

Eye colour	Tally	Frequency
blue	||||	4
brown	⊬⊬ |	6
green	||	2

(b) brown

5. (a)

	Male	Female
Junior management	51	42
Senior management	28	32

(b) A higher proportion of female managers are in senior management, than for male managers.

6. How many hours of television do you watch each week?
Less than 20 ☐ 20 to 30 ☐ More than 30 ☐
How many days a week do you watch TV?
Every day ☐   4 to 6 ☐   1 to 3 ☐   0 ☐

7. Only males asked.   No-one under 11.
Mainly adults surveyed.

8. (a)

Time (t seconds)	Tally	Frequency
$0 \leqslant t < 5$	|||	3
$5 \leqslant t < 10$	⊬⊬ ||	7
$10 \leqslant t < 15$	⊬⊬ ||||	9
$15 \leqslant t < 20$	||||	4
$20 \leqslant t < 25$	||	2

(b) $10 \leqslant t < 15$

9. (a) **Q**   (b) **Z**
(c) (i) Too open (ii) Not enough boxes

10. How far do you travel to the superstore?
Less than 5 km ☐   5 km to 10 km ☐
More than 10 km ☐
How often do you come to the superstore each week? 1 ☐ 2 ☐ 3 ☐ More than 3 ☐
How much, on average, do you spend per visit?
Less than £20 ☐   £20 to £30 ☐
£50 or more ☐

11. Prove. Semi-detached 75%, Detached 80%.

12. Do not support.
Women 75% Men 75%   Same proportion

13. (a) 2   (b) 5   (c) 24   (d) 49

CHAPTER 29

Exercise **29.1**   Page 298

1. (a) 70   (b) 103

2. (a) 39   (b) 84

4. (a) 9   (b) 6   (c) White
(d) 37

1. (a) 7   (b) Brown   (c) 22
2. (a) 8   (b) 4   (c) 22
3. (a)

(c) 3

Score	Frequency
1	4
2	5
3	7
4	4
5	5
6	5
Total	30

4. (a) Saturday   (b) 5 hours   (c) 41 hours
   (d) Sunday   (e) $\frac{1}{4}$ (f) 6 hours
5. (b) £5   (c) £7   (d) 20%
6. (a) 15   (b) 1   (c) 5   (d) 20%
7. (b) 3   (c) 6
9. (a) 38   (b) Monday
   (c)

Date of birth	Number of boys
Sun	1
Mon	3
Tue	4
Wed	4
Thu	1
Fri	5
Sat	1

1. (a) 10   (b) 3   (c) 4   (d) $\frac{7}{10}$ (e) 75%
2. (a) 12   (b) 6   (c) Flu
3. (a) Brett   (b) Trent
   (c) 5 marks   (d) 13 marks
   (e) (i) Trent   (ii) Dexter
4. (a) 7 hours   (b) 5 hours
   (c) 3   (d) (i) 20   (ii) 20%
   (e) E.g. boys have higher mode and larger range.
5. (a) 5   (b) 7
   (c) (i) 15   (ii) $\frac{1}{3}$
   (d) 4   (e) 5
   (f) Boys have higher mode and larger range.

1.

Tree	Angle
Ash	120°
Beech	150°
Maple	90°

2.

Colour	Angle
Brown	160°
Blue	100°
Green	60°
Other	40°

3.

Car	Angle
Ford	90°
Rover	81°
Vauxhall	135°
BMW	54°

4.

Cereal	Angle
Cornflakes	125°
Muesli	100°
Porridge	60°
Bran Flakes	75°

5.

Ice Cream	Angle
Vanilla	144°
Strawberry	72°
99	90°
Raspberry Ripple	54°

6.

Takeaway	Angle
Fish & Chips	110°
Chicken & Chips	136°
Chinese Meal	52°
Pizza	62°

1. (a) 12   (b) 8   (c) Hotel
2. (a) 20   (b) 15   (c) Sauze d'Oulx
3. (a) France   (b) 45   (c) 55   (d) 20
4. (a) 5   (b) 2   (c) 18
5. (a) 14   (b) 72

6. (a) Heathrow (b) 540 (c) 1080

7. (a) Brown (b) 26 (c) 25%

8. (a) 288 (b) 174°

Exercise 29.6 Page 311

1.

```
            1 | 0 means 10 litres
1 | 0 2 6 6 7 9
2 | 3 3 4 5 5 6 7 9
3 | 1 3 5 5
4 | 1 2
```

2.

```
            3 | 2 means 3.2 seconds
1 | 5
2 | 4 4 5 6 7 8 8 9
3 | 0 1 2 2 3 5 5 6 7
4 | 2 2 3
5 | 6 6 8
```

3.

```
            1 | 6 means 16 press-ups
0 | 9
1 | 6 8
2 | 0 1 2 4 5 7 8
3 | 2 2 3 6 6 6
4 | 0 1
```

4.

```
            2 | 7 means 2.7 cm
1 | 8
2 | 0 1 4 5 6 6 7
3 | 1 4 5 5 6 9
4 | 0 2 2 5
5 | 4
6 | 0
```

5. (a) 12
(b) 23 pence
(c) 39 pence

Exercise 29.7 Page 313

1. (a) 9
(b) 50
(c) 17
(d) Highest mark scored by a boy.
Lowest mark scored by a girl.
Boys have a greater range of marks.

2. (a)

```
Adults |    | Children   4 | 7 means 4.7 mins
           4 | 7 9
       9 4 | 5 | 1 3 4 9
   7 5 4 1 0 | 6 | 2 3 4 5 5 6 8
 9 8 7 3 3 3 0 | 7 | 1 4 6 7 9
     2 2 0 | 8 | 0 2
       4 2 | 9
         1 | 10
```

(b) Adults have larger range.
Fastest time recorded by child,
slowest time recorded by adult.

Review Exercise 29 Page 314

1. (a) 50 (b) 35

2. (a) Saturday (b) 17 hours

3. (b) 21 (c) 3 eggs

4. (b) Bed & Breakfast
(c) 50 (d) 34%

5.

(a)		(b)
Activity	Frequency	Angle
Gym	12	144°
Swimming	3	36°
Squash	6	72°
Aerobics	9	108°

6. 112

7. (a) Maris Piper (b) 36 tonnes

8. (a)

```
            5 | 4 means 5.4 grams
2 | 8
3 | 5 9
4 | 2 4 6 6 7 8 8
5 | 0 1 4 4 6 6 8
6 | 0 3 7
```

(b) 3.9 grams

9. (a)

Poultry	Chicken	Turkey	Duck
Angle	210°	120°	30°

(b) 36

(c)

Poultry	Chicken	Turkey	Duck
Number sold	9	5	2

10. (a) 2 : 3   (b) 27%
     (c) Boys: mode 8, range 3.
        Girls: mode 10, range 6.
        Boys have a lower modal mark but a
        smaller range of marks than the girls.

CHAPTER 30

Exercise 30.1   Page 318

1. (a) 7   (b) 4   (c) 4

2. (a) 3   (b) 3

3. (a) 1   (b) 2   (c) 3

4. (a) 5   (b) 2   (c) 3

5. 21p

6. (a) 3   (b) 5   (c) 3.5   (d) 4

7. (a) 18 kg   (b) 74 kg   (c) 72.4 kg

8. (a) 135   (b) 135   (c) 133

9. (a) 39   (b) 23   (c) 38.8

10. 63   **11.** 4   **12.** 8   **13.** 129 cm

Exercise 30.2   Page 319

1. (a) (i) 60 g   (ii) 99 g
     (b) Premium more widely spread and heavier.

2. (a) (i) 9 minutes   (ii) 9.5 minutes
     (b) Buses are more variable, but less late on
        average.

3. (a) (i) 42 words per minute
        (ii) 60 words per minute
     (b) Second group equal on average, but a
        little more varied.

4. (a) (i) 5   (ii) 1.8
     (b) Third division - more goals on average
        and more spread.

5. (a) (i) 0.5 minutes   (ii) 1.95 minutes
     (b) Girls a little slower on average and more
        varied.

6. (a) Roman 1.6%, Chinese 1.9%,
        Egyptian 2.5%, Greek 1.6%
     (b) Roman 6.48%, Chinese 6.48%,
        Egyptian 6.48%, Greek 6.38%

7. (a) 28.3
     (b) Much bigger variation in the sizes of
        classes in Year 11.

Exercise 30.3   Page 322

1. (a) Entries are: 12, 10, 5, 3
     (b) 1   (c) 2   (d) 1.97

2. (a)

Number of keys	2	3	4	5	6
Frequency	2	3	8	5	2

     (b) 20   (c) 4   (d) 4   (e) 4.1

3. (a)

Wage (£)	15	20	25	30	35
Frequency	5	4	6	1	3

     (b) £20   (c) £25   (d) 19
     (e) £25   (f) £440   (g) £23.16

4. (a) 2, 2.5, 2.7   (b) 2, 2, 2.1
     (c) 0, 5, 4.5

Exercise 30.4   Page 323

1. (a) 5   (b) 4   (c) 5   (d) 5

2. (a) 6   (b) 5   (c) 4
     (d) 5.38. No shoe of this size.

3. (a) 6p, 31p   (b) 30p, 30.0p

4. (a) 9   (b) 9   (c) 30   (d) 8.5

Exercise 30.5   Page 325

1. Jays: mean 1.9, range 5
    Wasps: mean 2.4, range 3
    Wasps scored more on average and had less
    spread.

2. Women: mean 1.6, range 6
    Men: mean 1.5, range 2
    Women made more visits to the cinema,
    though the number of visits is more spread.

3. (a) Before: median 3, range 4
        After: median 3, range 5
        Would have been better to calculate the
        means. Before 2.2. After 3.0
     (b) Before: median 2, range 5
        After: median 2, range 4
        Less variation in number of faults after
        servicing.

4. Average: Boys 6.2, Girls 7.1
    Variation: Boys 4, Girls $4\frac{1}{2}$
    No. Girls' average greater than boys'.
    Correct about variation.

5. (a) MacQuick 20 - 29, Pizza Pit 30 - 39
     (b) MacQuick - mean 26 years
        (Pizza Pit 36.5 years)
     (c) Exact ages not known.

Exercise 30.6 — Page 327

1. Mode trainers. Cannot calculate others.

2. Mode 15s, median 12s, mean 22.15s
   Median most sensible, not affected by 200 as is mean, mode not much use.

3. Mode 81, median 83, mean 69.8
   Median most sensible, not affected by 5 and 6 as is mean, mode not much use.

4. Swimmer A.
   Mean is lower (A 30.88s, B 31.38s)
   Range less (A 1.7s, B 15s)
   Median is higher (A 30.9s, B 30.0s)

5. Batsman B.
   Higher median (B 31.5, A 21)
   Higher mean (B 36, A 35)

6. He should use the median mark.
   The median mark is the middle mark, so half of the students will get the median mark or higher.

Review Exercise 30 — Page 328

1. (a) 2   (b) 4

2. (a) £22   (b) £27
   (c) Mode is second lowest price.

3. (a) (i) 31 years old   (ii) 12 years
   (b) Larger spread of ages for English teachers.

4. (a) 29   (b) 9   (c) 6
   (d) 8   (e) 6

5. (a) No. Only 2 of the 4 cars that had one fault before servicing now have no faults.
   (b) Mode.
   (c) Mean.
       After servicing mean = 1.2 (1 d.p.).

6. (a) 7   (b) 6
   (c) Boys better.
       Higher median and smaller range.

7. (a) Mean weight of Phillip's friends is greater than Elizabeth's friends.
   (b) Both groups of friends have the same median height.

8. (a) 25   (b) 4   (c) 2
   (d) 2.2

9. (a) 8°C   (b) 3.1°C

CHAPTER 31

Exercise 31.1 — Page 331

1. (a) 15°C
   (b) Temperature variations during each day are not known.
       Line only indicates trend in midday temperatures.

2. (a) 8
   (b) Jan, Feb, June
   (c) No information given about when cars are sold during the month.

3. (b) (i) 154 cm   (ii) 15 years 4 months

4. (a) 82 kg   (b) 82 kg
   (c) 5 kg   (d) Week 4

5. (b) £118 - £119
   (c) Money was withdrawn

Exercise 31.2 — Page 334

1. (a) 36   (b) 24   (c) 40

2. (a)

Distance (m miles)	Frequency
$0 \leqslant m < 10\,000$	9
$10\,000 \leqslant m < 20\,000$	8
$20\,000 \leqslant m < 30\,000$	6
$30\,000 \leqslant m < 40\,000$	7

3. (a) Entries are: 4, 7, 9, 4
   (c) 6.00 and less than 6.50

4. (a) 3 but less than 4   (b) 31
   (c) 15   (d) 4
   (e) 190

5. (a) 14   (b) 70
   (c) £300 and less than £400
   (d) 210

Exercise 31.3 — Page 337

1.

Time (seconds)	Frequency
10 and less than 20	4
20 and less than 30	6
30 and less than 40	2

2. (a) 26   (b) 0
   (c) 27   (d) 95

3. (a)

Mark	Frequency
20 and less than 30	5
30 and less than 40	8
40 and less than 50	9
50 and less than 60	6
60 and less than 70	2

    (b) 40 and less than 50   (c) 22

4. (a) 16   (b) $2 \leqslant k < 4$

5. (c) English results have smaller range.
        English modal class is higher.

6. (b) 2000 results have a larger range.
        1999 results have higher modal class.

Exercise **31.4**   **Page 340**

1. Axes not labelled.

2. Bars not equal width.

3. Vertical axis does not begin at zero.

4. Pass rate not given.
    Advert implies you "pass" after 8 lessons.

5. 10% increase in price, disproportionate
    increase in diagram size.

6. Horizontal axis does not begin at zero and is
    not a uniform scale.

7. Vertical scale not uniform.
    Size of diagrams disproportionate to increase
    in sales.

8. Horizontal scale not uniform.
    Vertical scale not calibrated.

Review Exercise **31**   **Page 341**

1. (a) £400

2. (b) £87 000
    (c) Prices of houses rise and fall.
        Future prices unpredictable.

3. Vertical scale does not begin at zero.
    Horizontal scale is not uniform.

4. (a) 3 but less than 4   (b) 31   (c) 190

5. (a) 39   (b) $8 \leqslant f < 12$

6.

Time (seconds)	Frequency
10 and less than 20	4
20 and less than 30	6
30 and less than 40	2

7. (a)

Height (h cm)	Frequency
$5 \leqslant h < 10$	6
$10 \leqslant h < 15$	10
$15 \leqslant h < 20$	7
$20 \leqslant h < 25$	9
$25 \leqslant h < 30$	8

    (c) 16   (d) $10 \leqslant h < 15$

8. (a)

Class interval (Steepness°)	Tally	Frequency
1 - 10	||||	4
11 - 20	⊬⊢	5
21 - 30	||||	4
31 - 40	⊬⊢ ||	7

CHAPTER   **32**

Exercise **32.1**   **Page 344**

1. (a) 2   (b) 164 cm   (c) No
    (d) Taller girls usually have larger shoe sizes
        than shorter girls.

2. (a) 72
    (b) (i)   English 46, French 88
        (ii) French could be her first language.

3. (a) 4   (b) 43 kg
    (c) Tend to be higher

4. (a) 39 000 miles
    (b) Older cars tend to have higher mileages.
    (c) (i) 2 years, 40 000 miles   (ii) Hire car

5. (a) 6   (b) 8.2 years
    (c) Children who read more tend to have a
        higher reading age.

Exercise **32.2**   **Page 347**

1. (a) **B**   (b) **C**   (c) **D**

2. (a) Negative   (b) Positive
    (c) No correlation   (d) Positive
    (e) Negative

3. (b) Positive correlation

4. (b) Negative correlation
    (c) Points are close to a straight line.

Exercise **32.3**   **Page 349**

1. (b) Positive correlation
    (d) Points are close to the line of best fit.

2. (b) Negative correlation   (d) 38 minutes

3. (a) Positive correlation   (d) 4.8 to 4.9 kg

4. (b) Negative correlation

Review Exercise 32   Page 350

1. (a) 6   (b) 8.2 years
(c) Children who read more tend to have a higher reading age.
(d) 9.2 years

2. (b) Negative correlation   (c) £4500
(e) Points are close to the line of best fit.

3. (a) (i) **B, D** (ii) **A, C, E** (iii) **F**
(c) No. Points scattered, no linear correlation.

4. (b) Negative correlation.
As the average temperature increases, fewer units of electricity tend to be used.
(d) 28 units

CHAPTER 33

Exercise 33.1   Page 352

1. (a) Certain   (b) Impossible
(c) Evens   (d) Impossible
(e) Evens

2. (a) Unlikely   (b) Likely
(c) Likely   (d) Unlikely
(e) Unlikely   (f) Likely

3. (a) Certain   (b) Impossible
(c) Evens   (d) Evens
(e) Impossible   (f) Unlikely

Exercise 33.2   Page 354

1. (a) **A**   (b) **C**   (c) **B**

2. (a) **T**   (b) **P**   (c) **R**   (d) **S**

3.

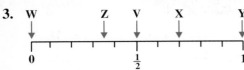

Exercise 33.3   Page 355

1. (a) $\frac{1}{6}$ (b) $\frac{1}{2}$ (c) $\frac{2}{3}$ (d) $\frac{1}{3}$

2. (a) $\frac{1}{3}$ (b) $\frac{2}{3}$ (c) $\frac{2}{3}$

3. (a) $\frac{3}{10}$ (b) $\frac{7}{10}$

4. (a) $\frac{1}{2}$ (b) $\frac{1}{2}$

5. (a) $\frac{1}{5}$ (b) $\frac{1}{5}$ (c) $\frac{2}{5}$

6. (a) $\frac{1}{11}$ (b) $\frac{4}{11}$ (c) $\frac{2}{11}$

7. (a) $\frac{1}{12}$ (b) $\frac{1}{6}$

8. (a) $\frac{1}{2}$ (b) $\frac{1}{4}$ (c) $\frac{1}{52}$

9. (a) $\frac{2}{5}$ (b) $\frac{3}{5}$ (c) 1   (d) 0

10. (a) $\frac{2}{3}$ (b) $\frac{1}{3}$ (c) $\frac{3}{4}$

11. (a) $\frac{2}{5}$ (b) $\frac{3}{5}$ (c) $\frac{4}{25}$ (d) $\frac{4}{15}$
(e) $\frac{2}{5}$

12. (a) $\frac{1}{3}$ (b) $\frac{1}{15}$ (c) $\frac{11}{24}$ (d) $\frac{17}{50}$
(e) $\frac{21}{25}$ (f) $\frac{4}{5}$

13. The events are not equally likely.

14. (a) $\frac{7}{15}$ (b) $\frac{1}{2}$ (c) $\frac{1}{16}$ (d) $\frac{3}{4}$

Exercise 33.4   Page 358

1. $\frac{7}{25}$ **2.** $\frac{9}{40}$ **3.** $\frac{3}{10}$

4. (a) $\frac{52}{100} = 0.52$ $\frac{102}{200} = 0.51$ $\frac{141}{300} = 0.47$
(b) 0.47

5. $\frac{21}{30} = \frac{7}{10}$ **6.** 8   **7.** 18   **8.** 25

9. (a) 300   (b) 120   (c) 150

Exercise 33.5   Page 360

1. $\frac{3}{5}$

2. 0.4   **5.** 0.6

3. 0.04   **6.** (a) 0.04   (b) 0.97

4. $\frac{47}{50}$ **7.** (a) 0.5   (b) 0.3

8. (a) (i) The probabilities add to 105%
(ii) 5%
(b) (i) 45%   (ii) 75%   (iii) 80%

9. (a) 0.4   (b) 0.6
(c) (i) Mutually exclusive - there are no blue cubes numbered 1
(ii) Not mutually exclusive - probability = 0.2
(d) (i) 0.6   (ii) 0.6

1. (a) RBG, RGB, GBR, GRB, BGR, BRG

    (b) $\frac{1}{3}$

2. (a)

	2nd dice					
	1	**2**	**3**	**4**	**5**	**6**
1	2	3	4	5	6	7
2	3	4	5	6	7	8
3	4	5	6	7	8	9
4	5	6	7	8	9	10
5	6	7	8	9	10	11
6	7	8	9	10	11	12

1st dice (left label)

    (b) (i) $\frac{1}{12}$ (ii) $\frac{1}{12}$ (iii) $\frac{5}{6}$

    (c) They cover all possible scores.

3.

	Dice					
	1	2	3	4	5	6
H	H1	H2	H3	H4	H5	H6
T	T1	T2	T3	T4	T5	T6

Coin (left label)

    (a) $\frac{1}{12}$ (b) $\frac{1}{4}$ (c) $\frac{1}{12}$ (d) $\frac{1}{4}$

    (e) $\frac{1}{6}$ (f) $\frac{1}{2}$

4. (a)

Stage 1	Stage 2
Bus	Bus
Bus	Walk
Train	Bus
Train	Walk
Lift	Bus
Lift	Walk

    (b) $\frac{1}{6}$

5. (a)

	2nd spin			
	1	**2**	**3**	**4**
1	2	3	4	5
2	3	4	5	6
3	4	5	6	7
4	5	6	7	8

1st spin (left label)

    (b) (i) $\frac{1}{16}$ (ii) $\frac{1}{8}$ (iii) $\frac{3}{16}$

6. (a)

	Bag A		
	R	R	W
W	RW	RW	WW
W	RW	RW	WW
R	RR	RR	WR

Bag B (left label)

    (c) $\frac{4}{9}$

7. (a)

A	1	1	2	2	3	3
B	2	3	2	3	2	3

    (b) (i) $\frac{2}{6} = \frac{1}{3}$ (ii) $\frac{4}{6} = \frac{2}{3}$ (c) $\frac{4}{5}$

8. (a) Maths, English
Maths, Science
Maths, Art
English, Science
English, Art
Science, Art

    (b) $\frac{3}{6} = \frac{1}{2}$ (c) $\frac{1}{3}$

9. (a)

	W	RW	GW	BW	YW	WW
	Y	RY	GY	BY	YY	WY
2nd spin	B	RB	GB	BB	YB	WB
	G	RG	GG	BG	YG	WG
	R	RR	GR	BR	YR	WR
		R	G	B	Y	W

1st spin

    (b) (i) $\frac{1}{25}$ (ii) $\frac{9}{25}$ (iii) $\frac{5}{25} = \frac{1}{5}$

10. (a)

	1	2	3	4	5	6
1	2	3	4	5	6	7
2	3	4	5	6	7	8
3	4	5	6	7	8	9

    (b) $\frac{1}{18}$ (c) $\frac{1}{6}$

1.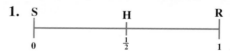

2. (a) Mint   (b) More mint than other prizes.

    (c) (d)

3. (a) $\frac{1}{5}$ (b) $\frac{4}{5}$

4. (a) $\frac{6}{11}$ (b) $\frac{5}{11}$

5. (a) Red 1,   Green 1,   Blue 1,
Red 2,   Green 2,   Blue 2,
Red 3,   Green 3,   Blue 3.

    (b) $\frac{2}{3}$ (c) 0.5

6. 0.15

7. (a)

	1	2	3	4
1	2	3	4	5
2	3	4	5	6
3	4	5	6	7

(b) (i) $\frac{2}{12} = \frac{1}{6}$ (ii) $\frac{10}{12} = \frac{5}{6}$

(c) $\frac{4}{12} = \frac{1}{3}$

8. (a) Red (b) (i) 0.1 (ii) 0

9. (a) $\frac{1}{6}$ (b) $\frac{1}{3}$

(c)

Dice \ Spinner	1	2	3
1	2	3	4
2	3	4	5
3	4	5	6
4	5	6	7
5	6	7	8
6	7	8	9

(d) $\frac{3}{18} = \frac{1}{6}$

(e) Decrease. There will be more possible outcomes, 24, but still only 3 ways of getting a total of 4.

10. (a) (i) $\frac{7}{20}$ (ii) $\frac{3}{4}$ (iii) $\frac{13}{20}$

(b) Red, Blue   Blue, Yellow
Red, Yellow   Blue, Blue
Red, Red   Yellow, Yellow

11. The events are not equally likely.

12. (a) $\frac{9}{30} = \frac{3}{10}$ (b) $\frac{3}{15} = \frac{1}{5}$

(c) 384

Section Review   Page 367

1. (a) 20 (b) 45 (c) 95
(d) Cod

2. (a) 6 (b) 21 (c) Football

3. (a) 28.8 (b) 4

4. (b)

(c) (i) $\frac{3}{20}$ (ii) $\frac{8}{20} = \frac{2}{5}$

5. (a) (i) 16 (ii) 38
(b) (i) Heathrow (ii) 40
(c) 120

6. (a)

Class interval	Tally	Frequency
0 - 9		0
10 - 19	.	0
20 - 29	$\|$	1
30 - 39	$\|\|\|$	3
40 - 49	||||$\|$	5
50 - 59	||||$\|$ $\|\|$	7
60 - 69	||||$\|$ $\|\|\|$	8
70 - 79	$\|\|\|$	3
80 - 89	$\|$	1
90 - 99	$\|\|$	2

(c) Median mark is in the 50s, the modal class is 60 - 69. Results have improved.

7.

Game	Angle
Badminton	64°
Basketball	120°
Squash	48°
Volleyball	128°

8. (a) 15 (b) 18 cm (c) 26 cm
(d) 23.7 cm

9. (a) $\frac{3}{20}$ (b) $\frac{7}{20}$

10. (a)

		Red	Red	Red
		A	1	2
	A	AA	A1	A2
Blue	2	2A	21	22
Blue	2	2A	21	22

(b) $\frac{2}{9}$

11. (a) 0.4 (b) 18

12. (a) 35 (b) 3 (c) 5.1
(d) Males have greater range, 7 compared with 3.
Females have greater average, 5.1 compared with 3.6.

13. Probably not, as 2 occurs twice as many times as any other number.

14. (a) $\frac{7}{9}$ (b) $\frac{6}{25}$
(c) Can swim: girls 0.76, boys 0.8.
Not true. 0.8 > 0.76

15. (a) **D.** Exact location known. Distances can be calculated later.
(b) Mainly after work shoppers.

429

16. (b) Positive correlation   (c) 32

17. 0.07

18. £380

1. (a) 7, 23, 56, 93, 234, 469, 614
   (b) Four hundred and sixty-nine

2. (a) 2139   (b) 570   (c) 2010

3. (a) 15, 20   (b) 20

4. (a) 3 thousands, 3000   (b) 4 tens, 40

5.

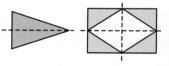

6. (a) £1.86   (b) £3.14

7. (a) 17
   (b) Add 4 to the last number.
   (c) No. All terms in the sequence are odd numbers.

8. (a) $\frac{3}{10}$ (b) 30%
   (c) Shade any 5 **more** squares

9. (a) 50%   (b) 0.4   (c) $\frac{2}{5}$, $\frac{1}{2}$, $\frac{2}{3}$, $\frac{3}{4}$

10. (a) 87   (b) 2.36   (c) 432

11. (a) 5   (b) 8   (c) 10

12. (a) Area = 9 cm², perimeter = 20 cm

13. (a) (i) 7431   (i) 1347
   (iii) **3 4 = 2× 1 7**
   (b) 6

14. (a) Units   (b) 4.5 kilograms

15. (a) 17.5   (b) 2.95   (c) 1.6

16. (a) $a = 155°$, supplementary angles
   (b) $b = 53°$, sum of angles in a triangle is 180°.

17. (a) b^3 (b) $35d$ pence   (c) 8

18. 14 pence   **19.** $\frac{5}{9}$

20. (a) 2.2   (b) 6   (c) 12
   (d) Kent had higher mean but lower spread. Murray had lower mean but larger spread.

21. 150 miles

22.

Not full size

23. (a) (i) $x = 10$ (ii) $x = 7$
   (b) $2a - 6$

24. (a) £12.48
   (b) (i) John
      (ii) $2000 \div 80 = 40$, 42 boxes are needed.

25. 76 cm

26. (a) 7   (b) 73

27. (a) 5 cm   (b) (i) 19 (ii) 8

28. (a) -14 (b) -4

29. 1, 0, $-\frac{1}{2}$

30. (a) 343   (b) 9   (c) 0.5

31. $\frac{60}{20 - 5} = 4$

32. (a) $x = 54°$
   (b) (i) $y = 63°$ (ii) alternate angles

33. (a)

A	B	Total	A	B	Total
1	5	6	3	5	8
1	6	7	3	6	9
1	7	8	3	7	10
2	5	7	4	5	9
2	6	8	4	6	10
2	7	9	4	7	11

   (b) $\frac{2}{12} = \frac{1}{6}$

34. (a) 18   (b) $2t - 3$ (c) $x = 7$

35. (b) 035°   (c) 215°

36. (a) $\frac{17}{20}$ (b) 8

37. (a) Reflection in the y axis
   (b) Rotation, 90° anticlockwise, about (0, 0)

38. (a) $\frac{1}{6}$ (b) $1\frac{11}{20}$

39. (a) $2(m - 2n)$ (b) $t(t - 2)$

40. (a) $x = 6$ (b) $y = -2$

41. (a) 48   (b) 90%

42. (a) (i) 11.40 am (ii) 20 minutes
(b) $12\frac{1}{2}$ miles
(c)

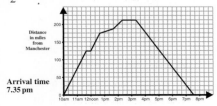

Calculator Paper **Page 376**

1. (a) Five thousand six hundred and twenty-four
(b) -15, -4, 3, 39, 120

2. (a) QR
(b) $\angle PSR = 100°$, $\angle QRS = 70°$
(c) $\angle QRS$
(d) 3.3 cm

3. (a) 3, 7, 9 (b) 2, 3, 6 (c) 24 (d) 9

4. (a) **R** (b) **A, C**

5. (a) 21 minutes (b) 6.06 pm

6. (a)

Result	Tally	Frequency
1	$\mathcal{HHT}$ |	6
2	$\mathcal{HHT}$ $\mathcal{HHT}$ ||	12
3	$\mathcal{HHT}$ $\mathcal{HHT}$ |	11
4	$\mathcal{HHT}$ |	6
5	$\mathcal{HHT}$	5

(c) 2

7. (a) £5586 (b) £6000

8. (a)

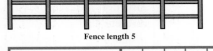

Fence length 5

(b)

Fence length	1	2	3	4	5	6
Number of pieces	4	7	10	13	16	19

(c) Multiply the fence length by 3, then add 1. $3 \times 25 + 1 = 76$

9. (a) $A(1, 4)$ (b) (ii) $D(-2, 1)$

10. (a) 230 cm (b) 41.6 km
(c) 40 gallons

11. (a) (i) 6 (ii) 4 (b) E.g. a rectangle

12. (a) £68.25 (b) 15 hours

13. (a) $-8°C$ (b) $9°C$
(c) 16 degrees

14. (a) $6t$ (b) (i) $w = 3$ (ii) $x = 2$
(c) 5

15. (a) (i) 0.125 (ii) 12.5% (b) £2815.75

16. $16\,cm^3$

17. (a) 2.4 (b) 21 **18.** 39p

19. (a)

x	-3	-2	-1	0	1	2	3
y	-1	0	1	2	3	4	5

(b)

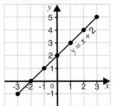

(c) $x = 0.5$

20. (a) 8 (b) $300\,cm^2$ (c) 240

21. £349.20 **22.** $x = 41°$, $y = 58°$

23. (a) $20x$ grams (b) 180 grams

24. 64%

25. (a) £5 (b) 2.25 m

26. (a) 90 (b) $40°$ (c) 0.22 (d) $\frac{3}{25}$

27. Size 1: 12.8 grams/penny
Size 2: 13.6 grams/penny
Size 2 gives more grams per penny.

28. (a) 12 (b) 2.5 cm (c) 5.89 cm

29. (a) 20.197 (b) $\frac{80 \times 10}{10 + 30} = 20$

30. £130.20

31. (a) (i) $p = 63°$
(ii) ΔABC is isosceles, $\angle BAC = \angle BCA$.
(b) (i) $m = 54°$ (ii) $r = 63°$
(c) (i) $t = 54°$
(ii) $\angle ABC = \angle CDE$ (alt. $\angle$s)

32. (a) $18\,000\,cm^3$ (b) 8%

33. (a) $\frac{8}{25}$ (b) $\frac{19}{25}$

34. 188.5 cm **35.** $200\,m^2$

36. How many hours a week do you listen to the radio?

Less than 10 ☐ 10 to 20 ☐ More than 20 ☐

On how many days each week do you listen to the radio?

Every day ☐ 4 to 6 ☐ 1 to 3 ☐ 0 ☐

37. (a) £4 (b) 35 g

38. (a) 36.66 (b) 512 (c) 0.325

39. (a) $x = 3.2$ (b) $3(a - 2b)$
(c) $7x + 6$

Index •••••••••••••••••••••••••••••••••